Blackstone's Statutes
Public Law & Human Rights

Blackstone's Statutes
Public Law & Human Rights

2005/2006

Fifteenth Edition

Edited by

Peter Wallington

MA, LLM, Barrister

11 King's Bench Walk Chambers

and

Robert G. Lee

LLB

Professor of Law, ESRC Centre for Business Relationships, Accountability,
Sustainability and Society, Cardiff Law School

OXFORD

UNIVERSITY PRESS

OXFORD

UNIVERSITY PRESS

Great Clarendon Street, Oxford OX2 6DP

Oxford University Press is a department of the University of Oxford.
It furthers the University's objective of excellence in research, scholarship,
and education by publishing worldwide in

Oxford New York

Auckland Cape Town Dar es Salaam Hong Kong Karachi
Kuala Lumpur Madrid Melbourne Mexico City Nairobi
New Delhi Shanghai Taipei Toronto

With offices in

Argentina Austria Brazil Chile Czech Republic France Greece
Guatemala Hungary Italy Japan Poland Portugal Singapore
South Korea Switzerland Thailand Turkey Ukraine Vietnam

Oxford is a registered trade mark of Oxford University Press
in the UK and in certain other countries

Published in the United States
by Oxford University Press Inc., New York

First published by Blackstone Press

First edition 1988	Sixth edition 1996	Twelfth edition 2002
Second edition 1990	Seventh edition 1997	Thirteenth edition 2003
Third edition 1992	Eighth edition 1998	Fourteenth edition 2004
Reprinted 1993	Ninth edition 1999	Fifteenth edition 2005
Fourth edition 1994	Tenth edition 2000	
Fifth edition 1995	Eleventh edition 2001	

British Library Cataloguing in Publication Data
Data available

Library of Congress Cataloging in Publication Data
Data applied for

ISBN 0–19–928314–1   978–0–19–928314–9

1 3 5 7 9 10 8 6 4 2

Typeset in ITC Stone Serif and ITC Stone Sans
by RefineCatch Limited, Bungay, Suffolk
Printed in Great Britain by Ashford Colour Press Ltd, Gosport, Hampshire

CONTENTS

ALPHABETICAL CONTENTS

EDITORS' PREFACE

The adage that Britain has no written constitution, while still technically true, is an increasingly unhelpful and unreal starting point for the study of Constitutional and Administrative Law. As in many other areas of the law, statute has assumed an increasingly pervasive role. In addition, the incorporation of the European Convention on Human Rights into domestic law provides a significant constitutional yardstick against which laws must be measured. Other international sources play an increasing part in the regulation of power in the UK, making it important to look for comparison at the constitutional approach of some other jurisdictions. The volume of statutory and analogous material to which students in the field of Public Law need to refer has become such that a separate set of materials is a necessary guide.

We have assembled here a collection of statutes on all aspects of Constitutional and Administrative Law and Human Rights. It is not intended to replace textbooks or cases and materials books, but to complement them and to provide necessary and quick reference to essential texts. Since it contains no commentary it is suitable—and we hope will be adopted—for reference in examinations in these subjects (but do check with your faculty or department whether this is so). We hope it will also encourage students to become more accustomed to reading and unravelling the language of Parliament—one of the most basic skills of a lawyer.

The selection of materials for a collection of statutes is a matter of sometimes arbitrary editorial judgement. Our selection is based on the knowledge that courses vary in content and an attempt to meet the major needs of a fairly broad range of undergraduate courses. This means the book will contain some material irrelevant to your particular course—but much that is central, or a valuable supplement, to any course in the Public Law area (including important parts of Legal System courses). The book is designed to be used by English, Welsh and Scottish students. It includes the legislation allowing significant devolution of power within the United Kingdom. The territorial extent of the Act is indicated for each statute. We have included those parts of Northern Irish legislation of most interest to students elsewhere in the UK. It should be noted that one consequence of the creation of a Scottish Parliament with legislative powers is that statutes extending to England and Wales and to Scotland may be amended in relation to one of the jurisdictions but not the other; for simplicity we have adopted the version applicable in England and Wales in such cases. The same problem also arises to a lesser extent in the application of legislation to Wales; when there are differences we have included the provisions as they apply in England only.

This edition sees the inclusion of some important material from 2004, which came too late for the Fourteenth Edition. This includes the Hunting Act 2004, included because of the controversy concerning the use of the Parliament Act 1949 in its passage, and the pending (at the time of going to press) challenge regarding its compatibility with the Human Rights Convention. The Civil Partnership Act 2004 and the Gender Recognition Act 2004 add to the materials with a human rights dimension. We have included yet more material of general constitutional and human rights importance on immigration and asylum (the Asylum and Immigration (Treatment of Claimants etc) Act 2004), and the Civil Contingencies Act 2004 with its extensive provision for emergency regulation. These are followed by a raft of important constitutional legislation passed before the dissolution of Parliament in April 2005. The long awaited Constitutional Reform Act 2005 allows for the creation of a new Supreme Court and makes other significant changes to the structure and appointment of the judiciary. The Prevention of Terrorism Act 2005 deals with the aftermath of the *Belmarsh* case in the House of Lords. Further reforms of the police and police powers are contained in the Serious Organised Crime and Police Act 2005, and the Inquiries Act 2005 gives wide ranging powers for ministers to convene and regulate inquiries into matters of public concern.

Part II of the book contains a range of non-UK material including constitutional material from elsewhere (including the USA and South Africa), relevant EU provisions and other relevant Treaties to which the UK is a party. There is also some domestic non-statutory material, in the form of the most important PACE Codes of Practice.

The amount of new material in this edition has required, once again, some editing of the previous text. We hope, however, that nothing vital has been lost. As always we are pleased to receive comments concerning the editorial judgements exercised. Because this is a text for students rather than practitioners, we have been able to be more selective in cutting material down to a manageable length. Omissions are indicated by a row of asterisks. Provisions as to commencement, etc. have also been omitted. The text is printed, where appropriate, as subsequently amended; new materials are shown by square brackets and repeals by dots. Statutes and Statutory Instruments are printed in chronological order (in alphabetical order within each year); other material is gathered together in Part II.

Another innovation, first introduced for the Fourteenth Edition, is a list of useful websites for further research. You can access any of these websites by hyperlinks from our new Online Resource Centre (*www.oup.com/uk/booksites/law/*), which will also give you updates on important developments affecting the materials in this book.

Significant legislation in the field of public law has been a defining feature of two immediately previous Labour Administrations, and this promises to be true for the Blair Government's third term of office. Dissolution of Parliament in April 2005, and the following hiatus in new statutory provisions, has allowed us to cover the significant provisions of public law as at 1 June 2005. All legislative changes enacted up to that date have been incorporated, whether or not yet in force.

We gratefully acknowledge the help we received from Clive Lewis, who advised on content and carefully checked the manuscript of the first edition, Tamara Egede and Elen Stokes for assistance with web based material, and Ruth Noble for research assistance for this edition. We are also indebted to Jeremy McBride of the University of Birmingham, both for suggestions as to inclusion and for the benefit of collaboration over the years in the internal production of statutory materials for students at Cambridge, Birmingham, Lancaster and Cardiff. Finally our thanks are due to our publishers for their speed and efficiency in production. The responsibility for errors is the editors' alone.

Peter Wallington
Robert G. Lee
June 2005

Legislation of the UK Parliament and other legislatures within the UK

Magna Carta
(Statute 25 Edw. 1, 1297)

Territorial extent: England and Wales, Northern Ireland

The Great Charter of the Liberties of England, and of the Liberties of the Forest; confirmed by King Edward, in the Twenty-fifth Year of his Reign.

Edward by the grace of God King of England, Lord of Ireland, and Duke of Guyan, to all archbishops, bishops, &c. We have seen the Great Charter of the Lord Henry sometimes King of England, our father, of the liberties of England in these words:

Henry by the grace of God King of England, Lord of Ireland, Duke of Normandy and Guyan, and Earl of Anjou, to all archbishops, bishops, abbots, priors, earls, barons, sheriffs, provosts, officers, and to all bailiffs, and other our faithful subjects, which shall see this present charter, greeting: Know ye, that we, unto the honour of Almighty God, and for the salvation of the souls of our progenitors and successors Kings of England, to the advancement of holy church and amendment of our realm, of our meer and free will, have given and granted to all archbishops, bishops, abbots, priors, earls, barons, and to all freemen of this our realm, these liberties following, to be kept in our kingdom of England for ever.

Chapter 1   Confirmation of liberties
First, we have granted to God, and by this our present charter have confirmed, for us and our heirs for ever, that the church of England shall be free, and shall have all her whole rights and liberties inviolable. We have granted also, and given to all the freemen of our realm, for us and our heirs for ever, these liberties underwritten, to have and to hold to them and their heirs, of us and our heirs for ever.

Chapters 2–28   . . .

Chapter 29   Imprisonment, etc. contrary to law
No freeman shall be taken or imprisoned, or be disseised of his freehold, or liberties, or free customs, or be outlawed, or exiled, or any other wise destroyed; nor will we not pass upon him, nor condemn him, but by lawful judgment of his peers, or by the law of the land. We will sell to no man, we will not deny or defer to any man either justice or right.

Chapters 30–36   . . .
[Chapter 37 (Escuage) omitted]

Treason Act 1351

(25 Edw. 3 Stat 5, c. 2)

Territorial extent: United Kingdom

Declaration what offences shall be adjudged treason

Item, whereas divers opinions have been before this time in what case treason shall be said, and in what not; the King, at the request of the lords and of the commons, hath made a declaration in the manner as hereafter followeth, that is to say; when a man doth compass or imagine the death of our lord the King, or of our lady his Queen or of their eldest son and heir; or if a man do violate the King's companion, or the King's eldest daughter unmarried, or the wife the King's eldest son and heir; or if a man do levy war against our lord the King in his realm, or be adherent to the King's enemies in his realm, giving to them aid and comfort in the realm, or elsewhere, and thereof be probably attainted of open deed by the people of their condition: . . . and if a man slea the chancellor, treasurer, or the King's justices of the one bench or the other, justices in eyre, or justices of assise, and all other justices assigned to hear and determine, being in their places, doing their offices: and it is to be understood, that in the cases above rehearsed, that ought to be judged treason which extends to our lord the King, and his royal majesty: . . .

Justices of the Peace Act 1361

(34 Edw. 3, c. 1)

Who shall be justices of the peace—Their jurisdiction over offenders; rioters; barrators; and vagabonds—Commissions of general inquiries to end—Fines to be reasonable

Territorial extent: England and Wales, Northern Ireland (in part—see Magistrates' Courts Act (Northern Ireland) 1964. Sch. 2)

First, that in every county of England shall be assigned for the keeping of the peace, one lord, and with him three or four of the most worthy in the county, with some learned in the law, and they shall have power to restrain the offenders, rioters, and all other barrators and to pursue, arrest, take, and chastise them according their trespass or offence; and to cause them to be imprisoned and duly punished according to the law and customs of the realm, and according to that which to them shall seem best to do by their discretions and good advisement; . . . and to take and arrest all those that they may find by indictment, or by suspicion, and to put them in prison; and to take of all them that be not of good fame, where they shall be found, sufficient surety and mainprise of their good behaviour towards the King and his people, and the other duly to punish; to the intent that the people be not by such rioters or rebels troubled nor endamaged, nor the peace blemished, nor merchants nor other passing by the highways of the realm disturbed, nor put in the peril which may happen of such offenders . . .

The Bill of Rights (1688)
(1 Will. & Mar. sess 2, c. 2)

An Act declaring the Rights and Liberties of the Subject and Setleing the Succession of the Crowne

Territorial extent: England and Wales, Northern Ireland (for Scotland see the equivalent Act of the Scottish Parliament, the Claim of Right 1689)

Whereas the lords spirituall and temporall and comons assembled at Westminster lawfully fully and freely representing all estates of the people of this realme did upon the thirteenth day of February in the yeare of our Lord one thousand six hundred eighty eight present unto their Majesties then called and known by the names and stile of William and Mary Prince and Princesse of Orange being present in their proper persons a certaine declaration in writeing made by the said lords and comons in the words following viz

The heads of declaration of lords and commons, recited—Whereas the late King James the Second by the assistance of diverse evill councillors judges and ministers imployed by him did endeavour to subvert and extirpate the Protestant religion and the lawes and liberties of this kingdome

Dispensing and suspending power—By assumeing and exerciseing a power of dispensing with and suspending of lawes and the execution of lawes without consent of Parlyament.

Committing prelates—By committing and prosecuting diverse worthy prelates for humbly petitioning to be excused from concurring to the said assumed power.

Ecclesiastical commission—By issueing and causeing to be executed a commission under the great seale for erecting a court called the court of commissioners for ecclesiasticall causes.

Levying money—By levying money for and to the use of the Crowne by pretence of prerogative for other time and in other manner then the same was granted by Parlyament.

Standing army—By raising and keeping a standing army within this kingdome in time of peace without consent of Parlyament and quartering soldiers contrary to law.

Disarming Protestants, etc.—By causing severall good subjects being protestants to be disarmed at the same time when papists were both armed and imployed contrary to law.

Violating elections—By violating the freedome of election of members to serve in Parlyament.

Illegal prosecutions—By prosecutions in the Court of King's Bench for matters and causes cognizable onely in Parlyament and by diverse other arbitrary and illegall courses.

Juries—And whereas of late yeares partiall corrupt and unqualifyed persons have beene returned and served on juryes in tryalls and particularly diverse jurors in tryalls for high treason which were not freeholders.

Excessive bail—And excessive baile hath beene required of persons committed in criminall cases to elude the benefitt of the lawes made for the liberty of the subjects.

Fines—And excessive fines have beene imposed.

Punishments—And illegall and cruell punishments inflicted.

Grants of fines, etc., before conviction, etc.—And severall grants and promises made of fines and forfeitures before any conviction or judgement against the persons upon whome the same were to be levyed.

All which are uterly and directly contrary to the knowne lawes and statutes and freedome of the realme.

And whereas the said late King James the Second haveing abdicated the government and the throne being thereby vacant his Highnesse the Prince of Orange (whome it hath pleased Almighty God to make the glorious instrument of delivering this kingdome from popery and arbitrary power) did (by the advice of the lords spirituall and temporall and diverse principall persons of the commons) cause letters to be written to the lords spirituall and temporall being protestants and other letters to the severall countyes cityes universities boroughss and cinque ports for the choosing of such persons to represent them as were of right to be sent to Parlyament to meete and sitt at Westminster upon the two and twentyeth day of January in this yeare one thousand six hundred eighty and eight in order to such an establishment as that their religion lawes and liberties might not againe be in danger of being subverted, upon which letters elections haveing beene accordingly made.

The subject's Rights – And thereupon the said lords spirituall and temporall and commons pursuant to their respective letters and elections being now assembled in a full and free representative of this nation takeing into their most serious consideration the best meanes for attaining the ends aforesaid doe in the first place (as their auncestors in like case have usually done) for the vindicating and asserting their auntient rights and liberties, declare

[1]   **Suspending power**—That the pretended power of suspending of laws or the execution of laws by regall authority without consent of Parlyament is illegall.

Late dispensing power—That the pretended power of dispensing with laws or the execution of laws by regall authoritie as it hath beene assumed and exercised of late is illegall.

Ecclesiastical courts illegal—That the commission for erecting the late court of commissioners for ecclesiasticall causes and all other commissions and courts of like nature are illegal and pernicious.

Levying money—That levying money for or to the use of the Crowne by pretence of prerogative without grant of Parlyament for longer time or in other manner than the same is or shall be granted is illegal.

Right to petition—That it is the right of the subjects to petition the King and all committments and prosecutions for such petitioning are illegal.

Standing army—That the raising or keeping a standing army within the kingdome in time of peace unlesse it be with consent of Parlyament is against law.

Subject's arms—That the subjects which are protestants may have arms for their defence suitable to their conditions and as allowed by law.

Freedom of election—That election of members of Parlyament ought to be free.

Freedom of speech—That the freedome of speech and debates or proceedings in Parlyament ought not to be impeached or questioned in any court or place out of Parlyament.

Excessive bail—That excessive baile ought not to be required nor excessive fines imposed nor cruell and unusuall punishments inflicted.

Juries—That jurors ought to be duly impannelled and returned . . .

Grants of forfeitures—That all grants and promises of fines and forfeitures of particular persons before conviction are illegal and void.

Frequent Parliaments—And that for redresse of all grievances and for the amending strengthening and preserving of the lawes Parlyaments ought to be held frequently.

The said right claimed, tender of the crown, regal power exercised, limitation of the crown, new oaths of allegiance, etc.—And they doe claime demand and insist upon all and singular the premises as their undoubted rights and liberties and that noe declarations judgements doeings or proceedings to the prejudice of the people in any of the said premises ought in any wise to be drawne hereafter into consequence or example. To which demand of their rights they are particularly encouraged by the declaration of his Highnesse the Prince of Orange as being the only meanes for obtaining a full redresse and remedy therein. Haveing therefore an intire confidence that his said Highnesse the Prince of Orange will perfect the deliverance soe farr advanced by him and will still preserve them from the violation of their rights which they have here asserted and from all other attempts upon their religion rights and liberties. The said lords spirituall and temporall and commons assembled at Westminster doe resolve that William and Mary Prince and Princesse of Orange be and be declared King and Queene of England France and Ireland and the dominions thereunto belonging to hold the crowne and royall dignity of the said kingdomes and dominions to them the said prince and princesse dureing their lives and the life of the survivour of them. And that the sole and full exercise of the regall power be onely in and executed by the said Prince of Orange in the names of the said prince and princesse dureing their joynt lives and after their deceases the said crowne and royall dignitie of the said kingdoms and dominions to be to the heires of the body of the said princesse and for default of such issue to the Princesse Anne of Denmarke and the heires of her body and for default of such issue to the heires of the body of the said Prince of Orange. And the lords spirituall and temporall and commons doe pray the said prince and princesse to accept the same accordingly. And that the oathes hereafter mentioned be taken by all persons of whome the oathes of allegiance and supremacy might be required by law instead of them and that the said oathes of allegiance and supremacy be abrogated.

I A B doe sincerely promise and sweare that I will be faithfull and beare true allegiance to their Majestyes King William and Queen Mary

Soe helpe me God

I A B doe sweare that I doe from my heart abhorr, detest and abjure as impious and hereticall this damnable doctrine and position that princes excommunicated or deprived by the Pope or any authority of the see of Rome may be deposed or murdered by their subjects or any other whatsoever. And I doe declare that noe forreigne prince person prelate, state or potentate hath or ought to have any jurisdiction power superiority preeminence or authoritie ecclesiasticall or spirituall within this realme.

Soe help me God

[Note: for the modern version of this effectively obsolete oath see the Accession Declaration Act 1910, Sch.]

Acceptance of the crown, the two Houses to sit, subjects' liberties to be allowed, and ministers hereafter to serve according to the same, William and Mary declared King and Queen, limitation of the crown, papists debarred the crown, every King, etc, shall make the declaration of 30 Car 2, if under 12 years old, to be done after attainment thereof, King's and Queen's assent. Upon which their said Majestyes did accept the crowne and royall dignitie of the kingdoms of England France and Ireland and the dominions thereunto belonging according to the resolution and desire of the said lords and commons contained in the said declaration. And thereupon their Majestyes were pleased that the said lords spirituall and temporall and commons being the two Houses of Parlyament should continue to sitt and with their Majesties royall concurrence make effectuall provision for the settlement of the religion lawes and liberties of this kingdome soe that the same for the future might not be in danger againe of being subverted, to which the said lords spirituall and temporall and commons did agree and proceede to act accordingly. Now in pursuance of the premises the said lords spirituall and temporall and commons in Parlyament assembled for the ratifying confirming and establishing the said declaration and the articles clauses matters and things therein contained by the force of a law made in due forme by authority of Parlyament doe pray that it may be declared and enacted that all and singular the rights and liberties asserted and claimed in the said declaration are the true auntient and indubitable rights and liberties of the people of this kingdome and soe shall be esteemed allowed adjudged deemed and taken to be and that all and every the paritculars aforesaid shall be firmly and strictly holden and observed as they are expressed in the said declaration. And all officers and ministers whatsoever shall serve their Majestyes and their successors according to the same in all times to come. And the said lords spirituall and temporall and commons seriously considering how it hath pleased Almighty God in his marvellous providence and mercifull goodness to this nation to provide and preserve their said Majestyes royall persons most happily to raigne over us upon the throne of their auncestors for which they render unto him from the bottome of their hearts their humblest thanks and praises doe truely firmly assuredly and in the sincerity of their hearts thinke and doe hereby recognize acknowledge and declare that King James the Second haveing abdicated the government and their Majestyes having accepted the crowne and royall dignity as aforesaid their said Majestyes did become were are and of right ought to be by the lawes of the realme our soveraigne liege lord and lady King and Queene of England France and Ireland and the dominions thereunto belonging in and to whose princely persons the royall state crowne and dignity of the said realmes with all honours stiles titles regalities prerogatives powers jurisdictions and authorities to the same belonging and appertaining are most fully and rightfully and intirely invested and incorporated united and annexed. And for preventing all questions and divisions in this realme by reason of any pretended titles to the crowne and for preserveing a certainty in the succession thereof in and upon which the unity peace tranquillity and safety of this nation doth under God wholly consist and depend the said lords spirituall and temporall and commons doe beseech their Majestyes that it may be enacted established and declared that the crowne and regall government of the said kingdoms and dominions with all and singular the premisses thereunto belonging and appertaining shall bee and continue to their said Majestyes and the survivour of them dureing their lives and the life of the survivour of them and that the entire perfect and full exercise of the regall power and government be onely in and executed by his Majestie in the names of both their Majestyes dureing their joynt lives and after their deceases the said crowne and premisses shall be and remaine to the heires of the body of her Majestie and for default of such issue to her royall Highnesse the Princess Anne of Denmarke and the heires of her body and for default of such issue to the heires of the body of his said Majestie And thereunto the said lords spirituall and temporall and commons doe in the name of all the people aforesaid most humbly and faithfully submitt themselves their heires and posterities for ever and doe faithfully promise that they will stand to maintaine and defend their said Majesties and alsoe the limitation and succession of the crowne herein specified and contained to the utmost of their powers with their lives and estates against all persons whatsoever that shall attempt any thing to the contrary. And whereas it hath beene found by experience that it is inconsistent with the safety and welfare of this protestant kingdome to be governed by a popish prince or by any King or Queene marrying a papist the said lords spirtuall and temporall and commons doe further pray that it may be enacted that all and every person and persons that is are or shall be reconciled to or shall hold communion with the see or church of Rome or shall professe the popish religion or shall marry a papist shall be excluded and be for ever uncapeable to inherit possesse or enjoy the crowne and government of this realme and Ireland and the dominions thereunto belonging or any part of the same or to have use or exercise any regall power authoritie or jurisdiction within the same And in all and every such case or cases the people of these realmes shall be and are hereby absolved of their allegiance and the said crowne and government shall from time to time descend to and be enjoyed by such person or persons being protestants as should have inherited and enjoyed the same in case the said person or persons soe reconciled holding communion or professing or marrying as aforesaid were naturally dead And that every King and Queene of this realme who at any time hereafter shall come to and succeede in the imperiall crowne of this kingdome shall on the first day of the meeting of the first Parlyament next after his or her comeing to the crowne sitting in his or her throne in the House of Peeres in the presence of the lords and commons therein assembled or at his or her coronation before such person or persons who shall administer the coronation oath to him or her at the time of his or her takeing the said oath (which shall first happen) make subscribe and audibly repeate the declaration mentioned in the Statute made in the thirtyeth yeare of the raigne of King Charles the Second entituled An Act for the more effectuall preserveing the Kings person and government by disableing papists from sitting in either House of Parlyament But if it shall happen that such King or Queene upon his or her succession to the crowne of this realme shall be under the age of twelve yeares then every such King or Queene shall make subscribe and audibly repeate the said declaration at his or her coronation or the first day of the meeting of the first Parlyament as aforesaid which shall first happen after such King or Queene shall have attained the said age of twelve years. All which their Majestyes are contented and pleased shall be declared enacted and established by authoritie of this present Parliament and shall stand remaine and be the law of this realme for ever And the same are by their said Majesties by and with the advice and consent of the lords spirituall and temporall and commons in Parlyament assembled and by the authoritie of the same declared enacted and established accordingly

2 Non obstantes made void
... noe dispensation by non obstante of or to any statute or any part thereof shall be allowed but ... the same shall be held void and of noe effect except a dispensation be allowed of in such statutes ...

3 ...

Crown and Parliament Recognition Act 1689
(2 Will. & Mar., c. 1)

An Act for Recognizing King William and Queene Mary and for avoiding all Questions touching the Acts made in the Parliament assembled at Westminster the thirteenth day of February one thousand six hundred eighty eight

Territorial extent: England and Wales, Northern Ireland (effectively extended to Scotland by the Union with Scotland Act 1706, below)

Wee your Majestyes most humble and loyall subjects the lords spirituall and temporall and commons in this present Parlyament assembled doe beseech your most excellent Majestyes that it may be publisehd and declared in this High Court of Parlyament and enacted by authoritie of the same that we doe recognize and acknowledge your Majestyes were are and of right ought to be by the laws of this realme our soveraigne liege lord and lady King and Queene of England France and Ireland and the dominions thereunto belonging in and to whose princely persons the royall state crowne and dignity of the said realms with all honours stiles tiles regalities prerogatives powers jurisdictions and authorities to the same belonging and appertaining are most fully rightfully and intirely invested and incorporated united and annexed. And for the avoiding of all disputes and questions concerning the being and authority of the late Parliament assembled at Westminster the thirteenth day of February one thousand six hundred eighty eight wee doe most humbly beseech your Majestyes that it may be enacted and bee it enacted by the King and Queenes most excellent Majestyes by and with the advice and consent of the lords spirituall and temporall and commons in this present Parlyament assembled and by authoritie of the same that all and singular the Acts made and enacted in the said Parlyament were and are laws and statutes of this kingdome and as such ought to be reputed taken and obeyed by all the people of this kingdome.

The Act of Settlement (1700)
(12 & 13 Will. 3, c. 2)

An Act for the further Limitation of the Crown and better securing the Rights and Liberties of the Subject

Territorial extent: England and Wales, Northern Ireland; effectively extended to Scotland by the Union with Scotland Act 1706.

Whereas in the first year of the reign of your Majesty and of our late most gracious soverign lady Queen Mary (of blessed memory) an Act of Parliament was made intituled (An Act for declaring the rights and liberties of the subject and for setling the succession of the crown) wherein it was (amongst other things) enacted established and declared that the crown and regall government of the kingdoms of England France and Ireland and the dominions thereunto belonging should be and continue to your Majestie and the said late Queen during the joynt lives of your Majesty and the said Queen and to the survivor and that after the decease of your Majesty and of the said Queen the said crown and regall government should be and remain to the heirs of the body of the said late Queen and for default of such issue to her royall Highness the Princess Ann of Denmark and the heirs of her body and for default of such issue to the heirs of the body of your Majesty And it was thereby further enacted that all and every person and persons that then were or afterwards should be reconciled to or shall hold communion with the see or church of Rome or should professe the popish religion or marry a papist should be excluded and are by that Act made for ever incapable to inherit possess or enjoy the crown and government of this realm and Ireland and the dominions thereunto belonging or any part of the same or to have use or exercise any regall power authority or jurisdiction within the same and in all and every such case and cases the people of these realms shall be and are thereby absolved of their allegiance and that the said crown and government shall from time to time descend to and be enjoyed by such person or persons being protestants as should have inherited and enjoyed the same in case the said person or persons so reconciled holding communion professing or marrying as aforesaid were naturally dead After the making of which Statute and the settlement therein contained your Majesties good subjects who were restored to the full and free possession and enjoyment of their religion rights and liberties by the providence of God giving success to your Majesties just undertakings and unwearied endeavours for that purpose had no greater temporall felicity to hope or wish for than to see a royall progeny descending from your Majesty to whom (under God) they owe their tranquility and whose ancestors have for many years been principall assertors of the reformed religion and the liberties of Europe and from our said most gracious sovereign lady whose memory will always be precious to the subjects of these realms And it having since pleased Almighty God to take away our said sovereign lady and also the most hopefull Prince William Duke of Gloucester (the only surviving issue of her royall Highness the Princess Ann of Denmark) to the unspeakable grief and sorrow of your Majesty and your said good subjects who under such losses being sensibly put in mind that it standeth wholly in the pleasure of Almighty God to prolong the lives of your Majesty and of her royall Highness and to grant to your Majesty or to her royall Highness such issue as may be inheritable to the crown and regall government aforesaid by the respective limitations in the said recited Act contained doe constantly implore the divine mercy for those blessings And your Majesties said subjects having daily experience of your royall care and concern for the present and future welfare of these kingdoms and particularly recommending from your throne a further provision to be made for the succession of the crown in the protestant line for the happiness of the nation and the security of our religion and it being absolutely necessary for the safety peace and quiet of this realm to obviate all doubts and contentions in the same by reason of any pretended titles to the crown and to maintain a certainty in the succession thereof to which your subjects may safely have recourse for their protection in case the limitations in the said recited Act should determine Therefore for a further provision of the succession of the crown in the protestant line we your Majesties most dutifull and loyal subjects the lords spirituall and temporall and commons in this present Parliament assembled do beseech your Majesty that it may be enacted and declared and be it enacted and declared by the Kings most excellent Majesty by and with the advice and consent of the lords spirituall and temporall and commons in this present Parliament assembled and by the authority of the same that

1   The Princess Sophia, Electress and Duchess dowager of Hanover, daughter of the late Queen of Bohemia, daughter of King James the First, to inherit after the King and the Princess Anne, in default of issue of the said princess and his Majesty, respectively; and the heirs of her body, being protestants

the most excellent Princess Sophia Electress and Dutchess dowager of Hanover daughter of the most excellent Princess Elizabeth late Queen of Bohemia daughter of our late sovereign lord King James the First of happy memory be and is hereby declared to be the next in succession in the protestant line to the imperiall crown and dignity of the [said] realms of England France and Ireland with the dominions and territories thereunto belonging after his Majesty and the Princess Ann of Denmark and in default of issue of the said Princess Ann and of his Majesty respectively and that from and after the deceases of his said Majesty our own soveriegn lord and of her royall Highness the Princess Ann of Denmark and for default of issue of the said Princess Ann and of his Majesty respectively the crown and regall government of the said kingdoms of England France and Ireland and of the dominions thereunto belonging with the royall state and dignity of the said realms and all honours stiles titles regalities prerogatives powers jurisdictions and authorities to the same belonging and appertaining shall be remain and continue to the said most excellent Princess Sophia and the heirs of her body being protestants And thereunto the said lords spirituall and temporall and commons shall and will in the name of all the people of this realm most humbly and faithfully submitt themselves their heirs and posterities and do faithfully promise that after the deceases of his Majesty and her royall Highness and the failure of the heirs of their respective bodies to stand to maintain and defend the said Princess Sophia and the heirs of her body being protestants according to the limitation and succession of the crown in this Act specified and contained to the utmost of their powers with their lives and estates against all persons whatsoever that shall attempt any thing to the contrary.

2   The persons inheritable by this Act, holding communion with the church of Rome, incapacitated as by the former Act; to take the oath at their coronation, according to Stat 1 W& M c. 6

Provided always and it is hereby enacted that all and every person and persons who shall or may take or inherit the said crownby vertue of the limitation of this present Act and is are or shall be reconciled to or shall hold communion with the see or church of Rome or shall profess the popish religion or shall marry a papist shall be subject to such incapacities as in such case or cases are by the said recited Act provided enacted and established. And that every King and Queen of this realm who shall come to and succeed in the imperiall crown of this kingdomby vertue of this Act shall have the coronation oath administered to him her or themat their respective coronations according to the Act of Parliament made in the first year of the reign of his Majesty and the said late Queen Mary intituled An Act for establishing the coronation oath and shall make subscribe and repeat the declaration in the Act first above recited mentioned or referred to in the manner and formthereby prescribed.

3   Further provisions for securing the religions, laws, and liberties of these realms

And whereas it is requisite and necessary that some further provision be made for securing our religion laws and liberties from and after the death of his Majesty and the Princess Ann of Denmark and in default of issue of the body of the said princess and of his Majesty respectively Be it enacted by the Kings most excellent Majesty by and with the advice and consent of the lords spirituall and temporall and commons in Parliament and by the authority of the same

That whosoever shall hereafter come to the possession of this crown shall joyn in communion with the Church of England as by law established

That in case the crown and imperiall dignity of this realm shall hereafter come to any person not being a native of this kingdom of England this nation be not obliged to ingage in any warr for the defence of any dominions or territories which do not belong to the crown of England without the consent of Parliament

· · · · ·

That after the said limitation shall take effect as aforesaid no person born out of the kingdoms of England Scotland or Ireland or the dominions thereunto belonging (although he be . . . made a denizen (except such as are born of English parents)) shall be capable to be of the privy councill or a member of either House of Parliament or to enjoy any office or place of trust either civill or military or to have any grant of lands tenements or hereditaments from the Crown to himself or to any other or others in trust for him.

· · · · ·

That no pardon under the great seal of England be pleadable to an impeachment by the commons in Parliament.

4   The laws and statutes of the realm confirmed

And whereas the laws of England are the birthright of the people thereof and all the Kings and Queens who shall ascend the throne of this realm ought to administer the government of the same according to the said laws and all their officers and ministers ought to serve them respectively according to the same The said lords spirituall and temporall and commons do therefore further humbly pray that all the laws and statutes of this realm for securing the established religion and the rights and liberties of the people thereof and all other laws and statutes of the same now in force may be ratified and confirmed And the same are by his Majesty by and with the advice and consent of the said lords spirituall and temporall and commons and by authority of the same ratified and confirmed accordingly.

Union with Scotland Act 1706
(6 Anne, c. 11)

An Act for an Union of the Two Kingdoms of England and Scotland

Territorial extent: England, Wales and Scotland (by the combined effect of this Act and the equivalent Act of the Parliament of Scotland (APS, XI, 406)); subsequently applied to Northern Ireland

Most Gracious Sovereign
Whereas articles of union were agreed on the twenty second day of July in the fifth year of your Majesties reign by the commissioners nominated on behalf of the kingdom of England under your Majesties great seal of England bearing date at Westminster the tenth day of April then last past in pursuance of an Act of Parliament made in England in the third year of your Majesties reign and the commissioners nominated on the behalf of the kingdom of Scotland under your Majesties great seal of Scotland bearing date the twenty-seventh day of February in the fourth year of your Majesties reign in pursuance of the fourth Act of the third session of the present Parliament of Scotland to treat of and concerning an union of the said kingdoms And whereas an Act hath passed in the Parliament of Scotland at Edinburgh the sixteenth day of January in the fifth year of your Majesties reign wherein "tis mentioned that the estates of Parliament considering the said articles of union of the two kingdoms had agreed to and approved of the said articles of union with some additions and explanations and that your Majesty with advice and consent of the estates of Parliament for establishing the Protestant religion and Presbyterian Church government within the kingdom of Scotland had passed in the same session of Parliament an Act intituled Act for securing of the Protestant religion and Presbyterian Church government which by the tenor thereof was appointed to be inserted in any Act ratifying the treaty and expresly declared to be a fundamental and essential condition of the said treaty or union in all times coming the tenor of which articles as ratified and approved of with additions and explanations by the said Act of Parliament of Scotland follows.

Article I

The kingdoms united; ensigns armorial—That the two kingdoms of England and Scotland shall upon the first day of May which shall be in the year one thousand seven hundred and seven and for ever after be united into one kingdom by the name of Great Britain and that the ensigns armorial of the said United Kingdom be such as her Majesty shall appoint and the crosses of St. George and St. Andrew be conjoyned in such manner as Her Majesty shall think fit and used in all flags banners standards and ensigns both at sea and land.

Article II

Succession to the monarchy—That the succession to the monarchy of the United Kingdom of Great Britain and of the dominions thereto belonging after her most sacred Majesty and in default of issue of her Majesty be remain and continue to the most excellent Princess Sophia Electoress and Dutchess dowager of Hanover and the heirs of her body being protestants upon whom the crown of England is settled by an Act of Parliament made in England in the twelfth year of the reign of his late Majesty King William the Third intituled An Act for the further limitation of the crown and better securing the right and liberties of the subject And that all papists and persons marrying papists shall be excluded from and for ever incapable to inherit possess or enjoy the imperial crown of Great Britain and the dominions thereunto belonging or any part thereof and in every such case the crown and government shall from time to time descend to and be enjoyed by such person being a protestant as should have inherited and enjoyed the same in case such papist or person marrying a papist was naturally dead according to the provision for the descent of the crown of England made by another Act of Parliament in England in the first year of the reign of their late Majesties King William and Queen Mary intituled An Act declaring the rights and liberties of the subject and settling the succession of the crown.

Article III

Parliament—That the United Kingdom of Great Britain be represented by one and the same Parliament to be stiled the Parliament of Great Britain.

Article IIII

Trade and navigation and other rights—That all the subjects of the United Kingdom of Great Britain shall from and after the union have full freedom and intercourse of trade and navigation to and from any port or place within the said United Kingdom and the dominions and plantations thereunto belonging and that there be a communication of all other rights privileges and advantages which do or may belong to the subjects of either kingdom except where it is otherwise expressly agreed in these articles.

Article V . . .

Article VI

Regulations of trade, duties, etc.—That all parts of the United Kingdom for ever from and after the union shall have the same allowances encouragements and drawbacks and be under the same prohibitions restrictions and regulations of trade and liable to the same customs and duties on import and export and that the allowances encouragements and drawbacks prohibitions restrictions and regulations of trade and the customs and duties on import and export settled in England when the union commences shall from and after the union take place throughout the whole United Kingdom . . .

Articles VII, XVI*****

Articles VIII–XV, XVII . . .

Article XVIII

Laws concerning public rights; private rights—That the laws concerning regulation of trade customs and such excises to which Scotland is by virtue of this treaty to be liable be the same in Scotland from and after the union as in England and that all other laws in use within the kingdom of Scotland do after the union and notwithstanding thereof remain in the same force as before (except such as are contrary to or inconsistent with this treaty) but alterable by the Parliament of Great Britain with this difference betwixt the laws concerning publick right policy and civil government and those which concern private right that the laws which concern publick right policy and civil government may be made the same throughout the whole United Kingdom. But that no alteration be made in laws which concern private right except for evident utility of the subjects within Scotland

*****

Article XXV

Laws inconsistent with the articles, void—That all laws and statutes in either kingdom so far as they are contrary to or inconsistent with the terms of these articles or any of them shall from and after the union cease and become void and shall be so declared to be by the respective Parliaments of the said kingdoms.

As by the said articles of union ratified and approved by the said Act of Parliament of Scotland relation being thereunto had may appear.

*****

5   Cap 8 ante, and the said Act of Parliament of Scotland to be observed as fundamental conditions of the said union; and the said articles and Acts of Parliament to continue the union

And it is hereby further enacted by the authority aforesaid that the said Act passed in this present session of Parliament intituled An Act for securing the Church of England as by law established and all and every the matters and things therein contained and also the said Act of Parliament of Scotland intituled Act for securing the Protestant religion and Presbyterian Church government with the establishment in the said Act contained be and shall for ever be held and adjudged to be and observed as fundamental and essential conditions of the said union and shall in all times coming be taken to be and are hereby declared to be essential and fundamental parts of the said articles and union and the said articles of union so as aforesaid ratified approved and confirmed by Act of Parliament of Scotland and by this present Act and the said Act passed in this present session of Parliament intituled an Act for securing the Church of England as by law established and also the said Act passed in the Parliament of Scotland intituled Act for securing the Protestant religion and Presbyterian Church government are hereby enacted and ordained to be and continue in all times coming the complete and intire union of the two kingdoms of England and Scotland.

*****

Metropolitan Police Act 1839

(2 & 3 Vict., c. 47)

An Act for further improving the Police in and near the Metropolis

Territorial extent: Metropolitan Police Area and City of London

*****

52   Commissioners may make regulations for the route of carriages, and persons, and for preventing obstruction of the streets during public processions, etc., or in the neighbourhood of public buildings, etc.

... It shall be lawful for the commissioners of police from time to time, and as occasion shall require, to make regulations for the route to be observed by all carts, carriages, horses, and persons, and for preventing obstruction of the streets and thoroughfares within the metropolitan police district, in all times of public processions, public rejoicings, or illuminations, and also to give directions to the constables for keeping order and for preventing any obstruction of the thoroughfares in the immediate neighbourhood of her Majesty's palaces and the public offices, the High Court of Parliament, the courts of law and equity, the [magistrates' courts], the theatres, and other places of public resort, and in any case when the streets or thoroughfares may be thronged or may be liable to be obstructed.

*****

Customs Consolidation Act 1876
(39 & 40 Vict., c. 36)

An Act to consolidate the Customs Laws

Territorial extent: United Kingdom

AS TO THE IMPORTATION, PROHIBITION, ENTRY, EXAMINATION, LANDING, AND WAREHOUSING OF GOODS

. . .

42   Prohibitions and restrictions
The goods enumerated and described in the following table of prohibitions and restrictions inwards are hereby prohibited to be imported or brought into the United Kingdom . . .

A TABLE OF PROHIBITIONS AND RESTRICTIONS INWARDS

Goods prohibited to be imported

. . .

Indecent or obscene prints, paintings, photographs, books, cards, lithographic or other engravings, or any other indecent or obscene articles.

*****

Riot (Damages) Act 1886
(49 & 50 Vict., c. 38)

An Act to provide compensation for Losses by Riots

Territorial extent: England and Wales. (For Scotland see the Riotous Assembly (Scotland) Act 1822.)

1   Short title
This Act may be cited for all purposes as the Riot (Damages) Act 1886.

2   Compensation to persons for damage by riot
(1) Where a house, shop, or building in [a police area] has been injured or destroyed, or the property therein has been injured, stolen, or destroyed, by any persons riotously and tumultuously assembled together, such compensation as herein-after mentioned shall be paid out of [the police fund] of [the area] to any person who has sustained loss by such injury, stealing, or destruction; but in fixing the amount of such compensation regard shall be had to the conduct of the said person, whether as respects the precautions taken by him or as respects his being a party or accessory to such riotous or tumultuous assembly, or as regards any provocation offered to the persons assembled or otherwise.

(2) Where any person having sustained such loss as aforesaid has received, by way of insurance or otherwise, any sum to recoup him, in whole or in part, for such loss, the compensation otherwise payable to him under this Act shall, if exceeding such sum, be reduced by the amount thereof, and in any other case shall not be paid to him, and the payer of such sum shall be entitled to compensation under this Act in respect of the sum so paid in like manner as if he had sustained the said loss, and any policy of insurance given by such payer shall continue in force as if he had made no such payment, and where such person was recouped as aforesaid otherwise than by payment of a sum, this enactment shall apply as if the value of such recoupment were a sum paid.

*****

Note: Section 10 of the Public Order Act 1986 provides that "riotous" and "riotously" in this Act are to be construed in accordance with the definition of "riot" in that Act.

Public Meeting Act 1908
(8 Edw. 7, c. 66)

An Act to prevent disturbance of Public Meetings

Territorial extent: England and Wales, Scotland

1   Penalty on endeavour to break up public meeting
(1) Any person who at a lawful public meeting acts in a disorderly manner for the purpose of preventing the transaction of the business for which the meeting was called together shall be guilty of an offence [and shall on summary conviction be liable to imprisonment for a term not exceeding six months or to a fine not exceeding [level 5 on the standard scale] or to both] . . .

(2) Any person who incites others to commit an offence under this section shall be guilty of a like offence.

[(3) If any constable reasonably suspects any person of committing an offence under the foregoing provisions of this section, he may if requested so to do by the chairman of the meeting require that person to declare to him immediately his name and address and, if that person refuses or fails so to declare his name and address or gives a false name and address he shall be guilty of an offence under this subsection and liable on summary conviction thereof to a fine not exceeding [level 1 on the standard scale], . . .]

[(4) This section does not apply as respects meetings to which section 97 of the Representation of the People Act 1983 applies.]

Official Secrets Act 1911
(1 & 2 Geo. 5, c. 28)

An Act to re-enact the Official Secrets Act 1889, with Amendments

Territorial extent: United Kingdom. See also s. 10(1)

Note: Printed as amended by the Official Secrets Act 1920; section 2 was repealed by the Official Secrets Act 1989 (below).

1 Penalties for spying
(1) If any person for any purpose prejudicial to the safety or interests of the State—
    (a) approaches [inspects, passes over] or is in the neighbourhood of, or enters any prohibited place within the meaning of this Act; or
    (b) makes any sketch, plan, model, or note which is calculated to be or might be or is intended to be directly or indirectly useful to an enemy; or
    (c) obtains, [collects, records, or publishes,] or communicates to any other person [any secret official code word or pass word, or] any sketch, plan, model, article, or note, or other document or information which is calculated to be or might be or is intended to be directly or indirectly useful to an enemy;
he shall be guilty of felony . . .

(2) On a prosecution under this section, it shall not be necessary to show that the accused person was guilty of any particular act tending to show a purpose prejudicial to the safety or interests of the State, and, notwithstanding that no such act is proved against him, he may be convicted if, from the circumstances of the case, or his conduct, or his known character as proved, it appears that his purpose was a purpose prejudicial to the safety or interests of the State; and if any sketch, plan, model, article, note, document, or information relating to or used in any prohibited place within the meaning of this Act, or anything in such a place [or any secret official code word or pass word], is made, obtained, [collected, recorded, published], or communicated by any person other than a person acting under lawful authority, it shall be deemed to have been made, obtained, [collected, recorded, published] or communicated for a purpose prejudicial to the safety or interests of the State unless the contrary is proved.

2 . . .

3 Definition of prohibited place
For the purposes of this Act, the expression "prohibited place" means—
    [(a) any work of defence, arsenal, naval or air force establishment or station, factory, dockyard, mine, minefield, camp, ship, or aircraft belonging to or occupied by or on behalf of His Majesty, or any telegraph, telephone, wireless or signal station, or office so belonging or occupied, and any place belonging to or occupied by or on behalf of His Majesty and used for the purpose of building, repairing, making, or storing any munitions of war, or any sketches, plans, models, or documents relating thereto, or for the purpose of getting any metals, oil, or minerals of use in time of war];
    (b) any place not belonging to His Majesty where any [munitions of war], or any [sketches, models, plans] or documents relating thereto, are being made, repaired, [gotten] or stored under contract with, or with any person on behalf of, His Majesty, or otherwise on behalf of His Majesty; and
    (c) any place belonging to [or used for the purposes of] His Majesty which is for the time being declared [by order of a Secretary of State] to be a prohibited place for the purposes of this section on the ground that information with respect thereto, or damage thereto, would be useful to an enemy; and

(d) any railway, road, way, or channel, or other means of communication by land or water (including any works or structures being part thereof or connected therewith), or any place used for gas, water, or electricity works or other works for purposes of a public character, or any place where any [munitions of war], or any [sketches, models, plans] or documents relating thereto, are being made, repaired, or stored otherwise than on behalf of His Majesty, which is for the time being declared [by order or a Secretary of State] to be a prohibited place for the purposes of this section, on the ground that information with respect thereto, or the destruction or obstruction thereof, or interference therewith, would be useful to an enemy.

4–6 . . .

7 *****

8 Restriction on prosecution
A prosecution for an offence under this Act shall not be instituted except by or with the consent of the Attorney-General:

. . . . .

9 Search warrants
(1) If a justice of the peace is satisfied by information on oath that there is reasonable ground for suspecting that an offence under this Act has been or is about to be committed, he may grant a search warrant authorising any constable . . . to enter at any time any premises or place named in the warrant, if necessary, by force, and to search the premises or place and every person found therein, and to seize any sketch, plan, model, article, note, or document, or anything of a like nature or anything which is evidence of an offence under this Act having been or being about to be committed, which he may find on the premises or place or on any such person, and with regard to or in connexion with which he has reasonable ground for suspecting that an offence under this Act has been or is about to be committed.

(2) Where it appears to a superintendent of police that the case is one of great emergency and that in the interests of the State immediate action is necessary, he may by a written order under his hand give to any constable the like authority as may be given by the warrant of a justice under the section.

10 Extent of Act and place of trial of offence
(1) This Act shall apply to all acts which are offences under this Act when committed in any part of His Majesty's dominions, or when committed by British officers or subjects elsewhere.

*****

Parliament Act 1911
(1 & 2 Geo. 5, c. 13)

An Act to make provision with respect to the powers of the House of Lords in relation of the House of Commons, and to limit the duration of Parliament

Territorial extent: United Kingdom

Note: The words in square brackets in s. 2 were substituted by the Parliament Act 1949.

Preamble
Whereas it is expedient that provision should be made for regulating the relations between the two Houses of Parliament:

And whereas it is intended to substitute for the House of Lords as it at present exists a Second Chamber constituted on a popular instead of hereditary basis, but such substitution cannot be immediately brought into operation:

And whereas provision will require hereafter to be made by Parliament in a measure effecting such substitution for limiting and defining the powers of the new Second Chamber, but it is expedient to make such provision as in this Act appears for restricting the existing powers of the House of Lords:

1 Powers of House of Lords as to Money Bills

(1) If a Money Bill, having been passed by the House of Commons, and sent up to the House of Lords at least one month before the end of the session, is not passed by the House of Lords without amendment within one month after it is so sent up to that House, the Bill shall, unless the House of Commons direct to the contrary, be presented to His Majesty and become an Act of Parliament on the Royal Assent being signified, notwithstanding that the House of Lords have not consented to the Bill.

(2) A Money Bill means a Public Bill which in the opinion of the Speaker of the House of Commons contains only provisions dealing with all or any of the following subjects, namely, the imposition, repeal, remission, alteration, or regulation of taxation; the imposition for the payment of debt or other financial purposes of charges on the Consolidated Fund, [the National Loans Fund] or on money provided by Parliament, or the variation or repeal of any such charges; supply; the appropriation, receipt, custody, issue or audit of accounts of public money; the raising or guarantee of any loan or the repayment thereof; or subordinate matters incidental to those subjects or any of them. In this subsection the expressions "taxation", "public money" and "loan" respectively do not include any taxation, money, or loan raised by local authorities or bodies for local purposes.

(3) There shall be endorsed on every Money Bill when it is sent up to the House of Lords and when it is presented to His Majesty for assent the certificate of the Speaker of the House of Commons signed by him that it is a Money Bill. Before giving his certificate, the Speaker shall consult, if practicable, two members to be appointed from the Chairmen's Panel at the beginning of each Session by the Committee of Selection.

2 Restriction of the powers of the House of Lords as to Bills other than Money Bills

(1) If any Public Bill (other than a Money Bill or a Bill containing any provision to extend the maximum duration of Parliament beyond five years) is passed by the House of Commons [in two successive sessions] (whether of the same Parliament or not), and, having been sent up to the House of Lords at least one month before the end of the session, is rejected by the House of Lords in each of those sessions, that Bill shall, on its rejection [for the second time] by the House of Lords, unless the House of Commons direct to the contrary, be presented to His Majesty and become an Act of Parliament on the Royal Assent being signified thereto, notwithstanding that the House of Lords have not consented to the Bill: Provided that this provision shall not take effect unless [one year has elapsed] between the date of the second reading in the first of those sessions of the Bill in the House of Commons and the date on which it passes the House of Commons [in the second of those sessions].

(2) When a Bill is presented to His Majesty for assent in pursuance of the provisions of this section, there shall be endorsed on the Bill the certificate of the Speaker of the House of Commons signed by him that the provisions of this section have been duly complied with.

(3) A Bill shall be deemed to be rejected by the House of Lords if it is not passed by the House of Lords either without amendment or with such amendments only as may be agreed to by both Houses.

(4) A Bill shall be deemed to be the same Bill as a former Bill sent up to the House of Lords in the preceding session if, when it is sent up to the House of Lords, it is identical with the

former Bill or contains only such alterations as are certified by the Speaker of the House of Commons to be necessary owing to the time which has elapsed since the date of the former Bill, or to represent any amendments which have been made by the House of Lords in the former Bill in the preceding sesion, and any amendments which are certified by the Speaker to have been made by the House of Lords [in the second session] and agreed to by the House of Commons shall be inserted in the Bill as presented for Royal Assent in pursuance of this section:

Provided that the House of Commons may, if they think fit, on the passage of such a Bill through the House [in the second session], suggest any further amendments without inserting the amendments in the Bill, and any such suggested amendments shall be considered by the House of Lords, and, if agreed to by that House, shall be treated as amendments made by the House of Lords and agreed to by the House of Commons; but the exercise of this power by the House of Commons shall not affect the operation of this section in the event of the Bill being rejected by the House of Lords.

3   Certificate of Speaker

Any certificate of the Speaker of the House of Commons given under this Act shall be conclusive for all purposes, and shall not be questioned in any court of law.

4   Enacting words

(1) In every Bill presented to His Majesty under the preceding provisions of this Act, the words of enactment shall be as follows, that is to say:–

"Be it enacted by the King's most Excellent Majesty, by and with the advice and consent of the Commons in this present Parliament assembled, in accordance with the provisions of [the Parliament Acts 1911 and 1949], and by authority of the same, as follows."

(2) Any alteration of a Bill necessary to give effect to this section shall not be deemed to be an amendment of the Bill.

5   Provisional Order Bills excluded

In this Act the expression "Public Bill" does not include any Bill for confirming a Provisional Order.

6   Saving for existing rights and privileges of the House of Commons

Nothing in this Act shall diminish or qualify the existing rights and privileges of the House of Commons.

7   Duration of Parliament

Five years shall be substituted for seven years as the time fixed for the maximum duration of Parliament under the Septennial Act, 1715.

Official Secrets Act 1920

(10 & 11 Geo. 5, c. 75)

An Act to amend the Official Secrets Act 1911

Territorial extent: United Kingdom

1   Unauthorised use of uniforms; falsification of reports, forgery, personation, and false documents

(1) If any person for the purpose of gaining admission, or of assisting any other person to gain admission, to a prohibited place, within the meaning of the Official Secrets Act 1911 (hereinafter referred to as "the principal Act"), or for any other purpose prejudicial to the safety or interests of the State within the meaning of the said Act—

(a) uses or wears, without lawful authority, any naval, military, air-force, police, or other official uniform, or any uniform so nearly resembling the same as to be calculated to deceive, or falsely represents himself to be a person who is or has been entitled to use or wear any such uniform; or

(b) orally, or in writing in any declaration or application, or in any document signed by him or on his behalf, knowingly makes or connives at the making of any false statement or any omission; or

(c) . . . tampers with any passport or any naval, military, air-force, police, or official pass, permit, certificate, licence, or other document of a similar character (herein-after in this section referred to as an official document), . . . or has in his possession any . . . forged, altered, or irregular official document; or

(d) personates, or falsely represents himself to be a person holding, or in the employ-ment of a person holding office under His Majesty, or to be or not to be a person to whom an official document or secret official code word or pass word has been duly issued or communicated, or with intent to obtain an official document, secret official code word or pass word, whether for himself or any other person, know-ingly makes any false statement; or

(e) uses, or has in his possession or under his control, without the authority of the Government Department or the authority concerned, any die, seal, or stamp of or belonging to, or used, made or provided by any Government Department, or by any diplomatic, naval, military, or air force authority appointed by or acting under the authority of His Majesty, or any die, seal or stamp so nearly resembling any such die, seal or stamp as to be calculated to deceive, or counterfeits any such die, seal or stamp, or uses, or has in his possession, or under his control, any such counterfeited die, seal or stamp;

he shall be guilty of a misdemeanour.

(2) If any person—

(a) retains for any purpose prejudicial to the safety or interests of the State any official document, whether or not completed or issued for use, when he has no right to retain it, or when it is contrary to his duty to retain it, or fails to comply with any directions issued by any Government Department or any person authorised by such department with regard to the return or disposal thereof; or

(b) allows any other person to have possession of any official document issued for his use alone, or communicates any secret official code word or pass word so issued, or, without lawful authority or excuse, has in his possession any official document or secret official code word or pass word issued for the use of some person other than himself, or on obtaining possession of any official document by finding or otherwise, neglects or fails to restore it to the person or authority by whom or for whose use it was issued, or to a police constable; or

(c) without lawful authority or excuse, manufactures or sells, or has in his possession for sale any such die, seal or stamp as aforesaid;

he shall be guilty of a misdemeanour.

(3) In the case of any prosecution under this section involving the proof of a purpose prejudicial to the safety or interests of the State, subsection (2) of section one of the principal Act shall apply in like manner as it applies to prosecutions under that section.

2–3   *****

4–5   . . .

6 Duty of giving information as to commission of offences

[(1) Where a chief officer of police is satisfied that there is reasonable ground for suspecting that an offence under section one of the principal Act has been committed and for believing that any person is able to furnish information as to the offence or suspected offence, he may apply to a Secretary of State for permission to exercise the powers conferred by this subsection and, if such permission is granted, he may authorise a superintendent of police, or any police officer not below the rank of inspector, to require the person believed to be able to furnish information to give any information in his power relating to the offence or suspected offence, and, if so required and on tender of his reasonable expenses, to attend at such reasonable time and place as may be specified by the superintendent or other officer; and if a person required in pursuance of such an authorisation to give information, or to attend as aforesaid, fails to comply with any such requirement or knowingly gives false information, he shall be guilty of a misdemeanour.

(2) Where a chief officer of police has reasonable grounds to believe that the case is one of great emergency and that in the interest of the State immediate action is necessary, he may exercise the powers conferred by the last foregoing subsection without applying for or being granted the permission of a Secretary of State, but if he does so shall forthwith report the circumstances to the Secretary of State.

(3) References in this section to a chief officer of police shall be construed as including references to any other officer of police expressly authorised by a chief officer of police to act on his behalf for the purposes of this section when by reason of illness, absence or other cause he is unable to do so.]

*****

The Statute of Westminster 1931
(22 & 23 Geo. 5, c. 4)

An Act to give effect to certain resolutions passed by Imperial Conferences held in the years 1926 and 1930

Territorial extent: As indicated in the Act (and see note to section 4)

Whereas the delegates of His Majesty's Governments in the United Kingdom, the Dominion of Canada, the Commonwealth of Australia, the Dominion of New Zealand, the Union of South Africa, the Irish Free State and Newfoundland, at Imperial Conferences holden at Westminster in the years of our Lord nineteen hundred and twenty-six and nineteen hundred and thirty did concur in making the declarations and resolutions set forth in the Reports of the said Conferences:

And whereas it is meet and proper to set out by way of preamble to this Act that, inasmuch as the Crown is the symbol of the free association of the members of the British Commonwealth of Nations, and as they are united by a common allegiance to the Crown, it would be in accord with the established constitutional position of all the members of the Commonwealth in relation to one another that any alteration in the law touching the Succession to the Throne or the Royal Style and Titles shall hereafter require the assent as well of the Parliaments of all the Dominions as of the Parliament of the United Kingdom:

And whereas it is in accord with the established constitutional position that no law hereafter made by the Parliament of the United Kingdom shall extend to any of the said Dominions as part of the law of that Dominion otherwise than at the request and with the consent of that Dominion:

And whereas it is necessary for the ratifying, confirming and establishing of certain of the said declarations and resolutions of the said Conferences that a law be made and enacted in due form by authority of the Parliament of the United Kingdom:

And whereas the Dominion of Canada, the Commonwealth of Australia, the Dominion of New Zealand, the Union of South Africa, the Irish Free State and Newfoundland have severally requested and consented to the submission of a measure to the Parliament of the United Kingdom for making such provision with regard to the matters aforesaid as is hereafter in this Act contained:

1   Meaning of "Dominion" in this Act

In this Act the expression "Dominion" means any of the following Dominions, that is to say, the Dominion of Canada, the Commonwealth of Australia, the Dominion of New Zealand, . . . the Irish Free State and Newfoundland.

2   Validity of laws made by Parliament of a Dominion

(1) The Colonial Laws Validity Act 1865 shall not apply to any law made after the commencement of this Act by the Parliament of a Dominion.

(2) No law and no provision of any law made after the commencement of this Act by the Parliament of a Dominion shall be void or inoperative on the ground that it is repugnant to the law of England, or to the provisions of any existing or future Act of Parliament of the United Kingdom, or to any order, rule or regulation made under any such Act, and the powers of the Parliament of a Dominion shall include the power to repeal or amend any such Act, order, rule or regulation in so far as the same is part of the law of the Dominion.

3   Power of Parliament of Dominion to legislate extra-territorally

It is hereby declared and enacted that the Parliament of a Dominion has full power to make laws having extra-territorial operation.

4   Parliament of United Kingdom not to legislate for Dominion except by consent

No Act of Parliament of the United Kingdom passed after the commencement of this Act shall extend, or be deemed to extend, to a Dominion as part of the law of that Dominion unless it is expressly declared in that Act that that Dominion has requested, and consented to, the enactment thereof.

Note: This section has been repealed in relation to Canada by the Canada Act 1982 s. 1, Sch B and in relation to Australia by the Australia Act 1986 s. 12.

*****

Public Order Act 1936
(1 Edw. 8 & 1 Geo. 6, c. 6)

An Act to prohibit the wearing of uniforms in connection with political objects and the maintenance by private persons of associations of military or similar character; and to make further provision for the preservation of public order on the occasion of public processions and meetings and in public places

Territorial extent: England and Wales, Scotland (s 8: Scotland only)

1   Prohibition of uniforms in connection with political objects

(1) Subject as hereinafter provided, any person who in any public place or at any public meeting wears uniform signifying his association with any political organisation or with the promotion of any political object shall be guilty of an offence:

Provided that, if the chief officer of police is satisfied that the wearing of any such uniform as aforesaid on any ceremonial, anniversary, or other special occasion will not be likely to involve risk of public disorder, he may, with the consent of a Secretary of State, by order permit the wearing of such uniform on that occasion either absolutely or subject to such conditions as may be specified in the order.

(2) Where any person is charged before any court with an offence under this section, no further proceedings in respect thereof shall be taken against him without the consent of the Attorney-General [except such as are authorised by [section 6 of the Prosecution of Offences Act 1979]] so, however, that if that person is remanded in custody he shall, after the expiration of a period of eight days from the date on which he was so remanded, be entitled to be [released on bail] without sureties unless within that period the Attorney-General has consented to such further proceedings as aforesaid.

2   Prohibition of quasi-military organisations

(1) If the members or adherents of any association of persons, whether incorporated or not, are—

(a) organised or trained or equipped for the purpose of enabling them to be employed in usurping the functions of the police or of the armed forces of the Crown; or

(b) organised and trained or organised and equipped either for the purpose of enabling them to be employed for the use or display of physical force in promoting any political object, or in such manner as to arouse reasonable apprehension that they are organised and either trained or equipped for that purpose;

then any person who takes part in the control or management of the association, or in so organising or training as aforesaid any members or adherents thereof, shall be guilty of an offence under this section:

Provided that in any proceedings against a person charged with the offence of taking part in the control or management of such an association as aforesaid it shall be a defence to that charge to prove that he neither consented to nor connived at the organisation, training, or equipment of members or adherents of the association in contravention of the provisions of this section.

(2) No prosecution shall be instituted under this section without the consent of the Attorney-General.

(3), (4) *****

(5) If a judge of the High Court is satisfied by information on oath that there is reasonable ground for suspecting that an offence under this section has been committed, and that evidence of the commission thereof is to be found at any premises or place specified in the information, he may, on an application made by an officer of police of a rank not lower than that of inspector, grant a search warrant authorising any such officer as aforesaid named in the warrant together with any other persons named in the warrant and any other officers of police to enter the premises or place at any time within [three months] from the date of the warrant, if necessary by force, and to search the premises or place and every person found therein, and to seize anything found on the premises or place or on any such person which the officer has reasonable ground for suspecting to be evidence of the commission of such an offence as aforesaid:

Provided that no woman shall, in pursuance of a warrant issued under this subsection, be searched except by a woman.

(6) Nothing in this section shall be construed as prohibiting the employment of a reasonable number of persons as stewards to assist in the preservation of order at any public meeting held upon private premises, or the making of arrangements for that purpose or the instruction of the persons to be so employed in their lawful duties as such stewards, or their being furnished with badges or other distinguishing signs.

3–5A   ...

6 (Amends the Public Meeting Act 1908, printed above as amended).

7 Enforcement

(1) Any person who commits an offence under section two of this Act shall be liable on summary conviction to imprisonment for a term not exceeding six months or to a fine not exceeding [the prescribed sum], or to both such imprisonment and fine, or, on conviction on indictment, to imprisonment for a term not exceeding two years or to a fine . . . or to both such imprisonment and fine.

(2) Any person guilty of [any offence under this Act other than an offence under section 2 . . .] shall be liable on summary conviction to imprisonment for a term not exceeding [51 weeks] or to a fine not exceeding [level 4 on the standard scale], or to both such imprisonment and fine.

(3) . . .

8 Application to Scotland

This Act shall apply to Scotland subject to the following modifications:—

(1) Subsection (2) of section one and subsection (2) of section two of this Act shall not apply.

(2) In subsection (3) of section two the Lord Advocate shall be substituted for the Attorney-General and the Court of Session shall be substituted for the High Court.

(3) Subsection (5) of section two shall have effect as if for any reference to a judge of the High Court there were substituted a reference to the Sheriff and any application for a search warrant under the said subsection shall be made by the procurator fiscal instead of such officer as is therein mentioned.

(4) The power conferred on the sheriff by subsection (5) of section two, as modified by the last foregoing paragraph, shall not be exercisable by [honorary sheriff].

(5), (6) . . .

9 Interpretation, etc.

(1) In this Act the following expressions have the meanings hereby respectively assigned to them, that is to say:—

. . .

"Meeting" means a meeting held for the purpose of the discussion of matters of public interest or for the purpose of the expression of views on such matters;

"Private premises" means premises to which the public have access (whether on payment or otherwise) only by permission of the owner, occupier, or lessee of the premises;

"Public meeting" includes any meeting in a public place and any meeting which the public or any section thereof are permitted to attend, whether on payment or otherwise;

["Public place" includes any highway and any other premises or place to which at the material time the public have or are permitted to have access, whether on payment or otherwise;]

. . .

*****

Statutory Instruments Act 1946

(9 & 10 Geo. 6, c. 36)

An Act to repeal the Rules Publication Act, 1893, and to make further provision as to the instruments by which statutory powers to make orders, rules, regulations and other subordinate legislation are exercised   [26 March 1946]

Territorial extent: United Kingdom

Note: By virtue of the Scotland Act (Transitory and Transitional Provisions) (Statutory Instruments) Order 1999 any reference in section 1 below to an Act includes a reference to an Act of the Scottish Parliament and later sections are to be read to apply to the Scottish Parliament. Similarly references to powers exercisable by Ministers of the Crown shall include the Scottish Ministers in accordance with the Order.

1   Definition of "Statutory Instrument"

(1) Where by this Act or any Act passed after the commencement of this Act power to make, confirm or approve orders, rules, regulations or other subordinate legislation is conferred on His Majesty in Council or on any Minister of the Crown then, if the power is expressed—

(a) in the case of a power conferred on His Majesty, to be exercisable by Order in Council;

(b) in the case of a power conferred on a Minister of the Crown, to be exercisable by statutory instrument,

any document by which that power is exercised shall be known as a "statutory instrument" and the provisions of this Act shall apply thereto accordingly.

[(1A) The References in subsection (1) to a Minister of the Crown shall be construed as including references to the National Assembly for Wales.]

(2) Where by any Act passed before the commencement of this Act power to make statutory rules within the meaning of the Rules Publication Act, 1893, was conferred on any rule-making authority within the meaning of that Act, any document by which that power is exercised after the commencement of this Act shall, save as is otherwise provided by regulations made under this Act, be known as a "statutory instrument" and the provisions of this Act shall apply thereto accordingly.

2   Numbering, printing, publication and citation

(1) Immediately after the making of any statutory instrument, it shall be sent to the King's printer of Acts of Parliament and numbered in accordance with regulations made under this Act, and except in such cases as may be provided by any Act passed after the commencement of this Act or prescribed by regulations made under this Act, copies thereof shall as soon as possible be printed and sold by [or under the authority of] the King's printer of Acts of Parliament.

(2) Any statutory instrument may, without prejudice to any other mode of citation, be cited by the number given to it in accordance with the provisions of this section, and the calendar year.

3   Supplementary provisions as to publication

(1) Regulations made for the purposes of this Act shall make provision for the publication by His Majesty's Stationery Office of lists showing the date upon which every statutory instrument printed and sold by [or under the authority of] the King's printer of Acts of Parliament was first issued by [or under the authority of] that office; and in any legal proceedings a copy of any list so published . . . shall be received in evidence as a true copy, and an entry therein shall be conclusive evidence of the date on which any statutory instrument was first issued by [or under the authority of] His Majesty's Stationery Office.

(2) In any proceedings against any person for an offence consisting of a contravention of any such statutory instrument, it shall be a defence to prove that the instrument had not been issued by [or under the authority of] His Majesty's Stationery Office at the date of the alleged contravention unless it is proved that at that date reasonable steps had been taken for the purpose of bringing the purport of the instrument to the notice of the public, or of persons likely to be affected by it, or of the person charged.

(3) Save as therein otherwise expressly provided, nothing in this section shall affect any enactment or rule of law relating to the time at which any statutory instrument comes into operation.

4   Statutory instruments which are required to be laid before Parliament

(1) Where by this Act or any Act passed after the commencement of this Act any statutory instrument is required to be laid before Parliament after being made, a copy of the instrument shall be laid before each House of Parliament and, subject as hereinafter provided, shall be so laid before the instrument comes into operation:

Provided that if it is essential that any such instrument should come into operation before copies thereof can be so laid as aforesaid, the instrument may be made so as to come into operation before it has been so laid; and where any statutory instrument comes into operation before it is laid before Parliament, notification shall forthwith be sent to [the Speaker of the House of Commons and the Speaker of the House of Lords] drawing attention to the fact that copies of the instrument have yet to be laid before Parliament and explaining why such copies were not so laid before the instrument came into operation.

(2) Every copy of any such statutory instrument sold by [or under the authority of] the King's printer of Acts of Parliament shall bear on the face thereof—

(a) a statement showing the date on which the statutory instrument came or will come into operation; and

(b) either a statement showing the date on which copies thereof were laid before Parliament or a statement that such copies are to be laid before Parliament.

(3) *****

5   Statutory instruments which are subject to annulment by resolution of either House of Parliament

(1) Where by this Act or any Act passed after the commencement of this Act, it is provided that any statutory instrument shall be subject to annulment in pursuance of resolution of either House of Parliament, the instrument shall be laid before Parliament after being made and the provisions of the last foregoing section shall apply thereto accordingly, and if either House, within the period of forty days beginning with the day on which a copy thereof is laid before it, resolves that an Address be presented to His Majesty praying that the instrument be annulled, no further proceedings shall be taken thereunder after the date of the resolution, and His Majesty may by Order in Council revoke the instrument, so, however, that any such resolution and revocation shall be without prejudice to the validity of anything previously done under the instrument or to the making of a new statutory instrument.

(2) *****

6   Statutory instruments of which drafts are to be laid before Parliament

(1) Where by this Act or any Act passed after the commencement of this Act it is provided that a draft of any statutory instrument shall be laid before Parliament, but the Act does not prohibit the making of the instrument without the approval of Parliament, then, in the case of an Order in Council the draft shall not be submitted to His Majesty in Council, and in any other case the statutory instrument shall not be made, until after the expiration of a period of forty days beginning with the day on which a copy of the draft is laid before each House of Parliament, or, if such copies are laid on different days, with the later of the two days, and if within that period either House resolves that the draft be not submitted to His Majesty or that the statutory instrument be not made, as the case may be, no further proceedings shall be taken thereon, but without prejudice to the laying before Parliament of a new draft.

(2) *****

*****

Crown Proceedings Act 1947

(10 & 11 Geo. 6, c. 44)

An Act to amend the law relating to the civil liabilities and rights of the Crown and to civil proceedings by and against the Crown, to amend the law relating to the civil liabilities of persons other than the Crown in certain cases involving the affairs or property of the Crown, and for purposes connected with the matters aforesaid   [31 July 1947]

Territorial extent: United Kingdom (ss. 2, 4, 11, 21, 40), England and Wales and Northern Ireland (ss. 1, 17, 25, 28), Scotland (ss. 41, 42, 43, 47)

PART I   SUBSTANTIVE LAW

1   Right to sue the Crown

Where any person has a claim against the Crown after the commencement of this Act, and, if this Act had not been passed, the claim might have been enforced, subject to the grant of His Majesty's fiat, by petition of right, or might have been enforced by a proceeding provided by any stautory provision repealed by this Act, then, subject to the provisions of this Act, the claim may be enforced as of right, and without the fiat of His Majesty, by proceedings taken against the Crown for that purpose in accordance with the provisions of this Act.

2   Liability of the Crown in tort

(1) Subject to the provisions of this Act, the Crown shall be subject to all those liabilities in tort to which, if it were a private person of full age and capacity, it would be subject–

    (a) in respect of torts committed by its servants or agents;

    (b) in respect of any breach of those duties which a person owes to his servants or agents at common law by reason of being their employer; and

    (c) in respect of any breach of the duties attaching at common law to the ownership, occupation, possession or control of property:

Provided that no proceedings shall lie against the Crown by virtue of paragraph (a) of this subsection in respect of any act or omission of a servant or agent of the Crown unless the act or omission would apart from the provisions of this Act have given rise to a cause of action in tort against that servant or agent or his estate.

(2) Where the Crown is bound by a statutory duty which is binding also upon persons other than the Crown and its officers, then, subject to the provisions of this Act, the Crown shall, in respect of a failure to comply with that duty, be subject to all those liabilities in tort (if any) to which it would be so subject if it were a private person of full age and capacity.

(3) Where any functions are conferred or imposed upon an officer of the Crown as such either by any rule of the common law or by statute, and that officer commits a tort while performing or purporting to perform those functions, the liabilities of the Crown in respect of the tort shall be such as they would have been if those functions had been conferred or imposed solely by virtue of instructions lawfully given by the Crown.

(4) *****

(5) No proceedings shall lie against the Crown by virtue of this section in respect of anything done or omitted to be done by any person while discharging or purporting to discharge any responsibilities of a judicial nature vested in him, or any responsibilities which he has in connection with the execution of judicial process.

(6) No proceedings shall lie against the Crown by virtue of this section in respect of any act, neglect or default of any officer of the Crown, unless that officer has been directly or indirectly appointed by the Crown and was at the material time paid in respect of his duties as an officer of the Crown wholly out of the Consolidated Fund of the United Kingdom, moneys provided by Parliament, [the Scottish Consolidated Fund] . . ., or any other Fund

certified by the Treasury for the purposes of this subsection or was at the material time holding an office in respect of which the Treasury certify that the holder thereof would normally be so paid.

3   *****

4   Application of law as to indemnity, contribution, joint and several tort-feasors, and contributory negligence

(1) Where the Crown is subject to any liability by virtue of this Part of this Act, the law relating to indemnity and contribution shall be enforceable by or against the Crown in respect of the liability to which it is so subject as if the Crown were a private person of full age and capacity.

(2) ...

(3) Without prejudice to the general effect of section one of this Act, the Law Reform (Contributory Negligence) Act 1945 (which amends the law relating to contributory negligence) shall bind the Crown.

5–9 ...

10   (Repealed by the Crown Proceedings (Armed Forces) Act 1987) . . .

11   Saving in respect of acts done under prerogative and statutory powers

(1) Nothing in Part I of this Act shall extinguish or abridge any powers or authorities which, if this Act had not been passed, would have been exercisable by virtue of the prerogative of the Crown, or any powers or authorities conferred on the Crown by any statute, and, in particular, nothing in the said Part I shall extinguish or abridge any powers or authorities exercisable by the Crown, whether in time of peace or of war, for the purpose of the defence of the realm or of training, or maintaining the efficiency of, any of the armed forces of the Crown.

(2) Where in any proceedings under this Act it is material to determine whether anything was properly done or omitted to be done in the exercise of the prerogative of the Crown, . . . a Secretary of State may, if satisfied that the act or omission was necessary for any such purpose as is mentioned in the last preceding subsection, issue a certificate to the effect that the act or omission was necessary for that purpose; and the certificate shall, in those precedings, be conclusive as to the matter so certified.

12–16   *****

PART II   JURISDICTION AND PROCEDURE

17   Parties to proceedings

(1) [The Minister for the Civil Service] shall publish a list specifying the several Government departments which are authorised departments for the purposes of this Act, and the name and address for service of the person who is, or is acting for the purposes of this Act as, the solicitor for each such department, and may from time to time amend or vary the said list.

Any document purporting to be a copy of a list published under this section and purporting to be printed under the superintendence or the authority of His Majesty's Stationery Office shall in any legal proceedings be received as evidence for the purpose of establishing what departments are authorised departments for the purposes of this Act, and what person is, or is acting for the purposes of this Act as, the solicitor for any such department.

(2) Civil proceedings by the Crown may be instituted either by an authorised Government department in its own name, whether that department was or was not at the commencement of this Act authorised to sue, or by the Attorney General.

(3) Civil proceedings against the Crown shall be instituted against the appropriate authorised Government department, or, if none of the authorised Government departments

is appropriate or the person instituting the proceedings has any reasonable doubt whether any and if so which of those departments is appropriate, against the Attorney General.

(4), (5) *****

18–20   ***

21   Nature of relief

(1) In any civil proceedings by or against the Crown the court shall, subject to the provisions of this Act, have power to make all such orders as it has power to make in proceedings between subjects, and otherwise to give such appropriate relief as the case may require:
Provided that:—

(a) where in any proceedings against the Crown any such relief is sought as might in proceedings between subjects be granted by way of injunction or specific performance, the court shall not grant an injunction or make an order for specific performance, but may in lieu thereof make an order declaratory of the rights of the parties; and

(b) in any proceedings against the Crown for the recovery of land or other property the court shall not make an order for the recovery of the land or the delivery of the property, but may in lieu thereof make an order declaring that the plaintiff is entitled as against the Crown to the land or property or to the possession thereof.

(2) The court shall not in any civil proceedings grant any injunction or make any order against an officer of the Crown if the effect of granting the injunction or making the order would be to give any relief against the Crown which could not have been obtained in proceedings against the Crown.

22–27   ***

PART IV   MISCELLANEOUS AND SUPPLEMENTAL

28–29, 31–33, 35, 37–38   ***

**30, 34, 36, 39   . . .

40   Savings

(1) Nothing in this Act shall apply to proceedings by or against, or authorise proceedings in tort to be brought against, His Majesty in His private capacity.

(2)–(5) *****

PART V   APPLICATION TO SCOTLAND

41   Application of Act to Scotland

The provisions of this Part of this Act shall have effect for the purpose of the application of this Act to Scotland.

42   Exclusion of certain provisions

Section one, Part II (except section thirteen so far as relating to proceedings mentioned in the First Schedule and section twenty-one), Part III (except section twenty-six) and section twenty-eight of this Act shall not apply to Scotland.

43   Interpretation for purposes of application to Scotland

In the application of this Act to Scotland:—

(a) for any reference to the High Court (except a reference to that Court as a prize court) there shall be substituted a reference to the Court of Session; for any reference to the county court there shall be substituted a reference to the sheriff court; the expression "plaintiff" means pursuer; the expression "defendant" means defender; the expression "county court rules" means Act of Sederunt applying to the sheriff court; and the expression "injunction" means interdict;

(b) the expression "tort" means any wrongful or negligent act or omission giving rise to liability in reparation, and any reference to liability or right or action or proceedings in tort shall be construed accordingly; and for any reference to Part II of the Law Reform (Married Women and Tortfeasors) Act, 1935, there shall be substituted a reference to section three of the Law Reform (Miscellaneous Provisions) (Scotland) Act, 1940.

44–54   *********

Life Peerages Act 1958
(6 & 7 Eliz. 2, c. 21)

An Act to make provision for the creation of life peerages carrying the right to sit and vote in the House of Lords   [30 April 1958]

Territorial extent: United Kingdom

1   Power to create life peerages carrying right to sit in the House of Lords

(1) . . . Her Majesty shall have power by letters patent to confer on any person a peerage for life having the incidents specified in subsection (2) of this section.

(2) A peerage conferred under this section shall, during the life of the person on whom it is conferred, entitle him–

(a) to rank as a baron under such style as may be appointed by the letters patent; and

(b) subject to subsection (4) of this section, to receive writs of summons to attend the House of Lords and sit and vote therein accordingly,

and shall expire on his death.

(3) A life peerage may be conferred under this section on a woman.

(4) Nothing in this section shall enable any person to receive a writ of summons to attend the House of Lords, or to sit and vote in that House, at any time when disqualified therefor by law.

*****

Obscene Publications Act 1959
(7 & 8 Eliz. 2, c. 66)

An Act to amend the law relating to the publication of obscene matter; to provide for the protection of literature; and to strengthen the law concerning pornography   [29 July 1959]

Territorial extent: England and Wales

1   Test of obscenity

(1) For the purposes of this Act an article shall be deemed to be obscene if its effect or (where the article comprises two or more distinct items) the effect of any one of its items is, if taken as a whole, such as to tend to deprave and corrupt persons who are likely, having regard to all relevant circumstances, to read, see or hear the matter contained or embodied in it.

(2) In this Act "article" means any description of article containing or embodying matter to be read or looked at or both, any sound record, and any film or other record of a picture or pictures.

(3) For the purposes of this Act a person publishes an article who—
  (a) distributes, circulates, sells, lets on hire, gives, or lends it, or who offers it for sale or for letting on hire; or
  (b) in the case of an article containing or embodying matter to be looked at or a record, shows, plays or projects it [, or, where the matter is data stored electronically, transmits that data.]
. . .

[(4) For the purposes of this Act a person also publishes an article to the extent that any matter recorded on it is included by him in a programme included in a programme service.

(5) Where the inclusion of any matter in a programme so included would, if that matter were recorded matter, constitute the publication of an obscene article for the purposes of this Act by virtue of subsection (4) above, this Act shall have effect in relation to the inclusion of that matter in that programme as if it were recorded matter.

(6) In this section "programme" and "programme service" have the same meaning as in the Broadcasting Act 1990.]

2   Prohibition of publication of obscene matter

(1) Subject as hereinafter provided, any person who, whether for gain or not, publishes an obscene article [or who has an obscene article for publication for gain (whether gain to himself or gain to another)] shall be liable—
  (a) on summary conviction to a fine not exceeding [the prescribed sum] or to imprisonment for a term not exceeding six months;
  (b) on conviction on indictment to a fine or to imprisonment for a term not exceeding three years or both.

(2) . . .

(3) A prosecution . . . for an offence against this section shall not be commenced more than two years after the commission of the offence.

[(3A) Proceedings for an offence under this section shall not be instituted except by or with the consent of the Director of Public Prosecutions in any case where the article in question is a moving picture film of a width of not less than sixteen millimetres and the relevant publication or the only other publication which followed or could reasonably have been expected to follow from the relevant publication took place or (as the case may be) was to take place in the course of [an exhibition of a film]; and in this subsection "the relevant publication" means—
  (a) in the case any proceedings under this section for publishing an obscene article, the publication in respect of which the defendant would be charged if the proceedings were brought; and
  (b) in the case of any proceedings under this section for having an obscene article for publication for gain, the publication which, if the proceedings were brought, the defendant would be alleged to have had in contemplation.]

(4) A person publishing an article shall not be proceeded against for an offence at common law consisting of the publication of any matter contained or embodied in the article where it is of the essence of the offence that the matter is obscene.

[(4A) Without prejudice to subsection (4) above, a person shall not be proceeded against for an offence at common law—
  (a) in respect of [an exhibition of a film] or anything said or done in the course of [an exhibition of a film], where it is of the essence of the common law offence that the exhibition or, as the case may be, what was said or done was obscene, indecent, offensive, disgusting or injurious to morality; or
  (b) in respect of an agreement to give [an exhibition of a film] or to cause anything to be said or done in the course of such an exhibition where the common law

offence consists of conspiring to corrupt public morals or to do any act contrary to public morals or decency.]

(5) A person shall not be convicted of an offence against this section if he proves that he had not examined the article in respect of which he is charged and had no reasonable cause to suspect that it was such that his publication of it would make him liable to be convicted of an offence against this section.

(6) In any proceedings against a person under this section the question whether an article is obscene shall be determined without regard to any publication by another person unless it could reasonably have been expected that the publication by the other person would follow from publication by the person charged.

[(7) In this section ["exhibition of a film"] has the [meaning given in paragraph 15 of Schedule 1 to the Licensing Act 2003].

3   Powers of search and seizure

(1) If a justice of the peace is satisfied by information on oath that there is reasonable ground for suspecting that, in any premises . . ., or on any stall or vehicle in that area, being premises or a stall or vehicle specified in the information, obscene articles are, or are from time to time, kept for publication for gain, the justice may issue a warrant under his hand empowering any constable to enter (if need be by force) and search the premises, or to search the stall or vehicle . . . and to seize and remove any articles found therein or thereon which the constable has reason to believe to be obscene articles and to be kept for publication for gain.

(2) A warrant under the foregoing subsection shall, if any obscene articles are seized under the warrant, also empower the seizure and removal of any documents found in the premises or, as the case may be, on the stall or vehicle which relate to a trade or business carried on at the premises or from the stall or vehicle.

(3) [Subject to subsection (3A) of this section] any articles seized under subsection (1) of this section shall be brought before a justice of the peace [in the local justice area in which the articles were seized, who] may thereupon issue a summons to the occupier of the premises or, as the case may be, the user of the stall or vehicle to appear on a day specified in the summons before a magistrates' court [acting in that local justice area] to show cause why the articles or any of them should not be forfeited; and if the court is satisfied, as respects any of the articles, that at the time when they were seized they were obscene articles kept for publication for gain, the court shall order those articles to be forfeited:

Provided that if the person summoned does not appear, the court shall not make an order unless service of the summons is proved.

[Provided also that this subsection does not apply in relation to any article seized under subsection (1) of this section which is returned to the occupier of the premises or, as the case may be, to the user of the stall or vehicle in or on which it was found.]

[(3A) Without prejudice to the duty of a court to make an order for the forfeiture of an article where section 1(4) of the Obscene Publications Act 1964 applies (orders made on conviction), in a case where by virtue of subsection (3A) of section 2 of this Act proceedings under the said section 2 for having an article for publication for gain could not be instituted except by or with the consent of the Director of Public Prosecutions, no order for the forfeiture of the article shall be made under this section unless the warrant under which the article was seized was issued on an information laid by or on behalf of the Director of Public Prosecutions.]

(4) In addition to the person summoned, any other person being the owner, author or maker of any of the articles brought before the court, or any other person through whose hands they had passed before being seized, shall be entitled to appear before the court on the day specified in the summons to show cause why they should not be forfeited.

(5)–(8) *****

4   Defence of public good

(1) [Subject to subsection (1A) of this section] a person shall not be convicted of an offence against section two of this Act, and an order for forfeiture shall not be made under the foregoing section, if it is proved that publication of the article in question is justified as being for the public good on the ground that it is in the interests of science, literature, art or learning, or of other objects of general concern.

[(1A) Subsection (1) of this section shall not apply where the article in question is a moving picture film or soundtrack, but—

(a) a person shall not be convicted of an offence against section 2 of this Act in relation to any such film or soundtrack, and

(b) an order for forfeiture of any such film or soundtrack shall not be made under section 3 of this Act,

if it is proved that publication of the film or soundtrack is justified as being for the public good on the ground that it is in the interests of drama, opera, ballet or any other art, or of literature or learning.]

(2) It is hereby declared that the opinion of experts as to the literary, artistic, scientific or other merits of an article may be admitted in any proceedings under this Act either to establish or to negative the said ground.

[(3) In this section "moving picture soundtrack" means any sound record designed for playing with a moving picture film, whether incorporated with the film or not.]

5   ***

War Damage Act 1965
(1965, c. 18)

An Act to abolish rights at common law to compensation in respect of damage to, or destruction of, property effected by, or on the authority of, the Crown during, or in contemplation of the outbreak of, war   [2 June 1965]

Territorial extent: United Kingdom

1   Abolition of rights at common law to compensation for certain damage to, or destruction of, property

(1) No person shall be entitled at common law to receive from the Crown compensation in respect of damage to, or destruction of, property caused (whether before or after the passing of this Act, within or outside the United Kingdom) by acts lawfully done by, or on the authority of, the Crown during, or in contemplation of the outbreak of, a war in which the Sovereign was, or is, engaged.

(2) . . .

Criminal Law Act 1967
(1967, c. 58)

An Act to amend the law of England and Wales by abolishing the division of crimes into felonies and misdemeanours and to amend and simplify the law in respect of matters arising from or related to that division or the abolition of it; to do away (within or without England and Wales) with certain obsolete crimes together with the torts of maintenance and champerty; and for purposes connected therewith   [21 July 1967]

Territorial extent: England and Wales

PART I   FELONY AND MISDEMEANOUR

1   *****

2   . . . (Repealed by the Police and Criminal Evidence Act 1984)

3   Use of force in making arrest, etc.

(1) A person may use such force as is reasonable in the circumstances in the prevention of crime, or in effecting or assisting in the lawful arrest of offenders or suspected offenders or of persons unlawfully at large.

(2) Subsection (1) above shall replace the rules of the common law on the question when force used for a purpose mentioned in the subsection is justified by that purpose.

*****

Parliamentary Commissioner Act 1967
(1967, c. 13)

An Act to make provision for the appointment and functions of a Parliamentary Commissioner for the investigation of administrative action taken on behalf of the Crown, and for purposes connected therewith [22 March 1967]

Territorial extent: United Kingdom

Note: This Act is printed as extensively amended by the Parliamentary and Health Service Commissioners Act 1987.

The Parliamentary Commissioner for Administration

1   Appointment and tenure of office

(1) For the purpose of conducting investigations in accordance with the following provisions of this Act there shall be appointed a Commissioner, to be known as the Parliamentary Commissioner for Administration.

(2) Her Majesty may by Letters Patent from time to time appoint a person to be the Commissioner, and any person so appointed shall (subject to [subsections (3) and (3A)] of this section) hold office during good behaviour.

(3) A person appointed to be the Commissioner may be relieved of office by Her Majesty at his own request, or may be removed from office by Her Majesty in consequence of Addresses from both Houses of Parliament, and shall in any case vacate office on completing the year of service in which he attains the age of sixty-five years.

[(3A) Her Majesty may declare the office of Commissioner to have been vacated if satisfied that the person appointed to be the Commissioner is incapable for medical reasons—

(a) of performing the duties of his office; and

(b) of requesting to be relieved of it.]

(4), (5) . . .

2   *****

3   Administrative provisions

(1) The Commissioner may appoint such officers as he may determine with the approval of the Treasury as to numbers and conditions of service.

(2), (3) *****

3A *****

[4 Departments etc. subject to investigation

(1) Subject to the provisions of this section and to the notes contained in Schedule 2 to this Act, this Act applies to the government departments, corporations and unincorporated bodies listed in that Schedule; and references in this Act to an authority to which this Act applies are references to any such corporation or body.

(2) Her Majesty may by Order in Council amend Schedule 2 to this Act by the alteration of any entry or note, the removal of any entry or note or the insertion of any additional entry or note.

(3) An Order in Council may only insert an entry if—
(a) it relates—
  (i) to a government department; or
  (ii) to a corporation or body whose functions are exercised on behalf of the Crown; or
(b) it relates to a corporation or body—
  (i) which is established by virtue of Her Majesty's prerogative or by an Act of Parliament or an Order in Council or order made under an Act of Parliament or which is established in any other way by a Minister of the Crown in his capacity as a Minister or by a government department;
  (ii) at least half of whose revenues derive directly from money provided by Parliament, a levy authorised by an enactment, a fee or charge of any other description so authorised or more than one of those sources; and
  (iii) which is wholly or partly constituted by appointment made by Her Majesty or a Minister of the Crown or government department.

[(3A) No entry shall be made if the result of making it would be that the Parliamentary Commissioner could investigate action which can be investigated [by the Public Services Ombudsman for Wales under the Public Services Ombudsman (Wales) Act 2005].]

[(3B) No entry shall be made in respect of—
(a) the Scottish Administration or any part of it;
(b) any Scottish public authority with mixed functions or no reserved functions within the meaning of the Scotland Act 1998; or
(c) the Scottish Parliamentary Corporate Body.]

(4) No entry shall be made in respect of a corporation or body whose sole activity is, or whose main activities are, included among the activities specified in subsection (5) below.

(5) The activities mentioned in subsection (4) above are—
(a) the provision of education, or the provision of training otherwise than under the Industrial Training Act 1982;
(b) the development of curricula, the conduct of examinations or the validation of educational courses;
(c) the control of entry to any profession or the regulation of the conduct of members of any profession;
(d) the investigation of complaints by members of the public regarding the actions of any person or body, or the supervision or review of such investigations or of steps taken following them.

(6) No entry shall be made in respect of a corporation or body operating in an exclusively or predominantly commercial manner or a corporation carrying on under national ownership an industry or undertaking or part of an industry or undertaking.

(7) Any statutory instrument made by virtue of this section shall be subject to annulment in pursuance of a resolution of either House of Parliament.]

(8) *****

5 Matters subject to investigation

(1) Subject to the provisions of this section, the Commissioner may investigate any action taken by or on behalf of a government department or other authority to which this Act applies, being action taken in the exercise of administrative functions of that department or authority, in any case where—

(a) a written complaint is duly made to a member of the House of Commons by a member of the public who claims to have sustained injustice in consequence of maladministration in connection with the action so taken; and

(b) the complaint is referred to the Commissioner, with the consent of the person who made it, by a member of that House with a request to conduct an investigation thereon.

(1A)–(1C) *****

(2) Except as hereinafter provided, the Commissioner shall not conduct an [investigation under subsection (1) of this section] in respect of any of the following matters, that is to say—

(a) any action in respect of which the person aggrieved has or had a right of appeal, reference or review to or before a tribunal constituted by or under any enactment or by virtue of Her Majesty's prerogative;

(b) any action in respect of which the person aggrieved has or had a remedy by way of proceedings in any court of law:

Provided that the Commissioner may conduct an investigation notwithstanding that the person aggrieved has or had such a right or remedy if satisfied that in the particular circumstances it is not reasonable to expect him to resort or have resorted to it.

(2A) *****

(3) Without prejudice to subsection (2) of this section, the Commisioner shall not conduct an investigation under this Act in respect of any such action or matter as is described in Schedule 3 to this Act.

(4) Her Majesty may by Order in Council amend the said Schedule 3 so as to exclude from the provisions of that Schedule such actions or matters as may be described in the Order; and any statutory instrument made by virtue of this subsection shall be subject to annulment in pursuance of a resolution of either House of Parliament.

(4A)–(4C) *****

(5) In determining whether to initiate, continue or discontinue an investigation under this Act, the Commissioner shall, subject to the foregoing provisions of this section, act in accordance with his own discretion; and any question whether a complaint is duly made under this Act shall be determined by the Commissioner.

(5A)–(9A) *****

6 Provisions relating to complaints

(1) A complaint under this Act may be made by any individual, or by any body of persons whether incorporated or not, not being—

(a) a local authority or other authority or body constituted for purposes of the public service or of local government or for the purposes of carrying on under national ownership any industry or undertaking or part of an industry or undertaking;

[(b) any other authority or body within subsection (1A) below.

(1A) An authority or body is within this subsection if—

(a) its members are appointed by—

(i) Her Majesty;

(ii) any Minister of the Crown;

(iii) any government department;

(iv) the Scottish Ministers;

(v) the First Minister; or

(vi) the Lord Advocate, or

(b) its revenues consist wholly or mainly of—
  (i) money provided by Parliament; or
  (ii) sums payable out of the Scottish Consolidated Fund (directly or indirectly).]

(2) Where the person by whom a complaint might have been made under the foregoing provisions of this Act has died or is for any reason unable to act for himself, the complaint may be made by his personal representative or by a member of his family or other individual suitable to represent him; but except as aforesaid a complaint shall not be entertained under this Act unless made by the person aggrieved himself.

(3) A complaint shall not be entertained under this Act unless it is made to a member of the House of Commons not later than twelve months from the day on which the person aggrieved first had notice of the matters alleged in the complaint; but the Commissioner may conduct an investigation pursuant to a complaint not made within that period if he considers that there are special circumstances which make it proper to do so.

(4) [Except as provided in subsection (5) below] a complaint shall not be entertained under this Act unless the person aggrieved is resident in the United Kingdom (or, if he is dead, was so resident at the time of his death) or the complaint relates to action taken in relation to him while he was present in the United Kingdom or on an installation in a designated area within the meaning of the Continental Shelf Act 1964 or on a ship registered in the United Kingdom or an aircraft so registered, or in relation to rights or obligations which accrued or arose in the United Kingdom or on such an installation, ship or aircraft.

(5) *****

7 Procedure in respect of investigations

(1) Where the Commissioner proposes to conduct an investigation pursuant to a complaint under [section 5(1) of] this Act, he shall afford to the principal officer of the department or authority concerned, and to any person who is alleged in the complaint to have taken or authorised the action complained of, an opportunity to comment on any allegations contained in the complaint.

(1A) *****

(2) Every [investigation under this Act] shall be conducted in private, but except as aforesaid the procedure for conducting an investigation shall be such as the Commissioner considers appropriate in the circumstances of the case; and without prejudice to the generality of the foregoing provision the Commissioner may obtain information from such persons and in such manner, and make such inquiries, as he thinks fit, and may determine whether any person may be represented, by counsel or solicitor or otherwise, in the investigation.

(3), (4) *****

8 Evidence

(1) For the purposes of an investigation under [section 5(1) of] this Act the Commissioner may require any Minister, officer or member of the department or authority concerned or any other person who in his opinion is able to furnish information or produce documents relevant to the investigation to furnish any such information or produce any such document.

(1A) *****

(2) For the purposes of any [investigation under this Act] the Commissioner shall have the same powers as the Court in respect of the attendance and examination of witnesses (including the administration of oaths or affirmations and the examination of witnesses abroad) and in respect of the production of documents.

(3) No obligation to maintain secrecy or other restriction upon the disclosure of information obtained by or furnished to persons in Her Majesty's service, whether imposed by any enactment or by any rule of law, shall apply to the disclosure of information for the purposes of an investigation under this Act; and the Crown shall not be entitled in relation to any such investigation to any such privilege in respect of the production of documents or the giving of evidence as is allowed by law in legal proceedings.

(4) No person shall be required or authorised by virtue of this Act to furnish any information or answer any question relating to proceedings of the Cabinet or of any committee of the Cabinet or to produce so much of any document as relates to such proceedings; and for the purposes of this subsection a certificate issued by the Secretary of the Cabinet with the approval of the Prime Minister and certifying that any information, question, document or part of a document so relates shall be conclusive.

(5) *****

9 Obstruction and contempt

(1) If any person without lawful excuse obstructs the Commissioner or any officer of the Commissioner in the performance of his functions under this Act, or is guilty of any act or omission in relation to any investigation under this Act which, if that investigation were a proceeding in the Court, would constitute contempt of court, the Commissioner may certify the offence to the Court.

(2) Where an offence is certified under this section, the Court may inquire into the matter and, after hearing any witnesses who may be produced against or on behalf of the person charged with the offence, and after hearing any statement that may be offered in defence, deal with him in any manner in which the court could deal with him if he had committed the like offence in relation to the Court.

(3) *****

10 Reports by Commissioner

(1) In any case where the Commissioner conducts an investigation under [section 5(1) of] this Act or decides not to conduct such an investigation, he shall send to the member of the House of Commons by whom the request for investigation was made (or if he is no longer a member of that House, to such member of that House as the Commissioner thinks appropriate) a report of the results of the investigation or, as the case may be, a statement of his reasons for not conducting an investigation.

(2) In any case where the Commissioner conducts an investigation under this Act, he shall also send a report of the results of the investigation to the principal officer of the department or authority concerned and to any other person who is alleged in the relevant complaint to have taken or authorised the action complained of.

(2A) *****

(3) If, after conducting an investigation under [section 5(1) of] this Act, it appears to the Commissioner that injustice has been caused to the person aggrieved in consequence of maladministration and that the injustice has not been, or will not be, remedied, he may, if he thinks fit, lay before each House of Parliament a special report upon the case.

(3A), (3B) *****

(4) The Commissioner shall annually lay before each House of Parliament a general report on the performance of his functions under this Act and may from time to time lay before each House of Parliament such other reports with respect to those functions as he thinks fit.

(5) For the purposes of the law of defamation, any such publication as is hereinafter mentioned shall be absolutely privileged, that is to say—

    (a) the publication of any matter by the Commissioner in making a report to either House of Parliament for the purposes of this Act;

    (b) the publication of any matter by a member of the House of Commons in communicating with the Commissioner or his officers for those purposes or by the Commissioner or his officers in communicating with such a member for those purposes;

    (c) the publication by such a member to the person by whom a complaint was made under this Act of a report or statement sent to the member in respect of the complaint in pursuance of section (1) of this section;

(d) the publication by the Commissioner to such a person as is mentioned in subsection (2) [or (2A)] of this section of a report to that person in pursuance of that subsection.

11, 11A, 11AA, 11B *****

Supplemental

12   Interpretation

(1), (2) *****

(3) It is hereby declared that nothing in this Act authorises or requires the Commissioner to question the merits of a decision taken without maladministration by a government department or other authority in the exercise of a discretion vested in that department or authority.

13–14 *****

Section 5   SCHEDULE 3
MATTERS NOT SUBJECT TO INVESTIGATION

1.   Action taken in matters certified by a Secretary of State or other Minister of the Crown to affect relations or dealings between the Government of the United Kingdom and any other Government or any international organisation of States or Governments.

2.   Action taken, in any country or territory outside the United Kingdom, by or on behalf of any officer representing or acting under the authority of Her Majesty in respect of the United Kingdom, or any other officer of the Government of the United Kingdom [other than action which is taken by an officer (not being an honorary consular officer) in the exercise of a consular function on behalf of the Government of the United Kingdom . . .].

3.   Action taken in connection with the administration of the goverment of any country or territory outside the United Kingdom which forms part of Her Majesty's dominions or in which Her Majesty has jurisdiction.

[4.   Action taken by the Secretary of State under the Extradition Act 2003].

5.   Action taken by or with the authority of the Secretary of State for the purposes of investigating crime or of protecting the security of the State, including action so taken with respect to passports.

6.   The commencement or conduct of civil or criminal proceedings before any court of law in the United Kingdom, of proceedings at any place under the Naval Discipline Act 1957, the Army Act 1955 or the Air Force Act 1955, or of proceedings before any international court or tribunal.

[6A.   Action taken by any person appointed by the Lord Chancellor as a member of the administrative staff of any court or tribunal, so far as that action is taken at the direction, or on the authority (whether express or implied) of any person acting in a judicial capacity or as a member of the tribunal.]

[6B.   (1) Action taken by any member of the administrative staff of a relevant tribunal so far as that action is taken at the direction, or on the authority (whether express or implied), of any person acting in his capacity as a member of the tribunal.

(2) In this paragraph, "relevant tribunal" has the meaning given by section 5(8) of this Act.]

[6C.   Action taken by any person appointed under section 5(3)(c) of the Criminal Injuries Compensation Act 1995, so far as that action is taken at the direction, or on the authority (whether express or implied) of any person acting as an adjudicator appointed under section 5 of that Act to determine appeals.]

7.   Any exercise of the prerogative of mercy or of the power of a Secretary of State to make

a reference in respect of any person to . . . the High Court of Justiciary or the Courts-Martial Appeal Court.

8.   [(1)] Action taken on behalf of the Minister of Health or the Secretary of State by [a Strategic Health Authority,] [a Health Authority, a Primary Care Trust, a Special Health Authority], [except the Rampton Hospital Review Board] [. . . the Rampton Hospital Board,] [the Broadmoor Hospital Board or the Moss Side and Park Lane Hospitals Board,] [. . . a Health Board or the Common Services Agency for the Scottish Health Service] [by the Dental Practice Board or the Scottish Dental Practice Board], . . .

[(2) For the purposes of this paragraph, action taken by a [Strategic Health Authority,] Health Authority, Special Health Authority or Primary Care Trust in the exercise of functions of the Secretary of State shall be regarded as action taken on his behalf.]

9.   Action taken in matters relating to contractual or other commercial transactions, whether within the United Kingdom or elsewhere, being transactions of a government department or authority to which this Act applies or of any such authority or body as is mentioned in paragraph (a) or (b) of subsection (1) of section 6 of this Act and not being transactions for or relating to—

(a) the acquisition of land compulsorily or in circumstances in which it could be acquired compulsorily;

(b) the disposal as surplus of land acquired compulsorily or in such circumstances as aforesaid.

10.   [(1)] Action taken in respect of appointments or removals, pay, discipline, super-annuation or other personnel matters, in relation to—

(a) service in any of the armed forces of the Crown, including reserve and auxiliary and cadet forces;

(b) service in any office or employment under the Crown or under any authority [(to which this Act applies)]; or

(c) service in any office or employment, or under any contract for services, in respect of which power to take action, or to determine or approve the action to be taken, in such matters is vested in Her Majesty, any Minister of the Crown or any such authority as aforesaid.

[(2) Sub-paragraph (1)(c) above shall not apply to any action (not otherwise excluded from investigation by this Schedule) which is taken by the Secretary of State in connection with—

(a) the provision of information relating to the terms and conditions of any employ-ment covered by an agreement entered into by him under section 12(1) of the Overseas Development and Cooperation Act 1980 [or pursuant to the exercise of his powers under Part 1 of the International Development Act 2002] or

(b) the provision of any allowance, grant or supplement or any benefit (other than those relating to superannuation) arising from the designation of any person in accordance with such an agreement.]

11.   The grant of honours, awards or privileges within the gift of the Crown, including the grant of Royal Charters.

*****

Foreign Compensation Act 1969

(1969, c. 20)

An Act to make provision with respect to certain property (including the proceeds thereof and any income or other property accruing therefrom) of persons formerly resident or carrying on business in Estonia, Latvia, Lithuania or a part of Czechoslovakia, Finland, Poland or Rumania which has been ceded to the Union of Soviet Socialist Republics, and to amend the Foreign Compensation Act 1950 [16 May 1969]

Territorial extent: United Kingdom

1–2 ...

3 Determination of the Foreign Compensation Commission and appeals against such determinations

(1) The Foreign Compensation Commission shall have power to determine any question as to the construction or interpretation of any provision of an Order in Council under section 3 of the Foreign Compensation Act 1950 with respect to claims falling to be determined by them.

(2) Subject to subsection (4) below, the Commission shall, if so required by a person mentioned in subsection (6) below who is aggrieved by any determination of the Commission on any question of law relating to the jurisdiction of the Commission or on any question mentioned in subsection (1) above, state and sign a case for the decision of the Court of Appeal.

(3) In this section "determination" includes a determination which under rules under section 4(2) of the Foreign Compensation Act 1950 (rules of procedure) is a provisional determination, and anything which purports to be a determination.

(4) Where the Court of Appeal decide a question on a case stated and signed by the Commission on a provisional determination in any proceedings, subsection (2) above shall not require the Commission to state and sign a case on a final determination by them of that question in those proceedings.

(5) Any person mentioned in subsection (6) below may, with a view to requiring the Commission to state and sign a case under this section, request the Commission to furnish a written statement of the reasons for any determination of theirs, but the Commission shall not be obliged to state the reasons for any determination unless it is given on a claim in which a question mentioned in subsection (2) above arises.

(6) The person who may make a request under subsection (5) above or a requirement under subsection (2) above in relation to any claim are the claimant and any person appointed by the Commission to represent the interests of any fund out of which the claim would, if allowed, be met.

(7) *****

(8) Notwithstanding anything in section 3 of the Appellate Jurisdiction Act 1876 (right of appeal to the House of Lords from decisions of the Court of Appeal), no appeal shall lie to the House of Lords from a decision of the Court of Appeal on an appeal under this section.

(9) Except as provided by subsection (2) above and subsection (10) below, no determination by the Commission on any claim made to them under the Foreign Compensation Act 1950 shall be called in question in any court of law.

(10) Subsection (9) above shall not affect any right of any person to bring proceedings questioning any determination of the Commission on the ground that it is contrary to natural justice.

(11), (12) ...

*****

Equal Pay Act 1970
(1970, c. 41)

An Act to prevent discrimination, as regards terms and conditions of employment between men and women   [29 May 1970]

Territorial extent: England and Wales, Scotland.

1   Requirement of equal treatment for men and women in same employment

[(1) If the terms of a contract under which a woman is employed at an establishment in Great Britain do not include (directly or by reference to a collective agreement or otherwise) an equality clause they shall be deemed to include one.

(2) An equality clause is a provision which relates to terms (whether concerned with pay or not) of a contract under which a woman is employed (the "woman's contract"), and has the effect that—

    (a) where the woman is employed on like work with a man in the same employment—

        (i) if (apart from the equality clause) any term of the woman's contract is or becomes less favourable to the woman than a term of a similar kind in the contract under which that man is employed, that term of the woman's contract shall be treated as so modified as not to be less favourable, and

        (ii) if (apart from the equality clause) at any time the woman's contract does not include a term corresponding to a term benefiting that man included in the contract under which he is employed, the woman's contract shall be treated as including such a term;

    (b) where the woman is employed on work rated as equivalent with that of a man in the same employment—

        (i) if (apart from the equality clause) any term of the woman's contract determined by the rating of the work is or becomes less favourable to the woman than a term of a similar kind in the contract under which that man is employed, that term of the woman's contract shall be treated as so modified as not to be less favourable, and

        (ii) if (apart from the equality clause) at any time the woman's contract does not include a term corresponding to a term benefiting that man included in the contract under which he is employed and determined by the rating of the work, the woman's contract shall be treated as including such a term;

    [(c) where a woman is employed on work which, not being work in relation to which paragraph (a) or (b) above applies, is, in terms of the demands made on her (for instance under such headings as effort, skill and decision), of equal value to that of a man in the same employment—

        (i) if (apart from the equality clause) any term of the woman's contract is or becomes less favourable to the woman than a term of a similar kind in the contract under which that man is employed, that term of the woman's contract shall be treated as so modified as not to be less favourable, and

        (ii) if (apart from the equality clause) at any time the woman's contract does not include a term corresponding to a term benefiting that man included in the contract under which he is employed, the woman's contract shall be treated as including such a term].]

[(3) An equality clause shall not operate in relation to a variation between the woman's contract and the man's contract if the employer proves that the variation is genuinely due to a material factor which is not the difference of sex and that factor—

    (a) in the case of an equality clause falling within subsection (2)(a) or (b) above, must be a material difference between the woman's case and the man's; and

(b) in the case of an equality clause falling within subsection (2)(c) above, may be such a material difference.]

(4) A woman is to be regarded as employed on like work with men if, but only if, her work and theirs is of the same or a broadly similar nature, and the differences (if any) between the things she does and the things they do are not of practical importance in relation to terms and conditions of employment; and accordingly in comparing her work with theirs regard shall be had to the frequency or otherwise with which any such differences occur in practice as well as to the nature and extent of the differences.

(5) A woman is to be regarded as employed on work rated as equivalent with that of any men if, but only if, her job and their job have been given an equal value, in terms of the demand made on a worker under various headings (for instance effort, skill, decision), on a study undertaken with a view to evaluating in those terms the jobs to be done by all or any of the employees in an undertaking or group of undertakings, or would have been given an equal value but for the evaluation being made on a system setting different values for men and women on the same demand under any heading.

(6) Subject to the following subsections, for purposes of this section—

(a) "employed" means employed under a contract of service or of apprenticeship or a contract personally to execute any work or labour, and related expressions shall be construed accordingly;

(b) . . .

(c) two employers are to be treated as associated if one is a company of which the other (directly or indirectly) has control or if both are companies of which a third person (directly or indirectly) has control,

[and men shall be treated as in the same employment with a woman if they are men employed by her employer or any associated employer at the same establishment or at establishments in Great Britain which include that one and at which common terms and conditions of employment are observed either generally or for employees of the relevant classes].

(7) . . .

[(8) This section shall apply to—

(a) service for purposes of a Minister of the Crown or government department, other than service of a person holding a statutory office, or

(b) service on behalf of the Crown for purposes of a person holding a statutory office or purposes of a statutory body,

as it applies to employment by a private person, and shall so apply as if references to a contract of employment included references to the terms of service.

(9) . . .

(10)–(12) *****

(13) Provisions of this section and [sections 2 [to 2A]] below framed with reference to women and their treatment relative to men are to be read as applying equally in a converse case to men and their treatment relative to women.]

2 Disputes as to, and enforcement of, requirement of equal treatment

[(1) Any claim in respect of the contravention of a term modified or included by virtue of an equality clause, including a claim for arrears of remuneration or damages in respect of the contravention, may be presented by way of a complaint to an [employment tribunal].]

[(1A) Where a dispute arises in relation to the effect of an equality clause the employer may apply to an [employment tribunal] for an order declaring the rights of the employer and the employee in relation to the matter in question.]

(2)–(5)*****

(6), (7) . . .

2ZA–2A *****

3–4 . . .

5 *****

6   Exclusion from ss 1 to 5 of pensions etc

[(1) [An equality clause shall not] operate in relation to terms—
- (a) affected by compliance with the laws regulating the employment of women, or
- (b) affording special treatment to women in connection with pregnancy or childbirth.]

(1B), (1C) *****

[7A   Service pay and conditions

(1) Sections 1 and 6 above shall apply, with the modifications mentioned in subsection (2) below and any other necessary modifications, to service by a woman in any of the armed forces as they apply to employment by a private person.

(2) In the application of those sections to service by a woman in any of the armed forces—
- (a) references to a contract of employment shall be regarded as references to the terms of service;
- (b) in section 1, in subsection (6), paragraph (c) and the words "or any associated employer" and subsections (8) to (11) (which have no application) [and subsection (13)] shall be omitted; and
- (c) references to an equality clause shall be regarded as referring to a corresponding term of service capable of requiring the terms of service applicable in her case to be treated as modified or as including other terms.

(3) Any claim in respect of the contravention of a term of service modified or included, in relation to a woman's service in any of the armed forces, by a term corresponding to an equality clause in a contract of employment (including a claim for arrears of pay or damages in respect of the contravention) may be presented by way of complaint to an [employment tribunal].

Any such contravention shall be regarded for the purposes of a claim under this subsection as if it were a breach of contract.

(4) Subsections (5) to (10) below apply in relation to any claim by a woman ("the claimant") arising from a contravention of a term of service referred to in subsection (3) above.

(5) No complaint in respect of the claim shall be presented to an [employment tribunal] unless—
- (a) the claimant has made a complaint to an officer under the service redress procedures applicable to her and has submitted that complaint to the Defence Council under those procedures; and
- (b) the Defence Council have made a determination with respect to the complaint.

(6)–(12)*****

[(13) Provisions of this section and sections 7AA to 7AC below, and provisions applied by this section, framed with reference to women and their treatment relative to men are to be read as applying equally in a converse case to men and their treatment relative to women.]]

7AA–7AC *****

[7B   Questioning of employer

[(1) For the purposes of this section—
- (a) a person who considers that she may have a claim under section 1 above is referred to as "the complainant", and
- (b) a person against whom the complainant may decide to make, or has made, a complaint under section 2(1) or 7A(3) above is referred to as "the respondent".

(2) With a view to helping a complainant to decide whether to institute proceedings and, if she does so, to formulate and present her case in the most effective manner, the Secretary of State shall by order prescribe—

(a) forms by which the complainant may question the respondent on any matter which is or may be relevant, and

(b) forms by which the respondent may if he so wishes reply to any questions.

(3) Where the complainant questions the respondent (whether in accordance with an order under subsection (2) above or not), the question and any reply by the respondent (whether in accordance with such an order or not) shall, subject to the following provisions of this section, be admissible as evidence in any proceedings under section 2(1) or 7A(3) above.

(4) If in any proceedings under section 2(1) or 7A(3) above it appears to the employment tribunal that the complainant has questioned the respondent (whether in accordance with an order under subsection (2) above or not) and that—

(a) the respondent deliberately and without reasonable excuse omitted to reply within such period as the Secretary of State may by order prescribe, or

(b) the respondent's reply is evasive or equivocal,

it may draw any inference which it considers it just and equitable to draw, including an inference that the respondent has contravened a term modified or included by virtue of the complainant's equality clause or corresponding term of service.

(5)–(10)*****

8, 10   . . .

9, 11   *****

Courts Act 1971

(1971, c. 23)

An Act to make further provision as respects the Supreme Court and county courts, judges and juries, to establish a Crown Court as part of the Supreme Court to try indictments and exercise certain other jurisdiction, to abolish courts of assize and certain other courts and to deal with their jurisdiction and other consequential matters, and to amend in other respects the law about courts and court proceedings   [12 May 1971]

Territorial extent: England and Wales

1–15   . . .

PART III   JUDGES

16   Appointment of Circuit Judges

(1) Her Majesty may from time to time appoint as Circuit judges, to serve in the Crown Court and county courts and to carry out such other judicial functions as may be conferred on them under this or any other enactment, such qualified persons as may be recommended to Her by the Lord Chancellor.

(2) The maximum number of Circuit judges shall be such as may be determined from time to time by the Lord Chancellor with the concurrence of the Minister for the Civil Service.

(3) No person shall be qualified to be appointed a Circuit judge [unless—

(a) he has a 10 year Crown Court or 10 year county court qualification within the meaning of section 71 of the Courts and Legal Services Act 1990;

(b) he is a Recorder; or

(c) he has held as a full-time appointment for at least 3 years one of the offices listed in Part IA of Schedule 2.]

(4) Before recommending any person to Her Majesty for appointment as a Circuit judge, the Lord Chancellor shall take steps to satisfy himself that that person's health is satisfactory.

(5) *****

17 Retirement, removal and disqualifications of Circuit Judges

[(1) Subject to subsection (4) below and to subsections (4) to (6) of Section 26 of the Judicial Pensions and Retirement Act 1993, a Circuit judge shall vacate his office on the day on which he attains the age of 70.]

(2), (3) . . .

(4) The Lord Chancellor may, if he thinks fit, [and if the Lord Chief Justice agrees], remove a Circuit judge from office on the ground of incapacity or misbehaviour.

(5), (6) . . .

*****

Immigration Act 1971
(1971, c. 77)

An Act to amend and replace the present immigration laws, to make certain related changes in the citizenship law and enable help to be given to those wishing to return abroad, and for purposes connected therewith   [28 October 1971]

Territorial extent: United Kingdom

Note: This Act is printed as extensively amended by the British Nationality Act 1981 and the Immigration and Asylum Act 1999. Provisions formerly in Part II have been replaced by the equivalent provisions of the latter Act.

PART I   REGULATION OF ENTRY INTO AND STAY IN UNITED KINGDOM

1 General principles

(1) All those who are in this Act expressed to have the right of abode in the United Kingdom shall be free to live in, and to come and go into and from, the United Kingdom without let or hindrance except such as may be required under and in accordance with this Act to enable their right to be established or as may be otherwise lawfully imposed on any person.

(2) Those not having that right may live, work and settle in the United Kingdom by permission and subject to such regulation and control of their entry into, stay in and departure from the United Kingdom as is imposed by this Act; and indefinite leave to enter or remain in the United Kingdom shall, by virtue of this provision, be treated as having been given under this Act to those in the United Kingdom at its coming into force, if they are then settled there (and not exempt under this Act from the provisions relating to leave to enter or remain).

(3) Arrival in and departure from the United Kingdom on a local journey from or to any of the Islands (that is to say, the Channel Islands and Isle of Man) or the Republic of Ireland shall not be subject to control under this Act, nor shall a person require leave to enter the United Kingdom on so arriving, except in so far as any of those places is for any purpose excluded from this subsection under the powers conferred by this Act; and in this Act the United Kingdom and those places, or such of them as are not so excluded, are collectively referred to as "the common travel area".

(4) The rules laid down by the Secretary of State as to the practice to be followed in the administration of this Act for regulating the entry into and stay in the United Kingdom of persons not having the right of abode shall include provision for admitting (in such cases and

subject to such restrictions as may be provided by the rules, and subject or not to conditions as to length of stay or otherwise) persons coming for the purpose of taking employment, or for purposes of study, or as visitors, or as dependants of persons lawfully in or entering the United Kingdom.

(5) . . .

[2   Statement of right of abode in United Kingdom

(1) A person is under this Act to have the right of abode in the United Kingdom if—

(a) he is a British citizen; or

(b) he is a Commonwealth citizen who—

(i)   immediately before the commencement of the British Nationality Act 1981 was a Commonwealth citizen having the right of abode in the United Kingdom by virtue of section 2(1)(d) or section 2(2) of this Act as then in force; and

(ii) has not ceased to be a Commonwealth citizen in the meanwhile.

(2) In relation to Commonwealth citizens who have the right of abode in the United Kingdom by virtue of subsection (1)(b) above, this Act, except this section and section [(5(2)] shall apply as if they were British citizens; and in this Act (except as aforesaid) "British citizen" shall be construed accordingly.]

[**Note:** Sections 2(1) and 2(2) as in force prior to the commencement of the 1981 Act provided as follows:

"(1) A person is under this Act to have the right of abode in the United Kingdom if—

(a) he is a citizen of the United Kingdom and Colonies who has that citizenship by his birth, adoption, naturalisation or (except as mentioned below) registration in the United Kingdom or in any of the Islands; or

(b) he is a citizen of the United Kingdom and Colonies born to or legally adopted by a parent who had that citizenship at the time of the birth or adoption, and the parent either—

(i)   then had that citizenship by his birth, adoption, naturalisation or (except as mentioned below) registration in the United Kingdom or in any of the Islands; or

(ii) had been born to or legally adopted by a parent who at the time of that birth or adoption so had it; or

(c) he is a citizen of the United Kingdom and Colonies who has at any time been settled in the United Kingdom and Islands and had at that time (and while such a citizen) been ordinarily resident there for the last five years or more; or

(d) he is a Commonwealth citizen born to or legally adopted by a parent who at the time of the birth or adoption had citizenship of the United Kingdom and Colonies by his birth in the United Kingdom or in any of the Islands.

(2) A woman is under this Act also to have the right of abode in the United Kingdom if she is a Commonwealth citizen and either—

(a) is the wife of any such citizen of the United Kingdom and Colonies as is mentioned in subsection (1)(a), (b) or (c) above or any such Commonwealth citizen as is mentioned in subsection (1)(d); or

(b) has at any time been the wife—

(i)   of a person then being such a citizen of the United Kingdom and Colonies or Commonwealth citizen; or

(ii) of a British subject who but for his death would on the date of commencement of the British Nationality Act 1948 have been such a citizen of the United Kingdom and Colonies as is mentioned in subsection (1)(a) or (b);

but in subsection (1)(a) and (b) above references to registration as a citizen of the United Kingdom and Colonies shall not, in the case of a woman, include registration after the passing of this Act under or by virtue of section 6(2) (wives) of the British Nationality Act 1948 unless she is so registered by virtue of her marriage to a citizen of the United Kingdom and Colonies before the passing of this Act."]

3   General provisions for regulation and control

(1) Except as otherwise provided by or under this Act, where a person is not [a British citizen]—

    (a) he shall not enter the United Kingdom unless given leave to do so in accordance with [the provisions of, or made under] this Act;

    (b) he may be given leave to enter the United Kingdom (or, when already there, leave to remain in the United Kingdom) either for a limited or for an indefinite period;

    [(c) if he is given limited leave to enter or remain in the United Kingdom, it may be given subject to [any or all of the following conditions, namely—

        (i)   a condition restricting his employment or occupation in the United Kingdom;

        (ii) a condition requiring him to maintain and accommodate himself, and any dependants of his, without recourse to public funds; and

        (iii) a condition requiring him to register with the police.]]

(2) The Secretary of State shall from time to time (and as soon as may be) lay before Parliament statements of the rules, or of any changes in the rules, laid down by him as to the practice to be followed in the administration of this Act for regulating the entry into and stay in the United Kingdom of persons required by this Act to have leave to enter, including any rules as to the period for which leave is to be given and the conditions to be attached in different circumstances; and section 1(4) above shall not be taken to require uniform provision to be made by the rules as regards admission of persons for a purpose or in a capacity specified in section 1(4) (and in particular, for this as well as other purposes of this Act, account may be taken of citizenship or nationality).

If a statement laid before either House of Parliament under this subsection is disapproved by a resolution of that House passed within the period of forty days beginning with the date of laying (and exclusive of any period during which Parliament is dissolved or prorogued or during which both Houses are adjourned for more than four days), then the Secretary of State shall as soon as may be make such changes or further changes in the rules as appear to him to be required in the circumstances, so that the statement of those changes be laid before Parliament at least by the end of the period of forty days beginning with the date of the resolution (but exclusive as aforesaid).

(3) In the case of a limited leave to enter or remain in the United Kingdom,—

    (a) a person's leave may be varied, whether by restricting, enlarging or removing the limit on its duration, or by adding, varying or revoking conditions, but if the limit on its duration is removed, any conditions attached to the leave shall cease to apply; and

    (b) the limitation on and any conditions attached to a person's leave [(whether imposed originally or on a variation) shall], if not superseded, apply also to any subsequent leave he may obtain after an absence from the United Kingdom within the period limited for the duration of the earlier leave.

(4) A person's leave to enter or remain in the United Kingdom shall lapse on his going to a country or territory outside the common travel area (whether or not he lands there), unless within the period for which he had leave he returns to the United Kingdom in circumstances in which he is not required to obtain leave to enter; but, if he does so return, his previous leave (and any limitation on it or conditions attached to it) shall continue to apply.

[(4A) For the purposes of subsection (4) above a person seeking to leave the United Kingdom through the tunnel system who is refused admission to France shall be treated as having gone to a country outside the common travel area.]

[(5) A person who is not a British citizen is liable to deportation from the United Kingdom if—

(a) the Secretary of State deems his deportation to be conducive to the public good; or

(b) another person to whose family he belongs is or has been ordered to be deported.]

(6) Without prejudice to the operation of subsection (5) above, a person who is not [a British citizen] shall also be liable to deportation from the United Kingdom if, after he has attained the age of seventeen, he is convicted of an offence for which he is punishable with imprisonment and on his conviction is recommended for deportation by a court empowered by this Act to do so.

(7) Where it appears to Her Majesty proper so to do by reason of restrictions or conditions imposed on [British citizens [, British overseas territories citizens] or British Overseas citizens] when leaving or seeking to leave any country or the territory subject to the government of any country, Her Majesty may by Order in Council make provision for prohibiting persons who are nationals or citizens of the country and are not [British citizens] from embarking in the United Kingdom, or from doing so elsewhere than at a port of exit, or for imposing restrictions or conditions on them when embarking or about to embark in the United Kingdom; and Her Majesty may also make provision by Order in Council to enable those who are not [British citizens] to be, in such cases as may be prescribed by the Order, prohibited in the interests of safety from so embarking on a ship or aircraft specified or indicated in the prohibition.

Any Order in Council under this subsection shall be subject to annulment in pursuance of a resolution of either House of Parliament.

[(7A) Any reference in an Order in Council under subsection (7) above to embarking or being about to embark shall be construed as including a reference to leaving or seeking to leave the United Kingdom through the tunnel system.]

(8) When any question arises under this Act whether or not a person is [a British citizen], or is entitled to any exemption under this Act, it shall lie on the person asserting it to prove that he is.

[(9) A person seeking to enter the United Kingdom and claiming to have the right of abode there shall prove that he has that right by means of either—

(a) a United Kingdom passport describing him as a British citizen or as a citizen of the United Kingdom and Colonies having the right of abode in the United Kingdom; or

(b) a certificate of entitlement . . .]

3A–3C, 4–5 *****

6 Recommendations by court for deportation

(1) Where under section 3(6) above a person convicted of an offence is liable to deportation on the recommendation of a court, he may be recommended for deportation by any court having power to sentence him for the offence unless the court commits him to be sentenced or further dealt with for that offence by another court:
*****

(2)–(4) *****

(5) Where a court recommends or purports to recommend a person for deportation, the validity of the recommendation shall not be called in question except on an appeal against the recommendation or against the conviction on which it is made; but—

(a) . . . the recommendation shall be treated as a sentence for the purpose of any . . . enactment providing an appeal against sentence; . . .

(6), (7) *****

7 Exemption from deportation for certain existing residents

(1) Notwithstanding anything in section 3(5) or (6) above but subject to the provisions of this section, a Commonwealth citizen or citizen of the Republic of Ireland who was such a citizen at the coming into force of this Act and was then ordinarily resident in the United Kingdom—

(a) ...
(b) [shall not be liable to deportation under section 3(5) if at the time of the Secretary of State's decision he had for the last five years been ordinarily resident in the United Kingdom and Islands]; and
(c) shall not on conviction of an offence be recommended for deportation under section 3(6) if at the time of the conviction he had for the last five years been ordinarily resident in the United Kingdom and Islands.

(2) A person who has at any time become ordinarily resident in the United Kingdom or in any of the Islands shall not be treated for the purposes of this section as having ceased to be so by reason only of his having remained there in breach of the immigration laws.

(3)–(5) *****

8–11 *****

12–21, 23 ...

22 *****

PART III   CRIMINAL PROCEEDINGS

24   Illegal entry and similar offences

(1) A person who is not [a British citizen] shall be guilty of an offence punishable on summary conviction with a fine of not more than [[level 5] on the standard scale] or with imprisonment for not more than six months, or with both, in any of the following cases:—
(a) if contrary to this Act he knowingly enters the United Kingdom in breach of a deportation order or without leave;
(aa) ...
(b) if, having only a limited leave to enter or remain in the United Kingdom, he knowingly either—
(i)   remains beyond the time limited by the leave; or
(ii) fails to observe a condition of the leave;
(c) if, having lawfully entered the United Kingdom without leave by virtue of section 8(1) above, he remains without leave beyond the time allowed by section 8(1);
(d) if, without reasonable excuse, he fails to comply with any requirement imposed on him under Schedule 2 to this Act to report to a medical officer of health, or to attend, or submit to a test or examination, as required by such an officer;
(e) if, without reasonable excuse, he fails to observe any restriction imposed on him under Schedule 2 or 3 to this Act as to residence [, as to his employment or occupation] or as to reporting to the police [, to an immigration officer or to the Secretary of State];
(f) if he [leaves a train in the United Kingdom] after being placed on board under Schedule 2 or 3 to this Act with a view to his removal from the United Kingdom;
(g) if he [leaves or seeks to leave the United Kingdom through the tunnel system] in contravention of a restriction imposed by or under an Order in Council under section 3(7) of this Act.

[(1A) A person commits an offence under subsection (1)(b)(i) above on the day when he first knows that the time limited by his leave has expired and continues to commit it throughout any period during which he is in the United Kingdom thereafter; but a person shall not be prosecuted under that provision more than once in respect of the same limited leave.]

(2) ...
(3), (4) *****

24A, 25–32 *****

PART IV   SUPPLEMENTARY

33   Interpretation

(1) For purposes of this Act, except in so far as the context otherwise requires—

*****

["certificate of entitlement" means a certificate under section 10 of the Nationality, Immigration and Asylum Act 2002 that a person has the right of abode in the United Kingdom;]

*****

["entrant" means a person entering or seeking to enter the United Kingdom, and "illegal entrant" means a person—

[(a) unlawfuly entering or seeking to enter in breach of a deportation order or of the immigration laws, or

(b) entering or seeking to enter by means which include deception by another person, and includes also a person who has entered as mentioned in paragraph (a) or (b) above;]

"entry clearance" means a visa, entry certificate or other document which, in accordance with the immigration rules, is to be taken as evidence [or the requisite evidence] of a person's eligibility, though not [a British citizen], for entry into the United Kingdom (but does not include a work permit);

"immigration laws" means this Act and any law for purposes similar to this Act which is for the time being or has (before or after the passing of this Act) been in force in any part of the United Kingdom and Islands;

"immigration rules" means the rules for the time being laid down as mentioned in section 3(2) above;

*****

"limited leave" and "indefinite leave" mean respectively leave under this Act to enter or remain in the United Kingdom which is, and one which is not, limited as to duration;

"settled" shall be construed in accordance [with subsection (2A) below];

*****

"work permit" means a permit indicating, in accordance with the immigration rules, that a person named in it is eligible, though not [a British citizen], for entry into the United Kingdom for the purpose of taking employment.

(1A) *****

(2) It is hereby declared that, except as otherwise provided in this Act, a person is not to be treated for the purposes of any provision of this Act as ordinarily resident in the United Kingdom or in any of the Islands at a time when he is there in breach of the immigration laws.

[(2A) Subject to section 8(5) above, references to a person being settled in the United Kingdom are references to his being ordinarily resident there without being subject under the immigration laws to any restriction on the period for which he may remain.]

(3), (4) *****

(5) This Act shall not be taken to supersede or impair any power exercisable by Her Majesty in relation to aliens by virtue of Her prerogative.

34–37 *****

Misuse of Drugs Act 1971

(1971, c. 38)

An Act to make new provision with respect to dangerous or otherwise harmful drugs and related matters, and for purposes connected therewith   [27 May 1971]

Territorial extent: United Kingdom

*****

Law enforcement and punishment of offences

23   Powers to search and obtain evidence

(1) A constable or other person authorised in that behalf by a general or special order of the Secretary of State . . . shall, for the purposes of the execution of this Act, have power to enter the premises of a person carrying on business as a producer or supplier of any controlled drugs and to demand the production of, and to inspect, any books or documents relating to dealings in any such drugs and to inspect any stocks of any such drugs.

(2) If a constable has reasonable grounds to suspect that any person is in possession of a controlled drug in contravention of this Act or of any regulations made thereunder, the constable may—

(a)   search that person, and detain him for the purpose of searching him;

(b)   search any vehicle or vessel in which the constable suspects that the drug may be found, and for that purpose require the person in control of the vehicle or vessel to stop it;

(c)   seize and detain, for the purposes of proceedings under this Act, anything found in the course of the search which appears to the constable to be evidence of an offence under this Act.

In this subsection "vessel" includes a hovercraft within the meaning of the Hovercraft Act 1968; and nothing in this subsection shall prejudice any power of search or any power to seize or detain property which is exercisable by a constable apart from this subsection.

(3) If a justice of the peace (or in Scotland a justice of the peace, a magistrate or a sheriff) is satisfied by information on oath that there is reasonable ground for suspecting—

(a)   that any controlled drugs are, in contravention of this Act or of any regulations made thereunder, in the possession of a person on any premises; or

(b)   that a document directly or indirectly relating to, or connected with, a transaction or dealing which was, or an intended transaction or dealing which would if carried out be, an offence under this Act, or in the case of a transaction or dealing carried out or intended to be carried out in a place outside the United Kingdom, an offence against the provision of a corresponding law in force in that place, is in the possession of a person on any premises,

he may grant a warrant authorising any constable acting for the police area in which the premises are situated at any time or times within one month from the date of the warrant, to enter, if need be by force, the premises named in the warrant, and to search the premises and any person found therein and, if there is reasonable ground for suspecting that an offence under this Act has been committed in relation to any controlled drugs found on the premises or in the possession of any such persons, or that a document so found is such a document as is mentioned in paragraph (b) above, to seize and detain those drugs or that document, as the case may be.

(3A) *******

(4) A person commits an offence if he—

(a)   intentionally obstructs a person in the exercise of his powers under this section; or

(b)   conceals from a person acting in the exercise of his powers under subsection (1) above any such books, documents, stocks or drugs as are mentioned in that subsection; or

(c)   without reasonable excuse (proof of which shall lie on him) fails to produce any such books or documents as are so mentioned where their production is demanded by a person in the exercise of his powers under that subsection.

(5) *****
*****

European Communities Act 1972
(1972, c. 68)

An Act to make provision in connection with the enlargement of the European Communities to include the United Kingdom, together with (for certain purposes) the Channel Islands, the Isle of Man and Gibraltar   [17 October 1972]

Territorial extent: United Kingdom

Note: In section 2, references to a statutory power or duty include a power or duty conferred by an Act of the Scottish Parliament or an instrument made thereunder, and section 2(2) is to be read as applying to regulations made by Scottish Ministers: see the Scotland Act 1998, Sch. 8, para. 5.

PART I   GENERAL PROVISIONS

1   Short title and interpretation
(1) This Act may be cited as the European Communities Act 1972.
(2) In this Act . . .
"the Communities" means the European Economic Community, the European Coal and Steel Community and the European Atomic Energy Community;
"the Treaties" or "the Community Treaties" means, subject to subsection (3) below, the pre-accession treaties, that is to say, those described in Part I of Schedule 1 to this Act, taken with—
***** [list omitted]
and any expression defined in Schedule 1 to this Act has the meaning there given to it.
(3) If Her Majesty by Order in Council declares that a treaty specified in the Order is to be regarded as one of the Community Treaties as herein defined, the Order shall be conclusive that it is to be so regarded; but a treaty entered into by the United Kingdom after the 22nd January 1972, other than a pre-accession treaty to which the United Kingdom accedes on terms settled on or before that date, shall not be so regarded unless it is so specified, nor be so specified unless a draft of the Order in Council has been approved by resolution of each House of Parliament.
(4) For purposes of subsections (2) and (3) above, "treaty" includes any international agreement, and any protocol or annex to a treaty or international agreement.
Note: The full list of Treaties in s. 1(2) includes those adopted and ratified by the UK since 1972 as well as the original treaties, so that major constitutional changes such as the incorporation of the Single European Act of 1986 and the Maastricht Treaty, 1992 are achieved by amendments to the subsection. Most recently, the European Communities (Amendment) Acts 2002 and 2003 add the Nice Treaty and the Treaty of Enlargement to the list in s. 1(2).

2   General implementation of Treaties
(1) All such rights, powers, liabilities, obligations and restrictions from time to time created or arising by or under the Treaties, and all such remedies and procedures from time to time provided for by or under the Treaties, as in accordance with the Treaties are without further enactment to be given legal effect or used in the United Kingdom shall be recognised and available in law, and be enforced, allowed and followed accordingly; and the expression "enforceable Community right" and similar expressions shall be read as referring to one to which this subsection applies.

(2) Subject to Schedule 2 to this Act, at any time after its passing Her Majesty may by Order in Council, and any designated Minister or department may by regulations, make provision—

(a) for the purpose of implementing any Community obligation of the United Kingdom, or enabling any such obligation to be implemented, or of enabling any rights enjoyed or to be enjoyed by the United Kingdom under or by virtue of the Treaties to be exercised; or

(b) for the purpose of dealing with matters arising out of or related to any such obligation or rights or the coming into force, or the operation from time to time, of subsection (1) above;

and in the exercise of any statutory power or duty, including any power to give directions or to legislate by means of orders, rules, regulations or other subordinate instrument, the person entrusted with the power or duty may have regard to the objects of the Communities and to any such obligation or rights as aforesaid.

In this subsection "designated Minister or Department" means such Minister of the Crown or government department as may from time to time be designated by Order in Council in relation to any matter or for any purpose, but subject to such restrictions or conditions (if any) as may be specified by the Order in Council.

(3) There shall be charged on and issued out of the Consolidated Fund or, if so determined by the Treasury, the National Loans Fund the amounts required to meet any Community obligation to make payments to any of the Communities or member States, or any Community obligation in respect of contributions to the capital or reserves of the European Investment Bank or in respect of loans to the Bank, or to redeem any notes or obligations issued or created in respect of any such Community obligation; and, except as otherwise provided by or under any enactment,—

(a) any other expenses incurred under or by virtue of the Treaties or this Act by any Minister of the Crown or government department may be paid out of moneys provided by Parliament; and

(b) any sums received under or by virtue of the Treaties or this Act by any Minister of the Crown or government department, save for such sums as may be required for disbursements permitted by any other enactment, shall be paid into the Consolidated Fund or, if so determined by the Treasury, the National Loans Fund.

(4) The provision that may be made under subsection (2) above includes, subject to Schedule 2 to this Act, any such provision (of any such extent) as might be made by Act of Parliament, and any enactment passed or to be passed, other than one contained in this Part of this Act, shall be construed and have effect subject to the foregoing provisions of this section; but, except as may be provided by any Act passed after this Act, Schedule 2 shall have effect in connection with the powers conferred by this and the following sections of this Act to make Orders in Council and regulations.

(5), (6) *****

3   Decisions on, and proof of, Treaties and Community instruments, etc.

(1) For the purposes of all legal proceedings any question as to the meaning or effect of any of the Treaties, or as to the validity, meaning or effect of any Community instrument, shall be treated as a question of law (and, if not referred to the European Court, be for determination as such in accordance with the principles laid down by and any relevant decision of the European Court [or any court attached thereto]).

(2) Judicial notice shall be taken of the Treaties, of the Official Journal of the Communities and of any decision of, or expression of opinion by, the European Court [or any court attached thereto] on any such question as aforesaid; and the Official Journal shall be admissible as evidence of any instrument or other act thereby communicated of any of the Communities or of any Community institution.

(3), (4), (5) *****

*****

Section 2   SCHEDULE 2
        PROVISIONS AS TO SUBORDINATE LEGISLATION

1.—(1) The powers conferred by section 2(2) of this Act to make provision for the purposes mentioned in section 2(2)(a) and (b) shall not include power—

    (a) to make any provision imposing or increasing taxation; or

    (b) to make any provision taking effect from a date earlier than that of the making of the instrument containing the provision; or

    (c) to confer any power to legislate by means of orders, rules regulations or other subordinate instrument, other than rules of procedure for any court or tribunal; or

    (d) to create any new criminal offence punishable with imprisonment for more than two years or punishable on summary conviction with imprisonment for more than [the prescribed term] or with a fine of more than [level 5 on the standard scale] (if not calculated on a daily basis) or with a fine of more than [£100 a day].

    (2) Sub-paragraph (1)(c) above shall not be taken to preclude the modification of a power to legislate conferred otherwise than under section 2(2), or the extension of any such power to purposes of the like nature as those for which it was conferred; and a power to give directions as to matters of administration is not to be regarded as a power to legislate within the meaning of sub-paragraph (1)(c).

    [(3) In sub-paragraph (1)(d), "the prescribed term" means—

    (a) in relation to England and Wales, where the offence is a summary offence, 51 weeks;

    (b) in relation to England and Wales, where the offence is triable either way, twelve months;

    (c) in relation to Scotland and Northern Ireland, three months.]

    2.—(1) Subject to paragraph 3 below, where a provision contained in any section of this Act confers power to make regulations (otherwise than by modification or extension of an existing power), the power shall be exercisable by statutory instrument.

    (2) Any statutory instrument containing an Order in Council or regulations made in the exercise of a power so conferred, if made without a draft having been approved by resolution of each House of Parliament, shall be subject to annulment in pursuance of a resolution of either House.

Local Government Act 1972
(1972, c. 70)

An Act to make provision with respect to local government and the functions of local authorities in England and Wales; to amend Part II of the Transport Act 1968; to confer rights of appeal in respect of decisions relating to licences under the Home Counties (Music and Dancing) Licensing Act 1926; to make further provision with respect to magistrates' courts committees; to abolish certain inferior courts of record; and for connected purposes   [26 October 1972]

Territorial extent: England and Wales

*****

[PART VA   ACCESS TO MEETINGS AND DOCUMENTS OF CERTAIN AUTHORITIES, COMMITTEES AND SUB-COMMITTEES

Note: This Part was added by the Local Government (Access to Information) Act 1985. It now also applies to Community Health Councils: Community Health Councils (Access to Information) Act 1988.

100A   Admission to meetings of principal councils

(1) A meeting of a principal council shall be open to the public except to the extent that they are excluded (whether during the whole or part of the proceedings) under subsection (2) below or by resolution under subsection (4) below.

(2) The public shall be excluded from a meeting of a principal council during an item of business whenever it is likely, in view of the nature of the business to be transacted or the nature of the proceedings, that, if members of the public were present during that item, confidential information would be disclosed to them in breach of the obligation of confidence; and nothing in this Part shall be taken to authorise or require the disclosure of confidential information in breach of the obligation of confidence.

(3) For the purposes of subsection (2) above, "confidential information" means—

    (a) information furnished to the council by a Government department upon terms (however expressed) which forbid the disclosure of the information to the public; and

    (b) information the disclosure of which to the public is prohibited by or under any enactment or by the order of a court;

and, in either case, the reference to the obligation of confidence is to be construed accordingly.

(4) A principal council may by resolution exclude the public from a meeting during an item of business whenever it is likely, in view of the nature of the business to be transacted or the nature of the proceedings, that if members of the public were present during that item there would be disclosure to them of exempt information, as defined in section 100I below.

(5), (6) *****

(7) Nothing in this section shall require a principal council to permit the taking of photographs of any proceedings, or the use of any means to enable persons not present to see or hear any proceedings (whether at the time or later), or the making of any oral report on any proceedings as they take place.

(8) This section is without prejudice to any power of exclusion to suppress or prevent disorderly conduct or other misbehaviour at a meeting.

100B   Access to agenda and connected reports

(1) Copies of the agenda for a meeting of a principal council and, subject to subsection (2) below, copies of any report for the meeting shall be open to inspection by members of the public at the offices of the council in accordance with subsection (3) below.

(2) If the proper officer thinks fit, there may be excluded from the copies of reports provided in pursuance of subsection (1) above the whole of any report which, or any part which, relates only to items during which, in his opinion, the meeting is likely not to be open to the public.

(3) Any document which is required by subsection (1) above to be open to inspection shall be so open at least [five] clear days before the meeting, except that—

    (a) where the meeting is convened at shorter notice, the copies of the agenda and reports shall be open to inspection from the time the meeting is convened, and

    (b) where an item is added to an agenda copies of which are open to inspection by the public, copies of the item (or of the revised agenda), and the copies of any report for the meeting relating to the item, shall be open to inspection from the time the item is added to the agenda;

but nothing in this subsection requires copies of any agenda, item or report to be open to inspection by the public until copies are available to members of the council.

(4) An item of business may not be considered at a meeting of a principal council unless either–

(a) a copy of the agenda including the item (or a copy of the item) is open to inspection by members of the public in pursuance of subsection (1) above for at least [five] clear days before the meeting or, where the meeting is convened at shorter notice, from the time the meeting is convened; or

(b) by reason of special circumstances, which shall be specified in the minutes, the chairman of the meeting is of the opinion that the item should be considered at the meeting as a matter of urgency.

(5)–(8) *****

100C   Inspection of minutes and other documents after meetings

(1) After a meeting of a principal council the following documents shall be open to inspection by members of the public at the offices of the council until the expiration of the period of six years beginning with the date of the meeting, namely—

(a) the minutes, or a copy of the minutes, of the meeting, excluding so much of the minutes of proceedings during which the meeting was not open to the public as discloses exempt information;

(b) where applicable, a summary under subsection (2) below;

(c) a copy of the agenda for the meeting; and

(d) a copy of so much of any report for the meeting as relates to any item during which the meeting was open to the public.

(2) *****

100D   Inspection of background papers

[(1) Subject, in the case of section 100C(1), to subsection (2) below, if and so long as copies of the whole or part of a report for a meeting of a principal council are required by section 100B(1) or 100C(1) above to be open to inspection by members of the public—

(a) those copies shall each include a copy of a list compiled by the proper officer, of the background papers for the report or the part of the report; and

(b) at least one copy of each of the documents included in that list shall also be open to inspection at the offices of the council.]

(2) Subsection (1) above does not require a copy . . . of any document included in the list, to be open to inspection after the expiration of the period of four years beginning with the date of the meeting.

(3)–(5) *****

100E   Application to committees and sub-committees

(1) Sections 100A to 100D above shall apply in relation to a committee or sub-committee of a principal council as they apply in relation to a principal council.

(2)–(4) *****

100F, G   *****

PART VI   DISCHARGE OF FUNCTIONS

101   Arrangements for discharge of functions by local authorities

(1) Subject to any express provision contained in this Act or any Act passed after this Act, a local authority may arrange for the discharge of any of their functions—

    (a) by a committee, a sub-committee or an officer of the authority; or

    (b) by any other local authority.

(1A), (1B), (1C) *****

(2) Where by virtue of this section any functions of a local authority may be discharged by a committee of theirs, then, unless the local authority otherwise direct, the committee may arrange for the discharge of any of those functions by a sub-committee or an officer of the authority and where by virtue of this section any functions of a local authority may be discharged by a sub-committee of the authority, then, unless the local authority or the committee otherwise direct, the sub-committee may arrange for the discharge of any of those functions by an officer of the authority.

(3) Where arrangements are in force under this section for the discharge of any functions of a local authority by another local authority, then, subject to the terms of the arrangements, that other authority may arrange for the discharge of those functions by a committee, sub-committee or officer of theirs and subsection (2) above shall apply in relation to those functions as it applies in relation to the functions of that other authority.

(4)–(5B) *****

(6) A local authority's functions with respect to levying, or issuing a precept for, a rate . . . shall be discharged only by the authority.

102–110   *****

111   Subsidiary powers of local authorities

(1) Without prejudice to any powers exercisable apart from this section but subject to the provisions of this Act and any other enactment passed before or after this Act, a local authority shall have power to do anything (whether or not involving the expenditure, borrowing or lending of money or the acquisition or disposal of any property or rights) which is calculated to facilitate, or is conducive or incidental to, the discharge of any of their functions.

(2) For the purposes of this section, transacting the business of a parish or community meeting or any other parish or community business shall be treated as a function of the parish or community council.

(3) A local authority shall not by virtue of this section raise money, whether by means of rates, precepts or borrowing, or lend money except in accordance with the enactments relating to those matters respectively.

(4) In this section "local authority" includes the Common Council.

112   Appointment of staff

(1) Without prejudice to section 111 above but subject to the provisions of this Act, a local authority shall appoint such officers as they think necessary for the proper discharge by the authority of such of their or another authority's functions as fall to be discharged by them and the carrying out of any obligations incurred by them in connection with an agreement made by them in pursuance of section 113 below.

(2) An officer appointed under subsection (1) above shall hold office on such reasonable terms and conditions, including conditions as to remuneration, as the authority appointing him think fit.

(3) Subject to subsection (4) below, any enactment or instrument made under an enactment which requires or empowers all local authorities or local authorities of any description or committees of local authorities to appoint a specified officer shall, to the extent that it makes any such provision, cease to have effect.

The reference in this section to committees of local authorities does not include a reference to any committee of which some members are required to be appointed by a body or person other than a local authority.

(4)–(6) *****

*****

PART XI   GENERAL PROVISIONS AS TO LOCAL AUTHORITIES

Legal proceedings

222   Power of local authorities to prosecute or defend legal proceedings

(1) Where a local authority consider it expedient for the promotion or protection of the interests of the inhabitants of their area—

(a) they may prosecute or defend or appear in any legal proceedings and, in the case of civil proceedings, may institute them in their own name, and

(b) they may, in their own name, make representations in the interests of the inhabitants at any public inquiry held by or on behalf of any Minister or public body under any enactment.

(2) In this section "local authority" includes the Common Council [and the London Fire and Emergency Planning Authority.]

*****

Byelaws

235   Power of councils to make byelaws for good rule and government and suppression of nuisances

(1) The council of a district [, the council of a principal area in Wales] and the council of a London borough may make byelaws for the good rule and government of the whole or any part of the district [principal area] or borough, as the case may be, and for the prevention and suppression of nuisances therein.

(2) The confirming authority in relation to byelaws made under this section shall be the Secretary of State.

(3) Byelaws shall not be made under this section for any purpose as respects any area if provision for that purpose as respects that area is made by, or is or may be made under, any other enactment.

*****

[SCHEDULE 12A   ACCESS TO INFORMATION: EXEMPT INFORMATION
PART I   DESCRIPTIONS OF EXEMPT INFORMATION

1. Information relating to a particular employee, former employee or applicant to become an employee of, or a particular office-holder, former office-holder or applicant to become an office-holder under, the authority.

2, 2A *****

3. Information relating to any particular occupier or former occupier of, or applicant for accommodation provided by or at the expense of the authority.

4. Information relating to any particular applicant for, or recipient or former recipient of, any service provided by the authority.

5. Information relating to any particular applicant for, or recipient or former recipient of, any financial assistance provided by the authority.

6. Information relating to the adoption, care, fostering or education of any particular child.

7. Information relating to the financial or business affairs of any particular person (other than the authority).

8. The amount of any expenditure proposed to be incurred by the authority under any particular contract for the acquisition of property or the supply of goods or services.

9. Any terms proposed or to be proposed by or to the authority in the course of negotiations for a contract for the acquisition or disposal of property or the supply of goods or services.

10. The identity of the authority (as well as of any other person, by virtue of paragraph 7 above) as the person offering any particular tender for a contract for the supply of goods or services.

11. Information relating to any consultations or negotiations, or contemplated consultations or negotiations, in connection with any labour relations matter arising between the authority or a Minister of the Crown and employees of, or office-holders under, the authority.

12. Any instructions to counsel and any opinion of counsel (whether or not in connection with any proceedings) and any advice received, information obtained or action to be taken in connection with—

    (a) any legal proceedings by or against the authority, or

    (b) the determination of any matter affecting the authority, (whether, in either case, proceedings have been commenced or are in contemplation).

13. Information which, if disclosed to the public, would reveal that the authority proposes—

    (a) to give under any enactment a notice under or by virtue of which requirements are imposed on a person; or

    (b) to make an order or direction under any enactment.

14. Any action taken or to be taken in connection with the prevention, investigation or prosecution of crime.

15.   The identity of a protected informant.]

*****

Local Government Act 1974

(1974, c. 7)

An Act to make further provision, in relation to England and Wales, with respect to the payment of grants to local authorities, rating and valuation, borrowing and lending by local authorities and the classification of highways; to extend the powers of the Countryside Commission to give financial assistance; to provide for the establishment of Commissions for the investigation of administrative action taken by or on behalf of local and other authorities; to restrict certain grants under the Transport Act 1968; to provide for the removal or relaxation of certain statutory controls affecting local government activities; to make provision in relation to the collection of sums by local authorities on behalf of water authorities; to amend section 259(3) of the Local Government Act 1972 and to make certain minor amendments of or consequential on that Act; and for connected purposes   **[8 February 1974]**

Territorial extent: England and Wales

PART III   LOCAL GOVERNMENT ADMINISTRATION

23   The Commissions for Local Administration

    (1) For the purpose of conducting investigations in accordance with this Part of this Act, there shall be—

        (a) a body of commissioners to be known as the Commission for Local Administration in England, . . .

[but [the Commission] may include persons appointed to act as advisers, not exceeding the number appointed to conduct investigations.]

(2) The Parliamentary Commissioner shall be a member of [the Commission].

(2A) . . .

(3) In the following provisions of this Part of this Act the expression "Local Commissioner" means a person, other than the Parliamentary Commissioner, [the Welsh Administration Ombudsman,] [or an advisory member] who is a member of [the Commission].

(3A) . . .

(4) Appointments to the office of . . . Commissioner shall be made by Her Majesty on the recommendation of the Secretary of State after consultation with [such persons as appear to the Secretary of State to represent authorities in England or, as the case may be, authorities in Wales to which this Part of this Act applies], and a person so appointed shall, subject to subsection (6) below, hold office during good behaviour.

(5) . . . Commissioners may be appointed to serve either as full-time commissioners or as part-time commissioners.

(6) A Commissioner may be relieved of office by Her Majesty at his own request or may be removed from office by Her Majesty on grounds of incapacity or misbehaviour, and shall in any case vacate office on completing the year of service in which he attains the age of sixty-five years.

(7) The Secretary of State shall designate two of the Local Commissioners for England as chairman and vice-chairman respectively of the Commission for Local Administration in England . . .

(8) The Commission for Local Administration in England shall divide England into areas and shall provide, in relation to each area, for one or more of the Local Commissioners to be responsible for the area; . . .

A Local Commissioner may, by virtue of this Subsection, be made responsible for more than one area.

(9)–(13) *****

23A *****

24 . . .

25 Authorities subject to investigation

(1) This Part of this Act applies to [the following authorities]—

(a)   any local authority,

[(aaa) the Greater London Authority,]

(aa)   . . .

[(ab) a National Park Authority [for a National Park in England];]

(b)   any joint board the constituent authorities of which are all local authorities,

[(ba) the Commission for the New Towns;

(bb)   any development corporation established for the purposes of a new town;

[(bbb) the London Development Agency,]

(bc)   . . .

(bd)   any urban development corporation established by an order under section 135 of the Local Government, Planning and Land Act 1980 [for an urban development area in England];]

[(be) any housing action trust established under Part III of the Housing Act 1988 [for a designated area in England];]

[(bf) the Urban Regeneration Agency;]

[(bg) [a fire and rescue authority [in England] constituted by a scheme under section 2 of the Fire and Rescue Services Act 2004 or a scheme to which section 4 of that Act applies];]

[(c)   any joint authority established by Part IV of the Local Government Act 1985;

[(cza) the London Fire and Emergency Planning Authority;]

[(ca)   any police authority established under [section 3 of the Police Act 1996 [for a police area in England]]]; . . .

[(caa) the Metropolitan Police Authority,]

(cb)   . . .

[(cc)   Transport for London . . .]

[(d)   in relation to the flood defence functions of the Environment Agency, within the meaning of the Water Resources Act 1991, the Environment Agency and any regional flood defence committee [for an area wholly or partly in England]] [; and

(e)   The London Transport Users' Committee.]

(2) Her Majesty may by Order in Council provide that this Part of this Act shall also apply, subject to any modifications or exceptions specified in the Order, to any authority specified in the Order, being an authority which is established by or under an Act of Parliament, and which has power to levy a rate, or to issue a precept.

(3)–(5) *****

26   Matters subject to investigation

(1) Subject to the provisions of this Part of this Act where a written complaint is made by or on behalf of a member of the public who claims to have sustained injustice in consequence of maladministration in connection with action taken by or on behalf of an authority to which this Part of this Act applies, being action taken in the exercise of administrative functions of that authority, a Local Commissioner may investigate that complaint.

(2) A complaint shall not be entertained under this Part of this Act unless [it is made in writing to the Local Commissioner, specifying the action alleged to constitute maladministration, or]

(a)   it is made inviting to a member of the authority, or of any other authority concerned, specifying the action alleged to constitute maladministration, and

(b)   it is referred to the Local Commissioner, with the consent of the person aggrieved, or of a person acting on his behalf, by that member, or by any other person who is a member of any authority concerned, with a request to investigate the complaint.

(3) If the Local Commissioner is satisfied that any member of any authority concerned has been requested to refer the complaint to a Local Commissioner, and has not done so, the Local Commissioner may, if he thinks fit, dispense with the requirements in subsection (2)(b) above.

(4) A complaint shall not be entertained unless it was made to [the Local Commissioner or] a member of any authority concerned within twelve months from the day on which the person aggrieved first had notice of the matters alleged in the complaint, but a Local Commissioner may conduct an investigation pursuant to a complaint not made within that period if he considers that [it is reasonable] to do so.

(5) Before proceeding to investigate a complaint, a Local Commissioner shall satisfy himself that the complaint has been brought, by or on behalf of the person aggrieved, to the notice of the authority to which the complaint relates and that that authority has been afforded a reasonable opportunity to investigate, and reply to, the complaint.

(6) A Local Commissioner shall not conduct an investigation under this Part of this Act in respect of any of the following matters, that is to say,—

(a)   any action in respect of which the person aggrieved has or had a right of appeal, reference or review to or before a tribunal constituted by or under any enactment;

(b)   any action in respect of which in the person aggrieved has or had a right of appeal to a Minister of the Crown . . . ; or

(c) any action in respect of which the person aggrieved has or had a remedy by way of proceedings in any court of law:

Provided that a Local Commissioner may conduct an investigation notwithstanding the existence of such a right or remedy if satisfied that in the particular circumstances it is not reasonable to expect the person aggrieved to resort or have resorted to it.

[(6A) A Local Commissioner shall not conduct an investigation under this Part of this Act in respect of any action taken in connection with the discharge by an authority of any of the authority's functions otherwise than in relation to England.]

(7) A Local Commissioner shall not conduct an investigation in respect of any action which in his opinion affects all or most of the inhabitants of the [following area:

[(aa)where the complaint relates to a National Park Authority, the area of the Park for which it is such an authority;]

(a) where the complaint relates to the Commission for the New Towns, the area of the new town or towns to which the complaint relates;

(b) . . .;

[(ba)where the complaint relates to the Urban Regeneration Agency, any designated area within the meaning of Part III of the Leasehold Reform, Housing and Urban Development Act 1993;]

(c) in any other case, the area of the authority concerned.]

(8) Without prejudice to the preceding provisions of this section, a Local Commissioner shall not conduct an investigation under this Part of this Act in respect of any such action or matter as is described in Schedule 5 to this Act.

(9) Her Majesty may by Order in Council amend the said Schedule 5 so as [to add to or to exclude from the provisions of that Schedule (as it has effect for the time being)] such actions or matters as may be described in the Order; and any Order made by virtue of this subsection shall be subject to annulment in pursuance of a resolution of either House of Parliament.

(10) In determining whether to initiate, continue or discontinue an investigation, a Local Commissioner shall, subject to the proceeding provisions of this section, act at discretion; and any question whether a complaint is duly made under this Part of this Act shall be determined by the Local Commissioner.

(11), (12), (13) *****

27 Provisions relating to complaints

(1) A complaint under this Part of this Act may be made by any individual, or by any body of persons whether incorporated or not, not being—

(a) a local authority or other authority or body constituted for purposes of the public service or of local government, [including the National Assembly for Wales,] or for the purposes of carrying on under national ownership any industry or undertaking or part of an industry or undertaking;

(b) any other authority or body whose members are appointed by Her Majesty or any Minister of the Crown or government department [or by the National Assembly for Wales], or whose revenues consist wholly or mainly of moneys provided by Parliament [or the National Assembly for Wales].

(2) *****

28 Procedure in respect of investigations

(1) Where a Local Commissioner proposes to conduct an investigation pursuant to a complaint, he shall afford to the authority concerned, and to any person who is alleged in the complaint to have taken or authorised the action complained of, an opportunity to comment on any allegations contained in the complaint.

(2) Every such investigation shall be conducted in private, but except as aforesaid the procedure for conducting an investigation shall be such as the Local Commissioner

considers appropriate in the circumstances of the case; and without prejudice to the generality of the preceding provision the Local Commissioner may obtain information from such persons and in such manner, and make such inquiries as he thinks fit, and may determine whether any person may be represented (by counsel or solicitor or otherwise) in the investigation.

(3) *****

(4) The conduct of an investigation under this Part of this Act shall not affect any action taken by the authority concerned, or any power or duty of that authority to take further action with respect to any matters subject to the investigation.

29   Investigations: further provisions

(1) For the purposes of an investigation under this Part of this Act a Local Commissioner may require any member or officer of the authority concerned, or any other person who in his opinion is able to furnish information or produce documents relevant to the investigation, to furnish any such information or produce any such documents.

(2) For the purposes of any such investigation a Local Commissioner shall have the same powers as the High Court in respect of the attendance and examination of witnesses, and in respect of the production of documents.

(3)–(10) *****

30   Reports on investigations

(1) In any case where a Local Commissioner conducts an investigation, or decides not to conduct an investigation, he shall send a report of the results of the investigation, or as the case may be a statement of his reasons for not conducting an investigation—

(a) to the person, if any, who referred the complaint to the Local Commissioner in accordance with section 26(2) above, and

(b) to the complainant, and

(c) to the authority concerned, and to any other authority or person who is alleged in the complaint to have taken or authorised the action complained of.

(2), (2AA), (2AB) *****

(2A) . . .

(3) Apart from identifying the authority or authorities concerned the report shall not . . . —

(a) mention the name of any person, or

(b) contain any particulars which, in the opinion of the Local Commissioner, are likely to identify any person and can be omitted without impairing the effectiveness of the report,

unless, after taking into account the public interest as well as the interests of the complainant and of persons other than the complainant, the Local Commissioner considers it necessary to mention the name of that person or to include in the report any such particulars.

[(3AA) Nothing in subsection (3) above prevents a report—

(a) mentioning the name of, or

(b) containing particulars likely to identify,

the Mayor of London or any member of the London Assembly.]

(3A) . . .

(4) Subject to the provisions of subsection (7) below, the authority concerned shall for a period of three weeks make copies of the report available for inspection by the public without charge at all reasonable hours at one or more of their offices; and any person shall be entitled to take copies of, or extracts from, the report when so made available.

[(4A) Subject to subsection (7) below, the authority concerned shall supply a copy of the report to any person on request if he pays such charge as the authority may reasonably require.

(5) Not later than [two weeks] after the report is received by the authority concerned, the

proper officer of the authority shall give public notice, by advertisement in the newspapers and such other ways as appear to him appropriate, that [copies of the report will be available as provided by subsections (4) and (4A)] above, and shall specify the date, being a date [not more than one week after the public notice is first given] from which the period of three weeks will begin.

(6) *****

(7) The Local Commissioner may, if he thinks fit after taking into account the public interest as well as the interests of the complainant and of persons other than the complainant, direct that a report specified in the direction shall not be subject to the provisions of subsections (4) [,(4A) and (5) above.]

(8) *****

31   Reports on investigations: further provisions

[(1) This section applies where a Local Commissioner reports that injustice has been caused to a person aggrieved in consequence of maladministration.

(2) The report shall be laid before the authority concerned and it shall be the duty of that authority to consider the report and, within the period of three months beginning with the date on which they received the report, or such longer period as the Local Commissioner may agree in writing, to notify the Local Commissioner of the action which the authority have taken or propose to take.

[(2A) If the Local Commissioner—

(a) does not receive the notification required by subsection (2) above within the period allowed by or under that subsection, or

(b) is not satisfied with the action which the authority concerned have taken or propose to take, or

(c) does not within a period of three months beginning with the end of the period so allowed, or such longer period as the Local Commissioner may agree in writing, receive confirmation from the authority concerned that they have taken action, as proposed, to the satisfaction of the Local Commissioner,

he shall make a further report setting out those facts and making recommendations.

(2B) Those recommendations are such recommendations as the Local Commissioner thinks fit to make with respect to action which, in his opinion, the authority concerned should take to remedy the injustice to the person aggrieved and to prevent similar injustice being caused in the future.

(2C) Section 30 above, with any necessary modifications, and subsection (2) above shall apply to a report under subsection (2A) above as they apply to a report under that section.

(2D) If the Local Commissioner—

(a) does not receive the notification required by subsection (2) above as applied by subsection (2C) above within the period allowed by or under that subsection or is satisfied before the period allowed by that subsection has expired that the authority concerned have decided to take no action, or

(b) is not satisfied with the action which the authority concerned have taken or propose to take, or

(c) does not within a period of three months beginning with the end of the period allowed by or under subsection (2) above as applied by subsection (2C) above, or such longer period as the Local Commissioner may agree in writing, receive confirmation from the authority concerned that they have taken action, as proposed, to the satisfaction of the Local Commissioner,

he may, by notice to the authority, require them to arrange for a statement to be published in accordance with subsections (2E) and (2F) below.

(2E) The statement referred to in subsection (2D) above is a statement, in such form as the authority concerned and the Local Commissioner may agree, consisting of—

(a) details of any action recommended by the Local Commissioner in his further report which the authority have not taken;

(b) such supporting material as the Local Commissioner may require; and

(c) if the authority so require, a statement of the reasons for their having taken no action on, or not the action recommended in, the report.]

(2F)–(2H) *****

[(3) In any case where—

(a) a report is laid before an authority under subsection [(2) or (2C)] above, and

(b) on consideration of the report, it appears to the authority that a payment should be made to, or some other benefit should be provided for, a person who has suffered injustice in consequence of maladministration [to which the report relates],

the authority may incur such expenditure as appears to them to be appropriate in making such a payment or providing such a benefit.]

(4) *****

31A, 32–33   *****

34   Interpretation of Part III

(1), (2) *****

(3) It is hereby declared that nothing in this Part of this Act authorises or requires a Local Commissioner to question the merits of a decision taken without maladministration by an authority in the exercise of a discretion vested in that authority.

Section 26   SCHEDULE 5
MATTERS NOT SUBJECT TO INVESTIGATION

1. The commencement or conduct of civil or criminal proceedings before any court of law.

2. Action taken by any [police] authority in connection with the investigation or prevention of crime.

3.–(1) Action taken in matters relating to contractual or other commercial transactions of any authority to which Part III of this Act applies, including transactions falling within sub-paragraph (2) below but excluding transactions falling within sub-paragraph (3) below.

(2) The transactions mentioned in sub-paragraph (1) above as included in the matters which, by virtue of that sub-paragraph, are not subject to investigation are all transactions of an authority to which Part III of this Act applies relating to the operation of public passenger transport, the carrying on of a dock or harbour undertaking, the provision of entertainment, or the provision and operation of industrial establishments and of markets, [other than transactions relating to the grant, renewal or revocation of a licence to occupy a pitch or stall in a fair or market, or the attachment of any condition to such a licence.]

(3) The transactions mentioned in sub-paragraph (1) above as not included in those matters are—

(a) transactions for or relating to the acquisition or disposal of land [or the provision of moorings (not being moorings provided in connection with a dock or harbour undertaking)]; and

(b) all transactions (not being transactions falling within sub-paragraph (2) above) in the discharge of functions exercisable under any public general Act, other than those required for the procurement of the goods and services necessary to discharge those functions.

4. Action taken in respect of appointments or removals, pay, discipline, superannuation or other personnel matters.

5.—(1) . . .

(2) Any action concerning—

   (a) the giving of instruction, whether secular or religious, or

   (b) conduct, curriculum, internal organisation, management or discipline, [in any school or other educational establishment maintained by the authority.]

[6. Any action taken by an authority mentioned in section 25(1)(ba) or (bb) or this Act which is not action in connection with functions in relation to housing.

7. Action taken by an authority mentioned in section 25(1)(bd) of this Act which is not action in connection with functions in relation to town and country planning.]

[8. Action taken by the Urban Regeneration Agency which is not action in connection with functions in relation to town and country planning.]

House of Commons Disqualification Act 1975
(1975, c. 24)

An Act to consolidate certain enactments relating to disqualification for membership of the House of Commons   [8 May 1975]

Territorial extent: United Kingdom

1 Disqualification of holders of certain offices and places

(1) Subject to the provisions of this Act, a person is disqualified for membership of the House of Commons who for the time being—

   [(za) is a Lord Spiritual;]

   (a) holds any of the judicial offices specified in Part I of Schedule 1 to this Act;

   (b) is employed in the civil service of the Crown, whether in an established capacity or not, and whether for the whole or part of his time;

   (c) is a member of any of the regular armed forces of the Crown or the Ulster Defence Regiment;

   (d) is a member of any police force maintained by a police authority; . . .

   (e) is a member of the legislature of any country or territory outside the Commonwealth [other than Ireland]; or

   (f) holds any office described in Part II or Part III of Schedule 1.

(2), (3) *****

(4) Except as provided by this Act, a person shall not be disqualified for membership of the House of Commons by reason of his holding an office or place of profit under the Crown or any other office or place; and a person shall not be disqualified for appointment to or for holding any office or place by reason of his being a member of that House.

2 Ministerial offices

(1) Not more than ninety-five persons being the holders of offices specified in Schedule 2 to this Act (in this section referred to as Ministerial offices) shall be entitled to sit and vote in the House of Commons at any one time.

(2) If at any time the number of members of the House of Commons who are holders of Ministerial offices exceeds the number entitled to sit and vote in that House under subsection (1) above, none except any who were both members of that House and holders of Ministerial offices before the excess occurred shall sit or vote therein until the number has been reduced, by death, resignation or otherwise, to the number entitled to sit and vote as aforesaid.

(3) A person holding a Ministerial office is not disqualified by this Act by reason of any office held by him ex officio as the holder of that Ministerial office.

3 *****

4 Stewardship of Chiltern Hundreds, etc.

For the purposes of the provisions of this Act relating to the vacation of the seat of a member of the House of Commons who becomes disqualified by this Act for membership of that House, the office of steward or bailiff of Her Majesty's three Chiltern Hundreds of Stoke, Desborough and Burnham, or of the Manor of Northstead, shall be treated as included among the offices described in Part III of Schedule 1 to this Act.

5 Power to amend Schedule 1

(1) If at any time it is resolved by the House of Commons that Schedule 1 to this Act be amended, whether by the addition or omission of any office or the removal of any office from one Part of the Schedule to another, or by altering the description of any office specified therein, Her Majesty may by Order in Council amend that Schedule accordingly.

(2) *****

6 Effects of disqualification and provision for relief

(1) Subject to any order made by the House of Commons under this section,—

    (a) if any person disqualified by this Act for membership of that House, or for membership for a particular constituency, is elected as a member of that House, or as a member for that constituency, as the case may be, his election shall be void; and

    (b) if any person being a member of that House becomes disqualified by this Act for membership for the constituency for which he is sitting, his seat shall be vacated.

(2) If, in a case falling or alleged to fall within subsection (1) above, it appears to the House of Commons that the grounds of disqualification or alleged disqualification under this Act which subsisted or arose at the material time have been removed, and that it is otherwise proper so to do, that House may by order direct that any such disqualification incurred on those grounds at that time shall be disregarded for the purposes of this section.

(3), (4) *****

7 Jurisdiction of Privy Council as to disqualification

(1) Any person who claims that a person purporting to be a member of the House of Commons is disqualified by this Act, or has been so disqualified at any time since his (election, may apply to Her Majesty in Council, in accordance with such rules as Her Majesty in Council may prescribe, for a declaration to that effect.

(2) Section 3 of the Judicial Committee Act 1833 (reference to the Judicial Committee of the Privy Council of appeals to Her Majesty in Council) shall apply to any application under this section as it applies to an appeal to Her Majesty in Council from a court.

(3)–(5) *****

8–9 *****

10 . . .

*****

Section 2   SCHEDULE 2
MINISTERIAL OFFICE

Prime Minister and First Lord of the Treasury.
[Leader of the House of Commons]

Lord Privy Seal.
Chancellor of the Duchy of Lancaster.
Paymaster General.
President of the Board of Trade.
Secretary of State.
Chancellor of the Exchequer.
. . .
Minister of State.
Chief Secretary to the Treasury.
Minister in charge of a public department of Her Majesty's Government in the United
     Kingdom (if not within the other provisions of this Schedule).
Attorney General.
. . .
Solicitor General.
[Advocate General for Scotland.]
. . .
Parliamentary Secretary to the Treasury.
Financial Secretary to the Treasury.
Parliamentary Secretary in a Government Department other than the Treasury, or not in a
department.
Junior Lord of the Treasury.
Treasurer of Her Majesty's Household.
Comptroller of Her Majesty's Household.
Vice-Chamberlain of Her Majesty's Household.
Assistant Government Whip.

Ministerial and Other Salaries Act 1975
(1975, c. 27)

*An Act to consolidate the enactments relating to the salaries of Ministers and Opposition Leaders
and Chief Whips and to other matters connected therewith*   [8 May 1975]

Territorial extent: United Kingdom

1   Salaries

(1) Subject to the provisions of this Act—
   (a) there shall be paid to the holder of any Ministerial office specified in Schedule 1
        to this Act such salary as is provided for by that Schedule; and
   (b) there shall be paid to the Leaders and Whips of the Opposition such salaries as are
        provided for by Schedule 2 to this Act.

(2) There shall be paid to the Lord Chancellor a salary (which shall be charged on and
paid out of the Consolidated Fund of the United Kingdom) at such rate as together with the
salary payable to him as Speaker of the House of Lords will amount to [[£2,500] a year more
than the salary payable to the Lord Chief Justice], . . .

(3) There shall be paid to the Speaker of the House of Commons a salary (which shall be
charged on and paid out of the Consolidated Fund of the United Kingdom) of [£60,000] a
year; and on a dissolution of Parliament the Speaker of the House of Commons at the time of
the dissolution shall for this purpose be deemed to remain Speaker until a Speaker is chosen by
the New Parliament.

(4) . . .

(5) *****

1A, 1B *****

2 Opposition Leaders and Whips
(1) In this Act "Leader of the Opposition" means, in relation to either House of Parliament, that Member of that House who is for the time being the Leader in that House of the party in opposition to Her Majesty's Government having the greatest numerical strength in the House of Commons; and "Chief Opposition Whip" means, in relation to either House of Parliament, the person for the time being nominated as such by the Leader of the Opposition in that House; and "Assistant Opposition Whip", in relation to the House of Commons, means a person for the time being nominated as such, and to be paid as such, by the Leader of the Opposition in the House of Commons.

(2) If any doubt arises as to which is or was at any material time the party in opposition to Her Majesty's Government having the greatest numerical strength in the House of Commons, or as to who is or was at any material time the leader in that House of such a party, the question shall be decided for the purposes of this Act by the Speaker of the House of Commons, and his decision, certified in writing under his hand, shall be final and conclusive.

(3) If any doubt arises as to who is or was at any material time the Leader in the House of Lords of the said party, the question shall be decided for the purposes of this Act by [the Speaker of the House of Lords] and his decision, certified in writing under his hand, shall be final and conclusive.

3 *****

4 Interpretation
(1) In this Act—
"Junior Lord of the Treasury" means any Lord Commissioner of the Treasury other than the First Lord and the Chancellor of the Exchequer;
"Minister of State" and "Parliamentary Secretary" have the same meanings as in the House of Commons Disqualification Act 1975.
(2) *****

Sex Discrimination Act 1975
(1975, c. 65)

An Act to render unlawful certain kinds of sex discrimination and discrimination on the ground of marriage, and establish a Commission with the function of working towards the elimination of such discrimination and promoting equality of opportunity between men and women generally; and for related purposes   [12 November 1975]

Territorial extent: England and Wales, Scotland (s. 35A applies only to England and Wales; the equivalent provisions are in s. 35B for Scotland)

PART I   DISCRIMINATION TO WHICH ACT APPLIES

[1   Direct and indirect discrimination against women
(1) In any circumstances relevant for the purposes of any provision of this Act, other than a provision to which subsection (2) applies, a person discriminates against a woman if—

    (a) on the ground of her sex he treats her less favourably than he treats or would treat a man, or

(b) he applies to her a requirement or condition which he applies or would apply equally to a man but—

    (i) which is such that the proportion of women who can comply with it is considerably smaller than the proportion of men who can comply with it, and

    (ii) which he cannot show to be justifiable irrespective of the sex of the person to whom it is applied, and

    (iii) which is to her detriment because she cannot comply with it.

(2) In any circumstances relevant for the purposes of a provision to which this subsection applies, a person discriminates against a woman if—

    (a) on the ground of her sex, he treats her less favourably than he treats or would treat a man, or

    (b) he applies to her a provision, criterion or practice which he applies or would apply equally to a man, but—

        (i) which is such that it would be to the detriment of a considerably larger proportion of women than of men, and

        (ii) which he cannot show to be justifiable irrespective of the sex of the person to whom it is applied, and

        (iii) which is to her detriment.

(3) Subsection (2) applies to—

    (a) any provision of Part 2,

    (b) sections 35A and 35B, and

    (c) any other provision of Part 3, so far as it applies to vocational training.]

(4) . . .

2   Sex discrimination against men

(1) Section 1, and the provisions of Parts II and III relating to sex discrimination against women, are to be read as applying equally to the treatment of men, and for that purpose shall have effect with such modifications as are requisite.

(2) In the application of subsection (1) no account shall be taken of special treatment afforded to women in connection with pregnancy or childbirth.

[2A   Discrimination on the grounds of gender reassignment

(1) A person ("A") discriminates against another person ("B") in any circumstances relevant for the purposes of—

    (a) any provision of Part II,

    (b) section 35A or 35B, or

    (c) any other provision of Part III, so far as it applies to vocational training,

if he treats B less favourably than he treats or would treat other persons, and does so on the ground that B intends to undergo, is undergoing or has undergone gender reassignment.

(2) Subsection (3) applies to arrangements made by any person in relation to another's absence from work or from vocational training.

(3) For the purposes of subsection (1), B is treated less favourably than others under such arrangements if, in the application of the arrangements to any absence due to B undergoing gender reassignment—

    (a) he is treated less favourably than he would be if the absence was due to sickness or injury, or . . .

    (b) he is treated less favourably than he would be if the absence was due to some other cause and, having regard to the circumstances of the case, it is reasonable for him to be treated no less favourably.

(4) In subsections (2) and (3) "arrangements" includes terms, conditions or arrangements on which employment, a pupillage or tenancy or vocational training is offered.

(5) For the purposes of subsection (1), a provision mentioned in that subsection framed

with reference to discrimination against women shall be treated as applying equally to the treatment of men with such modifications as are requisite.]

[3 Discrimination against married persons and civil partners in employment field

(1) In any circumstances relevant for the purposes of any provision of Part 2, a person discriminates against a person ("A") who fulfils the condition in subsection (2) if—

    (a) on the ground of the fulfilment of the condition, he treats A less favourably than he treats or would treat a person who does not fulfil the condition, or

    (b) he applies to A a provision, criterion or practice which he applies or would apply equally to a person who does not fulfil the condition, but—

        (i) which puts or would put persons fulfilling the condition at a particular disadvantage when compared with persons not fulfilling the condition, and

        (ii) which puts A at that disadvantage, and

        (iii) which he cannot show to be a proportionate means of achieving a legitimate aim.

(2) The condition is that the person is—

    (a) married, or

    (b) a civil partner.

(3) For the purposes of subsection (1), a provision of Part 2 framed with reference to discrimination against women is to be treated as applying equally to the treatment of men, and for that purpose has effect with such modifications as are requisite.]

4 Discrimination by way of victimisation

(1) A person ("the discriminator") discriminates against another person ("the person victimised") in any circumstances relevant for the purposes of any provision of this Act if he treats the person victimised less favourably than in those circumstances he treats or would treat other persons, and does so by reason that the person victimised has—

    (a) brought proceedings against the discriminator or any other person under this Act or the Equal Pay Act 1970 [or sections 62 to 65 of the Pensions Act 1995], or

    (b) given evidence or information in connection with proceedings brought by any person against the discriminator or any other person under this Act or the Equal Pay Act 1970 [or sections 62 to 65 of the Pensions Act 1995], or

    (c) otherwise done anything under or by reference to this Act or the Equal Pay Act 1970 [or sections 62 to 65 of the Pensions Act 1995] in relation to the discriminator or any other person, or

    (d) alleged that the discriminator or any other person has committed an act which (whether or not the allegation so states) would amount to a contravention of this Act or give rise to a claim under the Equal Pay Act 1970 [or under sections 62 to 65 of the Pensions Act 1995],

or by reason that the discriminator knows the person victimised intends to do any of those things, or suspects the person victimised has done, or intends to do, any of them.

(2) Subsection (1) does not apply to treatment of a person by reason of any allegation made by him if the allegation was false and not made in good faith.

(3) For the purposes of subsection (1), a provision of Part II or III framed with reference to discrimination against women shall be treated as applying equally to the treatment of men and for that purpose shall have effect with such modifications as are requisite.

5 Interpretation

(1) In this Act—

    (a) references to discrimination refer to any discrimination falling within sections 1 to 4; and

(b) references to sex discrimination refer to any discrimination falling within section 1 or 2,

and related expressions shall be construed accordingly.

(2) In this Act—

"woman" includes a female of any age, and

"man" includes a male of any age.

[(3) Each of the following comparisons, that is—

(a) a comparison of the cases of persons of different sex under section 1(1) or (2),

(b) a comparison of the cases of persons required for the purposes of section 2A, and

(c) a comparison of the cases of persons who do and who do not fulfil the condition in section 3(2),

must be such that the relevant circumstances in the one case are the same, or not materially different, in the other.]

PART II   DISCRIMINATION IN THE EMPLOYMENT FIELD

Discrimination by employers

6   Discrimination against applicants and employees

(1) It is unlawful for a person, in relation to employment by him at an establishment in Great Britain, to discriminate against a woman—

(a) in the arrangements he makes for the purpose of determining who should be offered that employment, or

(b) in the terms on which he offers her that employment, or

(c) by refusing or deliberately omitting to offer her that employment.

(2) It is unlawful for a person, in the case of a woman employed by him at an establishment in Great Britain, to discriminate against her—

(a) in the way he affords her access to opportunities for promotion, transfer or training, or to any other benefits, facilities or services, or by refusing or deliberately omitting to afford her access to them, or

(b) by dismissing her, or subjecting her to any other detriment.

(3) . . .

(4), (4A) *****

(5) Subject to section 8(3), subsection (1)(b) does not apply to any provision for the payment of money which, if the woman in question were given the employment, would be included (directly . . . or otherwise) in the contract under which she was employed.

(6) Subsection (2) does not apply to benefits consisting of the payment of money when the provision of those benefits is regulated by the woman's contract of employment.

(7) Subsection (2) does not apply to benefits, facilities or services of any description if the employer is concerned with the provision (for payment or not) of benefits, facilities or services of that description to the public, or to a section of the public comprising the woman in question, unless—

(a) that provision differs in a material respect from the provision of the benefits, facilities or services by the employer to his employees, or

(b) the provision of the benefits, facilities or services to the woman in question is regulated by her contract of employment, or

(c) the benefits, facilities or services relate to training.

[(8) In its application to any discrimination falling within section 2A, this section shall have effect with the omission of subsections (4) to (6).]

7   Exception where sex is a genuine occupational qualification

(1) In relation to sex discrimination—

(a) section 6(1)(a) or (c) does not apply to any employment where being a man is a genuine occupational qualification for the job, and

(b) section 6(2)(a) does not apply to opportunities for promotion or transfer to, or training for, such employment.

(2) Being a man is a genuine occupational qualification for a job only where—

(a) the essential nature of the job calls for a man for reasons of physiology (excluding physical strength or stamina) or, in dramatic performances or other entertainment, for reasons of authenticity, so that the essential nature of the job would be materially different if carried out by a woman; or

(b) the job needs to be held by a man to preserve decency or privacy because—

   (i) it is likely to involve physical contact with men in circumstances where they might reasonably object to its being carried out by a woman, or

   (ii) the holder of the job is likely to do his work in circumstances where men might reasonably object to the presence of a woman because they are in a state of undress or are using sanitary facilities; or

[(ba) the job is likely to involve the holder of the job doing his work, or living, in a private home and needs to be held by a man because objection might reasonably be taken to allowing to a woman—

   (i) the degree of physical or social contact with a person living in the home, or

   (ii) the knowledge of intimate details of such a person's life,

which is likely, because of the nature or circumstances of the job or of the home, to be allowed to, or available to, the holder of the job; or]

(c) the nature or location of the establishment makes it impracticable for the holder of the job to live elsewhere than in premises provided by the employer, and—

   (i) the only such premises which are available for persons holding that kind of job are lived in, or normally lived in, by men and are not equipped with separate sleeping accommodation for women and sanitary facilities which could be used by women in privacy from men, and

   (ii) it is not reasonable to expect the employer either to equip those premises with such accommodation and facilities or to provide other premises for women; or

(d) the nature of the establishment, or of the part of it within which the work is done, requires the job to be held by a man because—

   (i) it is, or is part of, a hospital, prison or other establishment for persons requiring special care, supervision or attention, and

   (ii) those persons are all men (disregarding any woman whose presence is exceptional), and

   (iii) it is reasonable, having regard to the essential character of the establishment or that part, that the job should not be held by a woman; or

(e) the holder of the job provides individuals with personal services promoting their welfare or education, or similar personal services, and those services can most effectively be provided by a man, or

(f) . . .

(g) the job needs to be held by a man because it is likely to involve the performance of duties outside the United Kingdom in a country whose laws or customs are such that the duties could not, or could not effectively, be performed by a woman, or

[(h) the job is one of two to be held

   (i) by a married couple,

   (ii) by a couple who are civil partners of each other, or

   (iii) by a married couple or a couple who are civil partners of each other.]

(3) Subsection (2) applies where some only of the duties of the job fall within paragraphs (a) to (g) as well as where all of them do.

(4) Paragraph (a), (b), (c), (d), (e) . . . or (g) of subsection (2) does not apply in relation to the filling of a vacancy at a time when the employer already has male employees—

(a) who are capable of carrying out the duties falling within that paragraph, and

(b) whom it would be reasonable to employ on those duties and

(c) whose numbers are sufficient to meet the employer's likely requirements in respect of those duties without undue inconvenience.

7A, 7B *****

8 Equal Pay Act 1970

(1) *****

(2) Section 1(1) of the Equal Pay Act 1970 (as set out in subsection (1) above) does not apply in determining for the purposes of section 6(1)(b) of this Act the terms on which employment is offered.

(3) Where a person offers a woman employment on certain terms, and if she accepted the offer then, by virtue of an equality clause, any of those terms would fall to be modified, or any additional term would fall to be included, the offer shall be taken to contravene section 6(1)(b).

(4) Where a person offers a woman employment on certain terms, and subsection (3) would apply but for the fact that, on her acceptance of the offer, section 1(3) of the Equal Pay Act 1970 (as set out in subsection (1) above) would prevent the equality clause from operating, the offer shall be taken not to contravene section 6(1)(b).

(5) An act does not contravene section 6(2) if—

(a) it contravenes a term modified or included by virtue of an equality clause, or

(b) it would contravene such a term but for the fact that the equality clause is prevented from operating by section 1(3) of the Equal Pay Act 1970.

(6), (7) *****

9 Discrimination against contract workers

(1) This section applies to any work for a person ("the principal") which is available for doing by individuals ("contract workers") who are employed not by the principal himself but by another person, who supplies them under a contract made with the principal.

(2) It is unlawful for the principal, in relation to work to which this section applies, to discriminate against a woman who is a contract worker—

(a) in the terms on which he allows her to do that work, or

(b) by not allowing her to do it or continue to do it, or

(c) in the way he affords her access to any benefits, facilities or services or by refusing or deliberately omitting to afford her access to them, or

(d) by subjecting her to any other detriment.

(3)–(3D), (4) *****

10 Meaning of employment at establishment in Great Britain

(1) For the purposes of this Part and section 1 of the Equal Pay Act 1970 ("the relevant purposes"), employment is to be regarded as being at an establishment in Great Britain unless the employee does his work wholly . . . outside Great Britain.

(2), (7) *****

Discrimination by other bodies

11 Partnerships

(1) It is unlawful for a firm . . ., in relation to a position as partner in the firm, to discriminate against a woman—

(a) in the arrangements they make for the purpose of determining who should be offered that position, or

(b) in the terms on which they offer her that position, or

(c) by refusing or deliberately omitting to offer her that position, or

(d) in a case where the woman already holds that position—

(i) in the way they afford her access to any benefits, facilities or services, or by refusing or deliberately omitting to afford her access to them, or

(ii) by expelling her from that position, or subjecting her to any other detriment.

(2) Subsection (1) shall apply in relation to persons proposing to form themselves into a partnership as it applies in relation to a firm.

(3) [Subject to subsection (3A),] subsection (1)(a) and (c) do not apply to a position as partner where, if it were employment, being a man would be a genuine occupational qualification for the job.

(3A)–(6) *****

12 Trade unions etc

(1) This section applies to an organisation of workers, an organisation of employers, or any other organisation whose members carry on a particular profession or trade for the purposes of which the organisation exists.

(2) It is unlawful for an organisation to which this section applies, in the case of a woman who is not a member of the organisation, to discriminate against her—

(a) in the terms on which it is prepared to admit her to membership, or

(b) by refusing, or deliberately omitting to accept, her application for membership.

(3) It is unlawful for an organisation to which this section applies, in the case of a woman who is a member of the organisation, to discriminate against her—

(a) in the way it affords her access to any benefits, facilities or services, or by refusing or deliberately omitting to afford her access to them, or

(b) by depriving her of membership, or varying the terms on which she is a member, or

(c) by subjecting her to any other detriment.

(4) This section does not apply to provision made in relation to the death or retirement from work of a member.

13 Qualifying bodies

(1) It is unlawful for an authority or body which can confer an authorisation or qualification which is needed for, or facilitates, engagement in a particular profession or trade to discriminate against a woman—

(a) in the terms on which it is prepared to confer on her that authorisation or qualification, or

(b) by refusing or deliberately omitting to grant her application for it, or

(c) by withdrawing it from her or varying the terms on which she holds it.

(2) Where an authority or body is required by law to satisfy itself as to his good character before conferring on a person an authorisation or qualification which is needed for, or facilitates, his engagement in any profession or trade then, without prejudice to any other duty to which it is subject, that requirement shall be taken to impose on the authority or body a duty to have regard to any evidence tending to show that he, or any of his employees, or agents (whether past or present), has practised unlawful discrimination in, or in connection with, the carrying on of any profession or trade.

(3), (4) ****

14–16 *****

Special cases

17 Police

(1) For the purposes of this Part, the holding of the office of constable shall be treated as employment—

(a) by the chief officer of police as respects any act done by him in relation to a constable or that office;

    (b) by the police authority as respects any act done by [it] in relation to a constable or that office.

  [(1A) For the purposes of section 41—

    (a) the holding of the office of constable shall be treated as employment by the chief officer of police (and as not being employment by any other person); and

    (b) anything done by a person holding such an office in the performance, or purported performance, of his functions shall be treated as done in the course of that employment.]

  (2), (3) *****

  (4) There shall be paid out of the police fund—

    (a) any compensation, costs or expenses awarded against a chief officer of police in any proceedings brought against him under this Act, and any costs or expenses incurred by him in any such proceedings so far as not recovered by him in the proceedings; and

    (b) any sum required by a chief officer of police for the settlement of any claim made against him under this Act if the settlement is approved by the police authority.

  (5)–(9) *****

18   *****

19 Ministers of religion etc

  (1) Nothing in this Part applies to employment for purposes of an organised religion where the employment is limited to one sex so as to comply with the doctrines of the religion or avoid offending the religious susceptibilities of a significant number of its followers.

  (2) Nothing in section 13 applies to an authorisation or qualification (as defined in that section) for purposes of an organised religion where the authorisation or qualification is limited to one sex so as to comply with the doctrines of the religion or avoid offending the religious susceptibilities of a significant number of its followers.

  [(3) In relation to discrimination falling within section 2A, this Part does not apply to employment for purposes of an organised religion where the employment is limited to persons who are not undergoing and have not undergone gender reassignment, if the limitation is imposed to comply with the doctrines of the religion or avoid offending the religious susceptibilities of a significant number of its followers.

  (4) In relation to discrimination falling within section 2A, section 13 does not apply to an authorisation or qualification (as defined in that section) for purposes of an organised religion where the authorisation or qualification is limited to persons who are not undergoing and have not undergone gender reassignment, if the limitation is imposed to comply with the doctrines of the religion or avoid offending the religious susceptibilities of a significant number of its followers.]

20   *****

[Relationships which have come to an end

20A   Relationships which have come to an end

  [(1) This section applies where—

    (a) there has been a relevant relationship between a woman and another person ("the relevant person"), and

    (b) the relationship has come to an end (whether before or after the commencement of this section).

  (2) In this section, a "relevant relationship" is a relationship during the course of which an act of discrimination by one party to the relationship against the other party to it is unlawful under any preceding provision of this Part.

  (3) It is unlawful for the relevant person to discriminate against the woman by subjecting

her to a detriment where the discrimination arises out of and is closely connected to the relevant relationship.]

21   *******

PART III   DISCRIMINATION IN OTHER FIELDS

Education

22   Discrimination by bodies in charge of educational establishments

It is unlawful, in relation to an educational establishment falling within column 1 of the following table, for a person indicated in relation to the establishment in column 2 (the "responsible body") to discriminate against a woman—

    (a) in the terms on which it offers to admit her to the establishment as a pupil, or

    (b) by refusing or deliberately omitting to accept an application for her admission to the establishment as a pupil, or

    (c) where she is a pupil of the establishment—

        (i)   in the way it affords her access to any benefits, facilities or services, or by refusing or deliberately omitting to afford her access to them, or

        (ii) by excluding her from the establishment or subjecting her to any other detriment.

[Table omitted]

[22A   Meaning of pupil in section 22

[For the purposes of section 22, "pupil" includes, in England and Wales, any person who receives education at a school or institution to which that section applies.]

23   Other discrimination by local education authorities

    (1) It is unlawful for a local education authority, in carrying out such of its functions under [the Education Acts] as do not fall under section 22, to do any act which constitutes sex discrimination.

    (2) It is unlawful for an education authority, in carrying out such of its functions under the Education (Scotland) [Act 1980] as do not fall under section 22, to do any act which constitutes sex discrimination.

[23A   Discrimination by Further Education and Higher Education Funding Councils

It is unlawful for [the Learning and Skills Council for England, the National Council for Education and Training for Wales,] the Higher Education Funding Council for England or the Higher Education Funding Council for Wales in carrying out their functions under [the Education Acts] [and the Learning and Skills Act 2000], to do any act which constitutes sex discrimination.]

[23B   Discrimination by Scottish Further and Higher Education Funding Councils

It is unlawful for the Scottish Further Education Funding Council or the Scottish Higher Education Funding Council in carrying out any of their functions to do any act which constitutes sex discrimination.]

23C   . . .

23D, 24   *******

25   General duty in public sector of education

    (1) Without prejudice to its obligation to comply with any other provision of this Act, a body to which this subsection applies shall be under a general duty to secure that facilities for

education provided by it, and any ancillary benefits or services, are provided without sex discrimination.

(2)–(5) *****

(6) Subsection (1) applies to—

(a) local education authorities in England and Wales;

(b) education authorities in Scotland;

(c)–(f)*****

25A ***

26 Exception for single-sex establishments

(1) Section 22(a) and (b)[, 25 and 25A] do not apply to the admission of pupils to any establishment (a "single-sex establishment") which admits pupils of one sex only, or which would be taken to admit pupils of one sex only if there were disregarded pupils of the opposite sex—

(a) whose admission is exceptional, or

(b) whose numbers are comparatively small and whose admission is confined to particular courses of instruction or teaching classes.

(2)–(4) *****

27–28 ***

Goods, facilities, services and premises

29 Discrimination in provision of goods, facilities or services

(1) It is unlawful for any person concerned with the provision (for payment or not) of goods, facilities or services to the public or a section of the public to discriminate against a woman who seeks to obtain or use those goods, facilities or services—

(a) by refusing or deliberately omitting to provide her with any of them, or

(b) by refusing or deliberately omitting to provide her with goods, facilities or services of the like quality, in the like manner and on the like terms as are normal in his case in relation to male members of the public or (where she belongs to a section of the public) to male members of that section.

(2) The following are examples of the facilities and services mentioned in subsection (1)—

(a) access to and use of any place which members of the public or a section of the public are permitted to enter;

(b) accommodation in a hotel, boarding house or other similar establishment;

(c) facilities by way of banking or insurance or for grants, loans, credit or finance;

(d) facilities for education;

(e) facilities for entertainment, recreation or refreshment;

(f) facilities for transport or travel;

(g) the services of any profession or trade, or any local or other public authority.

(3) For the avoidance of doubt it is hereby declared that where a particular skill is commonly exercised in a different way for men and for women it does not contravene subsection (1) for a person who does not normally exercise it for women to insist on exercising it for a woman only in accordance with his normal practice or, if he reasonably considers it impracticable to do that in her case, to refuse or deliberately omit to exercise it.

(4) *****

30–32 ***

33 Exception for political parties

(1) This section applies to a political party if—

(a) it has as its main object, or one of its main objects, the promotion of parliamentary candidatures for the Parliament of the United Kingdom, or

(b) it is an affiliate of, or has as an affiliate, or has similar formal links with, a political party within paragraph (a).

(2) Nothing in section 29(1) shall be construed as affecting any special provision for persons of one sex only in the constitution, organisation or administration of the political party.

(3) Nothing in section 29(1) shall render unlawful an act done in order to give effect to such a special provision.

34 Exception for voluntary bodies

(1) This section applies to a body—

(a) the activities of which are carried on otherwise than for profit, and

(b) which was not set up by any enactment.

(2) Sections 29(1) and 30 shall not be construed as rendering unlawful—

(a) the restriction of membership of any such body to persons of one sex (disregarding any minor exceptions), or

(b) the provision of benefits, facilities or services to members of any such body where the membership is so restricted,

even though membership of the body is open to the public, or to a section of the public.

(3), (4) *****

35 *****

Barristers

[35A Discrimination by, or in relation to, barristers

[(1) It is unlawful for a barrister or barrister's clerk, in relation to any offer of a pupillage or tenancy, to discriminate against a woman—

(a) in the arrangements which are made for the purpose of determining to whom it should be offered;

(b) in respect of any terms on which it is offered; or

(c) by refusing, or deliberately omitting, to offer it to her.

(2) It is unlawful for a barrister or barrister's clerk, in relation to a woman who is a pupil or tenant in the chambers in question, to discriminate against her—

(a) in respect of any terms applicable to her as a pupil or tenant;

(b) in the opportunities for training, or gaining experience, which are afforded or denied to her;

(c) in the benefits, facilities or services which are afforded or denied to her; or

(d) by terminating her pupillage or by subjecting her to any pressure to leave the chambers or other detriment.

(3) It is unlawful for any person, in relation to the giving, withholding or acceptance of instructions to a barrister, to discriminate against a woman.

(4), (5) *****

35B–36 ******

PART IV   OTHER UNLAWFUL ACTS

37 *****

38 Discriminatory advertisements

(1) It is unlawful to publish or cause to be published an advertisement which indicates, or might reasonably be understood as indicating, an intention by a person to do any act which is or might be unlawful by virtue of Part II or III.

(2) Subsection (1) does not apply to an advertisement if the intended act would not in fact be unlawful.

(3) For the purposes of subsection (1), use of a job description with a sexual connotation (such as "waiter", "salesgirl", "postman" or "stewardess") shall be taken to indicate an intention to discriminate, unless the advertisement contains an indication to the contrary.

(4) The publisher of an advertisement made unlawful by subsection (1) shall not be subject to any liability under that subsection in respect of the publication of the advertisement if he proves—

    (a) that the advertisement was published in reliance on a statement made to him by the person who caused it to be published to the effect that, by reason of the operation of subsection (2), the publication would not be unlawful, and

    (b) that it was reasonable for him to rely on the statement.

(5) A person who knowingly or recklessly makes a statement such as is referred to in subsection (4) which in a material respect is false or misleading commits an offence, and shall be liable on summary conviction to a fine not exceeding [level 5 on the standard scale].

39 Instructions to discriminate
It is unlawful for a person—

    (a) who has authority over another person, or

    (b) in accordance with whose wishes that other person is accustomed to act,

to instruct him to do any act which is unlawful by virtue of Part II or III, or procure or attempt to procure the doing by him of any such act.

40 Pressure to discriminate
(1) It is unlawful to induce, or attempt to induce, a person to do any act which contravenes Part II or III by—

    (a) providing or offering to provide him with any benefit, or

    (b) subjecting or threatening to subject him to any detriment.

(2) An offer or threat is not prevented from falling within subsection (1) because it is not made directly to the person in question, if it is made in such a way that he is likely to hear of it.

41 Liability of employers and principals
(1) Anything done by a person in the course of his employment shall be treated for the purposes of this Act as done by his employer as well as by him, whether or not it was done with the employer's knowledge or approval.

(2) Anything done by a person as agent for another person with the authority (whether express or implied, and whether precedent or subsequent) of that other person shall be treated for the purposes of this Act as done by that other person as well as by him.

(3) In proceedings brought under this Act against any person in respect of an act alleged to have been done by an employee of his it shall be a defence for that person to prove that he took such steps as were reasonably practicable to prevent the employee from doing that act, or from doing in the course of his employment acts of that description.

42 Aiding unlawful acts
(1) A person who knowingly aids another person to do an act made unlawful by this Act shall be treated for the purpose of this Act as himself doing an unlawful act of the like description.

(2) For the purposes of subsection (1) an employee or agent for whose act the employer or principal is liable under section 41 (or would be so liable but for section 41(3)) shall be deemed to aid the doing of the act by the employer or principal.

(3) A person does not under this section knowingly aid another to do an unlawful act if—

    (a) he acts in reliance on a statement made to him by that other person that, by reason of any provision of this Act, the act which he aids would not be unlawful, and

    (b) it is reasonable for him to rely on the statement.

(4) A person who knowingly or recklessly makes a statement such as is referred to in subsection (3)(a) which in a material respect is false or misleading commits an offence,

and shall be liable on summary conviction to a fine not exceeding [level 5 on the standard scale].

PART V   GENERAL EXCEPTIONS FROM PARTS II TO IV

[42A   Selection of candidates
    (1) Nothing in Parts 2 to 4 shall—
        (a) be construed as affecting arrangements to which this section applies, or
        (b) render unlawful anything done in accordance with such arrangements.
    (2) This section applies to arrangements made by a registered political party which—
        (a) regulate the selection of the party's candidates in a relevant election, and
        (b) are adopted for the purpose of reducing inequality in the numbers of men and women elected, as candidates of the party, to be members of the body concerned.
    (3) The following elections are relevant elections for the purposes of this section—
        (a) parliamentary elections;
        (b) elections to the European Parliament;
        (c) elections to the Scottish Parliament;
        (d) elections to the National Assembly for Wales;
        (e) local government elections within the meaning of section 191, 203 or 204 of the Representation of the People Act 1983 (excluding any election of the Mayor of London).
    (4) In this section "registered political party" means a party registered in the Great Britain register under Part 2 of the Political Parties, Elections and Referendums Act 2000).]

43–46   ***

47   Discriminatory training by certain bodies
    (1) Nothing in Parts II to IV shall render unlawful any act done in relation to particular work by [any person] in, or in connection with—
        (a) affording women only, or men only, access to facilities for training which would help to fit them for that work, or
        (b) encouraging women only, or men only, to take advantage of opportunities for doing that work,
where [it reasonably appears to that person] that at any time within the 12 months immediately preceding the doing of the act there were no persons of the sex in question doing that work in Great Britain, or the number of persons of that sex doing the work in Great Britain was comparatively small.
    (2) Where in relation to particular work [it reasonably appears to any person] that although the condition for the operation of subsection (1) is not met for the whole of Great Britain it is met for an area within Great Britain, nothing in Parts II to IV shall render unlawful any act done by [that person] in, or in connection with—
        (a) affording persons who are of the sex in question, and who appear likely to take up that work in that area, access to facilities for training which would help to fit them for that work, or
        (b) encouraging persons of that sex to take advantage of opportunities in the area for doing that work.
    (3) Nothing in Parts II to IV shall render unlawful any act done by [any person] in, or in connection with, affording persons access to facilities for training which would help to fit them for employment, where [it reasonably appears to that person] that those persons are in special need of training by reason of the period for which they have been discharging domestic or family responsibilities to the exclusion of regular full time employment.
    The discrimination in relation to which this subsection applies may result from confining

the training to persons who have been discharging domestic or family responsibilities, or from the way persons are selected for training, or both.

[(4) The preceding provisions of this section shall not apply in relation to any discrimination which is rendered unlawful by section 6.]

48   Other discriminatory training etc

(1) Nothing in Parts II to IV shall render unlawful any act done by an employer in relation to particular work in his employment, being an act done in, or in connection with,—

(a) affording his female employees only, or his male employees only, access to facilities for training which would help to fit them for that work, or

(b) encouraging women only, or men only, to take advantage of opportunities for doing that work,

where at any time within the twelve months immediately preceding the doing of the act there were no persons of the sex in question among those doing that work or the number of persons of that sex doing the work was comparatively small.

(2), (3) *****

49–50   *****

[51   Acts done for purposes of protection of women

(1) Nothing in the following provisions, namely—

(a) Part II,

(b) Part III so far as it applies to vocational training, or

(c) Part IV so far as it has effect in relation to the provisions mentioned in paragraphs (a) and (b),

shall render unlawful any act done by a person in relation to a woman if—

(i) it was necessary for that person to do it in order to comply with a requirement of an existing statutory provision concerning the protection of women, or

(ii) it was necessary for that person to do it in order to comply with a requirement of a relevant statutory provision (within the meaning of Part I of the Health and Safety at Work etc. Act 1974) and it was done by that person for the purpose of the protection of the woman in question (or of any class of women that included that woman).

(2) In subsection (1)—

(a) the reference in paragraph (i) of that subsection to an existing statutory provision concerning the protection of women is a reference to any such provision having effect for the purpose of protecting women as regards—

(i) pregnancy or maternity, or

(ii) other circumstances giving rise to risks specifically affecting women,

whether the provision relates only to such protection or to the protection of any other class of persons as well; and

(b) the reference in paragraph (ii) of that subsection to the protection of a particular woman or class of women is a reference to the protection of that woman or those women as regards any circumstances falling within paragraph (a)(i) or (ii) above.

(3), (4) *****

51A   *****

52   Acts safeguarding national security

(1) Nothing in Parts II to IV shall render unlawful an act done for the purpose of safeguarding national security.

(2), (3) *****

52A   *****

PART VI EQUAL OPPORTUNITIES COMMISSION

53 Establishment and duties of Commission

(1) There shall be a body of Commissioners named the Equal Opportunities Commission, consisting of at least eight but not more than fifteen individuals each appointed by the Secretary of State on a full-time or part-time basis, which shall have the following duties—

    (a) to work towards the elimination of discrimination,

    (b) to promote equality of opportunity between men and women generally, . . .

    [(ba) to promote equality of opportunity, in the field of employment and of vocational training, for persons who intend to undergo, are undergoing or have undergone gender reassignment, and]

    (c) to keep under review the working of this Act and the Equal Pay Act 1970 and, when they are so required by the Secretary of State or otherwise think it necessary, draw up and submit to the Secretary of State proposals for amending them.

    (2)–(4) *****

54–56 *****

[Codes of practice

56A Codes of practice

(1) The Commission may issue codes of practice containing such practical guidance as the Commission think fit for [one or more] of the following purposes, namely—

    (a) the elimination of discrimination in the field of employment;

    (b) the promotion of equality of opportunity in that field between men and women;

    [(ba) the promotion of equality of opportunity in that field for persons who intend to undergo, are undergoing or have undergone gender reassignment].

(2) When the Commission propose to issue a code of practice, they shall prepare and publish a draft of that code, shall consider any representations made to them about the draft and may modify the draft accordingly.

(3) In the course of preparing any draft code of practice for eventual publication under subsection (2) the Commission shall consult with—

    (a) such organisations or associations of organisations representative of employers or of workers; and

    (b) such other organisations, or bodies,

as appear to the Commission to be appropriate.

(4) If the Commission determine to proceed with the draft, they shall transmit the draft to the Secretary of State who shall—

    (a) if he approves of it, lay it before both Houses of Parliament; and

    (b) if he does not approve of it, publish details of his reasons for withholding approval.

    (5)–(9) *****

(10) A failure on the part of any person to observe any provision of a code of practice shall not of itself render him liable to any proceedings; but in any proceedings under this Act [or the Equal Pay Act 1970] before an [employment tribunal] any code of practice issued under this section shall be admissible in evidence, and if any provision of such a code appears to the tribunal to be relevant to any question arising in the proceedings it shall be taken into account in determining that question.

(11) Without prejudice to subsection (1), a code of practice issued under this section may include such practical guidance as the Commission think fit as to what steps it is reasonably practicable for employers to take for the purpose of preventing their employees from doing in the course of their employment acts made unlawful by this Act.]

57–61 *****

PART VII   ENFORCEMENT

General

[62   Restriction of proceedings for breach of Act

(1) Except as provided by this Act no proceedings, whether civil or criminal, shall lie against any person in respect of an act by reason that the act is unlawful by virtue of a provision of this Act.

(2) Subsection (1) does not preclude the making of an order of certiorari, mandamus or prohibition.

(3) In Scotland, subsection (1) does not preclude the exercise of the jurisdiction of the Court of Session to entertain an application for reduction or suspension of any order or determination, or otherwise to consider the validity of any order or determination, or to require reasons for any order or determination to be stated.]

Enforcement in employment field

63   Jurisdiction of [employment tribunals]

(1) A complaint by any person ("the complainant") that another person ("the respondent")—

(a) has committed an act of discrimination against the complainant which is unlawful by virtue of Part II, or

(b) is by virtue of section 41 or 42 to be treated as having committed such an act of discrimination against the complainant,

may be presented to an [employment tribunal].

(2) Subsection (1) does not apply to a complaint under section 13(1) of an act in respect of which an appeal, or proceedings in the nature of an appeal, may be brought under any enactment.

[63A   Burden of proof: employment tribunals

(1) This section applies to any complaint presented under section 63 to an employment tribunal.

(2) Where, on the hearing of the complaint, the complainant proves facts from which the tribunal could, apart from this section, conclude in the absence of an adequate explanation that the respondent—

(a) has committed an act of discrimination against the complainant which is unlawful by virtue of Part 2, or

(b) is by virtue of section 41 or 42 to be treated as having committed such an act of discrimination against the complainant,

the tribunal shall uphold the complaint unless the respondent proves that he did not commit, or, as the case may be, is not to be treated as having committed, that act.]

64   ...

65   Remedies on complaint under section 63

(1) Where an [employment tribunal] finds that a complaint presented to it under section 63 is well-founded the tribunal shall make such of the following as it considers just and equitable—

(a) an order declaring the rights of the complainant and the respondent in relation to the act to which the complaint relates;

(b) an order requiring the respondent to pay to the complainant compensation of an amount corresponding to any damages he could have been ordered by a county court or by a sheriff court to pay to the complainant if the complaint had fallen to be dealt with under section 66;

(c) a recommendation that the respondent take within a specified period action appearing to the tribunal to be practicable for the purpose of obviating or reducing the adverse effect on the complainant of any act of discrimination to which the complaint relates.

[(1A) In applying section 66 for the purposes of subsection (1)(b), no account shall be taken of subsection (3) of that section.

(1B) As respects an unlawful act of discrimination falling within [section 1(2)(b)] or section 3(1)(b), if the respondent proves that the [provision, criterion or practice] in question was not applied with the intention of treating the complainant unfavourably on the ground of his sex [or (as the case may be) fulfilment of the condition in section 3(2)], an order may be made under subsection (1)(b) only if the [employment tribunal]—

(a) makes such order under subsection (1)(a) and such recommendation under subsection (1)(c) (if any) as it would have made if it had no power to make an order under subsection (1)(b); and

(b) (where it makes an order under subsection (1)(a) or a recommendation under subsection (1)(c) or both) considers that it is just and equitable to make an order under subsection (1)(b) as well.]

(2) . . .

(3) If without reasonable justification the respondent to a complaint fails to comply with a recommendation made by an [employment tribunal] under subsection (1)(c), then, if they think it just and equitable to do so—

(a) the tribunal may [. . .] increase the amount of compensation required to be paid to the complainant in respect of the complaint by an order made under subsection (1)(b), or

(b) if an order under subsection (1)(b) [was not made], the tribunal may make such an order.

Enforcement of Part III

66   Claims under Part III

(1) A claim by any person ("the claimant") that another person ("the respondent")—

(a) has committed an act of discrimination against the claimant which is unlawful by virtue of Part III, or

(b) is by virtue of section 41 or 42 to be treated as having committed such an act of discrimination against the claimant,

may be made the subject of civil proceedings in like manner as any other claim in tort or (in Scotland) in reparation for breach of statutory duty.

(2) Proceedings under subsection (1)—

(a) shall be brought in England and Wales only in a county court, and

(b) shall be brought in Scotland only in a sheriff court.

but all such remedies shall be obtainable in such proceedings as, apart from this subsection [and section 62(1)], would be obtainable in the High Court or the Court of Session, as the case may be.

(3) As respects an unlawful act of discrimination falling within section 1(1)(b) . . . no award of damages shall be made if the respondent proves that the requirement or condition in question was not applied with the intention of treating the claimant unfavourably on the ground of his sex . . .

[(3A) Subsection (3) does not affect the award of damages in respect of an unlawful act of discrimination falling within section 1(2)(b).]

(4) For the avoidance of doubt it is hereby declared that damages in respect of an unlawful act of discrimination may include compensation for injury to feelings whether or not they include compensation under any other head.

(5)–(8) *****

66A–70 *****

Other enforcement by the Commission

71   Persistent discrimination

(1) If, during the period of five years beginning on the date on which either of the following became final in the case of any person, namely,—

    (a) a non-discrimination notice served on him,

    (b) a finding by a court or tribunal under section 63 or 66, or section 2 of the Equal Pay Act 1970, that he has done an unlawful discriminatory act or an act in breach of a term modified or included by virtue of an equality clause,

it appears to the Commission that unless restrained he is likely to do one or more acts falling within paragraph (b), or contravening section 37, the Commission may apply to a county court for an injunction, or to the sheriff court for an order, restraining him from doing so; and the court, if satisfied that the application is well-founded, may grant the injunction or order in the terms applied for or in more limited terms.

(2) In proceedings under this section the Commission shall not allege that the person to whom the proceedings relate has done an act which is within the jurisdiction of an [employment tribunal] unless a finding by an [employment tribunal] that he did that act has become final.

72   Enforcement of ss 38 to 40

(1) Proceedings in respect of a contravention of section 38, 39, or 40 shall be brought only by the Commission in accordance with the following provisions of this section.

(2) The proceedings shall be—

    (a) an application for a decision whether the alleged contravention occurred, or

    (b) an application under subsection (4) below,

or both.

(3) An application under subsection (2)(a) shall be made—

    (a) in a case based on any provision of Part II, to an [employment tribunal], and

    (b) in any other case to a county court or sheriff court.

(4) If it appears to the Commission—

    (a) that a person has done an act which by virtue of section 38, 39 or 40 was unlawful, and

    (b) that unless restrained he is likely to do further acts which by virtue of that section are unlawful,

the Commission may apply to a county court for an injunction, or to a sheriff court for an order, restraining him from doing such acts; and the court, if satisfied that the application is well-founded, may grant the injunction or . . . order in the terms applied for or more limited terms.

(5) *****

73   *****

Help for persons suffering discrimination

74   Help for aggrieved persons in obtaining information etc

(1) With a view to helping a person ("the person aggrieved") who considers he may have been discriminated against in contravention of this Act to decide whether to institute proceedings and, if he does so, to formulate and present his case in the most effective manner, the Secretary of State shall by order prescribe—

    (a) forms by which the person aggrieved may question the respondent on his reasons for doing any relevant act, or on any other matter which is or may be relevant;

    (b) forms by which the respondent may if he so wishes reply to any questions.

(2) Where the person aggrieved questions the respondent (whether in accordance with an order under subsection (1) or not)—

(a) the question, and any reply by the respondent (whether in accordance with such an order or not) shall, subject to the following provisions of this section, be admissible as evidence in the proceedings;

(b) if it appears to the court or tribunal that the respondent deliberately, and without reasonable excuse omitted to reply within a reasonable period or that his reply is evasive or equivocal, the court or tribunal may draw any inference from that fact that it considers it just and equitable to draw, including an inference that he committed an unlawful act.

(3)–(6) *****

75 Assistance by Commission

(1) Where, in relation to proceedings or prospective proceedings either under this Act or in respect of an equality clause, an individual who is an actual or prospective complainant or claimant applies to the Commission for assistance under this section, the Commission shall consider the application and may grant it if they think fit to do so on the ground that—

(a) the case raises a question of principle, or

(b) it is unreasonable, having regard to the complexity of the case or the applicant's position in relation to the respondent or another person involved or any other matter, to expect the applicant to deal with the case unaided,

or by reason of any other special consideration.

(2) Assistance by the Commission under this section may include—

(a) giving advice;

(b) procuring or attempting to procure the settlement of any matter in dispute;

(c) arranging for the giving of advice or assistance by a solicitor or counsel;

(d) arranging for representation by any person including all such assistance as is usually given by a solicitor or counsel in the steps preliminary or incidental to any proceedings, or in arriving at or giving effect to a compromise to avoid or bring to an end any proceedings;

[(e) any other form of assistance which the Commission may consider appropriate,]

but paragraph (d) shall not affect the law and practice regulating the descriptions of persons who may appear in, conduct, defend and address the Court in, any proceedings.

(3)–(5) *****

Period within which proceedings to be brought

76 Period within which proceedings to be brought

(1) An [employment tribunal] shall not consider a complaint under section 63 unless it is presented to the tribunal before the end of]—

(a) the period of three months beginning when the act complained of was done; or

(b) in a case to which section 85(9A) applies, the period of six months so beginning.]

(2) A county court or a sheriff court shall not consider a claim under section 66 unless proceedings in respect of the claim are instituted before the end of—

[(a) the period of six months beginning when the act complained of was done; or

(b) in a case to which section 66(5) applies, the period of eight months so beginning].

(2A)–(4) *****

(5) A court or tribunal may nevertheless consider any such complaint, claim or application which is out of time if, in all the circumstances of the case, it considers that it is just and equitable to do so.

(6) For the purposes of this section—

(a) where the inclusion of any term in a contract renders the making of the contract an unlawful act that act shall be treated as extending throughout the duration of the contract, and

(b) any act extending over a period shall be treated as done at the end of that period, and

(c) a deliberate omission shall be treated as done when the person in question decided upon it,

and in the absence of evidence establishing the contrary a person shall be taken for the purposes of this section to decide upon an omission when he does an act inconsistent with doing the omitted act or, if he has done no such inconsistent act, when the period expires within which he might reasonably have been expected to do the omitted act if it was to be done.

77–84 *****

85   Application to Crown

(1) This Act applies—

(a) to an act done by or for purposes of a Minister of the Crown or government department, or

(b) to an act done on behalf of the Crown by a statutory body, or a person holding a statutory office,

as it applies to an act done by a private person.

(2) Parts II and IV apply to—

(a) service for purposes of a Minister of the Crown or government department, other than service of a person holding a statutory office, or

(b) service on behalf of the Crown for purposes of a person holding a statutory office or purposes of a statutory body, [or

(c) service in the armed forces,]

as they apply to employment by a private person, and shall so apply as if references to a contract of employment included references to the terms of service.

(3) Subsections (1) and (2) have effect subject to section 17.

[(4) Nothing in this Act shall render unlawful an act done for the purpose of ensuring the combat effectiveness of the [armed forces.]]

(5)–(9) *****

[(9A) This subsection applies to any complaint by a person ("the complainant") that another person—

(a) has committed an act of discrimination against the complainant which is unlawful by virtue of section 6; or

(b) is by virtue of section 41 or 42 to be treated as having committed such an act of discrimination against the complainant,

if at the time when the act complained of was done the complainant was serving in the armed forces and the discrimination in question relates to his service in those forces.

(9B) No complaint to which subsection (9A) applies shall be presented to an [employment tribunal] under section 63 unless—

(a) the complainant has made a complaint to an officer under the service redress procedures applicable to him and has submitted that complaint to the Defence Council under those procedures; and

(b) the Defence Council have made a determination with respect to the complaint.

(9C)–(10)*****

*****

Race Relations Act 1976

(1976, c. 74)

An Act to make fresh provision with respect to discrimination on racial grounds and relations between people of different racial groups; and to make in the Sex Discrimination Act 1975 amendments for bringing provisions in that Act relating to its administration and enforcement into conformity with the corresponding provisions in this Act [22 November 1976]

Territorial extent: England and Wales, Scotland. (s. 26A applies only to England and Wales; the equivalent provision applying to Scotland is s. 26B)

PART I DISCRIMINATION TO WHICH ACT APPLIES

1 Racial discrimination

(1) A person discriminates against another in any circumsntances relevant for the purposes of any provision of this Act if—

    (a) on racial grounds he treats that other less favourably than he treats or would treat other persons; or

    (b) he applies to that other a requirement or condition which he applies or would apply equally to persons not of the same racial group as that other but—

        (i) which is such that the proportion of persons of the same racial group as that other who can comply with it is considerably smaller than the proportion of persons not of that racial group who can comply with it; and

        (ii) which he cannot show to be justifiable irrespective of the colour, race, nationality or ethnic or national origins of the person to whom it is applied; and

        (iii) which is to the detriment of that other because he cannot comply with it.

[(1A) A person also discriminates against another if, in any circumstances relevant for the purposes of any provision referred to in subsection (1B), he applies to that other a provision, criterion or practice which he applies or would apply equally to persons not of the same race or ethnic or national origins as that other, but—

    (a) which puts or would put persons of the same race or ethnic or national origins as that other at a particular disadvantage when compared with other persons,

    (b) which puts that other at that disadvantage, and

    (c) which he cannot show to be a proportionate means of achieving a legitimate aim.

(1B) The provisions mentioned in subsection (1A) are—

    (a) Part II;

*****

(1C) Where, by virtue of subsection (1A), a person discriminates against another, subsection (1)(b) does not apply to him.]

(2) It is hereby declared that, for the purposes of this Act, segregating a person from other persons on racial grounds is treating him less favourably than they are treated.

2 Discrimination by way of victimisation

(1) A person ("the discriminator") discriminates against another person ("the person victimised") in any circumstances relevant for the purposes of any provision of this Act if he treats the person victimised less favourably than in those circumstances he treats or would treat other persons, and does so by reason that the person victimised has—

    (a) brought proceedings against the discriminator or any other person under this Act; or

    (b) given evidence or information in connection with proceedings brought by any person against the discriminator or any other person under this Act; or

    (c) otherwise done anything under or by reference to this Act in relation to the dis-
        criminator or any other person; or

    (d) alleged that the discriminator or any other person has committed an act which
        (whether or not the allegation so states) would amount to a contravention of this
        Act,

or by reason that the discriminator knows that the person victimised intends to do any of
those things, or suspects that the person victimised has done, or intends to do, any of them.

    (2) Subsection (1) does not apply to treatment of a person by reason of any allegation
made by him if the allegation was false and not made in good faith.

3   Meaning of "racial grounds", "racial group" etc

    (1) In this Act, unless the context otherwise requires—

    "racial grounds" means any of the following grounds, namely colour, race, nationality or
ethnic or national origins;

    "racial group" means a group of persons defined by reference to colour, race, nationality
or ethnic or national origins, and references to a person's racial group refer to any racial group
into which he falls.

    (2) The fact that a racial group comprises two or more distinct racial groups does not
prevent it from constituting a particular racial group for the purposes of this Act.

    (3) In this Act—

    (a) references to discrimination refer to any discrimination falling within section 1
        or 2; and

    (b) references to racial discrimination refer to any discrimination falling within
        section 1,

and related expressions shall be construed accordingly.

    (4) A comparison of the case of a person of a particular racial group with that of a person
not of that group under section 1(1) [or (1A)] must be such that the relevant circumstances in
the one case are the same, or not materially different, in the other.

[3A   Harassment

    (1) A person subjects another to harassment in any circumstances relevant for the pur-
poses of any provision referred to in section 1(1B) where, on grounds of race or ethnic or
national origins, he engages in unwanted conduct which has the purpose or effect of—

    (a) violating that other person's dignity, or

    (b) creating an intimidating, hostile, degrading, humiliating or offensive environ-
        ment for him.

    (2) Conduct shall be regarded as having the effect specified in paragraph (a) or (b) of
subsection (1) only if, having regard to all the circumstances, including in particular the
perception of that other person, it should reasonably be considered as having that effect.]

PART II   DISCRIMINATION IN THE EMPLOYMENT FIELD

Discrimination by employers

4   ... Applicants and employees

    (1) It is unlawful for a person, in relation to employment by him at an establishment in
Great Britain, to discriminate against another—

    (a) in the arrangements he makes for the purpose of determining who should be
        offered that employment; or

    (b) in the terms on which he offers him that employment; or

    (c) by refusing or deliberately omitting to offer him that employment.

    (2) It is unlawful for a person, in the case of a person employed by him at an establish-
ment in Great Britain, to discriminate against that employee—

(a) in the terms of employment which he affords him; or

(b) in the way he affords him access to opportunities for promotion, transfer or training, or to any other benefits, facilities or services, or by refusing or deliberately omitting to afford him access to them; or

(c) by dismissing him, or subjecting him to any other detriment.

[(2A) It is unlawful for an employer, in relation to employment by him at an establishment in Great Britain, to subject to harassment a person whom he employs or who has applied to him for employment.]

(3) Except in relation to discrimination falling within section 2 [or discrimination on grounds of race or ethnic or national origins], subsections (1) and (2) do not apply to employment for the purposes of a private household.

(4), (5) *****

[4A   Exception for genuine occupational requirement

(1) In relation to discrimination on grounds of race or ethnic or national origins—

(a) section 4(1)(a) or (c) does not apply to any employment; and

(b) section 4(2)(b) does not apply to promotion or transfer to, or training for, any employment; and

(c) section 4(2)(c) does not apply to dismissal from any employment;

where subsection (2) applies.

(2) This subsection applies where, having regard to the nature of the employment or the context in which it is carried out—

(a) being of a particular race or of particular ethnic or national origins is a genuine and determining occupational requirement;

(b) it is proportionate to apply that requirement in the particular case; and

(c) either—

(i) the person to whom that requirement is applied does not meet it, or

(ii) the employer is not satisfied, and in all the circumstances it is reasonable for him not to be satisfied, that that person meets it.]

5   Exceptions for genuine occupational qualifications

(1) In relation to racial discrimination [in cases where section 4A does not apply]—

(a) section 4(1)(a) or (c) does not apply to any employment where being of a particular racial group is a genuine occupational qualification for the job; and

(b) section 4(2)(b) does not apply to opportunities for promotion or transfer to, or training for, such employment.

(2) Being of a particular racial group is a genuine occupational qualification for a job only where—

(a) the job involves participation in a dramatic performance or other entertainment in a capacity for which a person of that racial group is required for reasons of authenticity; or

(b) the job involves participation as an artist's or photographic model in the production of a work of art, visual image or sequence of visual images for which a person of that racial group is required for reasons of authenticity; or

(c) the job involves working in a place where food or drink is (for payment or not) provided to and consumed by members of the public or a section of the public in a particular setting for which, in that job, a person of that racial group is required for reasons of authenticity; or

(d) the holder of the job provides persons of that racial group with personal services promoting their welfare, and those services can most effectively be provided by a person of that racial group.

(3) Subsection (2) applies where some only of the duties of the job fall within paragraph (a), (b), (c) or (d) as well as where all of them do.

(4) Paragraph (a), (b), (c) or (d) of subsection (2) does not apply in relation to the filling of a vacancy at a time when the employer already has employees of the racial group in question—

    (a) who are capable of carrying out the duties falling within that paragraph; and

    (b) whom it would be reasonable to employ on those duties; and

    (c) whose numbers are sufficient to meet the employer's likely requirements in respect of those duties without undue inconvenience.

6 *****

7 . . . Contract workers

(1) This section applies to any work for a person ("the principal") which is available for doing by individuals ("contract workers") who are employed not by the principal himself but by another person, who supplies them under a contract made with the principal.

(2) It is unlawful for the principal, in relation to work to which this section applies, to discriminate against a contract worker—

    (a) in the terms on which he allows him to do that work; or

    (b) by not allowing him to do it or continue to do it; or

    (c) in the way he affords him access to any benefits, facilities or services or by refusing or deliberately omitting to afford him access to them; or

    (d) by subjecting him to any other detriment.

(3)–(5) *****

8–9 *****

Discrimination by other bodies

10 Partnerships

(1) It is unlawful for a firm consisting of six or more partners, in relation to a position as partner in the firm, to discriminate against a person—

    (a) in the arrangements they make for the purpose of determining who should be offered that position; or

    (b) in the terms on which they offer him that position; or

    (c) by refusing or deliberately omitting to offer him that position; or

    (d) in a case where the person already holds that position—

        (i) in the way they afford him access to any benefits, facilities or services, or by refusing or deliberately omitting to afford him access to them; or

        (ii) by expelling him from that position, or subjecting him to any other detriment.

[(1A) The limitation of subsection (1) to six or more partners does not apply in relation to discrimination on grounds of race or ethnic or national origins.

(1B) It is unlawful for a firm, in relation to a position as a partner in the firm, to subject to harassment a person who holds or has applied for that position.]

(2)–(6) *****

11 Trade unions etc

(1) This section applies to an organisation of workers, an organisation of employers, or any other organisation whose members carry on a particular profession or trade for the purposes of which the organisation exists.

(2) It is unlawful for an organisation to which this section applies, in the case of a person who is not a member of the organisation, to discriminate against him—

    (a) in the terms on which it is prepared to admit him to membership; or

    (b) by refusing, or deliberately omitting to accept, his application for membership.

(3) It is unlawful for an organisation to which this section applies, in the case of a person who is a member of the organisation, to discriminate against him—

(a) in the way it affords him access to any benefits, facilities or services, or by refusing or deliberately omitting to afford him access to them; or

(b) by depriving him of membership, or varying the terms on which he is a member; or

(c) by subjecting him to any other detriment.

[(4) It is unlawful for an organisation to which this section applies, in relation to a person's membership or application for membership of that organisation, to subject him to harassment.]

12   Qualifying bodies

(1) It is unlawful for an authority or body which can confer an authorisation or qualification which is needed for, or facilitates, engagement in a particular profession or trade to discriminate against a person—

(a) in the terms on which it is prepared to confer on him that authorisation or qualification; or

(b) by refusing, or deliberately omitting to grant, his application for it; or

(c) by withdrawing it from him or varying the terms on which he holds it.

[(1A) It is unlawful for an authority or body to which subsection (1) applies, in relation to an authorisation or qualification conferred by it, to subject to harassment a person who holds or applies for such an authorisation or qualification.]

(2), (3) *****

13–15   *****

16   . . .

PART III   DISCRIMINATION IN OTHER FIELDS

Education

17   . . . Bodies in charge of educational establishments

[(1)] It is unlawful, in relation to an educational establishment falling within column 1 of the following table, for a person indicated in relation to the establishment in column 2 (the "responsible body") to discriminate against a person—

(a) in the terms on which it offers to admit him to the establishment as a pupil; or

(b) by refusing or deliberately omitting to accept an application for his admission to the establishment as a pupil; or

(c) where he is a pupil of the establishment—

(i) in the way it affords him access to any benefits, facilities or services, or by refusing or deliberately omitting to afford him access to them; or

(ii) by excluding him from the establishment or subjecting him to any other detriment.

[Table omitted]

(2) *****

[17A   Meaning of pupil in section 17

For the purposes of section 17, "pupil" includes, in England and Wales, any person who receives education at a school or institution to which that section applies.]

18   Other discrimination [etc] by local education authorities

(1) It is unlawful for a local education authority, in carrying out such of its functions under [the Education Acts] as do not fall under section 17, to do any act which constitutes racial discrimination [or harassment].

(2) It is unlawful for an education authority, in carrying out such of its functions under

the Education (Scotland) [Act 1980] as do not fall under section 17, to do any act which constitutes racial discrimination [or harassment].

[18A   . . . Further Education and Higher Education Funding Councils

It is unlawful for [the Learning and Skills Council for England, the National Council for Education and Training for Wales,] the Higher Education Funding Council for England or the Higher Education Funding Council for Wales in carrying out their functions under [the Education Acts] [and the Learning and Skills Act 2000], to do any act which constitutes racial discrimination [or harassment].]

[18B   . . . Scottish Further and Higher Education Funding Councils

It is unlawful for the Scottish Further Education Funding Council or the Scottish Higher Education Funding Council in carrying out any of their functions to do any act which constitutes racial discrimination [or harassment].]

18C, 19, 19ZA . . .

18D, 19A   *****

19B   . . . Public authorities

(1) It is unlawful for a public authority in carrying out any functions of the authority to do any act which constitutes discrimination.

[(1A) It is unlawful for a public authority to subject a person to harassment in the course of carrying out any functions of the authority which consist of the provision of—

(a) any form of social security;

(b) healthcare;

(c) any other form of social protection; or

(d) any form of social advantage,

which does not fall within section 20.]

(2) In this section "public authority"—

(a) includes any person certain of whose functions are functions of a public nature; but

(b) does not include any person mentioned in subsection (3).

(3) The persons mentioned in this subsection are—

(a) either House of Parliament;

(b) a person exercising functions in connection with proceedings in Parliament;

(c) the Security Service;

(d) the Secret Intelligence Service;

(e) the Government Communications Headquarters; and

(f) any unit or part of a unit of any of the naval, military or air forces of the Crown which is for the time being required by the Secretary of State to assist the Government Communications Headquarters in carrying out its functions.

(4) In relation to a particular act, a person is not a public authority by virtue only of subsection (2)(a) if the nature of the act is private.

(5), (6) *****

19C–19F   *****

Goods, facilities, services and premises

20   . . . Provision of goods, facilities or services

(1) It is unlawful for any person concerned with the provision (for payment or not) of goods, facilities or services to the public or a section of the public to discriminate against a person who seeks to obtain or use those goods, facilities or services—

(a) by refusing or deliberately omitting to provide him with any of them; or

(b) by refusing or deliberately omitting to provide him with goods, facilities or services of the like quality, in the like manner and on the like terms as are normal in the first-mentioned person's case in relation to other members of the public or (where the person so seeking belongs to a section of the public) to other members of that section.

(2) The following are examples of the facilities and services mentioned in subsection (1)—

(a) access to and use of any place which members of the public are permitted to enter;

(b) accommodation in a hotel, boarding house or other similar establishment;

(c) facilities by way of banking or insurance or for grants, loans, credit or finance;

(d) facilities for education;

(e) facilities for entertainment, recreation or refreshment;

(f) facilities for transport or travel;

(g) the services of any profession or trade, or any local or other public authority.

[(3) It is unlawful for any person concerned with the provision of goods, facilities or services as mentioned in subsection (1), in relation to such provision, to subject to harassment—

(a) a person who seeks to obtain or use those goods, facilities or services, or

(b) a person to whom he provides those goods, facilities or services.]

21   Disposal or management of premises

(1) It is unlawful for a person, in relation to premises in Great Britain of which he has power to dispose, to discriminate against another—

(a) in the terms on which he offers him those premises; or

(b) by refusing his application for those premises; or

(c) in his treatment of him in relation to any list of persons in need of premises of that description.

(2) It is unlawful for a person, in relation to premises managed by him, to discriminate against a person occupying the premises—

(a) in the way he affords him access to any benefits or facilities, or by refusing or deliberately omitting to afford him access to them; or

(b) by evicting him, or subjecting him to any other detriment.

[(2A) It is unlawful for a person, in relation to such premises as are referred to in subsection (1) or (2), to subject to harassment a person who applies for or, as the case may be, occupies such premises.]

(3) Subsection (1) does not apply to [discrimination, on grounds other than those of race or ethnic or national origins, by] a person who owns an estate or interest in the premises and wholly occupies them unless he uses the services of an estate agent for the purposes of the disposal of the premises, or publishes or causes to be published an advertisement in connection with the disposal.

22–24   *****

25   Discrimination: associations not within s 11

(1) This section applies to any association of persons (however described, whether corporate or unincorporate, and whether or not its activities are carried on for profit) if—

(a) it has twenty-five or more members; and

(b) admission to membership is regulated by its constitution and is so conducted that the members do not constitute a section of the public within the meaning of section 20(1); and

(c) it is not an organisation to which section 11 applies.

(2) It is unlawful for an association to which this section applies, in the case of a person who is not a member of the association, to discriminate against him—

(a) in the terms on which it is prepared to admit him to membership; or

(b) by refusing or deliberately omitting to accept his application for membership.

(3) It is unlawful for an association to which this section applies, in the case of a person who is a member or associate of the association, to discriminate against him—

    (a) in the way it affords him access to any benefits, facilities or services, or by refusing or deliberately omitting to afford him access to them; or

    (b) in the case of a member, by depriving him of membership, or varying the terms on which he is a member; or

    (c) in the case of an associate, by depriving him of his rights as an associate, or varying those rights; or

    (d) in either case, by subjecting him to any other detriment.

    (4) *****

26   Exception from s 25 for certain associations

(1) An association to which section 25 applies is within this subsection if the main object of the association is to enable the benefits of membership (whatever they may be) to be enjoyed by persons of a particular racial group defined otherwise than by reference to colour; and in determining whether that is the main object of an association regard shall be had to the essential character of the association and to all relevant circumstances including, in particular, the extent to which the affairs of the association are so conducted that the persons primarily enjoying the benefits of membership are of the racial group in question.

(2) In the case of an association within subsection (1), nothing in section 25 shall render unlawful any act not involving discrimination on the ground of colour.

[Barristers

26A   Barristers

(1) It is unlawful for a barrister or barrister's clerk, in relation to any offer of a pupillage or tenancy, to discriminate against a person—

    (a) in the arrangements which are made for the purpose of determining to whom it should be offered;

    (b) in respect of any terms on which it is offered; or

    (c) by refusing, or deliberately omitting, to offer it to him.

(2) It is unlawful for a barrister or barrister's clerk, in relation to a pupil or tenant in the chambers in question, to discriminate against him—

    (a) in respect of any terms applicable to him as a pupil or tenant;

    (b) in the opportunities for training, or gaining experience, which are afforded or denied to him;

    (c) in the benefits, facilities or services which are afforded or denied to him; or

    (d) by terminating his pupillage or by subjecting him to any pressure to leave the chambers or other detriment.

(3) It is unlawful for any person, in relation to the giving, withholding or acceptance of instructions to a barrister, to discriminate against any person [or to subject any person to harassment].

[(3A) It is unlawful for a barrister or barrister's clerk, in relation to a pupillage or tenancy in the set of chambers in question, to subject to harassment a person who is, or has applied to be, a pupil or tenant.]

    (4), (5) *****

26B, 27   *****

PART IV   OTHER UNLAWFUL ACTS

[27A   Relationships which have come to an end

(1) In this section a "relevant relationship" is a relationship during the course of which,

by virtue of any provision referred to in section 1(1B), taken with section 1(1) or (1A), or (as the case may be) by virtue of section 3A—

(a) an act of discrimination by one party to the relationship ("the relevant party") against another party to the relationship, on grounds of race or ethnic or national origins, or

(b) harassment of another party to the relationship by the relevant party,

is unlawful.

(2) Where a relevant relationship has come to an end it is unlawful for the relevant party—

(a) to discriminate against another party, on grounds of race or ethnic or national origins, by subjecting him to a detriment, or

(b) to subject another party to harassment,

where the discrimination or harassment arises out of and is closely connected to that relationship.

(3), (4) *****

28 *****

29 Discriminatory advertisements

(1) It is unlawful to publish or to cause to be published an advertisement which indicates, or might reasonably be understood as indicating, an intention by a person to do an act of discrimination, whether the doing of that act by him would be lawful or, by virtue of Part II or III, unlawful.

(2) Subsection (1) does not apply to an advertisement—

(a) if the intended act would be lawful by virtue of any of sections 5, 6, 7(3) and (4), 10(3), 26, 34(2)(b), 35 to 39 and 41; or

(b) if the advertisement relates to the services of an employment agency (within the meaning of section 14(1)) and the intended act only concerns employment which the employer could by virtue of section 5, 6 or 7(3) or (4) lawfully refuse to offer to persons against whom the advertisement indicates an intention to discriminate.

(3) Subsection (1) does not apply to an advertisement which indicates that persons of any class defined otherwise than by reference to colour, race or ethnic or national origins are required for employment outside Great Britain.

(4) The publisher of an advertisement made unlawful by subsection (1) shall not be subject to any liability under that subsection in respect of the publication of the advertisement if he proves—

(a) that the advertisement was published in reliance on a statement made to him by the person who caused it to be published to the effect that, by reason of the operation of subsection (2) or (3), the publication would not be unlawful; and

(b) that it was reasonable for him to rely on the statement.

(5) A person who knowingly or recklessly makes a statement such as is mentioned in subsection (4)(a) which in a material respect is false or misleading commits an offence, and shall be liable on summary conviction to a fine not exceeding [level 5 on the standard scale].

30 Instructions to [commit unlawful acts]

It is unlawful for a person—

(a) who has authority over another person; or

(b) in accordance with whose wishes that other person is accustomed to act,

to instruct him to do any act which is unlawful by virtue of Part II or III, [section 76ZA or, where it renders an act unlawful on grounds of race or ethnic or national origins, section 76,] or procure or attempt to procure the doing by him of any such act.

31 Pressure to [commit unlawful acts]

(1) It is unlawful to induce, or attempt to induce, a person to do any act which

contravenes Part II or III[, section 76ZA or, where it renders an act unlawful on grounds of race or ethnic or national origins, section 76].

(2) An attempted inducement is not prevented from falling within subsection (1) because it is not made directly to the person in question, if it is made in such a way that he is likely to hear of it.

32   Liability of employers and principals

(1) Anything done by a person in the course of his employment shall be treated for the purposes of this Act (except as regards offences thereunder) as done by his employer as well as by him, whether or not it was done with the employer's knowledge or approval.

(2) Anything done by a person as agent for another person with the authority (whether express or implied, and whether precedent or subsequent) of that other person shall be treated for the purposes of this Act (except as regards offences thereunder) as done by that other person as well as by him.

(3) In proceedings brought under this Act against any person in respect of an act alleged to have been done by an employee of his it shall be a defence for that person to prove that he took such steps as were reasonably practicable to prevent the employee from doing that act, or from doing in the course of his employment acts of that description.

33   Aiding unlawful acts

(1) A person who knowingly aids another person to do an act made unlawful by this Act shall be treated for the purposes of this Act as himself doing an unlawful act of the like description.

(2) For the purposes of subsection (1) an employee or agent for whose act the employer or principal is liable under section 32 (or would be so liable but for section 32(3)) shall be deemed to aid the doing of the act by the employer or principal.

(3) A person does not under this section knowingly aid another to do an unlawful act if—
    (a) he acts in reliance on a statement made to him by that other person that, by reason of any provision of this Act, the act which he aids would not be unlawful; and
    (b) it is reasonable for him to rely on the statement.

(4) A person who knowingly or recklessly makes a statement such as is mentioned in subsection (3)(a) which in a material respect is false or misleading commits an offence, and shall be liable on summary conviction to a fine not exceeding [level 5 on the standard scale].

34   *****

PART VI   GENERAL EXCEPTIONS FROM PARTS II TO IV

35   Special needs of racial groups in regard to education, training or welfare

Nothing in Parts II to IV shall render unlawful any act done in affording persons of a particular racial group access to facilities or services to meet the special needs of persons of that group in regard to their education, training or welfare, or any ancillary benefits.

36   Provision of education or training for persons not ordinarily resident in Great Britain

Nothing in Parts II to IV shall render unlawful any act done by a person[, on grounds other than race or ethnic or national origins,] for the benefit of persons not ordinarily resident in Great Britain in affording them access to facilities for education or training or any ancillary benefits, where it appears to him that the persons in question do not intend to remain in Great Britain after their period of education or training there.

37   Discriminatory training by certain bodies

(1) Nothing in Parts II to IV shall render unlawful any act done in relation to particular work by [any person] in or in connection with—

(a) affording only persons of a particular racial group access to facilities for training which would help to fit them for that work; or

(b) encouraging only persons of a particular racial group to take advantage of opportunities for doing that work,

where [it reasonably appears to that person] that at any time within the twelve months immediately preceding the doing of the act—

(i) there were no persons of that group among those doing that work in Great Britain; or

(ii) the proportion of persons of that group among those doing that work in Great Britain was small in comparison with the proportion of persons of that group among the population of Great Britain.

(2) Where in relation to particular work [it reasonably appears to any person] that although the condition for the operation of subsection (1) is not met for the whole of Great Britain it is met for an area within Great Britain, nothing in Parts II to IV shall render unlawful any act done by [that person] in or in connection with—

(a) affording persons who are of the racial group in question, and who appear likely to take up that work in that area, access to facilities for training which would help to fit them for that work; or

(b) encouraging persons of that group to take advantage of opportunities in the area for doing that work.

[(3) The preceding provisions of this section shall not apply to any discrimination which is rendered unlawful by section 4(1) or (2).]

38   Other discriminatory training etc

(1) Nothing in Parts II to IV shall render unlawful any act done by an employer in relation to particular work in his employment at a particular establishment in Great Britain, being an act done in or in connection with—

(a) affording only those of his employees working at that establishment who are of a particular racial group access to facilities for training which would help to fit them for that work; or

(b) encouraging only persons of a particular racial group to take advantage of opportunities for doing that work at that establishment,

where any of the conditions in subsection (2) was satisfied at any time within the twelve months immediately preceding the doing of the act.

(2) Those conditions are—

(a) that there are no persons of the racial group in question among those doing that work at that establishment; or

(b) that the proportion of persons of that group among those doing that work at that establishment is small in comparison with the proportion of persons of that group—

(i) among all those employed by that employer there; or

(ii) among the population of the area from which that employer normally recruits persons for work in his employment at that establishment.

(3)–(6) *****

39–40   *****

41   Acts done under statutory authority etc

(1) Nothing in Parts II to IV shall render unlawful any act of discrimination done—

(a) in pursuance of any enactment or Order in Council; or

(b) in pursuance of any instrument made under any enactment by a Minister of the Crown; or

(c) in order to comply with any condition or requirement imposed by a Minister of the Crown (whether before or after the passing of this Act) by virtue of any enactment.

References in this [section] to an enactment, Order in Council or instrument include an enactment, Order in Council or instrument passed or made after the passing of this Act.

[(1A) Subsection (1) does not apply to an act which is unlawful, on grounds of race or ethnic or national origins, by virtue of a provision referred to in section 1(1B).]

(2) *****

42 Acts safeguarding national security

Nothing in Parts II to IV shall render unlawful an act done for the purpose of safeguarding national security [if the doing of the act was justified by that purpose].

PART VII   THE COMMISSION FOR RACIAL EQUALITY

General

43 Establishment and duties of Commission

(1) There shall be a body of Commissioners named the Commission for Racial Equality consisting of at least eight but not more than fifteen individuals each appointed by the Secretary of State on a full-time or part-time basis, which shall have the following duties—

(a) to work towards the elimination of discrimination [and harassment];

(b) to promote equality of opportunity, and good relations, between persons of different racial groups generally; and

(c) to keep under review the working of this Act and, when they are so required by the Secretary of State or otherwise think it necessary, draw up and submit to the Secretary of State proposals for amending it.

(1A)–(4) *****

(5) . . .

44–46   *****

Codes of practice

47 Codes of practice

(1) The Commission may issue codes of practice containing such practical guidance as the Commission think fit for [all or any] of the following purposes, namely—

(a) the elimination of discrimination [and harassment] in the field of employment;

(b) the promotion of equality of opportunity in that field between persons of different racial groups

[(c) the elimination of discrimination [and harassment] in the field of housing . . .;

(d) the promotion of equality of opportunity in the field of . . . housing between persons of different racial groups].

(2) When the Commission propose to issue a code of practice, they shall prepare and publish a draft of that code, shall consider any representations made to them about the draft and may modify the draft accordingly.

(3), (3A) *****

(4) If the Commission determine to proceed with [a draft code of practice], they shall transmit the draft to the Secretary of State who shall—

(a) if he approves of it, lay it before both Houses of Parliament; and

(b) if he does not approve of it, publish details of his reasons for withholding approval.

(5)–(9) *****

(10) A failure on the part of any person to observe any provision of a code of practice

shall not of itself render him liable to any proceedings; but in any proceedings under this Act before an [employment tribunal] [a county court or, in Scotland, a sheriff court] any code of practice issued under this section shall be admissible in evidence, and if any provision of such a code appears to the tribunal [or the court] to be relevant to any question arising in the proceedings it shall be taken into account in determining that question.

(11) Without prejudice to subsection (1), a code of practice issued under this section may include such practical guidance as the Commission think fit as to what steps it is reasonably practicable for employers to take for the purpose of preventing their employees from doing in the course of their employment acts made unlawful by this Act.

48–52 *****

PART VIII   ENFORCEMENT

General

53   Restriction of proceedings for breach of Act

(1) Except as provided by this Act [or the Special Immigration Appeals Commission Act 1997 or [Part 5 of the Nationality, Immigration and Asylum Act 2002]] no proceedings, whether civil or criminal, shall lie against any person in respect of an act by reason that the act is unlawful by virtue of a provision of this Act.

(2) Subsection (1) does not preclude the making of an order of certiorari, mandamus or prohibition.

(3) In Scotland, subsection (1) does not preclude the exercise of the jurisdiction of the Court of Session to entertain an application for reduction or suspension of any order or determination or otherwise to consider the validity of any order or determination, or to require reasons for any order or determination to be stated.

[(4) Subsections (2) and (3) do not, except so far as provided by section 76, apply to any act which is unlawful by virtue of section 76(5) or (9) or by virtue of section 76(10)(b)[, (11) and (11B)].]

Enforcement in employment field

54   Jurisdiction of [employment tribunals]

(1) A complaint by any person ("the complainant") that another person ("the respondent")—

    (a) has committed an act . . . against the complainant which is unlawful by virtue of Part II[, section 76ZA or, in relation to discrimination on grounds of race or ethnic or national origins, or harassment, section 26A, 26B or 76]; or

    (b) is by virtue of section 32 or 33 to be treated as having committed such an act . . . against the complainant,

may be presented to an [employment tribunal].

(2) Subsection (1) does not apply to a complaint under section 12(1) of an act in respect of which an appeal, or proceedings in the nature of an appeal, may be brought under any enactment . . .

[54A   Burden of proof: employment tribunals

(1) This section applies where a complaint is presented under section 54 and the complaint is that the respondent—

    (a) has committed an act of discrimination, on grounds of race or ethnic or national origins, which is unlawful by virtue of any provision referred to in section 1(1B)(a), (e) or (f), or Part IV in its application to those provisions, or

    (b) has committed an act of harassment.

(2) Where, on the hearing of the complaint, the complainant proves facts from which the tribunal could, apart from this section, conclude in the absence of an adequate explanation that the respondent—

    (a) has committed such an act of discrimination or harassment against the complainant, or

    (b) is by virtue of section 32 or 33 to be treated as having committed such an act of discrimination or harassment against the complainant,

the tribunal shall uphold the complaint unless the respondent proves that he did not commit or, as the case may be, is not to be treated as having committed, that act.]

55 ...

56   Remedies on complaint under s 54

(1) Where an [employment tribunal] finds that a complaint presented to it under section 54 is well-founded, the tribunal shall make such of the following as it considers just and equitable—

    (a) an order declaring the rights of the complainant and the respondent in relation to the act to which the complaint relates;

    (b) an order requiring the respondent to pay to the complainant compensation of an amount corresponding to any damages he could have been ordered by a county court or by a sheriff court to pay to the complainant if the complaint had fallen to be dealt with under section 57;

    (c) a recommendation that the respondent take within a specified period action appearing to the tribunal to be practicable for the purpose of obviating or reducing the adverse effect on the complainant of any act of discrimination to which the complaint relates.

(2), (3) ...

(4) If without reasonable justification the respondent to a complaint fails to comply with a recommendation made by an [employment tribunal] under subsection (1)(c), then, if it thinks it just and equitable to do so—

    (a) the tribunal may ... increase the amount of compensation required to be paid to the complainant in respect of the complaint by an order made under subsection (1)(b); or

    (b) if an order under subsection (1)(b) could have been made but was not, the tribunal may make such an order.

(5), (6) *****

Enforcement of Part III

57   Claims under Part III [etc]

(1) A claim by any person ("the claimant") that another person ("the respondent")—

    (a) has committed an act ... against the claimant which is unlawful by virtue of Part III [other than, in relation to discrimination on grounds of race or ethnic or national origins, or harassment, section 26A or 26B]; or

    (b) is by virtue of section 32 or 33 to be treated as having committed such an act ... against the claimant, may be made the subject of civil proceedings in like manner as any other claim in tort or (in Scotland) in reparation for breach of statutory duty.

(2) Proceedings under subsection (1)—

    (a) shall, in England and Wales, be brought only in a designated county court; and

    (b) shall, in Scotland, be brought only in a sheriff court.

(3) As respects an unlawful act of discrimination falling within section 1(1)(b), no award of damages shall be made if the respondent proves that the requirement or condition in

question was not applied with the intention of treating the claimant unfavourably on racial grounds.

(4) For the avoidance of doubt it is hereby declared that damages in respect of an unlawful act of discrimination may include compensation for injury to feelings whether or not they include compensation under any other head.

(4A)–(7) *****

57ZA–61   *****

62   Persistent discrimination

(1) If, during the period of five years beginning on the date on which any of the following became final in the case of any person, namely—

   (a) a non-discrimination notice served on him; or

   (b) a finding by a tribunal or court under section 54 or 57; that he has done an unlawful [act of discrimination or harassment]; or

   [(ba) a finding under the Special Immigration Appeals Commission Act 1997 or [Part 5 of the Nationality, Immigration and Asylum Act 2002] that he has done an act which was unlawful by virtue of section 19B; or]

   (c) a finding by a court in proceedings under section 19 or 20 of the Race Relations Act 1968 that he has done an act which was unlawful by virtue of any provision of Part I of that Act,

it appears to the Commission that unless restrained he is likely to do one or more acts falling within paragraph (b), or contravening section 28, the Commission may apply to a designated county court for an injunction, or to a sheriff court for an order, restraining him from doing so; and the court, if satisfied that the application is well-founded, may grant the injunction or order in the terms applied for or in more limited terms.

(2) In proceedings under this section the Commission shall not allege that the person to whom the proceedings relate has done an act falling within subsection (1)(b) or contravening section 28 which is within the jurisdiction of an [employment tribunal] unless a finding by an [employment tribunal] that he did that act has become final.

63   Enforcement of ss 29 to 31

(1) Proceedings in respect of a contravention of section 29, 30 or 31 shall be brought only by the Commission in accordance with the following provisions of this section.

(2) The proceedings shall be—

   (a) an application for a decision whether the alleged contravention occurred; or

   (b) an application under subsection (4),

or both.

(3) An application under subsection (2)(a) shall be made—

   (a) in a case based on any provision of Part II, to an [employment tribunal]; and

   (b) in any other case, to a designated county court or a sheriff court.

(4) If it appears to the Commission—

   (a) that a person has done an act which by virtue of section 29, 30 or 31 was unlawful; and

   (b) that unless restrained he is likely to do further acts which by virtue of that section are unlawful,

the Commission may apply to a designated county court for an injunction, or to a sheriff court for an order, restraining him from doing such acts; and the court, if satisfied that the application is well-founded, may grant the injunction or order in the terms applied for or more limited terms.

(5) In proceedings under subsection (4) the Commission shall not allege that the person to whom the proceedings relate has done an act which is unlawful under this Act and within the jurisdiction of an [employment tribunal] unless a finding by an [employment tribunal] that he did that act has become final.

Help for persons suffering discrimination

65   Help for aggrieved persons in obtaining information etc

(1) With a view to helping a person ("the person aggrieved") who considers he may have been discriminated against [or subjected to harassment] in contravention of this Act to decide whether to institute proceedings and, if he does so, to formulate and present his case in the most effective manner, the Secretary of State shall by order prescribe—

   (a) forms by which the person aggrieved may question the respondent on his reasons for doing any relevant act, or on any other matter which is or may be relevant; and

   (b) forms by which the respondent may if he so wishes reply to any questions.

(2) Where the person aggrieved questions the respondent (whether in accordance with an order under subsection (1) or not)—

   (a) the question, and any reply by the respondent (whether in accordance with such an order or not) shall, subject to the following provisions of this section, be admissible as evidence in the proceedings;

   (b) if it appears to the court or tribunal that the respondent deliberately, and without reasonable excuse, omitted to reply within a reasonable period [or, where the question relates to discrimination on grounds of race or ethnic or national origins, or to harassment, the period of eight weeks beginning with the day on which the question was served on him] or that his reply is evasive or equivocal, the court or tribunal may draw any inference from that fact that it considers it just and equitable to draw, including an inference that he committed an unlawful act.

(3)–(7) *****

66   Assistance by Commission

(1) Where, in relation to proceedings or prospective proceedings under this Act, an individual who is an actual or prospective complainant or claimant applies to the Commission for assistance under this section, the Commission shall consider the application and may grant it if they think fit to do so—

   (a) on the ground that the case raises a question of principle; or

   (b) on the ground that it is unreasonable, having regard to the complexity of the case, or to the applicant's position in relation to the respondent or another person involved, or to any other matter, to expect the applicant to deal with the case unaided; or

   (c) by reason of any other special consideration.

(2) Assistance by the Commission under this section may include—

   (a) giving advice;

   (b) procuring or attempting to procure the settlement of any matter in dispute;

   (c) arranging for the giving of advice or assistance by a solicitor or counsel;

   (d) arranging for representation by any person, including all such assistance as is usually given by a solicitor or counsel in the steps preliminary or incidental to any proceedings, or in arriving at or giving effect to a compromise to avoid or bring to an end any proceedings;

   (e) any other form of assistance which the Commission may consider appropriate,

but paragraph (d) shall not affect the law and practice regulating the descriptions of persons who may appear in, conduct, defend, and address the court in, any proceedings.

(3)–(9) *****

67–67A *****

Period within which proceedings to be brought

68   Period within which proceedings to be brought

(1) An [employment tribunal] shall not consider a complaint under section 54 unless it is presented to the tribunal before the end of[—

    (a) the period of three months beginning when the act complained of was done; or

    (b) in a case to which section 75(8) applies, the period of six months so beginning.]

(2) [Subject to subsection (2A)] a county court or a sheriff court shall not consider a claim under section 57 unless proceedings in respect of the claim are instituted before the end of—

    (a) the period of six months beginning when the act complained of was done; . . .

    (b) . . .

(2A)–(5) *****

(6) A court or tribunal may nevertheless consider any such complaint, claim or application which is out of time if, in all the circumstances of the case, it considers that it is just and equitable to do so.

(7) For the purposes of this section—

    (a) when the inclusion of any term in a contract renders the making of the contract an unlawful act, that act shall be treated as extending throughout the duration of the contract; and

    (b) any act extending over a period shall be treated as done at the end of that period; and

    (c) a deliberate omission shall be treated as done when the person in question decided upon it;

and in the absence of evidence establishing the contrary a person shall be taken for the purposes of this section to decide upon an omission when he does an act inconsistent with doing the omitted act or, if he has done no such inconsistent act, when the period expires within which he might reasonably have been expected to do the omitted act if it was to be done.

69 *****

70 . . .

PART X   SUPPLEMENTAL

[71   Specified authorities: general statutory duty

(1) Every body or other person specified in Schedule 1A or of a description falling within that Schedule shall, in carrying out its functions, have due regard to the need—

    (a) to eliminate unlawful racial discrimination; and

    (b) to promote equality of opportunity and good relations between persons of different racial groups.

(2) The Secretary of State may by order impose, on such persons falling within Schedule 1A as he considers appropriate, such duties as he considers appropriate for the purpose of ensuring the better performance by those persons of their duties under subsection (1).]

    (3)–(7) *****

71A–E, 72–74   *****

75   Application to Crown etc

(1) This Act applies—

    (a) to an act done by or for purposes of a Minister of the Crown or government department; or

    (b) to an act done on behalf of the Crown by a statutory body, or a person holding a statutory office,

as it applies to an act done by a private person.

(2) Parts II and IV apply to—

    (a) service for purposes of a Minister of the Crown or government department, other than service of a person holding a statutory office; or

    (b) service on behalf of the Crown for purposes of a person holding a statutory office or purposes of a statutory body; or

(c) service in the armed forces,

as they apply to employment by a private person, and shall so apply as if references to a contract of employment included references to the terms of service.

(3), (4) *****

(5) Nothing in this Act shall—

    (a) invalidate any rules (whether made before or after the passing of this Act) restricting employment in the service of the Crown or by any public body prescribed for the purposes of this subsection by regulations made by the Minister for the Civil Service to persons of particular birth, nationality, descent or residence; or

    (b) render unlawful the publication, display or implementation of any such rules, or the publication of advertisements stating the gist of any such rules.

In this subsection "employment" includes service of any kind, and "public body" means a body of persons, whether corporate or unincorporate, carrying on a service or undertaking of a public nature.

(6), (7) *****

(8) This subsection applies to any complaint by a person ("the complainant") that another person—

    (a) has committed an act of discrimination against the complainant which is unlawful by virtue of section 4; or

    (b) is by virtue of section 32 or 33 to be treated as having committed such an act of discrimination against the complainant,

if at the time when the act complained of was done the complainant was serving in the armed forces and the discrimination in question relates to his service in those forces.

[(9) No complaint to which subsection (8) applies shall be presented to an [employment tribunal] under section 54 unless—

    (a) the complainant has made a complaint to an officer under the service redress procedures applicable to him and has submitted that complaint to the Defence Council under those procedures; and

    (b) the Defence Council have made a determination with respect to the complaint.]

(9A)–(10) *****

75A–76ZA *****

[*Police*

76A   Police forces

(1) In this section, "relevant police office" means—

    (a) the office of constable held—

        (i) as a member of a police force; or

        (ii) on appointment as a special constable for a police area; or

    (b) an appointment as police cadet to undergo training with a view to becoming a member of a police force.

(2) For the purposes of Part II, the holding of a relevant police office shall be treated as employment—

    (a) by the chief officer of police as respects any act done by him in relation to that office or a holder of it;

    (b) by the police authority as respects any act done by it in relation to that office or a holder of it.

(3) For the purposes of section 32—

    (a) the holding of a relevant police office shall be treated as employment by the chief officer of police (and as not being employment by any other person); and

    (b) anything done by a person holding such an office in the performance, or purported performance, of his functions shall be treated as done in the course of that employment.

(4) There shall be paid out of the police fund—

(a) any compensation, costs or expenses awarded against a chief officer of police in any proceedings brought against him under this Act, and any costs or expenses incurred by him in any such proceedings so far as not recovered by him in the proceedings; and

(b) any sum required by a chief officer of police for the settlement of any claim made against him under this Act if the settlement is approved by the police authority.]

(5), (6) *****

Highways Act 1980
(1980, c. 66)

An Act to consolidate the Highways Acts 1959 to 1971 and related enactments with amendments to give effect to recommendations of the Law Commission   [13 November 1980]

Territorial extent: England and Wales

Obstruction of highways and streets

137 Penalty for wilful obstruction

(1) If a person, without lawful authority or excuse, in any way wilfully obstructs the free passage along a highway he is guilty of an offence and liable to a fine not exceeding [level 3 on the standard scale].

(2) . . .

Magistrates' Courts Act 1980
(1980, c. 43)

An Act to consolidate certain enactments relating to the jurisdiction of, and the practice and procedure before, magistrates' courts and the functions of justices' clerks, and to matters connected therewith, with amendments to give effect to recommendations of the Law Commission

[1 August 1980]

Territorial extent: England and Wales

PART I   CRIMINAL JURISDICTION AND PROCEDURE

Jurisdiction to issue process and deal with charges

1 Issue of summons to accused or warrant for his arrest

[(1) On an information being laid before a justice of the peace that a person has, or is suspected of having, committed an offence, the justice may issue—

(a) a summons directed to that person requiring him to appear before a magistrates' court to answer the information, or

(b) a warrant to arrest that person and bring him before a magistrates' court.]

(2) . . .

(3) No warrant shall be issued under this section [upon an information being laid] unless the information is in writing . . .

(4) No warrant shall be issued under this section for the arrest of any person who has attained [the age of 18 years] unless—

    (a) the offence to which the warrant relates is an indictable offence or is punishable with imprisonment, or

    (b) the person's address is not sufficiently established for a summons [, or a written charge and requisition,] to be served on him.

(5) . . .

(6)–(7) *****

(8) . . .

*****

PART VI   RECOGNIZANCES

Recognizances to keep the peace or be of good behaviour

115   Binding over to keep the peace or be of good behaviour

(1) The power of a magistrates' court on the complaint of any person to adjudge any other person to enter into a recognizance, with or without sureties, to keep the peace or to be of good behaviour towards the complaint shall be exercised by order on complaint.

(2) *****

(3) If any person ordered by a magistrates' court under subsection (1) above to enter into a recognizance, with or without sureties, to keep the peace or to be of good behaviour fails to comply with the order, the court may commit him to custody for a period not exceeding 6 months or until he sooner complies with the order.

*****

British Nationality Act 1981
(1981, c. 61)

An Act to make fresh provision about citizenship and nationality, and to amend the Immigration Act 1971 as regards the right of abode in the United Kingdom   [30 October 1981]

Territorial extent: United Kingdom

PART I   BRITISH CITIZENSHIP

Acquisition after commencement

1   Acquisition by birth or adoption

(1) A person born in the United Kingdom after commencement [, or in a qualifying territory on or after the appointed day] shall be a British citizen if at the time of the birth his father or mother is—

    (a) a British citizen; or

    (b) settled in the United Kingdom [or that territory].

(2) A new-born infant who, after commencement, is found abandoned in the United Kingdom [, or on or after the appointed day is found abandoned in a qualifying territory] shall, unless the contrary is shown, be deemed for the purposes of subsection (1)—

    (a) to have been born in the United Kingdom after commencement [or in that territory on or after the appointed day]; and

(b) to have been born to a parent who at the time of the birth was a British citizen or settled in the United Kingdom [or that territory].

(3) A person born in the United Kingdom after commencement who is not a British citizen by virtue of subsection (1) or (2) shall be entitled to be registered as a British citizen if, while he is a minor—

(a) his father or mother becomes a British citizen or becomes settled in the United Kingdom; and

(b) an application is made for his registration as a British citizen.

(4) A person born in the United Kingdom after commencement who is not a British citizen by virtue of subsection (1) or (2) shall be entitled, on an application for his registration as a British citizen made at any time after he has attained the age of ten years, to be registered as such a citizen if, as regards each of the first ten years of that person's life, the number of days on which he was absent from the United Kingdom in that year does not exceed 90.

(5)–(8) *****

2 Acquisition by descent

(1) A person born outside the United Kingdom [and the qualifying territories] after commencement shall be a British citizen if at the time of the birth his father or mother—

(a) is a British citizen otherwise than by descent; or

(b) is a British citizen and is serving outside the United Kingdom [and the qualifying territories] in service to which this paragraph applies, his or her recruitment for that service having taken place in the United Kingdom [or a qualifying territory]; or

(c) is a British citizen and is serving outside the United Kingdom [and the qualifying territories] in service under a Community institution, his or her recruitment for that service having taken place in a country which at the time of the recruitment was a member of the Communities.

(2) Paragraph (b) of subsection (1) applies to—

(a) Crown service under the government of the United Kingdom [or of a qualifying territory]; and

(b) service of any description for the time being designated under subsection (3).

(3) For the purposes of this section the Secretary of State may by order made by statutory instrument designate any description of service which he considers to be closely associated with the activities outside the United Kingdom [and the qualifying territories] of Her Majesty's government in the United Kingdom [or in a qualifying territory].

(4) Any order made under subsection (3) shall be subject to annulment in pursuance of a resolution of either House of Parliament.

3 Acquisition by registration: minors

(1) If while a person is a minor an application is made for his registration as a British citizen, the Secretary of State may, if he thinks fit, cause him to be registered as such a citizen.

(2) A person born outside the United Kingdom [and the qualifying territories] shall be entitled, on an application for his registration as a British citizen made within the period of twelve months from the date of the birth, to be registered as such a citizen if the requirements specified in subsection (3) or, in the case of a person born stateless, the requirements specified in paragraphs (a) and (b) of that subsection, are fulfilled in the case of either that person's father or his mother ("the parent in question").

(3) The requirements referred to in subsection (2) are—

(a) that the parent in question was a British citizen by descent at the time of the birth; and

(b) that the father or mother of the parent in question—

(i) was a British citizen otherwise than by descent at the time of the birth of the parent in question; or

(ii) became a British citizen otherwise than by descent at commencement, or would have become such a citizen otherwise than by descent at commencement but for his or her death; and

(c) that, as regards some period of three years ending with a date not later than that date of the birth—

(i) the parent in question was in the United Kingdom [or a qualifying territory] at the beginning of that period; and

(ii) the number of days on which the parent in question was absent from the United Kingdom [and the qualifying territories] in the period does not exceed 270.

(4) If in the special circumstances of any particular case the Secretary of State thinks fit, he may treat subsection (2) as if the reference to twelve months were a reference to six years.

(5) A person born outside the United Kingdom [and the qualifying territories] shall be entitled, on an application for his registration as a British citizen made while he is a minor, to be registered as such a citizen if the following requirements are satisfied, namely—

(a) that at the time of that person's birth his father or mother was a British citizen by descent; and

(b) subject to subsection (6), that that person and his father and mother were in the United Kingdom [or a qualifying territory] at the beginning of the period of three years ending with the date of the application and that, in the case of each of them, the number of days on which the person in question was absent from the United Kingdom [and the qualifying territories] in that period does not exceed 270; and

(c) subject to subsection (6), that the consent of his father and mother to the registration has been signified in the prescribed manner.

(6) In the case of an application under subsection (5) of the registration of a person as a British citizen—

(a) if his father or mother died, or their marriage [or civil partnership] was terminated, on or before the date of the application, or his father and mother were legally separated on that date, the references to his father and mother in paragraph (b) of that subsection shall be read either as references to his father or as references to his mother; [and]

(b) if his father or mother died on or before that date, the reference to his father and mother in paragraph (c) of that subsection shall be read as a reference to either of them. . . .

4, 4A–C ***

5 Acquisition by registration: nationals for purposes of the Community treaties

A [British overseas territories citizen] who falls to be treated as a national of the United Kingdom for the purposes of the Community Treaties shall be entitled to be registered as a British citizen if an application is made for his registration as such a citizen.

6 Acquisition by naturalisation

(1) If, on an application for naturalisation as a British citizen made by a person of full age and capacity, the Secretary of State is satisfied that the applicant fulfils the requirements of Schedule 1 for naturalisation as such a citizen under this subsection, he may, if he thinks fit, grant to him a certificate of naturalisation as such a citizen.

(2) If, on an application for naturalisation as a British citizen made by a person of full age and capacity who on the date of the application is married to a British citizen [or is the civil partner of a British citizen], the Secretary of State is satisfied that the applicant fulfils the requirements of Schedule 1 for naturalisation as such a citizen under this subsection, he may, if he thinks fit, grant to him a certificate of naturalisation as such a citizen.

7–9 . . .

10 *****

Acquisition at commencement

11 Citizens of UK and Colonies who are to become British citizens at commencement

(1) Subject to subsection (2), a person who immediately before commencement—

(a) was a citizen of the United Kingdom and Colonies; and

(b) had the right of abode in the United Kingdom under the Immigration Act 1971 as then in force,

shall at commencement become a British citizen.

(2) A person who was registered as a citizen of the United Kingdom and Colonies under section 1 of the British Nationality (No 2) Act 1964 (stateless persons) on the ground mentioned in subsection (1)(a) of that section (namely that his mother was a citizen of the United Kingdom and Colonies at the time when he was born) shall not become a British citizen under subsection (1) unless—

(a) his mother becomes a British citizen under subsection (1) or would have done so but for her death; or

(b) immediately before commencement he had the right of abode in the United Kingdom by virtue of section 2(1)(c) of the Immigration Act 1971 as then in force (settlement in United Kingdom, combined with five or more years' ordinary residence there as a citizen of the United Kingdom and Colonies).

(3) *****

Renunciation and resumption

12 Renunciation

(1) If any British citizen of full age and capacity makes in the prescribed manner a declaration of renunciation of British citizenship, then, subject to subsection (3) and (4), the Secretary of State shall cause the declaration to be registered.

(2) On the registration of a declaration made in pursuance of this section the person who made it shall cease to be a British citizen.

(3) A declaration made by a person in pursuance of this section shall not be registered unless the Secretary of State is satisfied that the person who made it will after the registration have or acquire some citizenship or nationality other than British citizenship; and if that person does not have any such citizenship or nationality on the date of registration and does not acquire some such citizenship or nationality within six months from that date, he shall be, and be deemed to have remained, a British citizen notwithstanding the registration.

(4) The Secretary of State may withhold registration of any declaration made in pursuance of this section if it is made during any war in which Her Majesty may be engaged in right of Her Majesty's government in the United Kingdom.

(5) For the purposes of this section any person who has been married[, or has formed a civil partnership,] shall be deemed to be of full age.

13–14 *****

PART II   BRITISH [OVERSEAS TERRITORIES] CITIZENSHIP

Acquisition after commencement

15 Acquisition by birth or adoption

(1) A person born in a [British overseas territory] after commencement shall be a [British overseas territories citizen] if at the time of the birth his father or mother is—

(a) a [British overseas territories citizen]; or

(b) settled in a [British overseas territory].

(2) A new-born infant who, after commencement, is found abandoned in a [British overseas territory] shall, unless the contrary is shown, be deemed for the purposes of subsection (1)—

(a) to have been born in that territory after commencement; and

(b) to have been born to a parent who at the time of the birth was a [British overseas territories citizen] or settled in a [British overseas territory].

(3) A person born in a [British overseas territory] after commencement who is not a [British overseas territories citizen] by virtue of subsection (1) or (2) shall be entitled to be registered as such a citizen if, while he is a minor—

(a) his father or mother becomes such a citizen or becomes settled in a [British overseas territory]; and

(b) an application is made for his registration as such a citizen.

(4) A person born in a [British overseas territory] after commencement who is not a [British overseas territories citizen] by virtue of subsection (1) or (2) shall be entitled, on an application for registration as a [British overseas territories citizen] made at any time after he has attained the age of ten years, to be registered as such a citizen if, as regards each of the first ten years of that person's life, the number of days on which he was absent from the territory in that year does not exceed 90.

(5)–(7) *****

16 Acquisition by descent

(1) A person born outside the [British overseas territories] after commencment shall be a [British overseas territories citizen] if at the time of the birth his father or mother—

(a) is such a citizen otherwise than by descent; or

(b) is such a citizen and is serving outside the [British overseas territories] in service to which this paragraph applies, his or her recruitment for that service having taken place in a [British overseas territory].

(2) Paragraph (b) of subsection (1) applies to—

(a) Crown service under the government of a [British overseas territory]; and

(b) service of any description for the time being designated under subsection (3).

(3) For the purposes of this section the Secretary of State may by order made by statutory instrument designate any description of service which he considers to be closely associated with the activities outside the [British overseas territories] of the government of any [British overseas territory].

(4) Any order made under subsection (3) shall be subject to annulment in pursuance of a resolution of either House of Parliament.

17–18, 22–25 *****

19–21 . . .

PART III BRITISH OVERSEAS CITIZENSHIP

26 Citizens of UK and Colonies who are to become British Overseas citizens at commencement

Any person who was a citizen of the United Kingdom and Colonies immediately before commencement and who does not at commencement become either a British citizen or a [British overseas territories citizen] shall at commencement become a British Overseas citizen.

27–35 *****

PART V   MISCELLANEOUS AND SUPPLEMENTARY

36 *****

37   Commonwealth citizenship

(1) Every person who—

(a) under [the British Nationality Acts 1981 and 1983] [or the British Overseas Territories Act 2002] is a British citizen, a [British overseas territories citizen], [a British National (Overseas),] a British Overseas citizen or a British subject; or

(b) under any enactment for the time being in force in any country mentioned in Schedule 3 is a citizen of that country,

shall have the status of a Commonwealth citizen.

(2) Her Majesty may by Order in Council amend Schedule 3 by the alteration of any entry, the removal of any entry, or the insertion of any additional entry.

(3) Any Order in Council made under this section shall be subject to annulment in pursuance of a resolution of either House of Parliament.

(4) After commencement no person shall have the status of a Commonwealth citizen or the status of a British subject otherwise than under this Act.

Note: Schedule 3 (not printed) lists those countries currently members of the Commonwealth.

38–39 *****

[40   Deprivation of citizenship

(1) In this section a reference to a person's "citizenship status" is a reference to his status as—

(a) a British citizen,

(b) a British overseas territories citizen,

(c) a British Overseas citizen,

(d) a British National (Overseas),

(e) a British protected person, or

(f) a British subject.

(2) The Secretary of State may by order deprive a person of a citizenship status if the Secretary of State is satisfied that the person has done anything seriously prejudicial to the vital interests of—

(a) the United Kingdom, or

(b) a British overseas territory.

(3) The Secretary of State may by order deprive a person of a citizenship status which results from his registration or naturalisation if the Secretary of State is satisfied that the registration or naturalisation was obtained by means of—

(a) fraud,

(b) false representation, or

(c) concealment of a material fact.

(4) The Secretary of State may not make an order under subsection (2) if he is satisfied that the order would make a person stateless.

(5) Before making an order under this section in respect of a person the Secretary of State must give the person written notice specifying—

(a) that the Secretary of State has decided to make an order,

(b) the reasons for the order, and

(c) the person's right of appeal under section 40A(1) or under section 2B of the Special Immigration Appeals Commission Act 1997].

(6) *****

[40A   Deprivation of citizenship: appeal

(1) A person who is given notice under section 40(5) of a decision to make an order in

respect of him under section 40 may appeal against the decision to an adjudicator appointed under section 81 of the Nationality, Immigration and Asylum Act 2002 (immigration appeal).

(2) Subsection (1) shall not apply to a decision if the Secretary of State certifies that it was taken wholly or partly in reliance on information which in his opinion should not be made public—

(a) in the interests of national security,

(b) in the interests of the relationship between the United Kingdom and another country, or

(c) otherwise in the public interest.]

(3) *****

(4)–(8) . . .

41 *****

[42   Registration and naturalisation: citizenship ceremony, oath and pledge

(1) A person of full age shall not be registered under this Act as a British citizen unless he has made the relevant citizenship oath and pledge specified in Schedule 5 at a citizenship ceremony.

(2) A certificate of naturalisation as a British citizen shall not be granted under this Act to a person of full age unless he has made the relevant citizenship oath and pledge specified in Schedule 5 at a citizenship ceremony.

(3) A person of full age shall not be registered under this Act as a British overseas territories citizen unless he has made the relevant citizenship oath and pledge specified in Schedule 5.

(4) A certificate of naturalisation as a British overseas territories citizen shall not be granted under this Act to a person of full age unless he has made the relevant citizenship oath and pledge specified in Schedule 5.

(5) A person of full age shall not be registered under this Act as a British Overseas citizen or a British subject unless he has made the relevant citizenship oath specified in Schedule 5.

(6) Where the Secretary of State thinks it appropriate because of the special circumstances of a case he may—

(a) disapply any of subsections (1) to (5), or

(b) modify the effect of any of those subsections.

(7) Sections 5 and 6 of the Oaths Act 1978 (c. 19) (affirmation) apply to a citizenship oath; and a reference in this Act to a citizenship oath includes a reference to a citizenship affirmation.]

42A, B, 43 *****

44   Decisions involving exercise of discretion

(1) Any discretion vested by or under this Act in the Secretary of State, a Governor or a Lieutenant-Governor shall be exercised without regard to the race, colour or religion of any person who may be affected by its exercise.

(2), (3) . . .

45–48 *****

49 . . .

50   Interpretation

(1) In this Act, unless the context otherwise requires–

"the 1948 Act" means the British Nationality Act 1948:

"alien" means a person who is neither a Commonwealth citizen nor a British protected person nor a citizen of the Republic of Ireland;

*****

"association" means an unincorporated body of persons;

["British National (Overseas)" means a person who is a British National (Overseas) under the Hong Kong (British Nationality) Order 1986, and "status of a British National (Overseas)" shall be construed accordingly;

"British Overseas citizen" includes a person who is a British Overseas citizen under the Hong Kong (British Nationality) Order 1986;]

["British overseas territory" means a territory mentioned in Schedule 6;]

"British protected person" means a person who is a member of any class of person declared to be British protected persons by an Order in Council for the time being in force under section 38 or is a British protected person by virtue of the Solomon Islands Act 1978;
*****

"Crown service" means the service of the Crown, whether within Her Majesty's dominions or elsewhere;

"Crown service under the government of the United Kingdom" means Crown service under Her Majesty's government in the United Kingdom or under Her Majesty's government in Northern Ireland [or under the Scottish Administration];
*****

"enactment" includes an enactment comprised in Northern Ireland legislation;

"foreign country" means a country other than the United Kingdom, a [British overseas territory], a country mentioned in Schedule 3 and the Republic of Ireland;
*****

"immigration laws"—

    (a) in relation to the United Kingdom, means the Immigration Act 1971 and any law for purposes similar to that Act which is for the time being or has at any time been in force in any part of the United Kingdom;

    (b) in relation to a [British overseas territory], means any law for purposes similar to the Immigration Act 1971 which is for the time being or has at any time been in force in that territory;

"the Islands" means the Channel Islands and the Isle of Man;

"minor" means a person who has not attained the age of eighteen years;

"prescribed" means prescribed by regulations made under section 41;

["qualifying territory" means a British Overseas Territory other than the Sovereign Base Areas of Akrotiri and Dhekelia.]

"settled" shall be construed in accordance with subsections (2) to (4);

"ship" includes a hovercraft;
*****

"United Kingdom consulate" means the office of a consular officer of Her Majesty's government in the United Kingdom where a register of births is kept or, where there is no such office, such office as may be prescribed.

(2) Subject to subsection (3), references in this Act to a person being settled in the United Kingdom or in a [British overseas territory] are references to his being ordinarily resident in the United Kingdom or, as the case may be, in that territory without being subject under the immigration laws to any restriction on the period for which he may remain.

(3), (4) *****

(5) It is hereby declared that a person is not to be treated for the purpose of any provision of this Act as ordinarily resident in the United Kingdom or in a [British overseas territory] at a time when he is in the United Kingdom or, as the case may be, in that territory in breach of the immigration laws.

(6)–(13) *****

51–53 *****

SCHEDULE 1
                       REQUIREMENTS FOR NATURALISATION

Naturalisation as a British citizen under section 6(1)

1.—(1) Subject to paragraph 2, the requirements for naturalisation as a British citizen under section 6(1) are, in the case of any person who applies for it—

    (a) the requirements specified in sub-paragraph (2) of this paragraph, or the alternative requirement specified in sub-paragraph (3) of this paragraph; and

    (b) that he is of good character; and

    (c) that he has a sufficient knowledge of the English, Welsh or Scottish Gaelic language; and

    [(ca) that he has sufficient knowledge about life in the United Kingdom; and]

    (d) that either–

        (i) his intentions are such that, in the event of a certificate of naturalisation as a British citizen being granted to him, his home or (if he has more than one) his principal home will be in the United Kingdom; or

        (ii) he intends, in the event of such a certificate being granted to him, to enter into, or continue in, Crown service under the government of the United Kingdom, or service under an international organisation of which the United Kingdom or Her Majesty's government therein is a member, or service in the employment of a company or association established in the United Kingdom.

  (2) The requirements referred to in sub-paragraph (1)(a) of this paragraph are—

    (a) that the applicant was in the United Kingdom at the beginning of the period of five years ending with the date of the application, and that the number of days on which he was absent from the United Kingdom in that period does not exceed 450; and

    (b) that the number of days on which he was absent from the United Kingdom in the period of twelve months so ending does not exceed 90; and

    (c) that he was not at any time in the period of twelve months so ending subject under the immigration laws to any restriction on the period for which he might remain in the United Kingdom; and

    (d) that he was not at any time in the period of five years so ending in the United Kingdom in breach of the immigration laws.

  (3) The alternative requirement referred to in sub-paragraph (1)(a) of this paragraph is that on the date of the application he is serving outside the United Kingdom in Crown service under the government of the United Kingdom.

  2. *****

Naturalisation as a British citizen under section 6(2)

  3. Subject to paragraph 4, the requirements for naturalisation as a British citizen under section 6(2) are, in the case of any person who applies for it—

    (a) that he was in the United Kingdom at the beginning of the period of three years ending with the date of the application, and that the number of days on which he was absent from the United Kingdom in that period does not exceed 270; and

    (b) that the number of days on which he was absent from the United Kingdom in the period of twelve months so ending does not exceed 90; and

    (c) that on the date of the application he was not subject under the immigration laws to any restriction on the period for which he might remain in the United Kingdom; and

    (d) that he was not at any time in the period of three years ending with the date of the application in the United Kingdom in breach of the immigration laws; and

(e) the [requirements specified in paragraph 1(1)(b), (c) and (ca)].

*****

[SCHEDULE 5   CITIZENSHIP OATH AND PLEDGE

1.   The form of citizenship oath and pledge is as follows for registration of or naturalisation as a British citizen—

Oath

"I, *[name]*, swear by Almighty God that, on becoming a British citizen, I will be faithful and bear true allegiance to Her Majesty Queen Elizabeth the Second, Her Heirs and Successors according to law."

Pledge

"I will give my loyalty to the United Kingdom and respect its rights and freedoms. I will uphold its democratic values. I will observe its laws faithfully and fulfil my duties and obligations as a British citizen.]

*****

Contempt of Court Act 1981
(1981, c. 49)

An Act to amend the law relating to contempt of court and related matters   [27 July 1981]

Territorial extent: United Kingdom (ss. 1–6, 8–11, Sch. 1); England and Wales (ss. 12–14); Scotland (s. 15); England, Wales and Northern Ireland (s. 7). For additional provisions applying to Northern Ireland see Sch. 4

Strict liability

1   The strict liability rule
In this Act "the strict liability rule" means the rule of law whereby conduct may be treated as a contempt of court as tending to interfere with the course of justice in particular legal proceedings regardless of intent to do so.

2   Limitation of scope of strict liability
(1) The strict liability rule applies only in relation to publications, and for this purpose "publication" includes any speech, writing, [programme included in a programme service] or other communication in whatever form, which is addressed to the public at large or any section of the public.

(2) The strict liability rule applies only to a publication which creates a substantial risk that the course of justice in the proceedings in question will be seriously impeded or prejudiced.

(3) The strict liability rule applies to a publication only if the proceedings in question are active within the meaning of this section at the time of the publication.

(4) Schedule 1 applies for determining the times at which proceedings are to be treated as active within the meaning of this section.

[(5) In this section, "programme service" has the same meaning as in the Broadcasting Act 1990.]

3 Defence of innocent publication or distribution

(1) A person is not guilty of contempt of court under the strict liability rule as the publisher of any matter to which that rule applies if at the time of publication (having taken all reasonable care) he does not know and has no reason to suspect that relevant proceedings are active.

(2) A person is not guilty of contempt of court under the strict liability rule as the distributor of a publication containing any such matter if at the time of distribution (having taken all reasonable care) he does not know that it contains such matter and has no reason to suspect that it is likely to do so.

(3) The burden of proof of any fact tending to establish a defence afforded by this section to any person lies upon that person.

(4) *****

4 Contemporary reports of proceedings

(1) Subject to this section a person is not guilty of contempt of court under the strict liability rule in respect of a fair and accurate report of legal proceedings held in public, published contemporaneously and in good faith.

(2) In any such proceedings the court may, where it appears to be necessary for avoiding a substantial risk of prejudice to the administration of justice in those proceedings, or in any other proceedings pending or imminent, order that the publication of any report of the proceedings, or any part of the proceedings, be postponed for such period as the court thinks necessary for that purpose.

(2A), (3) *****

(4) . . .

5 Discussion of public affairs

A publication made as or as part of a discussion in good faith of public affairs or other matters of general public interest is not to be treated as a contempt of court under the strict liability rule if the risk of impediment or prejudice to particular legal proceedings is merely incidental to the discussion.

6 Savings

Nothing in the foregoing provisions of this Act—

  (a) prejudices any defence available at common law to a charge of contempt of court under the strict liability rule;

  (b) implies that any publication is punishable as contempt of court under that rule which would not be so punishable apart from those provisions;

  (c) restricts liability for contempt of court in respect of conduct intended to impede or prejudice the administration of justice.

7 Consent required for institution of proceedings

Proceedings for a contempt of court under the strict liability rule (other than Scottish proceedings) shall not be instituted except by or with the consent of the Attorney General or on the motion of a court having jurisdiction to deal with it.

Other aspects of law and procedure

8 Confidentiality of jury's deliberations

(1) Subject to subsection (2) below, it is a contempt of court to obtain, disclose or solicit any particulars of statements made, opinions expressed, arguments advanced or votes cast by members of a jury in the course of their deliberations in any legal proceedings.

(2) This section does not apply to any disclosure of any particulars—

  (a) in the proceedings in question for the purpose of enabling the jury to arrive at their verdict, or in connection with the delivery of that verdict, or

(b) in evidence in any subsequent proceedings for an offence alleged to have been committed in relation to the jury in the first mentioned proceedings,

or to the publication of any particulars so disclosed.

(3) Proceedings for a contempt of court under this section (other than Scottish proceedings) shall not be instituted except by or with the consent of the attorney general or on the motion of a court having jurisdiction to deal with it.

9   Use of tape recorders

(1) Subject to subsection (4) below, it is a contempt of court–

(a) to use in court, or bring into court for use, any tape recorder or other instrument for recording sound, except with the leave of the court;

(b) to publish a recording of legal proceedings made by means of any such instrument, or any recording derived directly or indirectly from it, by playing it in the hearing of the public or any section of the public, or to dispose of it or any recording so derived, with a view to such publication;

(c) to use any such recording in contravention of any conditions of leave granted under paragraph (a).

(2) Leave under paragraph (a) of subsection (1) may be granted or refused at the discretion of the court, and if granted may be granted subject to such conditions as the court thinks proper with respect to the use of any recording made pursuant to the leave; and where leave has been granted the court may at the like discretion withdraw or amend it either generally or in relation to any particular part of the proceedings.

(3), (4) ******

10   Sources of information

No court may require a person to disclose, nor is any person guilty of contempt of court for refusing to disclose, the source of information contained in a publication for which he is responsible, unless it be established to the satisfaction of the court that disclosure is necessary in the interests of justice or national security or for the prevention of disorder or crime.

11   Publication of matters exempted from disclosure in court

In any case where a court (having power to do so) allows a name or other matter to be withheld from the public in proceedings before the court, the court may give such directions prohibiting the publication of that name or matter in connection with the proceedings as appear to the court to be necessary for the purpose of which it was so withheld.

12   Offences of contempt of magistrates' courts

(1) A magistrates' court has jurisdiction under this section to deal with any person who—

(a) wilfully insults the justice or justices, any witness before or officer of the court or any solicitor or counsel having business in the court, during his or their sitting or attendance in court or in going to or returning from the court; or

(b) wilfully interrupts the proceedings of the court or otherwise misbehaves in court.

(2) In any such case the court may order any officer of the court, or any constable, to take the offender into custody and detain him until the rising of the court; and the court may, if it thinks fit, commit the offender to custody for a specified period not exceeding one month or impose on him a fine not exceeding [£2,500], or both.

(2A) ******

(3) . . .

(4), (5) ******

13   . . .

Penalties for contempt and kindred offences

14   Proceedings in England and Wales

(1) In any case where a court has power to commit a person to prison for contempt of court and (apart from this provision) no limitation applies to the period of committal, the committal shall (without prejudice to the power of the court to order his earlier discharge) be for a fixed term, and that term shall not on any occasion exceed two years in the case of committal by a superior court, or one month in the case of committal by an inferior court.

(2) In any case where an inferior court has power to fine a person for contempt of court and (apart from the provision) no limit applies to the amount of the fine, the fine shall not on any occasion exceed [£2,500].

(2A)–(4), (4A) *****

[(4A) For the purposes of the preceding provisions of this section a county court shall be treated as a superior court and not as an inferior court.]

(5) *****

Note: This section, as amended, contains two subsections numbered (2A) and two numbered (4A).

15   Penalties for contempt of court in Scottish proceedings

(1) In Scottish proceedings, when a person is committed to prison for contempt of court the committal shall (without prejudice to the power of the court to order his earlier discharge) be for a fixed term.

(2) The maximum penalty which may be imposed by way of imprisonment or fine for contempt of court in Scottish proceedings shall be two years' imprisonment or a fine or both, except that—

    (a) where the contempt is dealt with by the sheriff in the course of or in connection with proceedings other than criminal proceedings on indictment, such penalty shall not exceed three months' imprisonment or a fine [of level 4 on the standard scale] or both; and

    (b) where the contempt is dealt with by the district court, such penalty shall not exceed sixty days' imprisonment or a fine of [level 4 on the standard scale] or both.

(3)–(5) *****

(6) . . .

16–21   *****

Section 2

SCHEDULE 1
TIMES WHEN PROCEEDINGS ARE ACTIVE FOR PURPOSES OF SECTION 2

Preliminary

1. In this Schedule "criminal proceedings" means proceedings against a person in respect of an offence, not being appellate proceedings or proceedings commenced by motion for committal or attachment in England and Wales or Northern Ireland; and "appellate proceedings" means proceedings on appeal from or for the review of the decision of a court in any proceedings.

2. Criminal, appellate and other proceedings are active within the meaning of section 2 at the times respectively prescribed by the following paragraphs of this Schedule; and in relation to proceedings in which more than one of the steps described in any of those paragraphs is taken, the reference in that paragraph is a reference to the first of those steps.

Criminal proceedings

3. Subject to the following provisions of this Schedule, criminal proceedings are active from the relevant initial step specified in paragraph 4 [or 4A] until concluded as described in paragraph 5.

4. The initial steps of criminal proceedings are:–

   (a) arrest without warrant;

   (b) the issue, or in Scotland the grant, of a warrant for arrest;

   (c) the issue of a summons to appear, or in Scotland the grant of a warrant to cite;

   (d) the service of an indictment or other document specifying the charge;

   (e) except in Scotland, oral charge.

[4A. Where as a result of an order under section 54 of the Criminal Procedure and Investigations Act 1996 (acquittal tainted by administration of justice offence) proceedings are brought against a person for an offence of which he has previously been acquitted, the initial step of the proceedings is a certification under subsection (2) of that section; and paragraph 4 has effect subject to this.]

5. Criminal proceedings are concluded—

   (a) by acquittal or, as the case may be, by sentence;

   (b) by any other verdict, finding, order or decision which puts an end to the proceedings;

   (c) by discontinuance or by operation of law.

6. The reference in paragraph 5(a) to sentence includes any order or decision consequent on conviction or finding of guilt which disposes of the case, either absolutely or subject to future events, and a deferment of sentence under [section 1 of the Powers of Criminal Courts (Sentencing) Act 2000], section 219 or 432 of the Criminal Procedure (Scotland) Act 1975 or Article 14 of the Treatment of Offenders (Northern Ireland) Order 1976.

7. Proceedings are discontinued within the meaning of paragraph 5(c)—

   (a)   in England and Wales or Northern Ireland, if the charge or summons is withdrawn or a *nolle prosequi* entered;

   [(aa) in England and Wales, if they are discontinued by virtue of section 23 of the Prosecution of Offences Act 1985;]

   (b)   in Scotland, if the proceedings are expressly abandoned by the prosecutor or are deserted *simpliciter*;

   (c)   in the case of proceedings in England and Wales or Northern Ireland commenced by arrest without warrant, if the person arrested is released, otherwise than on bail, without having been charged.

8.–10. *****

11. Criminal proceedings against a person which become active on the issue or the grant of a warrant for his arrest cease to be active at the end of the period of twelve months beginning with the date of the warrant unless he has been arrested within that period, but become active again if he is subsequently arrested.

Other proceedings at first instance

12. Proceedings other than criminal proceedings and appellate proceedings are active from the time when arrangements for the hearing are made or, if no such arrangements are previously made, from the time the hearing begins, until the proceedings are disposed of or discontinued or withdrawn; and for the purposes of this paragraph any motion or application made in or for the purposes of any proceedings, and any pre-trial review in the county court, is to be treated as a distinct proceeding.

13. In England and Wales or Northern Ireland arrangements for the hearing of proceedings to which paragraph 12 applies are made within the meaning of that paragraph—

(a) in the case of proceedings in the High Court for which provision is made by rules of court for setting down for trial, when the case is set down;

(b) in the case of any proceedings, when a date for the trial or hearing is fixed.

14. In Scotland arrangements for the hearing of proceedings to which paragraph 12 applies are made within the meaning of that paragraph—

(a) in the case of an ordinary action in the Court of Session or in the sheriff court, when the record is closed;

(b) in the case of a motion or application, when it is enrolled or made;

(c) in any other case, when the date for a hearing is fixed or a hearing is allowed.

Appellate proceedings

15. Appellate proceedings are active from the time when they are commenced—

(a) by application for leave to appeal or apply for review, or by notice of such an application;

(b) by notice of appeal or of application for review;

(c) by other originating process,

until disposed of or abandoned, discontinued or withdrawn.

16. Where, in appellate proceedings relating to criminal proceedings, the court—

(a) remits the case to the court below; or

(b) orders a new trial or a *venire de novo*, or in Scotland grants authority to bring a new prosecution,

any further or new proceedings which result shall be treated as active from the conclusion of the appellate proceedings.

*****

Indecent Displays (Control) Act 1981

(1981, c. 42)

An Act to make fresh provision with respect to the public display of indecent matter; and for purposes connected therewith   [27 July 1981]

Territorial extent: England and Wales, Scotland

1   Indecent displays

(1) If any indecent matter is publicly displayed the person making the display and any person causing or permitting the display to be made shall be guilty of an offence.

(2) Any matter which is displayed in or so as to be visible from any public place shall, for the purposes of this section, be deemed to be publicly displayed.

(3) In subsection (2) above, "public place", in relation to the display of any matter, means any place to which the public have or are permitted to have access (whether on payment or otherwise) while that matter is displayed except—

(a) a place to which the public are permitted to have access only on payment which is or includes payment for that display; or

(b) a shop or any part of a shop to which the public can only gain access by passing beyond an adequate warning notice;

but the exclusions contained in paragraphs (a) and (b) above shall only apply where persons under the age of 18 years are not permitted to enter while the display in question is continuing.

(4) Nothing in this section applies in relation to any matter—

[(a) included by any person in a television broadcasting service or other television programme service (within the meaning of Part I of the Broadcasting Act 1990);] or

(b) included in the display of an art gallery or museum and visible only from within the gallery or museum; or

(c) displayed by or with the authority of, and visible only from within a building occupied by, the Crown or any local authority; or

[(d) included in a performance of a play (within the meaning of paragraph 14(1) of Schedule 1 to the Licensing Act 2003) in England and Wales or of a play (within the meaning of the Theatres Act 1968 in Scotland;] or

[(e) included in [an exhibition of a film, within the meaning of paragraph 15 of Schedule 1 to the Licensing Act 2003, in England and Wales, or a film exhibition, as defined in the Cinemas Act 1985, in Scotland]—

    (i) given in a place which as regards that exhibition is required to be licensed under section 1 of the Act or by virtue only of section 5, 7 or 8 of that Act is not required to be so licensed; or

    (ii) which is an exhibition to which section 6 of that Act applies given by an exempted organisation as defined by subsection (6) of that section.]

(5) In this section "matter" includes anything capable of being displayed, except that it does not include an actual human body or any part thereof; and in determining for the purpose of this section whether any displayed matter is indecent—

(a) there shall be disregarded any part of that matter which is not exposed to view; and

(b) account may be taken of the effect of juxtaposing one thing with another.

(6) A warning notice shall not be adequate for the purposes of this section unless it complies with the following requirements—

(a) The warning notice must contain the following words, and no others—

"WARNING

Persons passing beyond this notice will find material on display which they may consider indecent. No admittance to persons under 18 years of age."

(b) The word "WARNING" must appear as a heading.

(c) No pictures or other matter shall appear on the notice.

(d) The notice must be so situated that no one could reasonably gain access to the shop or part of the shop in question without being aware of the notice and it must be easily legible by any person gaining such access.

*****

Senior Courts Act 1981

(1981, c. 54)

An Act to consolidate with amendments the Supreme Court of Judicature (Consolidation) Act 1925 and other enactments relating to the Supreme Court in England and Wales and the administration of justice therein; to repeal certain obsolete or unnecessary enactments so relating; to amend Part VIII of the Mental Health Act 1959, the Courts-Martial (Appeals) Act 1968, the Arbitration Act 1979 and the law relating to county courts; and for connected purposes   **[28 July 1981]**

Territorial extent: England and Wales

1–3 *****

The High Court

4   The High Court

(1) The High Court shall consist of—

(a) ...;

(b) the Lord Chief Justice;

[(ba) the President of the Queen's Bench Division;

(c) the President of the Family Division;

(d) the Chancellor of the High Court;]

[(dd) the Senior Presiding Judge;]

[(ddd) the vice-president of the Queen's Bench Division;] and

(e) not more than [108] puisne judges of that court.

(2) The puisne judges of the High Court shall be styled "Justices of the High Court".

(3) All the judges of the High Court shall, except where this Act expressly provides otherwise, have in all respects equal power, authority and jurisdiction.

(4)–(6) *****

5–9 *****

10   Appointment of judges of Senior Courts

(1) Whenever the office of Lord Chief Justice, Master of the Rolls, [President of the Queen's Bench Division, President of the Family Division or Chancellor of the High Court] is vacant, Her Majesty may [on the recommendation of the Lord Chancellor] by letters patent appoint a qualified person to that office.

(2) Subject to the limits on numbers for the time being imposed by sections 2(1) and 4(1), Her Majesty may [on the recommendation of the Lord Chancellor] from time to time by letters patent appoint qualified persons as Lords Justices of Appeal or as puisne judges of the High Court.

(3) No person shall be qualified for appointment—

(a) as Lord Chief Justice, Master of the Rolls, [President of the Queen's Bench Division, President of the Family Division or Chancellor of High Court], unless he is qualified for appointment as a Lord Justice of Appeal or is a judge of the Court of Appeal;

(b) as a Lord Justice of Appeal, [unless—

(i) he has a 10 year High Court qualification within the meaning of section 71 of the Courts and Legal Services Act 1990; or

(ii) he is a judge of the High Court;] or

(c) as a puisne judge of the High Court, [unless—

(i) he has a 10 year High Court qualification within the meaning of section 71of the Courts and Legal Services Act 1990; or

(ii) he is a Circuit Judge who has held that office for at least 2 years.]

(4)–(8) *****

11   Tenure of office of judges of Senior Courts

(1) This section applies to the office of any judge of the [Senior Courts] ...

(2) A person appointed to an office to which this section applies shall vacate it on the day on which he attains the age of [seventy] years unless by virtue of this section he has ceased to hold it before then.

(3) A person appointed to an office to which this section applies shall hold that office during good behaviour, subject to a power of removal by Her Majesty on an address presented to Her by both Houses of Parliament.

[(3A) It is for the Lord Chancellor to recommend to Her Majesty the exercise of the power of removal under subsection (3).]

(4)–(6) *****

(7) A person who holds an office to which this section applies may at any time resign it by giving the Lord Chancellor notice in writing to that effect.

(8) The Lord Chancellor, if satisfied by means of a medical certificate that a person holding an office to which this section applies—

(a) is disabled by permanent infirmity from the performance of the duties of his office; and

(b) is for the time being incapacitated from resigning his office, may, subject to subsection (9), by instrument under his hand declare that person's office to have been vacated; and the instrument shall have the like effect for all purposes as if that person had on the date of the instrument resigned his office.

(9) A declaration under subsection (8) with respect to a person shall be of no effect unless it is made—

(a) in the case of any of the Lord Chief Justice, the Master of the Rolls, [the President of the Queen's Bench Division, the President of the Family Division and the Chancellor of the High Court], with the concurrence of two others of them;

(b) in the case of a Lord Justice of Appeal, with the concurrence of the Master of the Rolls;

(c) in the case of a puisne judge of any Division of the High Court, with the concurrence of the senior judge of that Division.

(10) . . .

12 Salaries etc of judges of Senior Courts

(1) Subject to subsections (2) and (3), there shall be paid to judges of the [Senior Courts] . . . such salaries as may be determined by the Lord Chancellor with the concurrence of the Minister for the Civil Service.

(2) Until otherwise determined under this section, there shall be paid to the judges mentioned in subsection (1) the same salaries as at the commencement of this Act.

(3) Any salary payable under this section may be increased, but not reduced, by a determination or further determination under this section.

(4) . . .

(5)–(7) *****

13–18 *****

PART II   JURISDICTION THE HIGH COURT

General jurisdiction

19 General jurisdiction

(1) The High Court shall be a superior court of record.

(2) Subject to the provisions of this Act, there shall be exercisable by the High Court—

(a) all such jurisdiction (whether civil or criminal) as is conferred on it by this or any other Act; and

(b) all such other jurisdiction (whether civil or criminal) as was exercisable by it immediately before the commencment of this Act (including jurisdiction conferred on a judge of the High Court by any statutory provision).

(3), (4) *****

*****

Other particular fields of jurisdiction

29   Orders of mandamus, prohibition and certiorari

(1) [Subject to subsection (3A), the] High Court shall have jurisdiction to make orders of mandamus, prohibition and certiorari in those classes of cases in which it had power to do so immediately before the commencement of this Act.

(2) Every such order shall be final, subject to any right of appeal therefrom.

(3) In relation to the jurisdiction of the Crown Court, other than its jurisdiction in matters relating to trial on indictment, the High Court shall have all such jurisdiction to make orders of mandamus, prohibition or certiorari as the High Court possesses in relation to the jurisdiction of an inferior court.

(3A) *****

(4) The power of the High Court under any enactment to require justices of the peace or a judge or officer of a county court to do any act relating to the duties of their respective offices, or to require a magistrates' court to state a case for the opinion of the High Court, in any case where the High Court formerly had by virtue of any enactment jurisdiction to make a rule absolute, or an order, for any of those purposes, shall be exercisable by order of mandamus.

(5) In any enactment—

(a) references to a writ of mandamus, of prohibition or of certiorari shall be read as references to the corresponding order; and

(b) references to the issue or award of any such writ shall be read as references to the making of the corresponding order.

[(6) In subsection (3) the reference to the Crown Court's jurisdiction in matters relating to trial on indictment does not include its jurisdiction relating to orders under section 17 of the Access to Justice Act 1999.]

30   *****

31   Application for judicial review

(1) An application to the High Court for one or more of the following forms of relief, namely—

(a) an order of mandamus, prohibition or certiorari;

(b) a declaration or injunction under subsection (2); or

(c) an injunction under section 30 restraining a person not entitled to do so from acting in an office to which that section applies,

shall be made in accordance with rules of court by a procedure to be known as an application for judicial review.

(2) A declaration may be made or an injunction granted under this subsection in any case where an application for judicial review, seeking that relief, has been made and the High Court considers that, having regard to—

(a) the nature of the matters in respect of which relief may be granted by orders of mandamus, prohibition or certiorari;

(b) the nature of the persons and bodies against whom relief may be granted by such orders; and

(c) all the circumstances of the case,

it would be just and convenient for the declaration to be made or for the injunction to be granted, as the case may be.

(3) No application for judicial review shall be made unless the leave of the High Court has been obtained in accordance with rules of court; and the court shall not grant leave to make such an application unless it considers that the applicant has a sufficient interest in the matter to which the application relates.

(4) On an application for judicial review the High Court may award damages to the applicant if—

    (a) he has joined with his application a claim for damages arising from any matter to which the application relates; and

    (b) the court is satisfied that, if the claim had been made in an action begun by the applicant at the time of making his application, he would have been awarded damages.

(5) If, on an application for judicial review seeking an order of certiorari, the High Court quashes the decision to which the application relates, the High Court may remit the matter to the court, tribunal or authority concerned, with a direction to reconsider it and reach a decision in accordance with the findings of the High Court.

(6) Where the High Court considers that there has been undue delay in making an application for judicial review, the court may refuse to grant—

    (a) leave for the making of the application; or

    (b) any relief sought on the application,

if it considers that the granting of the relief sought would be likely to cause substantial hardship to, or substantially prejudice the rights of, any person or would be detrimental to good administration.

(7) Subsection (6) is without prejudice to any enactment or rule of court which has the effect of limiting the time within which an application for judicial review may be made.

Note: The provisions of s. 31 are implemented by Part 54 of the Civil Procedure Rules 1998 (replacing Order 53 of the Rules of the Supreme Court), printed below.

*****

Canada Act 1982

(1982, c. 11)

An Act to give effect to a request by the Senate and House of Commons of Canada
[29 March 1982]

Territorial extent: Canada

Whereas Canada has requested and consented to the enactment of an Act of the Parliament of the United Kingdom to give effect to the provisions hereinafter set forth and the Senate and the House of Commons of Canada in Parliament assembled have submitted an address to Her Majesty requesting that Her Majesty may graciously be pleased to cause a Bill to be laid before the Parliament of the United Kingdom for that purpose:

Be it therefore enacted by the Queen's Most Excellent Majesty, by and with the advice and consent of the Lords Spiritual and Temporal, and Commons, in this present Parliament assembled, and by the authority of the same, as follows:

1 Constitution Act, 1982 enacted
The Constitution Act, 1982 set out in Schedule B to this Act is hereby enacted for and shall have the force of law in Canada and shall come into force as provided in that Act.

2 Termination of power to legislate for Canada
No Act of the Parliament of the United Kingdom passed after the Constitution Act, 1982 comes into force shall extend to Canada as part of its law.

3 French version
So far as it is not contained in Schedule B, the French version of this Act is set out in Schedule A to this Act and has the same authority in Canada as the English version thereof.

4   Short title

This Act may be cited as the Canada Act 1982.

*****

SCHEDULE B   CONSTITUTION ACT, 1982

PART I   CANADIAN CHARTER OF RIGHTS AND FREEDOMS

Whereas Canada is founded upon principles that recognize the supremacy of God and the rule of law:

Guarantee of Rights and Freedoms

1   Rights and freedoms in Canada

The *Canadian Charter of Rights and Freedoms* guarantees the rights and freedoms set out in it subject only to such reasonable limits prescribed by law as can be demonstrably justified in a free and democratic society.

Fundamental Freedoms

2   Fundamental freedoms

Everyone has the following fundamental freedoms:
- (a) freedom of conscience and religion;
- (b) freedom of thought, belief, opinion and expression, including freedom of the press and other media of communication;
- (c) freedom of peaceful assembly; and
- (d) freedom of association.

Democratic Rights

3   Democratic rights of citizens

Every citizen of Canada has the right to vote in an election of members of the House of Commons or of a legislative assembly and to be qualified for membership therein.

4   Maximum duration of legislative bodies

(1) No House of Commons and no legislative assembly shall continue for longer than five years from the date fixed for the return of the writs at a general election of its members.

Continuation in special circumstances

(2) In time of real or apprehended war, invasion or insurrection, a House of Commons may be continued by Parliament and a legislative assembly may be continued by the legislature beyond five years if such continuation is not opposed by the votes of more than one-third of the members of the House of Commons or the legislative assembly, as the case may be.

5   Annual sitting of legislative bodies

There shall be a sitting of Parliament and of each legislature at least once every twelve months.

Mobility Rights

6   Mobility of citizens

(1) Every citizen of Canada has the right to enter, remain in and leave Canada.

Rights to move and gain livelihood

(2) Every citizen of Canada and every person who has the status of a permanent resident of Canada has the right

(a) to move to and take up residence in any province; and

(b) to pursue the gaining of a livelihood in any province.

Limitation

(3) The rights specified in subsection (2) are subject to

(a) any laws or practices of general application in force in a province other than those that discriminate among persons primarily on the basis of province of present or previous residence; and

(b) any laws providing for reasonable residency requirements as a qualification for the receipt of publicly provided social services.

Affirmative action programs

(4) Subsections (2) and (3) do not preclude any law, program or activity that has as its object the amelioration in a province of conditions of individuals in that province who are socially or economically disadvantaged if the rate of employment in that province is below the rate of employment in Canada.

Legal Rights

7   Life, liberty and security of person

Everyone has the right to life, liberty and security of the person and the right not to be deprived thereof except in accordance with the principles of fundamental justice.

8   Search or seizure

Everyone has the right to be secure against unreasonable search or seizure.

9   Detention or imprisonment

Everyone has the right not to be arbitrarily detained or imprisoned.

10   Arrest or detention

Everyone has the right on arrest or detention

(a) to be informed promptly of the reasons therefor;

(b) to retain and instruct counsel without delay and to be informed of that right;

and

(c) to have the validity of the detention determined by way of *habeas corpus* and to be released if the detention is not lawful.

11   Proceedings in criminal and penal matters

Any person charged with an offence has the right

(a) to be informed without unreasonable delay of the specific offence;

(b) to be tried within a reasonable time;

(c) not to be compelled to be a witness in proceedings against that person in respect of the offence;

(d) to be presumed innocent until proven guilty according to law in a fair and public hearing by an independent and impartial tribunal;

(e) not to be denied reasonable bail without just cause;

(f) except in the case of an offence under military law tried before a military tribunal, to the benefit of trial by jury where the maximum punishment for the offence is imprisonment for five years or a more severe punishment;

(g) not to be found guilty on account of any act or omission unless, at the time of the act or omission, it constituted an offence under Canadian or international law or was criminal according to the general principles of law recognized by the community of nations;

(h) if finally acquitted of the offence, not to be tried for it again and, if finally found guilty and punished for the offence, not to be tried or punished for it again; and

(i) if found guilty of the offence and if the punishment for the offence has been varied between the time of commission and the time of sentencing, to the benefit of the lesser punishment.

12   Treatment or punishment

Everyone has the right not to be subjected to any cruel and unusual treatment or punishment.

13   Self-crimination

A witness who testifies in any proceedings has the right not to have any incriminating evidence so given used to incriminate that witness in any other proceedings, except in a prosecution for perjury or for the giving of contradictory evidence.

14   Interpreter

A party or witness in any proceedings who does not understand or speak the language in which the proceedings are conducted or who is deaf has the right to the assistance of an interpreter.

Equality Rights

15   Equality before and under law and equal protection and benefit of law

(1) Every individual is equal before and under the law and has the right to the equal protection and equal benefit of the law without discrimination and, in particular, without discrimination based on race, national or ethnic origin, colour, religion, sex, age or mental or physical disability.

Affirmative action programs

(2) Subsection (1) does not preclude any law, program or activity that has as its object the amelioration of conditions of disadvantaged individuals or groups including those that are disadvantaged because of race, national or ethnic origin, colour, religion, sex, age or mental or physical disability.

Official Languages of Canada

16   Official languages of Canada

(1) English and French are the official languages of Canada and have equality of status and equal rights and privileges as to their use in all institutions of the Parliament and government of Canada.

(2), (3) *****

17–23   *****

Enforcement

24   Enforcement of guaranteed rights and freedoms

(1) Anyone whose rights or freedoms, as guaranteed by this Charter, have been infringed or denied may apply to a court of competent jurisdiction to obtain such remedy as the court considers appropriate and just in the circumstances.

Exclusion of evidence bringing administration of justice into disrepute

(2) Where, in proceedings under subsection (1), a court concludes that evidence was obtained in a manner that infringed or denied any rights or freedoms guaranteed by this Charter, the evidence shall be excluded if it is established that, having regard to all the circumstances, the admission of it in the proceedings would bring the administration of justice into disrepute.

General

25   Aboriginal rights and freedoms not affected by Charter

The guarantee in this Charter of certain rights and freedoms shall not be construed so as to abrogate or derogate from any aboriginal, treaty or other rights or freedoms that pertain to the aboriginal peoples of Canada including

    (a) any rights or freedoms that have been recognised by the Royal Proclamation of October 7, 1763; and

    (b) any rights or freedoms that may be acquired by the aboriginal peoples of Canada by way of land claims settlement.

26   Other rights and freedoms not affected by Charter

The guarantee in this Charter of certain rights and freedoms shall not be construed as denying the existence of any other rights or freedoms that exist in Canada.

27   Multicultural heritage

This Charter shall be interpreted in a manner consistent with the preservation and enhancement of the multicultural heritage of Canadians.

28   Rights guaranteed equally to both sexes

Notwithstanding anything in this Charter, the rights and freedoms referred to in it are guaranteed equally to male and female persons.

29   Rights respecting certain schools preserved

Nothing in this Charter abrogates or derogates from any rights or privileges guaranteed by or under the Constitution of Canada in respect of denominational, separate or dissentient schools.

30   *****

31   Legislative powers not extended

Nothing in this Charter extends the legislative powers of any body or authority.

Application of Charter

32   Application of Charter

    (1) This Charter applies

        (a) to the Parliament and government of Canada in respect of all matters within the authority of Parliament including all matters relating to the Yukon Territory and Northwest Territories; and

        (b) to the legislature and government of each province in respect of all matters within the authority of the legislature of each province.

Exception

    (2) Notwithstanding subsection (1), section 15 shall not have effect until three years after this section comes into force.

33   Exceptions where express declaration

    (1) Parliament or the legislature of a province may expressly declare in an Act of Parliament or of the legislature, as the case may be, that the Act or a provision thereof shall operate notwithstanding a provision included in section 2 or sections 7 to 15 of this Charter.

Operation of exception

    (2) An Act or a provision of an Act in respect of which a declaration made under this section is in effect shall have such operation as it would have but for the provision of this Charter referred to in the declaration.

Five year limitation
    (3) A declaration made under subsection (1) shall cease to have effect five years after it comes into force or on such earlier date as may be specified in the declaration.

Re-enactment
    (4) Parliament or the legislature of a province may re-enact a declaration made under subsection (1).

Five year limitation
    (5) Subsection (3) applies in respect of a re-enactment made under subsection (4).

Citation

34   Citation
This Part may be cited as the *Canadian Charter of Rights and Freedoms*.

*****

Note: Schedule A to this Act is a French language version of the Act, and Schedule B is also printed in English and French. Both texts have equal status.

Representation of the People Act 1983
(1983, c. 2)

An Act to consolidate the Representation of the People Acts of 1949, 1969, 1977, 1978 and 1980, The Electoral Registers Acts of 1949 and 1953, the Elections (Welsh Forms) Act 1964, Part III of the Local Government Act 1972, sections 6 to 10 of the Local Government (Scotland) Act 1973, the Representation of the People (Armed Forces) Act 1976, the Returning Officers (Scotland) Act 1977, section 3 of the Representation of the People Act 1981, section 62 of and Schedule 2 to the Mental Health (Amendment) Act 1982, and connected provisions; and to repeal as obsolete the Representation of the People Act 1979 and other enactments related to the Representation of the People Acts
[8 February 1983]

Territorial extent: United Kingdom

PART I   PARLIAMENTARY AND LOCAL GOVERNMENT FRANCHISE AND ITS EXERCISE

Parliamentary and local government franchise

[1   Parliamentary electors
    (1) A person is entitled to vote as an elector at a parliamentary election in any constituency if on the date of the poll he—
    (a) is registered in the register of parliamentary electors for that constituency;
    (b) is not subject to any legal incapacity to vote (age apart);
    (c) is either a Commonwealth citizen or a citizen of the Republic of Ireland; and
    (d) is of voting age (that is, 18 years or over).
    (2) A person is not entitled to vote as an elector—
    (a) more than once in the same constituency at any parliamentary election; or
    (b) in more than one constituency at a general election.]

*****

75 Prohibition of expenses not authorised by election agent
[(1) No expenses shall, with a view to promoting or procuring the election of a candidate (or, in the case of an election of the London members of the London Assembly at an ordinary election, a registered political party or candidates of that party) at an election, be incurred by any person other than the candidate. his election agent and persons authorised in writing by the election agent on account—
(a) of holding public meetings or organising any public display; or
(b) of issuing advertisements, circulars or publications; or
(c) of otherwise presenting to the electors the candidate or his views or the extent or nature of his backing or disparaging another candidate, or
(d) in the case of an election of the London members of the London Assembly at an ordinary election, of otherwise presenting to the electors the candidate's registered political party (if any) or the views of that party or the extent or nature of that party's backing or disparaging any other registered political party
but paragraph (c) or (d) of this subsection shall not—
(i) restrict the publication of any matter relating to the election in a newspaper or other periodical or in a broadcast made by the British Broadcasting Corporation or or by Sianel Pedwar Cymru or in a programme included in any service licensed under Part I or III of the Broadcasting Act 1990 or Part I or II of the Broadcasting Act 1996;
(ii) apply to any expenses incurred by any person which do not exceed in the aggregate the permitted sum (and are not incurred by that person as part of a concerted plan of action), or to expenses incurred by any person in travelling or in living away from home or similar personal expenses.]
[(1ZA) For the purposes of subsection (1)(ii) above, "the permitted sum" means—
(a) in respect of a candidate at a parliamentary election, £500;
(b) in respect of a candidate at a local government election, £50 together with an additional 0.5p for every entry in the register of local government electors for the electoral area in question as it has effect on the last day for publication of notice of the election;
and expenses shall be regarded as incurred by a person "as part of a concerted plan of action" if they are incurred by that person in pursuance of any plan or other arrangement whereby that person and one or more other persons are to incur, with a view to promoting or procuring the election of the same candidate, expenses which (disregarding subsection (1)(ii)) fall within subsection (1) above.]
[(1A) In the application of subsection (1) above in relation to an election of the London members of the London Assembly at an ordinary election, any reference to the candidate includes a reference to all or any of the candidates of a registered political party; and in the application of subsection (1ZA) above in relation to such an election the reference to the same candidate includes a reference to all or any of the candidates of the same registered political party.]
(1B), (1C) . . .
(2) Where a person incurs any expenses required by this section to be authorised by the election agent—
(a) that person shall within 21 days after the day on which the result of the election is declared deliver to the appropriate officer a return of the amount of those expenses, stating the election at which and the candidate in whose support they were incurred, and
(b) the return shall be accompanied by a declaration made by that person (or in the case of an association or body of persons, by a director, general manager, secretary or other similar officer of the association or body) verifying the return and giving particulars of the matters for which the expenses were incurred,

but this subsection does not apply to any person engaged or employed for payment or promise of payment by the candidate or his election agent.

(3), (4) *****

(5) If a person—

(a) incurs, or aids, abets, counsels or procures any other person to incur. any expenses in contravention of this section, or

(b) knowingly makes the declaration required by subsection (2) falsely, he shall be guilty of a corrupt practice; and if a person fails to deliver or send any declaration or return or a copy of it as required by this section he shall be guilty of an illegal practice, but—

(i) the court before whom a person is convicted under this subsection may, if they think it just in the special circumstances of the case, mitigate or entirely remit any incapacity imposed by virtue of section 173 below; and

(ii) a candidate shall not be liable, nor shall his election be avoided, for a corrupt or illegal practice under this subsection committed by an agent without his consent or connivance.

(6), (7) *****

92   Broadcasting from outside United Kingdom

[(1) No person shall, with intent to influence persons to give or refrain from giving their votes at a parliamentary or local government election, include, or aid, abet, counsel or procure the inclusion of, any matter relating to the election in any programme service (within the meaning of the Broadcasting Act 1990) provided from a place outside the United Kingdom otherwise than in pursuance of arrangements made with—

(a)   the British Broadcasting Corporation;

(b)   Sianel Pedwar Cymru; or

(c)   the holder of any licence granted by [the Office of Communications].

for the reception and re-transmission of that matter by that body or the holder of that licence.]

(2) An offence under this section shall be an illegal practice, but the court before whom a person is convicted of an offence under this section may, if they think it just in the special circumstances of the case, mitigate or entirely remit any incapacity imposed by virtue of section [160(5)] below.

(3) *****

[93   Broadcasting of local items during election period

(1) Each broadcasting authority shall adopt a code of practice with respect to the participation of candidates at a parliamentary or local government election in items about the constituency or electoral area in question which are included in relevant services during the election period.

(2) The code for the time being adopted by a broadcasting authority under this section shall be either—

(a)   a code drawn up by that authority, whether on their own or jointly with one or more other broadcasting authorities, or

(b)   a code drawn up by one or more other such authorities;

and a broadcasting authority shall from time to time consider whether the code for the time being so adopted by them should be replaced by a further code falling within paragraph (a) or (b).

(3) Before drawing up a code under this section a broadcasting authority shall have regard to any views expressed by the Electoral Commission for the purposes of this subsection; and any such code may make different provision for different cases.

(4) The [Office of Communications shall] do all that they can to secure that the code for the time being adopted by them under this section is observed in the provision of relevant

services; and the British Broadcasting Corporation and Sianel Pedwar Cymru shall each observe in the provision of relevant services the code so adopted by them.

(5) For the purposes of subsection (1) "the election period", in relation to an election, means the period beginning—

(a) (if a parliamentary general election) with the date of the dissolution of Parliament or any earlier time at which Her Majesty's intention to dissolve Parliament is announced,

(b) (if a parliamentary by-election) with the date of the issue of the writ for the election or any earlier date on which a certificate of the vacancy is notified in the London Gazette in accordance with the Recess Elections Act 1975, or

(c) (if a local government election) with the last date for publication of notice of the election,

and ending with the close of the poll.]

(6) *****

94–96 *****

97   Disturbances at election meetings

(1) A person who at a lawful public meeting to which this section applies acts, or incites others to act, in a disorderly manner for the purpose of preventing the transaction of the business for which the meeting was called together shall be guilty of an illegal practice.

[(2) This section applies to a political meeting held in an electoral region in connection with a European parliamentary election between the last date on which notice of election may be published in accordance with the elections rules and the date of the poll.]

(3) If a constable reasonably suspects any person of committing an offence under subsection (1) above, he may if requested so to do by the chairman of the meeting require that person to declare to him immediately his name and address and, if that person refuses or fails so to declare his name and address or gives a false name and address, he shall be liable on summary conviction to a fine not exceeding [level 1 on the standard scale,] . . .

This subsection does not apply in Northern Ireland.

98   . . .

99   *****

100   Illegal canvassing by police officers

(1) No member of a police force shall by word, message, writing or in any other manner, endeavour to persuade any person to give, or dissuade any person from giving, his vote, whether as an elector or as proxy—

(a) at any parliamentary election for a constituency, or

(b) at any local government election for any electoral area, wholly or partly within the police area.

(2) A person acting in contravention of subsection (1) above shall be liable [on summary conviction to a fine not exceeding level 3 on the standard scale, but] nothing in that subsection shall subject a member of a police force to any penalty for anything done in the discharge of his duty as a member of the force.

(3) In this section references to a member of a police force and to a police area are to be taken in relation to Northern Ireland as references to a member of the [Police Service of Northern Ireland] and to Northern Ireland.

*****

Police and Criminal Evidence Act 1984

(1984, c. 60)

An Act to make further provision in relation to the powers and duties of the police, persons in police detention, criminal evidence, police discipline and complaints against the police; to provide for arrangements for obtaining the views of the community on policing and for a rank of deputy chief constable; to amend the law relating to the Police Federations and Police Forces and Police Cadets in Scotland; and for connected purposes   [31 October 1984]

Territorial extent: England and Wales

Note: For the application of this Act to investigating officers of the Customs and Excise see the Police and Criminal Evidence Act 1984 (Application to Customs and Excise) Order 1985 (SI 1985 No 1800) and for its application to the investigation of offences conducted by officers of the armed services police see the Police and Criminal Evidence (Application to the Armed Forces) Order 1997 (SI 1997 No 15).

PART I   POWERS TO STOP AND SEARCH

1   Power of constable to stop and search persons, vehicles etc
  (1) A constable may exercise any power conferred by this section—
    (a) in any place to which at the time when he proposes to exercise the power the public or any section of the public has access, on payment or otherwise, as of right or by virtue of express or implied permission; or
    (b) in any other place to which people have ready access at the time when he proposes to exercise the power but which is not a dwelling.
  (2) Subject to subsection (3) to (5) below, a constable—
    (a) may search—
      (i)   any person or vehicle;
      (ii) anything which is in or on a vehicle,
for stolen or prohibited articles [any article to which subsection (8A) below applies or any firework to which subsection (8B) below applies]; and
    (b) may detain a person or vehicle for the purpose of such a search.
  (3) This section does not give a constable power to search a person or vehicle or anything in or on a vehicle unless he has reasonable grounds for suspecting that he will find stolen or prohibited articles [any article to which subsection (8A) below applies or any firework to which subsection (8B) below applies].
  (4), (5) *****
  (6) If in the course of such a search a constable discovers an article which he has reasonable grounds for suspecting to be a stolen or prohibited article [, an article to which subsection (8A) applies or a firework to which subsection (8B) applies], he may seize it.
  (7) An article is prohibited for the purposes of this Part of this Act if it is—
    (a) an offensive weapon; or
    (b) an article—
      (i)   made or adapted for use in the course of or in connection with an offence to which this sub-paragraph applies; or
      (ii) intended by the person having it with him for such use by him or by some other person.
  (8) The offences to which subsection (7)(b)(i) above applies are—
    (a) burglary;
    (b) theft;

(c)　offences under section 12 of the Theft Act 1968 (taking motor vehicle or other conveyance without authority); . . .

(d)　offences under section 15 of that Act (obtaining property by deception); [and

(e)　offences under section 1 of the Criminal Damage Act 1971 (destroying or damaging property).]

[(8A) This subsection applies to any article in relation to which a person has committed, or is committing or is going to commit an offence under section 139 of the Criminal Justice Act 1988.]

(8B), (8C) *****

(9)　In this Part of this Act "offensive weapon" means any article—

(a)　made or adapted for use for causing injury to persons; or

(b)　intended by the person having it with him for such use by him or by some other person.

2　Provisions relating to search under section 1 and other powers

(1)　A constable who detains a person or vehicle in the exercise—

(a)　of the power conferred by section 1 above; or

(b)　of any other power—

(i)　to search a person without first arresting him; or

(ii)　to search a vehicle without making an arrest,

need not conduct a search if it appears to him subsequently—

(i)　that no search is required; or

(ii)　that a search is impracticable.

(2)　If a constable contemplates a search, other than a search of an unattended vehicle, in the exercise—

(a)　of the power conferred by section 1 above; or

(b)　of any other power, except the power conferred by section 6 below and the power conferred by section 27(2) of the Aviation Security Act 1982—

(i)　to search a person without first arresting him; or

(ii)　to search a vehicle without making an arrest,

it shall be his duty, subject to subsection (4) below, to take reasonable steps before he commences the search to bring to the attention of the appropriate person–

(i)　if the constable is not in uniform, documentary evidence that he is a constable; and

(ii)　whether he is in uniform or not, the matters specified in subsection (3) below;

and the constable shall not commence the search until he has performed that duty.

(3)　The matters referred to in subsection (2)(ii) above are—

(a)　the constable's name and the name of the police station to which he is attached;

(b)　the object of the proposed search;

(c)　the constable's grounds for proposing to make it; and

(d)　the effect of section 3(7) or (8) below, as may be appropriate.

(4)　A constable need not bring the effect of section 3(7) or (8) below to the attention of the appropriate person if it appears to the constable that it will not be practicable to make the record in section 3(1) below.

(5)　In this section "the appropriate person" means—

(a)　if the constable proposes to search a person, that person; and

(b)　if he proposes to search a vehicle, or anything in or on a vehicle, the person in charge of the vehicle.

(6)　On completing a search of an unattended vehicle or anything in or on such a vehicle in the exercise of any such power as is mentioned in subsection (2) above a constable shall leave a notice—

(a)　stating that he has searched it;

(b) giving the name of the police station to which he is attached;

(c) stating that an application for compensation for any damage caused by the search may be made to that police station; and

(d) stating the effect of section 3(8) below.

(7) *****

(8) The time for which a person or vehicle may be detained for the purposes of such a search is such time as is reasonably required to permit a search to be carried out either at the place where the person or vehicle was first detained or nearby.

(9) Neither the power conferred by section 1 above nor any other power to detain and search a person without first arresting him or to detain and search a vehicle without making an arrest is to be construed—

(a) as authorising a constable to require a person to remove any of his clothing in public other than an outer coat, jacket or gloves; or

(b) as authorising a constable not in uniform to stop a vehicle.

(10) *****

3 Duty to make records concerning searches

(1) Where a constable has carried out a search in the exercise of any such power as is mentioned in section 2(1) above, other than a search—

(a) under section 6 below; or

(b) under section 27(2) of the Aviation Security Act 1982,

he shall make a record of it in writing unless it is not practicable to do so.

(2) If—

(a) a constable is required by subsection (1) above to make a record of a search; but

(b) it is not practicable to make the record on the spot,

he shall make it as soon as practicable after the completion of the search.

(3) The record of a search of a person shall include a note of his name, if the constable knows it, but a constable may not detain a person to find out his name.

(4) If a constable does not know the name of the person whom he has searched, the record of the search shall include a note otherwise describing that person.

(5) The record of a search of a vehicle shall include a note describing the vehicle.

(6) The record of a search of a person or a vehicle—

(a) shall state—

(i) the object of the search;

(ii) the grounds for making it;

(iii) the date and time when it was made;

(iv) the place where it was made;

(v) whether anything, and if so what, was found;

(vi) whether any, and if so what, injury to a person or damage to property appears to the constable to have resulted from the search; and

(b) shall identify the constable making it.

(7) If a constable who conducted a search of a person made a record of it, the person who was searched shall be entitled to a copy of the record if he asks for one before the end of the period specified in subsection (9) below.

(8) If—

(a) the owner of a vehicle which has been searched or the person who was in charge of the vehicle at the time when it was searched asks for a copy of the record of the search before the end of the period specified in subsection (9) below; and

(b) the constable who conducted the search made a record of it,

the person who made the request shall be entitled to a copy.

(9) The period mentioned in subsections (7) and (8) above is the period of 12 months beginning with the date on which the search was made.

(10) *****

4 Road checks

(1) This section shall have effect in relation to the conduct of road checks by police officers for the purpose of ascertaining whether a vehicle is carrying—

    (a) a person who has committed an offence other than a road traffic offence or a [vehicle] excise offence;

    (b) a person who is a witness to such an offence;

    (c) a person intending to commit such an offence; or

    (d) a person who is unlawfully at large.

(2) For the purposes of this section a road check consists of the exercise in a locality of the power conferred by section [163 of the Road Traffic Act 1988] in such a way as to stop during the period for which its exercise in that way in that locality continues all vehicles or vehicles selected by any criterion.

(3) Subject to subsection (5) below, there may only be such a road check if a police officer of the rank of superintendent or above authorises it in writing.

(4) An officer may only authorise a road check under subsection (3) above—

    (a) for the purpose specified in subsection (1)(a) above, if he has reasonable grounds—

        (i) for believing that the offence is [an indictable offence]; and

        (ii) for suspecting that the person is, or is about to be, in the locality in which vehicles would be stopped if the road check were authorised;

    (b) for the purpose specified in subsection (1)(b) above, if he has reasonable grounds for believing that the offence is [an indictable offence];

    (c) for the purpose specified in subsection (1)(c) above, if he has reasonable grounds—

        (i) for believing that the offence would be [an indictable offence]; and

        (ii) for suspecting that the person is, or is about to be, in the locality in which vehicles would be stopped if the road check were authorised;

    (d) for the purpose specified in subsection (1)(d) above, if he has reasonable grounds for suspecting that the person is, or is about to be, in that locality.

(5) An officer below the rank of superintendent may authorise such a road check if it appears to him that it is required as a matter of urgency for one of the purposes specified in subsection (1) above.

(6)–(14) *****

(15) Where a vehicle is stopped in a road check, the person in charge of the vehicle at the time when it is stopped shall be entitled to obtain a written statement of the purpose of the road check if he applies for such a statement not later than the end of the period of twelve months from the day on which the vehicle was stopped.

(16) Nothing in this section affects the exercise by police officers of any power to stop vehicles for purposes other than those specified in subsection (1) above.

5–7 *****

PART II POWERS OF ENTRY, SEARCH AND SEIZURE

Search warrants

8 Power of justice of the peace to authorise entry and search of premises

(1) If on an application made by a constable a justice of the peace is satisfied that there are reasonable grounds for believing—

    (a) that [an indictable offence] has been committed; and

    (b) that there is material on premises [mentioned in subsection (1A) below] which is likely to be of substantial value (whether by itself or together with other material) to the investigation of the offence; and

(c) that the material is likely to be relevant evidence; and

(d) that it does not consist of or include items subject to legal privilege, excluded material or special procedure material; and

(e) that any of the conditions specified in subsection (3) below applies, [in relation to each set of premises specified in the application,]

he may issue a warrant authorising a constable to enter and search the premises.

[(1A) The premises referred to in subsection (1)(b) above are—

(a) one or more sets of premises specified in the application (in which case the application is for a "specific premises warrant"); or

(b) any premises occupied or controlled by a person specified in the application, including such sets of premises as are so specified (in which case the application is for an "all premises warrant").

(1B) If the application is for an all premises warrant, the justice of the peace must also be satisfied—

(a) that because of the particulars of the offence referred to in paragraph (a) of subsection (1) above, there are reasonable grounds for believing that it is necessary to search premises occupied or controlled by the person in question which are not specified in the application in order to find the material referred to in paragraph (b) of that subsection; and

(b) that it is not reasonably practicable to specify in the application all the premises which he occupies or controls and which might need to be searched.]

[(1C) The warrant may authorise entry to and search of premises on more than one occasion if, on the application, the justice of the peace is satisfied that it is necessary to authorise multiple entries in order to achieve the purpose for which he issues the warrant.

(1D) If it authorises multiple entries, the number of entries authorised may be unlimited, or limited to a maximum.]

(2) A constable may seize and retain anything for which a search has been authorised under subsection (1) above.

(3) The conditions mentioned in subsection (1)(e) above are—

(a) that it is not practicable to communicate with any person entitled to grant entry to the premises;

(b) that it is practicable to communicate with a person entitled to grant entry to the premises but it is not practicable to communicate with any person entitled to grant access to the evidence;

(c) that entry to the premises will not be granted unless a warrant is produced;

(d) that the purpose of a search may be frustrated or seriously prejudiced unless a constable arriving at the premises can secure immediate entry to them.

(4) In this Act "relevant evidence", in relation to an offence, means anything that would be admissible in evidence at a trial for the offence.

(5) The power to issue a warrant conferred by this section is in addition to any such power otherwise conferred.

(6) *****

9 Special provisions as to access

(1) A constable may obtain access to excluded material or special procedure material for the purposes of a criminal investigation by making an application under Schedule 1 below and in accordance with that Schedule.

(2) Any Act (including a local Act) passed before this Act under which a search of premises for the purposes of a criminal investigation could be authorised by the issue of a warrant to a constable shall cease to have effect so far as it relates to the authorisation of searches—

    (a) for items subject to legal privilege; or

    (b) for excluded material; or

    (c) for special procedure material consisting of documents or records other than documents.

(2A) *****

10 Meaning of "items subject to legal privilege"

(1) Subject to subsection (2) below, in this Act "items subject to legal privilege" means—

    (a) communications between a professional legal adviser and his client or any person representing his client made in connection with the giving of legal advice to the client;

    (b) communications between a professional legal adviser and his client or any person representing his client or between such an adviser or his client or any such representative and any other person made in connection with or in contemplation of legal proceedings and for the purposes of such proceedings; and

    (c) items enclosed with or referred to in such communications and made—

        (i) in connection with the giving of legal advice; or

        (ii) in connection with or in contemplation of legal proceedings and for the purposes of such proceedings,

when they are in the possession of a person who is entitled to possession of them.

(2) Items held with the intention of furthering a criminal purpose are not items subject to legal privilege.

11 Meaning of "excluded material"

(1) Subject to the following provisions of this section, in this Act "excluded material" means—

    (a) personal records which a person has acquired or created in the course of any trade, business, profession or other occupation or for the purposes of any paid or unpaid office and which he holds in confidence;

    (b) human tissue or tissue fluid which has been taken for the purposes of diagnosis or medical treatment and which a person holds in confidence;

    (c) journalistic material which a person holds in confidence and which consists—

        (i) of documents; or

        (ii) of records other than documents.

(2) A person holds material other than journalistic material in confidence for the purposes of this section if he holds it subject—

    (a) to an express or implied undertaking to hold it in confidence; or

    (b) to a restriction on disclosure or an obligation of secrecy contained in any enactment, including an enactment contained in an Act passed after this Act.

(3) A person holds journalistic material in confidence for the purposes of this section if—

    (a) he holds it subject to such an undertaking, restriction or obligation; and

    (b) it has been continuously held (by one or more persons) subject to such an undertaking, restriction or obligation since it was first acquired or created for the purposes of journalism.

12 Meaning of "personal records"

In this Part of this Act "personal records" means documentary and other records concerning an individual (whether living or dead) who can be identified from them and relating—

    (a) to his physical or mental health;

    (b) to spiritual counselling or assistance given or to be given to him; or

    (c) to counselling or assistance given or to be given to him, for the purposes of his personal welfare, by any voluntary organisation or by any individual who—

        (i) by reason of his office or occupation has responsibilities for his personal welfare; or

(ii) by reason of an order of a court has responsibilities for his supervision.

13   Meaning of "journalistic material"

(1) Subject to subsection (2) below, in this Act "journalistic material" means material acquired or created for the purposes of journalism.

(2) Material is only journalistic material for the purposes of this Act if it is in the possession of a person who acquired or created it for the purposes of journalism.

(3) A person who receives material from someone who intends that the recipient shall use it for the purposes of journalism is to be taken to have acquired it for those purposes.

14   Meaning of "special procedure material"

(1) In this Act "special procedure material" means—
    (a) material to which subsection (2) below applies; and
    (b) journalistic material, other than excluded material.

(2) Subject to the following provisions of this section, this subsection applies to material, other than items subject to legal privilege and excluded material, in the possession of a person who—
    (a) acquired or created it in the course of any trade, business, profession or other occupation or for the purposes of any paid or unpaid office; and
    (b) holds it subject—
        (i) to an express or implied undertaking to hold it in confidence; or
        (ii) to a restriction or obligation such as is mentioned in section 11(2)(b) above.

(3)–(6) *****

15   Search warrants—safeguards

(1) This section and section 16 below have effect in relation to the issue to constables under any enactment, including an enactment contained in an Act passed after this Act, of warrants to enter and search premises; and an entry on or search of premises under a warrant is unlawful unless it complies with this section and section 16 below.

(2) Where a constable applies for any such warrant, it shall be his duty—
    (a) to state—
        (i) the ground on which he makes the application; . . .
        (ii) the enactment under which the warrant would be issued [; and
        (iii) if the application is for a warrant authorising entry and search on more than one occasion, the ground on which he applies for such a warrant, and whether he seeks a warrant authorising an unlimited number of entries, or (if not) the maximum number of entries desired;]
    [(b) to specify the matters set out in subsection (2A) below; and]
    (c) to identify, so far as is practicable, the articles or persons to be sought.

[(2A) The matters which must be specified pursuant to subsection (2)(b) above are—
    (a) if the application is for a specific premises warrant made by virtue of section 8(1A)(a) above or paragraph 12 of Schedule 1 below, each set of premises which it is desired to enter and search;
    (b) if the application is for an all premises warrant made by virtue of section 8(1A)(b) above or paragraph 12 of Schedule 1 below—
        (i) as many sets of premises which it is desired to enter and search as it is reasonably practicable to specify;
        (ii) the person who is in occupation or control of those premises and any others which it is desired to enter and search;
        (iii) why it is necessary to search more premises than those specified under subparagraph (i); and
        (iv) why it is not reasonably practicable to specify all the premises which it is desired to enter and search.]

(3) An application for such a warrant shall be made ex parte and supported by an information in writing.

(4) The constable shall answer on oath any question that the justice of the peace or judge hearing the application asks him.

(5) A warrant shall authorise an entry on one occasion only [unless it specifies that it authorises multiple entries].

[(5A) If it specifies that it authorises multiple entries, it must also specify whether the number of entries authorised is unlimited, or limited to a specified maximum.]

(6) A warrant—

    (a) shall specify—

        (i) the name of the person who applies for it;

        (ii) the date on which it is issued;

        (iii) the enactment under which it is issued; and

        [(iv) each set of premises to be searched, or (in the case of an all premises warrant) the person who is in occupation or control of premises to be searched, together with any premises under his occupation or control which can be specified and which are to be searched; and]

    (b) shall identify, so far as is practicable, the articles or persons to be sought.

(7), (8) *****

Note: This section, and sections 16, 21 and 22, are modified in relation to confiscation and money laundering investigations under the Proceeds of Crime Act 2002, by SI 2003/174, Arts 2 5 respectively.

16 Execution of warrants

(1) A warrant to enter and search premises may be executed by any constable.

(2) Such a warrant may authorise persons to accompany any constable who is executing it.

[(2A) A person so authorised has the same powers as the constable whom he accompanies in respect of—

    (a) the execution of the warrant, and

    (b) the seizure of anything to which the warrant relates.

(2B) But he may exercise those powers only in the company, and under the supervision, of a constable.]

(3) Entry and search under a warrant must be within [three months] from the date of its issue.

[(3A) If the warrant is an all premises warrant, no premises which are not specified in it may be entered or searched unless a police officer of at least the rank of inspector has in writing authorised them to be entered.]

(3B) *****

(4) Entry and search under a warrant must be at a reasonable hour unless it appears to the constable executing it that the purpose of a search may be frustrated on an entry at a reasonable hour.

(5) Where the occupier of premises which are to be entered and searched is present at the time when a constable seeks to execute a warrant to enter and search them, the constable—

    (a) shall identify himself to the occupier and, if not in uniform, shall produce to him documentary evidence that he is a constable;

    (b) shall produce the warrant to him; and

    (c) shall supply him with a copy of it.

(6) Where—

    (a) the occupier of such premises is not present at the time when a constable seeks to execute such a warrant; but

    (b) some other person who appears to the constable to be in charge of the premises is present, subsection (5) above shall have effect as if any reference to the occupier were a reference to that other person.

(7) If there is no person present who appears to the constable to be in charge of the premises, he shall leave a copy of the warrant in a prominent place on the premises.

(8) A search under a warrant may only be a search to the extent required for the purpose for which the warrant was issued.

(9) A constable executing a warrant shall make an endorsement on it stating–

(a) whether the articles or persons sought were found; and

(b) whether any articles were seized, other than articles which were sought [and, unless the warrant is a specific premises warrant specifying one set of premises only, he shall do so separately in respect of each set of premises entered and searched which he shall in each case stated in the endorsement.]

(10)–(12) *****

Entry and search without search warrant

17   Entry for purpose of arrest etc.

(1) Subject to the following provisions of this section, and without prejudice to any other enactment, a constable may enter and search any premises for the purpose—

(a) of executing—

(i) a warrant of arrest issued in connection with or arising out of criminal proceedings; or

(ii) a warrant of commitment issued under section 76 of the Magistrates' Courts Act 1980;

(b) of arresting a person for an [indictable] offence;

(c) of arresting a person for an offence under—

(i) section 1 (prohibition of uniforms in connection with political objects) . . . of the Public Order Act 1936;

(ii) any enactment contained in sections 6 to 8 or 10 of the Criminal Law Act 1977 (offences relating to entering and remaining on property);

[(iii) section 4 of the Public Order Act 1986 (fear or provocation of violence)];

[(iiia) [section 4 (driving etc. when   under influence of drink or drugs) or 163 (failure to stop when required to do so by a constable in uniform) of the Road Traffic Act 1988; or]

[(iiib) section 27 of the Transport and Works Act 1992 (which relates to offences involving drink or drugs);]

(iv) section 76 of the Criminal Justice and Public Order Act 1994 (failure to comply with an interim possession order);]

[(ca) of arresting, in pursuance of section 32(1A) of the Children and Young Persons Act 1969, any child or young person who has been remanded or committed to local authority accommodation under section 23(1) of that Act;

[(caa) of arresting a person for an offence to which section 61 of the Animal Health Act 1981 applies;]

(cb) of recapturing any person who is, or is deemed for any purpose to be, unlawfully at large while liable to be detained—

(i) in a prison, remand centre, young offender institution or secure training centre, or

(ii) in pursuance of [section 92 of the Powers of Criminal Courts (Sentencing) Act 2000] (dealing with children and young persons guilty of grave crimes), in any other place;]

(d) of recapturing [any person whatever] who is unlawfully at large and whom he is pursuing; or

(e) of saving life or limb or preventing serious damage to property.

(2) Except for the purpose specified in paragraph (e) of subsection (1) above, the powers of entry and search conferred by this section—

(a) are only exercisable if the constable has reasonable grounds for believing that the person whom he is seeking is on the premises; and

(b) are limited, in relation to premises consisting of two or more separate dwellings, to powers to enter and search—

(i) any parts of the premises which the occupiers of any dwelling comprised in the premises use in common with the occupiers of any other such dwelling; and

(ii) any such dwelling in which the constable has reasonable grounds for believing that the person whom he is seeking may be.

(3) The powers of entry and search conferred by this section are only exercisable for the purposes specified in subsection (1)(c)(ii) [or (iv)] above by a constable in uniform.

(4) The power of search conferred by this section is only a power to search to the extent that is reasonably required for the purpose for which the power of entry is exercised.

(5) Subject to subsection (6) below, all the rules of common law under which a constable has power to enter premises without a warrant are hereby abolished.

(6) Nothing in subsection (5) above affects any power of entry to deal with or prevent a breach of the peace.

18   Entry and search after arrest

(1) Subject to the following provisions of this section, a constable may enter and search any premises occupied or controlled by a person who is under arrest for an [indictable] offence, if he has reasonable grounds for suspecting that there is on the premises evidence, other than items subject to legal privilege, that relates—

(a) to that offence; or

(b) to some other arrestable offence which is connected with or similar to that offence.

(2) A constable may seize and retain anything for which he may search under subsection (1) above.

(3) The power to search conferred by subsection (1) above is only a power to search to the extent that is reasonably required for the purpose of discovering such evidence.

(4) Subject to subsection (5) below, the powers conferred by this section may not be exercised unless an officer of the rank of inspector or above has authorised them in writing.

[(5) A constable may conduct a search under subsection (1)—

(a) before the person is taken to a police station or released on bail under section 30A, and

(b) without obtaining an authorisation under subsection (4),

if the condition in subsection (5A) is satisfied.

(5A) The condition is that the presence of the person at a place (other than a police station) is necessary for the effective investigation of the offence.]

(6)–(8) *****

Seizure etc.

19   General power of seizure etc.

(1) The powers conferred by subsections (2), (3) and (4) below are exercisable by a constable who is lawfully on any premises.

(2) The constable may seize anything which is on the premises if he has reasonable grounds for believing—

(a) that it has been obtained in consequence of the commission of an offence; and

(b) that it is necessary to seize it in order to prevent it being concealed, lost, damaged, altered or destroyed.

(3) The constable may seize anything which is on the premises if he has reasonable grounds for believing—

(a) that it is evidence in relation to an offence which he is investigating or any other offence; and

(b) that it is necessary to seize it in order to prevent the evidence being concealed, lost, altered or destroyed.

(4) The constable may require any information which is [stored in any electronic form] and is accessible from the premises to be produced in a form in which it can be taken away [or from which it can readily be produced in a visible and legible form] if he has reasonable grounds for believing—

(a) that—

(i) it is evidence in relation to an offence which he is investigating or any other offence; or

(ii) it has been obtained in consequence of the commission of an offence; and

(b) that it is necessary to do so in order to prevent it being concealed, lost, tampered with or destroyed.

(5) The powers conferred by this section are in addition to any power otherwise conferred.

(6) No power of seizure conferred on a constable under any enactment (including an enactment contained in an Act passed after this Act) is to be taken to authorise the seizure of an item which the constable exercising the power has reasonable grounds for believing to be subject to legal privilege.

20   Extension of powers of seizure to computerised information

(1) Every power of seizure which is conferred by an enactment to which this section applies on a constable who has entered premises in the exercise of a power conferred by an enactment shall be construed as including a power to require any information [stored in any electronic form] and accessible from the premises to be produced in a form in which it can be taken away [or from which it can readily be produced in a visible and legible form].

(2) This section applies—

(a) to any enactment contained in an Act passed before this Act;

(b) to sections 8 and 18 above;

(c) to paragraph 13 of Schedule 1 to this Act; and

(d) to any enactment contained in an Act passed after this Act.

21   Access and copying

(1) A constable who seizes anything in the exercise of a power conferred by any enactment, including an enactment contained in an Act passed after this Act, shall, if so requested by a person showing himself—

(a) to be the occupier of premises on which it was seized; or

(b) to have had custody or control of it immediately before the seizure,

provide that person with a record of what he seized.

(2) The officer shall provide the record within a reasonable time from the making of the request for it.

(3) Subject to subsection (8) below, if a request for permission to be granted access to anything which—

(a) has been seized by a constable; and

(b) is retained by the police for the purpose of investigating an offence,

is made to the officer in charge of the investigation by a person who had custody or control of the thing immediately before it was so seized or by someone acting on behalf of such a person the officer shall allow the person who made the request access to it under the supervision of a constable.

(4) Subject to subsection (8) below, if a request for a photograph or copy of any such thing is made to the officer in charge of the investigation by a person who had custody or control

of the thing immediately before it was so seized, or by someone acting on behalf of such a person, the officer shall—

    (a) allow the person who made the rquest access to it under the supervision of a constable for the purpose of photographing or copying it; or

    (b) photograph or copy it, or cause it to be photographed or copied.

(5) A constable may also photograph or copy, or have photographed or copied, anything which he has power to seize, without a request being made under subsection (4) above.

(6) Where anything is photographed or copied under subsection (4)(b) above, the photograph or copy shall be supplied to the person who made the request.

(7) The photograph or copy shall be so supplied within a reasonable time from the making of the request.

(8) There is no duty under this section to grant access to, or to supply a photograph or copy of, anything if the officer in charge of the investigation for the purposes of which it was seized has reasonable grounds for believing that to do so would prejudice—

    (a) that investigation;

    (b) the investigation of an offence other than the offence for the purposes of investigating which the thing was seized; or

    (c) any criminal proceedings which may be brought as a result of—

        (i) the investigation of which he is in charge; or

        (ii) any such investigation as is mentioned in paragraph (b) above.

[(9) The references to a constable in subsections (1), (2), (3)(a) and (5) include a person authorised under section 16(2) to accompany a constable executing a warrant.]

22 Retention

(1) Subject to subsection (4) below, anything which has been seized by a constable or taken away by a constable following a requirement made by virtue of section 19 or 20 above may be retained so long as is necessary in all the circumstances.

(2) Without prejudice to the generality of subsection (1) above—

    (a) anything seized for the purposes of a criminal investigation may be retained, except as provided by subsection (4) below—

        (i) for use as evidence at a trial for an offence; or

        (ii) for forensic examination or for investigation in connection with an offence; and

    (b) anything may be retained in order to establish its lawful owner, where there are reasonable grounds for believing that it has been obtained in consequence of the commission of an offence.

(3) *****

(4) Nothing may be retained for either of the purposes mentioned in subsection (2)(a) above if a photograph or copy would be sufficient for that purpose.

(5)–(7) *****

23–23A *****

PART III   ARREST

[24   Arrest without warrant: constables

(1) A constable may arrest without a warrant—

    (a) anyone who is about to commit an offence;

    (b) anyone who is in the act of committing an offence;

    (c) anyone whom he has reasonable grounds for suspecting to be about to commit an offence;

    (d) anyone whom he has reasonable grounds for suspecting to be committing an offence.

(2) If a constable has reasonable grounds for suspecting that an offence has been committed, he may arrest without a warrant anyone whom he has reasonable grounds to suspect of being guilty of it.

(3) If an offence has been committed, a constable may arrest without a warrant—

    (a) anyone who is guilty of the offence;

    (b) anyone whom he has reasonable grounds for suspecting to be guilty of it.

(4) But the power of summary arrest conferred by subsection (1), (2) or (3) is exercisable only if the constable has reasonable grounds for believing that for any of the reasons mentioned in subsection (5) it is necessary to arrest the person in question.

(5) The reasons are—

    (a) to enable the name of the person in question to be ascertained (in the case where the constable does not know, and cannot readily ascertain, the person's name, or has reasonable grounds for doubting whether a name given by the person as his name is his real name);

    (b) correspondingly as regards the person's address;

    (c) to prevent the person in question—

        (i) causing physical injury to himself or any other person;

        (ii) suffering physical injury;

        (iii) causing loss of or damage to property;

        (iv) committing an offence against public decency (subject to subsection (6)); or

        (v) causing an unlawful obstruction of the highway;

    (d) to protect a child or other vulnerable person from the person in question;

    (e) to allow the prompt and effective investigation of the offence or of the conduct of the person in question;

    (f) to prevent any prosecution for the offence from being hindered by the disappearance of the person in question.

(6) Subsection (5)(c)(iv) applies only where members of the public going about their normal business cannot reasonably be expected to avoid the person in question.

24A   Arrest without warrant: other persons

(1) A person other than a constable may arrest without a warrant—

    (a) anyone who is in the act of committing an indictable offence;

    (b) anyone whom he has reasonable grounds for suspecting to be committing an indictable offence.

(2) Where an indictable offence has been committed, a person other than a constable may arrest without a warrant—

    (a) anyone who is guilty of the offence;

    (b) anyone whom he has reasonable grounds for suspecting to be guilty of it.

(3) But the power of summary arrest conferred by subsection (1) or (2) is exercisable only if—

    (a) the person making the arrest has reasonable grounds for believing that for any of the reasons mentioned in subsection (4) it is necessary to arrest the person in question; and

    (b) it appears to the person making the arrest that it is not reasonably practicable for a constable to make it instead.

(4) The reasons are to prevent the person in question—

    (a) causing physical injury to himself or any other person;

    (b) suffering physical injury;

    (c) causing loss of or damage to property; or

    (d) making off before a constable can assume responsibility for him.]

25   . . .

26–27   *****

28   Information to be given on arrest

(1) Subject to subsection (5) below, where a person is arrested, otherwise than by being informed that he is under arrest, the arrest is not lawful unless the person arrested is informed that he is under arrest as soon as is practicable after his arrest.

(2) Where a person is arrested by a constable, subsection (1) above applies regardless of whether the fact of the arrest is obvious.

(3) Subject to subsection (5) below, no arrest is lawful unless the person arrested is informed of the ground for the arrest at the time of, or as soon as is practicable after, the arrest.

(4) Where a person is arrested by a constable, subsection (3) above applies regardless of whether the ground for the arrest is obvious.

(5) Nothing in this section is to be taken to require a person to be informed—

(a) that he is under arrest; or

(b) of the ground for the arrest,

if it was not reasonably practicable for him to be so informed by reason of his having escaped from arrest before the information could be given.

29   Voluntary attendance at police station etc.

Where for the purpose of assisting with an investigation a person attends voluntarily at a police station or at any other place where a constable is present or accompanies a constable to a police station or any such other place without having been arrested—

(a) he shall be entitled to leave at will unless he is placed under arrest;

(b) he shall be informed at once that he is under arrest if a decision is taken by a constable to prevent him from leaving at will.

30   Arrest elsewhere than at police station

[(1) Subsection (1A) applies where a person is, at any place other than a police station—

(a) arrested by a constable for an offence, or

(b) taken into custody by a constable after being arrested for an offence by a person other than a constable.

(1A) The person must be taken by a constable to a police station as soon as practicable after the arrest.

(1B) Subsection (1A) has effect subject to section 30A (release on bail) and subsection (7) (release without bail).]

(2) Subject to subsections (3) and (5) below, the police station to which an arrested person is taken under [subsection (1A)] above shall be a designated police station.

(3)–(5) *****

(6) If the first police station to which an arrested person is taken after his arrest is not a designated police station, he shall be taken to a designated police station not more than six hours after his arrival at the first police station unless he is released previously.

[(7) A person arrested by a constable at any place other than a police station must be released without bail if the condition in subsection (7A) is satisfied.

(7A) The condition is that, at any time before the person arrested reaches a police station, a constable is satisfied that there are no grounds for keeping him under arrest or releasing him on bail under section 30A.]

(8), (9) *****

[(10) Nothing in subsection (1A) or in section 30A prevents a constable delaying taking a person to a police station or releasing him on bail if the condition in subsection (10A) is satisfied.

(10A) The condition is that the presence of the person at a place (other than a police station) is necessary in order to carry out such investigations as it is reasonable to carry out immediately.

(11) Where there is any such delay the reasons for the delay must be recorded when the person first arrives at the police station or (as the case may be) is released on bail.]

(12), (13) *****

[30A   Bail elsewhere than at police station

(1) A constable may release on bail a person who is arrested or taken into custody in the circumstances mentioned in section 30(1).

(2) A person may be released on bail under subsection (1) at any time before he arrives at a police station.

(3) A person released on bail under subsection (1) must be required to attend a police station.

(4) No other requirement may be imposed on the person as a condition of bail.

(5) The police station which the person is required to attend may be any police station.]

[30B   Bail under section 30A: notices

[(1) Where a constable grants bail to a person under section 30A, he must give that person a notice in writing before he is released.

(2) The notice must state—

(a) the offence for which he was arrested, and

(b) the ground on which he was arrested.

(3) The notice must inform him that he is required to attend a police station.

(4) It may also specify the police station which he is required to attend and the time when he is required to attend.

(5) If the notice does not include the information mentioned in subsection (4), the person must subsequently be given a further notice in writing which contains that information.

(6) The person may be required to attend a different police station from that specified in the notice under subsection (1) or (5) or to attend at a different time.

(7) He must be given notice in writing of any such change as is mentioned in subsection (6) but more than one such notice may be given to him.]

[30C   Bail under section 30A: supplemental

(1) A person who has been required to attend a police station is not required to do so if he is given notice in writing that his attendance is no longer required.

(2) If a person is required to attend a police station which is not a designated police station he must be—

(a) released, or

(b) taken to a designated police station,

not more than six hours after his arrival.

(3) Nothing in the Bail Act 1976 applies in relation to bail under section 30A.

(4) Nothing in section 30A or 30B or in this section prevents the re-arrest without a warrant of a person released on bail under section 30A if new evidence justifying a further arrest has come to light since his release.]

[30D   Failure to answer to bail under section 30A

(1) A constable may arrest without a warrant a person who—

(a) has been released on bail under section 30A subject to a requirement to attend a specified police station, but

(b) fails to attend the police station at the specified time.

(2) A person arrested under subsection (1) must be taken to a police station (which may be the specified police station or any other police station) as soon as practicable after the arrest.

(3) In subsection (1), "specified" means specified in a notice under subsection (1) or (5) of section 30B or, if notice of change has been given under subsection (7) of that section, in that notice.

(4) For the purposes of—

(a) section 30 (subject to the obligation in subsection (2)), and

(b) section 31,

an arrest under this section is to be treated as an arrest for an offence.]

31   Arrest for further offence

Where—
- (a) a person—
  - (i)   has been arrested for an offence; and
  - (ii) is at a police station in consequence of that arrest; and
- (b) it appears to a constable that, if he were released from that arrest, he would be liable to arrest for some other offence,

he shall be arrested for that other offence.

32   Search upon arrest

(1) A constable may search an arrested person, in any case where the person to be searched has been arrested at a place other than a police station, if the constable has reasonable grounds for believing that the arrested person may present a danger to himself or others.

(2) Subject to subsections (3) to (5) below, a constable shall also have power in any such case—
- (a) to search the arrested person for anything—
  - (i)   which he might use to assist him to escape from lawful custody; or
  - (ii) which might be evidence relating to an offence; and
- (b) [if the offence for which he has been arrested is an indictable offence, to enter and search any premises in which he was when arrested or immediately before he was arrested for evidence relating to the offence].

(3) The power to search conferred by subsection (2) above is only a power to search to the extent that is reasonably required for the purpose of discovering any such thing or any such evidence.

(4) The powers conferred by this section to search a person are not to be construed as authorising a constable to require a person to remove any of his clothing in public other than an outer coat, jacket or gloves [but they do authorise a search of a person's mouth].

(5) A constable may not search a person in the exercise of the power conferred by subsection (2)(a) above unless he has reasonable grounds for believing that the person to be searched may have concealed on him anything for which a search is permitted under that paragraph.

(6) A constable may not search premises in the exercise of the power conferred by subsection (2)(b) above unless he has reasonable grounds for believing that there is evidence for which a search is permitted under that paragraph on the premises.

(7) In so far as the power of search conferred by subsection (2)(b) above relates to premises consisting of two or more separate dwellings, it is limited to a power to search–
- (a) any dwelling in which the arrest took place or in which the person arrested was immediately before his arrest; and
- (b) any parts of the premises which the occupier of any such dwelling uses in common with the occupiers of any other dwellings comprised in the premises.

(8) A constable searching a person in the exercise of the power conferred by subsection (1) above may seize and retain anything he finds, if he has reasonable grounds for believing that the person searched might use it to cause physical injury to himself or to any other person.

(9) A constable searching a person in the exercise of the power conferred by subsection (2)(a) above may seize and retain anything he finds, other than an item subject to legal privilege, if he has reasonable grounds for believing—
- (a) that he might use it to assist him to escape from lawful custody; or
- (b) that it is evidence of an offence or has been obtained in consequence of the commission of an offence.

(10) Nothing in this section shall be taken to affect the power conferred by [section 43 of the Terrorism Act 2000.]

33 ...

PART IV   DETENTION

Detention—conditions and duration

34   Limitations on police detention

(1) A person arrested for an offence shall not be kept in police detention except in accordance with the provisions of this Part of this Act.

(2) Subject to subsection (3) below, if at any time a custody officer—

    (a) becomes aware, in relation to any person in police detention, that the grounds for the detention of that person have ceased to apply; and

    (b) is not aware of any other grounds on which the continued detention of that person could be justified under the provisions of this Part of this Act,

it shall be the duty of the custody officer, subject to subsection (4) below, to order his immediate release from custody.

(3) No person in police detention shall be released except on the authority of a custody officer at the police station where his detention was authorised or, if it was authorised at more than one station, a custody officer at the station where it was last authorised.

(4) A person who appears to the custody officer to have been unlawfully at large when he was arrested is not to be released under subsection (2) above.

(5)–(7) *****

35   Designated police stations

(1) The chief officer of police for each police area shall designate the police stations in his area which, subject to [sections 30(3) and (5), 30A(5) and 30D(2)] above, are to be the stations in that area to be used for the purpose of detention arrested persons.

(2) A chief officer's duty under subsection (1) above is to designate police stations appearing to him to provide enough accommodation for that purpose.

(2A), (3), (4) *****

36   Custody officers at police stations

(1) One or more custody officers shall be appointed for each designated police station.

(2) A custody officer for [a police station designated under s 35(1) above] shall be appointed—

    (a) by the chief officer of police for the area in which the designated police station is situated; or

    (b) by such other police officer as the chief officer of police for that area may direct.

[(2A)] *****

[(3) No person may be appointed a custody officer unless—

    (a) he is a police officer of at least the rank of sergeant; or

    (b) he is a staff custody officer.]

(4) An officer of any rank may perform the functions of a custody officer at a designated police station if a custody officer is not readily available to perform them.

(5)–(10) *****

37   Duties of custody officer before charge

(1) Where—

    (a) a person is arrested for an offence—

        (i) without a warrant; or

        (ii) under a warrant not endorsed for bail, ...

(b) ...

the custody officer at each police station where he is detained after his arrest shall determine whether he has before him sufficient evidence to charge that person with the offence for which he was arrested and may detain him at the police station for such period as is necessary to enable him to do so.

(2) If the custody officer determines that he does not have such evidence before him, the person arrested shall be released either on bail or without bail, unless the custody officer has reasonable grounds for believing that his detention without being charged is necessary to secure or preserve evidence relating to an offence for which he is under arrest or to obtain such evidence by questioning him.

(3) If the custody officer has reasonable grounds for so believing, he may authorise the person arrested to be kept in police detention.

(4) Where a custody officer authorises a person who has not been charged to be kept in police detention, he shall, as soon as is practicable, make a written record of the grounds for the detention.

(5) Subject to subsection (6) below, the written record shall be made in the presence of the person arrested who shall at that time be informed by the custody officer of the grounds for his detention.

(6) Subsection (5) above shall not apply where the person arrested is, at the time when the written record is made—

    (a) incapable of understanding what is said to him;

    (b) violent or likely to become violent; or

    (c) in urgent need of medical attention.

(7)–(10), (15) *****

(11)–(14) ...

37A–37D *****

38 Duties of custody officer after charge

(1) Where a person arrested for an offence otherwise than under a warrant endorsed for bail is charged with an offence, the custody officer shall[, subject to section 25 of the Criminal Justice and Public Order Act 1994,] order his release from police detention, either on bail or without bail, unless—

    (a) if the person arrested is not an arrested juvenile—

        (i) his name or address cannot be ascertained or the custody officer has reasonable grounds for doubting whether a name or address furnished by him as his name or address is his real name or address;

        [(ii) the custody officer has reasonable grounds for believing that the person arrested will fail to appear in court to answer to bail;

        (iii) in the case of a person arrested for an imprisonable offence, the custody officer has reasonable grounds for believing that the detention of the person arrested is necessary to prevent him from committing an offence;

        [(iiia) in a case where a sample may be taken from the person under section 63B below, the custody officer has reasonable grounds for believing that the detention of the person is necessary to enable a sample to be taken from him;]

        (iv) in the case of a person arrested for an offence which is not an imprisonable offence, the custody officer has reasonable grounds for believing that the detention of the person arrested is necessary to prevent him from causing physical injury to any other person or from causing loss of or damage to property;

        (v) the custody officer has reasonable grounds for believing that the detention of the person arrested is necessary to prevent him from interfering with the administration of justice or with the investigation of offences or of a particular offence; or

(vi)   the custody officer has reasonable grounds for believing that the detention of the person arrested is necessary for his own protection;]

(b) if he is an arrested juvenile—

(i)   any of the requirements of paragraph (a) above is satisfied [(but, in the case of paragraph (a)(ii) only if the arrested juvenile has attained the minimum age)]; or

(ii)   the custody officer has reasonable grounds for believing that he ought to be detained in his own interests.

(2) If the release of a person arrested is not required by subsection (1) above, the custody officer may authorise him to be kept in police detention [but may not authorise a person to be kept in police detention by virtue of subsection (1)(a)(iiia) after the end of the period of six hours beginning when he was charged with the offence.].

(2A) *****

(3) Where a custody officer authorises a person who has been charged to be kept in police detention, he shall, as soon as practicable, make a written record of the grounds for the detention.

(4) Subject to subsection (5) below, the written record shall be made in the presence of the person charged who shall at that time be informed by the custody officer of the grounds for his detention.

(5) Subsection (4) above shall not apply where the person charged is, at the time when the written record is made—

(a) incapable of understanding what is said to him;

(b) violent or likely to become violent; or

(c) in urgent need of medical attention.

(6)–(8) *****

39   Responsibilities in relation to persons detained

(1) Subject to subsection (2) and (4) below, it shall be the duty of the custody officer at a police station to ensure—

(a) that all persons in police detention at that station are treated in accordance with this Act and any code of practice issued under it and relating to the treatment of persons in police detention; and

(b) that all matters relating to such persons which are required by this Act or by such codes of practice to be recorded are recorded in the custody records relating to such persons.

(2)–(5) *****

(6) Where—

(a) an officer of higher rank than the custody officer [or, if the custody officer is a staff custody officer, any police officer or police employee] gives directions relating to a person in police detention; and

(b) the directions are at variance—

(i)   with any decision made or action taken by the custody officer in the performance of a duty imposed on him under this Part of this Act; or

(ii)   with any decision or action which would be for the directions have been made or taken by him in the performance of such a duty,

the custody officer shall refer the matter at once to an officer of the rank of superintendent or above who is responsible for the police station for which the custody officer is acting as custody officer.

(7) *****

40   Review of police detention

(1) Reviews of the detention of each person in police detention in connection with the investigation of an offence shall be carried out periodically in accordance with the following provisions of this section—

(a) in the case of a person who has been arrested and charged, by the custody officer; and

(b) in the case of a person who has been arrested but not charged, by an officer of at least the rank of inspector who has not been directly involved in the investigation.

(2) The officer to whom it falls to carry out a review is referred to in this section as a "review officer".

(3) Subject to subsection (4) below—

(a) the first review shall be not later than six hours after the detention was first authorised;

(b) the second review shall be not later than nine hours after the first;

(c) subsequent reviews shall be at intervals of not more than nine hours.

(4) A review may be postponed—

(a) if, having regard to all the circumstances prevailing at the latest time for it specified in subsection (3) above, it is not practicable to carry out the review at that time;

(b) without prejudice to the generality of paragraph (a) above—

(i) if at that time the person in detention is being questioned by a police officer and the review officer is satisfied that an interruption of the questioning for the purpose of carrying out the review would prejudice the investigation in connection with which he is being questioned; or

(ii) if at that time no review officer is readily available.

(5) If a review is postponed under subsection (4) above it shall be carried out as soon as practicable after the latest time specified for it in subsection (3) above.

(6) If a review is carried out after postponement under subsection (4) above, the fact that it was so carried out shall not affect any requirement of this section as to the time at which any subsequent review is to be carried out.

(7) The review officer shall record the reasons for any postponement of a review in the custody record.

(8)–(14) *****

40A   ***

41   Limits on period of detention without charge

(1) Subject to the following provisions of this section and to sections 42 and 43 below, a person shall not be kept in police detention for more than 24 hours without being charged.

(2) The time from which the period of detention of a person is to be calculated (in this Act referred to as "the relevant time")—

(a) in the case of a person to whom this paragraph applies, shall be—

(i) the time at which that person arrives at the relevant police station; or

(ii) the time 24 hours after the time of that person's arrest,

whichever is the earlier;

(b) in the case of a person arrested outside England and Wales, shall be—

(i) the time at which that person arrives at the first police station to which he is taken in the police area in England or Wales in which the offence for which he was arrested is being investigated; or

(ii) the time 24 hours after the time of that person's entry into England and Wales,

whichever is the earlier;

(c) in the case of a person who—

(i) attends voluntarily at a police station; or

(ii) accompanies a constable to a police station without having been arrested, and is arrested at the police station, the time of his arrest;

[(ca) in the case of a person who attends a police station to answer bail granted under section 30A, the time when he arrives at the police station;]

(d) in any other case, except where subsection (5) below applies, shall be the time at which the person arrested arrives at the first police station to which he is taken after his arrest.

(3)–(6) *****

(7) Subject to subsection (8) below, a person who at the expiry of 24 hours after the relevant time is in police detention and has not been charged shall be released at that time either on bail or without bail.

(8) Subsection (7) above does not apply to a person whose detention for more than 24 hours after the relevant time has been authorised or is otherwise permitted in accordance with section 42 or 43 below.

(9) *****

42   Authorisation of continued detention

(1) Where a police officer of the rank of superintendent or above who is responsible for the police station at which a person is detained has reasonable grounds for believing that—

(a) the detention of that person without charge is an arrestable offence evidence relating to an offence for which he is under arrest or to obtain such evidence by questioning him;

[(b) an offence for which he is under arrest is an [indictable] offence; and]

(c) the investigation is being conducted diligently and expeditiously,

he may authorise the keeping of that person in police detention for a period expiring at or before 36 hours after the relevant time.

(2) Where an officer such as is mentioned in subsection (1) above has authorised the keeping of a person in police detention for a period expiring less than 36 hours after the relevant time, such an officer may authorise the keeping of that person in police detention for a further period expiring not more than 36 hours after that time if the conditions specified in subsection (1) above are still satisfied when he gives the authorisation.

(3) If it is proposed to transfer a person in police detention to another police area, the officer determining whether or not to authorise keeping him in detention under subsection (1) above shall have regard to the distance and the time the journey would take.

(4)–(5) *****

(6) Before determining whether to authorise the keeping of a person in detention under subsection (1) or (2) above, an officer shall give—

(a) that person; or

(b) any solicitor representing him who is available at the time when it falls to the officer to determine whether to give the authorisation,

an opportunity to make representations to him about the detention.

(7)–(9) *****

(10) Where an officer has authorised the keeping of a person who has not been charged in detention under subsection (1) or (2) above, he shall be released from detention, either on bail or without bail, not later than 36 hours after the relevant time, unless—

(a) he has been charged with an offence; or

(b) his continued detention is authorised or otherwise permitted in accordance with section 43 below.

(11) A person released under subsection (10) above shall not be re-arrested without a warrant for the offence for which he was previously arrested unless new evidence justifying

a further arrest has come to light since his release [; but this subsection does not prevent an arrest under section 46A below].

43   Warrants of further detention

(1) Where, on an application on oath made by a constable and supported by an information, a magistrate's court is satisfied that there are reasonable grounds for believing that the further detention of the person to whom the application relates is justified, it may issue a warrant of further detention authorising the keeping of that person in police detention.

(2) A court may not hear an application for a warrant of further detention unless the person to whom the application relates—

(a) has been furnished with a copy of the information; and

(b) has been brought before the court for the hearing.

(3) The person to whom the application relates shall be entitled to be legally represented at the hearing and, if he is not so represented but wishes to be so represented—

(a) the court shall adjourn the hearing to enable him to obtain representation; and

(b) he may be kept in police detention during the adjournment.

(4) A person's further detention is only justified for the purposes of this section or section 44 below if—

(a) his detention without charge is necessary to secure or preserve evidence relating to an offence for which he is under arrest or to obtain such evidence by questioning him;

(b) an offence for which he is under arrest is [an indictable offence]; and

(c) the investigation is being conducted diligently and expeditiously.

(5) Subject to subsection (7) below, an application for a warrant of further detention may be made—

(a) at any time before the expiry of 36 hours after the relevant time; or

(b) in a case where—

(i)   it is not practicable for the magistrates' court to which the application will be made to sit at the expiry of 36 hours after the relevant time; but

(ii) the court will sit during the 6 hours following the end of that period,

at any time before the expiry of the said 6 hours.

(6) In a case to which subsection (5)(b) above applies—

(a) the person to whom the application relates may be kept in police detention until the application is heard; and

(b) the custody officer shall make a note in that person's custody record—

(i)   of the fact that he was kept in police detention for more than 36 hours after the relevant time; and

(ii) of the reason why he was so kept.

(7) If—

(a) an application for a warrant of further detention is made after the expiry of 36 hours after the relevant time; and

(b) it appears to the magistrates' court that it would have been reasonable for the police to make it before the expiry of that period,

the court shall dismiss the application.

(8) Where on an application such as is mentioned in subsection (1) above a magistrates' court is not satisfied that there are reasonable grounds for believing that the further detention of the person to whom the application relates is justified, it shall be its duty—

(a) to refuse the application; or

(b) to adjourn the hearing of it until a time not later than 36 hours after the relevant time.

(9) The person to whom the application relates may be kept in police detention during the adjournment.

(10) A warrant of further detention shall—
   (a) state the time at which it is issued;
   (b) authorise the keeping in police detention of the person to whom it relates for the period stated in it.

(11) Subject to subsection (12) below, the period stated in a warrant of further detention shall be such period as the magistrates' court thinks fit, having regard to the evidence before it.

(12) The period shall not be longer than 36 hours.

(13), (14) *****

(15) Where an application under this section is refused, the person to whom the application relates shall forthwith be charged or, subject to subsection (16) below, released, either on bail or without bail.

(16) A person need not be released under subsection (15) above—
   (a) before the expiry of 24 hours after the relevant time; or
   (b) before the expiry of any longer period for which his continued detention is or has been authorised under section 42 above.

(17) Where an application under this section is refused, no further application shall be made under this section in repect of the person to whom the refusal relates, unless supported by evidence which has come to light since the refusal.

(18), (19) *****

44   Extension of warrants of further detention

(1) On an application on oath made by a constable and supported by an information a magistrates' court may extend a warrant of further detention issued under section 43 above if it is satisfied that there are reasonable grounds for believing that the further detention of the person to whom the application relates is justified.

(2) Subject to subsection (3) below, the period for which a warrant of further detention may be extended shall be such period as the court thinks fit, having regard to the evidence before it.

(3) The period shall not—
   (a) be longer than 36 hours; or
   (b) end later than 96 hours after the relevant time.

(4) Where a warrant of further detention has been extended under subsection (1) above, or further extended under this subsection, for a period ending before 96 hours after the relevant time, on an application such as is mentioned in that subsection a magistrates' court may further extend the warrant if it is satisfied as there mentioned; and subsections (2) and (3) above apply to such further extensions as they apply to extensions under subsection (1) above.

(5) A warrant of further detention shall, if extended or further extended under this section, be endorsed with a note of the period of the extension.

(6) Subsections (2), (3), and (14) of section 43 above shall apply to an application made under this section as they apply to an application made under that section.

(7), (8) *****

45   Detention before charge—supplementary

(1) In sections 43 and 44 of this Act "magistrates' court" means a court consisting of two or more justices of the peace sitting otherwise than in open court.

(2) Any reference in this Part of this Act to a period of time or a time of day is to be treated as approximate only.

45A   *****

Detention—miscellaneous

46   Detention after charge

(1) Where a person—

(a) is charged with an offence; and

(b) after being charged—

    (i) is kept in police detention; or

    (ii) is detained by a local authority in pursuance of arrangements made under section 38(6) above,

he shall be brought before a magistrates' court in accordance with the provisions of this section.

(2) If he is to be brought before a magistrates' court [in the local justice] area in which the police station at which he was charged is situated, he shall be brought before such a court as soon as is practicable and in any event not later than the first sitting after he is charged with the offence.

(3) If no magistrates' court [in that area] is due to sit either on the day on which he is charged or on the next day, the custody officer for the police station at which he was charged shall inform the [designated officer] for the area that there is a person in the area to whom subsection (2) above applies.

(4) If the person charged is to be brought before a magistrates' court [in a local justice] area other than that in which the police station at which he was charged is situated, he shall be removed to that area as soon as is practicable and brought before such a court as soon as is practicable after this arrival in the area and in any event not later than the first sitting of a magistrates' court [in that area] after this arrival in the area.

(5)–(9) *****

[46A Power of arrest for failure to answer to police bail

(1) A constable may arrest without a warrant any person who, having been released on bail under this Part of this Act subject to a duty to attend at a police station, fails to attend at that police station at the time appointed for him to do so.

[(1A) A person who has been released on bail under section 37(7)(a) or 37C(2)(b) above may be arrested without warrant by a constable if the constable has reasonable grounds for suspecting that the person has broken any of the conditions of bail.]

(2) A person who is arrested under this section shall be taken to the police station appointed as the place at which he is to surrender to custody as soon as practicable after the arrest.

(3) For the purpose of—

(a) section 30 above (subject to the obligation in subsection (2) above), and

(b) section 31 above,

an arrest under the section shall be treated as an arrest for an offence.]

47 Bail after arrest

(1) [Subject to the following provisions of this section], a release on bail of a person under this Part of this Act shall be a release on bail granted in accordance with [sections 3, 3A, 5 and 5A of the Bail Act 1976 as they apply to bail granted by a constable].

[(1A) The normal powers to impose conditions of bail shall be available to him where a custody officer releases a person on bail under section [37(7)(a) above or section] 38(1) above (including that subsection as applied by section 40(10) above) but not in any other cases.]

[(1B) No application may be made under section 5B of the Bail Act 1976 if a person is released on bail under section 37(7)(a) or 37C(2)(b) above.

(1C) Subsections (1D) to (1F) below apply where a person released on bail under section 37(7)(a) or 37C(2)(b) above is on bail subject to conditions.

(1D) The person shall not be entitled to make an application under section 43B of the Magistrates' Courts Act 1980.

(1E) A magistrates' court may, on an application by or on behalf of the person, vary the conditions of bail; and in this subsection "vary" has the same meaning as in the Bail Act 1976.

(1F) Where a magistrates' court varies the conditions of bail under subsection (1E) above, that bail shall not lapse but shall continue subject to the conditions as so varied.]

(2) Nothing in the Bail Act 1976 shall prevent the re-arrest without warrant of a person released on bail subject to a duty to attend at a police station if new evidence justifying a further arrest has come to light since his release.

(3), (3A), (4), (6), (7) *****

(5), (8) . . .

47A–51 *****

52 . . .

PART V   QUESTIONING AND TREATMENT OF PERSONS BY POLICE

53   Abolition of certain powers of constables to search persons

(1) Subject to subsection (2) below, there shall cease to have effect any Act (including a local Act) passed before this Act in so far as it authorises—

(a) any search by a constable of a person in police detention at a police station; or

(b) an intimate search of a person by a constable; and any rule of common law which authorises a search such as is mentioned in paragraph (a) or (b) above is abolished.

(2) . . .

54   Search of detained persons

(1) The custody officer at a police station shall ascertain . . . everything which a person has with him when he is—

(a) brought to the station after being arrested elsewhere or after being committed to custody by an order or sentence of a court; or

[(b) arrested at the station or detained there [, as a person falling within section 34(7), under section 37 above].]

[(2) The custody officer may record or cause to be recorded all or any of the things which he ascertains under subsection (1).

(2A) In the case of an arrested person, any such record may be made as part of his custody record.]

(3) Subject to subsection (4) below, a custody officer may seize and retain any such thing or cause any such thing to be seized and retained.

(4) Clothes and personal effects may only be seized if the custody officer—

(a) believes that the person from whom they are seized may use them—

(i) to cause physical injury to himself or any other person;

(ii) to damage property;

(iii) to interfere with evidence; or

(iv) to assist him to escape; or

(b) has reasonable grounds for believing that they may be evidence relating to an offence.

(5) Where anything is seized, the person from whom it is seized shall be told the reason for the seizure unless he is—

(a) violent or likely to become violent; or

(b) incapable of understanding what is said to him.

(6) Subject to subsection (7) below, a person may be searched if the custody officer considers it necessary to enable him to carry out his duty under subsection (1) above and to the extent that the custody officer considers necessary for that purpose.

[(6A) A person who is in custody at a police station or is in police detention otherwise than at a police station may at any time be searched in order to ascertain whether he has with him anything which he could use for any of the purposes specified in subsection (4)(a) above.

(6B) Subject to subsection (6C) below, a constable may seize and retain, or cause to be seized and retained, anything found on such a search.

(6C) A constable may only seize clothes and personal effects in the circumstances specified in subsection (4) above.]

(7) An intimate search may not be conducted under this section.

(8) A search under this section shall be carried out by a constable.

(9) The constable carrying out a search shall be of the same sex as the person searched.

[54A Searches and examination to ascertain identity

(1) If an officer of at least the rank of inspector authorises it, a person who is detained in a police station may be searched or examined, or both—

    (a) for the purpose of ascertaining whether he has any mark that would tend to identify him as a person involved in the commission of an offence; or

    (b) for the purpose of facilitating the ascertainment of his identity.

(2) An officer may only give an authorisation under subsection (1) for the purpose mentioned in paragraph (a) of that subsection if—

    (a) the appropriate consent to a search or examination that would reveal whether the mark in question exists has been withheld; or

    (b) it is not practicable to obtain such consent.

(3) An officer may only give an authorisation under subsection (1) in a case in which subsection (2) does not apply if—

    (a) the person in question has refused to identify himself; or

    (b) the officer has reasonable grounds for suspecting that that person is not who he claims to be.

(4) An officer may give an authorisation under subsection (1) orally or in writing but, if he gives it orally, he shall confirm it in writing as soon as is practicable.

(5) Any identifying mark found on a search or examination under this section may be photographed—

    (a) with the appropriate consent; or

    (b) if the appropriate consent is withheld or it is not practicable to obtain it, without it.

(6) Where a search or examination may be carried out under this section, or a photograph may be taken under this section, the only persons entitled to carry out the search or examination, or to take the photograph, are [constables].

(7) A person may not under this section carry out a search or examination of a person of the opposite sex or take a photograph of any part of the body of a person of the opposite sex.

(8) An intimate search may not be carried out under this section.

(9) A photograph taken under this section—

    (a) may be used by, or disclosed to, any person for any purpose related to the prevention or detection of crime, the investigation of an offence or the conduct of a prosecution; and

    (b) after being so used or disclosed, may be retained but may not be used or disclosed except for a purpose so related.]

(10)–(13) *****

55 Intimate searches

(1) Subject to the following provisions of this section, if an officer of at least the rank of [inspector] has reasonable grounds for believing—

    (a) that a person who has been arrested and is in police detention may have concealed on him anything which—

        (i) he could use to cause physical injury to himself or others; and

        (ii) he might so use while he is in police detention or in the custody of a court; or

    (b) that such a person—

(i)   may have a Class A drug concealed on him; and

(ii) was in possession of it with the appropriate criminal intention before his arrest,
he may authorise [an intimate] search of that person.

(2) An officer may not authorise an intimate search of a person for anything unless he has
reasonable grounds for believing that it cannot be found without his being intimately searched.

(3) *****

(4) An intimate search which is only a drug offence search shall be by way of examination
by a suitably qualified person.

(5) Except as provided by subsection (4) above, an intimate search shall be by way of
examination by a suitably qualified person unless an officer of at least the rank of [inspector]
considers that this is not practicable.

(6) An intimate search which is not carried out as mentioned in subsection (5) above shall
be carried out by a constable.

(7) A constable may not carry out an intimate search of a person of the opposite sex.

(8) No intimate search may be carried out except—

(a) at a police station;

(b) at a hospital;

(c) at a registered medical practitioner's surgery; or

(d) at some other place used for medical purposes.

(9) An intimate search which is only a drug offence search may not be carried out at a
police station.

(10) If an intimate search of a person is carried out, the custody record relating to him
shall state—

(a) which parts of his body were searched; and

(b) why they were searched.

(11) *****

(12) This custody officer at a police station may seize and retain anything which is found
on an intimate search of a person, or cause any such thing to be seized and retained—

(a) if he believes that the person from whom it is seized may use it—

(i)   to cause physical injury to himself or any other person;

(ii) to damage property;

(iii) to interfere with evidence; or

(iv) to assist him to escape; or

(b) if he has reasonable grounds for believing that it may be evidence relating to an
offence.

(13) Where anything is seized under this section, the person from whom it is seized shall
be told the reason for the seizure unless he is—

(a) violent or likely to become violent; or

(b) incapable of understanding what is said to him.

(14)–(16) *****

(17) In this section—
*****

"Class A drug" has the meaning assigned to it by section 2(1)(b) of the Misuse of Drugs Act
1971;

"drug offence search" means an intimate search for a Class A drug which an officer has
authorised by virtue of subsection (1)(b) above; and

"suitably qualified person" means—

(a) a registered medical practitioner; or

(b) a registered nurse.

56   Right to have someone informed when arrested

(1) Where a person has been arrested and is being held in custody in a police station or

other premises, he shall be entitled, if he so requests, to have one friend or relative or other person who is known to him or who is likely to take an interest in his welfare told, as soon as is practicable except to the extent that delay is permitted by this section, that he has been arrested and is being detained there.

(2) Delay is only permitted—

(a) in the case of a person who is in police detention for [an indictable offence]; and

(b) if an officer of at least the rank of [inspector] authorises it.

(3) In any case the person in custody must be permitted to exercise the right conferred by subsection (1) above within 36 hours from the relevant time as defined in section 41(2) above.

(4)–(5B) *****

(6) If a delay is authorised—

(a) the detained person shall be told the reason for it; and

(b) the reason shall be noted on his custody record.

(7)–(10) *****

57   ***

58   Access to legal advice

(1) A person arrested and held in custody in a police station or other premises shall be entitled, if he so requests, to consult a solicitor privately at any time.

(2) Subject to subsection (3) below, a request under subsection (1) above and the time at which it was made shall be recorded in the custody record.

(3) Such a request need not be recorded in the custody record of a person who makes it at a time while he is at a court after being charged with an offence.

(4) If a person makes such a request, he must be permitted to consult a solicitor as soon as is practicable except to the extent that delay is permitted by this section.

(5) In any case he must be permitted to consult a solicitor within 36 hours from the relevant time, as defined in section 41(2) above.

(6) Delay in compliance with a request is only permitted—

(a) in the case of a person who is in police detention for [an indictable offence]; and

(b) if an officer of at least the rank of superintendent authorises it.

(7)–(8B) *****

(9) If delay is authorised—

(a) the detained person shall be told the reason for it; and

(b) the reason shall be noted on his custody record.

(10) The duties imposed by subsection (9) above shall be performed as soon as is practicable.

(11) There may be no further delay in permitting the exercise of the right conferred by subsection (1) above once the reason for authorising delay ceases to subsist.

[(12) Nothing in this section applies to a person arrested or detained under the terrorism provisions.]

59   . . .

60   Tape-recording of interviews

(1) It shall be the duty of the Secretary of State—

(a) to issue a code of practice in connection with the tape-recording of interviews of persons suspected of the commission of criminal offences which are held by police officers at police stations; and

(b) to make an order requiring the tape-recording of interviews of persons suspected of the commission of criminal offences, or of such descriptions of criminal offences as may be specified in the order, which are so held, in accordance with the code as it has effect for the time being.

(2) An order under subsection (1) above shall be made by statutory instrument and shall be subject to annulment in pursuance of a resolution of either House of Parliament.

[60A   Visual recording of interviews
(1) The Secretary of State shall have power—
    (a) to issue a code of practice for the visual recording of interviews held by police officers at police stations; and
    (b) to make an order requiring the visual recording of interviews so held, and requiring the visual recording to be in accordance with the code for the time being in force under this section.]
(2)–(4) *****

61   Fingerprinting
(1) Except as provided by this section no person's fingerprints may be taken without the appropriate consent.
(2) Consent to the taking of a person's fingerprints must be in writing if it is given at a time when he is at a police station.
[(3) The fingerprints of a person detained at a police station may be taken without the appropriate consent if—
    (a) he is detained in consequence of his arrest for a recordable offence; and
    (b) he has not had his fingerprints taken in the course of the investigation of the offence by the police.]
[(3A) [Where a person mentioned in paragraph (a) of subsection (3) or (4) has already had his fingerprints taken in the course of the investigation of the offence by the police], that fact shall be disregarded for the purposes of that subsection if—
    (a) the fingerprints taken on the previous occasion do not constitute a complete set of his fingerprints; or
    (b) some or all of the fingerprints taken on the previous occasion are not of sufficient quality to allow satisfactory analysis, comparison or matching (whether in the case in question or generally).]
[(4) The fingerprints of a person detained at a police station may be taken without the appropriate consent if—
    (a) he has been charged with a recordable offence or informed that he will be reported for such an offence; and
    (b) he has not had his fingerprints taken in the course of the investigation of the offence by the police.]
[(4A) The fingerprints of a person who has answered to bail at a court or police station may be taken without the appropriate consent at the court or station if—
    (a) the court, or
    (b) an officer of at least the rank of inspector,
authorises them to be taken.
(4B) A court or officer may only give an authorisation under subsection (4A) if—
    (a) the person who has answered to bail has answered to it for a person whose fingerprints were taken on a previous occasion and there are reasonable grounds for believing that he is not the same person; or
    (b) the person who has answered to bail claims to be a different person from a person whose fingerprints were taken on a previous occasion.]
(5) An officer may give an authorisation under [subsection (4A)] above orally or in writing but, if he gives it orally, he shall confirm it in writing as soon as is practicable.
(6)–(10) *****

61A–63C *****

64   Destruction of fingerprints and samples

[(1A) Where—

(a) fingerprints [, impressions of footwear] or samples are taken from a person in connection with the investigation of an offence, and

(b) subsection (3) below does not require them to be destroyed, the fingerprints [, impressions of footwear] or samples may be retained after they have fulfilled the purposes for which they were taken but shall not be used by any person except for purposes related to the prevention or detection of crime, the investigation of an offence [, the conduct of a prosecution or the identification of a deceased person or of the person from whom a body part came.]

(1B), (1BA) *****

(2) ...

(3) If—

(a) fingerprints [, impressions of footwear] or samples are taken from a person in connection with the investigation of an offence; and

(b) that person is not suspected of having committed the offence,

they must [except as provided in [the following subsections of this section]] be destroyed as soon as they have fulfilled the purpose for which they were taken.

(3AA)–(3AD) *****

(4) ...

(5)–(7) *****

[64A   Photographing of suspects etc.

(1) A person who is detained at a police station may be photographed—

(a) with the appropriate consent; or

(b) if the appropriate consent is withheld or it is not practicable to obtain it, without it.

(1A), (1B) *****

(2) A person proposing to take a photograph of any person under this section—

(a) may, for the purpose of doing so, require the removal of any item or substance worn on or over the whole or any part of the head or face of the person to be photographed; and

(b) if the requirement is not complied with, may remove the item or substance himself.

(3) Where a photograph may be taken under this section, the only persons entitled to take the photograph are [constables].

(4) A photograph taken under this section—

(a) may be used by, or disclosed to, any person for any purpose related to the prevention or detection of crime, the investigation of an offence or the conduct of a prosecution [or to the enforcement of a sentence]; and

(b) after being so used or disclosed, may be retained but may not be used or disclosed except for a purpose so related.]

(5)–(7) *****

65   Part V—supplementary

(1) In this Part of this Act—

["analysis", in relation to a skin impression, includes comparison and matching;]

"appropriate consent" means—

(a) in relation to a person who has attained the age of 17 years, the consent of that person;

(b) in relation to a person who has not attained that age but has attained the age of 14 years, the consent of that person and his parent or guardian; and

(c) in relation to a person who has not attained the age of 14 years, the consent of his parent or guardian;

*****

["fingerprints", in relation to any person, means a record (in any form and produced by any method) of the skin pattern and other physical characteristics or features of—
  (a) any of that person's fingers; or
  (b) either of his palms;];
["intimate sample" means—
  (a) a sample of blood, semen or any other tissue fluid, urine or pubic hair;
  (b) a dental impression;
  (c) [a swab taken from any part of a person's genitals (including pubic hair) or from a person's body orifice other than the mouth;]
"intimate search" means a search which consists of the physical examination of a person's body orifices other than the mouth;
"non-intimate sample" means—
  (a) a sample of hair other than pubic hair;
  (b) a sample taken from a nail or from under a nail;
  (c) [a swab taken from any part of a person's body other than a part from which a swab taken would be an intimate sample;]
  (d) saliva;
  [(e) a skin impression;]]

*****

. . .

(1A), (1B), (2) *****

PART VI   CODES OF PRACTICE—GENERAL

66   Codes of practice

(1) The Secretary of State shall issue codes of practice in connection with—
  (a) the exercise by police officers of statutory powers—
    (i) to search a person without first arresting him;
    (ii) to search a vehicle without making an arrest; [or
    (iii) to arrest a person.]
  (b) the detention, treatment, questioning and indication of persons by police officers;
  (c) searches of premises by police officers; and
  (d) the seizure of property found by police officers on persons or premises.
  [(2) Codes shall (in particular) include provisions in connection with the exercise by police officers of powers under section 63B, above.]

67   Codes of practice—supplementary

[(1) In this section, "code" means a code of practice under section 60, 60A or 66.
(2) The Secretary of State may at any time revise the whole or any part of a code.
(3) A code may be made, or revised, so as to—
  (a) apply only in relation to one or more specified areas,
  (b) have effect only for a specified period,
  (c) apply only in relation to specified offences or descriptions of offender.
(4) Before issuing a code, or any revision of a code, the Secretary of State must consult—
  (a) persons whom he considers to represent the interests of police authorities,
  (b) persons whom he considers to represent the interests of chief officers of police,

    (c) the General Council of the Bar,

    (d) the Law Society of England and Wales,

    (e) the Institute of Legal Executives, and

    (f) such other persons as he thinks fit.

(5) A code, or a revision of a code, does not come into operation until the Secretary of State by order so provides.

(6) The power conferred by subsection (5) is exercisable by statutory instrument.

(7) An order bringing a code into operation may not be made unless a draft of the order has been laid before Parliament and approved by a resolution of each House.

(7A) An order bringing a revision of a code into operation must be laid before Parliament if the order has been made without a draft having been so laid and approved by a resolution of each House.

(7B) When an order or draft of an order is laid, the code or revision of a code to which it relates must also be laid.

(7C) No order or draft of an order may be laid until the consultation required by subsection (4) has taken place.

(7D) An order bringing a code, or a revision of a code, into operation may include transitional or saving provisions.]

(8) . . .

(9) Persons other than police officers who are charged with the duty of investigating offences or charging offenders shall in the discharge of that duty have regard to any relevant provision of such a code.

[(9A) Persons on whom powers are conferred by—

    (a) any designation under section 38 or 39 of the Police Reform Act 2002 (c 30) (police powers for police authority employees), or

    (b) any accreditation under section 41 of that Act (accreditation under community safety accreditation schemes),

shall have regard to any relevant provision of a code of practice to which this section applies in the exercise or performance of the powers and duties conferred or imposed on them by that designation or accreditation.]

(10) A failure on the part—

    (a) of a police officer to comply with any provision of such a code; or

    (b) of any person other than a police officer who is charged with the duty of investigating offences or charging offenders to have regard to any relevant provision of . . . a code in the discharge of the duty; [or

    (c) of a person designated under section 38 or 39 or accredited under section 41 of the Police Reform Act 2002 to have regard to any relevant provision of . . . a code in the exercise or performance of the powers and duties conferred or imposed on him by that designation or accreditation,]

shall not of itself render him liable to any criminal or civil proceedings.

(11) In all criminal and civil proceedings any . . . code shall be admissible in evidence; and if any provision of . . . a code appears to the court or tribunal conducting the proceedings to be relevant to any question arising in the proceedings it shall be taken into account in determining that question.

(12) *****

Note: Extracts from the Codes of Practice issued under this section (as revised) are printed at the end of this book.

PART VIII   EVIDENCE IN CRIMINAL PROCEEDINGS—GENERAL

68 . . .

69–75   ***

Confessions

76   Confessions

(1) In any proceedings a confession made by an accused person may be given in evidence against him in so far as it is relevant to any matter in issue in the proceedings and is not excluded by the court in pursuance of this section.

(2) If, in any proceedings where the prosecution proposes to give in evidence a confession made by an accused person, it is represented to the court that the confession was or may have been obtained—

    (a) by oppression of the person who made it; or

    (b) in consequence of anything said or done which was likely, in the circumstances existing at the time, to render unreliable any confession which might be made by him in consequence thereof,

the court shall not allow the confession to be given in evidence against him except in so far as the prosecution proves to the court beyond reasonable doubt that the confession (notwithstanding that it may be true) was not obtained as aforesaid.

(3) In any proceedings where the prosecution proposes to give in evidence a confession made by an accused person, the court may of its own motion require the prosecution, as a condition of allowing it to do so, to prove that the confession was not obtained as mentioned in subsection (2) above.

(4) The fact that a confession is wholly or partly excluded in pursuance of this section shall not affect the admissibility in evidence—

    (a) of any facts discovered as a result of the confession; or

    (b) where the confession is relevant as showing that the accused speaks, writes or expresses himself in a particular way, of so much of the confession as is necessary to show that he does so.

(5) Evidence that a fact to which this subsection applies was discovered as a result of a statement made by an accused person shall not be admissible unless evidence of how it was discovered is given by him or on his behalf.

(6) Subsection (5) above applies—

    (a) to any fact discovered as a result of a confession which is wholly excluded in pursuance of this section; and

    (b) to any fact discovered as a result of a confession which is partly so excluded, if that fact is discovered as a result of the excluded part of the confession.

(7) Nothing in Part VII of this Act shall prejudice the admissibility of a confession made by an accused person.

(8) In this section "oppression" includes torture, inhuman or degrading treatment, and the use or threat of violence (whether or not amounting to torture).

(9) . . .

[76A   Confessions may be given in evidence for co-accused

(1) In any proceedings a confession made by an accused person may be given in evidence for another person charged in the same proceedings (a co-accused) in so far as it is relevant to any matter in issue in the proceedings and is not excluded by the court in pursuance of this section.

(2) If, in any proceedings where a co-accused proposes to give in evidence a confession made by an accused person, it is represented to the court that the confession was or may have been obtained—

(a) by oppression of the person who made it; or

(b) in consequence of anything said or done which was likely, in the circumstances existing at the time, to render unreliable any confession which might be made by him in consequence thereof,

the court shall not allow the confession to be given in evidence for the co-accused except in so far as it is proved to the court on the balance of probabilities that the confession (notwithstanding that it may be true) was not so obtained.

(3) Before allowing a confession made by an accused person to be given in evidence for a co-accused in any proceedings, the court may of its own motion require the fact that the confession was not obtained as mentioned in subsection (2) above to be proved in the proceedings on the balance of probabilities.

(4) The fact that a confession is wholly or partly excluded in pursuance of this section shall not affect the admissibility in evidence—

(a) of any facts discovered as a result of the confession; or

(b) where the confession is relevant as showing that the accused speaks, writes or expresses himself in a particular way, of so much of the confession as is necessary to show that he does so.

(5) Evidence that a fact to which this subsection applies was discovered as a result of a statement made by an accused person shall not be admissible unless evidence of how it was discovered is given by him or on his behalf.

(6) Subsection (5) above applies—

(a) to any fact discovered as a result of a confession which is wholly excluded in pursuance of this section; and

(b) to any fact discovered as a result of a confession which is partly so excluded, if the fact is discovered as a result of the excluded part of the confession.

(7) In this section "oppression" includes torture, inhuman or degrading treatment, and the use or threat of violence (whether or not amounting to torture).]

77   Confessions by mentally handicapped persons

(1) Without prejudice to the general duty of the court at a trial on indictment [with a jury] to direct the jury on any matter on which it appears to the court appropriate to do so, where at such a trial—

(a) the case against the accused depends wholly or substantially on a confession by him; and

(b) the court is satisfied—

(i) that he is mentally handicapped; and

(ii) that the confession was not made in the presence of an independent person, the court shall warn the jury that there is special need for caution before convicting the accused in reliance on the confession, and shall explain that the need arises because of the circumstances mentioned in paragraphs (a) and (b) above, but in doing so shall not be required to use any particular form of words.

(2) In any case where at the summary trial of a person for an offence it appears to the court that a warning under subsection (1) above would be required if the trial were on indictment, the court shall treat the case as one in which there is a special need for caution before convicting the accused on his confession.

(2A) *****

(3) In this section—

"independent person" does not include a police officer or a person employed for, or engaged on police purposes;

"mentally handicapped", in relation to a person, means that he is in a state of arrested or incomplete development of mind which includes significant impairment of intelligence and social functioning; and "police purposes" has the meaning assigned to it by [section 101(2) of the Police Act 1996.] **Note:** The Police and Criminal Evidence Act 1984 (Application to Customs and Excise) Order 1985 (SI 1985 No. 1800), Art. 10, provides that subsection (3) above "shall be modified to the extent that the definition of 'independent person' shall, in addition to the persons mentioned therein, also include an officer or any other person acting under the authority of the Commissioners of Customs and Excise".

Miscellaneous

78   Exclusion of unfair evidence

(1) In any proceedings the court may refuse to allow evidence on which the prosecution proposes to rely to be given if it appears to the court that, having regard to all the circumstances, including the circumstances in which the evidence was obtained, the admission of the evidence would have such an adverse effect on the fairness of the proceedings that the court ought not to admit it.

(2) Nothing in this section shall prejudice any rule of law requiring a court to exclude evidence.

(3) . . .

79–81   ***

PART VIII—SUPPLEMENTARY

82   Part VIII—interpretation

(1) In this Part of this Act—

"confession" includes any statement wholly or partly adverse to the person who made it, whether made to a person in authority or not and whether made in words or otherwise;
*****

(2) *****

(3) Nothing in this Part of this Act shall prejudice any power of a court to exclude evidence (whether by preventing questions from being put or otherwise) at its discretion.

83–106   (Repealed and re-enacted by the Police Act 1996, see below.) . . .

PART XI   MISCELLANEOUS AND SUPPLEMENTARY

107–108, 110–111, 113–115   ***

**109, 112, 116   . . .

117   Power of constable to use reasonable force

Where any provision of this Act—

    (a) confers a power on a constable; and

    (b) does not provide that the power may only be exercised with the consent of some person, other than a police officer,

the officer may use reasonable force, if necessary, in the exercise of the power.

118   General interpretation

(1) *****

(2) [Subject to subsection (2A)] a person is in police detention for the purposes of this Act if—

    [(a) he has been taken to a police station after being arrested for an offence or after being arrested under section 41 of the Terrorism Act 2000]]; or

    (b) he is arrested at a police station after attending voluntarily at the station or accompanying a constable to it, and is detained there or is detained elsewhere in the charge of a constable, except that a person who is at a court after being charged is not in police detention for those purposes.

[(2A) Where a person is in another's lawful custody by virtue of paragraph 22, 34(1) or 35(3) of Schedule 4 to the Police Reform Act 2002, he shall be treated as in police detention.]

*****

Section 9   SCHEDULE 1
                         SPECIAL PROCEDURE

Making of orders by circuit judge

1. If on an application made by a constable a [judge] is satisfied that one or other of the sets of access conditions is fulfilled, he may make an order under paragraph 4 below.

2. The first set of access conditions is fulfilled if—
   (a) there are reasonable grounds for believing—
       (i) that [an indictable offence] has been committed;
       (ii) that there is material which consists of special procedure material or includes special procedure material and does not also include excluded material on premises specified in the application [, or on premises occupied or controlled by a person specified in the application (including all such premises on which there are reasonable grounds for believing that there is such material as it is reasonably practicable so to specify);];
       (iii) that the material is likely to be of substantial value (whether by itself or together with other material) to the investigation in connection with which the application is made; and
       (iv) that the material is likely to be relevant evidence;
   (b) other methods of obtaining the material—
       (i) have been tried without success; or
       (ii) have not been tried because it appeared that they were bound to fail; and
   (c) it is in the public interest, having regard—
       (i) to the benefit likely to accrue to the investigation if the material is obtained; and
       (ii) to the circumstances under which the person in possession of the material holds it,
that the material should be produced or that access to it should be given.

3. The second set of access conditions is fulfilled if—
   (a) there are reasonable grounds for believing that there is material which consists of or includes excluded material or special procedure material on premises specified in the application [, or on premises occupied or controlled by a person specified in the application (including all such premises on which there are reasonable grounds for believing that there is such material as it is reasonably practicable so to specify)];
   (b) but for section 9(2) above a search of [such premises] for that material could have been authorised by the issue of a warrant to a constable under an enactment other than this Schedule; and
   (c) the issue of such a warrant would have been appropriate.

4. An order under this paragraph is an order that the person who appears to the [judge] to be in possession of the material to which the application relates shall—
   [(a) produce it to a constable for him to take away; or]
   (b) give a constable access to it,
not later than the end of the period of seven days from the date of the order or the end of such longer period as the order may specify.

5. Where the material consists of information [stored in any electronic form]—

(a) an order under paragraph 4(a) above shall have effect as an order to produce the material in a form in which it can be taken away and in which it is visible and legible [or from which it can readily be produced in a visible and legible form]; and

(b) an order under paragraph 4(b) above shall have effect as an order to give a constable access to the material in a form in which it is visible and legible.

6. For the purposes of sections 21 and 22 above material produced in pursuance of an order under paragraph 4(a) above shall be treated as if it were material seized by a constable.

Notices of applications for orders

7. An application for an order under paragraph 4 above shall be made inter partes.

8. Notice of an application for such an order may be served on a person either by delivering it to him or by leaving it at his proper address or by sending it by post to him in a registered letter or by the recorded delivery service.

9. Such a notice may be served—

(a) on a body corporate, by serving it on the body's secretary or clerk or other similar officer; and

(b) on a partnership, by serving it on one of the partners.

10. For the purposes of this Schedule, and of section 7 of the Interpretation Act 1978 in its application to this Schedule, the proper address of a person, in the case of secretary or clerk or other similar officer of a body corporate, shall be that of the registered or principal office of that body, in the case of a partner of a firm shall be that of the principal office of the firm, and in any other case shall be the last known address of the person to be served.

11. Where notice of an application for an order under paragraph 4 above has been served on a person, he shall not conceal, destroy, alter or dispose of the material to which the application relates except—

(a) with the leave of a judge; or

(b) with the written permission of a constable,

until—

(i) the application is dismissed or abandoned; or

(ii) he has complied with an order under paragraph 4 above made on the application.

Issue of warrants by [a judge]

12. If on an application made by a constable a [judge]—

(a) is satisfied—

(i) that either set of access conditions is fulfilled; and

(ii) that any of the further conditions set out in paragraph 14 below is also fulfilled [in relation to each set of premises specified in the application]; or

(b) is satisfied—

(i) that the second set of access conditions is fufilled; and

(ii) that an order under paragraph 4 above relating to the material has not been complied with,

he may issue a warrant authorising a constable to enter and search the premises [or (as the case may be) all premises occupied or controlled by the person referred to in paragraph 2(a)(ii) or 3(a), including such sets of premises as are specified in the application (an "all premises warrant")].

12A   *****

13. A constable may seize and retain anything for which a search has been authorised under paragraph 12 above.

14. The further conditions mentioned in paragraph 12(a)(ii) above are—

(a) that it is not practicable to communicate with any person entitled to grant entry to the premises . . . ;

(b) that it is practicable to communicate with a person entitled to grant entry to the premises but it is not practicable to communicate with any person entitled to grant access to the material;

(c) that the material contains information which–

    (i) is subject to a restriction or obligation such as is mentioned in section 11(2)(b) above; and

    (ii) is likely to be disclosed in breach of it if a warrant is not issued;

(d) that service of notice of an application for an order under paragraph 4 above may seriously prejudice the investigation.

15.—(1) If a person fails to comply with an order under paragraph 4 above, a [judge] may deal with him as if he had committed a contempt of the Crown Court.

(2) Any enactment relating to contempt of the Crown Court shall have effect in relation to such a failure as if it were such a contempt.

16. *****

[Interpretation

17.—In this Schedule "judge" means [a judge of the High Court,] a Circuit Judge or a [Recorder].]

*****

Video Recordings Act 1984
(1984, c. 39)

An Act to make provision for regulating the distribution of video recordings and for connected purposes   [12 July 1984]

Territorial extent: United Kingdom

Preliminary

1 Interpretation of terms

(1) The provisions of this section shall have effect for the interpretation of terms used in this Act.

(2) "Video work" means any series of visual images (with or without sound)—

(a) produced electronically by the use of information contained on any disc . . . magnetic tape [or any other device capable of storing data electronically], and

(b) shown as a moving picture.

(3) "Video recording" means any disc . . . magnetic tape [or any other device capable of storing data electronically] containing information by the use of which the whole or a part of a video work may be produced.

(4) "Supply" means supply in any manner, whether or not for reward, and, therefore, includes supply by way of sale, letting on hire, exchange or loan; and references to a supply are to be interpreted accordingly.

2 Exempted works

(1) Subject to subsection (2) [or (3)] below, a video work is for the purposes of this Act an exempted work if, taken as a whole—

(a) it is designed to inform, educate or instruct;

(b) it is concerned with sport, religion or music; or

(c) it is a video game.

(2) A video work is not an exempted work for those purposes if, to any significant extent, it depicts—

    (a) human sexual activity or acts of force or restraint associated with such activity;

    (b) mutilation or torture of, or other acts of gross violence towards, humans or animals;

    (c) human genital organs or human urinary or excretory functions;

    [(d) techniques likely to be useful in the commission of offences;]

or is [likely] to any significant extent to stimulate or encourage anything falling within paragraph (a) or, in the case of anything falling within paragraph (b), is [likely] to any extent to do so.

[(3) A video work is not an exempted work for those purposes if, to any significant extent, it depicts criminal activity which is likely to any significant extent to stimulate or encourage the commission of offences.]

3 Exempted supplies

(1) The provisions of this section apply to determine whether or not a supply of a video recording is an exempted supply for the purposes of this Act.

(2) The supply of a video recording by any person is an exempted supply if it is neither—

    (a) a supply for reward, nor

    (b) a supply in the course or furtherance of a business.

(3)–(12) *****

Designated authority

4 Authority to determine suitability of video works for classification

(1) The Secretary of State may by notice under this section designate any person as the authority responsible for making arrangements—

    (a) for determining for the purposes of this Act whether or not video works are suitable for classification certificates to be issued in respect of them, having special regard to the likelihood of video works in respect of which such certificates have been issued being viewed in the home,

    (b) in the case of works which are determined in accordance with the arrangements to be so suitable—

        [(ia) for assigning a unique title to each video work in respect of which a classification certificate is to be issued,]

        (i) for making such other determinations as are required for the issue of classification certificates, and

        (ii) for issuing such certificates, and

    (c) for maintaining a record of such determinations (whether determinations made in pursuance of arrangements made by that person or by any person previously designated under this section), . . .

(1A), (1B), (2) *****

(3) The Secretary of State shall not make any designation under this section unless he is satisfied that adequate arrangements will be made for an appeal by any person against a determination that a video work submitted by him for the issue of a classification certificate—

    (a) is not suitable for a classification certificate to be issued in respect of it, or

    (b) is not suitable for viewing by persons who have not attained a particular age,

or against a determination that no video recording containing the work is to be supplied other than in a licensed sex shop.

(4)–(8) *****

[4A Criteria for suitability to which special regard to be had

(1) The designated authority shall, in making any determination as to the suitability of

a video work, have special regard (among the other relevant factors) to any harm that may be caused to potential viewers or, through their behaviour, to society by the manner in which the work deals with—

    (a) criminal behaviour;

    (b) illegal drugs;

    (c) violent behaviour or incidents;

    (d) horrific behaviour or incidents; or

    (e) human sexual activity.

  (2) For the purposes of this section—

"potential viewer" means any person (including a child or young person) who is likely to view the video work in question if a classification certificate or a classification certificate of a particular description were issued;

"suitability" means suitability for the issue of a classification certificate or suitability for the issue of a certificate of a particular description;

"violent behaviour" includes any act inflicting or likely to result in the infliction of injury; and any behaviour or activity referred to in subsection (1)(a) to (e) above shall be taken to include behaviour or activity likely to stimulate or encourage it.]

4B, 5–6 *****

Classification and labelling

7 Classification certificates

  (1) In this Act "classification certificate" means a certificate—

    (a) issued in respect of a video work in pursuance of arrangements made by the designated authority; and

    (b) satisfying the requirements of subsection (2) below.

  (2) Those requirements are that the certificate must contain [the title assigned to the video work in accordance with section 4(1)(b)(ia) of this Act and]—

    (a) a statement that the video work concerned is suitable for general viewing and unrestricted supply (with or without any advice as to the desirability of parental guidance with regard to the viewing of the work by young children or as to the particular suitability of the work for viewing by children [or young children]); or

    (b) a statement that the video work concerned is suitable for viewing only by persons who have attained the age (not being more than eighteen years) specified in the certificate and that no video recording containing that work is to be supplied to any person who has not attained the age so specified; or

    (c) the statement mentioned in paragraph (b) above together with a statement that no video recording containing that work is to be supplied other than in a licensed sex shop.

*****

Prosecution of Offences Act 1985
(1985, c. 23)

An Act to provide for the establishment of a Crown Prosecution Service for England and Wales; to make provision as to costs in criminal cases; to provide for the imposition of time limits in relation to preliminary stages of criminal proceedings; to amend section 42 of the Supreme Court Act 1981

and section 3 of the Children and Young Persons Act 1969; to make provision with respect to consents to prosecutions; to repeal section 9 of the Perjury Act 1911; and for connected purposes
[23 May 1985]

Territorial extent: England and Wales

PART I   THE CROWN PROSECUTION SERVICE

Constitution and functions of Service

1   The Crown Prosecution Service

(1) There shall be a prosecuting service for England and Wales (to be known as the "Crown Prosecution Service") consisting of—

(a) the Director of Public Prosecutions, who shall be head of the Service;

(b) the Chief Crown Prosecutors, designated under subsection (4) below, each of whom shall be the member of the Service responsible to the Director for supervising the operation of the service in his area; and

(c) the other staff appointed by the Director under this section.

(2) The Director shall appoint such staff for the Service as, with the approval of the Treasury as to numbers, remuneration and other terms and conditions of service, he considers necessary for the discharge of his functions.

(3) The Director may designate any member of the Service [who has a general qualification (within the meaning of section 71 of the Courts and Legal Services Act 1990)] for the purposes of this subsection, and any person so designated shall be known as a Crown Prosecutor.

(4) The Director shall divide England and Wales into areas and, for each of those areas, designate a Crown Prosecutor for the purposes of this subsection and any person so designated shall be known as a Chief Crown Prosecutor.

(5) The Director may, from time to time, vary the division of England and Wales made for the purpose of subsection (4) above.

(6) Without prejudice to any functions which may have been assigned to him in his capacity as a member of the Service, every Crown Prosecutor shall have all the powers of the Director as to the institution and conduct of proceedings but shall exercise those powers under the direction of the Director.

(7) Where any enactment (whenever passed)—

(a) prevents any step from being taken without the consent of the Director or without his consent or the consent of another; or

(b) requires any step to be taken by or in relation to the Director; any consent given by or, as the case may be, step taken by or in relation to, a Crown Prosecutor shall be treated, for the purposes of that enactment, as given by or, as the case may be, taken by or in relation to the Director.

2   The Director of Public Prosecutions

(1) The Director of Public Prosecutions shall be appointed by the Attorney General.

(2) The Director must be a [person who has a 10 year general qualification, within the meaning of section 71 of the Courts and Legal Services Act 1990.]

(3) *****

3   Functions of the Director

(1) The Director shall discharge his functions under this or any other enactment under the superintendence of the Attorney General.

(2) It shall be the duty of the Director [, subject to any provisions contained in the Criminal Justice Act 1987]—

(a) to take over the conduct of all criminal proceedings, other than specified proceedings, instituted on behalf of a police force (whether by a member of that force or by any other person);

[(aa) to take over the conduct of any criminal proceedings instituted by an immigration officer (as defined for the purposes of the Immigration Act 1971) acting in his capacity as such an officer;]

(b) to institute and have the conduct of criminal proceedings in any case where it appears to him that—
  (i) the importance or difficulty of the case makes it appropriate that proceedings should be instituted by him; or
  (ii) it is otherwise appropriate for proceedings to be instituted by him;

[(ba) to institute and have the conduct of any criminal proceedings in any case where the proceedings relate to the subject matter of a report a copy of which has been sent to him under paragraph 23 or 24 of Schedule 3 to the Police Reform Act 2002 (reports or investigations into conduct of persons serving with the police);]

(c) to take over the conduct of all binding over proceedings instituted on behalf of a police force (whether by a member of that force or by any other person);
  *****

(g) to discharge such other functions as may from time to time be assigned to him by the Attorney General in pursuance of this paragraph.

(2A), (3), (4) *****

4–5 *****

6 Prosecutions instituted and conducted otherwise than by the Service

(1) Subject to subsection (2) below, nothing in this Part shall preclude any person from instituting any criminal proceedings or conducting any criminal proceedings to which the Director's duty to take over the conduct of proceedings does not apply.

(2) Where criminal proceedings are instituted in circumstances in which the Director is not under a duty to take over their conduct, he may nevertheless do so at any stage.

7–9 *****

Guidelines

10 Guidelines for Crown Prosecutors

(1) The Director shall issue a Code for Crown Prosecutors giving guidance on general principles to be applied by them—
  (a) in determining, in any case—
    (i) whether proceedings for an offence should be instituted or, where proceedings have been instituted, whether they should be discontinued; or
    (ii) what charges should be preferred; and
  (b) in considering, in any case, representations to be made by them to any magistrates' court about the mode of trial suitable for that case.

(2) The Director may from time to time make alterations in the Code.

(3) The provisions of the Code shall be set out in the Director's report under section 9 of this Act for the year in which the Code is issued; and any alteration in the Code shall be set out in his report under that section for the year in which the alteration is made.

*****

Parliamentary Constituencies Act 1986
(1986, c. 56)

An Act to consolidate the House of Commons (Redistribution of Seats) Acts 1949 to 1979 and certain related enactments   [7 November 1986]

Territorial extent: United Kingdom

1   Parliamentary constituencies
(1) There shall for the purpose of parliamentary elections be the county and borough constituencies (or in Scotland the county and burgh constituencies), each returning a single member, which are described in Orders in Council made under this Act.

(2) In this Act and, except where the context otherwise requires, in any Act passed after the Representation of the People Act 1948, "constituency" means an area having separate representation in the House of Commons.

2   . . .

3   [Reports of the Electoral Commission]
(1) [The Electoral Commission shall keep under review the representation in the House of Commons of each of England, Scotland, Wales and Northern Ireland and shall, in accordance with subsection (2) below, submit to the Secretary of State separate reports with respect to the whole or each of these parts] of the United Kingdom, either—

(a) showing the constituencies into which they recommend that it should be divided in order to give effect to the rules set out in paragraphs 1 to 6 of Schedule 2 to this Act (read with paragraph 7 of that Schedule), or

(b) stating that, in the opinion of the Commission, no alteration is required to be made in respect of that part of the United Kingdom in order to give effect to the said rules (read with paragraph 7).

(2) Reports under subsection (1) above [with respect to a particular part of the United Kingdom] shall be submitted by [the Electoral Commission [not less than eight nor more than twelve years] from the date of the last report under that subsection with respect to that part of the United Kingdom.]

[(2A) A failure by [the Electoral Commission] to submit a report within the time limit which is appropriate to that report shall not be regarded as invalidating the report for the purpose of any enactment.]

(3) [The Electoral Commission] may also from time to time submit to the Secretary of State reports with respect to the area comprised in any particular constituency or constituencies in [any part of the United Kingdom], showing the constituencies into which they recommend that that area should be divided in order to give effect to the rules set out in paragraphs 1 to 6 of Schedule 2 to this Act (read with paragraph 7 of that Schedule).

(4) A report of [the Electoral Commission] under this Act showing the constituencies into which they recommend that any area should be divided shall state, as respects each constituency, the name by which they recommend that it should be known, and whether they recommend that it should be a county constituency or a borough constituency (or in Scotland a county constituency or a burgh constituency).

[(5) As soon as practicable after the Electoral Commission have submitted a report to the Secretary of State under this Act, he shall lay before Parliament:

(a) the report; and

(b) (except where the report states that no alteration is required to be made in respect of the part of the United Kingdom to which it relates) the draft of an Order in Council for giving effect to the recommendation contained in the report.]

(6) Schedule 2 to this Act which contains the rules referred to above and related provisions shall have effect.

(7), (8) *****

*****

Section 3   SCHEDULE 2
        RULES FOR REDISTRIBUTION OF SEATS

The rules

1.—(1) The number of constituencies in Great Britain shall not be substantially greater or less than 613.

(2) . . .

(3) The number of constituencies in Wales shall not be less than 35.

(4) The number of constituencies in Northern Ireland shall not be greater than 18 or less than 16, and shall be 17 unless it appears to [the Electoral Commission or (as the case may be) the Boundary Committee] for Northern Ireland that Northern Ireland should for the time being be divided into 16 or (as the case may be) into 18 constituencies.

2. Every constituency shall return a single member.

3. There shall continue to be a constituency which shall include the whole of the City of London and the name of which shall refer to the City of London.

3A. *****

4.—(1) So far as is practicable having regard to rules 1 to [3A]—

(a) in England and Wales,—

   (i) no county or part of a county shall be included in a constituency which includes the whole or part of any other county or the whole or part of a London borough,

   (ii) no London borough or any part of a London borough shall be included in a constituency which includes the whole or part of any other London borough,

(b) in Scotland, regard shall be had to the boundaries of local authority areas,

(c) in Northern Ireland, no ward shall be included partly in one constituency and partly in another.

[(1A) In sub-paragraph (1)(a) above "county" means in relation to Wales, a preserved county (as defined by section 64 of the Local Government (Wales) Act 1994).]

(2) In sub-paragraph (1)(b) above "area" and "local authority" have the same meanings as in the Local Government (Scotland) Act 1973.

5. The electorate of any constituency shall be as near the electoral quota as is practicable having regard to rules 1 to 4; and [the Electoral Commission (as the case may be) a Boundary Committee] may depart from the strict application of rule 4 if it appears to them that a departure is desirable to avoid an excessive disparity between the electorate of any constituency and the electoral quota, or between the electorate of any constituency and that of neighbouring constituencies in the part of the United Kingdom with which they are concerned.

6. [The Electoral Commission or (as the case may be) a Boundary Committee] may depart from the strict application of rules 4 and 5 if special geographical considerations, including in particular the size, shape and accessibility of a constituency, appear to them to render a departure desirable.

General and supplementary

7. It shall not be the duty of [the Electoral Commission or (as the case may be) a Boundary Committee] to aim at giving full effect in all circumstances to the above rules [(except rule 3A)], but they shall take account, so far as they reasonably can—

(a) of the inconveniences attendant on alterations of constituencies other than alterations made for the purposes of rule 4, and

(b) of any local ties which would be broken by such alterations.

8., 9. *****

Public Order Act 1986
(1986, c. 64)

An Act to abolish the common law offences of riot, rout, unlawful assembly and affray and certain statutory offences relating to public order; to create new offences relating to public order; to control public processions and assemblies; to control the stirring up of racial hatred; to provide for the exclusion of certain offenders from sporting events; to create a new offence relating to the con-tamination of or interference with goods; to confer power to direct certain trespassers to leave land; to amend section 7 of the Conspiracy and Protection of Property Act 1875, section 1 of the Prevention of Crime Act 1953, Part V of the Criminal Justice (Scotland) Act 1980 and the Sporting Events (Control of Alcohol etc.) Act 1985; to repeal certain obsolete or unnecessary enactments; and for connected purposes   *[7 November 1986]*

Territorial extent: England and Wales (ss. 1–9, 13, 39, 40(4)); England and Wales, Scotland (remainder)

PART I   NEW OFFENCES

1   Riot

(1) Where 12 or more persons who are present together use or threaten unlawful violence for a common purpose and the conduct of them (taken together) is such as would cause a person of reasonable firmness present at the scene to fear for his personal safety, each of the persons using unlawful violence for the common purpose is guilty of riot.

(2) It is immaterial whether or not the 12 or more use or threaten unlawful violence simultaneously.

(3) The common purpose may be inferred from conduct.

(4) No person of reasonable firmness need actually be, or be likely to be, present at the scene.

(5) Riot may be committed in private as well as in public places.

(6) A person guilty of riot is liable on conviction on indictment to imprisonment for a term not exceeding ten years or a fine or both.

2   Violent disorder

(1) Where 3 or more persons who are present together use or threaten unlawful violence and the conduct of them (taken together) is such as would cause a person of reasonable firmness present at the scene to fear for his personal safety, each of the persons using or threatening unlawful violence is guilty of violent disorder.

(2) It is immaterial whether or not the 3 or more use or threaten unlawful violence simultaneously.

(3) No person of reasonable firmness need actually be, or be likely to be, present at the scene.

(4) Violent disorder may be committed in private as well as in public places.

(5) A person guilty of violent disorder is liable on conviction on indictment to imprison-ment for a term not exceeding 5 years or a fine or both, or on summary conviction to imprisonment for a term not exceeding 6 months or a fine not exceeding the statutory maximum or both.

3 Affray

(1) A person is guilty of affray if he uses or threatens unlawful violence towards another and his conduct is such as would cause a person of reasonable firmness present at the scene to fear for his personal safety.

(2) Where 2 or more persons use or threaten the unlawful violence, it is the conduct of them taken together that must be considered for the purposes of subsection (1).

(3) For the purposes of this section a threat cannot be made by the use of words alone.

(4) No person of reasonable firmness need actually be, or be likely to be, present at the scene.

(5) Affray may be committed in private as well as in public places.

(6) . . .

(7) A person guilty of affray is liable on conviction on indictment to imprisonment for a term not exceeding 3 years or a fine or both, or on summary conviction to imprisonment for a term not exceeding 6 months or a fine not exceeding the statutory maximum or both.

4 Fear or provocation of violence

(1) A person is guilty of an offence if he—

   (a) uses towards another person threatening, abusive or insulting words or behaviour, or

   (b) distributes or displays to another person any writing, sign or other visible representation which is threatening, abusive or insulting,

with intent to cause that person to believe that immediate unlawful violence will be used against him or another by any person, or to provoke the immediate use of unlawful violence by that person or another, or whereby that person is likely to believe that such violence will be used or it is likely that such violence will be provoked.

(2) An offence under this section may be committed in a public or a private place, except that no offence is committed where the words or behaviour are used, or the writing, sign or other visible representation is distributed or displayed, by a person inside a dwelling and the other person is also inside that or another dwelling.

(3) . . .

(4) A person guilty of an offence under this section is liable on summary conviction to imprisonment for a term not exceeding 6 months or a fine not exceeding level 5 on the standard scale or both.

[4A Intentional harassment, alarm or distress

(1) A person is guilty of an offence if, with intent to cause a person harassment, alarm or distress, he—

   (a) uses threatening, abusive or insulting words or behaviour, or disorderly behaviour, or

   (b) displays any writing, sign or other visible representation which is threatening, abusive or insulting,

thereby causing that or another person harassment, alarm or distress.

(2) An offence under this section may be committed in a public or a private place, except that no offence is committed where the words or behaviour are used, or the writing, sign or other visible representation is displayed, by a person inside a dwelling and the person who is harassed, alarmed or distressed is also inside that or another dwelling.

(3) It is a defence for the accused to prove—

   (a) that he was inside a dwelling and had no reason to believe that the words or behaviour used, or the writing, sign or other visible representation displayed, would be heard or seen by a person outside that or any other dwelling, or

   (b) that his conduct was reasonable.

(4) . . .

(5) A person guilty of an offence under this section is liable on summary conviction to imprisonment for a term not exceeding 6 months or a fine not exceeding level 5 on the standard scale or both.]

5   Harassment, alarm or distress

(1) A person is guilty of an offence if he—

    (a) uses threatening, abusive or insulting words or behaviour, or disorderly behaviour, or

    (b) displays any writing, sign or other visible representation which is threatening, abusive or insulting,

within the hearing or sight of a person likely to be caused harassment, alarm or distress thereby.

(2) An offence under this section may be committed in a public or a private place, except that no offence is committed where the words or behaviour are used, or the writing, sign or other visible representation is displayed, by a person inside a dwelling and the other person is also inside that or another dwelling.

(3) It is a defence for the accused to prove—

    (a) that he had no reason to believe that there was any person within hearing or sight who was likely to be caused harassment, alarm or distress, or

    (b) that he was inside a dwelling and had no reason to believe that the words or behaviour used, or the writing, sign or other visible representation displayed, would be heard or seen by a person outside that or any other dwelling, or

    (c) that his conduct was reasonable.

(4), (5) . . .

(6) A person guilty of an offence under this section is liable on summary conviction to a fine not exceeding level 3 on the standard scale.

6   Mental element: miscellaneous

(1) A person is guilty of riot only if he intends to use violence or is aware that his conduct may be violent.

(2) A person is guilty of violent disorder or affray only if he intends to use or threaten violence or is aware that his conduct may be violent or threaten violence.

(3) A person is guilty of an offence under section 4 only if he intends his words or behaviour, or the writing, sign or other visible representation, to be threatening, abusive or insulting, or is aware that it may be threatening, abusive or insulting.

(4) A person is guilty of an offence under section 5 only if he intends his words or behaviour, or the writing, sign or other visible representation, to be threatening, abusive or insulting, or is aware that it may be threatening, abusive or insulting or (as the case may be) he intends his behaviour to be or is aware that it may be disorderly.

(5) For the purposes of this section a person whose awareness is impaired by intoxication shall be taken to be aware of that of which he would be aware if not intoxicated, unless he shows either that his intoxication was not self-induced or that it was caused solely by the taking or administration of a substance in the course of medical treatment.

(6) In subsection (5) "intoxication" means any intoxication, whether caused by drink, drugs or other means, or by a combination of means.

(7) Subsections (1) and (2) do not affect the determination for the purposes of riot or violent disorder of the number of persons who use or threaten violence.

7   Procedure: miscellaneous

(1) No prosecution for an offence of riot or incitement to riot may be instituted except by or with the consent of the Director of Public Prosecutions.

(2)–(4) *****

8   Interpretation

In this Part—

"dwelling" means any structure or part of a structure occupied as a person's home or as other living accommodation (whether the occupation is separate or shared with others) but does not include any part not so occupied, and for this purpose "structure" includes a tent, caravan, vehicle, vessel or other temporary or movable structure;

"violence" means any violent conduct, so that–

(a) except in the context of affray, it includes violent conduct towards property as well as violent conduct towards persons, and

(b) it is not restricted to conduct causing or intended to cause injury or damage but includes any other violent conduct (for example, throwing at or towards a person a missile of a kind capable of causing injury which does not hit or falls short).

9   Offences abolished

(1) The Common Law offences of riot, rout, unlawful assembly and affray are abolished.

(2) *****

10   ***

PART II   PROCESSIONS AND ASSEMBLIES

11   Advance notice of public processions

(1) Written notice shall be given in accordance with this section of any proposal to hold a public procession intended—

(a) to demonstrate support for or opposition to the views or actions of any person or body of persons,

(b) to publicise a cause or campaign, or

(c) to mark or commemorate an event, unless it is not reasonably practicable to give any advance notice of the procession.

(2) Subsection (1) does not apply where the procession is one commonly or customarily held in the police area (or areas) in which it is proposed to be held or is a funeral procession organised by a funeral director acting in the normal course of his business.

(3) The notice must specify the date when it is intended to hold the procession, the time when it is intended to start it, its proposed route, and the name and address of the person (or of one of the persons) proposing to organise it.

(4) Notice must be delivered to a police station—

(a) in the police area in which it is proposed the procession will start, or

(b) where it is proposed the procession will start in Scotland and cross into England, in the first police area in England on the proposed route.

(5) If delivered not less than 6 clear days before the date when the procession is intended to be held, the notice may be delivered by post by the recorded delivery service; but section 7 of the Interpretation Act 1978 (under which a document sent by post is deemed to have been served when posted and to have been delivered in the ordinary course of post) does not apply.

(6) If not delivered in accordance with subsection (5), the notice must be delivered by hand not less than 6 clear days before the date when the procession is intended to be held or, if that is not reasonably practicable, as soon as delivery is reasonably practicable.

(7) Where a public procession is held, each of the persons organising it is guilty of an offence if—

(a) the requirements of this section as to notice have not been satisfied, or

(b) the date when it is held, the time when it starts, or its route, differs from the date, time or route specified in the notice.

(8) It is a defence for the accused to prove that he did not know of, and neither suspected nor had reason to suspect, the failure to satisfy the requirements or (as the case may be) the difference of date, time or route.

(9) To the extent that an alleged offence turns on a difference of date, time or route, it is a defence for the accused to prove that the difference arose from circumstances beyond his control or from something done with the agreement of a police officer or by his direction.

(10) A person guilty of an offence under subsection (7) is liable on summary conviction to a fine not exceeding level 3 on the standard scale.

12 Imposing conditions on public processions

(1) If the senior police officer, having regard to the time or place at which and the circumstances in which any public procession is being held or is intended to be held and to its route or proposed route, reasonably believes that—

    (a) it may result in serious public disorder, serious damage to property or serious disruption to the life of the community, or

    (b) the purpose of the persons organising it is the intimidation of others with a view to compelling them not to do an act they have a right to do, or to do an act they have a right not to do,

he may give directions imposing on the persons organising or taking part in the procession such conditions as appear to him necessary to prevent such disorder, damage, disruption or intimidation, including conditions as to the route of the procession or prohibiting it from entering any public place specified in the directions.

(2) In subsection (1) "the senior police officer" means—

    (a) in relation to a procession being held, or to a procession intended to be held in a case where persons are assembling with a view to taking part in it, the most senior in rank of the police officers present at the scene, and

    (b) in relation to a procession intended to be held in a case where paragraph (a) does not apply, the chief officer of police.

(3) A direction given by a chief officer of police by virtue of subsection (2)(b) shall be given in writing.

(4) A person who organises a public procession and knowingly fails to comply with a condition imposed under this section is guilty of an offence, but it is a defence for him to prove that the failure arose from circumstances beyond his control.

(5) A person who takes part in a public procession and knowingly fails to comply with a condition imposed under this section is guilty of an offence, but it is a defence for him to prove that the failure arose from circumstances beyond his control.

(6) A person who incites another to commit an offence under subsection (5) is guilty of an offence.

(7) . . .

(8) A person guilty of an offence under subsection (4) is liable on summary conviction to imprisonment for a term not exceeding [51 weeks] or a fine not exceeding level 4 on the standard scale or both.

(9) A person guilty of an offence under subsection (5) is liable on summary conviction to a fine not exceeding level 3 on the standard scale.

(10) A person guilty of an offence under subsection (6) is liable on summary conviction to imprisonment for a term not exceeding [51 weeks] or a fine not exceeding level 4 on the standard scale or both, notwithstanding section 45(3) of the Magistrates' Courts Act 1980 (inciter liable to same penalty as incited).

(11) In Scotland this section applies only in relation to a procession being held, and to a procession intended to be held in a case where persons are assembling with a view to taking part in it.

13 Prohibiting public processions

(1) If at any time the chief officer of police reasonably believes that, because of particular circumstances existing in any district or part of a district, the powers under section 12 will not be sufficient to prevent the holding of public processions in that district or part from resulting

in serious public disorder, he shall apply to the council of the district for an order prohibiting for such period not exceeding 3 months as may be specified in the application the holding of all public processions (or of any class of public procession so specified) in the district or part concerned.

(2) On receiving such an application, a council may with the consent of the Secretary of State make an order either in the terms of the application or with such modifications as may be approved by the Secretary of State.

(3) Subsection (1) does not apply in the City of London or the metropolitan police district.

(4) If at any time the Commissioner of Police for the City of London or the Commissioner of Police of the Metropolis reasonably believes that, because of particular circumstances existing in his police area or part of it, the powers under section 12 will not be sufficient to prevent the holding of public processions in that area or part from resulting in serious public disorder, he may with the consent of the Secretary of State make an order prohibiting for such period not exceeding 3 months as may be specified in the order the holding of all public processions (or of any class of public procession so specified) in the area or part concerned.

(5) An order made under this section may be revoked or varied by a subsequent order made in the same way, that is, in accordance with subsections (1) and (2) or subsection (4), as the case may be.

(6) An order under this section shall, if not made in writing, be recorded in writing as soon as practicable after being made.

(7) A person who organises a public procession the holding of which he knows is prohibited by virtue of an order under this section is guilty of an offence.

(8) A person who takes part in a public procession the holding of which he knows is prohibited by virtue of an order under this section is guilty of an offence.

(9) A person who incites another to commit an offence under subsection (8) is guilty of an offence.

(10) . . .

(11) A person guilty of an offence under subsection (7) is liable on summary conviction to imprisonment for a term not exceeding [51 weeks] or a fine not exceeding level 4 on the standard scale or both.

(12) A person guilty of an offence under subsection (8) is liable on summary conviction to a fine not exceeding level 3 on the standard scale.

(13) A person guilty of an offence under subsection (9) is liable on summary conviction to imprisonment for a term not exceeding [51 weeks] or a fine not exceeding level 4 on the standard scale or both, notwithstanding section 45(3) of the Magistrates' Courts Act 1980.

14 Imposing conditions on public assemblies

(1) If the senior police officer, having regard to the time or place at which and the circumstances in which any public assembly is being held or is intended to be held, reasonably believes that—

(a) it may result in serious public disorder, serious damage to property or serious disruption to the life of the community, or

(b) the purpose of the persons organising it is the intimidation of others with a view to compelling them not to do an act they have a right to do, or to do an act they have a right not to do,

he may give directions imposing on the persons organising or taking part in the assembly such conditions as to the place at which the assembly may be (or continue to be) held, its maximum duration, or the maximum number of persons who may constitute it, as appear to him necessary to prevent such disorder, damage, disruption or intimidation.

(2) In subsection (1) "the senior police officer" means—

(a) in relation to an assembly being held, the most senior in rank of the police officers present at the scene, and

(b) in relation to an assembly intended to be held, the chief officer of police.

(3) A direction given by a chief officer of police by virtue of subsection (2)(b) shall be given in writing.

(4) A person who organises a public assembly and knowingly fails to comply with a condition imposed under this section is guilty of an offence, but it is a defence for him to prove that the failure arose from circumstances beyond his control.

(5) A person who takes part in a public assembly and knowingly fails to comply with a condition imposed under this section is guilty of an offence, but it is a defence for him to prove that the failure arose from circumstances beyond his control.

(6) A person who incites another to commit an offence under subsection (5) is guilty of an offence.

(7) . . .

(8) A person guilty of an offence under subsection (4) is liable on summary conviction to imprisonment for a term not exceeding [51 weeks] or a fine not exceeding level 4 on the standard scale or both.

(9) A person guilty of an offence under subsection (5) is liable on summary conviction to a fine not exceeding level 3 on the standard scale.

(10) A person guilty of an offence under subsection (6) is liable on summary conviction to imprisonment for a term not exceeding [51 weeks] or a fine not exceeding level 4 on the standard scale or both, notwithstanding section 45(3) of the Magistrates' Courts Act 1980.

[14A Prohibiting trespassory assemblies

(1) If at any time the chief officer of police reasonably believes that an assembly is intended to be held in any district at a place on land to which the public has no right of access or only a limited right of access and that the assembly—
  (a) is likely to be held without the permission of the occupier of the land or to conduct itself in such a way as to exceed the limits of any permission of his or the limits of the public's right of access, and
  (b) may result—
    (i) in serious disruption to the life of the community, or
    (ii) where the land, or a building or monument on it, is of historical, architectural, archaeological or scientific importance, in significant damage to the land, building or monument,
he may apply to the council of the district for an order prohibiting for a specified period the holding of all trespassory assemblies in the district or a part of it, as specified.

(2) On receiving such an application, a council may—
  (a) in England and Wales, with the consent of the Secretary of State make an order either in the terms of the application or with such modifications as may be approved by the Secretary of State; or
  (b) in Scotland, make an order in the terms of the application.

(3), (4) *****

(5) An order prohibiting the holding of trespassory assemblies operates to prohibit any assembly which—
  (a) is held on land to which the public has no right of access or only a limited right of access, and
  (b) takes place in the prohibited circumstances, that is to say, without the permission of the occupier of the land or so as to exceed the limits of any permission of his or the limits of the public as right of access.

(6) No order under this section shall prohibit the holding of assemblies for a period exceeding 4 days or in an area exceeding an area represented by a circle with a radius of 5 miles from a specified centre.

(7) An order made under this section may be revoked or varied by a subsequent order

made in the same way, that is, in accordance with subsection (1) and (2) or subsection (4), as the case may be.

(8) Any order under this section shall, if not made in writing, be recorded in writing as soon as practicable after being made.

(9) In this section and sections 14B and 14C—

"assembly" means an assembly of 20 or more persons;

"land", means land in the open air;

*****

(9A), (10), (11) *****

14B Offences in connection with trespassory assemblies and arrest therefor

(1) A person who organises an assembly the holding of which he knows is prohibited by an order under section 14A is guilty of an offence.

(2) A person who takes part in an assembly which he knows is prohibited by an order under section 14A is guilty of an offence.

(3) In England and Wales, a person who incites another to commit an offence under subsection (2) is guilty of an offence.

(4) . . .

(5)–(8) *****

14C Stopping persons from proceeding to trespassory assemblies

(1) If a constable in uniform reasonably believes that a person is on his way to an assembly within the area to which an order under section 14A applies which the constable reasonably believes is likely to be an assembly which is prohibited by that order, he may, subject to subsection (2) below—

(a) stop that person, and

(b) direct him not to proceed in the direction of the assembly.

(2) The power conferred by subsection (1) may only be exercised within the area to which the order applies.

(3) A person who fails to comply with a direction under subsection (1) which he knows has been given to him is guilty of an offence.

(4) . . .

(5) A person guilty of an offence under subsection (3) is liable on summary conviction to a fine not exceeding level 3 on the standard scale.]

15 *****

16 Interpretation

In this Part—

*****

"public assembly" means an assembly of [2] or more persons in a public place which is wholly or partly open to the air;

"public place" means—

(a) any highway, or in Scotland any road within the meaning of the Roads (Scotland) Act 1984, and

(b) any place to which at the material time the public or any section of the public has access, on payment or otherwise, as of right or by virtue of express or implied permission;

"public procession" means a procession in a public place.

PART III   RACIAL HATRED

Meaning of "racial hatred"

17   Meaning of "racial hatred"

In this Part "racial hatred" means hatred against a group of persons . . . defined by reference to colour, race, nationality (including citizenship) or ethnic or national origins.

Acts intended or likely to stir up racial hatred

18   Use of words or behaviour or display of written material

(1) A person who uses threatening, abusive or insulting words or behaviour, or displays any written material which is threatening, abusive or insulting, is guilty of an offence if—

(a) he intends thereby to stir up racial hatred, or

(b) having regard to all the circumstances racial hatred is likely to be stirred up thereby.

(2) An offence under this section may be committed in a public or a private place, except that no offence is committed where the words or behaviour are used, or the written material is displayed, by a person inside a dwelling and are not heard or seen except by other persons in that or another dwelling.

(3) . . .

(4) In proceedings for an offence under this section it is a defence for the accused to prove that he was inside a dwelling and had no reason to believe that the words or behaviour used, or the written material displayed, would be heard or seen by a person outside that or any other dwelling.

(5) A person who is not shown to have intended to stir up racial hatred is not guilty of an offence under this section if he did not intend his words or behaviour, or the written material, to be, and was not aware that it might be, threatening, abusive or insulting.

(6) This section does not apply to words or behaviour used, or written material displayed, solely for the purpose of being [included in a programme service].

19   Publishing or distributing written material

(1) A person who publishes or distributes written material which is threatening, abusive or insulting is guilty of an offence if—

(a) he intends thereby to stir up racial hatred, or

(b) having regard to all the circumstances racial hatred is likely to be stirred up thereby.

(2) In proceedings for an offence under this section it is a defence for an accused who is not shown to have intended to stir up racial hatred to prove that he was not aware of the content of the material and did not suspect, and had no reason to suspect, that it was threatening, abusive or insulting.

(3) References in this Part to the publication or distribution of written material are to its publication or distribution to the public or a section of the public.

20   Public performance of play

(1) If a public performance of a play is given which involves the use of threatening, abusive or insulting words or behaviour, any person who presents or directs the performance is guilty of an offence if—

(a) he intends thereby to stir up racial hatred, or

(b) having regard to all the circumstances (and, in particular, taking the performance as a whole) racial hatred is likely to be stirred up thereby.

(2)–(6) *****

21   Distributing, showing or playing a recording

(1) A person who distributes, or shows or plays, a recording of visual images or sounds which are threatening, abusive or insulting is guilty of an offence if—

    (a) he intends thereby to stir up racial hatred, or

    (b) having regard to all the circumstances racial hatred is likely to be stirred up thereby.

(2) In this Part "recording" means any record from which visual images or sounds may, by any means, be reproduced; and references to the distribution, showing or playing of a recording are to its distribution, showing or playing to the public or a section of the public.

(3) In proceedings for an offence under this section it is a defence for an accused who is not shown to have intended to stir up racial hatred to prove that he was not aware of the content of the recording and did not suspect, and had no reason to suspect, that it was threatening, abusive or insulting.

(4) This section does not apply to the showing or playing of a recording solely for the purpose of enabling the recording to be [included in a programme service.]

22 Broadcasting or including programme in cable programme service

(1) If a programme involving threatening, abusive or insulting visual images or sounds is [included in a programme service], each of the persons mentioned in subsection (2) is guilty of an offence if—

    (a) he intends thereby to stir up racial hatred, or

    (b) having regard to all the circumstances racial hatred is likely to be stirred up thereby.

(2) The persons are—

    (a) the person providing the . . . programme service,

    (a) any person by whom the programme is produced or directed, and

    (c) any person by whom offending words or behaviour are used.

(3)–(6) *****

(7), (8) . . .

Racially inflammatory material

23 Possession of racially inflammatory material

(1) A person who has in his possession written material which is threatening, abusive or insulting, or a recording of visual images or sounds which are threatening, abusive or insulting, with a view to—

    (a) in the case of written material, its being displayed, published, distributed, [or included in a programme service], whether by himself or another, or

    (b) in the case of a recording, its being distributed, shown, played, [or included in a programme service], whether by himself or another,

is guilty of an offence if he intends racial hatred to be stirred up thereby or, having regard to all the circumstances, racial hatred is likely to be stirred up thereby.

(2) For this purpose regard shall be had to such display, publication, distribution, show-ing, playing, [or inclusion in a programme service] as he has, or it may reasonably be inferred that he has, in view.

(3) In proceedings for an offence under this section it is a defence for an accused who is not shown to have intended to stir up racial hatred to prove that he was not aware of the content of the written material or recording and did not suspect, and had no reason to suspect, that it was threatening, abusive or insulting.

(4) . . .

24 Powers of entry and search

(1) If in England and Wales a justice of the peace is satisfied by information on oath laid by a constable that there are reasonable grounds for suspecting that a person has possession of written material or a recording in contravention of section 23, the justice may issue a warrant under his hand authorising any constable to enter and search the premises where it is suspected the material or recording is situated.

(2) If in Scotland a sheriff or justice of the peace is satisfied by evidence on oath that there are reasonable grounds for suspecting that a person has possession of written material or a recording in contravention of section 23, the sheriff or justice may issue a warrant authorising any constable to enter and search the premises where it is suspected the material or recording is situated.

(3) A constable entering or searching premises in pursuance of a warrant issued under this section may use reasonable force if necessary.

(4) *****

25   *****

Supplementary provisions

26   Savings for reports of parliamentary or judicial proceedings

(1) Nothing in this Part applies to a fair and accurate report of proceedings in Parliament [or the Scottish Parliament].

(2) Nothing in this Part applies to a fair and accurate report of proceedings publicly heard before a court or tribunal exercising judicial authority where the report is published contemporaneously with the proceedings or, if it is not reasonably practicable or would be unlawful to publish a report of them contemporaneously, as soon as publication is reasonably practicable and lawful.

27   Procedure and punishment

(1) No proceedings for an offence under this Part may be instituted in England and Wales except by or with the consent of the Attorney General.

(2) For the purposes of the rules in England and Wales against charging more than one offence in the same count or information, each of sections 18 to 23 creates one offence.

(3) A person guilty of an offence under this Part is liable—

  (a) on conviction on indictment to imprisonment for a term not exceeding [seven] years or a fine or both;

  (b) on summary conviction to imprisonment for a term not exceeding six months or a fine not exceeding the statutory maximum or both.

28–29   *****
Note: Section 29 provides that "programme service" has the same meaning as in the Broadcasting Act 1990.

30–34, 36, 39   . . .

35, 37–38   *****

40   Amendments repeals and savings

(1)–(3) *****

(4) Nothing in this Act affects the common law powers in England and Wales to deal with or prevent a breach of the peace.

(5) As respects Scotland, nothing in this Act affects any power of a constable under any rule of law.

*****

Criminal Justice Act 1988

(1988, c. 33)

An Act to make fresh provision for extradition; to amend the rules of evidence in criminal proceedings; to provide for the reference by the Attorney General of certain questions relating to sentencing to the Court of Appeal; to amend the law with regard to the jurisdiction and powers of criminal courts, the collection, enforcement and remission of fines imposed by coroners, juries, supervision orders, the detention of children and young persons, probation and the probation service, criminal appeals, anonymity in cases of rape and similar cases, orders under sections 4 and 11 of the Contempt of Court Act 1981 relating to trials on indictment, orders restricting the access of the public to the whole or any part of a trial on indictment or to any proceedings ancillary to such a trial and orders restricting the publication of any report of the whole or any part of a trial on indictment or any such ancillary proceedings, the alteration of names of petty sessions areas, officers of inner London magistrates' courts and the costs and expenses of prosecution witnesses and certain other persons; to make fresh provision for the payment of compensation by the Criminal Injuries Compensation Board; to make provision for the payment of compensation for a miscarriage of justice which has resulted in a wrongful conviction; to create an offence of torture and an offence of having an article with a blade or point in a public place; to create further offences relating to weapons; to create a summary offence of possession of an indecent photograph of a child; to amend the Police and Criminal Evidence Act 1984 in relation to searches, computer data about fingerprints and bail for persons in customs detention; to make provision in relation to the taking of body samples by the police in Northern Ireland; to amend the Bail Act 1976; to give a justice of the peace power to authorise entry and search of premises for offensive weapons; to provide for the enforcement of the Video Recordings Act 1984 by officers of a weights and measures authority and in Northern Ireland by Officers of the Department of Economic Development; to extend to the purchase of easements and other rights over land the power to purchase land conferred on the Secretary of State by section 36 of the Prison Act 1952; and for connected purposes   [29 July 1988]

Territorial extent: England and Wales; Northern Ireland (except section 160)

PART XI   MISCELLANEOUS

Miscarriages of justice

133   Compensation for miscarriages of justice

(1) Subject to subsection (2) below, when a person has been convicted of a criminal offence and when subsequently his conviction has been reversed or he has been pardoned on the ground that a new or newly discovered fact shows beyond reasonable doubt that there has been a miscarriage of justice, the Secretary of State shall pay compensation for the miscarriage of justice to the person who has suffered punishment as a result of such conviction or, if he is dead, to his personal representatives, unless the non-disclosure of the unknown fact was wholly or partly attributable to the person convicted.

(2) No payment of compensation under this section shall be made unless an application for such compensation has been made to the Secretary of State.

(3) The question whether there is a right to compensation under this section shall be determined by the Secretary of State.

(4) If the Secretary of State determines that there is a right to such compensation, the amount of the compensation shall be assessed by an assessor appointed by the Secretary of State.

[(4A) In assessing so much of any compensation payable under this section to or in respect of a person as is attributable to suffering, harm to reputation or similar damage, the assessor shall have regard in particular to–

   (a) the seriousness of the offence of which the person was convicted and the severity of the punishment resulting from the conviction;
   (b) the conduct of the investigation and prosecution of the offence; and
   (c) any other convictions of the person and any punishment resulting from them.]

   (5)–(7) *****

Torture

134 Torture

   (1) A public official or person acting in an official capacity, whatever his nationality, commits the offence of torture if in the United Kingdom or elsewhere he intentionally inflicts severe pain or suffering on another in the performance or purported performance of his official duties.

   (2) A person not falling within subsection (1) above commits the offence of torture, whatever his nationality, if—

   (a) in the United Kingdom or elsewhere he intentionally inflicts severe pain or suffering on another at the instigation or with the consent or acquiescence—
      (i) of a public official; or
      (ii) of a person acting in an official capacity; and
   (b) the official or other person is performing or purporting to perform his official duties when he instigates the commission of the offence or consents to or acquiesces in it.

   (3) It is immaterial whether the pain or suffering is physical or mental and whether it is caused by an act or an omission.

   (4) It shall be a defence for a person charged with an offence under this section in respect of any conduct of his to prove that he had lawful authority, justification or excuse for that conduct.

   (5), (6) *****

135 Requirement of Attorney General's consent for prosecutions

Proceedings for an offence under section 134 above shall not be begun—

   (a) in England and Wales, except by, or with the consent of, the Attorney General; or
   (b) in Northern Ireland, except by, or with the consent of, the [Advocate General for Northern Ireland].

136–158 *****

159 Crown Court proceedings—orders restricting or preventing reports or restricting public access

   (1) A person aggrieved may appeal to the Court of Appeal, if that court grants leave, against—

   (a) an order under section 4 or 11 of the Contempt of Court Act 1981 made in relation to a trial on indictment;
   [(aa) An order made by the Crown Court under section 58(7) or (8) of the Criminal Procedure and Investigations Act 1996 in a case where the court has convicted a person on a trial on indictment;]
   (b) any order restricting the access of the public to the whole or any part of a trial on indictment or to any proceedings ancillary to such a trial; and
   (c) any order restricting the publication of any report of the whole or any part of a trial on indictment or any such ancillary proceedings;

and the decision of the Court of Appeal shall be final.

(2) Subject to Rules of Court, the jurisdiction of the Court of Appeal under this section shall be exercised by the criminal division of the Court, and references to the Court of Appeal in this section shall be construed as references to that division.

(3)–(7) *****

*****

Elected Authorities (Northern Ireland) Act 1989
(1989, c. 3)

An Act to amend the law relating to the franchise at elections to district councils in Northern Ireland, to make provision in relation to a declaration against terrorism to be made by candidates at such elections and at elections to the Northern Ireland Assembly and by persons co-opted as members of district councils, to amend sections 3 and 4 of the Local Government Act (Northern Ireland) 1972, and for connected purposes   [15 March 1989]

Territorial extent: Northern Ireland

1–2 *****

Disqualification for breach of declaration against terrorism or in consequence of imprisonment or detention

3   Declaration against terrorism: local elections

(1) A person is not validly nominated as a candidate at a local election unless his consent to nomination includes a declaration in the form set out in Part I of Schedule 2 to this Act.

(2) *****

4   *****

5   Declaration against terrorism: Assembly elections

A person is not validly nominated as a candidate at an election to the Northern Ireland Assembly unless his consent to nomination includes a declaration in the form set out in Part I of Schedule 2 to this Act.

6   Breach of terms of declaration

(1) A person who has made a declaration required for the purposes of section 3, 4 or 5 of this Act in connection with a local election, an election to the Northern Ireland Assembly or the filling of a casual vacancy in a district council acts in breach of the terms of the declaration if at any time after he is declared to be elected at that election or is chosen to fill that vacancy and while he remains a member of the district council or of the Assembly—

  (a) he expresses support for or approval of—
    (i)   a proscribed organisation, or
    (ii) acts of terrorism (that is to say, violence for political ends) connected with the affairs of Northern Ireland, and
  (b) he does so—
    (i)   at a public meeting, or
    (ii) knowing, or in such circumstances that he can reasonably be expected to know, that the fact that he has made that expression of support or approval is likely to become known to the public.

(2) For the purposes of subsection (1) above a person shall be taken to express support for, or approval of, any matter if his words or actions could reasonably be understood as expressing support for, or approval of, it.

(3) It is immaterial for the purposes of subsection (1) above—
  (a) whether the expression of support or approval is made by spoken or written words, by the display of written matter or by other behaviour, and
  (b) whether it is made in the United Kingdom or elsewhere.

(4), (5) *****

7 *****

8 ***** (allows disqualification for breach of declaration)

9–13 *****

SCHEDULE 1

*****

SCHEDULE 2   DECLARATION AGAINST TERRORISM

PART I   FORM FOR INCLUSION IN CONSENT TO NOMINATION

I declare that, if elected, I will not by word or deed express support for or approval of—
  (a) any organisation that is for the time being a proscribed organisation specified in [Schedule 2 to the Terrorism Act 2000]; or
  (b) acts of terrorism (that is to say, violence for political ends) connected with the affairs of Northern Ireland.

*****

Official Secrets Act 1989

(1989, c. 6)

An Act to replace section 2 of the Official Secrets Act 1911 by provisions protecting more limited classes of official information   [11 May 1989]

Territorial extent: United Kingdom

1   Security and intelligence

(1) A person who is or has been—
  (a) a member of the security and intelligence services; or
  (b) a person notified that he is subject to the provisions of this subsection,
is guilty of an offence if without lawful authority he discloses any information, document or other article relating to security or intelligence which is or has been in his possession by virtue of his position as a member of any of those services or in the course of his work while the notification is or was in force.

(2) The reference in subsection (1) above to disclosing information relating to security or intelligence includes a reference to making any statement which purports to be a disclosure of such information or is intended to be taken by those to whom it is addressed as being such a disclosure.

(3) A person who is or has been a Crown Servant or government contractor is guilty of an offence if without lawful authority he makes a damaging disclosure of any information, document or other article relating to security or intelligence which is or has been in his possession by virtue of his position as such but otherwise than as mentioned in subsection (1) above.

(4) For the purposes of subsection (3) above a disclosure is damaging if—

(a) it causes damage to the work of, or of any part of, the security and intelligence service; or

(b) it is of information or a document or other article which is such that its unauthorised disclosure would be likely to cause such damage or which falls within a class or description of information, documents or articles the unauthorised disclosure of which would be likely to have that effect.

(5) It is a defence for a person charged with an offence under this section to prove that at the time of the alleged offence he did not know, and had no reasonable cause to believe, that the information, document or article in question related to security or intelligence or, in the case of an offence under subsection (3), that the disclosure would be damaging within the meaning of that subsection.

(6)–(8) *****

(9) In this section "security or intelligence" means the work of, or in support of, the security and intelligence services or any part of them, and references to information relating to security or intelligence include references to information held or transmitted by those services or by persons in support of, or of any part of, them.

2 Defence

(1) A person who is or has been a Crown servant or government contractor is guilty of an offence if without lawful authority he makes a damaging disclosure of any information, document or other article relating to defence which is or has been in his possession by virtue of his position as such.

(2) For the purposes of subsection (1) above a disclosure is damaging if—

(a) it damages the capability of, or of any part of, the armed forces of the Crown to carry out their tasks or leads to loss of life or injury to members of those forces or serious damage to the equipment or installations of those forces; or

(b) otherwise than as mentioned in paragraph (a) above, it endangers the interests of the United Kingdom abroad, seriously obstructs the promotion or protection by the United Kingdom of those interests or endangers the safety of British citizens abroad; or

(c) it is of information or of a document or article which is such that its unauthorised disclosure would be likely to have any of those effects.

(3) It is a defence for a person charged with an offence under this section to prove that at the time of the alleged offence he did not know, and had no reasonable cause to believe, that the information, document or article in question related to defence or that its disclosure would be damaging within the meaning of subsection (1) above.

(4) *****

3 International relations

(1) A person who is or has been a Crown servant or government contractor is guilty of an offence if without lawful authority he makes a damaging disclosure of–

(a) any information, document or other article relating to international relations; or

(b) any confidential information, document or other article which was obtained from a State other than the United Kingdom or an international organisation,

being information or a document or article which is or has been in his possession by virtue of his position as a Crown servant or government contractor.

(2) For the purposes of subsection (1) above a disclosure is damaging if—

(a) it endangers the interests of the United Kingdom abroad, seriously obstructs the promotion or protection by the United Kingdom of those interests or endangers the safety of British citizens abroad; or

(b) it is of information or of a document or article which is such that its unauthorised disclosure would be likely to have any of those effects.

(3) In the case of information or a document or article within subsection (1)(b) above—

(a) the fact that it is confidential, or

(b) its nature or contents,

may be sufficient to establish for the purposes of subsection (2)(b) above that the information, document or article is such that its unauthorised disclosure would be likely to have any of the effects there mentioned.

(4) It is a defence for a person charged with an offence under this section to prove that at the time of the alleged offence he did not know, and had no reasonable cause to believe, that the information, document or article in question was such as is mentioned in subsection (1) above or that its disclosure would be damaging within the meaning of that subsection.

(5), (6) *****

4 Crime and special investigation powers

(1) A person who is or has been a Crown servant or government contractor is guilty of an offence if without lawful authority he discloses any information, document or other article to which this section applies and which is or has been in his possession by virtue of his position as such.

(2) This section applies to any information, document or other article—

(a) the disclosure of which—

(i) results in the commission of an offence; or

(ii) facilitates an escape from legal custody or the doing of any other act prejudicial to the safekeeping of persons in legal custody; or

(iii) impedes the prevention or detection of offences or the apprehension or prosecution of suspected offenders; or

(b) which is such that its unauthorised disclosure would be likely to have any of those effects.

(3) *****

(4) It is a defence for a person charged with an offence under this section in respect of a disclosure falling within subsection (2)(a) above to prove that at the time of the alleged offence he did not know, and had no reasonable cause to believe, that the disclosure would have any of the effects there mentioned.

(5) It is a defence for a person charged with an offence under this section in respect of any other disclosure to prove that at the time of the alleged offence he did not know, and had no reasonable cause to believe, that the information, document or article in question was information or a document or article to which this section applies.

(6) In this section "legal custody" includes detention in pursuance of any enactment or any instrument made under an enactment.

5–6 *****

7 Authorised disclosures

(1) For the purposes of this Act a disclosure by—

(a) a Crown servant; or

(b) a person, not being a Crown servant or government contractor, in whose case a notification for the purposes of section 1(1) above is in force,

is made with lawful authority if, and only if, it is made in accordance with his official duty.

(2) For the purposes of this Act a disclosure by a government contractor is made with lawful authority if, and only if, it is made—

(a) in accordance with an official authorisation; or

(b) for the purposes of the functions by virtue of which he is a government contractor and without contravening an official restriction.

(3) For the purposes of this Act a disclosure made by any other person is made with lawful authority if, and only if, it is made—

(a) to a Crown servant for the purposes of his functions as such; or

(b) in accordance with an official authorisation.

(4) It is a defence for a person charged with an offence under any of the foregoing provisions of this Act to prove that at the time of the alleged offence he believed that he had lawful authority to make the disclosure in question and had no reasonable cause to believe otherwise.

(5), (6) *****

8 Safeguarding of information

(1) Where a Crown servant or government contractor, by virtue of his position as such, has in his possession or under his control any document or other article which it would be an offence under any of the foregoing provisions of this Act for him to disclose without lawful authority he is guilty of an offence if—

(a) being a Crown servant, he retains the document or article contrary to his official duty; or

(b) being a government contractor, he fails to comply with an official direction for the return or disposal of the document or article,

or if he fails to take such care to prevent the unauthorised disclosure of the document or article as a person in his position may reasonably be expected to take.

(2) It is a defence for a Crown servant charged with an offence under subsection (1)(a) above to prove that at the time of the alleged offence he believed that he was acting in accordance with his official duty and had no reasonable cause to believe otherwise.

(3)–(9) *****

9 Prosecutions

(1) Subject to subsection (2) below, no prosecution for an offence under this Act shall be instituted in England and Wales or in Northern Ireland except by or with the consent of the Attorney General or, as the case may be, the [Advocate General for Northern Ireland].

(2) *****

10 Penalties

(1) A person guilty of an offence under any provision of this Act other than section 8(1), (4) or (5) shall be liable—

(a) on conviction on indictment, to imprisonment for a term not exceeding two years or a fine or both;

(b) on summary conviction, to imprisonment for a term not exceeding six months or a fine not exceeding the statutory maximum or both.

(2) A person guilty of an offence under section 8(1), (4) or (5) above shall be liable on summary conviction to imprisonment for a term not exceeding [51 weeks] or a fine not exceeding level 5 on the standard scale or both.

11 Arrest, search and trial

(1) ...

(2) *****

(3) Section 9(1) of the Official Secrets Act 1911 (search warrants) shall have effect as if references to offences under that Act included references to offences under any provision of this Act other than section 8(1), (4) or (5); and the following provisions of the Police and Criminal Evidence Act 1984, that is to say—

(a) section 9(2) (which excludes items subject to legal privilege and certain other material from powers of search conferred by previous enactments); and

(b) paragraph 3(b) of Schedule 1 (which prescribes access conditions for the special procedure laid down in that Schedule), shall apply to section 9(1) of the said Act of 1911 as extended by this subsection as they apply to that section as originally enacted.

(4) Section 8(4) of the Official Secrets Act 1920 (exclusion of public from hearing on grounds of national safety) shall have effect as if references to offences under that Act included references to offences under any provision of this Act other than section 8(1), (4) or (5).

(5) Proceedings for an offence under this Act may be taken in any place in the United Kingdom.

12   "Crown servant" and "government contractor"

(1) In this Act "Crown servant" means—

(a) a Minister of the Crown;

[(aa) a member of the Scottish Executive or a Junior Scottish Minister;]

(b) . . .

(c) any person employed in the civil service of the Crown, including Her Majesty's Diplomatic Service, Her Majesty's Overseas Civil Service, the civil service of Northern Ireland and the Northern Ireland Court Service;

(d) any member of the naval, military or air forces of the Crown, including any person employed by an association established for the purposes of [Part XI the Reserve Forces Act 1996];

(e) any constable and any other person employed or appointed in or for the purposes of any police force [(including the Police Service of Northern Ireland and the Police Service of Northern Ireland Reserve)] [or of the Serious Organised Crime Agency];

(f) any person who is member or employee of a prescribed body or a body of a pre-scribed class and either is prescribed for the purposes of this paragraph or belongs to a prescribed class of members or employees of any such body;

(g) any person who is the holder of a prescribed office or who is an employee of such a holder and either is prescribed for the purposes of this paragraph or belongs to a prescribed class of such employees.

(2) In this Act "government contractor" means, subject to subsection (3) below, any person who is not a Crown servant but who provides, or is employed in the provision of, goods or services—

(a) for the purposes of any Minister or person mentioned in paragraph (a) or (b) of subsection (1) above [, of any office-holder in the Scottish Administration], of any of the services, forces or bodies mentioned in that subsection or of the holder of any office prescribed under that subsection;

[(aa) for the purposes of the National Assembly for Wales; or]

(b) under an agreement or arrangement certified by the Secretary of State as being one to which the government of a State other than the United Kingdom or an inter-national organisation is a party or which is subordinate to, or made for the purposes of implementing, any such agreement or arrangement.

(3)–(5) *****

13   Other interpretation provisions

(1) In this Act—

"disclose" and "disclosure", in relation to a document or other article, include parting with possession of it;

"international organisation" means, subject to subsections (2) and (3) below, an organisa-tion of which only States are members and includes a reference to any organ of such an organisation;

"prescribed" means prescribed by an order made by the Secretary of State;

"State" includes the government of a State and any organ of its government and references to a State other than the United Kingdom include references to any territory outside the United Kingdom.

(2) In section 12(2)(b) above the reference to an international organisation includes a reference to any such organisation whether or not one of which only States are members and includes a commercial organisation.

(3) In determining for the purposes of subsection (1) above whether only States are members of an organisation, any member which is itself an organisation of which only States are members, or which is an organ of such an organisation, shall be treated as a State.
*****

Security Service Act 1989
(1989, c. 5)

An Act to place the Security Service on a statutory basis; to enable certain actions to be taken on the authority of warrants issued by the Secretary of State, with provision for the issue of such warrants to be kept under review by a Commissioner; to establish a procedure for the investigation by a Tribunal or, in some cases, by the Commissioner of complaints about the Service; and for connected purposes   [27 April 1989]

Territorial extent: United Kingdom

1   The Security Service
(1) There shall continue to be a Security Service (in this Act referred to as "the Service") under the authority of the Secretary of State.

(2) The function of the Service shall be the protection of national security and, in particular, its protection against threats from espionage, terrorism and sabotage, from the activities of agents of foreign powers and from actions intended to overthrow or undermine parliamentary democracy by political, industrial or violent means.

(3) It shall also be the function of the Service to safeguard the economic well-being of the United Kingdom against threats posed by the actions or intentions of persons outside the British Islands.

[(4) It shall also be the function of the Service to act in support of the activities of police forces [, the Serious Organised Crime Agency,] and other law enforcement agencies in the prevention and detection of serious crime.]

(5) *****

2   The Director-General
(1) The operations of the Service shall continue to be under the control of a Director-General appointed by the Secretary of State.

(2) The Director-General shall be responsible for the efficiency of the Service and it shall be his duty to ensure—

(a) that there are arrangements for securing that no information is obtained by the Service except so far as necessary for the proper discharge of its functions or disclosed by it except so far as necessary for that purpose or for the purpose of [the prevention or detection of] serious crime [or for the purpose of any criminal proceedings]; and

(b) that the Service does not take any action to further the interests of any political party; [and

(c) that there are arrangements, agreed with [the Director General of the Serious Organised Crime Agency], for co-ordinating the activities of the Service in pursuance of section 1(4) of this Act with the activities of police forces [, the Serious Organised Crime Agency] and other law enforcement agencies.]

(3) The arrangements mentioned in subsection (2)(a) above shall be such as to ensure that information in the possession of the Service is not disclosed for use in determining whether a person should be employed, or continue to be employed, by any person, or in any office or capacity, except in accordance with provisions in that behalf approved by the Secretary of State.

(3A) *****

(3B) ...

(4) The Director-General shall make an annual report on the work of the Service to the Prime Minister and the Secretary of State and may at any time report to either of them on any matter relating to its work.

3–5 ...

*****

Trade Union and Labour Relations (Consolidation) Act 1992

(1992, c. 52)

An Act to consolidate the enactments relating to collective labour relations, that is to say, to trade unions, employers' associations, industrial relations and industrial action   [16 July 1992]

Territorial extent: Great Britain (but see section 242 below)

*****

PART V   INDUSTRIAL ACTION

220   Peaceful picketing

(1) It is lawful for a person in contemplation or furtherance of a trade dispute to attend—

   (a) at or near his own place of work, or

   (b) if he is an official of a trade union, at or near the place of work of a member of the union whom he is accompanying and whom he represents,

for the purpose only of peacefully obtaining or communicating information, or peacefully persuading any person to work or abstain from working.

(2) If a person works or normally works—

   (a) otherwise than at any one place, or

   (b) at a place the location of which is such that attendance there for a purpose mentioned in subsection (1) is impracticable,

his place of work for the purposes of that subsection shall be any premises of his employer from which he works or from which his work is administered.

(3) In the case of a worker not in employment where—

   (a) his last employment was terminated in connection with a trade dispute, or

   (b) the termination of his employment was one of the circumstances giving rise to a trade dispute,

in relation to that dispute his former place of work shall be treated for the purposes of subsection (1) as being his place of work.

(4) A person who is an official of a trade union by virtue only of having been elected or appointed to be a representative of some of the members of the union shall be regarded for the purposes of subsection (1) as representing only those members; but otherwise an official of a union shall be regarded for those purposes as representing all its members.

221–239   ***

Criminal offences

240   Breach of contract involving injury to persons or property

(1) A person commits an offence who wilfully and maliciously breaks a contract of service or hiring, knowing or having reasonable cause to believe that the probable consequences of his so doing, either alone or in combination with others, will be—

    (a) to endanger human life or cause serious bodily injury, or

    (b) to expose valuable property, whether real or personal, to destruction or serious injury.

(2) Subsection (1) applies equally whether the offence is committed from malice conceived against the person endangered or injured or, as the case may be, the owner of the property destroyed or injured, or otherwise.

(3) A person guilty of an offence under this section is liable on summary conviction to imprisonment for a term not exceeding three months or to a fine not exceeding level 2 on the standard scale or both.

(4) This section does not apply to seamen.

241   Intimidation or annoyance by violence or otherwise

(1) A person commits an offence who, with a view to compelling another person to abstain from doing or to do any act which that person has a legal right to do or abstain from doing, wrongfully and without legal authority—

    (a) uses violence to or intimidates that person or his [spouse or civil partner] or children, or injures his property,

    (b) persistently follows that person about from place to place,

    (c) hides any tools, clothes or other property owned or used by that person, or deprives him of or hinders him in the use thereof,

    (d) watch or besets the house or other place where the person resides, works, carries on business or happens to be, or the approach to any such house or place, or

    (e) follows that person with two or more other persons in a disorderly manner in or through any street or road.

(2) A person guilty of an offence under this section is liable on summary conviction to imprisonment for a term not exceeding six months or a fine not exceeding level 5 on the standard scale, or both.

(3) . . .

242   Restriction of offence of conspiracy: England and Wales

(1) Where in pursuance of any such agreement as is mentioned in section 1(1) of the Criminal Law Act 1977 (which provides for the offence of conspiracy) the acts in question in relation to an offence are to be done in contemplation or furtherance of a trade dispute, the offence shall be disregarded for the purposes of that subsection if it is a summary offence which is not punishable with imprisonment.

(2) This section extends to England and Wales only.

*****

Tribunals and Inquiries Act 1992

(1992, c. 53)

An Act to consolidate the Tribunals and Inquiries Act 1971 and certain other enactments relating to tribunals and inquiries   [16 July 1992]

Territorial extent: United Kingdom

The Council on Tribunals and their functions

1   The Council on Tribunals
   (1) There shall continue to be a council entitled the Council on Tribunals (in this Act referred to as "the Council")—
   (a) to keep under review the constitution and working of the tribunals specified in Schedule 1 (being the tribunals constituted under or for the purposes of the statutory provisions specified in that Schedule) and, from time to time, to report on their constitution and working;
   (b) to consider and report on such particular matters as may be referred to the Council under this Act with respect to tribunals other than the ordinary courts of law, whether or not specified in Schedule 1, or any such tribunal; and
   (c) to consider and report on such matters as may be referred to the Council under this Act, or as the council may determine to be of special importance, with respect to administrative procedures involving, or which may involve, the holding by or on behalf of a Minister of a statutory inquiry, or any such procedure.
   (2) Nothing in this section authorises or requires the Council to deal with any matter with respect to which the Parliament of Northern Ireland had power to make laws.

2   Composition of the Council and the Scottish Committee
   (1) Subject to subsection (3), the Council shall consist of not more than fifteen nor less than ten members appointed by the Lord Chancellor and the [Scottish Ministers], and one of the members shall be so appointed to be chairman of the Council.
   (2) There shall be a Scottish Committee of the Council (in this Act referred to as "the Scottish Committee") which, subject to subsection (3), shall consist of–
   (a) either two or three members of the Council designated by the [Scottish Ministers], and
   (b) either three or four persons, not being members of the Council, appointed by the [Scottish Ministers];
and the [Scottish Ministers] shall appoint one of the members of the Scottish Committee (being a member of the Council) to be chairman of the Scottish Committee.
   (3) In addition to the persons appointed or designated under subsection (1) or (2), the Parliamentary Commissioner for Administration [and the Scottish Public Services Ombudsman shall by virtue of their offices be members] of the Council and of the Scottish Committee.
   (4) In appointing members of the Council regard shall be had to the need for representation of the interests of persons in Wales.

3–4   ***

Composition and procedure of tribunals and inquiries

5   Recommendations of Council as to appointment of members of tribunals
   (1) Subject to section 6 but without prejudice to the generality of section 1(1)(a), the Council may make to the appropriate Minister general recommendations as to the making of appointments to membership of any tribunals mentioned in Schedule 1 or of panels constituted for the purposes of any such tribunals; and (without prejudice to any statutory provisions having effect with respect to such appointments) the appropriate Minister shall have regard to recommendations under this section.
   (2) In this section "the appropriate Minister", in relation to appointments of any description, means the Minister making the appointments or, if they are not made by a Minister, the Minister in charge of the government department concerned with the tribunals in question.

(3) *****

6 Appointment of chairmen of certain tribunals

(1) The chairman, or any person appointed to act as chairman, of any of the tribunals to which this subsection applies shall (without prejudice to any statutory provisions as to qualifications) be selected by the appropriate authority from a panel of persons appointed by the Lord Chancellor.

(2) Members of panels constituted under this section shall hold and vacate office under the terms of the instruments under which they are appointed, but may resign office by notice in writing to the Lord Chancellor; and any such member who ceases to hold office shall be eligible for re-appointment.

(3)–(9) *****

7 Concurrence required for removal of members of certain tribunals

(1) Subject to subsection (2), the power of a Minister . . . to terminate a person's membership of any tribunal specified in Schedule 1, or of a panel constituted for the purposes of any such tribunal, shall be exercisable only with the consent of—

(a) the Lord Chancellor, [(unless he is the minister terminating the person's membership)] the Lord President of the Court of Session and the Lord Chief Justice of Northern Ireland, if the tribunal sits in all parts of the United Kingdom;

(b) the Lord Chancellor [(unless he is the minister terminating the person's membership)] and the Lord President of the Court of Session, if the tribunal sits in all parts of Great Britain;

(c) the Lord Chancellor [(unless he is the minister terminating the person's membership)] and the Lord Chief Justice of Northern Ireland, if the tribunal sits both in England and Wales and in Northern Ireland;

(d) the Lord Chancellor [(unless he is the minister terminating the person's membership) and the Lord Chief Justice of England and Wales] if the tribunal does not sit outside England and Wales;

(e) the Lord President of the Court of Session, if the tribunal sits only in Scotland;

(f) the Lord Chief Justice of Northern Ireland, if the tribunal sits only in Northern Ireland.

(2) *****

(3) . . .

8–9 *****

Judicial control of tribunals etc.

10 Reasons to be given for decisions of tribunals and Ministers

(1) Subject to the provisions of this section and of section 14, where—

(a) any tribunal specified in Schedule 1 gives any decision, or

(b) any Minister notifies any decision taken by him—

(i) after a statutory inquiry has been held by him or on his behalf, or

(ii) in a case in which a person concerned could (whether by objecting or otherwise) have required a statutory inquiry to be so held,

it shall be the duty of the tribunal or Minister to furnish a statement, either written or oral, of the reasons for the decision if requested, on or before the giving or notification of the decision, to state the reasons.

(2) The statement referred to in subsection (1) may be refused, or the specification of the reasons restricted, on grounds of national security.

(3), (4) *****

(5) Subsection (1) does not apply—

(a) to decisions in respect of which any statutory provision has effect, apart from this section, as to the giving of reasons,

(b) to decisions of a Minister in connection with the preparation, making, approval, confirmation, or concurrence in regulations, rules or bye-laws, or orders or schemes of a legislative and not executive character; . . .

(6) Any statement of the reasons for a decision referred to in paragraph (a) or (b) of subsection (1), whether given in pursuance of that subsection or of any other statutory provision, shall be taken to form part of the decision and accordingly to be incorporated in the record.

(7), (8) *****

11 *****

12   Supervisory functions of superior courts not excluded by Acts passed before 1st August 1958

(1) As respects England and Wales—

(a) any provision in an Act passed before 1st August 1958 that any order or determination shall not be called into question in any court, or

(b) any provision in such an Act which by similar words excludes any of the powers of the High Court,

shall not have effect so as to prevent the removal of the proceedings into the High Court by order of certiorari or to prejudice the powers of the High Court to make orders of mandamus.

(2) As respects Scotland—

(a) any provision in an Act passed before 1st August 1958 that any order or determination shall not be called into question in any court, or

(b) any provision in such an Act which by similar words excludes any jurisdiction which the Court of Session would otherwise have to entertain an application for reduction or suspension of any order or determination, or otherwise to consider the validity of any order or determination,

shall not have effect so as to prevent the exercise of any such jurisdiction.

(3) Nothing in this section shall apply—

(a) to any order or determination of a court of law, or

(b) where an Act makes special provision for application to the High Court or the Court of Session within a time limited by the Act.

13–19, Schedules *****

European Communities (Amendment) Act 1993

(1993, c. 32)

An Act to make provision consequential on the Treaty on European Union signed at Maastricht on 7th February 1992   [20 July 1993]

Territorial extent: United Kingdom

1 *****

2   Economic and monetary union

No notification shall be given to the Council of the European Communities that the United Kingdom intends to move to the third stage of economic and monetary union (in accordance with the Protocol on certain provisions relating to the United Kingdom adopted at Maastricht on 7th February 1992) unless a draft of the notification has first been approved by Act of Parliament and unless Her Majesty's Government has reported to Parliament on its proposals for the co-ordination of economic policies, its role in the European Council of Finance Ministers (ECOFIN) in pursuit of the objectives of Article 2 of the Treaty establishing the European Community as provided for in Articles 103 and 102a, and the work of the European Monetary Institute in preparation for economic and monetary union.

*****

Criminal Justice and Public Order Act 1994
(1994, c. 33)

An Act to make further provision in relation to criminal justice (including employment in the prison service); to amend or extend the criminal law and powers for preventing crime and enforcing that law; to amend the Video Recordings Act 1984; and for purposes connected with those purposes   [3 November 1994]

Territorial extent: England and Wales, Scotland (ss. 61–66, 163), United Kingdom (ss. 68, 69), England and Wales (remaining provisions printed here). Sections 34–37 (below) have been applied, with modifications, to the armed forces by the Criminal Justice and Public Order Act 1994 (Application to the Armed Forces) Order 1997 (SI 1997/16)

Inferences from accused's silence

34   Effect of accused's failure to mention facts when questioned or charged
   (1) Where, in any proceedings against a person for an offence, evidence is given that the accused—
   (a) at any time before he was charged with the offence, on being questioned under caution by a constable trying to discover whether or by whom the offence had been committed, failed to mention any fact relied on in his defence in those proceedings; or
   (b) on being charged with the offence or officially informed that he might be prosecuted for it, failed to mention any such fact,
being a fact which in the circumstances existing at the time the accused could reasonably have been expected to mention when so questioned, charged or informed, as the case may be, subsection (2) below applies.
   (2) Where this subsection applies—
   [(a) ...
   (b) a judge, in deciding whether to grant an application made by the accused under [paragraph 2 of Schedule 3 to the Crime and Disorder Act 1998];
   (c) the court, in determining whether there is a case to answer; and
   (d) the court or jury, in determining whether the accused is guilty of the offence charged,
may draw such inferences from the failure as appear proper.
   [(2A) Where the accused was at an authorised place of detention at the time of the failure, subsections (1) and (2) above do not apply if he had not been allowed an opportunity to consult a solicitor prior to being questioned, charged or informed as mentioned in subsection (1) above.]
   (3) Subject to any directions by the court, evidence tending to establish the failure may be given before or after evidence tending to establish the fact which the accused is alleged to have failed to mention.
   (4) This section applies in relation to questioning by persons (other than constables) charged with the duty of investigating offences or charging offenders as it applies in relation

to questioning by constables; and in subsection (1) above "officially informed" means informed by a constable or any such person.

(5) This section does not—

(a) prejudice the admissibility in evidence of the silence or other reaction of the accused in the face of anything said in his presence relating to the conduct in respect of which he is charged, in so far as evidence thereof would be admissible apart from this section; or

(b) preclude the drawing of any inference from any such silence or other reaction of the accused which could properly be drawn apart from this section.

(6) *****

(7) . . .

35   Effect of accused's silence at trial

(1) At the trial of any person . . . for an offence, subsections (2) and (3) below apply unless—

(a) the accused's guilt is not in issue; or

(b) it appears to the court that the physical or mental condition of the accused makes it undesirable for him to give evidence;

but subsection (2) below does not apply if, at the conclusion of the evidence for the prosecution, his legal representative informs the court that the accused will give evidence or, where he is unrepresented, the court ascertains from him that he will give evidence.

(2) Where this subsection applies, the court shall, at the conclusion of the evidence for the prosecution, satisfy itself (in the case of proceedings on indictment [with a jury], in the presence of the jury) that the accused is aware that the stage has been reached at which evidence can be given for the defence and that he can, if he wishes, give evidence and that, if he chooses not to give evidence, or having been sworn, without good cause refuses to answer any question, it will be permissible for the court or jury to draw such inferences as appear proper from his failure to give evidence or his refusal, without good cause, to answer any question.

(3) Where this subsection applies, the court or jury, in determining whether the accused is guilty of the offence charged, may draw such inferences as appear proper from the failure of the accused to give evidence or his refusal, without good cause, to answer any question.

(4) This section does not render the accused compellable to give evidence on his own behalf, and he shall accordingly not be guilty of contempt of court by reason of a failure to do so.

(5) For the purposes of this section a person who, having been sworn, refuses to answer any question shall be taken to do so without good cause unless—

(a) he is entitled to refuse to answer the question by virtue of any enactment, whenever passed or made, or on the ground of privilege; or

(b) the court in the exercise of its general discretion excuses him from answering it.

(6) . . .

(7) *****

36   Effect of accused's failure or refusal to account for objects, substances or marks

(1) Where—

(a) a person is arrested by a constable, and there is—

(i)   on his person; or

(ii) in or on his clothing or footwear; or

(iii) otherwise in his possession; or

(iv) in any place in which he is at the time of his arrest,

any object, substance or mark, or there is any mark on any such object; and

(b) that or another constable investigating the case reasonably believes that the presence of the object, substance or mark may be attributable to the participation of the person arrested in the commission of an offence specified by the constable; and

(c) the constable informs the person arrested that he so believes, and requests him to account for the presence of the object, substance or mark; and

(d) the person fails or refuses to do so, then if, in any proceedings against the person for the offence so specified, evidence of those matters is given,

subsection (2) below applies.

(2) Where this subsection applies–

(a) . . .

(b) a judge, in deciding whether to grant an application made by the accused under [paragraph 2 of Schedule 3 to the Crime and Disorder Act 1998];

(c) the court, in determining whether there is a case to answer, and

(d) the court or jury, in determining whether the accused is guilty of the offence charged,

may draw such inferences from the failure or refusal as appear proper.

(3) Subsections (1) and (2) above apply to the condition of clothing or footwear as they apply to a substance or mark thereon.

(4) Subsections (1) and (2) above do not apply unless the accused was told in ordinary language by the constable when making the request mentioned in subsection (1)(c) above what the effect of this section would be if he failed or refused to comply with the request.

[(4A) Where the accused was at an authorised place of detention at the time of the failure or refusal, subsections (1) and (2) above do not apply if he had not been allowed an opportunity to consult a solicitor prior to the request being made.]

(5) *****

(6) This section does not preclude the drawing of any inference from a failure or refusal of the accused to account for the presence of an object, substance or mark or from the condition of clothing or footwear which could properly be drawn apart from this section.

(7) *****

(8) . . .

37 Effect of accused's failure or refusal to account for presence at a particular place

(1) Where—

(a) a person arrested by a constable was found by him at a place at or about the time the offence for which he was arrested is alleged to have been committed; and

(b) that or another constable investigating the offence reasonably believes that the presence of the person at that place and at that time may be attributable to his participation in the commission of the offence; and

(c) the constable informs the person that he so believes, and requests him to account for that presence; and

(d) the person fails or refuses to do so,

then if, in any proceedings against the person for the offence, evidence of those matters is given, subsection (2) below applies.

(2) Where this subsection applies—

(a) . . . .

(b) a judge, in deciding whether to grant an application made by the accused under [paragraph 2 of Schedule 3 to the Crime and Disorder Act 1998];

(c) the court, in determining whether there is a case to answer; and

(d) the court or jury, in determining whether the accused is guilty of the offence charged,

may draw such inferences from the failure or refusal as appear proper.

(3) Subsections (1) and (2) do not apply unless the accused was told in ordinary language by the constable when making the request mentioned in subsection (1)(c) above what the effect of this section would be if he failed or refused to comply with the request.

[(3A) Where the accused was at an authorised place of detention at the time of the failure or refusal, subsections (1) and (2) do not apply if he had not been allowed an opportunity to consult a solicitor prior to the request being made.]

(4) *****

(5) This section does not preclude the drawing of any inference from a failure or refusal of the accused to account for his presence at a place which could properly be drawn apart from this section.

(6) *****

(7) . . .

38–59 *****

Powers of police to stop and search

60 Powers to stop and search in anticipation of violence

[(1) If a police officer of or above the rank of inspector reasonably believes—
- (a) that incidents involving serious violence may take place in any locality in his police area, and that it is expedient to give an authorisation under this section to prevent their occurrence, or
- (b) that persons are carrying dangerous instruments or offensive weapons in any locality in his police area without good reason,

he may give an authorisation that the powers conferred by this section are to be exercisable at any place within that locality for a specified period not exceeding 24 hours.]

(2) . . .

(3) If it appears to [an officer of or above the rank of] superintendent that it is expedient to do so, having regard to offences which have, or are reasonably suspected to have, been committed in connection with any [activity] falling within the authorisation, he may direct that the authorisation shall continue in being for a further [24] hours.

(3A) *****

(4) This section confers on any constable in uniform power—
- (a) to stop any pedestrian and search him or anything carried by him for offensive weapons or dangerous instruments,
- (b) to stop any vehicle and search the vehicle, its driver and any passenger for offensive weapons or dangerous instruments.

(4A) . . .

(5) A constable may, in the exercise of [the powers conferred by subsection (4) above], stop any person or vehicle and make any search he thinks fit whether or not he has any grounds for suspecting that the person or vehicle is carrying weapons or articles of that kind.

(6) If in the course of a search under this section a constable discovers a dangerous instrument or an article which he has reasonable grounds for suspecting to be an offensive weapon, he may seize it.

(7)–(10A) *****

(11) In this section—
*****

"dangerous instruments" means instruments which have a blade or are sharply pointed;

"offensive weapon" has the meaning given by section 1(9) of the Police and Criminal Evidence Act 1984 [or, in relation to Scotland, section 47(4) of the Criminal Law (Consolidation) (Scotland) Act 1995]; and
*****

"vehicle" includes a caravan as defined in section 29(1) of the Caravan Sites and Control of Development Act 1960.

[(11A) For the purposes of this section, a person carries a dangerous instrument or an offensive weapon if he has it in his possession.]

(12) The powers conferred by this section are in addition to, and not in derogation of, any power otherwise conferred.

[60AA   Powers to require removal of disguises

(1) Where—

(a) an authorisation under section 60 is for the time being in force in relation to any locality for any period, or

(b) an authorisation under subsection (3) that the powers conferred by subsection (2) shall be exercisable at any place in a locality is in force for any period,

those powers shall be exercisable at any place in that locality at any time in that period.

(2) This subsection confers power on any constable in uniform—

(a) to require any person to remove any item which the constable reasonably believes that person is wearing wholly or mainly for the purpose of concealing his identity;

(b) to seize any item which the constable reasonably believes any person intends to wear wholly or mainly for that purpose.

(3) If a police officer of or above the rank of inspector reasonably believes—

(a) that activities may take place in any locality in his police area that are likely (if they take place) to involve the commission of offences, and

(b) that it is expedient, in order to prevent or control the activities, to give an author-isation under this subsection, he may give an authorisation that the powers con-ferred by this section shall be exercisable at any place within that locality for a specified period not exceeding twenty-four hours.

(4), (5) *****

(7) A person who fails to remove an item worn by him when required to do so by a constable in the exercise of his power under this section shall be liable, on summary convic-tion, to imprisonment for a term not exceeding [51 weeks] or to a fine not exceeding level 3 on the standard scale or both.

(8), (9) *****

(10) The powers conferred by this section are in addition to, and not in derogation of, any power otherwise conferred.

(11) This section does not extend to Scotland.]

60A, 60B   *****

PART V   PUBLIC ORDER: COLLECTIVE TRESPASS OR NUISANCE ON LAND

Powers to remove trespassers on land

61   Power to remove trespassers on land

(1) If the senior police officer present at the scene reasonably believes that two or more persons are trespassing on land and are present there with the common purpose of residing there for any period, that reasonable steps have been taken by or on behalf of the occupier to ask them to leave and—

(a) that any of those persons has caused damage to the land or to property on the land or used threatening, abusive or insulting words or behaviour towards the occupier, a member of his family or an employee or agent of his, or

(b) that those persons have between them six or more vehicles on the land, he may direct those persons, or any of them, to leave the land and to remove any vehicles or other property they have with them on the land.

(2) Where the persons in question are reasonably believed by the senior police officer to be persons who were not originally trespassers but have become trespassers on the land, the officer must reasonably believe that the other conditions specified in subsection (1) are satisfied after those persons become trespassers before he can exercise the power conferred by that subsection.

(3) A direction under subsection (1) above, if not communicated to the persons referred to in subsection (1) by the police officer giving the direction, may be communicated to them by any constable at the scene.

(4) If a person knowing that a direction under subsection (1) above has been given which applies to him—

(a) fails to leave the land as soon as reasonably practicable, or

(b) having left again enters the land as a trespasser within the period of [51 weeks] beginning with the day on which the direction was given,

he commits an offence and is liable on summary conviction to imprisonment for a term not exceeding [51 weeks] or a fine not exceeding level 4 on the standard scale, or both.

(4A), (4B) *****

(5) . . .

(6) In proceedings for an offence under this section it is a defence for the accused to show—

(a) that he was not trespassing on the land, or

(b) that he had a reasonable excuse for failing to leave the land as soon as reasonably practicable or, as the case may be, for again entering the land as a trespasser.

(7)–(9) *****

62   Supplementary powers of seizure

(1) If a direction has been given under section 61 and a constable reasonably suspects that any person to whom the direction applies has, without reasonable excuse—

(a) failed to remove any vehicle on the land which appears to the constable to belong to him or to be in his possession or under his control; or

(b) entered the land as a trespasser with a vehicle within the period of three months beginning with the day on which the direction was given,

the constable may seize and remove that vehicle.

(2) *****

[62A   Power to remove trespassers: alternative site available

(1) If the senior police officer present at a scene reasonably believes that the conditions in subsection (2) are satisfied in relation to a person and land, he may direct the person—

(a) to leave the land;

(b) to remove any vehicle and other property he has with him on the land.

(2) The conditions are—

(a) that the person and one or more others ("the trespassers") are trespassing on the land;

(b) that the trespassers have between them at least one vehicle on the land;

(c) that the trespassers are present on the land with the common purpose of residing there for any period;

(d) if it appears to the officer that the person has one or more caravans in his possession or under his control on the land, that there is a suitable pitch on a relevant caravan site for that caravan or each of those caravans;

(e) that the occupier of the land or a person acting on his behalf has asked the police to remove the trespassers from the land.

(3) A direction under subsection (1) may be communicated to the person to whom it applies by any constable at the scene.

(4) Subsection (5) applies if—

(a) a police officer proposes to give a direction under subsection (1) in relation to a person and land, and

(b) it appears to him that the person has one or more caravans in his possession or under his control on the land.

(5) The officer must consult every local authority within whose area the land is situated as to whether there is a suitable pitch for the caravan or each of the caravans on a relevant caravan site which is situated in the local authority's area.

(6), (7) *****

62B   Failure to comply with direction under section 62A: offences

(1) A person commits an offence if he knows that a direction under section 62A(1) has been given which applies to him and—

(a) he fails to leave the relevant land as soon as reasonably practicable, or

(b) he enters any land in the area of the relevant local authority as a trespasser before the end of the relevant period with the intention of residing there.

(2) The relevant period is the period of 3 months starting with the day on which the direction is given.

(3) A person guilty of an offence under this section is liable on summary conviction to imprisonment for a term not exceeding [51 weeks] or a fine not exceeding level 4 on the standard scale or both.

(4) . . .

(5) In proceedings for an offence under this section it is a defence for the accused to show—

(a) that he was not trespassing on the land in respect of which he is alleged to have committed the offence, or

(b) that he had a reasonable excuse—

(i) for failing to leave the relevant land as soon as reasonably practicable, or

(ii) for entering land in the area of the relevant local authority as a trespasser with the intention of residing there, or

(c) that, at the time the direction was given, he was under the age of 18 years and was residing with his parent or guardian.

62C   Failure to comply with direction under section 62A: seizure

(1) This section applies if a direction has been given under section 62A(1) and a constable reasonably suspects that a person to whom the direction applies has, without reasonable excuse—

(a) failed to remove any vehicle on the relevant land which appears to the constable to belong to him or to be in his possession or under his control; or

(b) entered any land in the area of the relevant local authority as a trespasser with a vehicle before the end of the relevant period with the intention of residing there.

(2) The relevant period is the period of 3 months starting with the day on which the direction is given.

(3) The constable may seize and remove the vehicle.]

62D–67   *****

68   Offence of aggravated trespass

(1) A person commits the offence of aggravated trespass if he trespasses on land . . . and, in relation to any lawful activity which persons are engaging in or are about to engage in on that or adjoining land . . ., does there anything which is intended by him to have the effect—

     (a) of intimidating those persons or any of them so as to deter them or any of them from engaging in that activity,

     (b) of obstructing that activity, or

     (c) of disrupting that activity.

  (1A) *****

  (2) Activity on any occasion on the part of a person or persons on land is "lawful" for the purposes of this section if he or they may engage in the activity on the land on that occasion without committing an offence or trespassing on the land.

  (3) A person guilty of an offence under this section is liable on summary conviction to imprisonment for a term not exceeding [51 weeks] or a fine not exceeding level 4 on the standard scale, or both.

  (4) . . .

  (5) In this section "land" does not include—

     (a) the highways and roads excluded from the application of section 61 by paragraph (b) of the definition of "land" in subsection (9) of that section; or

     (b) a road within the meaning of the Roads (Northern Ireland) Order 1993.

69   Powers to remove persons committing or participating in aggravated trespass

  (1) If the senior police officer present at the scene reasonably believes—

     (a) that a person is committing, has committed or intends to commit the offence of aggravated trespass on land . . .; or

     (b) that two or more persons are trespassing on land . . . and are present there with the common purpose of intimidating persons so as to deter them from engaging in a lawful activity or of obstructing or disrupting a lawful activity, he may direct that person or (as the case may be) those persons (or any of them) to leave the land.

  (2) A direction under subsection (1) above, if not communicated to the persons referred to in subsection (1) by the police officer giving the direction, may be communicated to them by any constable at the scene.

  (3) If a person knowing that a direction under subsection (1) above has been given which applies to him—

     (a) fails to leave the land as soon as practicable, or

     (b) having left again enters the land as a trespasser within the period of three months beginning with the day on which the direction was given, he commits an offence and is liable on summary conviction to imprisonment for a term not exceeding [51 weeks] or a fine not exceeding level 4 on the standard scale, or both.

  (4) In proceedings for an offence under subsection (3) it is a defence for the accused to show—

     (a) that he was not trespassing on the land, or

     (b) that he had a reasonable excuse for failing to leave the land as soon as practicable or, as the case may be, for again entering the land as a trespasser.

  (5) . . .

  (6) In this section "lawful activity" and "land" have the same meaning as in section 68.

70–162   *****

Closed-circuit television by local authorities

163   Local authority powers to provide closed-circuit television

  (1) Without prejudice to any power which they may exercise for those purposes under any other enactment, a local authority may take such of the following steps as they consider will, in relation to their area, promote the prevention of crime or the welfare of the victims of crime—

(a) providing apparatus for recording visual images of events occurring on any land in their area;

[(b) providing within their area an electronic communications service which is distributed—

   (i) only to persons on a single set of premises; and

   (ii) by an electronic communications network which is wholly within those premises and is not connected to an electronic communications network any part of which is outside those premises;]

(c) arranging for the provision of any other description of telecommunications system [electronic communications network or electronic communications service] within their area or between any land in their area and any building occupied by a public authority.

(2) Any power to provide, or to arrange for the provision of, any apparatus includes power to maintain, or operate, or, as the case may be, to arrange for the maintenance or operation of, that apparatus.

(3) Before taking such a step under this section, a local authority shall consult the chief officer of police for the police area in which the step is to be taken.

(3A), (4), (5) *****

*****

Intelligence Services Act 1994
(1994, c. 13)

An Act to make provision about the Secret Intelligence Service and the Government Communications Headquarters, including provision for the issue of warrants and authorisations enabling certain actions to be taken and for the issue of such warrants and authorisations to be kept under review; to make further provision about warrants issued on applications by the Security Service; to establish a procedure for the investigation of complaints about the Secret Intelligence Service and the Government Communications Headquarters; to make provision for the establishment of an Intelligence and Security Committee to scrutinise all three of those bodies; and for connected purposes
[26 May 1994]

Territorial extent: United Kingdom. Sections 5(1) and 11(1) also apply to the Colonies listed in the Intelligence Services Act 1994 (Dependent Territories) Order 1995 (SI 1995/752)

The Secret Intelligence Service

1 The Secret Intelligence Service

(1) There shall continue to be a Secret Intelligence Service (in this Act referred to as "the Intelligence Service") under the authority of the Secretary of State; and, subject to subsection (2) below, its functions shall be—

(a) to obtain and provide information relating to the actions or intentions of persons outside the British Islands; and

(b) to perform other tasks relating to the actions or intentions of such persons.

(2) The functions of the Intelligence Service shall be exercisable only—

(a) in the interests of national security, with particular reference to the defence and foreign policies of Her Majesty's Government in the United Kingdom; or

(b) in the interests of the economic well-being of the United Kingdom; or

(c) in support of the prevention or detection of serious crime.

2   The Chief of the Intelligence Service

(1) The operations of the Intelligence Service shall continue to be under the control of a Chief of that Service appointed by the Secretary of State.

(2) The Chief of the Intelligence Service shall be responsible for the efficiency of that Service and it shall be his duty to ensure—

   (a) that there are arrangements for securing that no information is obtained by the Intelligence Service except so far as necessary for the proper discharge of its functions and that no information is disclosed by it except so far as necessary—
      (i)   for that purpose;
      (ii) in the interests of national security;
      (iii) for the purpose of the prevention or detection of serious crime; or
      (iv) for the purpose of any criminal proceedings; and
   (b) that the Intelligence Service does not take any action to further the interests of any United Kingdom political party.

(3), (4) *****

GCHQ

3   The Government Communications Headquarters

(1) There shall continue to be a Government Communications Headquarters under the authority of the Secretary of State; and, subject to subsection (2) below, its functions shall be—

   (a) to monitor or interfere with electromagnetic, acoustic and other emissions and any equipment producing such emissions and to obtain and provide information derived from or related to such emissions or equipment and from encrypted material; and
   (b) to provide advice and assistance about—
      (i) languages, including terminology used for technical matters, and
      (ii) cryptography and other matters relating to the protection of information and other material,
      to the armed forces of the Crown, to Her Majesty's Government in the United Kingdom or to a Northern Ireland Department or to any other organisation which is determined for the purposes of this section in such manner as may be specified by the Prime Minister.

(2) The functions referred to in subsection (1)(a) above shall be exercisable only—

   (a) in the interests of national security, with particular reference to the defence and foreign policies of Her Majesty's Government in the United Kingdom; or
   (b) in the interests of the economic well-being of the United Kingdom in relation to the actions or intentions of persons outside the British Islands; or
   (c) in support of the prevention or detection of serious crime.

(3) In this Act the expression "GCHQ" refers to the Government Communications Headquarters and to any unit or part of a unit of the armed forces of the Crown which is for the time being required by the Secretary of State to assist the Government Communications Headquarters in carrying out its functions.

4   The Director of GCHQ

(1) The operations of GCHQ shall continue to be under the control of a Director appointed by the Secretary of State.

(2) The Director shall be responsible for the efficiency of GCHQ and it shall be his duty to ensure—

   (a) that there are arrangements for securing that no information is obtained by GCHQ except so far as necessary for the proper discharge of its functions and that no information is disclosed by it except so far as necessary for that purpose or for the purpose of any criminal proceedings; and

(b) that GCHQ does not take any action to further the interests of any United Kingdom political party.

(3), (4) *****

Authorisation of certain actions

5 Warrants: general

(1) No entry on or interference with property or with wireless telegraphy shall be unlawful if it is authorised by a warrant issued by the Secretary of State under this section.

(2) The Secretary of State may, on an application made by the Security Service, the Intelligence Service or GCHQ, issue a warrant under this section authorising the taking, subject to subsection (3) below, of such action as is specified in the warrant in respect of any property so specified or in respect of wireless telegraphy so specified if the Secretary of State—

(a) thinks it necessary for the action to be taken [for the purpose of] assisting, as the case may be,—

(i) the Security Service in carrying out any of its functions under the 1989 Act; or

(ii) the Intelligence Service in carrying out any of its functions under section 1 above; or

(iii) GCHQ in carrying out any function which falls within section 3(1)(a) above; and

[(b) is satisfied that the taking of the action is proportionate to what the action seeks to achieve;] and

(c) is satisfied that satisfactory arrangements are in force under section 2(2)(a) of the 1989 Act (duties of the Director-General of the Security Service), section 2(2)(a) above or section 4(2)(a) above with respect to the disclosure of information obtained by virtue of this section and that any information obtained under the warrant will be subject to those arrangements.

[(2A) The matters to be taken into account in considering whether the requirements of subsection (2)(a) and (b) and satisfied in the case of any warrant shall include whether what it is thought necessary to achieve by the conduct authorised by the warrant could reasonably be achieved by other means.]

[(3) A warrant issued on the application of the Intelligence Service or GCHQ for the purposes of the exercise of their functions by virtue of section 1(2)(c) or 3(2)(c) above may not relate to property in the British Islands.

(3A) A warrant issued on the application of the Security Service for the purposes of the exercise of their function under section 1(4) of the Security Service Act 1989 may not relate to property in the British Islands unless it authorises the taking of action in relation to conduct within subsection (3B) below.

(3B) Conduct is within this subsection if it constitutes (or, if it took place in the United Kingdom, would constitute) one or more offences, and either—

(a) it involves the use of violence, results in substantial financial gain or is conduct by a large number of persons in pursuit of a common purpose; or

(b) the offence or one of the offences is an offence for which a person who has attained the age of twenty-one [(eighteen in relation to England and Wales)] and has no previous convictions could reasonably be expected to be sentenced to imprisonment for a term of three years or more.]

(4), (5) *****

6 *****

7 Authorisation of acts outside the British Islands

(1) If, apart from this section, a person would be liable in the United Kingdom for any act

done outside the British Islands, he shall not be so liable if the act is one which is authorised to be done by virtue of an authorisation given by the Secretary of State under this section.

(2) In subsection (1) above "liable in the United Kingdom" means liable under the criminal or civil law of any part of the United Kingdom.

(3) The Secretary of State shall not give an authorisation under this section unless he is satisfied—

(a) that any acts which may be done in reliance on the authorisation or, as the case may be, the operation in the course of which the acts may be done will be necessary for the proper discharge of a function of the Intelligence Service [or GCHQ]; and

(b) that there are satisfactory arrangements in force to secure—

(i) that nothing will be done in reliance on the authorisation beyond what is necessary for the proper discharge of a function of the Intelligence Service [or GCHQ]; and

(ii) that, in so far as any act may be done in reliance on the authorisation, their nature and likely consequences will be reasonable, having regard to the purposes for which they are carried out; and

(c) that there are satisfactory arrangements in force under section 2(2)(a) [or 4(2)(a)] above with respect to the disclosure of information obtained by virtue of this section and that any information obtained by virtue of anything done in reliance on the authorisation will be subject to those arrangements.

(4)–(9) *****

8–9 . . .

10 The Intelligence and Security Committee

(1) There shall be a Committee, to be known as the Intelligence and Security Committee and in this section referred to as "the Committee", to examine the expenditure, administration and policy of—

(a) the Security Service;

(b) the Intelligence Service; and

(c) GCHQ.

(2) The Committee shall consist of nine members—

(a) who shall be drawn both from the members of the House of Commons and from the members of the House of Lords; and

(b) none of whom shall be a Minister of the Crown.

(3) The members of the Committee shall be appointed by the Prime Minister after consultation with the Leader of the Opposition, within the meaning of the Ministerial and other Salaries Act 1975; and one of those members shall be so appointed as Chairman of the Committee.

(4)–(7) *****

11–12 *****

Criminal Appeal Act 1995
(1995, c. 35)

An Act to amend provisions relating to appeals and references to the Court of Appeal in criminal cases; to establish a Criminal Cases Review Commission and confer functions on, and make other provision in relation to, the Commission; to amend section 142 of the Magistrates' Courts Act 1980 and introduce in Northern Ireland provision similar to those of that section; to amend section 133 of the Criminal Justice Act 1988; and for connected purposes   [19 July 1995]

Territorial extent: England and Wales, Northern Ireland (except ss. 9, 11)

Note: The "1968 Act" refers to the Criminal Appeal Act 1968 and the "1980 Act" refers to the Criminal Appeal (Northern Ireland) Act 1980.

PART II   THE CRIMINAL CASES REVIEW COMMISSION

The Commission

8   The Commission

(1) There shall be a body corporate to be known as the Criminal Cases Review Commission.

(2) The Commission shall not be regarded as the servant or agent of the Crown or as enjoying any status, immunity or privilege of the Crown; and the Commission's property shall not be regarded as property of, or held on behalf of, the Crown.

(3) The Commission shall consist of not fewer than eleven members.

(4) The members of the Commission shall be appointed by Her Majesty on the recommendation of the Prime Minister.

(5) At least one third of the members of the Commission shall be persons who are legally qualified; and for this purpose a person is legally qualified if—

(a) he has a ten year general qualification, within the meaning of section 71 of the Courts and Legal Services Act 1990, or

(b) he is a member of the Bar of Northern Ireland, or solicitor of the Supreme Court of Northern Ireland, of at least ten years' standing.

(6) At least two thirds of the members of the Commission shall be persons who appear to the Prime Minister to have knowledge or experience of any aspect of the criminal justice system and of them at least one shall be a person who appears to him to have knowledge or experience of any aspect of the criminal justice system in Northern Ireland; and for the purposes of this subsection the criminal justice system includes, in particular, the investigation of offences and the treatment of offenders.

(7) *****

References to court

9   Cases dealt with on indictment in England and Wales

(1) Where a person has been convicted of an offence on indictment in England and Wales, the Commission—

(a) may at any time refer the conviction to the Court of Appeal, and

(b) (whether or not they refer the conviction) may at any time refer to the Court of Appeal any sentence (not being a sentence fixed by law) imposed on, or in subsequent proceedings relating to, the conviction.

(2) A reference under subsection (1) of a person's conviction shall be treated for all purposes as an appeal by the person under section 1 of the 1968 Act against the conviction.

(3) A reference under subsection (1) of a sentence imposed on, or in subsequent proceedings relating to, a person's conviction on an indictment shall be treated for all purposes as an appeal by the person under section 9 of the 1968 Act against—

(a) the sentence, and

(b) any other sentence (not being a sentence fixed by law) imposed on, or in subsequent proceedings relating to, the conviction or any other conviction on the indictment.

(4) On a reference under subsection (1) of a person's conviction on an indictment the Commission may give notice to the Court of Appeal that any other conviction on the indict-

ment which is specified in the notice is to be treated as referred to the Court of Appeal under subsection (1).

(5), (6) *****

10 *****

11   Cases dealt with summarily in England and Wales

(1) Where a person has been convicted of an offence by a magistrates' court in England and Wales, the Commission—

(a) may at any time refer the conviction to the Crown Court, and

(b) (whether or not they refer the conviction) may at any time refer to the Crown Court any sentence imposed on, or in subsequent proceedings relating to, the conviction.

(2) A reference under subsection (1) of a person's conviction shall be treated for all purposes as an appeal by the person under section 108(1) of the Magistrates' Courts Act 1980 against the conviction (whether or not he pleaded guilty).

(3) A reference under subsection (1) of a sentence imposed on, or in subsequent proceedings relating to, a person's conviction shall be treated for all purposes as an appeal by the person under section 108(1) of the Magistrates' Courts Act 1980 against—

(a) the sentence, and

(b) any other sentence imposed on, or in subsequent proceedings relating to, the conviction or any related conviction.

(4) On a reference under subsection (1) of a person's conviction the Commission may give notice to the Crown Court that any related conviction which is specified in the notice is to be treated as referred to the Crown Court under subsection (1).

(5) For the purposes of this section convictions are related if they are convictions of the same person by the same court on the same day.

(6) On a reference under this section the Crown Court may not award any punishment more severe than that awarded by the court whose decision is referred.

(7) The Crown Court may grant bail to a person whose conviction or sentence has been referred under this section; and any time during which he is released on bail shall not count as part of any term of imprisonment or detention under his sentence.

12 *****

13   Conditions for making of references

(1) A reference of a conviction, verdict, finding or sentence shall not be made under any of sections 9 to 12 unless—

(a) the Commission consider that there is a real possibility that the conviction, verdict, finding or sentence would not be upheld were the reference to be made,

(b) the Commission so consider—

(i) in the case of a conviction, verdict or finding, because of an argument, or evidence, not raised in the proceedings which led to it or on any appeal or application for leave to appeal against it, or

(ii) in the case of a sentence, because of an argument on a point of law, or information, not so raised, and

(c) an appeal against the conviction, verdict, finding or sentence has been determined or leave to appeal against it has been refused.

(2) Nothing in subsection (1)(b)(i) or (c) shall prevent the making of a reference if it appears to the Commission that there are exceptional circumstances which justify making it.

14   Further provisions about references

(1) A reference of a conviction, verdict, finding or sentence may be made under any of sections 9 to 12 either after an application has been made by or on behalf of the person to whom it relates or without an application having been so made.

(2) In considering whether to make a reference of a conviction, verdict, finding or sentence under any of sections 9 to 12 the Commission shall have regard to—

    (a) any application or representations made to the Commission by or on behalf of the person to whom it relates,

    (b) any other representations made to the Commission in relation to it, and

    (c) any other matters which appear to the Commission to be relevant.

(3) In considering whether to make a reference under section 9 or 10 the Commission may at any time refer any point on which they desire the assistance of the Court of Appeal to that Court for the Court's opinion on it; and on a reference under this subsection the Court of Appeal shall consider the point referred and furnish the Commission with the Court's opinion on the point.

    (4)–(5) *****

15 *****

16 Assistance in connection with prerogative of mercy

(1) Where the Secretary of State refers to the Commission any matter which arises in the consideration of whether to recommend the exercise of Her Majesty's prerogative of mercy in relation to a conviction and on which he desires their assistance, the Commission shall—

    (a) consider the matter referred, and

    (b) give to the Secretary of State a statement of their conclusions on it; and the Secretary of State shall, in considering whether so to recommend, treat the Commission's statement as conclusive of the matter referred.

(2) Where in any case the Commission are of the opinion that the Secretary of State should consider whether to recommend the exercise of Her Majesty's prerogative of mercy in relation to the case they shall give him the reasons for their opinion.

*****

Criminal Procedure (Scotland) Act 1995

(1995, c. 46)

An Act to consolidate certain enactments relating to criminal procedure in Scotland

[8 November 1995]

Territorial extent: Scotland

*****

PART II POLICE FUNCTIONS

Lord Advocate's instructions

12 Instructions by Lord Advocate as to reporting of offences

The Lord Advocate may, from time to time, issue instructions to a chief constable with regard to the reporting, for consideration of the question of prosecution, of offences alleged to have been committed within the area of such chief constable, and it shall be the duty of a chief constable to whom any such instruction is issued to secure compliance therewith.

13 Powers relating to suspects and potential witnesses

(1) Where a constable has reasonable grounds for suspecting that a person has committed or is committing an offence at any place, he may require—

(a) that person, if the constable finds him at that place or at any place where the constable is entitled to be, to give his name and address and may ask him for an explanation of the circumstances which have given rise to the constable's suspicion;

(b) any other person whom the constable finds at that place or at any place where the constable is entitled to be and who the constable believes has information relating to the offence, to give his name and address.

(2) The constable may require the person mentioned in paragraph (a) of subsection (1) above to remain with him while he (either or both)—

(a) subject to subsection (3) below, verifies any name and address given by the person;

(b) notes any explanation proffered by the person.

(3) The constable shall exercise his power under paragraph (a) of subsection (2) above only where it appears to him that such verification can be obtained quickly.

(4) A constable may use reasonable force to ensure that the person mentioned in paragraph (a) of subsection (1) above remains with him.

(5) A constable shall inform a person, when making a requirement of that person under—

(a) paragraph (a) of subsection (1) above, of his suspicion and of the general nature of the offence which he suspects that the person has committed or is committing;

(b) paragraph (b) of subsection (1) above, of his suspicion, of the general nature of the offence which he suspects has been or is being committed and that the reason for the requirement is that he believes the person has information relating to the offence;

(c) subsection (2) above, why the person is being required to remain with him;

(d) either of the said subsections, that failure to comply with the requirement may constitute an offence.

(6), (7) *****

14 Detention and questioning at police station

(1) Where a constable has reasonable grounds for suspecting that a person has committed or is committing an offence punishable by imprisonment, the constable may, for the purpose of facilitating the carrying out of investigations—

(a) into the offence; and

(b) as to whether criminal proceedings should be instigated against the person, detain that person and take him as quickly as is reasonably practicable to a police station or other premises and may thereafter for that purpose take him to any other place and, subject to the following provisions of this section, the detention may continue at the police station or, as the case may be, the other premises or place.

(2) Detention under subsection (1) above shall be terminated not more than six hours after it begins or (if earlier)—

(a) when the person is arrested;

(b) when he is detained in pursuance of any other enactment; or

(c) where there are no longer such grounds as are mentioned in the said subsection (1), and when a person has been detained under subsection (1) above, he shall be informed immediately upon the termination of his detention in accordance with this subsection that his detention has been terminated.

(3) Where a person has been released at the termination of a period of detention under subsection (1) above he shall not thereafter be detained, under that subsection, on the same grounds or on any grounds arising out of the same circumstances.

(4)–(6) *****

(7) Where a person is detained under subsection (1) above, a constable may—

(a) without prejudice to any relevant rule of law as regards the admissibility in evidence of any answer given, put questions to him in relation to the suspected offence;

(b) exercise the same powers of search as are available following an arrest.

(8) A constable may use reasonable force in exercising any power conferred by subsection (1), or by paragraph (b) of subsection (7), above.

(9) A person detained under subsection (1) above shall be under no obligation to answer any question other than to give his name and address, and a constable shall so inform him both on so detaining him and on arrival at the police station or other premises.

15 Rights of person arrested or detained

(1) Without prejudice to section 17 of this Act, a person who, not being a person in respect of whose custody or detention subsection (4) below applies—

(a) has been arrested and is in custody in a police station or other premises, shall be entitled to have intimation of his custody and of the place where he is being held sent to a person reasonably named by him;

(b) is being detained under section 14 of this Act and has been taken to a police station or other premises or place, shall be entitled to have intimation of his detention and of the police station or other premises or place sent to a solicitor and to one other person reasonably named by him,

without delay or, where some delay is necessary in the interest of the investigation or the prevention of crime or the apprehension of offenders, with no more delay than is so necessary.

(2) A person shall be informed of his entitlement under subsection (1) above—

(a) on arrival at the police station or other premises; or

(b) where he is not arrested, or as the case may be detained, until after such arrival, on such arrest or detention.

(3)–(6) *****

16 *****

17 Right of accused to have access to solicitor

(1) Where an accused has been arrested on any criminal charge, he shall be entitled immediately upon such arrest—

(a) to have intimation sent to a solicitor that his professional assistance is required by the accused, and informing the solicitor—

(i) of the place where the person is being detained;

(ii) whether the person is to be liberated; and

(iii) if the person is not to be liberated, the court to which he is to be taken and the date when he is to be so taken; and

(b) to be told what rights there are under—

(i) paragraph (a)above;

(ii) subsection (2) below; and

(iii) section 35(1) and (2) of this Act.

(2) The accused and the solicitor shall be entitled to have a private interview before the examination or, as the case may be, first appearance.

17A–21 *****

22 Liberation by police

(1) Where a person has been arrested and charged with an offence which may be tried summarily, the officer in charge of a police station may—

(a) liberate him upon a written undertaking, signed by him and certified by the officer, in terms of which the person undertakes to appear at a specified court at a specified time; or

(b) liberate him without any such undertaking; or

(c) refuse to liberate him;

(2) A person in breach of an undertaking given by him under subsection (1) above without reasonable excuse shall be guilty of an offence and liable on summary conviction to the following penalties—

(a) a fine not exceeding level 3 on the standard scale; and
(b) imprisonment for a period—
(i)   where conviction is in the district court, not exceeding 60 days; or
(ii) where conviction is in the sheriff court, not exceeding 3 months.

(3) The refusal of the officer in charge to liberate a person under subsection (1)(c) above and the detention of that person until his case is tried in the usual form shall not subject the officer to any claim whatsoever.

(4) The penalties provided for in subsection (2) above may be imposed in addition to any other penalty which it is competent for the court to impose, notwithstanding that the total of penalties imposed may exceed the maximum penalty which it is competent to impose in respect of the original offence.

(5) In any proceedings relating to an offence under this section, a writing, purporting to be such an undertaking as is mentioned in subsection (1)(a) above and bearing to be signed and certified, shall be sufficient evidence of the terms of the undertaking given by the arrested person.

22A–34 *****

35 Judicial examination

(1) The accused's solicitor shall be entitled to be present at the examination.

(2) The sheriff may delay the examination for a period not exceeding 48 hours from and after the time of the accused's arrest, in order to allow time for the attendance of the solicitor.

(3) Where the accused is brought before the sheriff for examination on any charge and he or his solicitor intimates that he does not desire to emit a declaration in regard to such a charge, it shall be unnecessary to take a declaration, and, subject to section 36 of this Act, the accused may be committed for further examination or until liberated in due course of law without a declaration being taken.

(4) Nothing in subsection (3) above shall prejudice the right of the accused subsequently to emit a declaration on intimating to the prosecutor his desire to do so; and that declaration shall be taken in further examination.

(4A)–(8) *****

36 Judicial examination: questioning by prosecutor

(1) Subject to the following provisions of this section, an accused on being brought before the sheriff for examination on any charge (whether the first or a further examination) may be questioned by the prosecutor in so far as such questioning is directed towards eliciting any admission, denial, explanation, justification or comment which the accused may have as regards anything to which subsections (2) to (4) below apply.

(2) This subsection applies to matters averred in the charge, and the particular aims of a line of questions under this subsection shall be to determine—

(a) whether any account which the accused can give ostensibly discloses a defence; and
(b) the nature and particulars of that defence.

(3) This subsection applies to the alleged making by the accused, to or in the hearing of a constable, of an extrajudicial confession (whether or not a full admission) relevant to the charge, and questions under this subsection may only be put if the accused has, before the examination, received from the prosecutor or from a constable a written record of the confession allegedly made.

(4) This subsection applies to what is said in any declaration emitted in regard to the charge by the accused at examination.

(5) The prosecutor shall, in framing questions in exercise of his power under subsection (1) above, have regard to the following principles—

    (a) the question should not be designed to challenge the truth of anything said by the accused;

    (b) there should be no reiteration of a question which the accused has refused to answer at the examination; and

    (c) there should be no leading questions,

and the sheriff shall ensure that all questions are fairly put to, and understood by, the accused.

(6) The accused shall be told by the sheriff—

    (a) where he is represented by a solicitor at the judicial examination, that he may consult that solicitor before answering any question; and

    (b) that if he answers any question put to him at the examination under this section in such a way as to disclose an ostensible defence, the prosecutor shall be under the duty imposed by subsection (10) below.

(7) With the permission of the sheriff, the solicitor for the accused may ask the accused any question the purpose of which is to clarify any ambiguity in an answer given by the accused to the prosecutor at the examination or to give the accused an opportunity to answer any question which he has previously refused to answer.

(8) An accused may decline to answer a question under subsection (1) above; and, where he is subsequently tried on the charge mentioned in that subsection or on any other charge arising out of the circumstances which gave rise to the charge so mentioned, his having so declined may be commented upon by the prosecutor, the judge presiding at the trial, or any co-accused, only where and in so far as the accused (or any witness called on his behalf) in evidence avers something which could have been stated appropriately in answer to that question.

(9)–(11) *****

37 Judicial examination: record of proceedings

(1) The prosecutor shall provide for a verbatim record to be made by means of shorthand notes or by mechanical means of all questions to and answers and declarations by the accused in examination, or further examination, under sections 35 and 36 of this Act.

(2)–(10) *****

*****

Disability Discrimination Act 1995

(1995, c. 50)

An Act to make it unlawful to discriminate against disabled persons in connection with employment, the provision of goods, facilities and services or the disposal or management of premises; to make provision about the employment of disabled persons; and to establish a National Disability Council   *[8 November 1995]*

Territorial extent: England and Wales, Scotland

Note. This Act was extensively amended by the Disability Discrimination Act 1995 (Amendment) Regulations 2003, SI 2003/1673 (implementing EU Directive 2000/78), and is reproduced here as amended. The amendments took effect on 1 October 2004.

PART I   DISABILITY

1   Meaning of "disability" and "disabled person"

(1) Subject to the provisions of Schedule 1, a person has a disability for the purposes of this Act if he has a physical or mental impairment which has a substantial and long-term adverse effect on his ability to carry out normal day-to-day activities.

(2) In this Act "disabled person" means a person who has a disability.

2   Past disabilities

(1) The provisions of this Part and Parts II [to 4 and 5A] apply in relation to a person who has had a disability as they apply in relation to a person who has that disability.

(2) Those provisions are subject to the modifications made by Schedule 2.

(3) Any regulations or order made under this Act [by the Secretary of State, the Scottish Ministers or the National Assembly for Wales] may include provision with respect to persons who have had a disability.

(4) In any proceedings under Part [2, 3, 4 or 5A] of this Act, the question whether a person had a disability at a particular time ("the relevant time") shall be determined, for the purposes of this section, as if the provisions of, or made under, this Act in force when the act complained of was done had been in force at the relevant time.

(5) The relevant time may be a time before the passing of this Act.

3   ***

PART II   [THE EMPLOYMENT FIELD] [AND MEMBERS OF LOCALLY-ELECTABLE AUTHORITIES]

[Meaning of "discrimination" and "harassment"]

3A   Meaning of "discrimination"

(1) For the purposes of this Part, a person discriminates against a disabled person if—

   (a) for a reason which relates to the disabled person's disability, he treats him less favourably than he treats or would treat others to whom that reason does not or would not apply, and

   (b) he cannot show that the treatment in question is justified.

(2) For the purposes of this Part, a person also discriminates against a disabled person if he fails to comply with a duty to make reasonable adjustments imposed on him in relation to the disabled person.

(3) Treatment is justified for the purposes of subsection (1)(b) if, but only if, the reason for it is both material to the circumstances of the particular case and substantial.

(4) But treatment of a disabled person cannot be justified under subsection (3) if it amounts to direct discrimination falling within subsection (5).

(5) A person directly discriminates against a disabled person if, on the ground of the disabled person's disability, he treats the disabled person less favourably than he treats or would treat a person not having that particular disability whose relevant circumstances, including his abilities, are the same as, or not materially different from, those of the disabled person.

(6) If, in a case falling within subsection (1), a person is under a duty to make reasonable adjustments in relation to a disabled person but fails to comply with that duty, his treatment of that person cannot be justified under subsection (3) unless it would have been justified even if he had complied with that duty.]

[3B   Meaning of "harassment"

(1) For the purposes of this Part, a person subjects a disabled person to harassment where, for a reason which relates to the disabled person's disability, he engages in unwanted conduct which has the purpose or effect of—

(a) violating the disabled person's dignity, or

(b) creating an intimidating, hostile, degrading, humiliating or offensive environment for him.

(2) Conduct shall be regarded as having the effect referred to in paragraph (a) or (b) of subsection (1) only if, having regard to all the circumstances, including in particular the perception of the disabled person, it should reasonably be considered as having that effect.]

[Employment

4 Employers: discrimination and harassment

(1) It is unlawful for an employer to discriminate against a disabled person—

(a) in the arrangements which he makes for the purpose of determining to whom he should offer employment;

(b) in the terms on which he offers that person employment; or

(c) by refusing to offer, or deliberately not offering, him employment.

(2) It is unlawful for an employer to discriminate against a disabled person whom he employs—

(a) in the terms of employment which he affords him;

(b) in the opportunities which he affords him for promotion, a transfer, training or receiving any other benefit;

(c) by refusing to afford him, or deliberately not affording him, any such opportunity; or

(d) by dismissing him, or subjecting him to any other detriment.

(3) It is also unlawful for an employer, in relation to employment by him, to subject to harassment—

(a) a disabled person whom he employs; or

(b) a disabled person who has applied to him for employment.]

(4)–(6) *****

[4A Employers: duty to make adjustments

(1) Where—

(a) a provision, criterion or practice applied by or on behalf of an employer, or

(b) any physical feature of premises occupied by the employer,

places the disabled person concerned at a substantial disadvantage in comparison with persons who are not disabled, it is the duty of the employer to take such steps as it is reasonable, in all the circumstances of the case, for him to have to take in order to prevent the provision, criterion or practice, or feature, having that effect.

(2) In subsection (1), "the disabled person concerned" means—

(a) in the case of a provision, criterion or practice for determining to whom employment should be offered, any disabled person who is, or has notified the employer that he may be, an applicant for that employment;

(b) in any other case, a disabled person who is—

(i) an applicant for the employment concerned, or

(ii) an employee of the employer concerned.

(3) Nothing in this section imposes any duty on an employer in relation to a disabled person if the employer does not know, and could not reasonably be expected to know—

(a) in the case of an applicant or potential applicant, that the disabled person concerned is, or may be, an applicant for the employment; or

(b) in any case, that that person has a disability and is likely to be affected in the way mentioned in subsection (1).]

4B–14D, 15A–15C *****

15–16 ...

Other unlawful acts

16A   Relationships which have come to an end
  (1) This section applies where—
      (a) there has been a relevant relationship between a disabled person and another person ("the relevant person"), and
      (b) the relationship has come to an end.
  (2) In this section a "relevant relationship" is—
      (a) a relationship during the course of which an act of discrimination against, or harassment of, one party to the relationship by the other party to it is unlawful under any preceding provision of this Part [, other than sections 15B and 15C]; or
      (b) a relationship between a person providing employment services . . . and a person receiving such services.
  (3) It is unlawful for the relevant person—
      (a) to discriminate against the disabled person by subjecting him to a detriment, or
      (b) to subject the disabled person to harassment,
where the discrimination or harassment arises out of and is closely connected to the relevant relationship.
  (4)–(7) *****

[16B   Discriminatory advertisements
  [(1) It is unlawful for a person to publish or cause to be published an advertisement which—
      (a) invites applications for a relevant appointment or benefit; and
      (b) indicates, or might reasonably be understood to indicate, that an application will or may be determined to any extent by reference to—
          (i) the applicant not having any disability, or any particular disability,
          (ii) the applicant not having had any disability, or any particular disability, or
          (iii) any reluctance of the person determining the application to comply with a duty to make reasonable adjustments or (in relation to employment services) with the duty imposed by section 21(1) as modified by section 21A(6).]
  (2) Subsection (1) does not apply where it would not in fact be unlawful under this Part or, to the extent that it relates to the provision of employment services, Part 3 for an application to be determined in the manner indicated (or understood to be indicated) in the advertisement.
  (2A)–(4) *****

[16C   Instructions and pressure to discriminate
  (1) It is unlawful for a person—
      (a) who has authority over another person, or
      (b) in accordance with whose wishes that other person is accustomed to act,
to instruct him to do any act which is unlawful under this Part or, to the extent that it relates to the provision of employment services, Part 3, or to procure or attempt to procure the doing by him of any such act.
  (2), (3) *****

17   . . .

Enforcement etc

[17A   Enforcement, remedies and procedure]
  [(1) A complaint by any person that another person—
      (a) has discriminated against him[, or subjected him to harassment,] in a way which is unlawful under this Part, or

(b) is, by virtue of section 57 or 58, to be treated as having [done so],
may be presented to an [employment tribunal].

[(1A) Subsection (1) does not apply to a complaint under section 14A(1) or (2) of an act in respect of which an appeal, or proceedings in the nature of an appeal, may be brought under any enactment.

(1B) . . .

(1C) Where, on the hearing of a complaint under subsection (1), the complainant proves facts from which the tribunal could, apart from this subsection, conclude in the absence of an adequate explanation that the respondent has acted in a way which is unlawful under this Part, the tribunal shall uphold the complaint unless the respondent proves that he did not so act.]

(2) Where an [employment tribunal] finds that a complaint presented to it under this section is well-founded, it shall take such of the following steps as it considers just and equitable—

(a) making a declaration as to the rights of the complainant and the respondent in relation to the matters to which the complaint relates;

(b) ordering the respondent to pay compensation to the complainant;

(c) recommending that the respondent take, within a specified period, action appearing to the tribunal to be reasonable, in all the circumstances of the case, for the purpose of obviating or reducing the adverse effect on the complainant of any matter to which the complaint relates.

(3) Where a tribunal orders compensation under subsection (2)(b), the amount of the compensation shall be calculated by applying the principles applicable to the calculation of damages in claims in tort or (in Scotland) in reparation for breach of statutory duty.

(4) For the avoidance of doubt it is hereby declared that compensation in respect of discrimination in a way which is unlawful under this Part may include compensation for injury to feelings whether or not it includes compensation under any other head.

(5) If the respondent to a complaint fails, without reasonable justification, to comply with a recommendation made by an [employment tribunal] under subsection (2)(c) the tribunal may, if it thinks it just and equitable to do so—

(a) increase the amount of compensation required to be paid to the complainant in respect of the complaint, where an order was made under subsection (2)(b); or

(b) make an order under subsection (2)(b).]

(6)–(8) *****

[17B   Enforcement of sections 16B(1) and 16C

(1) Only the Disability Rights Commission may bring proceedings in respect of a contravention of section [16B(1)] (discriminatory advertisements) or section 16C (instructions and pressure to discriminate).

(2) The Commission shall bring any such proceedings in accordance with subsection (3) or (4).

(3) The Commission may present to an employment tribunal a complaint that a person has done an act which is unlawful under section [16B(1)] or 16C; and if the tribunal finds that the complaint is well-founded it shall make a declaration to that effect.

(4) Where—

(a) a tribunal has made a finding pursuant to subsection (3) that a person has done an act which is unlawful under section [16B(1)] or 16C,

(b) that finding has become final, and

(c) it appears to the Commission that, unless restrained, he is likely to do a further act which is unlawful under [section 16B(1) or (as the case may be) section 16C],

the Commission may apply to a county court for an injunction, or (in Scotland) to a sheriff court for an interdict, restraining him from doing such an act; and the court, if satisfied that the application is well-founded, may grant the injunction or interdict in the terms applied for or in more limited terms.

17C–18A   ***

[**18B   Reasonable adjustments: supplementary**
(1) In determining whether it is reasonable for a person to have to take a particular step in order to comply with a duty to make reasonable adjustments, regard shall be had, in particular, to—
  (a) the extent to which taking the step would prevent the effect in relation to which the duty is imposed;
  (b) the extent to which it is practicable for him to take the step;
  (c) the financial and other costs which would be incurred by him in taking the step and the extent to which taking it would disrupt any of his activities;
  (d) the extent of his financial and other resources;
  (e) the availability to him of financial or other assistance with respect to taking the step;
  (f) the nature of his activities and the size of his undertaking;
  (g) where the step would be taken in relation to a private household, the extent to which taking it would—
    (i) disrupt that household, or
    (ii) disturb any person residing there.
(2) The following are examples of steps which a person may need to take in relation to a disabled person in order to comply with a duty to make reasonable adjustments—
  (a) making adjustments to premises;
  (b) allocating some of the disabled person's duties to another person;
  (c) transferring him to fill an existing vacancy;
  (d) altering his hours of working or training;
  (e) assigning him to a different place of work or training;
  (f) allowing him to be absent during working or training hours for rehabilitation, assessment or treatment;
  (g) giving, or arranging for, training or mentoring (whether for the disabled person or any other person);
  (h) acquiring or modifying equipment;
  (i) modifying instructions or reference manuals;
  (j) modifying procedures for testing or assessment;
  (k) providing a reader or interpreter;
  (l) providing supervision or other support.]
(3)–(6) *****

18C–18E   ***

PART III   DISCRIMINATION IN OTHER AREAS

Goods, facilities and services

19   Discrimination in relation to goods, facilities and services
(1) It is unlawful for a provider of services to discriminate against a disabled person—
  (a) in refusing to provide, or deliberately not providing, to the disabled person any service which he provides, or is prepared to provide, to members of the public;
  (b) in failing to comply with any duty imposed on him by section 21 in circumstances

in which the effect of that failure is to make it impossible or unreasonably difficult for the disabled person to make use of any such service;

(c) in the standard of service which he provides to the disabled person or the manner in which he provides it to him; or

(d) in the terms on which he provides a service to the disabled person.

(2) For the purposes of this section and sections 20 and 21—

(a) the provision of services includes the provision of any goods or facilities;

(b) a person is "a provider of services" if he is concerned with the provision, in the United Kingdom, of services to the public or to a section of the public; and

(c) it is irrelevant whether a service is provided on payment or without payment.

(3) The following are examples of services to which this section and sections 20 [to 21ZA] apply—

(a) access to and use of any place which members of the public are permitted to enter;

(b) access to and use of means of communication;

(c) access to and use of information services;

(d) accommodation in a hotel, boarding house or other similar establishment;

(e) facilities by way of banking or insurance or for grants, loans, credit or finance;

(f) facilities for entertainment, recreation or refreshment;

(g) facilities provided by employment agencies or under section 2 of the Employment and Training Act 1973;

(h) the services of any profession or trade, or any local or other public authority.

(4)–(6) *****

20 Meaning of "discrimination"

(1) For the purposes of section 19, a provider of services discriminates against a disabled person if—

(a) for a reason which relates to the disabled person's disability, he treats him less favourably than he treats or would treat others to whom that reason does not or would not apply; and

(b) he cannot show that the treatment in question is justified.

(2) For the purposes of section 19, a providers of services also discriminates against a disabled person if—

(a) he fails to comply with a section 21 duty imposed on him in relation to the disabled person; and

(b) he cannot show that his failure to comply with that duty is justified.

(3) For the purposes of this section, treatment is justified only if—

(a) in the opinion of the provider of services, one or more of the conditions mentioned in subsection (4) are satisfied; and

(b) it is reasonable, in all the circumstances of the case, for him to hold that opinion.

(4) The conditions are that—

(a) in any case, the treatment is necessary in order not to endanger the health or safety of any person (which may include that of the disabled person);

(b) in any case, the disabled person is incapable of entering into an enforceable agreement, or of giving an informed consent, and for that reason the treatment is reasonable in that case;

(c) in a case falling within section 19(1)(a), the treatment is necessary because the provider of services would otherwise be unable to provide the service to members of the public;

(d) in a case falling within section 19(1)(c) or (d), the treatment is necessary in order for the provider of services to be able to provide the service to the disabled person or to other members of the public;

(e) in a case falling within section 19(1)(d), the difference in the terms on which the service is provided to the disabled person and those on which it is provided to other members of the public reflects the greater cost to the provider of services in providing the service to the disabled person.

(5) Any increase in the cost of providing a service to a disabled person which results from compliance by a provider of services with a section 21 duty shall be disregarded for the purposes of subsection (4)(e).

(6)–(9) *****

21   Duty of providers of services to make adjustments

(1) Where a provider of services has a practice, policy or procedure which makes it impossible or unreasonably difficult for disabled persons to make use of a service which he provides, or is prepared to provide, to other members of the public, it is his duty to take such steps as it is reasonable, in all the circumstances of the case, for him to have to take in order to change that practice, policy or procedure so that it no longer has that effect.

(2) Where a physical feature (for example, one arising from the design or construction of a building or the approach or access to premises) makes it impossible or unreasonably difficult for disabled persons to make use of such a service, it is the duty of the provider of that service to take such steps as it is reasonable, in all the circumstances of the case, for him to have to take in order to—

    (a) remove the feature;

    (b) alter it so that it no longer has that effect;

    (c) provide a reasonable means of avoiding the feature; or

    (d) provide a reasonable alternative method of making the service in question available to disabled persons.

(3) *****

(4) Where an auxiliary aid or service (for example, the provision of information on audio tape or of a sign language interpreter) would—

    (a) enable disabled persons to make use of a service which a provider of services provides, or is prepared to provide, to members of the public, or

    (b) facilitate the use by disabled persons of such a service,

it is the duty of the provider of that service to take such steps as it is reasonable, in all the circumstances of the case, for him to have to take in order to provide that auxiliary aid or service.

(5) *****

(6) Nothing in this section requires a provider of services to take any steps which would fundamentally alter the nature of the service in question or the nature of his trade, profession or business.

(7) Nothing in this section requires a provider of services to take any steps which would cause him to incur expenditure exceeding the prescribed maximum.

(8)–(10)   *****

21A–24M   *****

Enforcement, etc

25   Enforcement, remedies and procedure

(1) A claim by any person that another person—

    (a) has discriminated against him in a way which is unlawful under this Part; or

    (b) is by virtue of section 57 or 58 to be treated as having discriminated against him in such a way,

may be made the subject of civil proceedings in the same way as any other claim in tort or (in Scotland) in reparation for breach of statutory duty.

(2) For the avoidance of doubt it is hereby declared that damages in respect of discrimination in a way which is unlawful under this Part may include compensation for injury to feelings whether or not they include compensation under any other head.

(3) Proceedings in England and Wales shall be brought only in a county court.

(4) Proceedings in Scotland shall be brought only in a sheriff court.

(5) The remedies available in such proceedings are those which are available in the High Court or (as the case may be) the Court of Session.

(6)–(9) *****

26–54 *****

55 Victimisation

(1) For the purposes of [Part 2 or Part 4, or Part 3 other than sections 24A to 24L], a person ("A") discriminates against another person ("B") if—

(a) he treats B less favourably than he treats or would treat other persons whose circumstances are the same as B's; and

(b) he does so for a reason mentioned in subsection (2).

(2) The reasons are that—

(a) B has—

(i)   brought proceedings against A or any other person under this Act; or

(ii) given evidence or information in connection with such proceedings brought by any person; or

(iii) otherwise done anything under [or by reference to] this Act in relation to A or any other person; or

(iv) alleged that A or any other person has (whether or not the allegation so states) contravened this Act; or

(b) A believes or suspects that B has done or intends to do any of those things.

(3) Where B is a disabled person, or a person who has had a disability, the disability in question shall be disregarded in comparing his circumstances with those of any other person for the purposes of subsection (1)(a).

(3A) *****

(4) Subsection (1) does not apply to treatment of a person because of an allegation made by him if the allegation was false and not made in good faith.

(5) *****

(6) . . .

[56 Help for aggrieved persons in obtaining information etc.

(1) For the purposes of this section—

(a) a person who considers that he may have been—

(i)   discriminated against in contravention of Part 2 or 3, or

(ii) subjected to harassment in contravention of Part 2 or section 21A(2), is referred to as "the person aggrieved"; and

(b) a person against whom the person aggrieved may decide to institute, or has instituted, proceedings in respect of such discrimination or harassment is referred to as "the respondent".

(2) With a view to helping the person aggrieved decide whether to institute proceedings and, if he does so, to formulate and present his case in the most effective manner, the Secretary of State shall by order prescribe—

(a) forms by which the person aggrieved may question the respondent on his reasons for doing any relevant act, or on any other matter which is or may be relevant; and

(b) forms by which the respondent may if he so wishes reply to any questions.

(3) Where the person aggrieved questions the respondent in accordance with forms prescribed by an order under subsection (2)—

(a) the question, and any reply by the respondent (whether in accordance with such an order or not), shall be admissible as evidence in any proceedings under Part 2 or 3;

(b) if it appears to the court or tribunal in any such proceedings—

(i) that the respondent deliberately, and without reasonable excuse, omitted to reply within the period of eight weeks beginning with the day on which the question was served on him, or

(ii) that the respondent's reply is evasive or equivocal,

it may draw any inference which it considers it just and equitable to draw, including an inference that the respondent committed an unlawful act.

(4) The Secretary of State may by order—

(a) prescribe the period within which questions must be duly served in order to be admissible under subsection (3)(a); and

(b) prescribe the manner in which a question, and any reply by the respondent, may be duly served.]

(5)–(9) *****

57 Aiding unlawful acts

(1) A person who knowingly aids another person to do an [unlawful act] is to be treated for the purposes of this Act as himself doing the same kind of unlawful act.

(2) For the purposes of subsection (1), an employee or agent for whose act the employer or principal is liable under section 58 (or would be so liable but for section 58(5)) shall be taken to have aided the employer or principal to do the act.

(3)–(6) *****

58 Liability of employers and principals

(1) Anything done by a person in the course of his employment shall be treated for the purposes of this Act as also done by his employer, whether or not it was done with the employer's knowledge or approval.

(2) Anything done by a person as agent for another person with the authority of that other person shall be treated for the purposes of this Act as also done by that other person.

(3) Subsection (2) applies whether the authority was—

(a) express or implied; or

(b) given before or after the act in question was done.

(4), (5) *****

59 Statutory authority and national security etc

(1) Nothing in this Act makes unlawful any act done—

(a) in pursuance of any enactment; or

[(b) in pursuance of any instrument made under any enactment by—

(i) a Minister of the Crown,

(ii) a member of the Scottish Executive, or

(iii) the National Assembly for Wales; or

(c) to comply with any condition or requirement—

(i) imposed by a Minister of the Crown (whether before or after the passing of this Act) by virtue of any enactment,

(ii) imposed by a member of the Scottish Executive (whether before or after the coming into force of this sub-paragraph) by virtue of any enactment, or

(iii) imposed by the National Assembly for Wales (whether before or after the coming into force of this sub-paragraph) by virtue of any enactment.]

(2) In subsection (1) "enactment" includes one passed or made after the date on which this Act is passed and "instrument" includes one made after that date.

[(2A) Nothing in—

(a) Part 2 of this Act, or

(b) Part 3 of this Act to the extent that it relates to the provision of employment services,

makes unlawful any act done for the purpose of safeguarding national security if the doing of the act was justified by that purpose.]

(3) Nothing in [any other provision of] this Act makes unlawful any act done for the purpose of safeguarding national security.

60–64 *****

[64A Police

(1) For the purposes of Part 2, the holding of the office of constable shall be treated as employment—

(a) by the chief officer of police as respects any act done by him in relation to a constable or that office;

(b) by the police authority as respects any act done by them in relation to a constable or that office.

(2) For the purposes of section 58—

(a) the holding of the office of constable shall be treated as employment by the chief officer of police (and as not being employment by any other person); and

(b) anything done by a person holding such an office in the performance, or purported performance, of his functions shall be treated as done in the course of that employment.

(3) There shall be paid out of the police fund—

(a) any compensation, costs or expenses awarded against a chief officer of police in any proceedings brought against him under Part 2 [or 3] and any costs or expenses incurred by him in any such proceedings so far as not recovered by him in the proceedings; and

(b) any sum required by a chief officer of police for the settlement of any claim made against him under Part 2 [or 3] if the settlement is approved by the police authority.

(4)–(8) *****]

*****

Asylum and Immigration Act 1996

(1996, c. 49)

An Act to amend and supplement the Immigration Act 1971 and the Asylum and Immigration Appeals Act 1993; to make further provision with respect to persons subject to immigration control and the employment of such persons; and for connected purposes [24 July 1996]

Territorial extent: United Kingdom. The Act extends, with modifications, to Jersey and Guernsey: see SI 1998 Nos 1070 and 1264

Note: "The 1993 Act": Asylum and Immigration Appeals Act 1993.

5–7 *****

Persons subject to immigration control

8 Restrictions on employment

(1) Subject to subsection (2) below, if any person ("the employer") employs a person

subject to immigration control ("the employee") who has attained the age of 16, the employer shall be guilty of an offence if—

(a) the employee has not been granted leave to enter or remain in the United Kingdom; or

(b) the employee's leave is not valid and subsisting, or is subject to a condition precluding him from taking up employment,

and (in either case) the employee does not satisfy such conditions as may be specified in an order made by the Secretary of State.

[(2) It is a defence for a person charged with an offence under this section to prove that before the employment began any relevant requirement of an order of the Secretary of State under subsection (2A) was complied with.

(2A) An order under this subsection may—

(a) require the production to an employer of a document of a specified description;

(b) require the production to an employer of one document of each of a number of specified descriptions;

(c) require an employer to take specified steps to retain, copy or record the content of a document produced to him in accordance with the order;

(d) make provision which applies generally or only in specified circumstances;

(e) make different provision for different circumstances.]

(3) The defence afforded by subsection (2) above shall not be available in any case where the employer knew that his employment of the employee would constitute an offence under this section.

[(4) A person guilty of an offence under this section shall be liable—

(a) on conviction on indictment, to a fine, or

(b) on summary conviction, to a fine not exceeding the statutory maximum.]

(5) Where an offence under this section committed by a body corporate is proved to have been committed with the consent or connivance of, or to be attributable to any neglect on the part of—

(a) any director, manager, secretary or other similar officer of the body corporate; or

(b) any person who was purporting to act in any such capacity, he as well as the body corporate shall be guilty of the offence and shall be liable to be proceeded against and punished accordingly.

(6)–(10) *****

[8A   Code of practice

(1) The Secretary of State must issue a code of practice as to the measures which an employer is to be expected to take, or not to take, with a view to securing that, while avoiding the commission of an offence under section 8, he also avoids unlawful discrimination.

(2) "Unlawful discrimination" means—

(a) discrimination in contravention of section 4(1) of the Race Relations Act 1976 ("the 1976 Act"); or

(b) in relation to Northern Ireland, discrimination in contravention of Article 6(1) of the Race Relations (Northern Ireland) Order 1997 ("the 1997 Order").

(3) Before issuing the code, the Secretary of State must–

(a) prepare and publish a draft of the proposed code; and

(b) consider any representations about it which are made to him.

(4) In preparing the draft, the Secretary of State must consult—

(a) the Commission for Racial Equality;

(b) the Equality Commission for Northern Ireland; and

(c) such organisations and bodies (including organisations or associations or organisations representative of employers or of workers) as he considers appropriate.

(5) If the Secretary of State decides to proceed with the code, he must lay a draft of the code before both Houses of Parliament.

(6) The draft code may contain modifications to the original proposals made in the light of representations to the Secretary of State.

(7) After laying the draft code before Parliament, the Secretary of State may bring the code into operation by an order made by statutory instrument.

(8) An order under subsection (7)—

(a) shall be subject to annulment in pursuance of a resolution of either House of Parliament;

(b) may contain such transitional provisions or savings as appear to the Secretary of State to be necessary or expedient in connection with the code.

(9) A failure on the part of any person to observe a provision of the code does not of itself make him liable to any proceedings.

(10) But the code is admissible in evidence—

(a) in proceedings under the 1976 Act before an employment tribunal;

(b) in proceedings under the 1997 Order before an industrial tribunal.

(11) If any provision of the code appears to the tribunal to be relevant to any question arising in such proceedings, that provision is to be taken into account in determining the question.

(12), (13) *****]

Broadcasting Act 1996
(1996, c. 55)

An Act to make new provision about the broadcasting in digital form of television and sound programme services and the broadcasting in that form on television or radio frequencies of other services; to amend the Broadcasting Act 1990; to make provision about rights to televise sporting or other events of national interest; to amend in other respects the law relating to the provision of television and sound programme services; to provide for the establishment and functions of a Broadcasting Standards Commission and for the dissolution of the Broadcasting Complaints Commission and the Broadcasting Standards Council; to make provision for the transfer to other persons of property, rights and liabilities of the British Broadcasting Corporation relating to their transmission network; and for connected purposes [24 July 1996]

Territorial extent: United Kingdom

PART I   DIGITAL TERRESTRIAL TELEVISION BROADCASTING

Introductory

1   Multiplex services and digital programme services

[(1) In this Part "multiplex service" means (except where the context otherwise requires) a television multiplex service.]

(1A), (2), (3) . . .

(4) In this Part "digital programme service" means a service consisting in the provision by any person of television programmes (together with any ancillary services, as defined by section 24(2)) with a view to their being broadcast in digital form [so as to be available for reception by members of the public], whether by him or by some other person, but does not include—

(a) a qualifying service,

(b) a teletext service, or

(c) any service in the case of which the visual images to be broadcast do not consist wholly or mainly of images capable of being seen as moving pictures,

except, in the case of a service falling within paragraph (b) or (c), to the extent that it is an ancillary service.

(4A)–(6) *****

(7) In this section–

["broadcast" means broadcast otherwise than from a satellite] . . .

2   *****

General provisions about licences

3   Licences under Part I

(1) Any licence granted by [OFCOM] under this Part shall be in writing and (subject to the provisions of this Part) shall continue in force for such period as is provided, in relation to a licence of the kind in question, by the relevant provision of this Part.

(2) A licence may be so granted for the provision of such a service as is specified in the licence or for the provision of a service of such a description as is so specified.

(3) [OFCOM]—

(a) shall not grant a licence to any person unless they are satisfied that he is a fit and proper person to hold it, and

(b) shall do all that they can to secure that, if they cease to be so satisfied in the case of any person holding a licence, that person does not remain the holder of the licence; and nothing in this Part shall be construed as affecting the operation of this subsection or of section 5(1) or (2)(b) or (c).

(4), (5) *****

(6) A licence granted to any person under this Part shall not be transferable to any other person without the previous consent in writing of [OFCOM].

(7) Without prejudice to the generality of subsection (6), [OFCOM] shall not give their consent for the purposes of that subsection unless they are satisfied that any such other person would be in a position to comply with all of the conditions included in the licence which would have effect during the periods for which it is to be in force.

(8) *****

4–17   *****

Digital programme services

18   Licensing of digital programme services

(1) An application for a licence to provide digital programme services (in this Part referred to as a "digital programme licence") shall—

(a) be made in such manner as [OFCOM] may determine, and

(b) be accompanied by such fee (if any) as they may determine.

(2) At any time after receiving such an application and before determining it, [OFCOM] may require the applicant to furnish such additional information as they may consider necessary for the purpose of considering the application.

(3) Any information to be furnished to [OFCOM] under this section shall, if they so require, be in such form or verified in such manner as they may specify.

(4) Where an application for a digital programme licence is made to [OFCOM] in accordance with the provisions of this section, they shall grant the licence unless precluded from doing so by section 3(3)(a) or 5(1).

(5), (6) . . .

19–39   *****

PART II   DIGITAL TERRESTRIAL SOUND BROADCASTING

Introductory

40–96   *****

PART IV   SPORTING AND OTHER EVENTS OF NATIONAL INTEREST

97   Listed events

[(1) The Secretary of State may, for the purposes of this Part, maintain a list of sporting and other events of national interest, and an event for the time being included in the list is referred to in this Part as a "listed event".

(1A) A list maintained under subsection (1) must be divided into two categories, and those categories are referred to in this Part as "Group A" and "Group B".

(1B) Each listed event must be allocated either to Group A or to Group B.

(2) Before drawing up such a list, or revising or ceasing to maintain it, the Secretary of State must consult—

(a) OFCOM,

(b) the BBC,

(c) the Welsh Authority, and

(d) in relation to a relevant event, the person from whom the rights to televise that event may be acquired.

(2A) For the purposes of subsection (2)(d), a relevant event is an event which the Secretary of State proposes—

(a) to include in a list maintained under subsection (1),

(b) to omit from such a list, or

(c) to move from one category in such a list to the other.]

(3) As soon as he has drawn up or revised such a list as is mentioned in subsection (1), the Secretary of State shall publish the list in such manner as he considers appropriate for bringing it to the attention of—

(a) the persons mentioned in subsection (2), and

(b) every person who is the holder of a licence granted . . . under Part I of the 1990 Act or a digital programme licence granted . . . under Part I of this Act.

(4) In this section "national interest" includes interest within England, Scotland, Wales or Northern Ireland.

(5) The [inclusion of any event in] such a list as is mentioned in subsection (1) shall not affect—

(a) the validity of any contract entered into before the date on which the Secretary of State consulted the persons mentioned in subsection (2) in relation to the proposed [inclusion], or

(b) the exercise of any rights acquired under such a contract.

[(5A) The allocation or transfer of an event to group A does not affect the validity of a contract entered into before the day on which the Secretary of State consulted the persons mentioned in subsection (2) in relation to the proposed allocation or transfer.

(5B) The Secretary of State may direct that, for the transitional purposes set out in the direction, the transfer of a Group B event to Group A is not to affect the application to that event of provisions of this Part relating to a Group B event.]

(6) The list drawn up by the Secretary of State for the purposes of section 182 of the 1990 Act, as that list is in force immediately before the commencement of this section, shall be taken to have been drawn up for the purposes of this Part.

*****

Criminal Procedure and Investigations Act 1996
(1996, c. 25)

An Act to make provision about criminal procedure and criminal investigations   [4 July 1996]

Territorial extent: England and Wales, Northern Ireland (ss. 22–24, 26, 41, 58); England and Wales, Scotland (ss. 37, 38, 40); England and Wales (s. 39); United Kingdom (ss. 59, 60). In its application to Northern Ireland the Act is subject to modifications as set out in Sch. 4 (not reprinted)

PART II   CRIMINAL INVESTIGATIONS

22   Introduction

(1) For the purposes of this Part a criminal investigation is an investigation conducted by police officers with a view to it being ascertained—

   (a) whether a person should be charged with an offence, or

   (b) whether a person charged with an offence is guilty of it.

(2) In this Part references to material are to material of all kinds, and in particular include references to—

   (a) information, and

   (b) objects of all descriptions.

(3) In this Part references to recording information are to putting it in a durable or retrievable form (such as writing or tape).

23   Code of practice

(1) The Secretary of State shall prepare a code of practice containing provisions designed to secure—

   (a) that where a criminal investigation is conducted all reasonable steps are taken for the purposes of the investigation and, in particular, all reasonable lines of inquiry are pursued;

   (b) that information which is obtained in the course of a criminal investigation and may be relevant to the investigation is recorded;

   (c) that any record of such information is retained;

   (d) that any other material which is obtained in the course of a criminal investigation and may be relevant to the investigation is retained;

   (e) that information falling within paragraph (b) and material falling within paragraph (d) is revealed to a person who is involved in the prosecution of criminal proceedings arising out of or relating to the investigation and who is identified in accordance with prescribed provisions;

   (f) that where such a person inspects information or other material in pursuance of a requirement that it be revealed to him, and he requests that it be disclosed to the accused, the accused is allowed to inspect it or is given a copy of it;

   (g) that where such a person is given a document indicating the nature of information or other material in pursuance of a requirement that it be revealed to him, and he requests that it be disclosed to the accused, the accused is allowed to inspect it or is given a copy of it;

   (h) that the person who is to allow the accused to inspect information or other material or to give him a copy of it shall decide which of those (inspecting or giving a copy) is appropriate;

   (i) that where the accused is allowed to inspect material as mentioned in paragraph (f) or (g) and he requests a copy, he is given one unless the person allowing the

inspection is of opinion that it is not practicable or not desirable to give him one;
- (j) that a person mentioned in paragraph (e) is given a written statement that prescribed activities which the code requires have been carried out.

(2)–(8) *****

24–25 *****

26 Effect of code

(1) A person other than a police officer who is charged with the duty of conducting an investigation with a view to it being ascertained—
- (a) whether a person should be charged with an offence, or
- (b) whether a person charged with an offence is guilty of it,

shall in discharging that duty have regard to any relevant provision of a code which would apply if the investigation were conducted by police officers.

(2) A failure—
- (a) by a police officer to comply with any provision of a code for the time being in operation by virtue of an order under section 25, or
- (b) by a person to comply with subsection (1),

shall not in itself render him liable to any criminal or civil proceedings.

(3) In all criminal and civil proceedings a code in operation at any time by virtue of an order under section 25 shall be admissible in evidence.

(4) If it appears to a court or tribunal conducting criminal or civil proceedings that—
- (a) any provision of a code in operation at any time by virtue of an order under section 25, or
- (b) any failure mentioned in subsection (2)(a) or (b),

is relevant to any question arising in the proceedings, the provision or failure shall be taken into account in deciding the question.

27–36 *****

Reporting restrictions

37 Restrictions on reporting

(1) Except as provided by this section—
- (a) no written report of proceedings falling within subsection (2) shall be published in [the United Kingdom];
- (b) no report of proceedings falling within subsection (2) shall be included in a relevant programme for reception in [the United Kingdom].

(2) The following proceedings fall within this subsection—
- (a) a preparatory hearing;
- (b) an application for leave to appeal in relation to such a hearing;
- (c) an appeal in relation to such a hearing.

(3) The judge dealing with a preparatory hearing may order that subsection (1) shall not apply, or shall not apply to a specified extent, to a report of—
- (a) the preparatory hearing, or
- (b) an application to the judge for leave to appeal to the Court of Appeal under section 35(1) in relation to the preparatory hearing.

(4)–(8) *****

(9) Subsection (1) does not apply to a report which contains only one or more of the following matters–
- (a) the identity of the court and the name of the judge;
- (b) the names, ages, home addresses and occupations of the accused and witnesses;
- (c) the offence or offences, or a summary of them, with which the accused is or are charged;

    (d) the names of counsel and solicitors in the proceedings;

    (e) where the proceedings are adjourned, the date and place to which they are adjourned;

    (f) any arrangements as to bail;

    (g) [whether a right to representation funded by the Legal Services Commission as part of the Criminal Defence Services was granted to the accused or any of the accused.]

(10)–(12) *****

38 Offences in connection with reporting

(1) If a report is published or included in a relevant programme in contravention of section 37 each of the following persons in guilty of an offence—

    (a) in the case of a publication of a written report as part of a newspaper or periodical, any proprietor, editor or publisher of the newspaper or periodical;

    (b) in the case of a publication of a written report otherwise than as part of a newspaper or periodical, the person who publishes it;

    (c) in the case of the inclusion of a report in a relevant programme, any body corporate which is engaged in providing the service in which the programme is included and any person having functions in relation to the programme corresponding to those of an editor of a newspaper.

(2) A person guilty of an offence under this section is liable on summary conviction to a fine of an amount not exceeding level 5 on the standard scale.

(3) Proceedings for an offence under this section shall not be instituted in England and Wales otherwise than by or with the consent of the Attorney General.

(3A), (4) *****

PART IV   RULINGS

39 Meaning of pre-trial hearing

(1) For the purposes of this Part a hearing is a pre-trial hearing if it relates to a trial on indictment and it takes place—

    [(a) after the accused has been sent for trial for the offence], and

    (b) before the start of the trial.

(2), (3) *****

40 Power to make rulings

(1) A judge may make at a pre-trial hearing a ruling as to—

    (a) any question as to the admissibility of evidence;

    (b) any other question of law relating to the case concerned.

(2) A ruling may be made under this section—

    (a) on an application by a party to the case, or

    (b) of the judge's own motion.

(3) Subject to subsection (4), a ruling made under this section has binding effect from the time it is made until the case against the accused or, if there is more than one, against each of them is disposed of; and the case against an accused is disposed of if—

    (a) he is acquitted or convicted, or

    (b) the prosecutor decides not to proceed with the case against him.

(4)–(7) *****

41 Restrictions on reporting

(1) Except as provided by this section—

    (a) no written report of matters falling within subsection (2) shall be published in Great Britain;

(b) no report of matters falling within subsection (2) shall be included in a relevant programme for reception in Great Britain.

(2) The following matters fall within this subsection—

(a) a ruling made under section 40;

(b) proceedings on an application for a ruling to be made under section 40;

(c) an order that a ruling made under section 40 be discharged or varied or further varied;

(d) proceedings on an application for a ruling made under section 40 to be discharged or varied or further varied.

(3) The judge dealing with any matter falling within subsection (2) may order that subsection (1) shall not apply, or shall not apply to a specified extent, to a report of the matter.

(4) Where there is only one accused and he objects to the making of an order under subsection (3) the judge shall make the order if (and only if) satisfied after hearing the representations of the accused that it is in the interests of justice to do so; and if the order is made it shall not apply to the extent that a report deals with any such objection or representations.

(5) Where there are two or more accused and one or more of them objects to the making of an order under subsection (3) the judge shall make the order if (and only if) satisfied after hearing the representations of each of the accused that it is in the interests of justice to do so; and if the order is made it shall not apply to the extent that a report deals with any such objection or representations.

(6) Subsection (1) does not apply to—

(a) the publication of a report of matters, or

(b) the inclusion in a relevant programme of a report of matters, at the conclusion of the trial of the accused or of the last of the accused to be tried.

(7), (8) *****

42–57 *****

Derogatory assertions

58 Orders in respect of certain assertions

(1) This section applies where a person has been convicted of an offence and a speech in mitigation is made by him or on his behalf before—

(a) a court determining what sentence should be passed on him in respect of the offence, or

(b) a magistrates' court determining whether he should be committed to the Crown Court for sentence.

(2) This section also applies where a sentence has been passed on a person in respect of an offence and a submission relating to the sentence is made by him or on his behalf before—

(a) a court hearing an appeal against or reviewing the sentence, or

(b) a court determining whether to grant leave to appeal against the sentence.

(3) Where it appears to the court that there is a real possibility that an order under subsection (8) will be made in relation to the assertion, the court may make an order under subsection (7) in relation to the assertion.

(4) Where there are substantial grounds for believing—

(a) that an assertion forming part of the speech or submission is derogatory to a person's character (for instance, because it suggests that his conduct is or has been criminal, immoral or improper), and

(b) that the assertion is false or that the facts asserted are irrelevant to the sentence, the court may make an order under subsection (8) in relation to the assertion.

(5) An order under subsection (7) or (8) must not be made in relation to an assertion if it appears to the court that the assertion was previously made—

(a) at the trial at which the person was convicted of the offence, or

(b) during any other proceedings relating to the offence.

(6) Section 59 has effect where a court makes an order under subsection (7) or (8).

(7) An order under this subsection—

(a) may be made at any time before the court has made a determination with regard to sentencing;

(b) may be revoked at any time by the court;

(c) subject to paragraph (b), shall cease to have effect when the court makes a determination with regard to sentencing.

(8) An order under this subsection—

(a) may be made after the court has made a determination with regard to sentencing, but only if it is made as soon as is reasonably practicable after the making of the determination;

(b) may be revoked at any time by the court;

(c) subject to paragraph (b), shall cease to have effect at the end of the period of 12 months beginning with the day on which it is made;

(d) may be made whether or not an order has been made under subsection (7) with regard to the case concerned.

59   Restriction on reporting of assertions

(1) Where a court makes an order under section 58(7) or (8) in relation to any assertion, at any time when the order has effect the assertion must not—

(a) be published in Great Britain in a written publication available to the public, or

(b) be included in a relevant programme for reception in Great Britain.

(2), (3) *****

60   Reporting of assertions: offences

(1) If an assertion is published or included in a relevant programme in contravention of section 59, each of the following persons is guilty of an offence—

(a) in the case of publication in a newspaper or periodical, any proprietor, any editor and any publisher of the newspaper or periodical;

(b) in the case of publication in any other form, the person publishing the assertion;

(c) in the case of an assertion included in a relevant programme, any body corporate engaged in providing the service in which the programme is included and any person having functions in relation to the programme corresponding to those of an editor of a newspaper.

(2) A person guilty of an offence under this section is liable on summary conviction to a fine of an amount not exceeding level 5 on the standard scale.

(3) Where a person is charged with an offence under this section it is a defence to prove that at the time of the alleged offence—

(a) he was not aware, and neither suspected nor had reason to suspect, that an order under section 58(7) or (8) had effect at that time, or

(b) he was not aware, and neither suspected nor had reason to suspect, that the publication or programme in question was of, or (as the case may be) included, the assertion in question.

(4)–(6) *****

*****

Defamation Act 1996

(1996, c. 31)

An Act to amend the law of defamation and to amend the law of limitation with respect to actions for defamation or malicious falsehood   [4 July 1996]

Territorial extent: United Kingdom

*****

Evidence concerning proceedings in Parliament

13 Evidence concerning proceedings in Parliament

(1) Where the conduct of a person in or in relation to proceedings in Parliament is in issue in defamation proceedings, he may waive for the purposes of those proceedings, so far as concerns him, the protection of any enactment or rule of law which prevents proceedings in Parliament being impeached or questioned in any court or place out of Parliament.

(2) Where a person waives that protection—

(a) any such enactment or rule of law shall not apply to prevent evidence being given, questions being asked or statements, submissions, comments or findings being made about his conduct, and

(b) none of those things shall be regarded as infringing the privilege of either House of Parliament.

(3) The waiver by one person of that protection does not affect its operation in relation to another person who has not waived it.

(4) Nothing in this section affects any enactment or rule of law so far as it protects a person (including a person who has waived the protection referred to above) from legal liability for words spoken or things done in the course of, or for the purposes of or incidental to, any proceedings in Parliament.

(5) Without prejudice to the generality of subsection (4), that subsection applies to—

(a) the giving of evidence before either House or a committee;

(b) the presentation or submission of a document to either House or a committee;

(c) the preparation of a document for the purposes of or incidental to the transacting of any such business;

(d) the formulation, making or publication of a document, including a report, by or pursuant to an order of either House or a committee; and

(e) any communication with the Parliamentary Commissioner for Standards or any person having functions in connection with the registration of Members' interests.

In this subsection "a committee" means a committee of either House or a joint committee of both Houses of Parliament.

Statutory privilege

14 Reports of court proceedings absolutely privileged

(1) A fair and accurate report of proceedings in public before a court to which this section applies, if published contemporaneously with the proceedings, is absolutely privileged.

(2) A report of proceedings which by an order of the court, or as a consequence of any statutory provision, is required to be postponed shall be treated as published contemporaneously if it is published as soon as practicable after publication is permitted.

(3) This section applies to—

(a) any court in the United Kingdom,

(b) the European Court of Justice or any court attached to that court,

(c) the European Court of Human Rights, and

(d) any international criminal tribunal established by the Security Council of the United Nations or by an international agreement to which the United Kingdom is a party.

In paragraph (a) "court" includes any tribunal or body exercising the judicial power of the State.

(4) *****

15 Reports, &c. protected by qualified privilege

(1) The publication of any report or other statement mentioned in Schedule 1 to this Act is privileged unless the publication is shown to be made with malice, subject as follows.

(2) In defamation proceedings in respect of the publication of a report or other statement mentioned in Part II of that Schedule, there is no defence under this section if the plaintiff shows that the defendant—

(a) was requested by him to publish in a suitable manner a reasonable letter or statement by way of explanation or contradiction, and

(b) refused or neglected to do so.

For this purpose "in a suitable manner" means in the same manner as the publication complained of or in a manner that is adequate and reasonable in the circumstances.

(3) This section does not apply to the publication to the public, or a section of the public, of matter which is not of public concern and the publication of which is not for the public benefit.

(4) Nothing in this section shall be construed—

(a) as protecting the publication of matter the publication of which is prohibited by law, or

(b) as limiting or abridging any privilege subsisting apart from this section.

16–19 *****

20 Short title and saving

(1) This Act may be cited as the Defamation Act 1996.

(2) Nothing in this Act affects the law relating to criminal libel.

Section 15   SCHEDULE 1
                        QUALIFIED PRIVILEGE

PART I   STATEMENTS HAVING QUALIFIED PRIVILEGE
WITHOUT EXPLANATION OR CONTRADICTION

1. A fair and accurate report of proceedings in public of a legislature anywhere in the world.

2. A fair and accurate report of proceedings in public before a court anywhere in the world.

3. A fair and accurate report of proceedings in public of a person appointed to hold a public inquiry by a government or legislature anywhere in the world.

4. A fair and accurate report of proceedings in public anywhere in the world of an international organisation or an international conference.

5. A fair and accurate copy of or extract from any register or other document required by law to be open to public inspection.

6. A notice or advertisement published by or on the authority of a court, or of a judge or officer of a court, anywhere in the world.

7. A fair and accurate copy of or extract from matter published by or on the authority of a government or legislature anywhere in the world.

8.   A fair and accurate copy of or extract from matter published anywhere in the world by an international organisation or an international conference.

PART II   STATEMENTS PRIVILEGED SUBJECT TO EXPLANATION
OR CONTRADICTION

9.—(1) A fair and accurate copy of or extract from a notice or other matter issued for the information of the public by or on behalf of—
   (a) a legislature in any member State or the European parliament;
   (b) the government of any member State, or any authority performing governmental functions in any member State or part of a member State, or the European Commission;
   (c) an international organisation or international conference.
   (2) In this paragraph "governmental functions" includes police functions.
   10.   A fair and accurate copy of or extract from a document made available by a court in any member State or the European Court of Justice (or any court attached to that court), or by a judge or officer of any such court.
   11.—(1) A fair and accurate report of proceedings at any public meeting or sitting in the United Kingdom of—
   (a) a local authority or local authority committee;
   [(aa) in the case of a local authority which are operating executive arrangements, the executive of that authority or a committee of that executive];
   (b) a justice or justices of the peace acting otherwise than as a court exercising judicial authority;
   (c) a commission, tribunal, committee or person appointed for the purposes of any inquiry by any statutory provision, by Her Majesty or by a Minister of the Crown [a minister of the Scottish Executive] or a Northern Ireland Department;
   (d) a person appointed by a local authority to hold a local inquiry in pursuance of any statutory provision;
   (e) any other tribunal, board, committee or body constituted by or under, and exercising functions under, any statutory provision.
   (1A)–(3) *****

*****

Education Act 1996

(1996, c. 56)

An Act to consolidate the Education Act 1944 and certain other enactments relating to education, with amendments to give effect to a recommendation of the Law Commission   [24 July 1996]

Territorial extent: England and Wales

*****

Sex education

403   Sex education: manner of provision
   (1) The . . . governing body and head teacher shall take such steps as are reasonably practicable to secure that where sex education is given to any registered pupils at a maintained

school, it is given in such a manner as to encourage those pupils to have due regard to moral considerations and the value of family life.

[(1A) The Secretary of State must issue guidance designed to secure that when sex education is given to registered pupils at maintained schools—

    (a) they learn the nature of marriage and its importance for family life and the bringing up of children, and

    (b) they are protected from teaching and materials which are inappropriate having regard to the age and the religious and cultural background of the pupils concerned.

(1B) In discharging their functions under subsection (1) governing bodies and head teachers must have regard to the Secretary of State's guidance.

(1C) Guidance under subsection (1A) must include guidance about any material which may be produced by NHS bodies for use for the purposes of sex education in schools.

(1D) The Secretary of State may at any time revise his guidance under subsection (1A).]

(2) In [this section] "maintained school" includes a [community or foundation special school] established in a hospital, [and "NHS Body" has the same meaning as in section 22 of the National Health Service Act 1977].

404   Sex education: statements of policy

(1) The governing body of a maintained school shall—

    (a) make, and keep up to date, a separate written statement of their policy with regard to the provision of sex education, and

    (b) make copies of the statement available for inspection (at all reasonable times) by parents of registered pupils at the school and provide a copy of the statement free of charge to any such parent who asks for one.

[(1A) A statement under subsection (1) must include a statement of the effect of section 405.]

(2) In subsection (1) "maintained school" includes, in relation to pupils who are provided with secondary education, a [community or foundation special school] established in a hospital.

(3) . . .

405   Exemption from sex education

If the parent of any pupil in attendance at a maintained school requests that he may be wholly or partly excused from receiving sex education at the school, the pupil shall, except so far as such education is comprised in the National Curriculum, be so excused accordingly until the request is withdrawn.

Politics

406   Political indoctrination

(1) The local education authority, governing body and head teacher shall forbid—

    (a) the pursuit of partisan political activities by any of those registered pupils at a maintained school who are junior pupils, and

    (b) the promotion of partisan political views in the teaching of any subject in the school.

(2) In the case of activities which take place otherwise than on the school premises, subsection (1)(a) applies only where arrangements for junior pupils to take part in the activities are made by—

    (a) any member of the school's staff (in his capacity as such), or

    (b) anyone acting on behalf of the school or of a member of the school's staff (in his capacity as such).

(3) In this section "maintained school" includes a [community or foundation special school] established in a hospital.

407   Duty to secure balanced treatment of political issues

(1) The local education authority, governing body and head teacher shall take such steps as are reasonably practicable to secure that where political issues are brought to the attention of pupils while they are—

(a) in attendance at a maintained school, or

(b) taking part in extra-curricular activities which are provided or organised for registered pupils at the school by or on behalf of the school, they are offered a balanced presentation of opposing views.

(2) In this section "maintained school" includes a [community or foundation special school] established in a hospital.

*****

Employment Rights Act 1996
(1996, c. 18)

An Act to consolidate enactments relating to employment rights   [22 May 1996]

Territorial extent: England and Wales, Scotland

Note: The sections in Part XIII which are printed here apply to the civil service, the armed forces and parliamentary staff the major provisions of the Act, relating to contracts of employment, time off and maternity rights. The earlier sections (Part IVA) are added by the Public Interest Disclosure Act 1998.

*****

[PART IVA   PROTECTED DISCLOSURES

43A   Meaning of "protected disclosure"

In this Act a "protected disclosure" means a qualifying disclosure (as defined by section 43B) which is made by a worker in accordance with any of sections 43C to 43H.

43B   Disclosures qualifying for protection

(1) In this Part a "qualifying disclosure" means any disclosure of information which, in the reasonable belief of the worker making the disclosure, tends to show one or more of the following–

(a) that a criminal offence has been committed, is being committed or is likely to be committed,

(b) that a person has failed, is failing or is likely to fail to comply with any legal obligation to which he is subject,

(c) that a miscarriage of justice has occurred, is occurring or is likely to occur,

(d) that the health or safety of any individual has been, is being or is likely to be endangered,

(e) that the environment has been, is being or is likely to be damaged, or

(f) that information tending to show any matter falling within any one of the preceding paragraphs has been, is being or is likely to be deliberately concealed.

(2) For the purposes of subsection (1), it is immaterial whether the relevant failure occurred, occurs or would occur in the United Kingdom or elsewhere, and whether the law applying to it is that of the United Kingdom or of any other country or territory.

(3) A disclosure of information is not a qualifying disclosure if the person making the disclosure commits an offence by making it.

(4) A disclosure of information in respect of which a claim to legal professional privilege (or, in Scotland, to confidentiality as between client and professional legal adviser) could be maintained in legal proceedings is not a qualifying disclosure if it is made by a person to whom the information had been disclosed in the course of obtaining legal advice.

(5) In this Part "the relevant failure", in relation to a qualifying disclosure, means the matter falling within paragraphs (a) to (f) of subsection (1).

43C   Disclosure to employer or other responsible person

(1) A qualifying disclosure is made in accordance with this section if the worker makes the disclosure in good faith—

(a) to his employer, or

(b) where the worker reasonably believes that the relevant failure relates solely or mainly to—

(i) the conduct of a person other than his employer, or

(ii) any other matter for which a person other than his employer has legal responsibility,

to that other person.

(2) A worker who, in accordance with a procedure whose use by him is authorised by his employer, makes a qualifying disclosure to a person other than his employer, is to be treated for the purposes of this Part as making the qualifying disclosure to his employer.

43D   Disclosure to legal adviser

A qualifying disclosure is made in accordance with this section if it is made in the course of obtaining legal advice.

43E   Disclosure to Minister of the Crown

A qualifying disclosure is made in accordance with this section if—

(a) the worker's employer is—

(i) an individual appointed under any enactment [including any enactment comprised in or in an instrument made under an Act of the Scottish Parliament] by a Minister of the Crown [or a member of the Scottish Executive], or

(ii) a body any of whose members are so appointed, and

(b) the disclosure is made in good faith to a Minister of the Crown [or a member of the Scottish Executive].

43F   Disclosure to prescribed person

(1) A qualifying disclosure is made in accordance with this section if the worker—

(a) makes the disclosure in good faith to a person prescribed by an order made by the Secretary of State for the purposes of this section, and

(b) reasonably believes—

(i) that the relevant failure falls within any description of matters in respect of which that person is so prescribed, and

(ii) that the information disclosed, and any allegation contained in it, are substantially true.

(2) An order prescribing persons for the purposes of this section may specify persons or descriptions of persons, and shall specify the descriptions of matters in respect of which each person, or persons of each description, is or are prescribed.

43G   Disclosure in other cases

(1) A qualifying disclosure is made in accordance with this section if—

(a) the worker makes the disclosure in good faith,

(b) he reasonably believes that the information disclosed, and any allegation contained in it, are substantially true,

(c) he does not make the disclosure for purposes of personal gain,

(d) any of the conditions in subsection (2) is met, and

(e) in all the circumstances of the case, it is reasonable for him to make the disclosure.

(2) The conditions referred to in subsection (1)(d) are—

(a) that, at the time he makes the disclosure, the worker reasonably believes that he will be subjected to a detriment by his employer if he makes a disclosure to his employer or in accordance with section 43F,

(b) that, in a case where no person is prescribed for the purposes of section 43F in relation to the relevant failure, the worker reasonably believes that it is likely that evidence relating to the relevant failure will be concealed or destroyed if he makes a disclosure to his employer, or

(c) that the worker has previously made a disclosure of substantially the same information—

(i) to his employer, or

(ii) in accordance with section 43F.

(3) In determining for the purposes of subsection (1)(c) whether it is reasonable for the worker to make the disclosure, regard shall be had, in particular, to—

(a) the identity of the person to whom the disclosure is made,

(b) the seriousness of the relevant failure,

(c) whether the relevant failure is continuing or is likely to occur in the future,

(d) whether the disclosure is made in breach of a duty of confidentiality owed by the employer to any other person,

(e) in a case falling within subsection (2)(c)(i) or (ii), any action which the employer or the person to whom the previous disclosure in accordance with section 43F was made has taken or might reasonably be expected to have taken as a result of the previous disclosure, and

(f) in a case falling within subsection (2)(c)(i), whether in making the disclosure to the employer the worker complied with any procedure whose use by him was authorised by the employer.

(4) For the purposes of this section a subsequent disclosure may be regarded as a disclosure of substantially the same information as that disclosed by a previous disclosure as mentioned in subsection (2)(c) even though the subsequent disclosure extends to information about action taken or not taken by any person as a result of the previous disclosure.

43H Disclosure of exceptionally serious failure

(1) A qualifying disclosure is made in accordance with this section if—

(a) the worker makes the disclosure in good faith,

(b) he reasonably believes that the information disclosed, and any allegation contained in it, are substantially true,

(c) he does not make the disclosure for purposes of personal gain,

(d) the relevant failure is of an exceptionally serious nature, and

(e) in all the circumstances of the case, it is reasonable for him to make the disclosure.

(2) In determining for the purposes of subsection (1)(e) whether it is reasonable for the worker to make the disclosure, regard shall be had, in particular, to the identity of the person to whom the disclosure is made.]

43J–43K   *****

[43KA Application of this part and related provisions to police

(1) For the purposes of—

(a) this Part,

(b) section 47B and sections 48 and 49 so far as relating to that section, and

(c) section 103A and the other provisions of Part 10 so far as relating to the right not to be unfairly dismissed in a case where the dismissal is unfair by virtue of section 103A,

a person who holds, otherwise than under a contract of employment, the office of constable or an appointment as a police cadet shall be treated as an employee employed by the relevant officer under a contract of employment; and any reference to a worker being "employed" and to his "employer" shall be construed accordingly.]

(2) *****

43L–47A   ***

[47B   Protected disclosures**

(1) A worker has the right not to be subjected to any detriment by any act, or any deliberate failure to act, by his employer done on the ground that the worker has made a protected disclosure.]

(2), (3) *****

48–103   ***

[103A   Protected Disclosure**

An employee who is dismissed shall be regarded for the purposes of this Part as unfairly dismissed if the reason (or, if more than one, the principal reason) for the dismissal is that the employee made a protected disclosure.]

104–190   ***

PART XIII   MISCELLANEOUS

CHAPTER I   PARTICULAR TYPES OF EMPLOYMENT

Crown employment etc.

191   Crown Employment

(1) Subject to sections 192 and 193, the provisions of this Act to which this section applies have effect in relation to Crown employment and persons in Crown employment as they have effect in relation to other employment and other employees or workers.

(2) This section applies to—
(a) Parts I to III,
[(aa) Part IVA,]
(b) Part V, apart from section 45,
(c) [Parts VI to VIIIA],
(d) in Part IX, sections 92 and 93,
(e) Part X, apart from section 101, and
(f) this Part and Parts XIV and XV.

(3) In this Act "Crown employment" means employment under or for the purposes of a government department or any officer or body exercising on behalf of the Crown functions conferred by a statutory provision.

(4) For the purposes of the application of provisions of this Act in relation to Crown employment in accordance with subsection (1)—
(a) references to an employee or a worker shall be construed as references to a person in Crown employment,
(b) references to a contract of employment, or a worker's contract, shall be construed as references to the terms of employment of a person in Crown employment,
(c) references to dismissal, or to the termination of a worker's contract, shall be construed as references to the termination of Crown employment,

(d) references to redundancy shall be construed as references to the existence of such circumstances as are treated, in accordance with any arrangements falling within section 177(3) for the time being in force, as equivalent to redundancy in relation to Crown employment, and

(e) references to an undertaking shall be construed—

(i) in relation to a Minister of the Crown, as references to his functions or (as the context may require) to the department of which he is in charge, and

(ii) in relation to a government department, officer or body, as references to the functions of the department, officer or body or (as the context may require) to the department, officer or body.

(5) Where the terms of employment of a person in Crown employment restrict his right to take part in—

(a) certain political activities, or

(b) activities which may conflict with his official functions, nothing in section 50 requires him to be allowed time off work for public duties connected with any such activities.

(6) *****

192 *****

193 National security

[Part IVA and section 47B of this Act do not apply in relation to employment for the purposes of—

(a) the Security Service,

(b) the Secret Intelligence Service, or

(c) the Government Communications Headquarters.]

*****

Police Act 1996

(1996, c. 16)

An Act to consolidate the Police Act 1964, Part IX of the Police and Criminal Evidence Act 1984, Chapter I of Part I of the Police and Magistrates' Courts Act 1994 and certain other enactments relating to the police   [22 May 1996]

Territorial extent: England and Wales (and in the case of Part III (ss. 59–64) Scotland)

PART I   ORGANISATION OF POLICE FORCES

Police areas

1 Police areas

(1) England and Wales shall be divided into police areas.

(2) The police areas referred to in subsection (1) shall be—

(a) those listed in Schedule 1 (subject to any amendment made to that Schedule by an order under section 32 below, section 58 of the Local Government Act 1972, or section 17 of the Local Government Act 1992),

(b) the metropolitan police district, and

(c) the City of London police area.

(3) References in Schedule 1 to any local government area are to that area as it is for the time being . . .

Forces outside London

2   Maintenance of police forces
A police force shall be maintained for every police area for the time being listed in Schedule 1.

3   Establishment of police authorities
(1) There shall be a police authority for every police area for the time being listed in Schedule 1.

(2) A police authority established under this section for any area shall be a body corporate to be known by the name of the area with the adddition of the words "Police Authority".

4   Membership of police authorities etc.
(1) Subject to subsection (2), each police authority established under section 3 shall consist of seventeen members.

(2) The Secretary of State may by order provide in relation to a police authority specified in the order that the number of its members shall be a specified odd number greater than seventeen.

(3) A statutory instrument containing an order under subsection (2) shall be laid before Parliament after being made.

(4) Schedules 2 and 3 shall have effect in relation to police authorities established under section 3 and the appointment of their members.

5   *****

[The metropolitan police force

5A   Maintenance of the metropolitan police force
A police force shall be maintained for the metropolitan police district.

5B   Establishment of the Metropolitan Police Authority
(1) There shall be a police authority for the metropolitan police district.

(2) The police authority established under this section shall be a body corporate to be known as the Metropolitan Police Authority.

5C   Membership etc. of the Metropolitan Police Authority
(1) The Metropolitan Police Authority shall consist of twenty three members (subject to subsection (2)).

(2) The Secretary of State may by order provide that the number of members of the Metropolitan Police Authority shall be a specified odd number not less than seventeen.

(3)–(6) *****

The metropolitan police and forces outside London]

6   General functions of police authorities
(1) Every police authority established under section 3 shall secure the maintenance of an efficient and effective police force for its area.

(2) In discharging its functions, every police authority established under section 3 shall have regard to—
    (a) any objectives determined by the Secretary of State under section 37,
    (b) any objectives determined by the authority under section 7,
    (c) any performance targets established by the authority, whether in compliance with a direction under section 38 or otherwise, and
    (d) any local policing plan issued by the authority under section 8.

(3) In discharging any function to which a code of practice issued under section 39 relates, a police authority established under section 3 shall have regard to the code.

(4) A police authority shall comply with any direction given to it by the Secretary of State under section 38 or 40.

[(5) This section shall apply in relation to the Metropolitan Police Authority as it applies in relation to a police authority established under section 3.]

[6A   Three-year strategy plans

(1) Every police authority maintaining a police force for a police area in England and Wales shall, before the beginning of every relevant three-year period, issue a plan ("a three-year strategy plan") which sets out the authority's medium and long term strategies for the policing of that area during that period.

(2) Before a three-year strategy plan for any period is issued by a police authority, a draft of a plan setting out medium and long term strategies for the policing of the authority's area during that period must have been—

    (a) prepared by the chief officer of police of the police force maintained by that authority; and

    (b) submitted by him to the police authority for its consideration.

(3) In preparing the draft plan, the chief officer of police of a police force shall have regard to the views, obtained in accordance with arrangements under section 96, of people in the police area in question.

(4) A police authority which has issued a three-year strategy plan for any period may modify that plan at any time during that period.

(5) It shall be the duty, in issuing, preparing or modifying a three-year strategy plan or a draft of such a plan, of every police authority or chief officer of police to have regard to the National Policing Plan in force at that time.

(6) The Secretary of State—

    (a) shall issue guidance to police authorities and chief officers of police as to the matters to be contained in any three-year strategy plan, and as to the form to be taken by any such plan; and

    (b) may from time to time revise and modify that guidance;

and it shall be the duty of every police authority and chief officer of police to take account of any guidance under this subsection when issuing, preparing or modifying any such plan or any draft plan prepared for the purposes of subsection (2).]

(7)–(15) *****

7   Local policing objectives

(1) Every police authority established under section 3 shall, before the beginning of each financial year, determine objectives for the policing of the authority's area during that year.

(2) Objectives determined under this section may relate to matters to which objectives determined under section 37 also relate, or to other matters, but in any event shall be so framed as to be consistent with the objectives determined under that section.

(3) Before determining objectives under this section, a police authority shall—

    (a) consult the chief constable for the area, and

    (b) consider any views obtained by the authority in accordance with arrangements made under section 96.

[(4) This section shall apply in relation to the Metropolitan Police Authority as it applies to a police authority established under section 3, but taking the reference to the chief constable for the area as a reference to the Commissioner of Police of the Metropolis.]

8   Local policing plans

(1) Every police authority established under section 3 shall, before the beginning of each financial year, issue a plan setting but the proposed arrangements for the policing of the authority's area during the year ("the local policing plan").

(2) The local policing plan shall include a statement of the authority's priorities for the year, of the financial resources expected to be available and of the proposed allocation of those resources, and shall give particulars of—

(a) any objectives determined by the Secretary of State under section 37,

(b) any objectives determined by the authority under section 7, . . .

(c) any performance targets established by the authority, whether in compliance with a direction under section 38 or otherwise[, and

(d) any action proposed for the purpose of complying with the requirements of Part 1 of the Local Government Act 1999 (best value)].

[(2A) The local policing plan for any financial year must be consistent with any three-year strategy plan under section 6A which sets out the authority's current strategies for the policing of its area during any period which includes the whole or any part of that financial year.]

(3) A draft of the local policing plan shall be prepared by the chief constable for the area and submitted by him to the police authority for it to consider.

(4) Before issuing a local policing plan which differs from the draft submitted by the chief constable under subsection (3), a police authority shall consult the chief constable.

(4A)–(6) *****

8A   *****

9   Annual reports by police authorities

(1) As soon as possible after the end of each financial year every police authority established under section 3 shall issue a report relating to the policing of the authority's area for the year.

(2)–(4) *****

[9A   General functions of the Commissioner of Police of the Metropolis

(1) The metropolitan police force shall be under the direction and control of the Commissioner of Police of the Metropolis appointed under section 9B.

(2) In discharging his functions, the Commissioner of Police of the Metropolis shall have regard to the local policing plan issued by the Metropolitan Police Authority under section 8.

9B   Appointment of Commissioner of Police of the Metropolis

(1) There shall be a Commissioner of Police of the Metropolis.

(2) Any appointment of a Commissioner of Police of the Metropolis shall be made by Her Majesty by warrant under Her sign manual.

(3) A person appointed as Commissioner of Police of the Metropolis shall hold office at Her Majesty's pleasure.

(4) Any appointment of a Commissioner of Police of the Metropolis shall be subject to regulations under section 50.

(5) Before recommending to Her Majesty that She appoint a person as the Commissioner of Police of the Metropolis, the Secretary of State shall have regard to—

(a) any recommendations made to him by the Metropolitan Police Authority; and

(b) any representations made to him by the Mayor of London.

(6) Any functions exercisable by the Mayor of London under subsection (5) may only be exercised by him personally.

9C–9D   *****

9E   Removal of Commissioner or Deputy Commissioner

(1) The Metropolitan Police Authority, acting with the approval of the Secretary of State, may call upon the Commissioner of Police of the Metropolis [in the interests of efficiency or effectiveness, to retire or to resign].

(2) Before seeking the approval of the Secretary of State under subsection (1), the Metropolitan Police Authority shall give the Commissioner of Police of the Metropolis [—

(a) an explanation in writing of the Authority's grounds for calling upon him, in the interests of efficiency or effectiveness, to retire or to resign; and

(b) an opportunity to make representations;

and the Authority shall consider any representations made by or on behalf of the Commissioner].

[(2A) The Metropolitan Police Authority, acting with the approval of the Secretary of State, may suspend the Commissioner of Police of the Metropolis from duty if—

(a) it is proposing to consider whether to exercise its power under subsection (1) to call upon the Commissioner to retire or to resign and is satisfied that, in the light of the proposal, the maintenance of public confidence in the metropolitan police force requires the suspension; or

(b) having been notified by the Secretary of State that he is proposing to consider whether to require the Authority to exercise that power, it is satisfied that, in the light of the Secretary of State's proposal, the maintenance of public confidence in that force requires the suspension; or

(c) it has exercised that power or been sent under section 42(2A) a copy of a notice of the Secretary of State's intention to require it to exercise that power, but the retirement or resignation has not yet taken effect;

and it shall be the duty of the Metropolitan Police Authority (without reference to the preceding provisions of this subsection) to suspend the Commissioner from duty if it is required to do so by the Secretary of State under section 42(1A).]

(3)–(5) *****

9F, 9FA, 9G   *****

9H   Other members of the metropolitan police force

(1) The ranks that may be held in the metropolitan police force shall be such as may be prescribed by regulations under section 50.

(2) The ranks so prescribed in the case of the metropolitan police force shall include, in addition to the ranks of—

(a) Commissioner of Police of the Metropolis,

(b) Deputy Commissioner of Police of the Metropolis,

(c) Assistant Commissioner of Police of the Metropolis,

[(ca) Deputy Assistant Commissioner of Police of the Metropolis, and]

(d) Commander,

those of [chief superintendent,] superintendent, chief inspector, inspector, sergeant and constable.

(3) In the metropolitan police force, appointments and promotions to any rank below that of Commander shall be made in accordance with regulations under section 50 by the Commissioner of Police of the Metropolis.]

10   General functions of chief constables

(1) A police force maintained under section 2 shall be under the direction and control of the chief constable appointed under section 11.

(2) In discharging his functions, every chief constable shall have regard to the local policing plan issued by the police authority for his area under section 8.

11   Appointment and removal of chief constables

(1) The chief constable of a police force maintained under section 2 shall be appointed by the police authority responsible for maintaining the force, but subject to the approval of the Secretary of State and to regulations under section 50.

(2) Without prejudice to any regulations under section 50 or under the Police Pensions Act 1976, the police authority, acting with the approval of the Secretary of State, may call upon the chief constable [in the interests of efficiency or effectiveness, to retire or to resign].

(3) Before seeking the approval of the Secretary of State under subsection (2), the police authority shall give the chief constable[—

(a) an explanation in writing of the authority's grounds for calling upon him, in the interests of efficiency or effectiveness, to retire or to resign; and

(b) an opportunity to make representations:

and the authority shall consider any representations made by or on behalf of the chief officer.

The opportunity given to the chief constable to make representations must include the opportunity to make them in person].

[(3A) A police authority maintaining a police force under section 2, acting with the approval of the Secretary of State, may suspend from duty the chief constable of that force if—

(a) it is proposing to consider whether to exercise its power under subsection (2) to call upon the chief constable to retire or to resign and is satisfied that, in the light of the proposal, the maintenance of public confidence in that force requires the suspension; or

(b) having been notified by the Secretary of State that he is proposing to consider whether to require the police authority to exercise that power, it is satisfied that, in the light of the Secretary of State's proposal, the maintenance of public confidence in that force requires the suspension; or

(c) it has exercised that power or been sent under section 42(2A) a copy of a notice of the Secretary of State's intention to require it to exercise that power, but the retirement or resignation has not yet taken effect;

and it shall be the duty of a police authority maintaining such a force (without reference to the preceding provisions of this subsection) to suspend the chief constable of that force from duty if it is required to do so by the Secretary of State under section 42(1A).]

(4) A chief constable who is called upon to [retire or resign under subsection (2) shall retire or resign with effect from such date as the police authority may specify, or with effect from such earlier date] as may be agreed upon between him and the authority.

11A–12A   *****

13   Other members of police forces

(1) The ranks that may be held in a police force maintained under section 2 shall be such as may be prescribed by regulations under section 50 and the ranks so prescribed shall include, in addition to chief constable [, deputy chief constable] and assistant chief constable, the ranks of [chief superintendent], superintendent, chief inspector, inspector, sergeant and constable.

(2) . . .

(3) Appointments and promotions to any rank below that of assistant chief constable in any police force maintained under section 2 shall be made, in accordance with regulations under section 50, by the chief constable.

14   Police fund

(1) Each police authority established under section 3 shall keep a fund to be known as the police fund.

(2) Subject to any regulations under the Police Pensions Act 1976, all receipts of the police authority shall be paid into the police fund and all expenditure of the authority shall be paid out of that fund.

(3) Accounts shall be kept by each police authority of payments made into or out of the police fund.

[(4) This section shall apply in relation to the Metropolitan Police Authority as it applies in relation to a police authority established under section 3.]

15–19   *****

20   Questions on police matters at council meetings

(1) Every relevant council shall make arrangements (whether by standing orders or otherwise) for enabling questions on the discharge of the functions of a police authority [established under section 3] to be put by members of the council at a meeting of the council for answer by a person nominated by the authority for that purpose.

(2) On being given reasonable notice by a relevant council of a meeting of that council at which questions on the discharge of the police authority's functions are to be put, the police authority shall nominate one or more of its members to attend the meeting to answer those questions.

(3) In this section "relevant council" has the same meaning as in Schedule 2.

20A–21   *****

General provisions

22   Reports by chief constables to police authorities

(1) Every [chief officer of police of a police force] shall, as soon as possible after the end of each financial year, submit to the police authority a general report on the policing during that year of the area for which his force is maintained.

(2) A [chief officer] shall arrange for a report submitted by him under subsection (1) to be published in such manner as appears to him to be appropriate.

(3) The [chief officer of police] of a police force shall, whenever so required by the police authority, submit to that authority a report on such matters as may be specified in the requirement, being matters connected with the policing of the area for which the force is maintained.

(4) A report submitted under subsection (3) shall be in such form as the police authority may specify.

(5) If it appears to the [chief officer] that a report in compliance with subsection (3) would contain information which in the public interest ought not to be disclosed, or is not needed for the discharge of the functions of the police authority, he may request that authority to refer the requirement to submit the report to the Secretary of State; and in any such case the requirement shall be of no effect unless it is confirmed by the Secretary of State.

(6) The police authority may arrange, or require the [chief officer] to arrange, for a report submitted under subsection (3) to be published in such manner as appears to the authority to be appropriate.

(7) . . .

23–24   *****

25   Provision of special services

(1) The chief officer of police of a police force may provide, at the request of any person, special police services at any premises or in any locality in the police area for which the force is maintained, subject to the payment to the police authority of charges on such scales as may be determined by the authority.

(1A) *****

(2) . . .

26–28   *****

29   Attestation of constables

Every member of a police force maintained for a police area and every special constable appointed for a police area shall, on appointment, be attested as a constable by making a declaration in the form set out in Schedule 4—

(a) ...

(b) ... before a justice of the peace having jurisdiction within the police area.

30   Jurisdiction of constables

(1) A member of a police force shall have all the powers and privileges of a constable throughout England and Wales and the adjacent United Kingdom waters.

(2) A special constable shall have all the powers and privileges of a constable in the police area for which he is appointed and, where the boundary of that area includes the coast, in the adjacent United Kingdom waters.

(3), (3A)–(6) *****

(4) *****

(5) ...

31–35   *****

PART II   CENTRAL SUPERVISION, DIRECTION AND FACILITIES

Functions of Secretary of State

36   General duty of Secretary of State

(1) The Secretary of State shall exercise his powers under the provisions of this Act referred to in subsection (2) in such manner and to such extent as appears to him to be best calculated to promote the efficiency and effectiveness of the police.

(2) The provisions of this Act mentioned in subsection (1) are—

(a) Part I;

(b) this Part;

(c) Part III (other than sections 61 and 62);

(d) in Chapter II of Part IV, section 85 and Schedule 6; and

(e) in Part V, section 95.

[36A   National policing plan

(1) It shall be the duty of the Secretary of State, before the beginning of each financial year, to prepare a National Policing Plan for that year.

(2) The Secretary of State shall lay the National Policing Plan for a financial year before Parliament.

(3) Subject to subsection (4), any such plan must be laid before Parliament not later than 30th November in the preceding financial year.

(4) If there are exceptional circumstances, any such plan may be laid before Parliament after the date mentioned in subsection (3); but it must be so laid before the beginning of the financial year to which it relates.

(5) If a plan is laid before Parliament after the date mentioned in subsection (3), the plan must contain a statement of the exceptional circumstances that gave rise to its being so laid.

(6) The National Policing Plan for a financial year—

(a) must set out whatever the Secretary of State considers to be the strategic policing priorities generally for the police forces maintained for police areas in England and Wales for the period of three years beginning with that year;

(b) *****

(c) may contain such other information, plans and advice as the Secretary of State considers relevant to the priorities set out in the plan.]

(7), (8) *****

37   Setting of objectives for police authorities

(1) The Secretary of State may by order determine objectives for the policing of the areas of all police authorities [to which this section applies].

[(1A) The police authorities to which this section applies are those established under section 3 and the Metropolitan Police Authority.]

(2) Before making an order under this section the Secretary of State shall consult—

(a) persons whom he considers to represent the interests of police authorities [to which this section applies], and

(b) persons whom he considers to represent the interests of [chief officers of police] of forces maintained by those authorities.

(3) A statutory instrument containing an order under this section shall be laid before Parliament after being made.

38   Setting of performance targets

(1) Where an objective has been determined under section 37, the Secretary of State may direct police authorities to establish levels of performance ("performance targets") to be aimed at in seeking to achieve the objective.

(2) A direction under this section may be given to all police authorities [to which section 37 applies] or to one or more particular authorities.

(3) A direction given under this section may impose conditions with which the performance targets must conform, and different conditions may be imposed for different authorities.

(4) The Secretary of State shall arrange for any direction given under this section to be published in such manner as appears to him to be appropriate.

39   Codes of practice

(1) The Secretary of State may issue codes of practice relating to the discharge by police authorities established under section 3 [and the Metropolitan Police Authority] of any of their functions.

(2) The Secretary of State may from time to time revise the whole or part of any code of practice issued under this section.

(3) The Secretary of State shall lay before Parliament a copy of any code of practice, and of any revision of a code of practice, issued by him under this section.

39A   *****

[40   Power to give directions to a police authority

(1) Where a report made to the Secretary of State on an inspection under section 54 states, in relation to any police force maintained under section 2, or in relation to the metropolitan police force—

(a) that, in the opinion of the person making the report, the whole or any part of the force inspected is, whether generally or in particular respects, not efficient or not effective, or

(b) that, in that person's opinion, the whole or a part of the force will cease to be efficient or effective, whether generally or in particular respects, unless remedial measures are taken,

the Secretary of State may direct the police authority responsible for maintaining that force to take such remedial measures as may be specified in the direction.

(2) Those remedial measures must not relate to any matter other than—

(a) a matter by reference to which the report contains a statement of opinion falling within subsection (1)(a) or (b); or

(b) a matter that the Secretary of State considers relevant to any matter falling within paragraph (a).

(3) If the Secretary of State exercises his power to give a direction under this section in relation to a police force—

(a) he shall prepare a report on his exercise of that power in relation to that force; and

(b) he shall lay that report before Parliament.

(4) *****

(5) The Secretary of State shall not give a direction under this section in relation to any police force unless—

- (a) the police authority maintaining that force and the chief officer of that force have each been given such information about the Secretary of State's grounds for proposing to give that direction as he considers appropriate for enabling them to make representations or proposals under the following paragraphs of this subsection;
- (b) that police authority and chief officer have each been given an opportunity of making representations about those grounds;
- (c) that police authority has had an opportunity of making proposals for the taking of remedial measures that would make the giving of the direction unnecessary; and
- (d) the Secretary of State has considered any such representations and any such proposals.]

(6)–(9) *****

41 Directions as to minimum budget

(1) The power of the Secretary of State to give directions under section 40 to a police authority established under section 3 shall include power to direct the authority that the amount of its budget requirement for any financial year (under section 43 of the Local Government Finance Act 1992) shall not be less than an amount specified in the direction.

(2)–(4) *****

41A–41B   *****

42 Removal of chief constables etc

[(1) The Secretary of State may—

- (a) require the Metropolitan Police Authority to exercise its power under section 9E to call upon the Commissioner or Deputy Commissioner, in the interests of efficiency or effectiveness, to retire or to resign; or
- (b) require a police authority maintaining a police force under section 2 to exercise its power under section 11 to call upon the chief constable of that force, in the interests of efficiency or effectiveness, to retire or to resign.

(1A) The Secretary of State may also, in any case falling within subsection (1B) in which he considers that it is necessary for the maintenance of public confidence in the force in question—

- (a) require the Metropolitan Police Authority to suspend the Commissioner or Deputy Commissioner from duty; or
- (b) require a police authority maintaining a police force under section 2 to suspend the chief constable of that force from duty.

(1B) The cases falling within this subsection are—

- (a) where the Secretary of State is proposing to exercise his power under subsection (1) in relation to the Metropolitan Police Authority or, as the case may be, the other police authority in question, or is proposing to consider so exercising that power;
- (b) where the Metropolitan Police Authority or the other police authority in question is itself proposing to exercise its power to call upon the Commissioner or Deputy Commissioner or, as the case may be, the chief constable of the force in question to retire or to resign, or is proposing to consider so exercising that power; and
- (c) where the power mentioned in paragraph (a) or (b) has been exercised but the retirement or resignation has not yet taken effect.

(2) Before requiring the exercise by the Metropolitan Police Authority or any other police authority of its power to call upon the Commissioner or Deputy Commissioner or the chief constable of the force in question to retire or to resign, the Secretary of State shall—

(a) give the officer concerned a notice in writing—
  (i) informing him of the Secretary of State's intention to require the exercise of that power; and
  (ii) explaining the Secretary of State's grounds for requiring the exercise of that power; and
(b) give that officer an opportunity to make representations to the Secretary of State.

(2A) Where the Secretary of State gives a notice under subsection (2)(a), he shall send a copy of the notice to the Metropolitan Police Authority or other police authority concerned.

(2B) The Secretary of State shall consider any representations made to him under subsection (2).]

(3) [Where the Secretary of State proposes to require the exercise of a power mentioned in subsection (1), he] shall, appoint one or more persons (one at least of whom shall be a person who is not an officer of police or of a Government department) to hold an inquiry and report to him and shall consider any report made under this subsection.

[(3A) At an inquiry held under subsection (3)—
  (a) the Commissioner, Deputy Commissioner or, as the case may be, the chief constable in question shall be entitled, in accordance with any regulations under section 42A, to make representations to the inquiry;
  (b) the Metropolitan Police Authority or, as the case may be, the police authority concerned shall be entitled, in accordance with any regulations made under section 42A, to make representations to the inquiry.

(3B) The entitlement of the Commissioner, Deputy Commissioner or, as the case may be, the chief constable in question to make representations shall include the entitlement to make them in person.]

(4) The costs incurred by [the Commissioner, the Deputy Commissioner or a chief constable] in respect of an inquiry under this section, taxed in such manner as the Secretary of State may direct, shall be defrayed out of the police fund.

(4A)–(4C) *****

(5) . . .

42A–45 *****

46 Police grant

(1) Subject to the following provisions of this section, the Secretary of State shall for each financial year make grants for police purposes to—
  (a) police authorities for areas other than the metropolitan police district, and
  (b) [the Greater London Authority];
[and in those provisions references to police authorities shall be taken as including references to the Greater London Authority].

(2) For each financial year the Secretary of State shall with the approval of the Treasury determine—
  (a) the aggregate amount of grants to be made under this section, and
  (b) the amount of the grant to be made to each authority; and any determination may be varied by further determinations under this subsection.

(3) The Secretary of State shall prepare a report setting out any determination under subsection (2), and stating the considerations which he took into account in making the determination.

(4) In determining the allocation among police authorities of the whole or any part of the aggregate amount of grants, the Secretary of State may exercise his discretion by applying such formulae or other rules as he considers appropriate.

(5) The considerations which the Secretary of State takes into account in making a determination under subsection (2), and the formulae and other rules referred to in subsection (4), may be different for different authorities or different classes of authority.

(6)–(8) *****

47–48 *****

49 ...

50 Regulations for police forces

(1) Subject to the provisions of this section, the Secretary of State may make regulations as to the government, administration and conditions or service of police forces.

(2) Without prejudice to the generality of subsection (1), regulations under this section may make provision with respect to—

    (a) the ranks to be held by members of police forces;

    (b) the qualifications for appointment and promotion of members of police forces;

    (c) periods of service on probation;

    (d) voluntary retirement of members of police forces;

    (e) the conduct, efficiency and effectiveness of members of police forces and the maintenance of discipline;

    (f) the suspension of members of a police force from membership of that force and from their office as constable;

    (g) the maintenance of personal records of members of police forces;

    (h) the duties which are or are not to be performed by members of police forces;

    (i) the treatment as occasions of police duty of attendance at meetings of the Police Federations and of any body recognised by the Secretary of State for the purposes of section 64;

    (j) the hours of duty, leave, pay and allowances of members of police forces; and

    (k) the issue, use and return of police clothing, personal equipment and accoutrements.

(3) Without prejudice to the powers conferred by this section, regulations under this section shall—

    (a) establish, or make provision for the establishment of, procedures for cases in which a member of a police force may be dealt with by dismissal, requirement to resign, reduction in rank, reduction in rate of pay, fine, reprimand or caution, and

    (b) make provision for securing that any case in which a senior officer may be dismissed or dealt with in any of the other ways mentioned in paragraph (a) is decided [by the police authority which maintains that force or by a committee of that authority].

For the purposes of this subsection "senior officer" means a member of a police force holding a rank above that of [chief] superintendent.

(4) In relation to any matter as to which provision may be made by regulations under this section, the regulations may, subject to subsection (3)(b),—

    (a) authorise or require provision to be made by, or confer discretionary powers on, the Secretary of State, police authorities, chief officers of police or other persons, or

    (b) authorise or require the delegation by any person of functions conferred on that person by or under the regulations.

(5) Regulations under this section for regulating pay and allowances may be made with retrospective effect to any date specified in the regulations, but nothing in this subsection shall be construed as authorising pay or allowances payable to any person to be reduced retrospectively.

(6) Regulations under this section as to conditions of service shall secure that appointments for fixed terms are not made except where the person appointed holds the rank of superintendent or a higher rank.

(7), (8) *****

51–53A *****

Inspectors of constabulary

54 Appointment and functions of inspectors of constabulary

(1) Her Majesty may appoint such number of inspectors (to be known as "Her Majesty's Inspectors of Constabulary") as the Secretary of State may with the consent of the Treasury determine, and of the persons so appointed one may be appointed as chief inspector of constabulary.

(2) The inspectors of constabulary shall inspect, and report to the Secretary of State on the efficiency and effectiveness of, every police force maintained for a police area [. . .] [and the Central Police Training and Development Authority].

(2A)–(5) *****

55 Publication of reports

(1) Subject to subsection (2), the Secretary of State shall arrange for any report received by him under section 54(2) [(2A) or (2C)] to be published in such manner as appears to him to be appropriate.

(2) The Secretary of State may exclude from publication under subsection (1) any part of a report if, in his opinion, the publication of that part—

    (a) would be against the interests of national security, or

    (b) might jeopardise the safety of any person.

(3)–(8) *****

56–58 *****

PART III   POLICE REPRESENTATIVE INSTITUTIONS

59 Police Federation

(1) There shall continue to be a Police Federation for England and Wales and a Police Federation of Scotland for the purpose of representing members of the police forces in those countries respectively in all matters affecting their welfare and efficiency, except for—

    (a) questions of promotion affecting individuals, and

    (b) (subject to subsection (2)) questions of discipline affecting individuals.

(2) A Police Federation may represent a member of a police force at any proceedings brought under regulations made in accordance with section 50(3) above or section 26(2A) of the Police (Scotland) Act 1967 or on an appeal from any such proceedings.

(3) Except on an appeal to a police appeals tribunal or as provided by section 84, a member of a police force may only be represented under subsection (2) by another member of a police force.

(4) The Police Federations shall act through local and central representative bodies.

(5) The Police Federations and every branch of a Federation shall be entirely independent of, and subject to subsection (6) unassociated with, any body or person outside the police service, but may employ persons outside the police service in an administrative or advisory capacity.

(6) The Secretary of State–

    (a) may authorise a Police Federation or a branch of a Federation to be associated with a person or body outside the police service in such cases and manner, and subject to such conditions and restrictions, as he may specify, and

    (b) may vary or withdraw an authorisation previously given; and anything for the time being so authorised shall not be precluded by subsection (5).

(7) This section applies to police cadets as it applies to members of police forces, and references to the police service shall be construed accordingly.

(8) . . .

60   Regulations for Police Federation

(1) The Secretary of State may by regulations–

  (a) prescribe the constitution and proceedings of the Police Federations, or
  (b) authorise the Federations to make rules concerning such matters relating to their constitution and proceedings as may be specified in the regulations.

(2) Without prejudice to the generality of subsection (1), regulations under this section may make provision–

  (a) with respect to the membership of the Federations;
  (b) with respect to the raising of funds by the Federations by voluntary subscription and the use and management of funds derived from such subscriptions;
  (c) with respect to the manner in which representations may be made by committees or bodies of the Federations to police authorities, chief officers of police and the Secretary of State;
  (d) for the payment by the Secretary of State of expenses incurred in connection with the Federations and for the use by the Federations of premises provided by police authorities for police purposes; and
  (e) for modifying any regulations under the Police Pensions Act 1976, section 50 above or section 26 of the Police (Scotland) Act 1967 in relation to any member of a police force who is the secretary or an officer of a Police Federation and for requiring the appropriate Federation to make contributions in respect of the pay, pension or allowances payable to or in respect of any such person.

(2A) . . .

(3)–(6) *****

61   The Police Negotiating Board for the United Kingdom

(1) There shall continue to be a Police Negotiation Board for the United Kingdom for the consideration by persons representing the interests of—

  (a) the authorities who between them maintain the police forces in Great Britain and the [Police Service of Northern Ireland,]
  [(aa) . . .]
  (b) the persons who are members of those police forces or of [the Police Service] or are police cadets,
  [(ba) . . .]
  (c) the Commissioner of Police of the Metropolis, . . .
  (d) the Secretary of State, [and
  (e) the Scottish Ministers],

of questions relating to hours of duty, leave, pay and allowances, pensions or the issue, use and return of police clothing, personal equipment and accoutrements.

(2) The Chairman and any deputy chairman or chairmen of the Board shall be appointed by the Prime Minister [after consultation with the Scottish Ministers].

(3)–(6) *****

62–63   *****

64   Membership of trade unions

(1) Subject to the following provisions of this section, a member of a police force shall not be a member of any trade union, or of any association having for its objects, or one of its objects, to control or influence the pay, pensions or conditions of service of any police force.

(2) Where a person was a member of a trade union before becoming a member of a police

force, he may, with the consent of the chief officer of police, continue to be a member of that union during the time of his service in the police force.

(3) ...

(4) This section applies to police cadets as it applies to members of a police force, and references to a police force or to service in a police force shall be construed accordingly.

(4A), (4B) ...

(5) Nothing in this section applies to membership of the Police Federations, or of any body recognised by the Secretary of State for the purposes of this section as representing members of police forces who are not members of those Federations.

PART IV   COMPLAINTS, DISCIPLINARY PROCEEDINGS ETC.

65–83 ...

CHAPTER II   DISCIPLINARY AND OTHER PROCEEDINGS

84   Representation at disciplinary and other proceedings

(1) A member of a police force of the rank of [chief] superintendent or below may not be dismissed, required to resign or reduced in rank by a decision taken in proceedings under regulations made in accordance with section 50(3)(a) unless he has been given an opportunity to elect to be legally represented at any hearing held in the course of those proceedings.

(2) Where a member of a police force makes an election to which subsection (1) refers, he may be represented at the hearing, at his option, either by counsel or by a solicitor.

(3) Except in a case where a member of a police force of the rank of [chief] superintendent or below has been given an opportunity to elect to be legally represented and has so elected, he may be represented at the hearing only by another member of a police force.

(4) Regulations under section 50 shall specify—

(a) a procedure for notifying a member of a police force of the effect of subsections (1) to (3) above,

(b) when he is to be notified of the effect of those subsections, and

(c) when he is to give notice whether he wishes to be legally represented at the hearing.

(5) If a member of a police force—

(a) fails without reasonable cause to give notice in accordance with the regulations that he wishes to be legally represented, or

(b) gives notice in accordance with the regulations that he does not wish to be legally represented,

he may be dismissed, required to resign or reduced in rank without his being legally represented.

(6) If a member of a police force has given notice in accordance with the regulations that he wishes to be legally represented, the case against him may be presented by counsel or a solicitor whether or not he is actually so represented.

85   Appeals against dismissal etc.

(1) A member of a police force who is dismissed, required to resign or reduced in rank by a decision taken in proceedings under regulations made in accordance with section 50(3) may appeal to a police appeals tribunal against the decision except where he has a right of appeal to some other person; and in that case he may appeal to a police appeals tribunal from any decision of that other person as a result of which he is dismissed, required to resign or reduced in rank.

(2) Where a police appeals tribunal allows an appeal it may, if it considers that it is appropriate to do so, make an order dealing with the appellant in a way—

(a) which appears to the tribunal to be less severe than the way in which he was dealt with by the decision appealed against, and

(b) in which he could have been dealt with by the person who made that decision.

(3) The Secretary of State may make rules as to the procedure on appeals to police appeals tribunals under this section.

(4)–(6) *****

86 . . .

87 *****

88   Liability for wrongful acts of constables

(1) The chief officer of police for a police area shall be liable in respect of [any unlawful conduct of] constables under his direction and control in the performance or purported performance of their functions in like manner as a master is liable in respect of [any unlawful conduct of] his servants in the course of their employment, and accordingly shall [, in the case of a tort,] be treated for all purposes as a joint tortfeasor.

(2) There shall be paid out of the police fund—

(a) any damages or costs awarded against the chief officer of police in any proceedings brought against him by virtue of this section and any costs incurred by him in any such proceedings so far as not recovered by him in the proceedings; and

(b) any sum required in connection with the settlement of any claim made against the chief officer of police by virtue of this section, if the settlement is approved by the police authority.

(3) Any proceedings in respect of a claim made by virtue of this section shall be brought against the chief officer of police for the time being or, in the case of a vacancy in that office, against the person for the time being performing the functions of the chief officer of police; and references in subsections (1) and (2) to the chief officer of police shall be construed accordingly.

(4) A police authority may, in such cases and to such extent as appear to it to be appropriate, pay out of the police fund—

(a) any damages or costs awarded against a person to whom this subsection applies in proceedings for [any lawful conduct of] that person,

(b) any costs incurred and not recovered by such a person in such proceedings, and

(c) any sum required in connection with the settlement of a claim that has or might have given rise to such proceedings.

(5) Subsection (4) applies to a person who is—

(a) a member of the police force maintained by the police authority,

(b) a constable for the time being required to serve with that force by virtue of section 24 or 98 [of this Act . . .], or

(c) a special constable appointed for the authority's police area.

(5A)–(8) *****

PART V   MISCELLANEOUS AND GENERAL

Offences

89   Assaults on constables

(1) Any person who assaults a constable in the execution of his duty, or a person assisting a constable in the execution of his duty, shall be guilty of an offence and liable on summary conviction to imprisonment for a term not exceeding six months or to a fine not exceeding level 5 on the standard scale, or to both.

(2) Any person who resists or wilfully obstructs a constable in the execution of his duty,

or a person assisting a constable in the execution of his duty, shall be guilty of an offence and liable on summary conviction to imprisonment for a term not exceeding [51 weeks] or to a fine not exceeding level 3 on the standard scale, or to both.

(3)–(6) *****

90   Impersonation, etc.

(1) Any person who with intent to deceive impersonates a member of a police force or special constable, or makes any statement or does any act calculated falsely to suggest that he is such a member or constable, shall be guilty of an offence and liable on summary conviction to imprisonment for a term not exceeding six months or to a fine not exceeding level 5 on the standard scale, or to both.

(2) Any person who, not being a constable, wears any article of police uniform in circumstances where it gives him an appearance so nearly resembling that of a member of a police force as to be calculated to deceive shall be guilty of an offence and liable on summary conviction to a fine not exceeding level 3 on the standard scale.

(3) Any person who, not being a member of a police force or special constable, has in his possession any article of police uniform shall, unless he proves that he obtained possession of that article lawfully and has possession of it for a lawful purpose, be guilty of an offence and liable on summary conviction to a fine not exceeding level 1 on the standard scale.

(4) *****

91   Causing disaffection

(1) Any person who causes, or attempts to cause, or does any act calculated to cause, disaffection amongst the members of any police force, or induces or attempts to induce, or does any act calculated to induce, any member of a police force to withhold his services, [or to commit breaches of discipline], shall be guilty of an offence and liable—

(a)   on summary conviction, to imprisonment for a term not exceeding six months or to a fine not exceeding the statutory maximum, or to both;

(b)   on conviction on indictment, to imprisonment for a term not exceeding two years or to a fine, or to both.

[(2)   This section applies in the case of—

(a)   special constables appointed for a police area,

(b)   members of the Civil Nuclear Constabulary, and

(c)   members of the British Transport Police Force,

as it applies in the case of members of a police force.]

92   *****

93   Acceptance of gifts and loans

(1) A police authority may, in connection with the discharge of any of its functions, accept gifts of money, and gifts or loans of other property, on such terms as appear to the authority to be appropriate.

(2) The terms on which gifts or loans are accepted under subsection (1) may include terms providing for the commercial sponsorship of any activity of the police authority or of the police force maintained by it.

(3) . . .

94–95   *****

96   Arrangements for obtaining the views of the community on policing

(1) Arrangements shall be made for each police area for obtaining—

(a)   the views of people in that area about matters concerning the policing of the area, and

(b)   their co-operation with the police in preventing crime in that area.

(2) Except as provided by [subsection (6)], arrangements for each police area shall be

made by the police authority after consulting the chief constable [or, in the case of the metropolitan police district, the Commissioner of Police of the Metropolis,] as to the arrangements that would be appropriate.

(3)–(5) . . .

(6) The Common Council of the City of London shall issue guidance to the Commissioner of Police for the City of London concerning arrangements for the City of London police area; and the Commissioner shall make arrangements under this section after taking account of that guidance.

(7)–(10) *****

*****

SCHEDULE 2   POLICE AUTHORITIES ESTABLISHED UNDER SECTION 3

Membership of police authorities

1.—(1) Where, by virtue of section 4, a police authority is to consist of seventeen members—

    (a) nine of those members shall be members of a relevant council appointed under paragraph 2,

    (b) five shall be persons appointed under paragraph 5, and

    (c) three shall be [lay justices] appointed under paragraph 8.

(2) Where, by virtue of an order under subsection (2) of that section, a police authority is to consist of more than seventeen members—

    (a) a number which is greater by one than the number of members provided for in paragraphs (b) and (c) below shall be members of a relevant council appointed under paragraph 2,

    (b) such number as may be prescribed by the order, not exceeding one third of the total membership, shall be persons appointed under paragraph 5, and

    (c) the remainder shall be [lay justices] appointed under paragraph 8.

Appointment of members by relevant councils

2.—(1) In the case of a police authority in relation to which there is only one relevant council, the members of the police authority referred to in paragraph 1(1)(a) or (2)(a) shall be appointed by that council.

(2) In any other case, those members shall be appointed by a joint committee consisting of persons appointed by the relevant councils from among their own members.

3. The number of members of the joint committee, and the number of those members to be appointed by each relevant council, shall be such as the councils may agree or, in the absence of agreement, as may be determined by the Secretary of State.

4.—(1) A council or joint committee shall exercise its power to appoint members of a police authority under paragraph 2 so as to ensure that, so far as practicable, [in the case of the members for whose appointment it is responsible the proportion who are members of any given party—

    (a) where it is a council that is responsible for their appointment, is the same as the proportion of the members of the council who are members of that party; and

    (b) where it is a joint committee that is so responsible, is the same as the proportion of the members of the relevant councils taken as a whole who are members of that party.]

(2) . . .

Appointment of independent members

5. The members of a police authority referred to in paragraph 1(1)(b) or (2)(b) shall be appointed—
   (a) by the members of the police authority appointed under paragraph 2 or 8,
   (b) from among persons on a short-list prepared by the Secretary of State in accordance with Schedule 3.

6.—(1) Every police authority shall arrange for a notice stating—
   (a) the name of each of its members appointed under paragraph 5, and
   (b) such other information relating to him as the authority considers appropriate, to be published in such manner as appears to it to be appropriate.

(2) A police authority shall send to the Secretary of State a copy of any notice which it has arranged to be published under sub-paragraph (1).

Appointment of magistrates

[7.—The members of a police authority referred to in paragraph 1(1)(c) or (2)(c) must be lay justices each of whom is assigned to a local justice area wholly or partly within the authority's area.

8.—They shall be appointed—
   (a) by the members of the police authority appointed under paragraph 2 or 5,
   (b) from among persons on a short-list prepared in accordance with Schedule 3A.]

9.–27. *******

[SCHEDULE 2A   THE METROPOLITAN POLICE AUTHORITY

Membership

1.—(1) Where the Metropolitan Police Authority is to consist of twenty three members—
   (a) twelve of those members shall be members of the London Assembly appointed under paragraph 2,
   (b) seven shall be persons appointed under paragraph 3, and
   (c) four shall be [lay justices] appointed under paragraph 5.

(2) Where, by virtue of an order under section 5C(2), the Metropolitan Police Authority is to consist of a number of members other than twenty three—
   (a) a number which is greater by one than the number of members provided for in paragraphs (b) and (c) shall be members of the London Assembly appointed under paragraph 2,
   (b) such number as may be prescribed by the order, not exceeding one third of the total membership, shall be persons appointed under paragraph 3, and
   (c) the remainder shall be [lay justices] appointed under paragraph 5.

Appointment of members by the Mayor

2.—(1) The members of the Metropolitan Police Authority referred to in paragraph 1(1)(a) or (2)(a) shall be appointed by the Mayor of London in accordance with this paragraph.

(2) One of those members must be the Deputy Mayor, except as provided by paragraphs 9(2)(b) and 17(b) of Schedule 4 to the Greater London Authority Act 1999 or unless the Deputy Mayor is disqualified from being appointed as or being a member of the Metropolitan Police Authority under paragraph 7 below.

(3) The Mayor (or, where paragraph 9(2)(b) or 17(b) of Schedule 4 to that Act applies, the Chair of the London Assembly) shall ensure that, so far as practicable, [in the case of the members of the Authority who are members of the London Assembly appointed under this

paragraph, the proportion who are members of any given party is the same as the proportion of the members of the London Assembly who are members of that party.]

Appointment of independent members

3.—(1) The members of the Metropolitan Police Authority referred to in paragraph 1(1)(b) or (2)(b) shall be appointed in accordance with this paragraph.

(2) One shall be appointed by the Secretary of State.

(3) The remainder shall be appointed—

(a) by the members of the Metropolitan Police Authority appointed under paragraph 2 or 5,

(b) from among persons on a short-list prepared by the Secretary of State in accordance with Schedule 3.

(4)–(6) *****

4. *****

Appointment of magistrates

[5.—(1) The members of the Metropolitan Police Authority referred to in paragraph 1(1)(c) or (2)(c) must be lay justices each of whom is assigned to a local justice area wholly or partly within the metropolitan police district.

(2) They shall be appointed—

(a) by the members of the Metropolitan Police Authority appointed under paragraph 2 or 3,

(b) from among persons on a short-list prepared in accordance with Schedule 3A.]

6.–20B. *****

Mayor's functions to be exercised by him personally

21. Any functions exercisable by the Mayor of London under this Schedule may only be exercised by him personally.

Interpretation

22. [In this Schedule, "lay justice" has the meaning given by section 9 of the Courts Act 2003.]

SCHEDULE 4   FORM OF DECLARATION

[I, ... of . . . . do solemnly and sincerely declare and affirm that I will well and truly serve the Queen in the office of constable, with fairness, integrity, diligence and impartiality, upholding fundamental human rights and according equal respect to all people; and that I will, to the best of my power, cause the peace to be kept and preserved, and prevent all offences against people and property; and that while I continue to hold the said office I will to the best of my skill and knowledge discharge all the duties thereof faithfully according to law.]
*****

Law Officers Act 1997
(1997, c. 60)

An Act to enable functions of the Attorney General and of the Attorney General for Northern Ireland to be exercised by the Solicitor General; and for connected purposes   [31 July 1997]

Territorial extent: United Kingdom

1   The Attorney General and the Solicitor General

(1) Any function of the Attorney General may be exercised by the Solicitor General.

(2) Anything done by or in relation to the Solicitor General in the exercise of or in connection with a function of the Attorney General has effect as if done by or in relation to the Attorney General.

(3) The validity of anything done in relation to the Attorney General, or done by or in relation to the Solicitor General, is not affected by a vacancy in the office of Attorney General.

(4) Nothing in this section—
- (a) prevents anything being done by or in relation to the Attorney General in the exercise of or in connection with any function of his; or
- (b) requires anything done by the Solicitor General to be done in the name of the Solicitor General instead of the name of the Attorney General.

(5) It is immaterial for the purposes of this section whether a function of the Attorney General arises under an enactment or otherwise.

*****

Local Government (Contracts) Act 1997
(1997, c. 65)

An Act to make provision about the powers of local authorities (including probation committees and the Receiver for the Metropolitan Police District) to enter into contracts; to enable expenditure of local authorities making administrative arrangements for magistrates' courts to be treated for some purposes as not being capital expenditure; and for connected purposes
[27 November 1997]

Territorial extent: England and Wales, Scotland (so far as reproduced here)

Contracts for provision of assets or services

1   Functions to include power to enter into contracts

(1) Every statutory provision conferring or imposing a function on a local authority confers power on the local authority to enter into a contract with another person for the provision or making available of assets or services, or both (whether or not together with goods) for the purposes of, or in connection with, the discharge of the function by the local authority.

(2) Where—
- (a) a local authority enters into a contract such as is mentioned in subsection (1) ("the provision contract") under any statutory provision, and
- (b) in connection with the provision contract, a person ("the financier") makes a loan to, or provides any other form of finance for, a party to the provision contract other than the local authority,

the statutory provision also confers power on the local authority to enter into a contract with the financier, or any insurer of or trustee for the financier, in connection with the provision contract.

(3)–(5) *****

Certified contracts

2   Certified contracts to be intra vires

(1) Where a local authority has entered into a contract, the contract shall, if it is a certified contract, have effect (and be deemed always to have had effect) as if the local authority had had power to enter into it (and had exercised that power properly in entering into it).

(2) For the purposes of this Act a contract entered into by a local authority is a certified contract if (and, subject to subsections (3) and (4), only if) the certification requirements have been satisfied by the local authority with respect to the contract and they were so satisfied before the end of the certification period.

(3) A contract entered into by a local authority shall be treated as a certified contract during the certification period if the contract provides that the certification requirements are intended to be satisfied by the local authority with respect to the contract before the end of that period.

(4) Where a local authority has entered into a contract which is a certified contract ("the existing contract") and the existing contract is replaced by a contract entered into by it with a person or persons not identical with the person or persons with whom it entered into the existing contract, the replacement contract is also a certified contract if—

(a) the period for which it operates or is intended to operate ends at the same time as the period for which the existing contract was to operate, and

(b) apart from that, its provisions are the same as those of the existing contract.

(5) In this Act "the certification period", in relation to a contract entered into by a local authority, means the period of six weeks beginning with the day on which the local authority entered into the contract.

(6), (7) *****

3   The certification requirements

(1) In this Act "the certification requirements", in relation to a contract entered into by a local authority, means the requirements specified in subsections (2) to (4).

(2) The requirement specified in this subsection is that the local authority must have issued a certificate (whether before or after the contract is entered into)—

(a) including details of the period for which the contract operates or is to operate,

(b) describing the purpose of the contract,

(c) containing a statement that the contract is or is to be a contract falling within section 4(3) or (4),

(d) stating that the local authority had or has power to enter into the contract and specifying the statutory provision, or each of the statutory provisions, conferring the power,

(e) stating that a copy of the certificate has been or is to be given to each person to whom a copy is required to be given by regulations,

(f) dealing in a manner prescribed by regulations with any matters required by regulations to be dealt with in certificates under this section, and

(g) confirming that the local authority has complied with or is to comply with any requirement imposed by regulations with respect to the issue of certificates under this section.

(3) The requirement specified in this subsection is that the local authority must have secured that the certificate is signed by any person who is required by regulations to sign it.

(4) The requirement specified in this subsection is that the local authority must have obtained consent to the issue of a certificate under this section from each of the persons with whom the local authority has entered, or is to enter, into the contract.

4 *****

5   Special provision for judicial reviews and audit reviews

(1) Section 2(1) does not apply for the purposes of determining any question arising on—

(a) an application for judicial review, or

(b) an audit review,

as to whether a local authority had power to enter into a contract (or exercised any power properly in entering into a contract).

(2) Section 2(1) has effect subject to any determination or order made in relation to a certified contract on—

(a) an application for judicial review, or

(b) an audit review.

(3) Where, on an application for judicial review or an audit review relating to a certified contract entered into by a local authority, a court—

(a) is of the opinion that the local authority did not have power to enter into the contract (or exercised any power improperly in entering into it), but

(b) (having regard in particular to the likely consequences for the financial provision of the local authority, and for the provision of services to the public, of a decision that the contract should not have effect) considers that the contract should have effect,

the court may determine that the contract has (and always has had) effect as if the local authority had had power to enter into it (and had exercised that power properly in entering into it).

(4) In this section and sections 6 and 7 references to an application for judicial review include any appeal (or further appeal) against a determination or order made on such an application.

*****

National Health Service (Private Finance) Act 1997

(1997, c. 56)

An Act to make provision about the powers of National Health Service trusts to enter into agreements   [15 July 1997]

Territorial extent: England and Wales, Northern Ireland (in accordance with section 2). A modified version of s 1 applies to Scotland: see the National Health Service Reform (Scotland) Act 2004 (asp 7), Sch 1 para 2 for details.

1   Powers of NHS trusts to enter into agreements

(1) The powers of a National Health Service trust include power to enter into externally financed development agreements.

(2) For the purposes of this section, an agreement is an externally financed development agreement if it is certified as such in writing by the Secretary of State.

(3) The Secretary of State may give a certificate under this section if—

(a) in his opinion the purpose or main purpose of the agreement is the provision of facilities in connection with the discharge by the trust of any of its functions; and

(b) a person proposes to make a loan to, or provide any other form of finance for, another party in connection with the agreement.

(4) If a National Health Service trust enters into an externally financed development agreement it may also, in connection with that agreement, enter into an agreement with a person who falls within subsection (3)(b) in relation to the externally financed development agreement.

(5) In subsection (3)—

"another party" means any party to the agreement other than the trust; and

"facilities" includes—

(a) works, buildings, plant, equipment or other property; and

(b) services.

(6) The fact that an agreement made by a National Health Service trust has not been certified under this section does not affect its validity.

*****

Police Act 1997

(1997, c. 50)

An Act to make provision for the National Criminal Intelligence Service and the National Crime Squad; to make provision about entry on and interference with property and with wireless telegraphy in the course of the prevention or detection of serious crime; to make provision for the Police Information Technology Organisation; to provide for the issue of certificates about criminal records; to make provision about the administration and organisation of the police; to repeal certain enactments about rehabilitation of offenders; and for connected purposes

[21 March 1997]

Territorial extent: United Kingdom (sections printed)

1–87, 89–90   ...

88   *****

PART III   AUTHORISATION OF ACTION IN RESPECT OF PROPERTY

The Commissioners

91   The Commissioners

(1) The Prime Minister [, after consultation with the Scottish Ministers] shall appoint for the purposes of this Part—

(a) a Chief Commissioner, and

(b) such number of other Commissioners as the Prime Minister thinks fit.

(2) The persons appointed under subsection (1) shall be persons who hold or have held high judicial office within the meaning of the Appellate Jurisdiction Act 1876.

(3) Subject to subsections (4) to (7), each Commissioner shall hold and vacate office in accordance with the terms of his appointment.

(4) Each Commissioner shall be appointed for a term of three years.

(5) A person who ceases to be a Commissioner (otherwise than under subsection (7)) may be reappointed under this section.

(6) Subject to subsection (7), a Commissioner shall not be removed from office before the end of the term for which he is appointed unless [–

(a) a resolution approving his removal has been passed by each House of Parliament; and

(b) a resolution approving his removal has been passed by the Scottish Parliament.]

(7)–(9A) *****

(10) The decisions of the Chief Commissioner or, subject to sections 104 and 106, any other Commissioner (including decisions as to his jurisdiction) shall not be subject to appeal or liable to be questioned in any court.

Authorisations

92   Effect of authorisation under Part III

No entry on or interference with property or with wireless telegraphy shall be unlawful if it is authorised by an authorisation having effect under this Part.

93   Authorisations to interfere with property etc.

(1) Where subsection (2) applies, an authorising officer may authorise—

(a) the taking of such action, in respect of such property in the relevant area, as he may specify,

[(ab) the taking of such action falling within subsection (1A) in respect of property outside the relevant area, as he may specify, or]

(b) the taking of such action in the relevant area as he may specify, in respect of wireless telegraphy.

[(1A) The action falling within this subsection is action for maintaining or retrieving any equipment, apparatus or device the placing or use of which in the relevant area has been authorised under this Part or Part II of the Regulation of Investigatory Powers Act 2000 or under any enactment contained in or made under an Act of the Scottish Parliament which makes provision equivalent to that made by Part II of that Act of 2000.

(1B) Subsection (1) applies where the authorising officer is a [member of the staff of the Serious Organised Crime Agency,] customs officer [or an officer of the Office of Fair Trading] with the omission of—

(a) the words "in the relevant area" in each place where they occur; and

(b) paragraph (ab).]

(2) This subsection applies where the authorising officer believes—

(a) that it is necessary for the action specified to be taken [for the purpose of preventing or detecting] serious crime, and

(b) [that the taking of the action is proportionate to what the action seeks to achieve.]

(2A)–(2B), (3) *****

(4) For the purposes of subsection (2), conduct which constitutes one or more offences shall be regarded as serious crime if, and only if,—

(a) it involves the use of violence, results in substantial financial gain or is conduct by a large number of persons in pursuit of a common purpose, or

(b) the offence or one of the offences is an offence for which a person who has attained the age of twenty-one [(eighteen in relation to England and Wales)] and has no previous convictions could reasonably be expected to be sentenced to imprisonment for a term of three years or more,

and, where the authorising officer is within subsection (5)(h), it relates to an assigned matter within the meaning of section 1(1) of the Customs and Excise Management Act 1979.

(5) In this section "authorising officer" means—

(a) the chief constable of a police force maintained under section 2 of the Police Act 1996 (maintenance of police forces for areas in England and Wales except London);

(b) the Commissioner, or an Assistant Commissioner, of Police of the Metropolis;

(c) the Commissioner of Police for the City of London;

(d) the chief constable of a police force maintained under or by virtue of section 1 of the Police (Scotland) Act 1967 (maintenance of police forces for areas in Scotland);

(e) the Chief Constable or a Deputy Chief Constable of the [Police Service of Northern Ireland];

[(ea) the Chief Constable of the Ministry of Defence Police;

(eb) the Provost Marshal of the Royal Navy Regulating Branch;

(ec) the Provost Marshal of the Royal Military Police;

(ed) the Provost Marshal of the Royal Air Force Police;

(ee) the Chief Constable of the British Transport Police;]

(f) [the Director General of the Serious Organised Crime Agency, or any member of the staff of that Agency who is designated for the purposes of this paragraph by that Director General;];

(g) . . .

(h) [any] customs officer designated by the Commissioners of Customs and Excise for the purposes of this paragraph [; or

(i) the chairman of the Office of Fair Trading].

(6), (6A), (6B) *****

(7) The powers conferred by, or by virtue of, this section are additional to any other powers which a person has as a constable either at common law or under or by virtue of any other enactment and are not to be taken to affect any of those other powers.

94 *****

95 Authorisations: form and duration etc.

(1) An authorisation shall be in writing, except that in an urgent case an authorisation (other than one given by virtue of section 94) may be given orally.

(2) An authorisation shall, unless renewed under subsection (3), cease to have effect—

(a) if given orally or by virtue of section 94, at the end of the period of 72 hours beginning with the time when it took effect;

(b) in any other case, at the end of the period of three months beginning with the day on which it took effect.

(3) If at any time before an authorisation would cease to have effect the authorising officer who gave the authorisation, or in whose absence it was given, considers it necessary for the authorisation to continue to have effect for the purpose for which it was issued, he may, in writing, renew it for a period of three months beginning with the day on which it would cease to have effect.

(4) A person shall cancel an authorisation given by him if satisfied that the [authorisation is one in relation to which the requirement of paragraphs (a) to (b) of section 93(2) are no longer satisfied.]

(5)–(7) *****

96 *****

Authorisations requiring approval

97 Authorisations requiring approval

(1) An authorisation to which this section applies shall not take effect until—

(a) it has been approved in accordance with this section by a Commissioner appointed under section 91(1)(b), and

(b) the person who gave the authorisation has been notified under subsection (4).

(2) Subject to subsection (3), this section applies to an authorisation if, at the time it is given, the person who gives it believes—

(a) that any of the property specified in the authorisation–
  (i) is used wholly or mainly as a dwelling or as a bedroom in a hotel, or
  (ii) constitutes office premises, or
(b) that the action authorised by it is likely to result in any person acquiring knowledge of—
  (i) matters subject to legal privilege,
  (ii) confidential personal information, or
  (iii) confidential journalistic material.

(3) This section does not apply to an authorisation where the person who gives it believes that the case is one of urgency.

(4) Where a Commissioner receives a notice under section 96 which specifies that this section applies to the authorisation, he shall as soon as is reasonably practicable–
  (a) decide whether to approve the authorisation or refuse approval, and
  (b) give written notice of his decision to the person who gave the authorisation.

(5) A Commissioner shall approve an authorisation if, and only if, he is satisfied that there are reasonable grounds for believing the matters specified in section 93(2).

(6)–(8) *****

98   Matters subject to legal privilege

(1) Subject to subsection (5) below, in section 97 "matters subject to legal privilege" means matters to which subsection (2), (3) or (4) below applies.

(2) This subsection applies to communications between a professional legal adviser and—
  (a) his client, or
  (b) any person representing his client, which are made in connection with the giving of legal advice to the client.

(3) This subsection applies to communications—
  (a) between a professional legal adviser and his client or any person representing his client, or
  (b) between a professional legal adviser or his client or any such representative and any other person,

which are made in connection with or in contemplation of legal proceedings and for the purposes of such proceedings.

(4) This subsection applies to items enclosed with or referred to in communications of the kind mentioned in subsection (2) or (3) and made—
  (a) in connection with the giving of legal advice, or
  (b) in connection with or in contemplation of legal proceedings and for the purposes of such proceedings.

(5) For the purposes of section 97—
  (a) communications and items are not matters subject to legal privilege when they are in the possession of a person who is not entitled to possession of them, and
  (b) communications and items held, or oral communications made, with the intention of furthering a criminal purpose are not matters subject to legal privilege.

99   Confidential personal information

(1) In section 97 "confidential personal information" means—
  (a) personal information which a person has acquired or created in the course of any trade, business, profession or other occupation or for the purposes of any paid or unpaid office, and which he holds in confidence, and
  (b) communications as a result of which personal information—
    (i) is acquired or created as mentioned in paragraph (a), and
    (ii) is held in confidence.

(2) For the purposes of this section "personal information" means information concerning an individual (whether living or dead) who can be identified from it and relating—

(a) to his physical or mental health, or

(b) to spiritual counselling or assistance given or to be given to him.

(3) A person holds information in confidence for the purposes of this section if he holds it subject—

(a) to an express or implied undertaking to hold it in confidence, or

(b) to a restriction on disclosure or an obligation of secrecy contained in any enactment (including an enactment contained in an Act passed after this Act).

100   Confidential journalistic material

(1) In section 97 "confidential journalistic material" means—

(a) material acquired or created for the purposes of journalism which—

(i)   is in the possession of persons who acquired or created it for those purposes,

(ii) is held subject to an undertaking, restriction or obligation of the kind mentioned in section 99(3), and

(iii) has been continuously held (by one or more persons) subject to such an undertaking, restriction or obligation since it was first acquired or created for the purposes of journalism, and

(b) communications as a result of which information is acquired for the purposes of journalism and held as mentioned in paragraph (a)(ii).

(2) For the purposes of subsection (1), a person who receives material, or acquires information, from someone who intends that the recipient shall use it for the purposes of journalism is to be taken to have acquired it for those purposes.

101–102   . . .

103   Quashing of authorisations etc.

(1) Where, at any time, a Commissioner appointed under section 91(1)(b) is satisfied that, at the time an authorisation was given or renewed, there were no reasonable grounds for believing the matters specified in section 93(2), he may quash the authorisation or, as the case may be, renewal.

(2) Where, in the case of an authorisation or renewal to which section 97 does not apply, a Commissioner appointed under section 91(1)(b) is at any time satisfied that, at the time the authorisation was given or, as the case may be, renewed,—

(a) there were reasonable grounds for believing any of the matters specified in subsection (2) of section 97, and

(b) there were no reasonable grounds for believing the case to be one of urgency for the purposes of subsection (3) of that section,

he may quash the authorisation or, as the case may be, renewal.

(3) Where a Commissioner quashes an authorisation or renewal under subsection (1) or (2), he may order the destruction of any records relating to information obtained by virtue of the authorisation (or, in the case of a renewal, relating wholly or partly to information so obtained after the renewal) other than records required for pending criminal or civil proceedings.

(4)–(9) *****

*****

Protection from Harassment Act 1997

(1997, c. 40)

An Act to make provision for protecting persons from harassment and similar conduct

[21 March 1997]

Territorial extent: England and Wales (sections printed). Sections 8–11 make corresponding provisions for Scotland; s. 13 provides for equivalent legislation by Order for Northern Ireland

England and Wales

1   Prohibition of harassment

(1) A person must not pursue a course of conduct—
- (a) which amounts to harassment of another, and
- (b) which he knows or ought to know amounts to harassment of the other.

[(1A) A person must not pursue a course of conduct—
- (a) which involves harassment of two or more persons, and
- (b) which he knows or ought to know involves harassment of those persons, and
- (c) by which he intends to persuade any person (whether or not one of those mentioned above)—
    - (i)   not to do something that he is entitled or required to do, or
    - (ii) to do something that he is not under any obligation to do.]

(2) For the purposes of this section, the person whose course of conduct is in question ought to know that it amounts to [or involves] harassment of another if a reasonable person in possession of the same information would think the course of conduct amounted to [or involved] harassment of the other.

(3) Subsection (1) [or (1A)] does not apply to a course of conduct if the person who pursued it shows—
- (a) that it was pursued for the purpose of preventing or detecting crime,
- (b) that it was pursued under any enactment or rule of law or to comply with any condition or requirement imposed by any person under any enactment, or
- (c) that in the particular circumstances the pursuit of the course of conduct was reasonable.

2   Offence of harassment

(1) A person who pursues a course of conduct in breach of [section 1(1) or (1A)] is guilty of an offence.

(2) A person guilty of an offence under this section is liable on summary conviction to imprisonment for a term not exceeding six months, or a fine not exceeding level 5 on the standard scale, or both.

(3) . . .

3   Civil remedy

(1) An actual or apprehended breach of [section 1(1)] may be the subject of a claim in civil proceedings by the person who is or may be the victim of the course of conduct in question.

(2) On such a claim, damages may be awarded for (among other things) any anxiety caused by the harassment and any financial loss resulting from the harassment.

(3) Where—
- (a) in such proceedings the High Court or a county court grants an injunction for the purpose of restraining the defendant from pursuing any conduct which amounts to harassment, and
- (b) the plaintiff considers that the defendant has done anything which he is prohibited from doing by the injunction,

the plaintiff may apply for the issue of a warrant for the arrest of the defendant.

(4) An application under subsection (3) may be made—
- (a) where the injunction was granted by the High Court, to a judge of that court, and

(b) where the injunction was granted by a county court, to a judge or district judge of that or any other county court.

(5) The judge or district judge to whom an application under subsection (3) is made may only issue a warrant if—

(a) the application is substantiated on oath, and

(b) the judge or district judge has reasonable grounds for believing that the defendant has done anything which he is prohibited from doing by the injunction.

(6) Where—

(a) the High Court or a county court grants an injunction for the purpose mentioned in subsection (3)(a), and

(b) without reasonable excuse the defendant does anything which he is prohibited from doing by the injunction,

he is guilty of an offence.

(7) Where a person is convicted of an offence under subsection (6) in respect of any conduct, that conduct is not punishable as a contempt of court.

(8) A person cannot be convicted of an offence under subsection (6) in respect of any conduct which has been punished as a contempt of court.

(9) A person guilty of an offence under subsection (6) is liable—

(a) on conviction on indictment, to imprisonment for a term not exceeding five years, or a fine, or both, or

(b) on summary conviction, to imprisonment for a term not exceeding six months, or a fine not exceeding the statutory maximum, or both.

[3A Injunctions to protect persons from harassment within section 1(1A)

(1) This section applies where there is an actual or apprehended breach of section 1(1A) by any person ("the relevant person").

(2) In such a case—

(a) any person who is or may be a victim of the course of conduct in question, or

(b) any person who is or may be a person falling within section 1(1A)(c),

may apply to the High Court or a county court for an injunction restraining the relevant person from pursuing any conduct which amounts to harassment in relation to any person or persons mentioned or described in the injunction.

(3) Section 3(3) to (9) apply in relation to an injunction granted under subsection (2) above as they apply in relation to an injunction granted as mentioned in section 3(3)(a).]

4 Putting people in fear of violence

(1) A person whose course of conduct causes another to fear, on at least two occasions, that violence will be used against him is guilty of an offence if he knows or ought to know that his course of conduct will cause the other so to fear on each of those occasions.

(2) For the purposes of this section, the person whose course of conduct is in question ought to know that it will cause another to fear that violence will be used against him on any occasion if a reasonable person in possession of the same information would think the course of conduct would cause the other so to fear on that occasion.

(3) It is a defence for a person charged with an offence under this section to show that—

(a) his course of conduct was pursued for the purpose of preventing or detecting crime,

(b) his course of conduct was pursued under any enactment or rule of law or to comply with any condition or requirement imposed by any person under any enactment, or

(c) the pursuit of his course of conduct was reasonable for the protection of himself or another or for the protection of his or another's property.

(4) A person guilty of an offence under this section is liable—

(a) on conviction on indictment, to imprisonment for a term not exceeding five years, or a fine, or both, or

    (b) on summary conviction, to imprisonment for a term not exceeding six months, or a fine not exceeding the statutory maximum, or both.

    (5), (6) *****

5 Restraining orders

(1) A court sentencing or otherwise dealing with a person ("the defendant") convicted of an offence under section 2 or 4 may (as well as sentencing him or dealing with him in any other way) make an order under this section.

(2) The order may, for the purpose of protecting the victim [or victims] of the offence, or any other person mentioned in the order, from further conduct which—

    (a) amounts to harassment, or

    (b) will cause a fear of violence,

prohibit the defendant from doing anything described in the order.

    (4)–(6) *****

6 *****

7 Interpretation of this group of sections

(1) This section applies for the interpretation of sections 1 to 5.

(2) References to harassing a person include alarming the person or causing the person distress.

[(3) A "course of conduct" must involve—

    (a) in the case of conduct in relation to a single person (see section 1(1)), conduct on at least two occasions in relation to that person, or

    (b) in the case of conduct in relation to two or more persons (see section 1(1A)), conduct on at least one occasion in relation to each of those persons.]

[(3A) A person's conduct on any occasion shall be taken, if aided, abetted, counselled or procured by another—

    (a) to be conduct on that occasion of the other (as well as conduct of the person whose conduct it is); and

    (b) to be conduct in relation to which the other's knowledge and purpose, and what he ought to have known, are the same as they were in relation to what was contemplated or reasonably foreseeable at the time of the aiding, abetting, counselling or procuring.]

(4) "Conduct" includes speech.

[(5) References to a person, in the context of the harassment of a person, are references to a person who is an individual.]

8–16 *****

Special Immigration Appeals Commission Act 1997
(1997, c. 68)

An Act to establish the Special Immigration Appeals Commission; to make provision with respect to its jurisdiction; and for connected purposes   [17 December 1997]

Territorial extent: United Kingdom

1 Establishment of the Commission

(1) There shall be a commission, known as the Special Immigration Appeals Commission, for the purpose of exercising the jurisdiction conferred by this Act.

(2) Schedule 1 to this Act shall have effect in relation to the Commission.

[(3) The Commission shall be a superior court of record.

(4) A decision of the Commission shall be questioned in legal proceedings only in accordance with—.

    (a) section 7 . . .]

2 Jurisdiction: appeals

[(1) A person may appeal to the Special Immigration Appeals Commission against a decision if—

    (a) he would be able to appeal against the decision under section 82(1) or 83(2) of the Nationality, Immigration and Asylum Act 2002 but for a certificate of the Secretary of State under section 97 of that Act (national security, &c), or

    (b) an appeal against the decision under section 82(1) or 83(2) of that Act lapsed under section 99 of that Act by virtue of a certificate of the Secretary of State under section 97 of that Act.

    (2), (3) *****

(4) An appeal against the rejection of a claim for asylum under this section shall be treated as abandoned if the appellant leaves the United Kingdom.

(5) A person may bring or continue an appeal against an immigration decision under this section while he is in the United Kingdom only if he would be able to bring or continue the appeal while he was in the United Kingdom if it were an appeal under section 82(1) of that Act.

(6) In this section "immigration decision" has the meaning given by section 82(2) of the Nationality, Immigration and Asylum Act 2002.]

2A   . . .

[2B

A person may appeal to the Special Immigration Appeals Commission against a decision to make an order under section 40 of the British Nationality Act 1981 (deprivation of citizenship) if he is not entitled to appeal under section 40A(1) of that Act because of a certificate under section 40A(2).]

3 *****

4 . . .

5 Procedure in relation to jurisdiction under sections 2 and 3

(1) The Lord Chancellor may make rules—

    (a) for regulating the exercise of the rights of appeal conferred by section 2 . . . [or 2B] above,

    (b) for prescribing the practice and procedure to be followed on or in connection with appeals under [section 2 . . . [or 2B] above], including the mode and burden of proof and admissibility of evidence on such appeals, and

    (c) for other matters preliminary or incidental to or arising out of such appeals, including proof of the decisions of the Special Immigration Appeals Commission.

(2) Rules under this section shall provide that an appellant has the right to be legally represented in any proceedings before the Commission on an appeal under section 2 . . . [or 2B] above, subject to any power conferred on the Commission by such rules.

[(2A) Rules under this section may, in particular, do anything which may be done by rules under section 106 of the Nationality, Immigration and Asylum Act 2002 (appeals: rules).]

(3) Rules under this section may, in particular—

    (a) make provision enabling proceedings before the Commission to take place without the appellant being given full particulars of the reasons for the decision which is the subject of the appeal,

    (b) make provision enabling the Commission to hold proceedings in the absence of any person, including the appellant and any legal representative appointed by him,

(c) make provision about the functions in proceedings before the Commission of persons appointed under section 6 below, and

(d) make provision enabling the Commission to give the appellant a summary of any evidence taken in his absence.

(4)–(9) *****

6 Appointment of person to represent the appellant's interests

(1) The relevant law officer may appoint a person to represent the interests of an appellant in any proceedings before the Special Immigration Appeals Commission from which the appellant and any legal representative of his are excluded.

(2) For the purposes of subsection (1) above, the relevant law officer is–

(a) in relation to proceedings before the Commission in England and Wales, the Attorney General,

(b) in relation to proceedings before the Commission in Scotland, the Lord Advocate, and

(c) in relation to proceedings before the Commission in Northern Ireland, the Attorney General for Northern Ireland.

(3) A person appointed under subsection (1) above—

(a) if appointed for the purposes of proceedings in England and Wales, shall have a general qualification for the purposes of section 71 of the Courts and Legal Services Act 1990,

(b) if appointed for the purposes of proceedings in Scotland, shall be—

(i) an advocate, or

(ii) a solicitor who has by virtue of section 25A of the Solicitors (Scotland) Act 1980 rights of audience in the Court of Session and the High Court of Justiciary, and

(c) if appointed for the purposes of proceedings in Northern Ireland, shall be a member of the Bar of Northern Ireland.

(4) A person appointed under subsection (1) above shall not be responsible to the person whose interests he is appointed to represent.

7 Appeals from the Commission

(1) Where the Special Immigration Appeals Commission has made a final determination of an appeal, any party to the appeal may bring a further appeal to the appropriate appeal court on any question of law material to that determination.

(2) An appeal under this section may be brought only with the leave of the Commission or, if such leave is refused, with the leave of the appropriate appeal court.

(3) In this section "the appropriate appeal court" means—

(a) in relation to a determination made by the Commission in England and Wales, the Court of Appeal,

(b) in relation to a determination made by the Commission in Scotland, the Court of Session, and

(c) in relation to a determination made by the Commission in Northern Ireland, the Court of Appeal in Northern Ireland.

(4) . . .

*****

Audit Commission Act 1998

(1998, c. 18)

An Act to consolidate Part III of the Local Government Finance Act 1982 and other enactments relating to the Audit Commission for Local Authorities and the National Health Service in England and Wales [11 June 1998]

Territorial extent: England and Wales

PART I THE AUDIT COMMISSION

1 The Audit Commission

(1) There shall continue to be a body known as the Audit Commission for Local Authorities and the National Health Service in England and Wales.

(2) The Commission shall consist of not less than 15 nor more than 20 members appointed by the Secretary of State.

(3) The Secretary of State shall appoint one of the members to be chairman and another to be deputy chairman.

(4) An appointment under subsection (2) or (3) shall be made after consultation with such organisations and other bodies as appear to the Secretary of State to be appropriate.

(5) *****

2–3 ***

4 Code of audit practice

(1) The Commission shall prepare, and keep under review, a code of audit practice prescribing the way in which auditors are to carry out their functions under this Act.

(2) A different code may be prepared with respect to the audit of the accounts of health service bodies as compared with the code applicable to the accounts of other bodies.

(3) A code prepared under this section shall embody what appears to the Commission to be the best professional practice with respect to the standards, procedures and techniques to be adopted by auditors.

(4) A code does not come into force until approved by a resolution of each House of Parliament, and its continuation in force is subject to its being so approved at intervals of not more than five years.

(5) Subsection (4) does not preclude alterations to a code being made by the Commission in the intervals between its being approved in accordance with that subsection.

(6)–(8) *****

5 General duties of auditors

(1) In auditing accounts required to be audited in accordance with this Act, an auditor shall by examination of the accounts and otherwise satisfy himself—

    (a) if they are accounts of a health service body, that they are prepared in accordance with directions under subsection (2), [or (2B)] of section 98 of the National Health Service Act 1997;

    (b) in any other case, that they are prepared in accordance with regulations under section 27;

    (c) that they comply with the requirements of all other statutory provisions applicable to the accounts;

    (d) that proper practices have been observed in the compilation of the accounts;

    (e) that the body whose accounts are being audited has made proper arrangements for securing economy, efficiency and effectiveness in its use of resources; and

(f) that that body, if required to publish information in pursuance of a direction under section 44 (performance information), has made such arrangements for collecting and recording the information and for publishing it as are required for the performance of its duties under that section.

(2) The auditor shall comply with the code of audit practice applicable to the accounts being audited as that code is for the time being in force.

6 Auditors' right to documents and information

(1) An auditor has a right of access at all reasonable times to every document relating to a body subject to audit which appears to him necessary for the purposes of his functions under this Act.

(2) An auditor may—

(a) require a person holding or accountable for any such document to give him such information and explanation as he thinks necessary for the purposes of his functions under this Act; and

(b) if he thinks it necessary, require the person to attend before him in person to give the information or explanation or to produce the document.

(3) . . .

(4)–(7) *****

7 *****

8 Immediate and other reports in public interest

In auditing accounts required to be audited in accordance with this Act, the auditor shall consider—

(a) whether, in the public interest, he should make a report on any matter coming to his notice in the course of the audit, in order for it to be considered by the body concerned or brought to the attention of the public, and

(b) whether the public interest requires any such matter to be made the subject of an immediate report rather than of a report to be made at the conclusion of the audit.

9 General report

(1) When an auditor has concluded his audit of the accounts of any body under this Act he shall, subject to subsection (2), enter on the relevant statement of accounts prepared pursuant to regulations under section 27 (or, where no such statement is required to be prepared, on the accounts)—

(a) a certificate that he has completed the audit in accordance with this Act, and

(b) his opinion on the statement (or, as the case may be, on the accounts).

(2) Where an auditor makes a report to the body concerned under section 8 at the conclusion of the audit, he may include the certificate and opinion referred to in subsection (1) in that report instead of making an entry on the statement or accounts.

10–13 *****

Public inspection etc. and action by the auditor

14 Inspection of statements of accounts and auditors' reports

(1) A local government elector for the area of a body subject to audit, other than a health service body, may—

(a) inspect and make copies of any statement of accounts prepared by the body pursuant to regulations under section 27;

(b) inspect and make copies of any report, other than an immediate report, made to the body by an auditor; and

    (c) require copies of any such statement or report to be delivered to him on payment of a reasonable sum for each copy.

(2) A document which a person is entitled to inspect under this section may be inspected by him at all reasonable times and without payment.

(3), (4) *****

15 Inspection of documents and questions at audit

(1) At each audit under this Act, other than an audit of accounts of a health service body, any persons interested may—

    (a) inspect the accounts to be audited and all books, deeds, contracts, bills, vouchers and receipts relating to them, and

    (b) make copies of all or any part of the accounts and those other documents.

(2) At the request of a local government elector for any area to which the accounts relate, the auditor shall give the elector, or any representative of his, an opportunity to question the auditor about the accounts.

(3) Nothing in this section entitles a person—

    (a) to inspect so much of any accounts or other document as contains personal information about a member of the staff of the body whose accounts are being audited; or

    (b) to require any such information to be disclosed in answer to any question.

(4), (5) *****

16 Right to make objections at audit

(1) At each audit of accounts under this Act, other than an audit of accounts of a health service body, a local government elector for an area to which the accounts relate, or any representative of his, may attend before the auditor and (in accordance with subsection (2)) make objections—

    (a) as to any matter in respect of which the auditor could take action under section 17 . . .

    (b) as to any other matter in respect of which the auditor could make a report under section 8.

(2) No objection may be made under subsection (1) unless the auditor has received written notice of the proposed objection and of the grounds on which it is to be made.

(3) An elector sending a notice to an auditor for the purposes of subsection (2) shall at the same time send a copy of the notice to the body whose accounts are being audited.

17, 19 *****

18, 20–23 . . .

24 Power of auditor to apply for judicial review

(1) Subject to section 31(3) of the Supreme Court Act 1981 (no application for judicial review without leave) the auditor appointed in relation to the accounts of a body other than a health service body may make an application for judicial review with respect to—

    (a) any decision of that body, or

    (b) any failure by that body to act,

which it is reasonable to believe would have an effect on the accounts of that body.

(2) The existence of the powers conferred on an auditor under this Act is not a ground for refusing an application falling within subsection (1) (or an application for leave to make such an application).

(3) On an application for judicial review made as mentioned in subsection (1), the court may make such order as it thinks fit for the payment, by the body to whose decision the application relates, of expenses incurred by the auditor in connection with the application.

*****

Bank of England Act 1998
(1998, c. 11)

An Act to make provision about the constitution, regulation, financial arrangements and functions of the Bank of England, including provision for the transfer of supervisory functions; to amend the Banking Act 1987 in relation to the provision and disclosure of information; to make provision relating to appointments to the governing body of a designated agency under the Financial Services Act 1986; to amend Schedule 5 to that Act; to make provision relating to the registration of Government stocks and bonds; to make provision about the application of section 207 of the Companies Act 1989 to bearer securities; and for connected purposes   [23 April 1998]

Territorial extent: United Kingdom

1   Court of directors
(1) There shall continue to be a court of directors of the Bank.

(2) The court shall consist of a Governor, 2 Deputy Governors and 16 directors of the Bank, all of whom shall be appointed by Her Majesty.

(3) On the day on which this Act comes into force, all persons who are, immediately before that day, holding office as director of the Bank shall vacate their office.

(4) *****

2   Functions of court of directors
(1) The court of directors of the Bank shall manage the Bank's affairs, other than the formulation of monetary policy.

(2) In particular, the court's functions under subsection (1) shall include determining the Bank's objectives (including objectives for its financial management) and strategy.

(3) In determining the Bank's objectives and strategy, the court's aim shall be to ensure the effective discharge of the Bank's functions.

(4) Subject to that, in determining objectives for the financial management of the Bank, the court's aim shall be to ensure the most efficient use of the Bank's resources.

3–10   *****

11   Objectives
In relation to monetary policy, the objectives of the Bank of England shall be—
   (a) to maintain price stability, and
   (b) subject to that, to support the economic policy of Her Majesty's Government, including its objectives for growth and employment.

12   Specification of matters relevant to objectives
(1) The Treasury may by notice in writing to the Bank specify for the purposes of section 11—
   (a) what price stability is to be taken to consist of, or
   (b) what the economic policy of Her Majesty's Government is to be taken to be.

(2) The Treasury shall specify under subsection (1) both of the matters mentioned there—
   (a) before the end of the period of 7 days beginning with the day on which this Act comes into force, and
   (b) at least once in every period of 12 months beginning on the anniversary of the day on which this Act comes into force.

(3) Where the Treasury give notice under this section they shall—
   (a) publish the notice in such manner as they think fit, and
   (b) lay a copy of it before Parliament.

13–18   *****

19   Reserve powers

(1) The Treasury, after consultation with the Governor of the Bank, may by order give the Bank directions with respect to monetary policy if they are satisfied that the directions are required in the public interest and by extreme economic circumstances.

(2) An order under this section may include such consequential modifications of the provisions of this Part relating to the Monetary Policy Committee as the Treasury think fit.

(3) A statutory instrument containing an order under this section shall be laid before Parliament after being made.

(4) Unless an order under this section is approved by resolution of each House of Parliament before the end of the period of 28 days beginning with the day on which it is made, it shall cease to have effect at the end of that period.

(5) In reckoning the period of 28 days for the purposes of subsection (4), no account shall be taken of any time during which Parliament is dissolved or prorogued or during which either House is adjourned for more than 4 days.

(6) An order under this section which does not cease to have effect before the end of the period of 3 months beginning with the day on which it is made shall cease to have effect at the end of that period.

(7) While an order under this section has effect, section 11 shall not have effect.

*****

Civil Procedure Rules 1998

PART 54   JUDICIAL REVIEW

54.1   Scope and interpretation

(1) This [section of this] Part contains rules about judicial review.

(2) In this [section]—

   (a) a "claim for judicial review" means a claim to review the lawfulness of—

      (i) an enactment; or

      (ii) a decision, action or failure to act in relation to the exercise of a public function;

   (b)–(d) . . .

   (e) "the judicial review procedure" means the Part 8 procedure as modified by this [section];

   (f) "interested party" means any person (other than the claimant and defendant) who is directly affected by the claim; and

   (g) "court" means the High Court, unless otherwise stated. (Rule 8.1(6)(b) provides that a rule or practice direction may, in relation to a specified type of proceedings, disapply or modify any of the rules set out in Part 8 as they apply to those proceedings)

54.2   When this [section] must be used

The judicial review procedure must be used in a claim for judicial review where the claimant is seeking—

   (a) a mandatory order;

   (b) a prohibiting order;

   (c) a quashing order; or

   (d) an injunction under section 30 of the Supreme Court Act 1981 (restraining a person from acting in any office in which he is not entitled to act).

54.3   When this [section] may be used

(1) The judicial review procedure may be used in a claim for judicial review where the claimant is seeking—

    (a) a declaration; or

    (b) an injunction. (Section 31(2) of the Supreme Court Act 1981 sets out the circumstances in which the court may grant a declaration or injunction in a claim for judicial review)

(Where the claimant is seeking a declaration or injunction in addition to one of the remedies listed in rule 54.2, the judicial review procedure must be used)

(2) A claim for judicial review may include a claim for damages [, restitution or the recovery of a sum due] but may not seek [such a remedy] alone.

(Section 31(4) of the Supreme Court Act 1981 sets out the circumstances in which the court may award damages [, restitution or a sum due] on a claim for judicial review)

54.4   Permission required

The court's permission to proceed is required in a claim for judicial review whether started under this [section] or transferred to the Administrative Court.

54.5   Time limit for filing claim form

(1) The claim form must be filed—

    (a) promptly; and

    (b) in any event not later than 3 months after the grounds to make the claim first arose.

(2) The time limit in this rule may not be extended by agreement between the parties.

(3) This rule does not apply when any other enactment specifies a shorter time limit for making the claim for judicial review.

54.6   Claim form

(1) In addition to the matters set out in rule 8.2 (contents of the claim form) the claimant must also state—

    (a) the name and address of any person he considers to be an interested party;

    (b) that he is requesting permission to proceed with a claim for judicial review;

    (c) any remedy (including any interim remedy) he is claiming.

(Part 25 sets out how to apply for an interim remedy)

(2) The claim form must be accompanied by the documents required by the relevant practice direction.

54.7   Service of claim form

The claim form must be served on—

    (a) the defendant; and

    (b) unless the court otherwise directs, any person the claimant considers to be an interested party,

within 7 days after the date of issue.

54.8   Acknowledgment of service

(1) Any person served with the claim form who wishes to take part in the judicial review must file an acknowledgment of service in the relevant practice form in accordance with the following provisions of this rule.

(2) Any acknowledgment of service must be—

    (a) filed not more than 21 days after service of the claim form; and

    (b) served on—

        (i) the claimant; and

        (ii) subject to any direction under rule 54.7(b), any other person named in the claim form, as soon as practicable and, in any event, not later than 7 days after it is filed.

(3) The time limits under this rule may not be extended by agreement between the parties.

(4) The acknowledgment of service—

    (a) must—

        (i) where the person filing it intends to contest the claim, set out a summary of his grounds for doing so; and

        (ii) state the name and address of any person the person filing it considers to be an interested party; and

    (b) may include or be accompanied by an application for directions.

(5) Rule 10.3(2) does not apply.

54.9–54.16 *****

54.17   Court's powers to hear any person

(1) Any person may apply for permission—

    (a) to file evidence; or

    (b) make representations at the hearing of the judicial review.

(2) An application under paragraph (1) should be made promptly.

54.18   Judicial review may be decided without a hearing

The court may decide the claim for judicial review without a hearing where all the parties agree.

54.19   Court's powers in respect of quashing orders

(1) This rule applies where the court makes a quashing order in respect of the decision to which the claim relates.

(2) The court may—

    (a) remit the matter to the decision-maker; and

    (b) direct it to reconsider the matter and reach a decision in accordance with the judgment of the court.

(3) Where the court considers that there is no purpose to be served in remitting the matter to the decision-maker it may, subject to any statutory provision, take the decision itself.

  (Where a statutory power is given to a tribunal, person or other body it may be the case that the court cannot take the decision itself.)

54.20   Transfer

The court may—

    (a) order a claim to continue as if it had not been started under this [section] and

    (b) where it does so, give directions about the future management of the claim. (Part 30 (transfer) applies to transfers to and from the Administrative Court.)

54.21–54.25 *****

Crime and Disorder Act 1998

(1998, c. 37)

An Act to make provision for preventing crime and disorder; to create certain racially-aggravated offences; to abolish the rebuttable presumption that a child is doli incapax and to make provision as to the effect of a child's failure to give evidence at his trial; to abolish the death penalty for treason and piracy; to make changes to the criminal justice system; to make further provision for dealing with offenders; to make further provision with respect to remands and committals for trial and the release and recall of prisoners; to amend Chapter I of Part II of the Crime (Sentences) Act 1997 and to repeal Chapter I of Part III of the Crime and Punishment (Scotland) Act 1997; to make amendments designed to facilitate, or otherwise desirable in connection with, the consolidation of certain enactments; and for connected purposes   [31 July 1998]

Territorial extent: England and Wales; ss. 12 and following, and 33, make equivalent provisions for Scotland to those reproduced. Certain provisions (not reproduced here) concerning the abolition of the death penalty for treason and piracy apply to Scotland and Northern Ireland

PART I: PREVENTION OF CRIME AND DISORDER

Crime and disorder: general

1   Anti-social behaviour orders

(1) An application for an order under this section may be made by a relevant authority if it appears to the authority that the following conditions are fulfilled with respect to any person aged 10 or over, namely—

   (a) that the person has acted, since the commencement date, in an anti-social manner, that is to say, in a manner that caused or was likely to cause harassment, alarm or distress to one or more persons not of the same household as himself; and

   [(b) that such an order is necessary to protect relevant persons from further anti-social acts by him.]

. . .

   (1A), (1B) *****

   (2) . . .

(3) Such an application shall be made by complaint to the magistrates' court whose commission area includes [the local government area or police area concerned].

(4) If, on such an application, it is proved that the conditions mentioned in subsection (1) above are fulfilled, the magistrates' court may make an order under this section (an "anti-social behaviour order") which prohibits the defendant from doing anything described in the order.

(5) For the purpose of determining whether the condition mentioned in subsection (1)(a) above is fulfilled, the court shall disregard any act of the defendant which he shows was reasonable in the circumstances.

[(6) The prohibitions that may be imposed by an anti-social behaviour order are those necessary for the purpose of protecting persons (whether relevant persons or persons elsewhere in England and Wales) from further anti-social acts by the defendant.]

(7) An anti-social behaviour order shall have effect for a period (not less than two years) specified in the order or until further order.

(8) Subject to subsection (9) below, the applicant or the defendant may apply by complaint to the court which made an anti-social behaviour order for it to be varied or discharged by a further order.

(9) Except with the consent of both parties, no anti-social behaviour order shall be discharged before the end of the period of two years beginning with the date of service of the order.

(10) If without reasonable excuse a person does anything which he is prohibited from doing by an anti-social behaviour order, he [is guilty of an offence and] liable—

   (a) on summary conviction, to imprisonment for a term not exceeding six months or to a fine not exceeding the statutory maximum, or to both; or

   (b) on conviction on indictment, to imprisonment for a term not exceeding five years or to a fine, or to both.

   (10A)–(12) *****

1A–1B *****

[1C   Orders on conviction in criminal proceedings

(1) This section applies where a person (the "offender") is convicted of a relevant offence.

(2) If the court considers—

(a) that the offender has acted, at any time since the commencement date, in an anti-social manner, that is to say in a manner that caused or was likely to cause harassment, alarm or distress to one or more persons not of the same household as himself, and

(b) that an order under this section is necessary to protect persons in any place in England and Wales from further anti-social acts by him,

it may make an order which prohibits the offender from doing anything described in the order.

(3) The court may make an order under this section—

[(a) if the prosecutor asks it to do so, or

(b) if the court thinks it is appropriate to do so.]

[(3A) For the purpose of deciding whether to make an order under this section the court may consider evidence led by the prosecution and the defence.

(3B) It is immaterial whether evidence led in pursuance of subsection (3A) would have been admissible in the proceedings in which the offender was convicted.]

(4) An order under this section shall not be made except—

(a) in addition to a sentence imposed in respect of the relevant offence; or

(b) in addition to an order discharging him conditionally.]

(5), (9), (10) *****

(6)–(8) . . .

1CA–10 *****

11   Child safety orders

(1) Subject to subsection (2) below, if a magistrates' court, on the application of a local authority, is satisfied that one or more of the conditions specified in subsection (3) below are fulfilled with respect to a child under the age of 10, it may make an order (a "child safety order") which—

(a) places the child, for a period (not exceeding the permitted maximum) specified in the order, under the supervision of the responsible officer; and

(b) requires the child to comply with such requirements as are so specified.

(2) A court shall not make a child safety order unless it has been notified by the Secretary of State that arrangements for implementing such orders are available in the area in which it appears that the child resides or will reside and the notice has not been withdrawn.

(3) The conditions are—

(a) that the child has committed an act which, if he had been aged 10 or over, would have constituted an offence;

(b) that a child safety order is necessary for the purpose of preventing the commission by the child of such an act as is mentioned in paragraph (a) above;

(c) that the child has contravened a ban imposed by a curfew notice; and

(d) that the child has acted in a manner that caused or was likely to cause harassment, alarm or distress to one or more persons not of the same household as himself.

(4) The maximum period permitted for the purposes of subsection (1)(a) above is [twelve months].

(5) The requirements that may be specified under subsection (1)(b) above are those which the court considers desirable in the interests of—

(a) securing that the child receives appropriate care, protection and support and is subject to proper control; or

(b) preventing any repetition of the kind of behaviour which led to the child safety order being made.

(6) Proceedings under this section or section 12 below shall be family proceedings for the purposes of the 1989 Act or section 65 of the Magistrates' Courts Act 1980 ("the 1980 Act"); and the standard of proof applicable to such proceedings shall be that applicable to civil proceedings.

(7), (8) *****

12–13E *****

14 Local child curfew schemes

(1) A local authority [or a chief officer of police] may make a scheme (a "local child curfew scheme") for enabling the authority [or (as the case may be) the officer]—

(a) subject to and in accordance with the provisions of the scheme; and

(b) if, after such consultation as is required by the scheme, the authority [or (as the case may be the officer] considers it necessary to do so for the purpose of maintaining order,

to give a notice imposing, for a specified period (not exceeding 90 days), a ban to which subsection (2) below applies.

(2) This subsection applies to a ban on children of specified ages [(under 16)] being in a public place within a specified area—

(a) during specified hours (between 9 am and 6 am); and

(b) otherwise than under the effective control of a parent or a responsible person aged 18 or over.

(3)–(4A) *****

(5) The Secretary of State—

(a) may confirm, or refuse to confirm, a local curfew scheme submitted under this section for confirmation; and

(b) may fix the date on which such a scheme is to come into operation; and if no date is so fixed, the scheme shall come into operation at the end of the period of one month beginning with the date of its confirmation.

(6) A notice given under a local child curfew scheme (a "curfew notice") may specify different hours in relation to children of different ages.

(7), (8) *****

15 Contravention of curfew notices

(1) Subsections (2) and (3) below apply where a constable has reasonable cause to believe that a child is in contravention of a ban imposed by a curfew notice.

(2) The constable shall, as soon as practicable, inform the local authority for the area that the child has contravened the ban.

(3) The constable may remove the child to the child's place of residence unless he has reasonable cause to believe that the child would, if removed to that place, be likely to suffer significant harm.

(4) *****

16–27 *****

PART II   CRIMINAL LAW

Racially [or religiously] aggravated offences: England and Wales

28   Meaning of "racially [or religiously] aggravated"

(1) An offence is racially [or religiously] aggravated for the purposes of sections 29 to 32 below if—

   (a) at the time of committing the offence, or immediately before or after doing so, the offender demonstrates towards the victim of the offence hostility based on the victim's membership (or presumed membership) of a racial [or religious] group; or

   (b) the offence is motivated (wholly or partly) by hostility towards members of a racial [or religious] group based on their membership of that group.

(2) In subsection (1)(a) above—

"membership", in relation to a racial [or religious] group, includes association with members of that group;

"presumed" means presumed by the offender.

(3) It is immaterial for the purposes of paragraph (a) or (b) of subsection (1) above whether or not the offender's hostility is also based, to any extent, on [any other factor not mentioned in that paragraph.]

(4) In this section "racial group" means a group of persons defined by reference to race, colour, nationality (including citizenship) or ethnic or national origins.

[(5) In this section "religious group" means a group of persons defined by reference to religious belief or lack of religious belief.]

29   Racially [or religiously] aggravated assaults

(1) A person is guilty of an offence under this section if he commits—

   (a) an offence under section 20 of the Offences Against the Person Act 1861 (malicious wounding or grievous bodily harm);

   (b) an offence under section 47 of that Act (actual bodily harm); or

   (c) common assault,

which is racially [or religiously] aggravated for the purposes of this section.

(2) A person guilty of an offence falling within subsection (1)(a) or (b) above shall be liable—

   (a) on summary conviction, to imprisonment for a term not exceeding six months or to a fine not exceeding the statutory maximum, or to both;

   (b) on conviction on indictment, to imprisonment for a term not exceeding seven years or to a fine, or to both.

(3) A person guilty of an offence falling within subsection (1)(c) above shall be liable—

   (a) on summary conviction, to imprisonment for a term not exceeding six months or to a fine not exceeding the statutory maximum, or to both;

   (b) on conviction on indictment, to imprisonment for a term not exceeding two years or to a fine, or to both.

30   Racially [or religiously] aggravated criminal damage

(1) A person is guilty of an offence under this section if he commits an offence under section 1(1) of the Criminal Damage Act 1971 (destroying or damaging property belonging to another) which is racially [or religiously] aggravated for the purposes of this section.

(2) A person guilty of an offence under this section shall be liable—

   (a) on summary conviction, to imprisonment for a term not exceeding six months or to a fine not exceeding the statutory maximum, or to both;

   (b) on conviction on indictment, to imprisonment for a term not exceeding fourteen years or to a fine, or to both.

(3) *****

31   Racially [or religiously] aggravated public order offences

(1) A person is guilty of an offence under this section if he commits—

    (a) an offence under section 4 of the Public Order Act 1986 (fear or provocation of violence);

    (b) an offence under section 4A of that Act (intentional harassment, alarm or distress); or

    (c) an offence under section 5 of that Act (harassment, alarm or distress),

which is racially [or religiously] aggravated for the purposes of this section.

(2), (3) . . .

(4) A person guilty of an offence falling within subsection (1)(a) or (b) above shall be liable—

    (a) on summary conviction, to imprisonment for a term not exceeding six months or to a fine not exceeding the statutory maximum, or to both;

    (b) on conviction on indictment, to imprisonment for a term not exceeding two years or to a fine, or to both.

(5) A person guilty of an offence falling within subsection (1)(c) above shall be liable on summary conviction to a fine not exceeding level 4 on the standard scale.

(6), (7) *****

32   Racially [or religiously] aggravated harassment etc.

(1) A person is guilty of an offence under this section if he commits—

    (a) an offence under section 2 of the Protection from Harassment Act 1997 (offence of harassment); or

    (b) an offence under section 4 of that Act (putting people in fear of violence),

which is racially [or religiously] aggravated for the purposes of this section.

(2) . . .

(3) A person guilty of an offence falling within subsection (1)(a) above shall be liable—

    (a) on summary conviction, to imprisonment for a term not exceeding six months or to a fine not exceeding the statutory maximum, or to both;

    (b) on conviction on indictment, to imprisonment for a term not exceeding two years or to a fine, or to both.

(4) A person guilty of an offence falling within subsection (1)(b) above shall be liable—

    (a) on summary conviction, to imprisonment for a term not exceeding six months or to a fine not exceeding the statutory maximum, or to both;

    (b) on conviction on indictment, to imprisonment for a term not exceeding seven years or to a fine, or to both.

(5)–(7) *****

*****

Government of Wales Act 1998

(1998, c. 38)

An Act to establish and make provision about the National Assembly for Wales and the Offices of Auditor General for Wales and Welsh Administration Ombudsman; to reform certain Welsh public bodies and abolish certain of the Welsh public bodies; and for connected purposes

[31 July 1998]

Territorial extent: United Kingdom (although many of the provisions will apply only in Wales)

PART I　THE NATIONAL ASSEMBLY FOR WALES

The Assembly

1　The Assembly

(1) There shall be an Assembly for Wales to be known as the National Assembly for Wales or Cynulliad Cenedlaethol Cymru (but referred to in this Act as the Assembly).

(2) The Assembly shall be a body corporate.

(3) The exercise by the Assembly of its functions is to be regarded as done on behalf of the Crown.

2　Membership

(1) The Assembly shall consist of—

    (a)　one member for each Assembly constituency, and

    (b)　members for each Assembly electoral region.

(2) The Assembly constituencies and Assembly electoral regions, and the number of Assembly seats for each Assembly electoral region, shall be as provided for by or in accordance with Schedule 1.

(3) Members of the Assembly (referred to in this Act as Assembly members) shall be returned in accordance with the provision made by and under this Act for—

    (a)　the holding of ordinary elections of Assembly members, and

    (b)　the filling of vacancies in Assembly seats.

(4) An ordinary election involves the holding of elections for the return of the entire Assembly.

(5) The term of office of an Assembly member—

    (a)　begins when he is declared to be returned as an Assembly member, and

    (b)　continues until the end of the day before the day of the poll at the next ordinary election.

(6) But an Assembly member may at any time resign his seat by giving notice to—

    (a)　the presiding officer, or

    (b)　any person authorised by the standing orders of the Assembly to receive the notice.

(7) The validity of anything done by the Assembly is not affected by any vacancy in its membership.

Ordinary elections

3　Time of ordinary elections

(1) The poll at the first ordinary election shall be held on a day appointed by order made by the Secretary of State.

(2) The poll at each subsequent ordinary election shall be held on the first Thursday in May in the fourth calendar year following that in which the previous ordinary election was held.

(3)–(6) *****

4　Voting at ordinary elections

(1) Each person entitled to vote at an ordinary election in an Assembly constituency shall have two votes.

(2) One (referred to in this Act as a constituency vote) is to be given for a candidate to be the Assembly member for the Assembly constituency.

(3) The other (referred to in this Act as an electoral region vote) is to be given for—

    (a)　a registered political party which has submitted a list of candidates to be Assembly members for the Assembly electoral region in which the Assembly constituency is included, or

    (b)　an individual who is a candidate to be an Assembly member for that Assembly electoral region.

(4) The Assembly member for the Assembly constituency shall be returned under the simple majority system.

(5) The Assembly members for the Assembly electoral region shall be returned under the additional member system of proportional representation in accordance with sections 5 to 7.

(6)–(8) *****

5   Party lists and individual candidates

(1) Any registered political party may submit a list of candidates to be Assembly members for the Assembly electoral region.

(2) The list is to be submitted to the regional returning officer.

(3) The list has effect in relation to—
  (a) the ordinary election, and
  (b) any vacancies in seats of Assembly members returned for Assembly electoral regions which occur after that election and before the next ordinary election.

(4) The list must not include more than twelve persons (but may include only one).

(5), (6) *****

6   Calculation of electoral region figures

(1) For each registered political party by which a list of candidates has been submitted for the Assembly electoral region—
  (a) there shall be added together the number of electoral region votes given for the party in the Assembly constituencies included in the Assembly electoral region, and
  (b) the number arrived at under paragraph (a) shall then be divided by the aggregate of one and the number of candidates of the party returned as Assembly members for any of those Assembly constituencies.

(2) For each individual candidate to be an Assembly member for the Assembly electoral region there shall be added together the number of electoral region votes given for him in the Assembly constituencies included in the Assembly electoral region.

(3) The number arrived at—
  (a) in the case of a registered political party, under subsection (1)(b), or
  (b) in the case of an individual candidate, under subsection (2),
is referred to in this Act as the electoral region figure for that party or individual candidate.

7   Return of electoral region members

(1) The first seat for the Assembly electoral region shall be allocated to the party or individual candidate with the highest electoral region figure.

(2) The second and subsequent seats for the Assembly electoral region shall be allocated to the party or individual candidate with the highest electoral region figure after any recalculation required by subsection (3) has been carried out.

(3) This subsection requires a recalculation under section 6(1)(b) in relation to a party—
  (a) for the first application of subsection (2), if the application of subsection (1) resulted in the allocation of a seat to the party, or
  (b) for any subsequent application of subsection (2), if the previous application of that subsection did so;
and a recalculation shall be carried out after adding one to the aggregate mentioned in section 6(1)(b).

(4) An individual candidate already returned as an Assembly member shall be disregarded.

(5) Seats for the Assembly electoral region which are allocated to a party shall be filled by the persons on the party's list in the order in which they appear on the list.

(6)–(10) *****

8–9 *****

The franchise and conduct of elections

10   Entitlement to vote

(1) The persons entitled to vote at an election of Assembly members (or of an Assembly member) in an Assembly constituency are those who on the day of the poll—

    (a) would be entitled to vote as electors at a local government election in an electoral area wholly or partly included in the Assembly constituency, and

    (b) are registered in the register of local government electors at an address within the Assembly constituency.

(2) But a person is not entitled as an elector—

    (a) to cast more than one constituency vote, or more than one electoral region vote, in the same Assembly constituency at any ordinary election.

    (b) to vote in more than one Assembly constituency at any ordinary election, or

    (c) to cast more than one vote in an election held under section 8.

11–20   *****

PART II   ASSEMBLY FUNCTIONS

Introduction

21   Introductory

The Assembly shall have the functions which are—

    (a) transferred to, or made exercisable by, the Assembly by virtue of this Act, or

    (b) conferred or imposed on the Assembly by or under this Act or any other Act.

Transfer of Ministerial functions to Assembly

22   Transfer of Ministerial functions

(1) Her Majesty may by Order in Council—

    (a) provide for the transfer to the Assembly of any function so far as exercisable by a Minister of the Crown in Relation to Wales,

    (b) direct that any function so far as so exercisable shall be exercisable by the Assembly concurrently with the Minister of the Crown, or

    (c) direct that any function so far as exercisable by a Minister of the Crown in relation to Wales shall be exercisable by the Minister only with the agreement of, or after consultation with, the Assembly.

(2) The Secretary of State shall, before the first ordinary election, lay before each House of Parliament the draft of an Order in Council under this section making provision for the transfer of such functions in each of the fields specified in Schedule 2 as the Secretary of State considers appropriate.

    (3)–(5) *****

23   General transfer of property, rights and liabilities etc.

(1) There shall be transferred to and vest in the Assembly by virtue of this subsection all property, rights and liabilities to which a Minister of the Crown is entitled or subject, at the coming into force of an Order in Council under section 22, in connection with any function exercisable by the Minister which is transferred by the Order in Council.

    (2), (3) *****

(4) the Assembly shall be substituted for any Minister of the Crown in any instruments, contracts or legal proceedings which relate to–

    (a) any function exercisable by the Minister which is transferred by an Order in Council under section 22, or

(b) any property, rights or liabilities transferred by subsection (1) as the result of the transfer of any such function by such an Order in Council,

and which are made or commenced before the coming into force of the Order in Council.

24–28 *****

29   Implementation of Community law

(1) The power to designate a Minister of the Crown or government department under section 2(2) of the European Communities Act 1972 may be exercised to designate the Assembly.

(2) Accordingly, the Assembly may exercise the power to make regulations conferred by section 2(2) of the European Communities Act 1972 in relation to any matter, or for any purpose, if the Assembly has been designated in relation to that matter or for that purpose, but subject to such restrictions or conditions (if any) as may be specified by the Order in Council designating the Assembly.

(3)–(5) *****

30   Consultation about public appointments

(1) Her Majesty may by Order in Council make provision requiring any Minister of the Crown or other person to consult the Assembly before—

(a) appointing a person to a specified public post,

(b) recommending, consenting to or approving the appointment of a person to a specified public post,

(c) nominating a person for appointment to a specified public post, or

(d) selecting persons with a view to the appointment of one or more of them to a specified public post (whether or not by the person subject to the requirement).

(2) In subsection (1) "a specified public post" means—

(a) a public office specified, or of a description specified, in the Order in Council, or

(b) membership, or membership of a description so specified, or a public body so specified or of a description so specified.

(3)–(9) *****

31   Consultation about government's legislative programme

(1) As soon as is reasonably practicable after the beginning of each session of Parliament, the Secretary of State for Wales shall undertake with the Assembly such consultation about the government's legislative programme for the session as appears to him to be appropriate but including attending and participating in proceedings of the Assembly relating to the programme on at least one occasion.

(2) For this purpose the government's legislative programme for a session of Parliament consists of the bills which (at the beginning of the session) are intended to be introduced into either House of Parliament during the session by a Minister of the Crown.

(3), (4) *****

32   Support of culture etc.

The Assembly may do anything it considers appropriate to support—

(a) museums, art galleries or libraries in Wales,

(b) buildings of historical or architectural interest, or other places of historical interest, in Wales,

(c) the Welsh language, or

(d) the arts, crafts, sport or other cultural or recreational activities in Wales.

33   Consideration of matters affecting Wales

The Assembly may consider, and make appropriate representations about, any matter affecting Wales.

34–37   *****

38   Legal proceedings

Where the Assembly considers it appropriate for the promotion or protection of the public interest it may institute in its own name, defend or appear in any legal proceedings relating to matters with respect to which any functions of the Assembly are exercisable.

39   Contracts

The Secretary of State may by order provide that the Local Government (Contracts) Act 1997 shall apply in relation to contracts entered into by the Assembly but subject to any appropriate modifications.

40   Supplementary powers

The Assembly may do anything (including the acquisition or disposal of any property or rights) which is calculated to facilitate, or is conducive or incidental to, the exercise of any of its functions.

41–45   *****

PART III   ASSEMBLY PROCEDURE

Introductory

46   Regulation of procedure

(1) The procedure of the Assembly (including that of committees of the Assembly and sub-committees of such committees) shall be regulated by the standing orders of the Assembly.

(2) But subsection (1) is subject to any other provision of this Act or any other enactment which regulates, or provides for the regulation of, the procedure of the Assembly (or of committees of the Assembly or sub-committees of such committees).

(3) The standing orders may make different provision for different circumstances.

(4) Section 50 makes provision for the making of standing orders to have effect when the Assembly first meets; but the Assembly may remake or revise the standing orders at any time.

(5) The Assembly may not delegate the function of remaking or revising the standing orders.

(6) The standing orders shall not be remade or revised unless a motion to approve the standing orders or revisions is passed by the Assembly on a vote in which at least two-thirds of the Assembly members voting support the motion.

47   Equal treatment of English and Welsh languages

(1) The Assembly shall in the conduct of its business give effect, so far as is both appropriate in the circumstances and reasonably practicable, to the principle that the English and Welsh languages should be treated on a basis of equality.

(2) In determining how to comply with subsection (1), the Assembly shall have regard to the spirit of any guidelines under section 9 of the Welsh Language Act 1993.

(3) the standing orders shall be made in both English and Welsh.

48   Equal opportunities in conduct of business

The Assembly shall make appropriate arrangements with a view to securing that its business is conducted with due regard to the principle that there should be equality of opportunity for all people.

49–51   *****

Offices and committees

52   Presiding officer and deputy

(1) The Assembly shall elect from among the Assembly members—

  (a) the presiding officer, and

  (b) the deputy presiding officer.

(2) The offices specified in subsection (1) shall be known by such titles as the standing orders may provide (but are referred to in this Act as the presiding officer and the deputy presiding officer).

(3) the presiding officer and the deputy presiding officer may not be Assembly members who represent the same party.

53 Assembly First Secretary and Assembly Secretaries

(1) The Assembly shall elect one of the Assembly members to be Assembly First Secretary or Prif Ysgrifennydd y Cynulliad.

(2) The Assembly First Secretary shall appoint Assembly Secretaries, or Ys-grifenyddion y Cynulliad, from among the Assembly members (and may at any time remove a person from office as an Assembly Secretary).

(3) The standing orders must specify the maximum number of Assembly Secretaries that may be appointed.

(4) The Assembly First Secretary, and each of the Assembly Secretaries, is a Crown servant for the purposes of the Official Secrets Act 1989.

54–55 ***

The statutory committees

56 Executive committee

(1) There shall be a committee of the Assembly whose members shall be—

  (a) the Assembly First Secretary, who shall chair it, and

  (b) the Assembly Secretaries.

(2) The Committee shall be known by such title as the standing orders may provide (but is referred to in this Act as the executive committee).

(3) The Assembly First Secretary shall allocate accountability in the fields in which the Assembly has functions to members of the executive committee so that, in the case of each of those fields, accountability in the field is allocated either to one of the Assembly Secretaries or to him.

(4) The Assembly First Secretary need not make an allocation under subsection (3) to every member of the executive committee; but the number of Assembly Secretaries to whom no such allocation in made shall not exceed such number as may be specified in, or determined in accordance with, the standing orders.

(5) For the purposes of this section and section 57 "accountability", in relation to a member of the executive committee and a field, means that he is the member of the executive committee accountable to the Assembly (in accordance with standing orders under subsection (7)) for the exercise of the Assembly's functions in that field, except the exercise of functions by the executive committee (or by the Assembly itself).

(6) The Assembly First Secretary is accountable to the Assembly (in accordance with standing orders under subsection (7)) for the exercise of functions by the executive committee.

(7) The standing orders must include provision for allowing Assembly members to question (orally or in writing, as Assembly members prefer)—

  (a) each member of the executive committee about the exercise of the Assembly's functions in the field or fields in which he is accountable, except the exercise of functions by the executive committee (or by the Assembly itself), and

  (8) *****

57 Subject committees

(1) The Assembly shall establish committees with responsibilities in the fields in which the Assembly has functions.

(2) The committees established under this section shall be known by such titles as the standing orders may provide (but are referred to in this Act as subject committees).

(3) There shall be the same number of—

    (a) subject committees, and

    (b) members of the executive committee to whom the Assembly First Secretary allocates accountability in any of the fields in which the Assembly has functions.

(4) The division between the subject committees of the fields in which those committees have responsibilities and the division between members of the executive committee of the fields in which accountability is allocated to members of that committee shall be the same; and the member of the executive committee who has accountability in the field or fields in which a subject committee has responsibilities shall be a member of that subject committee.

(5)–(8) *****

58 Subordinate legislation scrutiny committee

(1) The Assembly shall establish a committee with responsibilities relating to the scrutiny of relevant Welsh subordinate legislation.

(2) For the purposes of this section "relevant Welsh subordinate legislation" is any subordinate legislation—

    (a) which is made or proposed to be made, or

    (b) which, or a draft of which, is (or but for paragraph 2(4) of Schedule 7 would be) required to be confirmed or approved,

by the Assembly (whether or not jointly with a Minister of the Crown or government department).

(3) The committee established under this section shall be known by such title as the standing orders may provide (but is referred to in this Act as the subordinate legislation scrutiny committee).

(4) The subordinate legislation scrutiny committee shall—

    (a) consider any proposed Assembly general subordinate legislation when the draft statutory instrument containing it has been laid before the Assembly, and

    (b) report to the Assembly whether or not the special attention of the Assembly should be drawn to it on any of the grounds specified in the standing orders for the purposes of this subsection.

(5)–(7) *****

59–65 *****

66 Making of Assembly general subordinate legislation

(1) Assembly general subordinate legislation shall be made by being signed by the presiding officer, the deputy presiding officer, the Assembly First Secretary or such other person as may be authorised by the subordinate legislation procedures.

(2) Assembly general subordinate legislation may not be made until a draft of the statutory instrument containing it has been laid before, and approved by a resolution of, the Assembly.

(3) The subordinate legislation procedures must include provision for securing that Assembly general subordinate legislation may be made by being signed otherwise than by the presiding officer only in the absence of the presiding officer.

(4)–(7) *****

67–68 *****

Other provisions about standing orders

69 Preservation of order

(1) The standing orders must include provision for preserving order in proceedings of the

Assembly (including proceedings of a committee of the Assembly or of a sub-committee of such a committee).

(2) In particular, standing orders made for preserving order in such proceedings must include provision for—

(a) preventing conduct which would constitute a criminal offence, and

(b) a sub judice rule,

and may include provision for excluding Assembly members from the proceedings and for withdrawing their rights and privileges as Assembly members for the period of their exclusion.

70   Openness

(1) The standing orders must include provision—

(a) for all proceedings of the Assembly itself to be held in public, and

(b) for all proceedings of a committee of the Assembly, or a subcommittee of such a committee, to be held in public except where the standing orders otherwise provide.

(2) But the standing orders may include provision as to conditions to be complied with by any member of the public attending proceedings of the Assembly (including proceedings of a committee of the Assembly or of a sub-committee of such a committee) and, in particular, provision for excluding from the proceedings any member of the public who does not comply with the conditions.

(3) The standing orders must include provision for—

(a) the publication of a report of the proceedings of the Assembly itself, and

(b) the publication of a report of the proceedings of a committee of the Assembly, or a sub-committee of such a committee, unless the proceedings were not held in public, as soon as reasonably practicable after the day on which the proceedings take place.

(4) The standing orders must include provision for any documents in the possession or under the control of the Assembly which contain material relating to any proceedings of the Assembly (including proceedings of a committee of the Assembly or of a sub-committee of such a committee) which have taken place, or are to take place, to be open to inspection by members of the public except where the standing orders otherwise provide.

(5) The standing orders must include provision—

(a) establishing procedures for the investigation of complaints about actions or failures on the part of the Assembly and for dealing with reports by [the Public Services Ombudsman for Wales] of investigations pursuant to complaints relating to the Assembly, and

(b) for publicising details of those procedures.

71   *****

72   Integrity

(1) The standing orders must include provision for a register of interests of Assembly members and for—

(a) registrable interests (as defined in the standing orders) to be registered in it, and

(b) the publication of the register.

(2) The standing orders must include provision for requiring any Assembly member who has–

(a) a financial interest (as defined in the standing orders) in any matter, or

(b) any other interest, or an interest of any other kind, specified in the standing orders in any matter,

to declare that interest before taking part in any proceedings of the Assembly (including proceedings of a committee of the Assembly or of a sub-committee of such a committee) relating to that matter.

(3) The standing orders may include provision—

(a) for preventing or restricting the participation in any proceedings of the Assembly (including proceedings of a committee of the Assembly or of a sub-committee of such a committee) of an Assembly member if he has a registrable interest, or an interest mentioned in subsection (2), in any matter to which the proceedings relate, and

(b) for preventing or restricting the exercise of a function by a member of the executive committee, or the exercise of a function by an Assembly member by virtue of section 59(6), if he has a registrable interest, or an interest mentioned in subsection (2), in any matter to which the function relates.

(4) The standing orders must include provision prohibiting an Assembly member—

(a) from advocating or initiating any cause or matter on behalf of any person, by any means specified in the standing orders, in consideration of any payment or benefit in kind of a description so specified, or

(b) from urging, in consideration of any such payment or benefit in kind, another Assembly member to advocate or initiate any cause or matter on behalf of any person by any such means.

(5)–(8) *****

73–75 *****

Miscellaneous

76 Attendance of Secretary of State for Wales

(1) The Secretary of State for Wales shall be entitled to attend and participate in any proceedings of the Assembly.

(2) Subsection (1) does not confer on the Secretary of State for Wales—

(a) any right to vote, or

(b) a right to attend or participate in the proceedings of a committee of the Assembly or any sub-committee of such a committee.

(3) *****

77 Defamation

(1) For the purposes of the law of defamation—

(a) any statement made in, for the purposes of or for purposes incidental to proceedings of the Assembly (including proceedings of a committee of the Assembly or of a sub-committee), and

(b) the publication by or under the authority of the Assembly of a report of such proceedings,

is absolutely privileged.

(2)–(5) *****

78–105 *****

106 Community law

(1) A Community obligation of the United Kingdom is also an obligation of the Assembly if, and to the extent that, the obligation could be implemented (or enabled to be implemented) or complied with by the exercise by the Assembly of any of its functions.

(2) Subsection (1) does not apply in the case of a Community obligation of the United Kingdom if—

(a) it is an obligation to achieve a result defined by reference to a quantity (whether expressed as an amount, proportion or ratio or otherwise), and

(b) the quantity relates to the United Kingdom (or to an area including the United Kingdom or to an area consisting of a part of the United Kingdom which includes the whole or part of Wales).

(3)–(6) *****

107 Human rights

(1) The Assembly has no power—

  (a) to make, confirm or approve any subordinate legislation, or

  (b) to do any other act,

so far as the subordinate legislation or act is incompatible with any of the Convention rights.

(2)–(4) *****

(5) In this Act "the Convention rights" has the same meaning as in the Human Rights Act 1998 and in subsection (2) "the Convention" has the same meaning as in that Act.

108 International obligations

(1) If a Minister of the Crown considers that any action proposed to be taken by the Assembly would be incompatible with any international obligation, he may by order direct that the proposed action shall not be taken.

(2) If a Minister of the Crown considers that any action capable of being taken by the Assembly is required for the purpose of giving effect to any international obligation, he may by order direct the Assembly to take the action.

(3) If a Minister of the Crown considers that any subordinate legislation made, or which could be revoked, by the Assembly is incompatible with any international obligation, he may by order revoke the legislation.

(4)–(11) *****

Decisions about Assembly functions

109 Resolution of devolution issues

Schedule 8 (which makes provision about devolution issues) has effect.

Note: Schedule 8 is not included for reasons of space; there are broadly equivalent provisions relating to Scotland in Schedule 6 to the Scotland Act 1998 (q.v.).

110 Power to vary retrospective decisions

(1) This section applies where any court or tribunal decides that the Assembly did not have the power to make a provision of subordinate legislation which it has purported to make.

(2) The court or tribunal may make an order—

  (a) removing or limiting any retrospective effect of the decision, or

  (b) suspending the effect of the decision for any period and on any conditions to allow the defect to be corrected.

(3) In determining whether to make an order under this section, the court or tribunal shall (among other things) have regard to the extent to which persons who are not parties to the proceedings would otherwise be adversely affected by the decision.

(4)–(8) *****

111   . . .

112–118   *****

Miscellaneous

119   *****

120 Equality of opportunity

(1) The Assembly shall make appropriate arrangements with a view to securing that its functions are exercised with due regard to the principle that there should be equality of opportunity for all people.

(2) After each financial year the Assembly shall publish a report containing—

    (a) a statement of the arrangements made in pursuance of subsection (1) which had effect during that financial year, and

    (b) an assessment of how effective those arrangements were in promoting equality of opportunity.

*****

SCHEDULE 2   FIELDS IN WHICH FUNCTIONS ARE TO BE TRANSFERRED BY FIRST ORDER IN COUNCIL

1. Agriculture, forestry, fisheries and food.
2. Ancient monuments and historic buildings.
3. Culture (including museums, galleries and libraries).
4. Economic development.
5. Education and training.
6. The environment.
7. Health and health services.
8. Highways.
9. Housing.
10. Industry.
11. Local government.
12. Social services.
13. Sport and recreation.
14. Tourism.
15. Town and country planning.
16. Transport.
17. Water and flood defence.
18. The Welsh language.

Human Rights Act 1998

(1998, c. 42)

An Act to give further effect to rights and freedoms guaranteed under the European Convention on Human Rights; to make provision with respect to holders of certain judicial offices who become judges of the European Court of Human Rights; and for connected purposes   [9 November 1998]

Territorial extent: United Kingdom

Introduction

1   The Convention Rights

(1) In this Act "the Convention rights" means the rights and fundamental freedoms set out in—

    (a) Articles 2 to 12 and 14 of the Convention,

    (b) Articles 1 to 3 of the First Protocol, and

    (c) [Article 1 of the Thirteenth Protocol,]

as read with Articles 16 to 18 of the Convention.

(2) Those Articles are to have effect for the purposes of this Act subject to any designated derogation or reservation (as to which see sections 14 and 15).

(3) The Articles are set out in Schedule 1.

(4) The [Secretary of State] may by order make such amendments to this act as he considers appropriate to reflect the effect, in relation to the United Kingdom, of a protocol.

(5) In subsection (4) "protocol" means a protocol to the Convention—

(a) which the United Kingdom has ratified; or

(b) which the United Kingdom has signed with a view to ratification.

(6) No amendment may be made by an order under subsection (4) so as to come into force before the protocol concerned is in force in relation to the United Kingdom.

Note: Schedule 1 is omitted, as the relevant Articles of and Protocols to the Convention are printed as part of the Convention at pp. 512–515. Note that Article 13 of the Convention (effective remedy) is not incorporated by s 1.

2   Interpretation of Convention rights

(1) A court or tribunal determining a question which has arisen in connection with a Convention right must take into account any—

(a) judgment, decision, declaration or advisory opinion of the European Court of Human Rights

(b) opinion of the Commission given in a report adopted under Article 31 of the Convention,

(c) decision of the Commission in connection with Article 26 or 27(2) of the convention, or

(d) decision of the Committee of Ministers taken under Article 46 of the Convention.

whenever made or given, so far as, in the opinion of the court or tribunal, it is relevant to the proceedings in which that question has arisen.

(2), (3) *****

Legislation

3   Interpretation of legislation

(1) So far as it is possible to do so, primary legislation and subordinate legislation must be read and given effect in a way which is compatible with Convention rights.

(2) This section—

(a) applies to primary legislation and subordinate legislation whenever enacted;

(b) does not affect the validity, continuing operation or enforcement of any incompatible primary legislation; and

(c) does not affect the validity, continuing operation or enforcement of any incompatible subordinate legislation if (disregarding any possibility of revocation) primary legislation prevents removal of the incompatibility.

4   Declaration of incompatibility

(1) Subsection (2) applies in any proceedings in which a court determines whether a provision of primary legislation is compatible with a Convention right.

(2) If the court is satisfied that the provision is incompatible with a Convention right, it may make a declaration of that incompatibility.

(3) Subsection (4) applies in any proceedings in which a court determines whether a provision of subordinate legislation, made in the exercise of a power conferred by primary legislation, is compatible with a Convention right.

(4) If the court is satisfied—

(a) that the provision is incompatible with a Convention right, and

(b) that (disregarding any possibility of revocation) the primary legislation concerned prevents removal of the incompatibility,

it may make a declaration of that incompatibility.

(5) In this section "court" means—

(a) [the Supreme Court];

(b) the Judicial Committee of the Privy Council;

(c) the Courts-Martial Appeal Court;

(d) in Scotland, the High Court of Justiciary sitting otherwise than as a trial court or the Court of Session;

(e) in England and Wales or Northern Ireland, the High Court or the Court of Appeal;

[(f) the Court of Protection, in any matter being dealt with by the President of the Family Division, the Vice Chancellor or a puisne judge of the High Court.]

(6) A declaration under this section ("a declaration of incompatibility")—

(a) does not affect the validity, continuing operation or enforcement of the provision in respect of which it is given; and

(b) is not binding on the parties to the proceedings in which it is made.

5   ***

Public authorities

6   Acts of public authorities

(1) It is unlawful for a public authority to act in a way which is incompatible with a Convention right.

(2) Subsection (1) does not apply to an act if—

(a) as the result of one or more provisions of primary legislation, the authority could not have acted differently; or

(b) in the case of one or more provisions of, or made under, primary legislation which cannot be read or given effect in a way which is compatible with the Convention rights, the authority was acting so as to give effect to or enforce those provisions.

(3) In this section "public authority" includes–

(a) a court or tribunal, and

(b) any person certain of whose functions are functions of a public nature,

but does not include either House of Parliament or a person exercising functions in connection with proceedings in Parliament.

(4) ...

(5) In relation to a particular act, a person is not a public authority by virtue only of subsection (3)(b) if the nature of the act is private.

(6) "An act" includes a failure to act but does not include a failure to—

(a) introduce in, or lay before, Parliament a proposal for legislation; or

(b) make any primary legislation or remedial order.

7   Proceedings

(1) A person who claims that a public authority has acted (or proposes to act) in a way which is made unlawful by section 6(1) may—

(a) bring proceedings against the authority under this Act in the appropriate court or tribunal, or

(b) rely on the convention right or rights concerned in any legal proceedings,

but only if he is (or would be) a victim of the unlawful act.

(2) In subsection (1)(a) "appropriate court or tribunal" means such court or tribunal as may be determined in accordance with rules; and proceedings against an authority include a counterclaim or similar proceedings.

(3) If the proceedings are brought on an application for judicial review, the applicant is to be taken to have a sufficient interest in relation to the unlawful act only if he is, or would be, a victim of that act.

(4) If the proceedings are made by way of a petition for judicial review in Scotland, the

applicant shall be taken to have title and interest to sue in relation to the unlawful act only if he is, or would be, a victim of that act.

(5) Proceedings under subsection (1)(a) must be brought before the end of—

(a) the period of one year beginning with the date on which the act complained of took place; or

(b) such longer period as the court or tribunal considers equitable having regard to all the circumstances,

but that is subject to any rule imposing a stricter time limit in relation to the procedure in question.

(6) In subsection (1)(b) "legal proceedings" includes—

(a) proceedings brought by or at the instigation of a public authority; and

(b) an appeal against the decision of a court or tribunal.

(7) For the purposes of this section, a person is a victim of an unlawful act only if he would be a victim for the purposes of Article 34 of the Convention if proceedings were brought in the European Court of Human Rights in respect of that act.

(8) Nothing in this Act creates a criminal offence.

(9)–(13) *****

8 Judicial remedies

(1) In relation to any act (or proposed act) of a public authority which the court finds is (or would be) unlawful, it may grant such relief or remedy, or make such order, within its powers as it considers just and appropriate.

(2) But damages may be awarded only by a court which has power to award damages, or to order the payment of compensation, in civil proceedings.

(3) No award of damages is to be made unless, taking account of all the circumstances of the case, including—

(a) any other relief or remedy granted, or order made, in relation to the act in question (by that or any other court), and

(b) the consequences of any decision (of that or any other court) in respect of that act,

the court is satisfied that the award is necessary to afford just satisfaction to the person in whose favour it is made.

(4) In determining—

(a) whether to award damages, or

(b) the amount of an award,

the court must take into account the principles applied by the European Court of Human Rights in relation to the award of compensation under Article 41 of the Convention.

(5), (6) *****

9 Judicial acts

(1) Proceedings under section 7(1)(a) in respect of a judicial act may be brought only—

(a) by exercising a right of appeal;

(b) on an application (in Scotland a petition) for a judicial review; or

(c) in such other forum as may be prescribed by rules.

(2) That does not affect any rule of law which prevents a court from being the subject of judicial review.

(3) In proceedings under this Act in respect of a judicial act done in good faith, damages may not be awarded otherwise than to compensate a person to the extent required by Article 5(5) of the Convention.

(4) An award of damages permitted by subsection (3) is to be made against the Crown; but no award may be made unless the appropriate person, if not a party to the proceedings, is joined.

(5) In this section—

"appropriate person" means the minister responsible for the court concerned or a person or government department nominated by him;

"court" includes a tribunal;

"judge" includes a member of a tribunal, a justice of the peace [(or, in Northern Ireland, a lay magistrate)] and a clerk or other officer entitled to exercise the jurisdiction of a court;

"judicial act" means a judicial act of a court and includes an act done on the instructions, or on behalf, of a judge; and

"rules" has the same meaning as in section 7(9).

Remedial action

10   Power to take remedial action

(1) This section applies if—

    (a) a provision of legislation has been declared under section 4 to be incompatible with a Convention right and, if an appeal lies—

        (i)   all persons who may appeal have stated in writing that they do not intend to do so;

        (ii) the time for bringing an appeal has expired and no appeal has been brought within that time; or

        (iii) an appeal brought within that time has been determined or abandoned; or

    (b) it appears to a Minister of the Crown or Her Majesty in Council that, having regard to a finding of the European Court of Human Rights made after the coming into force of this section in proceedings against the United Kingdom, a provision of legislation is incompatible with an obligation of the United Kingdom arising from the Convention.

(2) If a Minister of the Crown considers that there are compelling reasons for proceedings under this section, he may by order make such amendments to the legislation as he considers necessary to remove the incompatibility.

(3) If, in the case of subordinate legislation, a Minister of the Crown considers—

    (a) that it is necessary to amend the primary legislation under which the subordinate legislation in question was made, in order to enable the incompatibility to be removed, and

    (b) that there are compelling reasons for proceeding under this section,

he may by order make such amendments to the primary legislation as he considers necessary.

(4)–(7) *****

Other rights and proceedings

11   Safeguard for existing human rights

A person's reliance on a Convention right does not restrict—

    (a) any other right or freedom conferred on him by or under any law having effect in any part of the United Kingdom; or

    (b) his right to make any claim or bring any proceedings which he could make or bring apart from sections 7 to 9.

12   Freedom of expression

(1) This section applies if a court is considering whether to grant any relief which, if granted, might affect the exercise of the Convention right to freedom of expression.

(2) If the person against whom the application for relief is made ("the respondent") is neither present nor represented, no such relief is to be granted unless the court is satisfied—

    (a) that the applicant has taken all practicable steps to notify the respondent; or

    (b) that there are compelling reasons why the respondent should not be notified.

(3) No such relief is to be granted so as to restrain publication before trial unless the court is satisfied that the applicant is likely to establish that publication should not be allowed.

(4) The court must have particular regard to the importance of the Convention right to freedom of expression and, where the proceedings relate to material which the respondent claims, or which appears to the court, to be journalistic, literary or artistic material (or to conduct connected with such material), to—

    (a) the extent to which—

        (i) the material has, or is about to, become available to the public; or

        (ii) it is, or would be, in the public interest for the material to be published;

    (b) any relevant privacy code.

(5) In this section—

"court" includes a tribunal; and

"relief" includes any remedy or order (other than in criminal proceedings).

13 Freedom of thought, conscience and religion

(1) If a court's determination of any question arising under this Act might affect the exercise by a religious organisation (itself or its members collectively) of the Convention right to freedom of thought, conscience and religion, it must have particular regard to the importance of that right.

(2) In this section "court" includes a tribunal.

14 Derogations

(1) In this Act "designated derogation" means . . . any derogation by the United Kingdom from an Article of the Convention, or of any protocol to the Convention, which is designated for the purposes of this Act in an order made by the [Secretary of State].

(2) . . .

Northern Ireland Act 1998
(1998, c. 47)

An Act to make provision for the government of Northern Ireland for the purpose of implementing the agreement reached at multi-party talks on Northern Ireland set out in Command Paper 3883   [19 November 1998]

Territorial extent: Northern Ireland

Note: Section 4 and Schedules 2 and 3 list the matters excepted, reserved and transferred to the Assembly but are not included in this text.

PART I   PRELIMINARY

1 Status of Northern Ireland

(1) It is hereby declared that Northern Ireland in its entirety remains part of the United Kingdom and shall not cease to be so without the consent of a majority of the people of Northern Ireland voting in an poll held for the purposes of this section in accordance with Schedule 1.

(2) But if the wish expressed by a majority in such a poll is that Northern Ireland should cease to be part of the United Kingdom and form part of a united Ireland the Secretary of State shall lay before Parliament such proposals to give effect to that wish as may be agreed between Her Majesty's Government in the United Kingdom and the Government of Ireland.

2–4 *********

PART II   LEGISLATIVE POWERS

General

5   Acts of the Northern Ireland Assembly

(1) Subject to sections 6 to 8, the Assembly may make laws, to be known as Acts.

(2) A Bill shall become an Act when it has been passed by the Assembly and has received Royal Assent.

(3) A Bill receives Royal Assent at the beginning of the day on which Letters Patent under the Great Seal of Northern Ireland signed with Her Majesty's own hand signifying Her Assent are notified to the Presiding Officer.

(4) The date of Royal Assent shall be written on the Act by the Presiding Officer, and shall form part of the Act.

(5) The validity of any proceedings leading to the enactment of an Act of the Assembly shall not be called into question in any legal proceedings.

(6) This section does not affect the power of the Parliament of the United Kingdom to make laws for Northern Ireland, but an Act of the Assembly may modify any provision made by or under an Act of Parliament in so far as it is part of the law of Northern Ireland.

6   Legislative competence

(1) A provision of an Act is not law if it is outside the legislative competence of the Assembly.

(2) A provision is outside that competence if any of the following paragraphs apply—

    (a) it would form part of the law of a country or territory other than Northern Ireland, or confer or remove functions exercisable otherwise than in or as regards Northern Ireland;

    (b) it deals with an excepted matter and is not ancillary to other provisions (whether in the Act or previously enacted) dealing with reserved or transferred matters;

    (c) it is incompatible with any of the Convention rights;

    (d) it is incompatible with Community law;

    (e) it discriminates against any person or class of person on the ground of religious belief or political opinion;

    (f) it modifies an enactment in breach of section 7.

(3)–(5) *****

7   Entrenched enactments

(1) Subject to subsection (2), the following enactments shall not be modified by an Act of the Assembly or subordinate legislation made, confirmed or approved by a Minister or Northern Ireland department—

    (a) the European Communities Act 1972;

    (b) the Human Rights Act 1998; ...

    (c) section 43(1) to (6) and (8), section 67, sections 84 to 86, section 95(3) and (4) and section 98 [; and

    (d) section 1 and section 84 of the Justice (Northern Ireland) Act 2002.]

(2) Subsection (1) does not prevent an Act of the Assembly or subordinate legislation modifying section 3(3) or (4) or 11(1) of the European Communities Act 1972.

(3) In this Act "Minister", unless the context otherwise requires, means the First Minister, the deputy First Minister or a Northern Ireland Minister.

8–67 *****

PART VII   HUMAN RIGHTS AND EQUAL OPPORTUNITIES

Human rights

68   The Northern Ireland Human Rights Commission

(1) There shall be a body corporate to be known as the Northern Ireland Human Rights Commission.

(2) The Commission shall consist of a Chief Commissioner and other Commissioners appointed by the Secretary of State.

(3) In making appointments under this section, the Secretary of State shall as far as practicable secure that the Commissioners, as a group, are representative of the community in Northern Ireland.

(4) Schedule 7 (which makes supplementary provision about the Commission) shall have effect.

69   The Commission's functions

(1) The Commission shall keep under review the adequacy and effectiveness in Northern Ireland of law and practice relating to the protection of human rights.

(2) The Commission shall, before the end of the period of two years beginning with the commencement of this section, make to the Secretary of State such recommendations as it thinks fit for improving—

  (a) its effectiveness;

  (b) the adequacy and effectiveness of the functions conferred on it by this Part;

and

  (c) the adequacy and effectiveness of the provisions of this Part relating to it.

(3) The Commission shall advise the Secretary of State and the Executive Committee of the Assembly of legislative and other measures which ought to be taken to protect human rights—

  (a) as soon as reasonably practicable after receipt of a general or specific request for advice; and

  (b) on such other occasions as the Commission thinks appropriate.

(4) The Commission shall advise the Assembly whether a Bill is compatible with human rights—

  (a) as soon as reasonably practicable after receipt of a request for advice; and

  (b) on such other occasions as the Commission thinks appropriate.

(5) The Commission may—

  (a) give assistance to individuals in accordance with section 70; and

  (b) bring proceedings involving law or practice relating to the protection of human rights.

(6) The Commission shall promote understanding and awareness of the importance of human rights in Northern Ireland; and for this purpose it may undertake, commission or provide financial or other assistance for—

  (a) research; and

  (b) educational activities.

(7)–(11) *****

*****

Public Interest Disclosure Act 1998
(1998, c. 23)

An Act to protect individuals who make certain disclosures of information in the public interest; to allow such individuals to bring action in respect of victimisation; and for connected purposes
[2 July 1998]

Territorial extent: England and Wales, Scotland

Note: This Act adds new sections to the Employment Rights Act 1996 and consists almost entirely of additions and textual amendments. The most important of the provisions added are printed as part of that Act, above.

Scotland Act 1998
(1998, c. 46)

An Act to provide for the establishment of a Scottish Parliament and Administration and other changes in the government of Scotland; to provide for changes in the constitution and functions of certain public authorities; to provide for the variation of the basic rate of income tax in relation to income of Scottish taxpayers in accordance with a resolution of the Scottish Parliament; to amend the law about parliamentary constituencies in Scotland; and for connected purposes
[19 November 1998]

Territorial extent: United Kingdom (although many of the provisions will apply only in Scotland) except for s. 25 which extends to Scotland alone

PART I   THE SCOTTISH PARLIAMENT

The Scottish parliament

1   The Scottish Parliament
   (1) There shall be a Scottish Parliament.
   (2) One member of the Parliament shall be returned for each constituency (under the simple majority system) at an election held in the constituency.
   (3) Members of the Parliament for each region shall be returned at a general election under the additional member system of proportional representation provided for in this part and vacancies among such members shall be filled in accordance with this Part.
   (4) The validity of any proceedings of the Parliament is not affected by any vacancy in its membership.
   (5) Schedule 1 (which makes provision for the constituencies and regions for the purposes of this Act and the number of regional members) shall have effect.

General elections

2   Ordinary general elections
   (1) The day on which the poll at the first ordinary general election for membership of the Parliament shall be held, and the day, time and place for the meeting of the Parliament following that poll, shall be appointed by order made by the Secretary of State.

(2) The poll at subsequent ordinary general elections shall be held on the first Thursday in May in the fourth calendar year following that in which the previous ordinary general election was held, unless the day of the poll is determined by a proclamation under sub-section (5).

(3)–(6) *****

3   Extraordinary general elections

(1) The Presiding Officer shall propose a day for the holding of a poll if—

(a) the Parliament resolves that it should be dissolved and, if the resolution is passed on a division, the number of members voting in favour of it is not less than two-thirds of the total number of seats for members of the Parliament, or

(b) any period during which the Parliament is required under section 46 to nominate one of its members for appointment as First Minister ends without such a nomination being made.

(2) If the Presiding Officer makes such a proposal, Her Majesty may by proclamation under the Scottish Seal—

(a) dissolve the Parliament and require an extraordinary general election to be held,

(b) require the poll at the election to be held on the day proposed, and

(c) require the Parliament to meet within the period of seven days beginning immediately after the day of the poll.

(3) If a poll is held under this section within the period of six months ending with the day on which the poll at the next ordinary general election would be held (disregarding section 2(5)), that ordinary general election shall not be held.

(4) Subsection (3) does not affect the year in which the subsequent ordinary general election is to be held.

4   *****

5   Candidates

(1) At a general election, the candidates may stand for return as constituency members or regional members.

(2) A person may not be a candidate to be a constituency member for more than one constituency.

(3) The candidates to be regional members shall be those included in a list submitted under subsection (4) or individual candidates.

(4) Any registered political party may submit to the regional returning officer a list of candidates to be regional members for a particular region (referred to in this Act, in relation to the region, as the party's "regional list").

(5) A registered political party's regional list has effect in relation to the general election and any vacancy occurring among the regional members after that election and before the next general election.

(6) Not more than twelve persons may be included in the list (but the list may include only one person).

(7)–(9) *****

6   Poll for regional members

(1) This section and sections 7 and 8 are about the return of regional members at a general election.

(2) In each of the constituencies for the Parliament, a poll shall be held at which each person entitled to vote as elector may give a vote (referred to in this Act as a "regional vote") for—

(a) a registered political party which has submitted a regional list, or

(b) an individual candidate to be a regional member for the region.

(3) The right conferred on a person by subsection (2) is in addition to any right the person may have to vote in any poll for the return of a constituency member.

7 Calculation of regional figures

(1) The persons who are to be returned as constituency members for constituencies included in the region must be determined before the persons who are to be returned as the regional members for the region.

(2) For each registered political party which has submitted a regional list, the regional figure for the purposes of section 8 is—

(a) the total number of regional votes given for the party in all the constituencies included in the region,

divided by

(b) the aggregate of one plus the number of candidates of the party returned as constituency members for any of those constituencies.

(3) Each time a seat is allocated to the party under section 8, that figure shall be recalculated by increasing (or further increasing) the aggregate in subsection (2)(b) by one.

(4) For each individual candidate to be a regional member for the region, the regional figure for the purposes of section 8 is the total number of regional votes given for him in all the constituencies included in the region.

8 Allocation of seats to regional members

(1) The first regional member seat shall be allocated to the registered political party or individual candidate with the highest regional figure.

(2) the second and subsequent regional member seats shall be allocated to the registered political party or individual candidate with the highest regional figure, after any recalculation required by section 7(3) has been carried out.

(3) An individual candidate already returned as a constituency or regional member shall be disregarded.

(4) Seats for the region which are allocated to a registered political party shall be filled by the persons in the party's regional list in the order in which they appear in the list.

(5) For the purposes of this section and section 10, a person in a registered political party's regional list who is returned as a member of the Parliament shall be treated as ceasing to be in the list (even if his return is void).

(6) Once a party's regional list has been exhausted (by the return of persons included in it as constituency members or by the previous application of subsection (1) or (2)) the party shall be disregarded.

(7)–(9) *****

Vacancies

9 Constituency vacancies

(1) Where the seat of a constituency member is vacant, an election shall be held to fill the vacancy (subject to subsection (4)).

(2) The date of the poll shall be fixed by the Presiding Officer.

(3) the date shall fall within the period of three months—

(a) beginning with the occurrence of the vacancy, or

(b) if the vacancy does not come to the notice of the Presiding Officer within the period of one month beginning with its occurrence, beginning when it does come to his notice.

(4) the election shall not be held if the latest date for holding the poll would fall within

the period of three months ending with the day on which the poll at the next ordinary general election would be held (disregarding section 2(5)).

(5), (6) *****

10   Regional vacancies

(1) This section applies where the seat of a regional member is vacant.

(2) If the regional member was returned as an individual candidate, or the vacancy is not filled in accordance with the following provisions, the seat shall remain vacant until the next general election.

(3) If the regional member was returned (under section 8 or this section) from a registered political party's regional list, the regional returning officer shall notify the Presiding Officer of the name of the person who is to fill the vacancy.

(4)–(7) ******

Franchise and conduct of elections

11   Electors

(1) The persons entitled to vote as electors at an election for membership of the parliament held in any constituency are those who on the day of the poll—

(a) would be entitled to vote as electors at a local government election in an electoral area falling wholly or partly within the constituency, and

(b) are registered in the register of local government electors at an address within the constituency.

(2) A person is not entitled to vote as elector in any constituency—

(a) more than once at a poll for the return of a constituency member, or

(b) more than once at a poll for the return of regional members,

or to vote as elector in more than one constituency at a general election.

12–18   *****

Presiding Officer and administration

19   Presiding Officer

(1) The Parliament shall, at its first meeting following a general election, elect from among its members a Presiding Officer and two deputies.

(2) A person elected Presiding Officer or deputy shall hold office until the conclusion of the next election for Presiding Officer under subsection (1) unless he previously resigns, ceases to be a member of the Parliament otherwise than by virtue of a dissolution or is removed from office by resolution of the Parliament.

(3) If the Presiding Officer or a deputy ceases to hold office before the Parliament is dissolved, the Parliament shall elect another from among its members to fill his place.

(4)–(7) *****

20   Clerk of the Parliament

(1) There shall be a Clerk of the Parliament.

(2) The Clerk shall be appointed by the Scottish Parliamentary Corporate Body (established under section 21).

(3), (4) *****

21   Scottish Parliamentary Corporate Body

(1) There shall be a body corporate to be known as "the Scottish Parliamentary Corporate Body" (referred to in this Act as the Parliamentary corporation) to perform the functions conferred on the corporation by virtue of this Act or any other enactment.

(2) the members of the corporation shall be—

(a) the Presiding Officer, and

(b) four members of the Parliament appointed in accordance with standing orders.

(3) The corporation shall provide the Parliament, or ensure that the Parliament is provided, with the property, staff and services required for the Parliament's purposes.

(4) The Parliament may give special or general directions to the corporation for the purpose of or in connection with the exercise of the corporation's functions.

(5)–(8) *****

Proceedings etc.

22   Standing orders

(1) The proceedings of the Parliament shall be regulated by standing orders.

(2) *****

23–27   *****

Legislation

28   Acts of the Scottish Parliament

(1) Subject to section 29, the Parliament may make laws, to be known as Acts of the Scottish Parliament.

(2) Proposed Acts of the Scottish Parliament shall be known as Bills; and a Bill shall become an Act of the Scottish Parliament when it has been passed by the Parliament and has received Royal Assent.

(3) A Bill receives Royal Assent at the beginning of the day on which Letters Patent under the Scottish Seal signed with Her Majesty's own hand signifying Her Assent are recorded in the Register of the Great Seal.

(4) The date of Royal Assent shall be written on the Act of the Scottish Parliament by the Clerk, and shall form part of the Act.

(5) The validity of an Act of the Scottish Parliament is not affected by any invalidity in the proceedings of the Parliament leading to its enactment.

(6) Every Act of the Scottish Parliament shall be judicially noticed.

(7) This section does not affect the power of the Parliament of the United Kingdom to make laws for Scotland.

29   Legislative competence

(1) An Act of the Scottish Parliament is not law so far as any provision of the Act is outside the legislative competence of the Parliament.

(2) A provision is outside the competence so far as any of the following paragraphs apply—

(a) it would form part of the law of a country or territory other than Scotland, or confer or remove functions exercisable otherwise than in or as regards Scotland,

(b) it relates to reserved matters,

(c) it is in breach of the restrictions in Schedule 4.

(d) it is incompatible with any of the Convention rights or with Community law,

(e) it would remove the Lord Advocate from his position as head of the systems of criminal prosecution and investigation of deaths in Scotland.

(3) For the purposes of this section, the question whether a provision of an Act of the Scottish Parliament relates to a reserved matter is to be determined, subject to subsection (4), by reference to the purpose of the provision, having regard (among other things) to its effect in all the circumstances.

(4) *****

30   Legislative competence: supplementary

(1) Schedule 5 (which defines reserved matters) shall have effect.

(2)–(4) *****

31   Scrutiny of Bills before introduction
(1) A member of the Scottish Executive in charge of a Bill shall, on or before introduction of the Bill in the Parliament state that in his view the provisions of the Bill would be within the legislative competence of the Parliament.

(2) The Presiding Officer shall, on or before the introduction of a Bill in the Parliament, decide whether or not in his view the provisions of the Bill would be within the legislative competence of the Parliament and state his decision.

(3) The form of any statement, and the manner in which it is to be made, shall be determined under standing orders, and standing orders may provide for any statement to be published.

32   Submission of Bills for Royal Assent
(1) It is for the Presiding Officer to submit Bills for Royal Assent.

(2) The Presiding Officer shall not submit a Bill for Royal Assent at any time when—
    (a) the Advocate General, the Lord Advocate or the Attorney General is entitled to make a reference in relation to the Bill under section 33,
    (b) any such reference has been made but has not been decided or otherwise disposed of by the [Supreme Court], or
    (c) an order may be made in relation to the Bill under section 35.

(3) The Presiding Officer shall not submit a Bill in its unamended form for Royal Assent if—
    (a) the [Supreme Court has] decided that the Bill or any provision of it would not be within the legislative competence of the Parliament, or
    (b) a reference made in relation to the Bill under section 33 has been withdrawn following a request for withdrawal of the reference under section 34(2)(b).

(4) In this Act—
"Advocate General" means the Advocate General for Scotland,
   . . .

33   Scrutiny of bills by the [Supreme Court]
(1) The Advocate General, the Lord Advocate or the Attorney General may refer the question of whether a Bill or any provision of a Bill would be within the legislative competence of the Parliament to the [Supreme Court] for decision.

(2), (3) *****

34   ECJ references
(1) This section applies where—
    (a) a reference has been made in relation to a Bill under section 33,
    (b) a reference for a preliminary ruling has been made by the [Supreme Court] in connection with that reference, and
    (c) neither of those references has been decided or otherwise disposed of.

(2) If the Parliament resolves that it wishes to reconsider the Bill—
    (a) the Presiding Officer shall notify the Advocate General, the Lord Advocate and the Attorney General of that fact, and
    (b) the person who made the reference in relation to the Bill under section 33 shall request the withdrawal of the reference.

(3) In this section "a reference for a preliminary ruling" means a reference of a question to the European Court under Article 177 of the Treaty establishing the European Community, Article 41 of the Treaty establishing the European Coal and Steel Community or Article 150 of the Treaty establishing the European Atomic Energy Community.

35   Power to intervene in certain cases
(1) If a Bill contains provisions—
    (a) which the Secretary of State has reasonable grounds to believe would be incompat-

ible with any international obligations or the interests of defence or national security, or

(b) which make modifications of the law as it applies to reserved matters and which the Secretary of State has reasonable grounds to believe would have an adverse effect on the operation of the law as it applies to reserved matters,

he may make an order prohibiting the Presiding Officer from submitting the Bill for Royal Assent.

(2)–(5) *****

36 *****

Other provisions

37 Acts of Union

The Union with Scotland Act 1706 and the Union with England Act 1707 have effect subject to this Act.

38 *****

39 Members' interests

(1) Provision shall be made for a register of interests of members of the Parliament and for the register to be published and made available for public inspection.

(2) Provision shall be made—

(a) requiring members of the Parliament to register in that register financial interests (including benefits in kind), as defined for the purposes of this paragraph,

(b) requiring that any member of the Parliament who has a financial interest (including benefits in kind), as defined for the purposes of this paragraph, in any matter declares that interest before taking part in any proceedings of the Parliament relating to that matter.

(3) Provision made in pursuance of subsection (2) shall include any provision which the Parliament considers appropriate for preventing or restricting the participation in proceedings of the Parliament of a member with an interest defined for the purposes of subsection (2)(a) or (b) in a matter to which the proceedings relate.

(4) Provision shall be made prohibiting a member of the Parliament from—

(a) advocating or initiating any cause or matter on behalf of any person, by any means specified in the provision, in consideration of any payment or benefit in kind of a description so specified, or

(b) urging, in consideration of any such payment or benefit in kind, any other member on behalf of any person by any such means.

(5) Provision made in pursuance of subsections (2) to (4) shall include any provision which the Parliament considers appropriate for excluding from proceedings of the Parliament any member who fails to comply with, or contravenes, any provision made in pursuance of those subsections.

(6)–(8) *****

Legal issues

40 *****

41 Defamatory statements

(1) For the purposes of the law of defamation—

(a) any statement made in proceedings of the Parliament, and

(b) the publication under the authority of the Parliament of any statement, shall be absolutely privileged.

(2) In subsection (1), "statement" has the same meaning as in the Defamation Act 1996.

42   Contempt of court

(1) The strict liability rule shall not apply in relation to any publication—

(a) made in proceedings of the Parliament in relation to a Bill or subordinate legislation, or

(b) to the extent that it consists of a fair and accurate report of such proceedings made in good faith.

(2) In subsection (1), "the strict liability rule" and "publication" have the same meanings as in the Contempt of Court Act 1981.

43   Corrupt practices

The Parliament shall be a public body for the purposes of the Prevention of Corruption Acts 1889 to 1916.

PART II   THE SCOTTISH ADMINISTRATION

Ministers and their staff

44   The Scottish Executive

(1) There shall be a Scottish Executive, whose members shall be—

(a) the First Minister,

(b) such Ministers as the First Minister may appoint under section 47, and

(c) the Lord Advocate and the Solicitor General for Scotland.

(2) The members of the Scottish Executive are referred to collectively as the Scottish Ministers.

(3) A person who holds a Ministerial office may not be appointed a member of the Scottish Executive; and if a member of the Scottish Executive is appointed to a Ministerial office he shall cease to hold office as a member of the Scottish Executive.

(4) In subsection (3), references to a member of the Scottish Executive include a junior Scottish Minister and "Ministerial office" has the same meaning as in section 2 of the House of Commons Disqualification Act 1975.

45   The First Minister

(1) The First Minister shall be appointed by Her Majesty from among the members of the Parliament and shall hold office at Her Majesty's pleasure.

(2) The First Minister may at any time tender his resignation to Her Majesty and shall do so if the Parliament resolves that the Scottish Executive no longer enjoys the confidence of the Parliament.

(3) The First Minister shall cease to hold office if a person is appointed in his place.

(4) If the office of First Minister is vacant or he is for any reason unable to act, the functions exercisable by him shall be exercisable by a person designated by the Presiding Officer.

(5)–(7) *****

46   Choice of the First Minister

(1) If one of the following events occurs, the Parliament shall within the period allowed nominate one of its members for appointment as First Minister.

(2) The events are—

(a) the holding of a poll at a general election,

(b) the First Minister tendering his resignation to Her Majesty,

(c) the office of First Minister becoming vacant (otherwise than in consequence of his so tendering his resignation),

(d) the First Minister ceasing to be a member of the Parliament otherwise than by virtue of a dissolution.

(3) The period allowed is the period of 28 days which begins with the day on which the event in question occurs; but—

    (a) if another of those events occurs within the period allowed, that period shall be extended (subject to paragraph (b)) so that it ends with the period of 28 days beginning with the day on which that other event occurred, and

    (b) the period shall end if the Parliament passes a resolution under section 3(1)(a) or when Her Majesty appoints a person as First Minister.

(4) The Presiding Officer shall recommend to Her Majesty the appointment of any member of the Parliament who is nominated by the Parliament under this section.

47 Ministers

(1) The First Minister may, with the approval of Her Majesty, appoint Ministers from among the members of the Parliament.

(2) The First Minister shall not seek Her Majesty's approval for any appointment under this section without the agreement of the Parliament.

(3) A Minister appointed under this section—

    (a) shall hold office at her Majesty's pleasure,

    (b) may be removed from office by the First Minister,

    (c) may at any time resign and shall do so if the Parliament resolves that the Scottish Executive no longer enjoys the confidence of the Parliament,

    (d) if he resigns, shall cease to hold office immediately, and

    (e) shall cease to hold office if he ceases to be a member of the Parliament otherwise than by virtue of a dissolution.

48–50 *****

51 The Civil Service

(1) The Scottish Ministers may appoint persons to be members of the staff of the Scottish Administration.

(2) Service as—

    (a) the holder of any office in the Scottish Administration which is not a ministerial office, or

    (b) a member of the staff of the Scottish Administration,

shall be service in the Home Civil Service.

(3)–(9) *****

Ministerial functions

52 *****

53 General transfer of functions

(1) The functions mentioned in subsection (2) shall, so far as they are exercisable within devolved competence, be exercisable by the Scottish Ministers instead of by a Minister of the Crown.

(2) Those functions are—

    (a) those of Her Majesty's prerogative and other executive functions which are exercisable on behalf of Her Majesty by a Minister of the Crown,

    (b) other functions conferred on a Minister of the Crown by a prerogative instrument, and

    (c) functions conferred on a Minister of the Crown by any pre-commencement enactment,

but do not include any retained functions of the Lord Advocate.

(3), (4) *****

54   Devolved competence

(1) References in this Act to the exercise of a function being within or outside devolved competence are to be read in accordance with this section.

(2) It is outside devolved competence—

    (a) to make any provision by subordinate legislation which would be outside the legislative competence of the Parliament if it were included in an Act of the Scottish Parliament, or

    (b) to confirm or approve any subordinate legislation containing such provision.

(3) In the case of any function other than a function of making, confirming or approving subordinate legislation, it is outside devolved competence to exercise the function (or exercise it in any way) so far as a provision of an Act of the Scottish Parliament conferring the function (or, as the case may be, conferring it so as to be exercisable in that way) would be outside the legislative competence of the Parliament.

55–56   *****

57   Community law and Convention rights

(1) Despite the transfer to the Scottish Ministers by virtue of section 53 of functions in relation to observing and implementing obligations under Community law, any function of a minister of the Crown in relation to any matter shall continue to be exercisable by him as regards Scotland for the purposes specified in section 2(2) of the European Communities Act 1972.

(2) A member of the Scottish Executive has no power to make any subordinate legislation, or to do any other act, so far as the legislation or act is incompatible with any of the Convention rights or with Community law.

(3) Subsection (2) does not apply to an act of the Lord Advocate—

    (a) in prosecuting any offence, or

    (b) in his capacity as head of the systems of criminal prosecution and investigation of deaths in Scotland,

which, because of subsection (2) of section 6 of the Human Rights Act 1998, is not unlawful under subsection (1) of that section.

58   Power to prevent or require action

(1) If the Secretary of State has reasonable grounds to believe that any action proposed to be taken by a member of the Scottish Executive would be incompatible with any international obligations, he may by order direct that the proposed action shall not be taken.

(2) If the Secretary of State has reasonable grounds to believe that any action capable of being taken by a member of the Scottish Executive is required for the purpose of giving effect to any such obligations, he may by order direct that the action shall be taken.

(3) In subsections (1) and (2), "action" includes making, confirming or approving subordinate legislation and, in subsection (2), includes introducing a Bill in the Parliament.

(4) If any subordinate legislation made or which could be revoked by a member of the Scottish Executive contains provisions—

    (a) which the Secretary of State has reasonable grounds to believe to be incompatible with any international obligations or the interests of defence or national security, or

    (b) which make modifications of the law as it applies to reserved matters and which the Secretary of State has reasonable grounds to believe to have an adverse effect on the operation of the law as it applies to reserved matters,

the Secretary of State may by order revoke the legislation.

(5) An order under this section must state the reasons for making the order.

59–72   *****

73   Power to fix basic rate for Scottish taxpayers

(1) Subject to section 74, this section applies for any year of assessment for which income tax is charged if—

    (a) the Parliament has passed a resolution providing for the percentage determined to be the basic rate for that year to be increased or reduced for Scottish taxpayers in accordance with the resolution,

    (b) the increase or reduction provided for is confined to an increase or reduction by a number not exceeding three which is specified in the resolution and is either a whole number or half of a whole number, and

    (c) the resolution has not been cancelled by a subsequent resolution of the Parliament.

(2) Where this section applies for any year of assessment the Income Tax Acts (excluding this Part) shall have effect in relation to the income of Scottish taxpayers as if any rate determined by the Parliament of the United Kingdom to be the basic rate for that year were increased or reduced in accordance with the resolution of the Scottish Parliament.

(3)–(5) *****

74–90   ***

Miscellaneous

91   Maladministration

(1) The Parliament shall make provision for the investigation of relevant complaints made to its members in respect of any action taken by or on behalf of—

    (a) a member of the Scottish Executive in the exercise of functions conferred on the Scottish Ministers, or

    (b) any other office-holder in the Scottish Administration.

(2) For the purposes of subsection (1), a complaint is a relevant complaint if it is a complaint of a kind which could be investigated under the Parliamentary Commissioner Act 1967 if it were made to a member of the House of Commons in respect of a government department or other authority to which that Act applies.

(3)–(6) *****

92–94   ***

95   Appointment and removal of judges

(1) It shall continue to be for the Prime Minister to recommend to Her Majesty the appointment of a person as Lord President of the Court of Session or Lord Justice Clerk.

(2) The Prime Minister shall not recommend to Her Majesty the appointment of any person who has not been nominated by the First Minister for such appointment.

(3) Before nominating persons for such appointment the First Minister shall consult the Lord President and the Lord Justice Clerk (unless, in either case, the office is vacant).

(4) It is for the First Minister, after consulting the Lord President, to recommend to Her Majesty the appointment of a person as—

    (a) a judge of the Court of Session (other than the Lord President or the Lord Justice Clerk), or

    (b) a sheriff principal or a sheriff.

(5) the First Minister shall comply with any requirement in relation to—

    (a) a nomination under subsection (2), or

    (b) a recommendation under subsection (4),

imposed by virtue of any enactment.

(6) A judge of the Court of Session and the Chairman of the Scottish Land Court may be removed from office only by Her Majesty; and any recommendation to Her Majesty for such removal shall be made by the First Minister.

(7) The First Minister shall make such a recommendation if (and only if) the Parliament, on a motion made by the First Minister, resolves that such a recommendation should be made.

(8) Provision shall be made for a tribunal constituted by the First Minister to investigate and report on whether a judge of the Court of Session or the Chairman of the Scottish Land Court is unfit for office by reason of inability, neglect of duty or misbehaviour and for the report to be laid before the Parliament.

(9)–(11) *****

96–97 *****

Juridical

98   Devolution issues
Schedule 6 (which makes provision in relation to devolution issues) shall have effect.

99   Rights and liabilities of the Crown in different capacities
(1) Rights and liabilities may arise between the Crown in right of Her Majesty's Government in the United Kingdom and the Crown in right of the Scottish Administration by virtue of a contract, by operation of law or by virtue of an enactment as they may arise between subjects.

(2) Property and liabilities may be transferred between the Crown in one of those capacities and the Crown in the other capacity as they may be transferred between subjects; and they may together create, vary or extinguish any property or liability as subjects may.

(3) Proceedings in respect of—
   (a) any property or liabilities to which the Crown in one of those capacities is entitled or subject under subsection (1) or (2), or
   (b) the exercise of, or failure to exercise, any function exercisable by an office-holder of the Crown in one of those capacities,
may be instituted by the Crown in either capacity; and the Crown in the other capacity may be a separate party in the proceedings.

(4) This section applies to a unilateral obligation as it applies to a contract.

(5) In this section—
"office-holder", in relation to the Crown in right of Her Majesty's Government in the United Kingdom, means any minister of the Crown or other office-holder under the Crown in that capacity and, in relation to the Crown in right of the Scottish Administration, means any office-holder in the Scottish Administration,
"subject" means a person not acting on behalf of the Crown.

100   Human rights
(1) This Act does not enable a person—
   (a) to bring any proceedings in a court or tribunal on the ground that an act is incompatible with the Convention rights, or
   (b) to rely on any of the Convention rights in any such proceedings,
unless he would be a victim for the purposes of Article 34 of the Convention (within the meaning of the Human Rights Act 1998) if proceedings in respect of the act were brought in the European Court of Human Rights.

(2) Subsection (1) does not apply to the Lord Advocate, the Advocate General, the Attorney General [, the Advocate General for Northern Ireland] or the Attorney General for Northern Ireland.

(3) This Act does not enable a court or tribunal to award any damages in respect of an act which is incompatible with any of the Convention rights which it could not award if section 8(3) and (4) of the Human Rights Act 1998 applied.

(4) In this section "act" means—

(a) making any legislation,
(b) any other act or failure to act, if it is the act or failure of a member of the Scottish Executive.

101 Interpretation of Acts of the Scottish Parliament etc.
(1) This section applies to—
(a) any provision of an Act of the Scottish Parliament, or of a Bill for such an Act, and
(b) any provision of subordinate legislation made, confirmed or approved, or purporting to be made, confirmed or approved, by a member of the Scottish Executive,
which could be read in such a way as to be outside competence.
(2) Such a provision is to be read as narrowly as is required for it to be within competence, if such a reading is possible, and is to have effect accordingly.
(3) In this section "competence"—
(a) in relation to an Act of the Scottish Parliament, or a Bill for such an Act, means the legislative competence of the Parliament, and
(b) in relation to subordinate legislation, means the powers conferred by virtue of this Act.

102 Powers of courts or tribunals to vary retrospective decisions
(1) This section applies where any court or tribunal decides that—
(a) an Act of the Scottish Parliament or any provision of such an Act is not within the legislative competence of the Parliament, or
(b) a member of the Scottish Executive does not have the power to make, confirm or approve a provision of subordinate legislation that he has purported to make, confirm or approve.
(2) The court or tribunal may make an order—
(a) removing or limiting any retrospective effect of the decision, or
(b) suspending the effect of the decision for any period and on any conditions to allow the defect to be corrected.
(3) In deciding whether to make an order under this section, the court or tribunal shall (among other things) have regard to the extent to which persons who are not parties to the proceedings would otherwise be adversely affected.
(4)–(7) *****
*****

Section 29 and 53(4)   SCHEDULE 4
ENACTMENTS ETC. PROTECTED FROM MODIFICATION

PART I   THE PROTECTED PROVISIONS

Particular enactments

1.—(1) An Act of the Scottish Parliament cannot modify, or confer power by subordinate legislation to modify, any of the following provisions.
(2) The provisions are—
(a) Articles 4 and 6 of the Union with Scotland Act 1706 and of the Union with England Act 1707 so far as they relate to freedom of trade,
(b) the Private Legislation Procedure (Scotland) Act 1936,
(c) the following provisions of the European Communities Act 1972—
Section 1 and Schedule 1,
Section 2, other than subsection (2), the words following "such Community obligation" in subsection (3) and the words "subject to Schedule 2 to this Act" in subsection (4),

Section 3(1) and (2),

Section 11(2),

(d) paragraphs 5(3)(b) and 15(4)(b) of Schedule 32 to the Local Government, Planning and Land Act 1980 (designation of enterprise zones),

(e) sections 140A to 140G of the Social Security Administration Act 1992 (rent rebate and rent allowance subsidy and council tax benefit),

(f) the Human Rights Act 1998.

The law on reserved matters

2.—(1) An Act of the Scottish Parliament cannot modify, or confer power by subordinate legislation to modify, the law on reserved matters.

(2) In this paragraph, "the law on reserved matters" means—

(a) any enactment the subject-matter of which is a reserved matter and which is comprised in an Act of Parliament or subordinate legislation under an Act of Parliament, and

(b) any rule of law which is not contained in an enactment and the subject-matter of which is a reserved matter,

and in this sub-paragraph "Act of Parliament" does not include this Act.

(3), (4) *****

3.—(1) Paragraph 2 does not apply to modifications which—

(a) are incidental to, or consequential on, provision made (whether by virtue of the Act in question or another enactment) which does not relate to reserved matters, and

(b) do not have a greater effect on reserved matters than is necessary to give effect to the purpose of the provision.

(2) In determining for the purposes of sub-paragraph (1)(b) what is necessary to give effect to the purpose of a provision, any power to make laws other than the power of the Parliament is to be disregarded.

This Act

4.—(1) An Act of the Scottish Parliament cannot modify, or confer power by subordinate legislation to modify, this Act.

(2) This paragraph does not apply to modifying sections 1(4), 17(5), 19(7), 21(5), 24(2), 28(5), 39(7), 40 to 43, 50, 69(3), 85, [93 and 97] and paragraphs 4(1) to (3) and 6(1) of Schedule 2.

(3)–(5) *****

5.–14. *****

Section 30   SCHEDULE 5
                      RESERVED MATTERS

PART I   GENERAL RESERVATIONS

The Constitution

1. The following aspects of the constitution are reserved matters, that is—

(a) the Crown, including succession to the Crown and a regency,

(b) the Union of the Kingdoms of Scotland and England,

(c) the Parliament of the United Kingdom,

(d) the continued existence of the High Court of Justiciary as a criminal court of first instance and of appeal,

    (e) the continued existence of the Court of Session as a civil court of first instance and of appeal.

2.–5. *****

Political parties

6. The registration and funding of political parties is a reserved matter [but this paragraph does not reserve making payments to any political party for the purpose of assisting members of the Parliament who are connected with the party to perform their Parliamentary duties].

Foreign affairs etc.

7.—(1) International relations, including relations with territories outside the United Kingdom, the European Communities (and their institutions) and other international organisations, regulation of international trade, and international development assistance and co-operation are reserved matters.

(2) Sub-paragraph (1) does not reserve—

    (a) observing and implementing international obligations, obligations under the Human Rights Convention and obligations under Community law,

    (b) assisting Ministers of the Crown in relation to any matter to which that sub-paragraph applies.

Public service

8.—(1) the Civil Service of the State is a reserved matter.

(2) Sub-paragraph (1) does not reserve the subject-matter of—

    (a) Part I of the Sheriff Courts and Legal Officers (Scotland) Act 1927 (appointment of sheriff clerks and procurators fiscal etc.),

    (b) Part III of the Administration of Justice (Scotland) Act 1933 (officers of the High Court of Justiciary and of the Court of Session).

Defence

9.—(1) The following are reserved matters—

    (a) the defence of the realm,

    (b) the naval, military or air forces of the Crown, including reserve forces,

    (c) visiting forces,

    (d) international headquarters and defence organisations,

    (e) trading with the enemy and enemy property.

(2) Sub-paragraph (1) does not reserve—

    (a) the exercise of civil defence functions by any person otherwise than as a member of any force or organisation referred to in sub-paragraph (1)(b) to (d) or any other force or organisation reserved by virtue of sub-paragraph (1)(a),

    (b) the conferral of enforcement powers in relation to sea fishing.

Treason

10. Treason (including constructive treason), treason felony and misprision of treason are reserved matters.

PART II   SPECIFIC RESERVATIONS

Preliminary

1. The matters to which any of the Sections in this Part apply are reserved matters for the purposes of this Act.

2. A Section applies to any matter described or referred to in it when read with any illustrations, exceptions or interpretation provisions in that Section.

3. Any illustrations, exceptions or interpretation provisions in a Section relate only to that Section (so that an entry under the heading "exceptions" does not affect any other Section).

Reservations

Head A – Financial and Economic Matters

Section A1   A1. Fiscal, economic and monetary policy

Fiscal, economic and monetary policy, including the issue and circulation of money, taxes and excise duties, government borrowing and lending, control over United Kingdom public expenditure, the exchange rate and the Bank of England.

Exception

Local taxes to fund local authority expenditure (for example, council tax and non-domestic rates).

Section A2   A2. The currency

Coinage, legal tender and bank notes.

Section A3   A3. Financial services

Financial services, including investment business, banking and deposit-taking, collective investment schemes and insurance.

Exception

The subject-matter of section 1 of the Banking and Financial Dealings Act 1971 (bank holidays).

Section A4   A4. Financial markets

Financial markets, including listing and public offers of securities and investments, transfer of securities and insider dealing.

Section A5   A5. Money laundering

The subject-matter of the Money Laundering Regulations 1993, but in relation to any type of business.
*****

Note: The text of remaining headings is omitted for reasons of space. The other headings are categorised as follows:

Head B – Home Affairs
Head C – Trade and Industry
Head D – Energy
Head E – Transport
Head F – Social Security
Head G – Regulation of the Professions
Head H – Employment
Head J – Health and Medicines
Head K – Media and Culture
Head L – Miscellaneous

Section 98

SCHEDULE 6
DEVOLUTION ISSUES

PART I   PRELIMINARY

1. In this Schedule "devolution issue" means—
   (a) a question whether an Act of the Scottish Parliament or any provision of an Act of the Scottish Parliament is within the legislative competence of the Parliament,
   (b) a question whether any function (being a function which any person has purported, or is proposing, to exercise) is a function of the Scottish Ministers, the First Minister or the Lord Advocate.
   (c) a question whether the purported or proposed exercise of a function by a member of the Scottish Executive is, or would be, within devolved competence,
   (d) a question whether a purported or proposed exercise of a function by a member of the Scottish Executive is, or would be incompatible with any of the Convention rights or with Community law,
   (e) a question whether a failure to act by a member of the Scottish Executive is incompatible with any of the Convention rights or with Community law,
   (f) any other question about whether a function is exercisable within devolved competence or in or as regards Scotland and any other question arising by virtue of this Act about reserved matters.

2. A devolution issue shall not be taken to arise in any proceedings merely because of any contention of a party to the proceedings which appears to the court or tribunal before which the proceedings take place to be frivolous or vexatious.

PART II   PROCEEDINGS IN SCOTLAND

Application of Part II

3. This Part of this Schedule applies in relation to devolution issues in proceedings in Scotland.

Institution of proceedings

4.—(1) Proceedings for the determination of a devolution issue may be instituted by the Advocate General or the Lord Advocate.

(2) The Lord Advocate may defend any such proceedings instituted by the Advocate General.

(3) This paragraph is without prejudice to any power to institute or defend proceedings exercisable apart from this paragraph by any person.

Intimation of devolution issue

5. Intimation of any devolution issue which arises in any proceedings before a court or tribunal shall be given to the Advocate General and the Lord Advocate (unless the person to whom the intimation would be given is a party to the proceedings).

6. A person to whom intimation is given in pursuance of paragraph 5 may take part as a party in the proceedings, so far as they relate to a devolution issue.

Reference of devolution issue to higher court

7. A court, other than the [Supreme Court] or any court consisting of three or more judges of the Court of Session, may refer any devolution issue which arises in proceedings (other than criminal proceedings) before it to the Inner House of the Court of Session.

8. A tribunal from which there is no appeal shall refer any devolution issue which arises in proceedings before it to the Inner House of the Court of Session; and any other tribunal may make such a reference.

9. A court, other than any court consisting of two or more judges of the High Court of Justiciary, may refer any devolution issue which arises in criminal proceedings before it to the High Court of Justiciary.

References from superior courts to [Supreme Court]

10. Any court consisting of three or more judges of the Court of Session may refer any devolution issue which arises in proceedings before it (otherwise than on a reference under paragraph 7 or 8) to the [Supreme Court].

11. Any court consisting of two or more judges of the High Court of Justiciary may refer any devolution issue which arises in proceedings before it (otherwise than on a reference under paragraph 9) to the [Supreme Court].

Appeals from superior courts to [Supreme Court]

12. An appeal against a determination of a devolution issue by the Inner House of the Court of Session on a reference under paragraph 7 or 8 shall lie to the [Supreme Court].

13. An appeal against a determination of a devolution issue by—
   (a) a court of two or more judges of the High Court of Justiciary (whether in the ordinary course of proceedings or on a reference under paragraph 9), or
   (b) a court of three or more judges of the Court of Session from which there is no appeal to the [Supreme Court apart from this paragraph],
shall lie to the [Supreme Court], but only with [permission] of the court [from which the appeal lies] or, failing such [permission], with [permission] of the [Supreme Court].

PART III   PROCEEDINGS IN ENGLAND AND WALES

Application of Part III

14. This Part of this Schedule applies in relation to devolution issues in proceedings in England and Wales.

Institution of proceedings

15.—(1) Proceedings for the determination of a devolution issue may be instituted by the Attorney General.

(2) The Lord Advocate may defend any such proceedings.

(3) This paragraph is without prejudice to any power to institute or defend proceedings exercisable apart from this paragraph by any person.

Notice of devolution issue

16. A court or tribunal shall order notice of any devolution issue which arises in any proceedings before it to be given to the Attorney General and the Lord Advocate (unless the person to whom the notice would be given is a party to the proceedings).

17. A person to whom notice is given in pursuance of paragraph 16 may take part as a party in the proceedings, so far as they relate to a devolution issue.

Reference of devolution issue to High Court or Court of Appeal

18. A magistrates' court may refer any devolution issue which arises in proceedings (other than criminal proceedings) before it to the High Court.

19.—(1) A court may refer any devolution issue which arises in proceedings (other than criminal proceedings) before it to the Court of Appeal.

(2) Sub-paragraph (1) does not apply to—

(a) a magistrates' court, the Court of Appeal or the [Supreme Court], or

(b) the High Court if the devolution issue arises in proceedings on a reference under paragraph 18.

20. A tribunal from which there is no appeal shall refer any devolution issue which arises in proceedings before it to the Court of Appeal; and any other tribunal may make such a reference.

21. A court, other than the [Supreme Court] or the Court of Appeal, may refer any devolution issue which arises in criminal proceedings before it to—

(a) the High Court (if the proceedings are summary proceedings), or

(b) the Court of Appeal (if the proceedings are proceedings on indictment).

References from Court of Appeal to [Supreme Court]

22. The Court of Appeal may refer any devolution issue which arises in proceedings before it (otherwise than on a reference under paragraph 19, 20 or 21) to the [Supreme Court].

Appeals from superior courts to [Supreme Court]

23. An appeal against a determination of a devolution issue by the High Court or the Court of Appeal on a reference under paragraph 18, 19, 20 or 21 shall lie to the [Supreme Court], but only with [permission] of the High Court or (as the case may be) the Court of Appeal or, failing such [permission], with [permission] of the [Supreme Court].

24–31   *****

(Equivalent provisions for issues arising in Northern Ireland)

PART V   GENERAL

32. . . .

Direct references to [Supreme Court]

33. The Lord Advocate, the Advocate General, the Attorney General or the [Advocate General for Northern Ireland] may require any court or tribunal to refer to the [Supreme Court] any devolution issue which has arisen in proceedings before it to which he is a party.

34. The Lord Advocate, the Attorney General, the Advocate General or the [Advocate General for Northern Ireland] may refer to the [Supreme Court] any devolution issue which is not the subject of proceedings.

35–38   *****

*****

Access to Justice Act 1999

(1999, c. 22)

An Act to establish the Legal Services Commission, the Community Legal Service and the Criminal Defence Service; to amend the law of legal aid in Scotland; to make further provision about legal services; to make provision about appeals, courts, judges and court proceedings; to amend the law about magistrates and magistrates' courts; and to make provision about immunity from action and costs and indemnities for certain officials exercising judicial functions   [27 July 1999]

Territorial extent: England and Wales

*****

PART III   PROVISION OF LEGAL SERVICES

Legal Services Complaints Commissioner

51 Commissioner

(1) The [Secretary of State] may appoint a person as Legal Services Complaints Commissioner.

(2) Any appointment of a person as Commissioner shall be for a period of not more than three years; and a person appointed as Commissioner shall hold and vacate office in accordance with the terms of his appointment.

(3) At the end of his term of appointment the Commissioner shall be eligible for re-appointment.

(4) The Commissioner shall not be an authorised advocate, authorised litigator, licensed conveyancer or authorised practitioner (within the meaning of the Courts and Legal Services Act 1990) or a notary.

(5) Schedule 8 (which makes further provision about the Commissioner) has effect.

52 Commissioner's functions

(1) If it appears to the [Secretary of State] that complaints about members of any professional body are not being handled effectively and efficiently, he may by direction require the Legal Services Complaints Commissioner to consider exercising in relation to the body such of the powers in subsection (2) as are specified in the direction.

(2) Those powers are—

    (a) to require a professional body to provide information, or make reports, to the Commissioner about the handling of complaints about its members,

    (b) to investigate the handling of complaints about the members of a professional body,

    (c) to make recommendations in relation to the handling of complaints about the members of a professional body,

    (d) to set targets in relation to the handling of complaints about the members of a professional body, and

    (e) to require a professional body to submit to the Commissioner a plan for the handling of complaints about its members.

(3) Where the Commissioner requires a professional body to submit to him a plan for the handling of complaints about its members but the body—

    (a) fails to submit to him a plan which he considers adequate for securing that such complaints are handled effectively and efficiently, or

    (b) submits to him such a plan but fails to handle complaints in accordance with it,

he may require the body to pay a penalty.

(4) Before requiring a professional body to pay a penalty under subsection (3) the Commissioner shall afford it a reasonable opportunity of appearing before him to make representations.

(5) The [Secretary of State] shall by order made by statutory instrument specify the maximum amount of any penalty under subsection (3).

(6) In determining the amount of any penalty which a professional body is to be required to pay under subsection (3) the Commissioner shall have regard to all the circumstances of the case, including in particular—

    (a) the total number of complaints about members of the body and, where the penalty is imposed in respect of a failure to handle complaints in accordance with a plan, the number of complaints not so handled, and

(b) the assets of the body and the number of its members.

(7) A penalty under subsection (3) shall be paid to the Commissioner who shall pay it to the [Secretary of State].

(8) Where a direction under subsection (1) in relation to a professional body has been given (and not revoked), section 24(1) of the Courts and Legal Services Act 1990 (power of Legal Services Ombudsman to make recommendations about arrangements for investigation of complaints) shall not have effect in relation to the body.

(9) No order shall be made under subsection (5) unless a draft of the order has been laid before, and approved by a resolution of, each House of Parliament.

(10) In this section "professional body" has the same meaning as in section 22 of the Courts and Legal Services Act 1990.

*****

Greater London Authority Act 1999
(1999, c. 29)

An Act to establish and make provision about the Greater London Authority, the Mayor of London and the London Assembly; to make provision in relation to London borough councils and the Common Council of the City of London with respect to matters consequential or the establishment of the Greater London Authority; to make provision with respect to the functions of other local authorities and statutory bodies exercising functions in Greater London; to make provision about transport and road traffic in and around Greater London; to make provision about policing in Greater London and to make an adjustment of the metropolitan police district; and for connected purposes   [11 November 1999]

Territorial extent: England, Scotland and Wales (but necessarily the substantive provisions apply only to London)

PART I   THE GREATER LONDON AUTHORITY

The Authority

1   The Authority

(1) There shall be an authority for Greater London, to be known as the Greater London Authority.

(2) The Authority shall be a body corporate.

(3) The Authority shall have the functions which are transferred to, or conferred or imposed on, the Authority by or under this Act or any other Act.

Membership

2   Membership of the Authority and the Assembly

(1) The Authority shall consist of—
  (a) the Mayor of London; and
  (b) an Assembly for London, to be known as the London Assembly.

(2) The Assembly shall consist of twenty five members, of whom–
  (a) fourteen shall be members of Assembly constituencies ("constituency members"); and

(b) eleven shall be members for the whole of Greater London ("London Members").

(3) There shall be one constituency member for each Assembly constituency.

(4) The Assembly constituencies shall be the areas, and shall be known by the names, specified in an order made by [statutory instrument by the Electoral Commission].

(5)–(11) *****

3–19 *****

Qualifications and disqualifications

20   Qualification to be the Mayor or an Assembly member

(1) Subject to any disqualification by virtue of this Act or any other enactment, a person is qualified to be elected and to be the Mayor or an Assembly member if he satisfies the requirements of subsections (2) to (4) below.

(2) The person must be—

(a) a Commonwealth citizen;

(b) a citizen of the Republic of Ireland; or

(c) a relevant citizen of the Union.

(3) On the relevant day, the person must have attained the age of 21 years.

(4) The person must satisfy at least one of the following conditions–

(a) on the relevant day he is, and from that day continues to be, a local government elector for Greater London;

(b) he has, during the whole of the twelve months preceding that day, occupied as owner or tenant any land or other premises in Greater London;

(c) his principal or only place of work during that twelve months has been in Greater London;

(d) he has during the whole of that twelve months resided in Greater London.

(5)–(8) *****

21–29 *****

PART II   GENERAL FUNCTIONS AND PROCEDURE

The general and subsidiary powers of the Authority

30   The general power of the Authority

(1) The Authority shall have power to do anything which it considers will further any one or more of its principal purposes.

(2) Any reference in this Act to the principal purposes of the Authority is a reference to the purposes of—

(a) promoting economic development and wealth creation in Greater London;

(b) promoting social development in Greater London; and

(c) promoting the improvement of the environment in Greater London.

(3) In determining whether or how to exercise the power conferred by subsection (1) above to further any one or more of its principal purposes, the Authority shall have regard to the desirability of so exercising that power as to—

(a) further the remaining principal purpose or purposes, so far as reasonably practicable to do so; and

(b) secure, over a period of time, a reasonable balance between furthering each of its principal purposes.

(4) In determining whether or how to exercise the power conferred by subsection (1) above, the Authority shall have regard to the effect which the proposed exercise of the power would have on—

(a) the health of persons in Greater London; and

(b) the achievement of sustainable development in the United Kingdom.

(5) Where the Authority exercises the power conferred by subsection (1) above, it shall do so in the way which it considers best calculated–

(a) to promote improvements in the health of persons in Greater London, and

(b) to contribute towards the achievement of sustainable development in the United Kingdom,

except to the extent that the Authority considers that any action that would need to be taken by virtue of paragraph (a) or (b) above is not reasonably practicable in all the circumstances of the case.

(6) In subsection (5)(a) above, the reference to promoting improvements in health includes a reference to mitigating any detriment to health which would otherwise be occasioned by the exercise of the power.

(7)–(10) *****

31–51 *****

Meetings and procedure of the Assembly

52   Meetings of the whole Assembly

(1) The Assembly may hold, in addition to any meetings required to be held by or under this section or any other enactment, such other meetings as it may determine.

(2) Before the expiration of the period of ten days following the day of the poll at an ordinary election, there shall be a meeting of the Assembly to elect—

(a) the Chair of the Assembly; and

(b) the Deputy Chair of the Assembly.

(3) On such ten occasions in each calendar year as the Assembly may determine, there shall be a meeting of the Assembly—

(a) to consider the written report submitted for the meeting by the Mayor under section 45 above,

(b) to enable Assembly members to put–

(i) oral or written questions to the Mayor, and

(ii) oral questions to any employees of the Authority who are required to attend such meetings and answer questions put to them by Assembly members; and

(c) to transact any other business on the agenda for the meeting.

(4)–(7) *****

(8) An extraordinary meeting of the Assembly may be called at any time by the chair of the Assembly.

(9), (10) *****

53 *****

54   Discharge of functions by committees or single members

(1) The Assembly may arrange for any of the functions exercisable by it to be discharged on its behalf—

(a) by a committee or sub-committee of the Assembly; or

(b) by a single member of the Assembly.

(2) The Assembly may arrange for a member of staff of the Authority appointed under section 67(2) below to exercise on the Assembly's behalf any function exercisable by the Assembly under section 67(2) or 70(2) below.

(3) Where by virtue of this section any functions exercisable by the Assembly may be discharged by a committee of the Assembly, then, unless the Assembly otherwise directs, the committee may arrange for the discharge of any of those functions by a sub-committee or by a single member of the Assembly.

(4) Where by virtue of this section any functions exercisable by the Assembly may be discharged by a sub-committee of the Assembly, then, unless the Assembly or the committee concerned otherwise directs, the sub-committee may arrange for the discharge of any of those functions by a single member of the Assembly.

(5)–(8) *****

*****

House of Lords Act 1999
(1999, c. 34)

An Act to restrict membership of the House of Lords by virtue of a hereditary peerage; to make related provision about disqualifications for voting at elections to and for membership of the House of Commons; and for connected purposes   [11 November 1999]

Territorial extent: United Kingdom

1   Exclusion of hereditary peers
No-one shall be a member of the House of Lords by virtue of a hereditary peerage.

2   Exception from section 1
(1) Section 1 shall not apply in relation to anyone excepted from it by or in accordance with Standing Orders of the House.

(2) At any time 90 people shall be excepted from section 1; but anyone excepted as holder of the office of Earl Marshal, or as performing the office of Lord Great Chamberlain, shall not count towards that limit.

(3) Once excepted from section 1, a person shall continue to be so throughout his life (until an Act of Parliament provides to the contrary).

(4) Standing Orders shall make provision for filling vacancies among the people excepted from section 1; and in any case where—

(a)   the vacancy arises on a death occurring after the end of the first Session of the next Parliament after that in which this Act is passed, and

(b)   the deceased person was excepted in consequence of an election, that provision shall require the holding of a by-election.

(5) A person may be excepted from section 1 by or in accordance with Standing Orders made in anticipation of the enactment or commencement of this section.

(6) Any question whether a person is excepted from section 1 shall be decided by the Clerk of the Parliaments, whose certificate shall be conclusive.

3   Removal of disqualifications in relation to the House of Commons
(1) The holder of a hereditary peerage shall not be disqualified by virtue of that peerage for–

(a)   voting at elections to the House of Commons, or

(b)   being, or being elected as, a member of that House.

(2) Subsection (1) shall not apply in relation to anyone excepted from section 1 by virtue of section 2.

4   *****

5   Commencement and transitional provision
(1) Sections 1 to 4 (including Schedules 1 and 2) shall come into force at the end of the Session of Parliament in which this Act is passed.

(2) Accordingly, any writ of summons issued for the present Parliament in right of a

hereditary peerage shall not have effect after that Session unless it has been issued to a person who, at the end of the Session, is excepted from section 1 by virtue of section 2.

6   Interpretation and short title

(1) In this Act "hereditary peerage" includes the principality of Wales and the earldom of Chester.

(2) This Act may be cited as the House of Lords Act 1999.

Immigration and Asylum Act 1999
(1999, c. 33)

An Act to make provision about immigration and asylum; to make provision about procedures in connection with marriage on superintendent registrar's certificate; and for connected purposes
[11 November 1999]

Territorial extent: United Kingdom

*****

10   Removal of certain persons unlawfully in the United Kingdom

(1) A person who is not a British citizen may be removed from the United Kingdom, in accordance with directions given by an immigration officer, if—

(a) having only a limited leave to enter or remain, he does not observe a condition attached to the leave or remains beyond the time limited by the leave;

[(b) he uses deception in seeking (whether successfully or not) leave to remain;

(ba) his indefinite leave to enter or remain has been revoked under section 76(3) of the Nationality, Immigration and Asylum Act 2002 (person ceasing to be refugee); or]

(c) directions . . . have been given for the removal, under this section, of a person . . . to whose family he belongs.

(2) Directions may not be given under subsection (1)(a) if the person concerned has made an application for leave to remain in accordance with regulations made under section 9.

[(3) Directions may not be given under subsection (1)(c) unless the Secretary of State has given the person concerned written notice, [of the intention to remove him.]

(4)–(10) *****

11–12, 15   . . .

13–14, 16–31   *****

PART II   CARRIERS' LIABILITY

Clandestine entrants

32   Penalty for carrying clandestine entrants

(1) A person is a clandestine entrant if—

(a) he arrives in the United Kingdom concealed in a vehicle, ship or aircraft,

[(aa) he arrives in the United Kingdom concealed in a rail freight wagon,]

(b) he passes, or attempts to pass, through immigration control concealed in a vehicle, or

(c) he arrives in the United Kingdom on a ship or aircraft, having embarked—

(i) concealed in a vehicle; and

(ii) at a time when the ship or aircraft was outside the United Kingdom, and claims, or indicates that he intends to seek, asylum in the United Kingdom or evades, or attempts to evade, immigration control.

[(2) The Secretary of State may require a person who is responsible for a clandestine entrant to pay—

(a) a penalty in respect of the clandestine entrant;

(b) a penalty in respect of any person who was concealed with the clandestine entrant in the same transporter.

(2A) In imposing a penalty under subsection (2) the Secretary of State—

(a) must specify an amount which does not exceed the maximum prescribed for the purpose of this paragraph,

(b) may, in respect of a clandestine entrant or a concealed person, impose separate penalties on more than one of the persons responsible for the clandestine entrant, and

(c) may not impose penalties in respect of a clandestine entrant or a concealed person which amount in aggregate to more than the maximum prescribed for the purpose of this paragraph.]

(3) A penalty imposed under this section must be paid to the Secretary of State before the end of the prescribed period.

(4)–(10) *****

[32A   Level of penalty: code of practice

(1) The Secretary of State shall issue a code of practice specifying matters to be considered in determining the amount of a penalty under section 32.

(2) The Secretary of State shall have regard to the code (in addition to any other matters he thinks relevant)—

(a) when imposing a penalty under section 32, and

(b) when considering a notice of objection under section 35(4).

(3) Before issuing the code the Secretary of State shall lay a draft before Parliament.

(4) After laying the draft code before Parliament the Secretary of State may bring the code into operation by order.

(5) The Secretary of State may from time to time revise the whole or any part of the code and issue the code as revised.

(6) Subsections (3) and (4) also apply to a revision or proposed revision of the code.]

33   *****

34   Defences to claim that penalty is due under section 32

[(1) A person ("the carrier") shall not be liable to the imposition of a penalty under section 32(2) if he has a defence under this section.]

(2) It is a defence for the carrier to show that he, or an employee of his who was directly responsible for allowing the clandestine entrant to be concealed, was acting under duress.

(3) It is also a defence for the carrier to show that—

(a) he did not know, and had no reasonable grounds for suspecting, that a clandestine entrant was, or might be, concealed in the transporter;

(b) an effective system for preventing the carriage of clandestine entrants was in operation in relation to the transporter; and

(c) ... on the occasion in question the person or persons responsible for operating that system did so properly.

(3A), (4) *****

(5) ...

[(6) Where a person has a defence under subsection (2) in respect of a clandestine entrant, every other responsible person in respect of the clandestine entrant is also entitled to the benefit of the defence.]

35   Procedure

(1) If the Secretary of State decides that a person ("P") is liable to one or more penalties under section 32, he must notify P of his decision.

(2) A notice under subsection (1) (a "penalty notice") must—

(a) state the Secretary of State's reasons for deciding that P is liable to the penalty (or penalties);

(b) state the amount of the penalty (or penalties) to which P is liable;

(c) specify the date before which, and the manner in which, the penalty (or penalties) must be paid; and

(d) include an explanation of the steps—

(i) that P [may] take if he objects to the penalty;

(ii) that the Secretary of State may take under this Part to recover any unpaid penalty.

[(3) Subsection (4) applies where a person to whom a penalty notice is issued objects on the ground that—

(a) he is not liable to the imposition of a penalty, or

(b) the amount of the penalty is too high.

(4) The person may give a notice of objection to the Secretary of State.

(5) A notice of objection must—

(a) be in writing,

(b) give the objector's reasons, and

(c) be given before the end of such period as may be prescribed.

(6) Where the Secretary of State receives a notice of objection to a penalty in accordance with this section he shall consider it and—

(a) cancel the penalty,

(b) reduce the penalty,

(c) increase the penalty, or

(d) determine to take no action under paragraphs (a) to (c).

(7) Where the Secretary of State considers a notice of objection under subsection (6) he shall—

(a) inform the objector of his decision before the end of such period as may be prescribed or such longer period as he may agree with the objector,

(b) if he increases the penalty, issue a new penalty notice under subsection (1), and

(c) if he reduces the penalty, notify the objector of the reduced amount.]

(8) . . .

(9)–(13) *****

[35A   Appeal

(1) A person may appeal to the court against a penalty imposed on him under section 32 on the ground that—

(a) he is not liable to the imposition of a penalty, or

(b) the amount of the penalty is too high.

(2) On an appeal under this section the court may—

(a) allow the appeal and cancel the penalty,

(b) allow the appeal and reduce the penalty, or

(c) dismiss the appeal.

(3) An appeal under this section shall be a re-hearing of the Secretary of State's decision to impose a penalty and shall be determined having regard to—

(a) any code of practice under section 32A which has effect at the time of the appeal,

(b) the code of practice under section 33 which had effect at the time of the events to which the penalty relates, and

(c) any other matters which the court thinks relevant (which may include matters of which the Secretary of State was unaware).]

(4), (5) *********

36   Power to detain vehicles etc in connection with penalties under section 32

(1) If a penalty notice has been [issued] under section 35, a senior officer may detain any relevant—

(a) vehicle,

(b) small ship, . . .

(c) small aircraft, [or

(d) rail freight wagon,]

until all penalties to which the notice relates, and any expenses reasonably incurred by the Secretary of State in connection with the detention, have been paid.

(2) That power—

(a) may be exercised only if, in the opinion of the senior officer concerned, there is a significant risk that the penalty (or one or more of the penalties) will not be paid before the end of the prescribed period if the transporter is not detained; and

(b) may not be exercised if alternative security which the Secretary of State considers is satisfactory, has been given.

(2A)–(5) *********

36A   *********

37   Effect of detention

(1) This section applies if a transporter is detained under [section 36(1)].

(2) The person to whom the penalty notice was addressed, or the owner or any other person, [whose interests may be affected by detention of the transporter,] may apply to the court for the transporter to be released.

(3) The court may release the transporter if it considers that—

(a) satisfactory security has been tendered in place of the transporter for the payment of the penalty alleged to be due and connected expenses;

(b) there is no significant risk that the penalty (or one or more of the penalties) and any connected expenses will not be paid; or

(c) there is a significant doubt as to whether the penalty is payable . . .

(3A)–(7) *********

38   *********

39   . . .

Passengers without proper documents

[40   Charge in respect of passenger without proper documents

(1) This section applies if an individual requiring leave to enter the United Kingdom arrives in the United Kingdom by ship or aircraft and, on being required to do so by an immigration officer, fails to produce—

(a) an immigration document which is in force and which satisfactorily establishes his identity and his nationality or citizenship, and

(b) if the individual requires a visa, a visa of the required kind.

(2) The Secretary of State may charge the owner of the ship or aircraft, in respect of the individual, the sum of £2,000.

(3) The charge shall be payable to the Secretary of State on demand.

(4) No charge shall be payable in respect of any individual who is shown by the owner to have produced the required document or documents to the owner or his employee

or agent when embarking on the ship or aircraft for the voyage or flight to the United Kingdom.

    (5) For the purpose of subsection (4) an owner shall be entitled to regard a document as—

      (a) being what it purports to be unless its falsity is reasonably apparent, and

      (b) relating to the individual producing it unless it is reasonably apparent that it does not relate to him.]

    (6)–(10) *****

[40A   Notification and objection

    (1) If the Secretary of State decides to charge a person under section 40, the Secretary of State must notify the person of his decision.

    (2) A notice under subsection (1) (a "charge notice") must—

      (a) state the Secretary of State's reasons for deciding to charge the person,

      (b) state the amount of the charge,

      (c) specify the date before which, and the manner in which, the charge must be paid,

      (d) include an explanation of the steps that the person may take if he objects to the charge, and

      (e) include an explanation of the steps that the Secretary of State may take under this Part to recover any unpaid charge.

    (3) Where a person on whom a charge notice is served objects to the imposition of the charge on him, he may give a notice of objection to the Secretary of State.

    (4) A notice of objection must—

      (a) be in writing,

      (b) give the objector's reasons, and

      (c) be given before the end of such period as may be prescribed.

    (5) Where the Secretary of State receives a notice of objection to a charge in accordance with this section, he shall—

      (a) consider it, and

      (b) determine whether or not to cancel the charge.]

    (6)–(9) *****

[40B   Appeal

    (1) A person may appeal to the court against a decision to charge him under section 40.

    (2) On an appeal under this section the court may—

      (a) allow the appeal and cancel the charge, or

      (b) dismiss the appeal.

    (3) An appeal under this section—

      (a) shall be a re-hearing of the Secretary of State's decision to impose a charge, and

      (b) may be determined having regard to matters of which the Secretary of State was unaware.]

    (4), (5) *****

*****

Local Government Act 1999

(1999, c. 27)

An Act to make provision imposing on local and certain other authorities requirements relating to economy, efficiency and effectiveness; and to make provision for the regulation of council tax and precepts   **[27 July 1999]**

Territorial extent: England and Wales (subject to certain modifications in Wales)

PART I   BEST VALUE

Best value authorities

1   Best value authorities

(1) For the purposes of this Part each of these is a best value authority—

    (a) a local authority;

    (b) a National Park authority;

    (c) the Broads Authority;

    (d) a police authority;

    [(e) a fire and rescue authority constituted by a scheme under section 2 of the Fire and Rescue Services Act 2004 or a scheme to which section 4 of that Act applies, and a metropolitan county fire and civil defence authority;]

    (f) the London Fire and Emergency Planning Authority;

    (g) a waste disposal authority;

    (h) a metropolitan county passenger transport authority;

    (i) Transport for London;

    (j) the London Development Agency.

(2) In relation to England "local authority" in subsection (1)(a) means—

    (a) a county council, a district council, a London borough council, a parish council or a parish meeting of a parish which does not have a separate parish council;

    (b) the Council of the Isles of Scilly;

    (c) the Common Council of the City of London in its capacity as a local authority;

    (d) the Greater London Authority so far as it exercises its functions through the Mayor.

(3) In relation to Wales "local authority" in subsection (1)(a) means a county council, a county borough council or a community council.

(4)–(5) *****

2   *****

Duties

3   The general duty

(1) A best value authority must make arrangements to secure continuous improvement in the way in which its functions are exercised, having regard to a combination of economy, efficiency and effectiveness.

(2) For the purpose of deciding how to fulfil the duty arising under subsection (1) an authority must consult—

    (a) representatives of persons liable to pay any tax, precept or levy to or in respect of the authority,

    (b) representatives of persons liable to pay non-domestic rates in respect of any area within which the authority carries out functions,

    (c) representatives of persons who use or are likely to use services provided by the authority, and

    (d) representatives of persons appearing to the authority to have an interest in any area within which the authority carries out functions.

(3) For the purposes of subsection (2) "representatives" in relation to a group of persons means persons who appear to the authority to be representative of that group.

(4) In deciding on—

    (a) the persons to be consulted, and

    (b) the form, content and timing of consultations, an authority must have regard to any guidance issued by the Secretary of State.

4   Performance indicators and standards
(1) The Secretary of State may by order specify—
(a) factors ("performance indicators") by reference to which a best value authority's performance in exercising functions can be measured;
(b) standards ("performance standards") to be met by best value authorities in relation to performance indicators specified under paragraph (a).
(2) An order may specify different performance indicators or standards—
(a) for different functions;
(b) for different authorities [or descriptions of authority];
(c) to apply at different times.
(3) Before specifying performance indicators or standards the Secretary of State shall consult—
(a) persons appearing to him to represent the best value authorities concerned, and
(b) such other persons (if any) as he thinks fit.
(4) In specifying performance indicators and standards, and in deciding whether to do so, the Secretary of State—
(a) shall aim to promote improvement of the way in which the functions of best value authorities are exercised, having regard to a combination of economy, efficiency and effectiveness, and
(b) shall have regard to any recommendations made to him by the Audit Commission.
(5) In exercising a function a best value authority must meet any applicable performance standard specified under subsection (1)(b).

*****

Youth Justice and Criminal Evidence Act 1999
(1999, c. 23)

An Act to provide for the referral of offenders under 18 to youth offender panels; to make provision in connection with the giving of evidence or information for the purposes of criminal proceedings; to amend section 51 of the Criminal Justice and Public Order Act 1994; to make pre-consolidation amendments relating to youth justice; and for connected purposes   [27 July 1999]

Territorial extent: England and Wales and, in relation to service courts, to Scotland, but the provisions of Part II Chapter IV extend also to Scotland and Northern Ireland

1–15 . . .

PART II   GIVING OF EVIDENCE OR INFORMATION FOR PURPOSES OF CRIMINAL PROCEEDINGS
CHAPTER I   SPECIAL MEASURES DIRECTIONS IN CASE OF VULNERABLE AND INTIMIDATED WITNESSES

Preliminary

16   Witnesses eligible for assistance on grounds of age or incapacity
(1) For the purposes of this Chapter a witness in criminal proceedings (other than the accused) is eligible for assistance by virtue of this section—

(a) if under the age of 17 at the time of the hearing; or

(b) if the court considers that the quality of evidence given by the witness is likely to be diminished by reason of any circumstances falling within sub-section (2).

(2) The circumstances falling within this subsection are—

(a) that the witness—

(i) suffers from mental disorder within the meaning of the Mental Health Act 1983, or

(ii) otherwise has a significant impairment of intelligence and social functioning;

(b) that the witness has a physical disability or is suffering from a physical disorder.

(3)–(5) *****

17 Witnesses eligible for assistance on grounds of fear or distress about testifying

(1) For the purposes of this Chapter a witness in criminal proceedings (other than the accused) is eligible for assistance by virtue of this subsection if the court is satisfied that the quality of evidence given by the witness is likely to be diminished by reason of fear or distress on the part of the witness in connection with testifying in the proceedings.

(2) In determining whether a witness falls within subsection (1) the court must take into account, in particular—

(a) the nature and alleged circumstances of the offence to which the proceedings relate;

(b) the age of the witness;

(c) such of the following matters as appear to the court to be relevant, namely—

(i) the social and cultural background and ethnic origins of the witness,

(ii) the domestic and employment circumstances of the witness, and

(iii) any religious beliefs or political opinions of the witness;

(d) any behaviour towards the witness on the part of—

(i) the accused,

(ii) members of the family or associates of the accused, or

(iii) any other person who is likely to be an accused or a witness in the proceedings.

(3) In determining that question the court must in addition consider any views expressed by the witness.

(4) Where the complainant in respect of a sexual offence is a witness in proceedings relating to that offence (or to that offence and any other offences), the witness is eligible for assistance in relation to those proceedings by virtue of this subsection unless the witness has informed the court of the witness's wish not to be so eligible by virtue of this subsection.

18 *****

Special measures directions

19 Special measures direction relating to eligible witness

(1) This section applies where in any criminal proceedings—

(a) a party to the proceedings makes an application for the court to give a direction under this section in relation to a witness in the proceedings other than the accused, or

(b) the court of its own motion raises the issue whether such a direction should be given.

(2) Where the court determines that the witness is eligible for assistance by virtue of section 16 or 17, the court must then—

(a) determine whether any of the special measures available in relation to the witness (or any combination of them) would, in its opinion, be likely to improve the quality of evidence given by the witness; and

   (b) if so—

      (i) determine which of those measures (or combination of them) would, in its opinion, be likely to maximise so far as practicable the quality of such evidence; and

      (ii) give a direction under this section providing for the measure or measures so determined to apply to evidence given by the witness.

(3) In determining for the purposes of this Chapter whether any special measure or measures would or would not be likely to improve, or to maximise so far as practicable, the quality of evidence given by the witness, the court must consider all the circumstances of the case, including in particular—

   (a) any views expressed by the witness; and

   (b) whether the measure or measures might tend to inhibit such evidence being effectively tested by a party to the proceedings.

(4) A special measures direction must specify particulars of the provision made by the direction in respect of each special measure which is to apply to the witness's evidence.

   (5), (6) *****

20–22 *****

Special measures

23   Screening witness from accused

(1) A special measures direction may provide for the witness, while giving testimony or being sworn in court, to be prevented by means of a screen or other arrangement from seeing the accused.

(2) But the screen or other arrangement must not prevent the witness from being able to see, and to be seen by—

   (a) the judge or justices (or both) and the jury (if there is one);

   (b) legal representatives acting in the proceedings; and

   (c) any interpreter or other person appointed (in pursuance of the direction or otherwise) to assist the witness.

   (3) *****

24   Evidence by live link

(1) A special measures direction may provide for the witness to give evidence by means of a live link.

(2) Where a direction provides for the witness to give evidence by means of a live link, the witness may not give evidence in any other way without the permission of the court.

(3) The court may give permission for the purposes of subsection (2) if it appears to the court to be in the interests of justice to do so, and may do so either—

   (a) on an application by a party to the proceedings, if there has been a material change of circumstances since the relevant time, or

   (b) of its own motion.

   (4), (8) *****

   (5)–(7) . . .

25   Evidence given in private

(1) A special measures direction may provide for the exclusion from the court, during the giving of the witness's evidence, of persons of any description specified in the direction.

(2) The persons who may be so excluded do not include—

   (a) the accused,

   (b) legal representatives acting in the proceedings, or

(c) any interpreter or other person appointed (in pursuance of the direction or otherwise) to assist the witness.

(3) A special measures direction providing for representatives of news gathering or reporting organisations to be so excluded shall be expressed not to apply to one named person who—

(a) is a representative of such an organisation, and

(b) has been nominated for the purpose by one or more such organisations, unless it appears to the court that no such nomination has been made.

(4) A special measures direction may only provide for the exclusion of persons under this section where—

(a) the proceedings relate to a sexual offence; or

(b) it appears to the court that there are reasonable grounds for believing that any person other than the accused has sought, or will seek, to intimidate the witness in connection with testifying in the proceedings.

(5) Any proceedings from which persons are excluded under this section (whether or not those persons include representatives of news gathering or reporting organisations) shall nevertheless be taken to be held in public for the purposes of any privilege or exemption from liability available in respect of fair, accurate and contemporaneous reports of legal proceedings held in public.

26–31 *********

Supplementary

32 Warning to jury

Where on a trial on indictment [with a jury] evidence has been given in accordance with a special measures direction, the judge must give the jury such warning (if any) as the judge considers necessary to ensure that the fact that the direction was given in relation to the witness does not prejudice the accused.

33 *********

CHAPTER II   PROTECTION OF WITNESSES FROM CROSS-EXAMINATION
BY ACCUSED IN PERSON

General prohibitions

34 Complainants in proceedings for sexual offences

No person charged with a sexual offence may in any criminal proceedings cross-examine in person a witness who is the complainant, either—

(a) in connection with that offence, or

(b) in connection with any other offence (of whatever nature) with which that person is charged in the proceedings.

35 *********

Prohibition imposed by court

36 Direction prohibiting accused from cross-examining particular witness

(1) This section applies where, in a case where neither of sections 34 and 35 operates to prevent an accused in any criminal proceedings from cross-examining a witness in person—

(a) the prosecutor makes an application for the court to give a direction under this section in relation to the witness, or

(b) the court of its own motion raises the issue whether such a direction should be given.

(2) If it appears to the court—
  (a) that the quality of evidence given by the witness on cross-examination—
    (i) is likely to be diminished if the cross-examination (or further cross-examination (or further cross-examination) is conducted by the accused in person, and
    (ii) would be likely to be improved if a direction were given under this section, and
  (b) that it would not be contrary to the interests of justice to give such a direction, the court may give a direction prohibiting the accused from cross-examining (or further cross-examining) the witness in person.

(3) In determining whether subsection (2)(a) applies in the case of a witness the court must have regard, in particular, to—
  (a) any views expressed by the witness as to whether or not the witness is content to be cross-examined by the accused in person;
  (b) the nature of the questions likely to be asked, having regard to the issues in the proceedings and the defence case advanced so far (if any);
  (c) any behaviour on the part of the accused at any stage of the proceedings, both generally and in relation to the witness;
  (d) any relationship (of whatever nature) between the witness and the accused;
  (e) whether any person (other than the accused) is or has at any time been charged in the proceedings with a sexual offence or an offence to which section 35 applies, and (if so) whether section 34 or 35 operates or would have operated to prevent that person from cross-examining the witness in person;
  (f) any direction under section 19 which the court has given, or proposes to give, in relation to the witness.

(4) For the purposes of this section—
  (a) "witness", in relation to an accused, does not include any other person who is charged with an offence in the proceedings; and
  (b) any reference to the quality of a witness's evidence shall be construed in accordance with section 16(5).

37 *****

Cross-examination on behalf of accused

38 Defence representation for purposes of cross-examination

(1) This section applies where an accused is prevented from cross-examining a witness in person by virtue of section 34, 35 or 36.

(2) Where it appears to the court that this section applies, it must—
  (a) invite the accused to arrange for a legal representative to act for him for the purpose of cross-examining the witness; and
  (b) require the accused to notify the court, by the end of such period as it may specify, whether a legal representative is to act for him for that purpose.

(3) If by the end of the period mentioned in subsection (2)(b) either—
  (a) the accused has notified the court that no legal representative is to act for him for the purpose of cross-examining the witness, or
  (b) no notification has been received by the court and it appears to the court that no legal representative is to so act,
the court must consider whether it is necessary in the interests of justice for the witness to be cross-examined by a legal representative appointed to represent the interests of the accused.

(4) If the court decides that it is necessary in the interests of justice for the witness to be so cross-examined, the court must appoint a qualified legal representative (chosen by the court) to cross-examine the witness in the interests of the accused.

(5) A person so appointed shall not be responsible to the accused.

(6)–(8) *****

39 Warning to jury

(1) Where on a trial on indictment [with a jury] an accused is prevented from cross-examining a witness in person by virtue of section 34, 35 or 36, the judge must give the jury such warning (if any) as the judge considers necessary to ensure that the accused is not prejudiced—

- (a) by any inferences that might be drawn from the fact that the accused has been prevented from cross-examining the witness in person;
- (b) where the witness has been cross-examined by a legal representative appointed under section 38(4), by the fact that the cross-examination was carried out, by such a legal representative and not by a person acting as the accused's own legal representative.

(2) Subsection (8)(a) of section 38 applies for the purposes of this section as it applies for the purposes of section 38.

40–43 *****

CHAPTER IV   REPORTING RESTRICTIONS

Reports relating to persons under 18

44 Restrictions on reporting alleged offences involving persons under 18

(1) This section applies (subject to subsection (3)) where a criminal investigation has begun in respect of—

- (a) an alleged offence against the law of—
  - (i)   England and Wales, or
  - (ii) Northern Ireland; or
- (b) an alleged civil offence (other than an offence falling within paragraph (a)) committed (whether or not in the United Kingdom) by a person subject to service law.

(2) No matter relating to any person involved in the offence shall while he is under the age of 18 be included in any publication if it is likely to lead members of the public to identify him as a person involved in the offence.

(3) The restrictions imposed by subsection (2) cease to apply once there are proceedings in a court (whether a court in England and Wales, a service court or a court in Northern Ireland) in respect of the offence.

(4) For the purposes of subsection (2) any reference to a person involved in the offence is to—

- (a) a person by whom the offence is alleged to have been committed; or
- (b) if this paragraph applies to the publication in question by virtue of subsection (5)—
  - (i)   a person against or in respect of whom the offence is alleged to have been committed, or
  - (ii) a person who is alleged to have been a witness to the commission of the offence;

except that paragraph (b)(i) does not include a person in relation to whom section 1 of the Sexual Offences (Amendment) Act 1992 (anonymity of victims of certain sexual offences) applies in connection with the offence.

(5)–(13) *****

45 Power to restrict reporting of criminal proceedings involving persons under 18

(1) This section applies (subject to subsection (2)) in relation to—

- (a) any criminal proceedings in any court (other than a service court) in England and Wales or Northern Ireland; and

(b) any proceedings (whether in the United Kingdom or elsewhere) in any service court.

(2) This section does not apply in relation to any proceedings to which section 49 of the Children and Young Persons Act 1933 applies.

(3) The court may direct that no matter relating to any person concerned in the proceedings shall while he is under the age of 18 be included in any publication if it is likely to lead members of the public to identify him as a person concerned in the proceedings.

(4) The court or an appellate court may by direction ("an excepting direction") dispense, to any extent specified in the excepting direction, with the restrictions imposed by a direction under subsection (3) if it is satisfied that it is necessary in the interests of justice to do so.

(5) The court or an appellate court may also by direction ("an excepting direction") dispense, to any extent specified in the excepting direction, with the restrictions imposed by a direction under subsection (3) if it is satisfied—

(a) that their effect is to impose a substantial and unreasonable restriction on the reporting of the proceedings, and

(b) that it is in the public interest to remove or relax that restriction; but no excepting direction shall be given under this subsection by reason only of the fact that the proceedings have been determined in any way or have been abandoned.

(6)–(11) *****

Reports relating to adult witnesses

46 Power to restrict reports about certain adult witnesses in criminal proceedings

(1) This section applies where—

(a) in any criminal proceedings in any court (other than a service court) in England and Wales or Northern Ireland, or

(b) in any proceedings (whether in the United Kingdom or elsewhere) in any service court,

a party to the proceedings makes an application for the court to give a reporting direction in relation to a witness in the proceedings (other than the accused) who has attained the age of 18.

In this section "reporting direction" has the meaning given by subsection (6).

(2) If the court determines—

(a) that the witness is eligible for protection, and

(b) that giving a reporting direction in relation to the witness is likely to improve—

(i) the quality of evidence given by the witness, or

(ii) the level of co-operation given by the witness to any party to the proceedings in connection with that party's preparation of its case,

the court may give a reporting direction in relation to the witness.

(3) For the purposes of this section a witness is eligible for protection if the court is satisfied—

(a) that the quality of evidence given by the witness, or

(b) the level of co-operation given by the witness to any party to the proceedings in connection with that party's preparation of its case,

is likely to be diminished by reason of fear or distress on the part of the witness in connection with being identified by members of the public as a witness in the proceedings.

(4) In determining whether a witness is eligible for protection the court must take into account, in particular—

(a) the nature and alleged circumstances of the offence to which the proceedings relate;

(b) the age of the witness;

     (c) such of the following matters as appear to the court to be relevant, namely—
        (i)   the social and cultural background and ethnic origins of the witness,
        (ii) the domestic and employment circumstances of the witness, and
        (iii) any religious beliefs or political opinions of the witness;
     (d) any behaviour towards the witness on the part of—
        (i)   the accused,
        (ii) members of the family or associates of the accused, or
        (iii) any other person who is likely to be an accused or a witness in the proceedings.

(5) In determining that question the court must in addition consider any views expressed by the witness.

(6) For the purposes of this section a reporting direction in relation to a witness is a direction that no matter relating to the witness shall during the witness's lifetime be included in any publication if it is likely to lead members of the public to identify him as being a witness in the proceedings.

(7)–(12) *****

*****

Freedom of Information Act 2000
(2000, c. 36)

An Act to make provision for the disclosure of information held by public authorities or by persons providing services for them and to amend the Data Protection Act 1998 and the Public Records Act 1958; and for connected purposes   [30 November 2000]

Territorial extent: England and Wales, Northern Ireland. The Act applies also to a limited extent to public bodies which operate also in Scotland, but not to purely Scottish public authorities such as the Scottish Parliament or Executive

PART I   ACCESS TO INFORMATION HELD BY PUBLIC AUTHORITIES

Right to information

1   General right of access to information held by public authorities

(1) Any person making a request for information to a public authority is entitled—
     (a) to be informed in writing by the public authority whether it holds information of the description specified in the request, and
     (b) if that is the case, to have that information communicated to him.

(2) Subsection (1) has effect subject to the following provisions of this section and to the provisions of sections 2, 9, 12 and 14.

(3) Where a public authority—
     (a) reasonably requires further information in order to identify and locate the information requested, and
     (b) has informed the applicant of that requirement,
the authority is not obliged to comply with subsection (1) unless it is supplied with that further information.

(4) The information—
     (a) in respect of which the applicant is to be informed under subsection (1)(a), or

(b) which is to be communicated under subsection (1)(b),

is the information in question held at the time when the request is received, except that account may be taken of any amendment or deletion made between that time and the time when the information is to be communicated under subsection (1)(b), being an amendment or deletion that would have been made regardless of the receipt of the request.

(5) A public authority is to be taken to have complied with subsection (1)(a) in relation to any information if it has communicated the information to the applicant in accordance with subsection (1)(b).

(6) In this Act, the duty of a public authority to comply with subsection (1)(a) is referred to as "the duty to confirm or deny".

2   Effect of the exemptions in Part II

(1) Where any provision of Part II states that the duty to confirm or deny does not arise in relation to any information, the effect of the provision is that where either—

    (a) the provision confers absolute exemption, or

    (b) in all the circumstances of the case, the public interest in maintaining the exclusion of the duty to confirm or deny outweighs the public interest in disclosing whether the public authority holds the information,

section 1(1)(a) does not apply.

(2) In respect of any information which is exempt information by virtue of any provision of Part II, section 1(1)(b) does not apply if or to the extent that—

    (a) the information is exempt information by virtue of a provision conferring absolute exemption, or

    (b) in all the circumstances of the case, the public interest in maintaining the exemption outweighs the public interest in disclosing the information.

(3) For the purposes of this section, the following provisions of Part II (and no others) are to be regarded as conferring absolute exemption—

    (a) section 21,

    (b) section 23,

    (c) section 32,

    (d) section 34,

    (e) section 36 so far as relating to information held by the House of Commons or the House of Lords,

    (f) in section 40—

        (i) subsection (1), and

        (ii) subsection (2) so far as relating to cases where the first condition referred to in that subsection is satisfied by virtue of subsection (3)(a)(i) or (b) of that section,

    (g) section 41, and

    (h) section 44.

3   Public authorities

(1) In this Act "public authority" means—

    (a) subject to section 4(4), any body which, any other person who, or the holder of any office which—

        (i) is listed in Schedule 1, or

        (ii) is designated by order under section 5, or

    (b) a publicly-owned company as defined by section 6.

(2) For the purposes of this Act, information is held by a public authority if—

    (a) it is held by the authority, otherwise than on behalf of another person, or

    (b) it is held by another person on behalf of the authority.

6   Publicly-owned companies

(1) A company is a "publicly-owned company" for the purposes of section 3(1)(b) if—

    (a) it is wholly owned by the Crown, or

    (b) it is wholly owned by any public authority listed in Schedule 1 other than—

        (i)   a government department, or

        (ii) any authority which is listed only in relation to particular information.

(2), (3) *****

7   *****

8   Request for information

(1) In this Act any reference to a "request for information" is a reference to such a request which—

    (a) is in writing,

    (b) states the name of the applicant and an address for correspondence, and

    (c) describes the information requested.

(2) For the purposes of subsection (1)(a), a request is to be treated as made in writing where the text of the request—

    (a) is transmitted by electronic means,

    (b) is received in legible form, and

    (c) is capable of being used for subsequent reference.

9   Fees

(1) A public authority to whom a request for information is made may, within the period for complying with section 1(1), give the applicant a notice in writing (in this Act referred to as a "fees notice") stating that a fee of an amount specified in the notice is to be charged by the authority for complying with section 1(1).

(2) Where a fees notice has been given to the applicant, the public authority is not obliged to comply with section 1(1) unless the fee is paid within the period of three months beginning with the day on which the fees notice is given to the applicant.

(3) Subject to subsection (5), any fee under this section must be determined by the public authority in accordance with regulations made by the [Secretary of State].

(4), (5) *****

10   Time for compliance with request

(1) Subject to subsections (2) and (3), a public authority must comply with section 1(1) promptly and in any event not later than the twentieth working day following the date of receipt.

(2) Where the authority has given a fees notice to the applicant and the fee is paid in accordance with section 9(2), the working days in the period beginning with the day on which the fees notice is given to the applicant and ending with the day on which the fee is received by the authority are to be disregarded in calculating for the purposes of subsection (1) the twentieth working day following the date of receipt.

(3)–(5) *****

11   Means by which communication to be made

(1) Where, on making his request for information, the applicant expresses a preference for communication by any one or more of the following means, namely—

    (a) the provision to the applicant of a copy of the information in permanent form or in another form acceptable to the applicant,

    (b) the provision to the applicant of a reasonable opportunity to inspect a record containing the information, and

    (c) the provision to the applicant of a digest or summary of the information in permanent form or in another form acceptable to the applicant,

the public authority shall so far as reasonably practicable give effect to that preference.

(2) In determining for the purposes of this section whether it is reasonably practicable to communicate information by particular means, the public authority may have regard to all the circumstances, including the cost of doing so.

(3) Where the public authority determines that it is not reasonably practicable to comply with any preference expressed by the applicant in making his request, the authority shall notify the applicant of the reasons for its determination.

(4) Subject to subsection (1), a public authority may comply with a request by communicating information by any means which are reasonable in the circumstances.

12 Exemption where cost of compliance exceeds appropriate limit

(1) Section 1(1) does not oblige a public authority to comply with a request for information if the authority estimates that the cost of complying with the request would exceed the appropriate limit.

(2) Subsection (1) does not exempt the public authority from its obligation to comply with paragraph (a) of section 1(1) unless the estimated cost of complying with that paragraph alone would exceed the appropriate limit.

(3) In subsections (1) and (2) "the appropriate limit" means such amount as may be prescribed, and different amounts may be prescribed in relation to different cases.

(4) The [Secretary of State] may by regulations provide that, in such circumstances as may be prescribed, where two or more requests for information are made to a public authority—

(a) by one person, or

(b) by different persons who appear to the public authority to be acting in concert or in pursuance of a campaign,

the estimated cost of complying with any of the requests is to be taken to be the estimated total cost of complying with all of them.

(5) The [Secretary of State] may by regulations make provision for the purposes of this section as to the costs to be estimated and as to the manner in which they are to be estimated.

13–16 *****

Refusal of request

17 Refusal of request

(1) A public authority which, in relation to any request for information, is to any extent relying on a claim that any provision of Part II relating to the duty to confirm or deny is relevant to the request or on a claim that information is exempt information must, within the time for complying with section 1(1), give the applicant a notice which—

(a) states that fact,

(b) specifies the exemption in question, and

(c) states (if that would not otherwise be apparent) why the exemption applies.

(2) *****

(3) A public authority which, in relation to any request for information, is to any extent relying on a claim that subsection (1)(b) or (2)(b) of section 2 applies must, either in the notice under subsection (1) or in a separate notice given within such time as is reasonable in the circumstances, state the reasons for claiming—

(a) that, in all the circumstances of the case, the public interest in maintaining the exclusion of the duty to confirm or deny outweighs the public interest in disclosing whether the authority holds the information, or

(b) that, in all the circumstances of the case, the public interest in maintaining the exemption outweighs the public interest in disclosing the information.

(4) A public authority is not obliged to make a statement under subsection (1)(c) or (3) if, or to the extent that, the statement would involve the disclosure of information which would itself be exempt information.

(5) A public authority which, in relation to any request for information, is relying on a claim that section 12 or 14 applies must, within the time for complying with section 1(1), give the applicant a notice stating that fact.

(6), (7) *****

The Information Commissioner and the Information Tribunal

18   The Information Commissioner and the Information Tribunal

(1) The Data Protection Commissioner shall be known instead as the Information Commissioner.

(2) The Data Protection Tribunal shall be known instead as the Information Tribunal.

(3) In this Act—

(a) the Information Commissioner is referred to as "the Commissioner", and

(b) the Information Tribunal is referred to as "the Tribunal".

(4)–(7) *****

Publication schemes

19   Publication schemes

(1) It shall be the duty of every public authority—

(a) to adopt and maintain a scheme which relates to the publication of information by the authority and is approved by the Commissioner (in this Act referred to as a "publication scheme"),

(b) to publish information in accordance with its publication scheme, and

(c) from time to time to review its publication scheme.

(2) A publication scheme must—

(a) specify classes of information which the public authority publishes or intends to publish,

(b) specify the manner in which information of each class is, or is intended to be, published, and

(c) specify whether the material is, or is intended to be, available to the public free of charge or on payment.

(3) in adopting or reviewing a publication scheme, a public authority shall have regard to the public interest—

(a) in allowing public access to information held by the authority, and

(b) in the publication of reasons for decisions made by the authority.

(4) A public authority shall publish its publication scheme in such manner as it thinks fit.

(5)–(7) *****

20   *****

PART II   EXEMPT INFORMATION

21   Information accessible to applicant by other means

(1) Information which is reasonably accessible to the applicant otherwise than under section 1 is exempt information.

(2) For the purposes of subsection (1)—

(a) information may be reasonably accessible to the applicant even though it is accessible only on payment, and

(b) information is to be taken to be reasonably accessible to the applicant if it is information which the public authority or any other person is obliged by or under any enactment to communicate (otherwise than by making the information available for inspection) to members of the public on request, whether free of charge or on payment.

(3) For the purposes of subsection (1), information which is held by a public authority and does not fall within subsection (2)(b) is not to be regarded as reasonably accessible to the applicant merely because the information is available from the public authority itself on request, unless the information is made available in accordance with the authority's publication scheme and any payment required is specified in, or determined in accordance with, the scheme.

22 *****

23 Information supplied by, or relating to, bodies dealing with security matters

(1) Information held by a public authority is exempt information if it was directly or indirectly supplied to the public authority by, or relates to, any of the bodies specified in subsection (3).

(2) A certificate signed by a Minister of the Crown certifying that the information to which it applies was directly or indirectly supplied by, or relates to, any of the bodies specified in subsection (3) shall, subject to section 60, be conclusive evidence of that fact.

(3) The bodies referred to in subsections (1) and (2) are—
  (a) the Security Service,
  (b) the Secret Intelligence Service,
  (c) the Government Communications Headquarters,
  (d) the special forces,
  (e) the Tribunal established under section 65 of the Regulation of Investigatory Powers Act 2000,
  (f) the Tribunal established under section 7 of the Interception of Communications Act 1985,
  (g) the Tribunal established under section 5 of the Security Service Act 1989,
  (h) the Tribunal established under section 9 of the Intelligence Services Act 1994,
  (i) the Security Vetting Appeals Panel,
  (j) the Security Commission,
  (k) the National Criminal Intelligence Service, . . .
  (l) the Service Authority for the National Criminal Intelligence Service [, and
  (m) the Serious Organised Crime Agency.]
(4), (5) *****

24 National security

(1) Information which does not fall within section 23(1) is exempt information if exemption from section 1(1)(b) is required for the purpose of safeguarding national security.

(2) The duty to confirm or deny does not arise if, or to the extent that, exemption from section 1(1)(a) is required for the purpose of safeguarding national security.

(3) A certificate signed by a Minister of the Crown certifying that exemption from section 1(1)(b), or from section 1(1)(a) and (b), is, or at any time was, required for the purpose of safeguarding national security shall, subject to section 60, be conclusive evidence of that fact.

(4) A certificate under subsection (3) may identify the information to which it applies by means of a general description and may be expressed to have prospective effect.

25 *****

26 Defence

(1) Information is exempt information if its disclosure under this Act would, or would be likely to, prejudice—
  (a) the defence of the British Islands or of any colony, or
  (b) the capability, effectiveness or security of any relevant forces.
(2) In subsection (1)(b) "relevant forces" means—
  (a) the armed forces of the Crown, and

(b) any forces co-operating with those forces,

or any part of any of those forces.

(3) The duty to confirm or deny does not arise if, or to the extent that, compliance with section 1(1)(a) would, or would be likely to, prejudice any of the matters mentioned in subsection (1).

27 International relations

(1) Information is exempt information if its disclosure under this Act would, or would be likely to, prejudice—

(a) relations between the United Kingdom and any other State,

(b) relations between the United Kingdom and any international organisation or international court,

(c) the interests of the United Kingdom abroad, or

(d) the promotion or protection by the United Kingdom of its interests abroad.

(2) Information is also exempt information if it is confidential information obtained from a State other than the United Kingdom or from an international organisation or international court.

(3) For the purposes of this section, any information obtained from a State, organisation or court is confidential at any time while the terms on which it was obtained require it to be held in confidence or while the circumstances in which it was obtained make it reasonable for the State, organisation or court to expect that it will be so held.

(4) The duty to confirm or deny does not arise if, or to the extent that, compliance with section 1(1)(a)—

(a) would, or would be likely to, prejudice any of the matters mentioned in subsection (1), or

(b) would involve the disclosure of any information (whether or not already recorded) which is confidential information obtained from a State other than the United Kingdom or from an international organisation or international court.

(5) *****

28 Relations within the United Kingdom

(1) Information is exempt information if its disclosure under this Act would, or would be likely to, prejudice relations between any administration in the United Kingdom and any other such administration.

(2) In subsection (1) "administration in the United Kingdom" means—

(a) the government of the United Kingdom,

(b) the Scottish Administration,

(c) the Executive Committee of the Northern Ireland Assembly, or

(d) the National Assembly for Wales.

(3) The duty to confirm or deny does not arise if, or to the extent that, compliance with section 1(1)(a) would, or would be likely to, prejudice any of the matters mentioned in subsection (1).

29 The economy

(1) Information is exempt information if its disclosure under this Act would, or would be likely to, prejudice—

(a) the economic interests of the United Kingdom or of any part of the United Kingdom, or

(b) the financial interests of any administration in the United Kingdom, as defined by section 28(2).

(2) The duty to confirm or deny does not arise if, or to the extent that, compliance with section 1(1)(a) would, or would be likely to, prejudice any of the matters mentioned in subsection (1).

30   Investigations and proceedings conducted by public authorities

(1) Information held by a public authority is exempt information if it has at any time been held by the authority for the purposes of—

    (a) any investigation which the public authority has a duty to conduct with a view to it being ascertained—

        (i) whether a person should be charged with an offence, or

        (ii) whether a person charged with an offence is guilty of it,

    (b) any investigation which is conducted by the authority and in the circumstances may lead to a decision by the authority to institute criminal proceedings which the authority has power to conduct, or

    (c) any criminal proceedings which the authority has power to conduct.

(2) *****

(3) The duty to confirm or deny does not arise in relation to information which is (or if it were held by the public authority would be) exempt information by virtue of subsection (1) or (2).

(4)–(6) *****

31   Law enforcement

(1) Information which is not exempt information by virtue of section 30 is exempt information if its disclosure under this Act would, or would be likely to, prejudice—

    (a) the prevention or detection of crime,

    (b) the apprehension or prosecution of offenders,

    (c) the administration of justice,

    (d) the assessment or collection of any tax or duty or of any imposition of a similar nature,

    (e) the operation of the immigration controls,

    (f) the maintenance of security and good order in prisons or in other institutions where persons are lawfully detained,

    (g) the exercise by any public authority of its functions for any of the purposes specified in subsection (2),

    (h) any civil proceedings which are brought by or on behalf of a public authority and arise out of an investigation conducted, for any of the purposes specified in subsection (2), by or on behalf of the authority by virtue of Her Majesty's prerogative or by virtue of powers conferred by or under an enactment, or

    (i) any inquiry held under the Fatal Accidents and Sudden Deaths Inquiries (Scotland) Act 1976 to the extent that the inquiry arises out of an investigation conducted, for any of the purposes specified in subsection(2), by or on behalf of the authority by virtue of Her Majesty's prerogative or by virtue of powers conferred by or under an enactment.

(2) The purposes referred to in subsection (1)(g) to (i) are—

    (a) the purpose of ascertaining whether any person has failed to comply with the law

    (b) the purpose of ascertaining whether any person is responsible for any conduct which is improper,

    (c) the purpose of ascertaining whether circumstances which would justify regulatory action in pursuance of any enactment exist or may arise,

    (d) the purpose of ascertaining a person's fitness or competence in relation to the management of bodies corporate or in relation to any profession or other activity which he is, or seeks to become, authorised to carry on,

    (e) the purpose of ascertaining the cause of an accident,

    (f) the purpose of protecting charities against misconduct or mismanagement (whether by trustees or other persons) in their administration,

    (g) the purpose of protecting the property of charities from loss or misapplication,

(h) the purpose of recovering the property of charities,

(i) the purpose of securing the health, safety and welfare of persons at work, and

(j) the purpose of protecting persons other than persons at work against risk to health or safety arising out of or in connection with the actions of persons at work.

(3) The duty to confirm or deny does not arise if, or to the extent that, compliance with section 1(1)(a) would, or would be likely to, prejudice any of the matters mentioned in subsection (1).

32–33 *****

34 Parliamentary privilege

(1) Information is exempt information if exemption from section 1(1)(b) is required for the purpose of avoiding an infringement of the privileges of either House of Parliament.

(2) The duty to confirm or deny does not apply if, or to the extent that, exemption from section 1(1)(a) is required for the purpose of avoiding an infringement of the privileges of either House of Parliament.

(3) A certificate signed by the appropriate authority certifying that exemption from section 1(1)(b), or from section 1(1)(a) and (b), is, or at any time was, required for the purpose of avoiding an infringement of the privileges of either House of Parliament shall be conclusive evidence of that fact.

(4) In subsection (3) "the appropriate authority" means—

(a) in relation to the House of Commons, the Speaker of that House, and

(b) in relation to the House of Lords, the Clerk of the Parliaments.

35 Formulation of government policy, etc.

(1) Information held by a government department or by the National Assembly for Wales is exempt information if it relates to—

(a) the formulation or development of government policy,

(b) Ministerial communications,

(c) the provision of advice by any of the Law Officers or any request for the provision of such advice, or

(d) the operation of any Ministerial private office.

(2) Once a decision as to government policy has been taken, any statistical information used to provide an informed background to the taking of the decision is not to be regarded—

(a) for the purposes of subsection (1)(a), as relating to the formulation or development of government policy, or

(b) for the purposes of subsection (1)(b), as relating to Ministerial communications.

(3) The duty to confirm or deny does not arise in relation to information which is (or if it were held by the public authority would be) exempt information by virtue of subsection (1).

(4), (5) *****

36 Prejudice to effective conduct of public affairs

(1) This section applies to—

(a) information which is held by a government department or by the National Assembly for Wales and is not exempt information by virtue of section 35, and

(b) information which is held by any other public authority.

(2) Information to which this section applies is exempt information if, in the reasonable opinion of a qualified person, disclosure of the information under this Act—

(a) would, or would be likely to, prejudice—

(i) the maintenance of the convention of the collective responsibility of Ministers of the Crown, or

(ii) the work of the Executive Committee of the Northern Ireland Assembly, or

(iii) the work of the executive committee of the National Assembly for Wales,

(b) would, or would be likely to, inhibit–

(i)   the free and frank provision of advice, or

(ii) the free and frank exchange of views for the purposes of deliberation, or

(c) would otherwise prejudice, or would be likely otherwise to prejudice, the effective conduct of public affairs.

(3) The duty to confirm or deny does not arise in relation to information to which this section applies (or would apply if held by the public authority) if, or to the extent that, in the reasonable opinion of a qualified person, compliance with section 1(1)(a) would, or would be likely to, have any of the effects mentioned in subsection (2).

(4) In relation to statistical information, subsections (2) and (3) shall have effect with the omission of the words "in the reasonable opinion of a qualified person".

(5) In subsections (2) and (3) "qualified person"—

(a) in relation to information held by a government department in the charge of a Minister of the Crown, means any Minister of the Crown,

(b) in relation to information held by a Northern Ireland department, means the Northern Ireland Minister in charge of the department,

(c) in relation to information held by any other government department, means the commissioners or other person in charge of that department,

(d) in relation to information held by the House of Commons, means the Speaker of that House,

(e) in relation to information held by the House of Lords, means the Clerk of the Parliaments,

(f) in relation to information held by the Northern Ireland Assembly, means the Presiding Officer,

(g) in relation to information held by the National Assembly for Wales, means the Assembly First Secretary,

(h)–(o) *****

(6), (7) *****

37 Communications with Her Majesty, etc. and honours

(1) Information is exempt information if it relates to—

(a) communications with Her Majesty, with other members of the Royal Family or with the Royal Household, or

(b) the conferring by the Crown of any honour or dignity.

(2) The duty to confirm or deny does not arise in relation to information which is (or if it were held by the public authority would be) exempt information by virtue of subsection (1).

38–41 *****

42 Legal professional privilege

(1) Information in respect of which a claim to legal professional privilege or, in Scotland, to confidentiality of communications could be maintained in legal proceedings is exempt information.

(2) The duty to confirm or deny does not arise if, or to the extent that, compliance with section 1(1)(a) would involve the disclosure of any information (whether or not already recorded) in respect of which such a claim could be maintained in legal proceedings.

43–44 *****

PART III   GENERAL FUNCTIONS OF . . . LORD CHANCELLOR AND INFORMATION COMMISSIONER

45   Issue of code of practice . . .

(1) The [Secretary of State] shall issue, and may from time to time revise, a code of practice providing guidance to public authorities as to the practice which it would, in his opinion, be desirable for them to follow in connection with the discharge of the authorities' functions under Part I.

(2), (3) *****

(4) Before issuing or revising any code under this section, the [Secretary of State] shall consult the Commissioner.

(5) The [Secretary of State] shall lay before each House of Parliament any code or revised code made under this section.

46–49   *****

PART IV   ENFORCEMENT

50   Application for decision by Commissioner

(1) Any person (in this section referred to as "the complainant") may apply to the Commissioner for a decision whether, in any specified respect, a request for information made by the complainant to a public authority has been dealt with in accordance with the requirements of Part I.

(2) On receiving an application under this section, the Commissioner shall make a decision unless it appears to him—

    (a) that the complainant has not exhausted any complaints procedure which is provided by the public authority in conformity with the code of practice under section 45,

    (b) that there has been undue delay in making the application,

    (c) that the application is frivolous or vexatious, or

    (d) that the application has been withdrawn or abandoned.

(3) Where the Commissioner has received an application under this section, he shall either—

    (a) notify the complainant that he has not made any decision under this section as a result of the application and of his grounds for not doing so, or

    (b) serve notice of his decision (in this Act referred to as a "decision notice") on the complainant and the public authority.

(4) Where the Commissioner decides that a public authority—

    (a) has failed to communicate information, or to provide confirmation or denial, in a case where it is required to do so by section 1(1), or

    (b) has failed to comply with any of the requirements of sections 11 and 17, the decision notice must specify the steps which must be taken by the authority for complying with that requirement and the period within which they must be taken.

(5) A decision notice must contain particulars of the right of appeal conferred by section 57.

(6), (7) *****

*****

Local Government Act 2000

(2000, c. 22)

An Act to make provision with respect to the functions and procedures of local authorities and provision with respect to local authority elections; to make provision with respect to grants and housing benefit in respect of certain welfare services; to amend section 29 of the Children Act 1989; and for connected purposes   [28 July 2000]

Territorial extent: England and Wales

PART I PROMOTION OF ECONOMIC, SOCIAL OR ENVIRONMENTAL WELL-BEING ETC.

Interpretation

1 Meaning of "local authority" in Part I

In this Part "local authority" means—
- (a) in relation to England—
    - (i) a county council,
    - (ii) a district council,
    - (iii) a London borough council,
    - (iv) the Common Council of the City of London in its capacity as a local authority,
    - (v) the Council of the Isles of Scilly,
- (b) in relation to Wales, a county council or a county borough council.

Promotion of well-being

2 Promotion of well-being

(1) Every local authority are to have power to do anything which they consider is likely to achieve any one or more of the following objects–
- (a) the promotion or improvement of the economic well-being of their area.
- (b) the promotion or improvement of the social well-being of their area, and
- (c) the promotion or improvement of the environmental well-being of their area.

(2) The power under subsection (1) may be exercised in relation to or for the benefit of—
- (a) the whole or any part of a local authority's area, or
- (b) all or any persons resident or present in a local authority's area.

(3) In determining whether or how to exercise the power under subsection (1), a local authority must have regard to their strategy under section 4.

(4) The power under subsection (1) includes power for a local authority to—
- (a) incur expenditure,
- (b) give financial assistance to any person,
- (c) enter into arrangements or agreements with any person,
- (d) co-operate with, or facilitate or co-ordinate the activities of, any person,
- (e) exercise on behalf of any person any functions of that person, and
- (f) provide staff, goods, services or accommodation to any person.

(5), (6) *****

3 Limits on power to promote well-being

(1) The power under section 2(1) does not enable a local authority to do anything which they are unable to do by virtue of any prohibition, restriction or limitation on their powers which is contained in any enactment (whenever passed or made).

(2) The power under section 2(1) does not enable a local authority to raise money (whether by precepts, borrowing or otherwise).

(3)–(8) *****

4   Strategies for promoting well-being

(1) Every local authority must prepare a strategy (referred to in this section as a community strategy) for promoting or improving the economic, social and environmental well-being of their area and contributing to the achievement of sustainable development in the United Kingdom.

(2) A local authority may from time to time modify their community strategy.

(3) In preparing or modifying their community strategy, a local authority–

(a) must consult and seek the participation of such persons as they consider appropriate, and

(b) must have regard to any guidance for the time being issued by the Secretary of State.

(4)–(5) *****

5   Power to amend or repeal enactments

(1) If the Secretary of State thinks that an enactment (whenever passed or made) prevents or obstructs local authorities from exercising their power under section 2(1) he may by order amend, repeal, revoke or disapply that enactment.

(2), (3) *****

6–9 *****

PART II   ARRANGEMENTS WITH RESPECT TO EXECUTIVES ETC.

Executive arrangements

10   Executive arrangements

(1) In this Part "executive arrangements" means arrangements by a local authority—

(a) for and in connection with the creation and operation of an executive of the authority, and

(b) under which certain functions of the authority are the responsibility of the executive.

(2) Executive arrangements by a local authority must conform with any provisions made by or under this Part which relate to such arrangements.

Local authority executives

11   Local authority executives

(1) The executive of a local authority must take one of the forms specified in subsections (2) to (5).

(2) It may consist of—

(a) an elected mayor of the authority, and

(b) two or more councillors of the authority appointed to the executive by the elected mayor.

Such an executive is referred to in this Part as a mayor and cabinet executive.

(3) It may consist of—

(a) a councillor of the authority (referred to in this Part as the executive leader) elected as leader of the executive by the authority, and

(b) two or more councillors of the authority appointed to the executive by one of the following—

(i) the executive leader, or

(ii) the authority.

Such an executive is referred to in this Part as a leader and cabinet executive.

(4) It may consist of—

(a) an elected mayor of the authority, and

(b) an officer of the authority (referred to in this Part as the council manager) appointed to the executive by the authority.

Such an executive is referred to in this Part as a mayor and council manager executive.

(5) It may take any such form as may be prescribed in regulations made by the Secretary of State.

(6) Regulations under subsection (5) may, in particular, provide for—

(a) a form of executive some or all of the members of which are elected by the local government electors for the authority's area to a specified post in the executive associated with the discharge of particular functions,

(b) a form of executive some or all of the members of which are elected by those electors but not to any such post,

(c) the system of voting that will be used for elections under paragraph (a) or (b).

(7) A local authority executive may not include the chairman or vice-chairman of the authority.

(8) The number of members of a mayor and cabinet executive or a leader and cabinet executive may not exceed 10.

(9), (10) *****

12   ***

Executive functions

13   Functions which are the responsibility of an executive

(1) This section has effect for the purposes of determining the functions of a local authority which are the responsibility of an executive of the authority under executive arrangements.

(2) Subject to any provision made by this Act or by any enactment which is passed or made after the day on which this Act is passed, any function of a local authority which is not specified in regulations under subsection (3) is to be the responsibility of an executive of the authority under executive arrangements.

(3) The Secretary of State may by regulations make provision for any function of a local authority specified in the regulations—

(a) to be a function which is not to be the responsibility of an executive of the authority under executive arrangements,

(b) to be a function which may be the responsibility of such an executive under such arrangements, or

(c) to be a function which—

(i) to the extent provided by the regulations is to be the responsibility of such an executive under such arrangements, and

(ii) to the extent provided by the regulations is not to be the responsibility of such an executive under such arrangements.

(4)–(14) *****

Provisions with respect to executive arrangements

14   Discharge of functions: mayor and cabinet executive

(1) Subject to any provision made under section 18, 19 or 20, any functions which, under executive arrangements. are the responsibility of a mayor and cabinet executive are to be discharged in accordance with this section.

(2) The elected mayor—

(a) may discharge any of those functions, or
(b) may arrange for the discharge of any of those functions—
        (i)   by the executive,
        (ii) by another member of the executive,
        (iii) by a committee of the executive, or
        (iv) by an officer of the authority.
    (3)–(6) *****

15–21   *****

22   Access to information etc.

(1) Meetings of a local authority executive, or a committee of such an executive, are to be open to the public or held in private.

(2) Subject to regulations under subsection (9), it is for a local authority executive to decide which of its meetings, and which of the meetings of any committee of the executive, are to be open to the public and which of those meetings are to be held in private.

(3) A written record must be kept of prescribed decisions made at meetings of local authority executives, or committees of such executives, which are held in private.

(4) A written record must be kept of prescribed decisions made by individual members of local authority executives.

(5) Written records under subsection (3) or (4) must include reasons for the decisions to which they relate.

(6) Written records under subsections (3) and (4), together with such reports, background papers or other documents as may be prescribed, must be made available to members of the public in accordance with regulations made by the Secretary of State.

    (7)–(13) *****

23–49   *****

50   Model code of conduct

(1) The Secretary of State may by order issue a model code as regards the conduct which is expected of members and co-opted members of relevant authorities in England and police authorities in Wales (referred to in this Part as a model code of conduct).

(2) The National Assembly for Wales may by order issue a model code as regards the conduct which is expected of members and co-opted members of relevant authorities in Wales other than police authorities (also referred to in this Part as a model code of conduct).

    (3)–(7) *****

51   Duty of relevant authorities to adopt codes of conduct

(1) It is the duty of a relevant authority, before the end of the period of six months beginning with the day on which the first order under section 50 which applies to them is made, to pass a resolution adopting a code as regards the conduct which is expected of members and co-opted members of the authority (referred to in this Part as a code of conduct).

    (2), (3) *****

(4) A code of conduct or revised code of conduct—
(a) must incorporate any mandatory provisions of the model code of conduct which for the time being applies to that authority,
(b) may incorporate any optional provisions of that model code, and
(c) may include other provisions which are consistent with that model code.

    (5)–(9) *****

52   Duty to comply with code of conduct

(1) A person who is a member or co-opted member of a relevant authority at a time when the authority adopt a code of conduct under section 51 for the first time—

(a) must, before the end of the period of two months beginning with the date on which the code of conduct is adopted, give to the authority a written undertaking that in performing his functions he will observe the authority's code of conduct for the time being under section 51, and

(b) if he fails to do so, is to cease to be a member or co-opted member at the end of that period.

(2)–(4) *****

Standards committees

53   Standards committees

(1) Subject to subsection (2), every relevant authority must establish a committee (referred to in this Part as a standards committee) which is to have the functions conferred on it by or under this Part.

(2) Subsection (1) does not apply to a parish council or community council.

(3) The number of members of a standards committee of a relevant authority in England or a police authority in Wales and their term of office are to be fixed by the authority (subject to any provision made by virtue of subsection (6)(a)).

(4) A standards committee of a relevant authority in England or a police authority in Wales must include—

(a) at least two members of the authority, and

(b) at least one person who is not a member, or an officer, of that or any other relevant authority.

(5) A standards committee of a relevant authority in England which are operating executive arrangements—

(a) may not include the elected mayor or executive leader, and

(b) may not be chaired by a member of the executive.

(6)–(12) *****

54   Functions of standards committees

(1) The general functions of a standards committee of a relevant authority are—

(a) promoting and maintaining high standards of conduct by the members and co-opted members of the authority, and

(b) assisting members and co-opted members of the authority to observe the authority's code of conduct.

(2) Without prejudice to its general functions, a standards committee of a relevant authority has the following specific functions—

(a) advising the authority on the adoption or revision of a code of conduct,

(b) monitoring the operation of the authority's code of conduct, and

(c) advising, training or arranging to train members and co-opted members of the authority on matters relating to the authority's code of conduct.

(3) A relevant authority may arrange for their standards committee to exercise such other functions as the authority consider appropriate.

(4)–(7) *****

54A, 55–56   *****

CHAPTER II   INVESTIGATIONS ETC: ENGLAND

Standards Board for England

57   Standards Board for England

(1) There is to be a body corporate known as the Standards Board for England.

(2) The Standards Board for England is to consist of not less than three members appointed by the Secretary of State.

(3) The Standards Board for England is to have the functions conferred on it by this Part and such other functions as may be conferred on it by order made by the Secretary of State under this subsection.

(4) In exercising its functions the Standards Board for England must have regard to the need to promote and maintain high standards of conduct by members and co-opted members of relevant authorities in England.

(5) The Standards Board for England—

   (a) must appoint employees known as ethical standards officers who are to have the functions conferred on them by this Part,

   (b) may issue guidance to relevant authorities in England and police authorities in Wales on matters relating to the conduct of members and co-opted members of such authorities,

   (c) may issue guidance to relevant authorities in England and police authorities in Wales in relation to the qualifications or experience which monitoring officers should possess, and

   (d) may arrange for any such guidance to be made public.

(6) Schedule 4 makes further provision in relation to the Standards Board for England.

58 Written allegations

(1) A person may make a written allegation to the Standards Board for England that a member or co-opted member (or former member or co-opted member) of a relevant authority in England has failed, or may have failed, to comply with the authority's code of conduct.

(2) If the Standards Board for England considers that a written allegation under subsection (1) should be investigated, it must refer the case to one of its ethical standards officers.

(3) *****

Functions of ethical standards officers

59 Functions of ethical standards officers

(1) The functions of ethical standards officers are to investigate—

   (a) cases referred to them by the Standards Board for England under section 58(2), and

   (b) other cases in which any such officer considers that a member or co-opted member (or former member or co-opted member) of a relevant authority in England has failed, or may have failed, to comply with the authority's code of conduct and which have come to the attention of any such officer as a result of an investigation under paragraph (a).

(2) The Standards Board for England may make arrangements in relation to the assignment of investigations under this section to particular ethical standards officers.

(3) The purpose of an investigation under this section is to determine which of the findings mentioned in subsection (4) is appropriate.

(4) Those findings are—

   (a) that there is no evidence of any failure to comply with the code of conduct of the relevant authority concerned,

   (b) that no action needs to be taken in respect of the matters which are the subject of the investigation,

   (c) that the matters which are the subject of the investigation should be referred to the monitoring officer of the relevant authority concerned, or

   (d) that the matters which are the subject of the investigation should be referred to the president of the Adjudication Panel for England for adjudication by a tribunal falling within section 76(1).

(5) *****

60–63 *****

Reports etc.

64   Reports etc.

(1) Where an ethical standards officer determines in relation to any case that a finding under section 59(4)(a) or (b) is appropriate—

(a) he may produce a report on the outcome of his investigation,

(b) he may provide a summary of any such report to any newspapers circulating in the area of the relevant authority concerned,

(c) he must send to the monitoring officer of the relevant authority concerned a copy of any such report, and

(d) where he does not produce any such report, he must inform the monitoring officer of the relevant authority concerned of the outcome of the investigation.

(2) Where an ethical standards officer determines in relation to any case that a finding under section 59(4)(c) is appropriate he must—

(a) produce a report on the outcome of his investigation,

(b) subject to subsection (4)(b), refer the matters which are the subject of the investigation to the monitoring officer of the relevant authority concerned, and

(c) send a copy of the report to the monitoring officer, and the standards committee, of the relevant authority concerned.

(3) Where an ethical standards officer determines in relation to any case that a finding under section 59(4)(d) is appropriate he must—

(a) produce a report on the outcome of his investigation,

(b) refer the matters which are the subject of the investigation to the president of the Adjudication Panel for England for adjudication by a tribunal falling within section 76(1), and

(c) send a copy of the report to the monitoring officer of the relevant authority concerned and to the president of the Adjudication Panel for England.

(4)–(6) *****

65–75 *****

Case tribunals and interim case tribunals

76   Case tribunals and interim case tribunals

(1) Adjudications in respect of matters referred to the president of the relevant Adjudication Panel under section 64(3) or 71(3) are to be conducted by tribunals (referred to in this Part as case tribunals) consisting of not less than three members of the Panel.

(2) Adjudications in respect of matters referred to the president of the relevant Adjudication Panel under section 65(4) or 72(4) are to be conducted by tribunals (referred to in this Part as interim case tribunals) consisting of not less than three members of the Panel.

(3) The president of the relevant Adjudication Panel (or in his absence the deputy president) is to appoint the members of any case tribunal or interim case tribunal.

(4)–(14) *****

Adjudications

77   Adjudications

(1) A person who is the subject of an adjudication conducted by a case tribunal or interim case tribunal may appear before the tribunal in person or be represented by—

(a) counsel or a solicitor, or

(b) any other person whom he desires to represent him.

(2) The Secretary of State may by regulations make such provision as appears to him to be

necessary or expedient with respect to adjudications by case tribunals or interim case tribunals drawn from the Adjudication Panel for England.

(3) The president of the Adjudication Panel for England may, after consultation with the Secretary of State, give directions as to the practice and procedure to be followed by tribunals drawn from the Panel.

(4) The National Assembly for Wales may by regulations make such provision as appears to it to be necessary or expedient with respect to adjudications by case tribunals or interim case tribunals drawn from the Adjudication Panel for Wales.

(5) The president of the Adjudication Panel for Wales may, after consultation with the National Assembly for Wales, give directions as to the practice and procedure to be followed by tribunals drawn from the Panel.

(6) Regulations under this section may, in particular, include provision—

(a) for requiring persons to attend adjudications to give evidence and produce documents and for authorising the administration of oaths to witnesses,

(b) for requiring persons to furnish further particulars,

(c) for prescribing the procedure to be followed in adjudications, including provision as to the persons entitled to appear and to be heard on behalf of persons giving evidence,

(d) for the award of costs or expenses (including provision with respect to interest and provision with respect to the enforcement of any such award),

(e) for taxing or otherwise settling any such costs or expenses (and for enabling such costs to be taxed in a county court),

(f) for the registration and proof of decisions and awards of tribunals.

(7) A person who without reasonable excuse fails to comply with any requirement imposed by virtue of subsection (6)(a) or (b) is guilty of an offence and liable on summary conviction to a fine not exceeding level 3 on the standard scale.

(8) In this section any reference to documents includes a reference to information held by means of a computer or in any other electronic form.

78   Decisions of interim case tribunals

(1) An interim case tribunal which adjudicates on any matters which are the subject of an interim report must reach one of the following decisions—

(a) that the person to whom the recommendation mentioned in section 65(3) or 72(3) relates should not be suspended or partially suspended from being a member or co-opted member of the relevant authority concerned,

(b) that that person should be suspended or partially suspended from being a member or co-opted member of the authority concerned for a period which does not exceed six months or (if shorter) the remainder of the person's term of office.

(2) An interim case tribunal must give notice of its decision to the standards committee of the relevant authority concerned.

(3) If the decision of an interim case tribunal is that a person should be suspended or partially suspended from being a member or co-opted member of the relevant authority concerned—

(a) the notice must give details of the suspension or partial suspension and specify the date on which the suspension or partial suspension is to begin, and

(b) the relevant authority must suspend or partially suspend the person in accordance with the notice.

(4)–(9) *****

(10) A person who is suspended or partially suspended under this section may appeal to the High Court—

(a) against the suspension or partial suspension, or

(b) against the length of the suspension or partial suspension.

79   Decisions of case tribunals

(1) A case tribunal which adjudicates on any matter must decide whether or not any person to which that matter relates has failed to comply with the code of conduct of the relevant authority concerned.

(2) Where a case tribunal decides that a person has not failed to comply with the code of conduct of the relevant authority concerned, it must give notice to that effect to the standards committee of the relevant authority concerned.

(3) Where a case tribunal decides that a person has failed to comply with the code of conduct of the relevant authority concerned, it must decide whether the nature of the failure is such that the person should be suspended or disqualified in accordance with subsection (4).

(4) A person may be—

(a) suspended or partially suspended from being a member or co-opted member of the relevant authority concerned, or

(b) disqualified for being, or becoming (whether by election or otherwise), a member of that or any other relevant authority.

(5) Where a case tribunal makes such a decision as is mentioned in subsection (4)(a), it must decide the period for which the person should be suspended or partially suspended (which must not exceed one year or, if shorter, the remainder of the person's term of office).

(6) Where a case tribunal makes such a decision as is mentioned in subsection (4)(b), it must decide the period for which the person should be disqualified (which must not exceed five years).

(7) Where a case tribunal decides that a person has failed to comply with the code of conduct of the relevant authority concerned but should not be suspended or disqualified as mentioned in subsection (4), it must give notice to the standards committee of the relevant authority concerned—

(a) stating that the person has failed to comply with that code of conduct, and

(b) specifying the details of that failure.

(8)–(14) *****

(15) Where a case tribunal decides under this section that a person has failed to comply with the code of conduct of the relevant authority concerned, that person may appeal to the High Court against that decision, or any other decision under this section which relates to him.

80   *****

CHAPTER V   SUPPLEMENTARY

Disclosure and registration of Members' interests etc.

81   Disclosure and registration of Members' interests etc.

(1) The monitoring officer of each relevant authority must establish and maintain a register of interests of the members and co-opted members of the authority.

(2) The mandatory provisions of the model code applicable to each relevant authority ("the mandatory provisions") must require the members and co-opted members of each authority to register in that authority's register maintained under subsection (1) such financial and other interests as are specified in the mandatory provisions.

(3)–(8) *****

Code of conduct for local government employees

82   Code of conduct for local government employees

(1) The Secretary of State may by order issue a code as regards the conduct which is expected of qualifying employees of relevant authorities in England and police authorities in Wales.

(2) The National Assembly for Wales may by order issue a code as regards the conduct which is expected of qualifying employees of relevant authorities in Wales (other than police authorities).

(3)–(6) *****

(7) The terms of appointment or conditions of employment of every qualifying employee of a relevant authority (whether appointed or employed before or after the commencement of this section) are to be deemed to incorporate any code for the time being under this section which is applicable.

(8) In this section "qualifying employee", in relation to a relevant authority, means an employee of the authority other than an employee falling within any description of employee specified in regulations under this subsection.

(9) The power to make regulations under subsection (8) is to be exercised—

(a) in relation to England. by the Secretary of State, and

(b) in relation to Wales, by the National Assembly for Wales.

*****

Police (Northern Ireland) Act 2000
(2000, c. 32)

An Act to make provision about policing in Northern Ireland, and for connected purposes
[23 November 2000]

Territorial extent: Northern Ireland

1 Name of the police in Northern Ireland

(1) The body of constables known as the Royal Ulster Constabulary shall continue in being as the Police Service of Northern Ireland (incorporating the Royal Ulster Constabulary).

(2) The body of constables referred to in subsection (1) shall be styled for operational purposes the "Police Service of Northern Ireland".

(3) The body of constables known as the Royal Ulster Constabulary Reserve shall continue in being as the Police Service of Northern Ireland Reserve (incorporating the Royal Ulster Constabulary Reserve).

(4) The body of constables referred to in subsection (3) shall be styled for operational purposes "The Police Service of Northern Ireland Reserve".

2–53 *****

54 Regulations as to emblems and flags

(1) The Secretary of State may make regulations—

(a) prescribing the design of an emblem for the police; and

(b) regulating the use of that or any other emblem—

(i)   on equipment or property used for the purposes of the police; or

(ii) otherwise in connection with the police.

(2) The Secretary of State may make regulations—

(a) prescribing the design of a flag for the police; and

(b) regulating the flying or carrying of that or any other flag—

(i)   on land or buildings used for the purposes of the police; or

(ii) otherwise in connection with the police.

(3) *****

*****

Political Parties, Elections and Referendums Act 2000
(2000, c. 41)

An Act to establish an Electoral Commission; to make provision about the registration and finances of political parties; to make provision about donations and expenditure for political purposes; to make provision about election and referendum campaigns and the conduct of referendums; to make provision about election petitions and other legal proceedings in connection with elections; to reduce the qualifying periods set out in sections 1 and 3 of the Representation of the People Act 1985; to make pre-consolidation amendments relating to European Parliamentary Elections; and for connected purposes [30 November 2000]

Territorial extent: United Kingdom, except that ss 50–69 do not apply to Northern Ireland (see SI 2001 No 446)

1   Establishment of the Electoral Commission
(1) There shall be a body corporate to be known as the Electoral Commission or, in Welsh, Comisiwn Etholiadol (in this Act referred to as "the Commission").

(2) The Commission shall consist of members to be known as Electoral Commissioners.

(3) There shall be not less than five, but not more than nine, Electoral Commissioners.

(4) The Electoral Commissioners shall be appointed by Her Majesty (in accordance with section 3).

(5) Her Majesty shall (in accordance with section 3) appoint one of the Electoral Commissioners to be the chairman of the Commission.

(6) Schedule 1, which makes further provision in relation to the Commission, shall have effect.

2   Speaker's Committee
(1) There shall be a Committee (to be known as "the Speaker's Committee") to perform the functions conferred on the Committee by this Act.

(2) The Speaker's Committee shall consist of the Speaker of the House of Commons, who shall be the chairman of the Committee, and the following other members, namely—
  (a) the Member of the House of Commons who is for the time being the Chairman of the Home Affairs Select Committee of the House of Commons;
  (b) [the Lord Chancellor];
  (c) a Member of the House of Commons who is a Minister of the Crown with responsibilities in relation to local government; and
  (d) five Members of the House of Commons who are not Ministers of the Crown.

(3) The member of the Committee mentioned in subsection (2)(c) shall be appointed to membership of the Committee by the Prime Minister.

(4) The members of the Committee mentioned in subsection (2)(d) shall be appointed to membership of the Committee by the Speaker of the House of Commons.

(5), (6) *****

3–21   *****

22   Parties to be registered in order to field candidates at elections
(1) Subject to subsection (4), no nomination may be made in relation to a relevant election unless the nomination is in respect of—
  (a) a person who stands for election in the name of a qualifying registered party; or
  (b) a person who does not purport to represent any party; or
  (c) a qualifying registered party, where the election is one for which registered parties may be nominated.

(2) For the purposes of subsection (1) a party (other than a minor party) is "qualifying registered party" in relation to a relevant election if—

    (a) the constituency, local government area or electoral region in which the election is held—

        (i) is in England, Scotland or Wales, or

        (ii) is the electoral region of Scotland or Wales,

and the party was, on the last day for publication of notice of the election, registered in respect of that part of Great Britain in the Great Britain register maintained by the Commission under section 23, or

    (b) the constituency, district electoral area or electoral region in which the election is held—

        (i) is in Northern Ireland, or

        (ii) is the electoral region of Northern Ireland,

and the party was, on that day, registered in the Northern Ireland register maintained by the Commission under that section.

    (3) For the purposes of subsection (1) a person does not purport to represent any party if either—

    (a) the description of the candidate given in his nomination paper, is—

        (i) "Independent", or

        (ii) where the candidate is the Speaker of the House of Commons seeking re-election, "The Speaker seeking re-election"; or

    (b) no description of the candidate is given in his nomination paper.

    (4) Subsection (1) does not apply in relation to any parish or community election.

    (5) The following elections are relevant elections for the purposes of this Part—

    (a) parliamentary elections,

    (b) elections to the European Parliament,

    (c) elections to the Scottish Parliament,

    (d) elections to the National Assembly for Wales,

    (e) elections to the Northern Ireland Assembly,

    (f) local government elections, and

    (g) local elections in Northern Ireland.

    (6) For the purposes of this Act a person stands for election in the name of a registered party if his nomination paper includes a description authorised by a certificate issued by or on behalf of the registered nominating officer of the party.

23 The new registers

    (1) In place of the register of political parties maintained by the registrar of companies under the Registration of Political Parties Act 1998, there shall be the new registers of political parties mentioned in subsection (2) which—

    (a) shall be maintained by the Commission, and

    (b) (subject to the provisions of this section) shall be so maintained in such form as the Commission may determine.

    (2) The new registers of political parties are—

    (a) a register of parties that intend to contest relevant elections in one or more of England, Scotland and Wales (referred to in this Act as "the Great Britain register"); and

    (b) a register of parties that intend to contest relevant elections in Northern Ireland (referred to in this Act as "the Northern Ireland register").

    (3)–(6) *****

24–36 *****

37 Party political broadcasts

    (1) A broadcaster shall not include in its broadcasting services any party political broadcast made on behalf of a party which is not a registered party.

(2) In this Act "broadcaster" means—
  (a) the holder of a licence under the Broadcasting Act 1990 or 1996,
  (b) the British Broadcasting Corporation, or
  (c) Sianel Pedwar Cymru.
(3) *****

38–53   ***

54   Permissible donors

(1) A donation received by a registered party must not be accepted by the party if—
  (a) the person by whom the donation would be made is not, at the time of its receipt by the party, a permissible donor; or
  (b) the party is (whether because the donation is given anonymously or by reason of any deception or concealment or otherwise) unable to ascertain the identity of that person.
(2) For the purposes of this Part the following are permissible donors—
  (a) an individual registered in an electoral register;
  (b) a company—
      (i) registered under the Companies Act 1985 or the Companies (Northern Ireland) Order 1986, and
      (ii) incorporated within the United Kingdom or another member State,
    which carries on business in the United Kingdom;
  (c) a registered party [, other than a Gibraltar party whose entry in the register includes a statement that it intends to contest one or more elections to the European Parliament in the combined region];
  (d) a trade union entered in the list kept under the Trade Union and Labour Relations (Consolidation) Act 1992 or the Industrial Relations (Northern Ireland) Order 1992;
  (e) a building society (within the meaning of the Building Societies Act 1986);
  (f) a limited liability partnership registered under the Limited Liability Partnerships Act 2000, or any corresponding enactment in force in Northern Ireland, which carries on business in the United Kingdom;
  (g) a friendly society registered under the Friendly Societies Act 1974 or a society registered (or deemed to be registered) under the Industrial and Provident Societies Act 1965 or the Industrial and Provident Societies Act (Northern Ireland) 1969; and
  (h) any unincorporated association of two or more persons which does not fall within any of the preceding paragraphs but which carries on business or other activities wholly or mainly in the United Kingdom and whose main office is there.
(2A)–(8) *****

55   ***

56   Acceptance or return of donations: general

(1) Where—
  (a) a donation is received by a registered party, and
  (b) it is not immediately decided that the party should (for whatever reason) refuse the donation,
all reasonable steps must be taken forthwith by or on behalf of the party to verify (or, so far as any of the following is not apparent, ascertain) the identity of the donor, whether he is a permissible donor, and (if that appears to be the case) all such details in respect of him as are required by virtue of paragraph 2 of Schedule 6 to be given in respect of the donor of a recordable donation.
(2) If a registered party receives a donation which it is prohibited from accepting by

virtue of section 54(1), or which it is decided that the party should for any other reason refuse, then—

    (a) unless the donation falls within section 54(1)(b), the donation, or a payment of an equivalent amount, must be sent back to the person who made the donation or any person appearing to be acting on his behalf,

    (b) if the donation falls within that provision, the required steps (as defined by section 57(1)) must be taken in relation to the donation,

within the period of 30 davs beginning with the date when the donation is received by the party.

  (3) Where—

    (a) subsection (2)(a) applies in relation to a donation, and

    (b) the donation is not dealt with in accordance with that provision,

the party and the treasurer of the party are each guilty of an offence.

  (4) Where—

    (a) subsection (2)(b) applies in relation to a donation, and

    (b) the donation is not dealt with in accordance with that provision,

the treasurer of the party is guilty of an offence.

  (5), (6) *****

57 Return of donations where donor unidentifiable

  (1) For the purposes of section 56(2)(b) the required steps are as follows—

    (a) if the donation mentioned in that provision was transmitted by a person other than the donor, and the identity of that person is apparent, to return the donation to that person;

    (b) if paragraph (a) does not apply but it is apparent that the donor has, in connection with the donation, used any facility provided by an identifiable financial institution, to return the donation to that institution; and

    (c) in any other case, to send the donation to the Commission.

  (2) In subsection (1) any reference to returning or sending a donation to any person or body includes a reference to sending a payment of an equivalent amount to that person or body.

  (3) Any amount sent to the Commission in pursuance of subsection (1)(c) shall be paid by them into the Consolidated Fund.

57A *****

58 Forfeiture of donations made by impermissible or unidentifiable donors

  (1) This section applies to any donation received by a registered party—

    (a) which, by virtue of section 54(1)(a) or (b), the party are prohibited from accepting, but

    (b) which has been accepted by the party.

  (2) The court may, on an application made by the Commission, order the forfeiture by the party of an amount equal to the value of the donation.

  (3) The standard of proof in proceedings on an application under this section shall be that applicable to civil proceedings.

  (4) An order may be made under this section whether or not proceedings are brought against any person for an offence connected with the donation.

  (5) In this section "the court" means—

    (a) in relation to England and Wales, a magistrates' court;

    (b) in relation to Scotland, the sheriff; and

    (c) in relation to Northern Ireland, a court of summary jurisdiction;

    [(d) in relation to Gibraltar, the Gibraltar Court;]

and proceedings on an application under this section to the sheriff shall be civil proceedings.

59–100 *****

101   Referendums to which this Part applies

(1) Subject to the following provisions of this section, this Part applies to any referendum held throughout—

    (a) the United Kingdom;

    (b) one or more of England, Scotland, Wales and Northern Ireland; or

    (c) any region in England specified in Schedule 1 to the Regional Development Agencies Act 1998.

(2) In this Part—

    (a) "referendum" means a referendum or other poll held, in pursuance of any provision made by or under an Act of Parliament, on one or more questions specified in or in accordance with any such provision;

    (b) "question" includes proposition (and "answer" accordingly includes response).

(3)–(5) *****

102–104 *****

105   Permitted participants

(1) In this Part "permitted participant", in relation to a particular referendum to which this Part applies, means—

    (a) a registered party by whom a declaration has been made under section 106 in relation to the referendum; or

    (b) any of the following by whom a notification has been given under section 106 in relation to the referendum, namely—

        (i) any individual resident in the United Kingdom or registered in an electoral register (as defined by section 54(8)), or

        (ii) any body falling within any of paragraphs (b) and (d) to (h) of section 54(2).

(2) In this Part "responsible person" means—

    (a) if the permitted participant is a registered party—

        (i) the treasurer of the party, or

        (ii) in the case of a minor party, the person for the time being notified to the Commission by the party in accordance with section 106(2)(b);

    (b) if the permitted participant is an individual, that individual; and

    (c) otherwise, the person or officer for the time being notified to the Commission by the permitted participant in accordance with section 106(4)(b)(ii).

106   Declarations and notifications for purposes of section 105

(1) For the purposes of section 105(1) a registered party makes a declaration to the Commission under this section if the party makes a declaration to the Commission which identifies—

    (a) the referendum to which it relates, and

    (b) the outcome or outcomes for which the party proposes to campaign.

(2) A declaration under this section—

    (a) must be signed by the responsible officers of the party (within the meaning of section 64); and

    (b) if made by a minor party, must be accompanied by a notification which states the name of the person who will be responsible for compliance on the part of the party with the provisions of Chapter II.

(3) For the purposes of section 105(1) an individual or body gives a notification to the Commission under this section if he or it gives the Commission a notification which identifies—

    (a) the referendum to which it relates, and

    (b) the outcome or outcomes for which the giver of the notification proposes to campaign.

(4) A notification under this section must—

    (a) if given by an individual, state—

        (i) his full name, and

        (ii) his home address in the United Kingdom, or (if he has no such address in the United Kingdom) his home address elsewhere,

and be signed by him;

    (b) if given by a body falling within any of paragraphs (b) and (d) to (h) of section 54(2), state—

        (i) all such details in respect of the body as are required by virtue of any of sub-paragraphs (4) and (6) to (10) of paragraph 2 of Schedule 6 to be given in respect of such a body as the donor of a recordable donation, and

        (ii) the name of the person or officer who will be responsible for compliance on the part of the body with the provisions of Chapter II,

and be signed by the body's secretary or a person who acts in a similar capacity in relation to the body.

    (5)–(7) *****

107 Register of declarations and notifications for purposes of section 105

(1) The Commission shall maintain a register of—

    (a) all declarations made to them under section 106; and

    (b) all notifications given to them under that section.

    (2)–(4) *****

108 Designation of organisations to whom assistance is available

(1) The Commission may, in respect of any referendum to which this Part applies, designate permitted participants as organisations to whom assistance is available in accordance with section 110.

(2) Where there are only two possible outcomes, in the case of a referendum to which this Part applies, the Commission—

    (a) may, in relation to each of those outcomes, designate one permitted participant as representing those campaigning for the outcome in question; but

    (b) otherwise shall not make any designation in respect of the referendum.

(3) Where there are more than two possible outcomes in the case of a referendum to which this Part applies, the Secretary of State may, after consulting the Commission, by order specify the possible outcomes in relation to which permitted participants may be designated in accordance with subsection (4).

(4) In such a case the Commission—

    (a) may, in relation to each of two or more outcomes specified in any such order, designate one permitted participant as representing those campaigning for the outcome in question; but

    (b) otherwise shall not make any designation in respect of the referendum.

109 *****

110 Assistance available to designated organisations

(1) Where the Commission have made any designations under section 108 in respect of a referendum, assistance shall be available to the designated organisations in accordance with this section.

(2) The Commission shall make to each designated organisation a grant of the same amount, which shall be an amount not exceeding £600,000 determined by the Commission.

(3) A grant under subsection (2) may be made subject to such conditions as the Commission consider appropriate.

(4) Each designated organisation (or, as the case may be, persons authorised by the organisation) shall have the rights conferred by or by virtue of Schedule 12, which makes provision as to—

    (a) the sending of referendum addresses free of charge;

    (b) the use of rooms free of charge for holding public meetings; and

    (c) referendum campaign broadcasts.

(5) In this section and Schedule 12 "designated organisation", in relation to a referendum, means a person or body designated by the Commission under section 108 in respect of that referendum.

111–112 *****

General restrictions relating to referendum expenses incurred by permitted participants

113   Restriction on incurring referendum expenses

(1) No amount of referendum expenses shall be incurred by or on behalf of a permitted participant unless it is incurred with the authority of—

    (a) the responsible person; or

    (b) a person authorised in writing by the responsible person.

(2) A person commits an offence if, without reasonable excuse, he incurs any expenses in contravention of subsection (1).

(3) Where, in the case of a permitted participant that is a registered party, any expenses are incurred in contravention of subsection (1), the expenses shall not count for the purposes of sections 117 to 123 or Schedule 14 as referendum expenses incurred by or on behalf of the permitted participant.

114–116 *****

Financial limits

117   General restriction on referendum expenses

(1) The total referendum expenses incurred by or on behalf of any individual or body during the referendum period in the case of a particular referendum to which this Part applies must not exceed £10,000 unless the individual or body is a permitted participant.

(2) Where—

    (a) during the referendum period any referendum expenses are incurred by or on behalf of any individual in excess of the limit imposed by subsection (1), and

    (b) he is not a permitted participant,

he is guilty of an offence if he knew, or ought reasonably to have known, that the expenses were being incurred in excess of that limit.

    (3)–(6) *****

118–126 *****

127   Referendum campaign broadcasts

(1) A broadcaster shall not include in its broadcasting services any referendum campaign broadcast made on behalf of any person or body other than one designated in respect of the referendum in question under section 108.

(2) In this section "referendum campaign broadcast" means any broadcast whose purpose (or main purpose) is or may reasonably be assumed to be—

    (a) to further any campaign conducted with a view to promoting or procuring a particular outcome in relation to any question asked in a referendum to which this Part applies, or

    (b) otherwise to promote or procure any such outcome.

*****

Regulation of Investigatory Powers Act 2000
(2000, c. 23)

An Act to make provision for and about the interception of communications, the acquisition and disclosure of data relating to communications, the carrying out of surveillance, the use of covert human intelligence sources and the acquisition of the means by which electronic data protected by encryption or passwords may be decrypted or accessed; to provide for Commissioners and a tribunal with functions and jurisdiction in relation to those matters, to entries on and interferences with property or with wireless telegraphy and to the carrying out of their functions by the Security Service, the Secret Intelligence Service and the Government Communications Headquarters; and for connected purposes   [28 July 2000]

Territorial extent: United Kingdom

1   Unlawful interception

(1) It shall be an offence for a person intentionally and without lawful authority to intercept, at any place in the United Kingdom, any communication in the course of its transmission by means of—

    (a) a public postal service; or

    (b) a public telecommunication system.

(2) It shall be an offence for a person—

    (a) intentionally and without lawful authority, and

    (b) otherwise than in circumstances in which his conduct is excluded by subsection
        (6) from criminal liability under this subsection,

to intercept, at any place in the United Kingdom, any communication in the course of its transmission by means of a private telecommunication system.

(3) Any interception of a communication which is carried out at any place in the United Kingdom by, or with the express or implied consent of, a person having the right to control the operation or the use of a private telecommunication system shall be actionable at the suit or instance of the sender or recipient, or intended recipient, of the communication if it is without lawful authority and is either—

    (a) an interception of that communication in the course of its transmission by means
        of that private system; or

    (b) an interception of that communication in the course of its transmission, by means
        of a public telecommunication system, to or from apparatus comprised in that
        private telecommunication system.

    (4) *****

(5) Conduct has lawful authority for the purposes of this section if, and only if—

    (a) it is authorised by or under section 3 or 4;

    (b) it takes place in accordance with a warrant under section 5 ("an interception
        warrant"); or

    (c) it is in exercise, in relation to any stored communication, of any statutory power
        that is exercised (apart from this section) for the purpose of obtaining information
        or of taking possession of any document or other property;

and conduct (whether or not prohibited by this section) which has lawful authority for the purposes of this section by virtue of paragraph (a) or (b) shall also be taken to be lawful for all other purposes.

(6) The circumstances in which a person makes an interception of a communication in the course of its transmission by means of a private telecommunication system are such that his conduct is excluded from criminal liability under subsection (2) if—

    (a) he is a person with a right to control the operation or the use of the system, or

(b) he has the express or implied consent of such a person to make the interception.

(7) A person who is guilty of an offence under subsection (1) or (2) shall be liable—

(a) on conviction on indictment, to imprisonment for a term riot exceeding two years or to a fine, or to both;

(b) on summary conviction, to a fine not exceeding the statutory maximum.

(8) *****

2   *****

3   Lawful interception without an interception warrant

(1) Conduct by any person consisting in the interception of a communication is authorised by this section if the communication is one which, or which that person has reasonable grounds for believing, is both—

(a) a communication sent by a person who has consented to the interception; and

(b) a communication the intended recipient of which has so consented.

(2) Conduct by any person consisting in the interception of a communication is authorised by this section if—

(a) the communication is one sent by, or intended for, a person who has consented to the interception; and

(b) surveillance by means of that interception has been authorised under Part II.

(3) Conduct consisting in the interception of a communication is authorised by this section if–

(a) it is conduct by or on behalf of a person who provides a postal service or a telecommunications service; and

(b) it takes place for purposes connected with the provision or operation of that service or with the enforcement, in relation to that service, of any enactment relating to the use of postal services or telecommunications services.

(4), (5) *****

4   Power to provide for lawful interception

(1) Conduct by any person ("the interceptor") consisting in the interception of a communication in the course of its transmission by means of a telecommunication system is authorised by this section if—

(a) the interception is carried out for the purpose of obtaining information about the communications of a person who, or who the interceptor has reasonable grounds for believing, is in a country or territory outside the United Kingdom;

(b) the interception relates to the use of a telecommunications service provided to persons in that country or territory which is either—

(i) a public telecommunications service; or

(ii) a telecommunications service that would be a public telecommunications service if the persons to whom it is offered or provided were members of the public in a part of the United Kingdom;

(c) the person who provides that service (whether the interceptor or another person) is required by the law of that country or territory to carry out, secure or facilitate the interception in question;

(d) the situation is one in relation to which such further conditions as may be prescribed by regulations made by the Secretary of State are required to be satisfied before conduct may be treated as authorised by virtue of this subsection; and

(e) the conditions so prescribed are satisfied in relation to that situation.

(2) Subject to subsection (3), the Secretary of State may by regulations authorise any such conduct described in the regulations as appears to him to constitute a legitimate practice reasonably required for the purpose, in connection with the carrying on of any business, of monitoring or keeping a record of—

    (a) communications by means of which transactions are entered into in the course of that business; or

    (b) other communications relating to that business or taking place in the course of its being carried on.

(3) Nothing in any regulations under subsection (2) shall authorise the interception of any communication except in the course of its transmission using apparatus or services provided by or to the person carrying on the business for use wholly or partly in connection with that business.

    (4)–(9) *****

5 Interception with a warrant

(1) Subject to the following provisions of this Chapter, the Secretary of State may issue a warrant authorising or requiring the person to whom it is addressed, by any such conduct as may be described in the warrant, to secure any one or more of the following—

    (a) the interception in the course of their transmission by means of a postal service or telecommunication system of the communications described in the warrant,

    (b) the making, in accordance with an international mutual assistance agreement, of a request for the provision of such assistance in connection with, or in the form of, an interception of communications as may be so described;

    (c) the provision, in accordance with an international mutual assistance agreement, to the competent authorities of a country or territory outside the United Kingdom of any such assistance in connection with, or in the form of, an interception of communications as may be so described;

    (d) the disclosure, in such manner as may be so described, of intercepted material obtained by any interception authorised or required by the warrant, and of related communications data.

(2) The Secretary of State shall not issue an interception warrant unless he believes—

    (a) that the warrant is necessary on grounds falling within subsection (3); and

    (b) that the conduct authorised by the warrant is proportionate to what is sought to be achieved by that conduct.

(3) Subject to the following provisions of this section, a warrant is necessary on grounds falling within this subsection if it is necessary—

    (a) in the interests of national security;

    (b) for the purpose of preventing or detecting serious crime;

    (c) for the purpose of safeguarding the economic well-being of the United Kingdom; or

    (d) for the purpose, in circumstances appearing to the Secretary of State to be equivalent to those in which he would issue a warrant by virtue of paragraph (b), of giving effect to the provisions of any international mutual assistance agreement.

(4) The matters to be taken into account in considering whether the requirements of subsection (2) are satisfied in the case of any warrant shall include whether the information which it is thought necessary to obtain under the warrant could reasonably be obtained by other means.

    (5), (6) *****

6–14 *****

15 General safeguards

(1) Subject to subsection (6), it shall be the duty of the Secretary of State to ensure, in relation to all interception warrants, that such arrangements are in force as he considers necessary for securing—

    (a) that the requirements of subsections (2) and (3) are satisfied in relation to the intercepted material and any related communications data; and

(b) in the case of warrants in relation to which there are section 8(4) certificates, that the requirements of section 16 are also satisfied.

(2) The requirements of this subsection are satisfied in relation to the intercepted material and any related communications data if each of the following—

(a) the number of persons to whom any of the material or data is disclosed or otherwise made available,

(b) the extent to which any of the material or data is disclosed or otherwise made available,

(c) the extent to which any of the material or data is copied, and

(d) the number of copies that are made,

is limited to the minimum that is necessary for the authorised purposes.

(3) The requirements of this subsection are satisfied in relation to the intercepted material and any related communications data if each copy made of any of the material or data (if not destroyed earlier) is destroyed as soon as there are no longer any grounds for retaining it as necessary for any of the authorised purposes.

(4)–(8) *****

16–58   *****

59   Intelligence Services Commissioner

(1) The Prime Minister shall appoint a Commissioner to be known as the Intelligence Services Commissioner.

(2) Subject to subsection (4), the Intelligence Services Commissioner shall keep under review, so far as they are not required to be kept under review by the Interception of Communications Commissioner—

(a) the exercise by the Secretary of State of his powers under sections 5 to 7 of [, or the Scottish Ministers (by virtue of provision made under section 63 of the Scotland Act 1998) of their powers under sections 5 and 6(3) and (4) of] the Intelligence Services Act 1994 (warrants for interference with wireless telegraphy, entry and interference with property etc.);

(b) the exercise and performance by the Secretary of State, [or the Scottish Ministers (by virtue of provision made under section 63 of the Scotland Act 1998)] in connection with or in relation to—

(i)   the activities of the intelligence services, and

(ii) the activities in places other than Northern Ireland of the officials of the Ministry of Defence and of members of Her Majesty's forces,

of the powers and duties conferred or imposed on him by Parts II and III of this Act [or on them by Part II of this Act];

(c) the exercise and performance by members of the intelligence services of the powers and duties conferred or imposed on them by or under Parts II and III of this Act;

(d) the exercise and performance in places other than Northern Ireland, by officials of the Ministry of Defence and by members of Her Majesty's forces, of the powers and duties conferred or imposed on such officials or members of Her Majesty's forces by or under Parts II and III; and

(e) the adequacy of the arrangements by virtue of which the duty imposed by section 55 is sought to be discharged—

(i)   in relation to the members of the intelligence services; and

(ii) in connection with any of their activities in places other than Northern Ireland, in relation to officials of the Ministry of Defence and members of Her Majesty's forces.

(3) The Intelligence Services Commissioner shall give the Tribunal all such assistance (including his opinion as to any issue falling to be determined by the Tribunal) as the Tribunal may require—

(a) in connection with the investigation of any matter by the Tribunal; or

(b) otherwise for the purposes of the Tribunal's consideration or determination of any matter.

(4) It shall not be the function of the Intelligence Services Commissioner to keep under review the exercise of any power of the Secretary of State to make, amend or revoke any subordinate legislation.

(5) A person shall not be appointed under this section as the Intelligence Services Commissioner unless he holds or has held a high judicial office (within the meaning of [Part 3 of the Constitutional Reform Act 2005) or is or has been a member of the Judicial Committee of the Privy Council].

(6)–(10) *****

60   Co-operation with and reports by s. 59 Commissioner

(1) It shall be the duty of—

(a) every member of an intelligence service,

(b) every official of the department of the Secretary of State [and every member of staff of the Scottish Administration (by virtue of provision under section 63 of the Scotland Act 1998)], and

(c) every member of Her Majesty's forces,

to disclose or provide to the Intelligence Services Commissioner all such documents and information as he may require for the purpose of enabling him to carry out his functions under section 59.

(2) As soon as practicable after the end of each calendar year, the Intelligence Services Commissioner shall make a report to the Prime Minister with respect to the carrying out of that Commissioner's functions.

(3) The Intelligence Services Commissioner may also, at any time, make any such other report to the Prime Minister on any matter relating to the carrying out of the Commissioner's functions as the Commissioner thinks fit.

(3A) *****

(4) The Prime Minister shall lay before each House of Parliament a copy of every annual report made by the Intelligence Services Commissioner under subsection (2), together with a statement as to whether any matter has been excluded from that copy in pursuance of subsection (5).

(4A)–(6) *****

61–64   *****

65   The Tribunal

(1) There shall, for the purpose of exercising the jurisdiction conferred on them by this section, be a tribunal consisting of such number of members as Her Majesty may by Letters Patent appoint.

(2) The jurisdiction of the Tribunal shall be—

(a) to be the only appropriate tribunal for the purposes of section 7 of the Human Rights Act 1998 in relation to any proceedings under subsection (1)(a) of that section (proceedings for actions incompatible with Convention rights) which fall within subsection (3) of this section;

(b) to consider and determine any complaints made to them which, in accordance with subsection (4), are complaints for which the Tribunal is the appropriate forum;

(c) to consider and determine any reference to them by any person that he has suffered detriment as a consequence of any prohibition or restriction, by virtue of section 17, on his relying in, or for the purposes of, any civil proceedings on any matter; and

    (d) to hear and determine any other such proceedings falling within subsection (3) as may be allocated to them in accordance with provision made by the Secretary of State by order.

(3) Proceedings fall within this subsection if—

    (a) they are proceedings against any of the intelligence services;

    (b) they are proceedings against any other person in respect of any conduct, or proposed conduct, by or on behalf of any of those services;

    (c) they are proceedings brought by virtue of section 55(4); or

    (d) they are proceedings relating to the taking place in any challengeable circumstances of any conduct falling within subsection (5).

(4) The Tribunal is the appropriate forum for any complaint if it is a complaint by a person who is aggrieved by any conduct falling within subsection (5) which he believes—

    (a) to have taken place in relation to him, to any of his property, to any communications sent by or to him, or intended for him, or to his use of any postal service, telecommunications service or telecommunication system; and

    (b) to have taken place in challengeable circumstances or to have been carried out by or on behalf of any of the intelligence services.

(5) Subject to subsection (6), conduct falls within this subsection if (whenever it occurred) it is—

    (a) conduct by or on behalf of any of the intelligence services;

    (b) conduct for or in connection with the interception of communications in the course of their transmission by means of a postal service or telecommunication system;

    (c) conduct to which Chapter II of Part I applies;

    [(ca) the carrying out of surveillance by a foreign police or customs officer (within the meaning of section 76A);]

    (d) [other] conduct to which Part II applies;

    (e) the giving of a notice under section 49 or any disclosure or use of a key to protected information;

    (f) any entry on or interference with property or any interference with wireless telegraphy.

(6) For the purposes only of subsection (3), nothing mentioned in paragraph (d) or (f) of subsection (5) shall be treated as falling, within that subsection unless it is conduct by or on behalf of a person holding any office, rank or position with—

    (a) any of the intelligence services;

    (b) any of Her Majesty's forces;

    (c) any police force;

    [(d) the Serious Organised Crime Agency; or]

    (f) the Commissioners of Customs and Excise;

and section 48(5) applies for the purposes of this subsection as it applies for the purposes of Part II.

(7) For the purposes of this section conduct takes place in challengeable circumstances if—

    (a) it takes place with the authority, or purported authority, of anything falling within subsection (8); or

    (b) the circumstances are such that (whether or not there is such authority) it would not have been appropriate for the conduct to take place without it, or at least without proper consideration having been given to whether such authority should be sought;

but conduct does not take place in challengeable circumstances to the extent that it is authorised by, or takes place with the permission of, a judicial authority.

[(7A) For the purposes of this section conduct also takes place in challengeable circumstances if it takes place, or purports to take place, under section 76A.]

(8) The following fall within this subsection—

(a) an interception warrant or a warrant under the Interception of Communications Act 1985;

(b) an authorisation or notice under Chapter II of Part I of this Act;

(c) an authorisation under Part II of this Act or under any enactment contained in or made under an Act of the Scottish Parliament which makes provision equivalent to that made by that Part;

(d) a permission for the purposes of Schedule 2 to this Act;

(e) a notice under section 49 of this Act; or

(f) an authorisation under section 93 of the Police Act 1997.

(9)–(11) *****

Terrorism Act 2000

(2000, c. 11)

An Act to make provision about terrorism; and to make temporary provision for Northern Ireland about the prosecution and punishment of certain offences, the preservation of peace and the maintenance of order   [20 July 2000]

Territorial extent: United Kingdom (with certain limited exceptions)

PART I   INTRODUCTORY

1   Terrorism: interpretation

(1) In this Act "terrorism" means the use or threat of action where—

(a) the action falls within subsection (2),

(b) the use or threat is designed to influence the government or to intimidate the public or a section of the public, and

(c) the use or threat is made for the purpose of advancing a political, religious or ideological cause.

(2) Action falls within this subsection if it—

(a) involves serious violence against a person,

(b) involves serious damage to property,

(c) endangers a person's life, other than that of the person committing the action,

(d) creates a serious risk to the health or safety of the public or a section of the public, or

(e) is designed seriously to interfere with or seriously to disrupt an electronic system.

(3) The use or threat of action falling within subsection (2) which involves the use of firearms or explosives is terrorism whether or not subsection (1)(b) is satisfied.

(4) In this section—

(a) "action" includes action outside the United Kingdom,

(b) a reference to any person or to property is a reference to any person, or to property, wherever situated,

(c) a reference to the public includes a reference to the public of a country other than the United Kingdom, and

(d) "the government" means the government of the United Kingdom, of a Part of the United Kingdom or of a country other than the United Kingdom.

(5) In this Act a reference to action taken for the purposes of terrorism includes a reference to action taken for the benefit of a proscribed organisation.

2   *****

PART II   PROSCRIBED ORGANISATIONS

Procedure

3   Proscription

(1) For the purposes of this Act an organisation is proscribed if—

(a) it is listed in Schedule 2, or

(b) it operates under the same name as an organisation listed in that Schedule.

(2) Subsection (1)(b) shall not apply in relation to an organisation listed in Schedule 2 if its entry is the subject of a note in that Schedule.

(3) The Secretary of State may by order—

(a) add an organisation to Schedule 2;

(b) remove an organisation from that Schedule,

(c) amend that Schedule in some other way.

(4) The Secretary of State may exercise his power under subsection (3)(a) in respect of an organisation only if he believes that it is concerned in terrorism.

(5) For the purposes of subsection (4) an organisation is concerned in terrorism if it—

(a) commits or participates in acts of terrorism,

(b) prepares for terrorism,

(c) promotes or encourages terrorism, or

(d) is otherwise concerned in terrorism.

4   Deproscription: application

(1) An application may be made to the Secretary of State for the exercise of his power under section 3(3)(b) to remove an organisation from Schedule 2.

(2) An application may be made by—

(a) the organisation, or

(b) any person affected by the organisation's proscription.

(3) The Secretary of State shall make regulations prescribing the procedure for applications under this section.

(4) The regulations shall, in particular—

(a) require the Secretary of State to determine an application within a specified period of time, and

(b) require an application to state the grounds on which it is made.

5   Deproscription: appeal

(1) There shall be a commission, to be known as the Proscribed Organisations Appeal Commission.

(2) Where an application under section 4 has been refused, the applicant may appeal to the Commission.

(3) The Commission shall allow an appeal against a refusal to deproscribe an organisation if it considers that the decision to refuse was flawed when considered in the light of the principles applicable on an application for judicial review.

(4)–(6) *****

6   Further appeal

(1) A party to an appeal under section 5 which the, Proscribed Organisations Appeal Commission has determined may bring a further appeal on a question of law to—

(a) the Court of Appeal, if the first appeal was heard in England and Wales,

(b) the Court of Session, if the first appeal was heard in Scotland, or

(c) the Court of Appeal in Northern Ireland, if the first appeal was heard in Northern Ireland.

(2) An appeal under subsection (1) may be brought only with the permission—

(a) of the Commission, or

(b) where the Commission refuses permission, of the court to which the appeal would be brought.

(3) An order under section 5(4) shall not require the Secretary of State to take any action until the final determination or disposal of an appeal under this section (including any appeal to the [Supreme Court]).

7–9 *****

10 Immunity

(1) The following shall not be admissible as evidence in proceedings for an offence under any of sections 11 to 13, 15 to 19 and 56—

(a) evidence of anything done in relation to an application to the Secretary of State under section 4,

(b) evidence of anything done in relation to proceedings before the Proscribed Organisations Appeal Commission under section 5 above or section 7(1) of the Human Rights Act 1998,

(c) evidence of anything done in relation to proceedings under section 6 (including that section as applied by section 9(2)), and

(d) any document submitted for the purposes of proceedings mentioned in any of paragraphs (a) to (c).

(2) But subsection (1) does not prevent evidence from being adduced on behalf of the accused.

Offences

11 Membership

(1) A person commits an offence if he belongs or professes to belong to a proscribed organisation.

(2) It is a defence for a person charged with an offence under subsection (1) to prove—

(a) that the organisation was not proscribed on the last (or only) occasion on which he became a member or began to profess to be a member, and

(b) that he has not taken part in the activities of the organisation at any time while it was proscribed.

(3) A person guilty of an offence under this section shall be liable—

(a) on conviction on indictment, to imprisonment for a term not exceeding ten years, to a fine or to both, or

(b) on summary conviction, to imprisonment for a term not exceeding six months, to a fine not exceeding the statutory maximum or to both.

(4) *****

12 Support

(1) A person commits an offence if—

(a) he invites support for a proscribed organisation, and

(b) the support is not, or is not restricted to, the provision of money or other property (within the meaning of section 15).

(2) A person commits an offence if he arranges, manages or assists in arranging or managing a meeting which he knows is—

(a) to support a proscribed organisation,

(b) to further the activities of a proscribed organisation, or

(c) to be addressed by a person who belongs or professes to belong to a proscribed organisation.

(3) A person commits an offence if he addresses a meeting and the purpose of his address is to encourage support for a proscribed organisation or to further its activities.

(4) Where a person is charged with an offence under subsection (2)(c) in respect of a private meeting it is a defence for him to prove that he had no reasonable cause to believe that the address mentioned in subsection (2)(c) would support a proscribed organisation or further its activities.

(5) In subsections (2) to (4)—

(a) "meeting" means a meeting of three or more persons, whether or not the public are admitted, and

(b) a meeting is private if the public are not admitted.

(6) A person guilty of an offence under this section shall be liable—

(a) on conviction on indictment, to imprisonment for a term not exceeding ten years, to a fine or to both, or

(b) on summary conviction, to imprisonment for a term not exceeding six months, to a fine not exceeding the statutory maximum or to both.

13   Uniform

(1) A person in a public place commits an offence if he—

(a) wears an item of clothing, or

(b) wears, carries or displays an article, in such a way or in such circumstances as to arouse reasonable suspicion that he is a member or supporter of a proscribed organisation.

(2) A constable in Scotland may arrest a person without a warrant if he has reasonable grounds to suspect that the person is guilty of an offence under this section.

(3) A person guilty of an offence under this section shall be liable on summary conviction to—

(a) imprisonment for a term not exceeding six months,

(b) a fine not exceeding level 5 on the standard scale, or

(c) both.

14   *****

Offences

15   Fund-raising

(1) A person commits an offence if he—

(a) invites another to provide money or other property, and

(b) intends that it should be used, or has reasonable cause to suspect that it may be used, for the purposes of terrorism.

(2) A person commits an offence if he—

(a) receives money or other property, and

(b) intends that it should be used, or has reasonable cause to suspect that it may be used, for the purposes of terrorism.

(3) A person commits an offence if he—

(a) provides money or other property, and

(b) knows or has reasonable cause to suspect that it will or may be used for the purposes of terrorism.

(4) In this section a reference to the provision of money or other property is a reference to its being given, lent or otherwise made available, whether or not for consideration.

16–18   *****

19   Disclosure of information: duty
(1) This section applies where a person—
   (a) believes or suspects that another person has committed an offence under any of sections 15 to 18, and
   (b) bases his belief or suspicion on information which comes to his attention in the course of a trade, profession, business or employment.
[(1A) But this section does not apply if the information came to the person in the course of a business in the regulated sector.]
(2) The person commits an offence if he does not disclose to a constable as soon as is reasonably practicable—
   (a) his belief or suspicion, and
   (b) the information on which it is based.
(3) It is a defence for a person charged with an offence under subsection (2) to prove that he had a reasonable excuse for not making the disclosure.
(4) Where—
   (a) a person is in employment,
   (b) his employer has established a procedure for the making of disclosures of the matters specified in subsection (2), and
   (c) he is charged with an offence under that subsection, it is a defence for him to prove that he disclosed the matters specified in that subsection in accordance with the procedure.
(5) Subsection (2) does not require disclosure by a professional legal adviser of—
   (a) information which he obtains in privileged circumstances, or
   (b) a belief or suspicion based on information which he obtains in privileged circumstances.
(6) For the purpose of subsection (5) information is obtained by an adviser in privileged circumstances if it comes to him, otherwise than with a view to furthering a criminal purpose—
   (a) from a client or a client's representative, in connection with the provision of legal advice by the adviser to the client,
   (b) from a person seeking legal advice from the adviser, or from the person's representative, or
   (c) from any person, for the purpose of actual or contemplated legal proceedings.
(7)–(8) *****

20–39 *****

PART V   COUNTER-TERRORIST POWERS

Suspected terrorists

40   Terrorist: interpretation
(1) In this Part "terrorist" means a person who—
   (a) has committed an offence under any of sections 11, 12, 15 to 18, 54 and 56 to 63, or
   (b) is or has been concerned in the commission, preparation or instigation of acts of terrorism.
(2) The reference in subsection (1)(b) to a person who has been concerned in the commission, preparation or instigation of acts of terrorism includes a reference to a person who has been, whether before or after the passing of this Act, concerned in the commission, preparation or instigation of acts of terrorism within the meaning given by section 1.

41   Arrest without warrant
(1) A constable may arrest without a warrant a person whom he reasonably suspects to be a terrorist.

(2) Where a person is arrested under this section the provisions of Schedule 8 (detention: treatment, review and extension) shall apply.

(3) Subject to subsections (4) to (7), a person detained under this section shall (unless detained under any other power) be released not later than the end of the period of 48 hours beginning—

(a) with the time of his arrest under this section, or

(b) if he was being detained under Schedule 7 when he was arrested under this section, with the time when his examination under that Schedule began.

(4) If on a review of a person's detention under Part II of Schedule 8 the review officer does not authorise continued detention, the person shall (unless detained in accordance with subsection (5) or (6) or under any other power) be released.

(5) Where a police officer intends to make an application for a warrant under paragraph 29 of Schedule 8 extending a person's detention, the person may be detained pending the making of the application.

(6) Where an application has been made under paragraph 29 or 36 of Schedule 8 in respect of a person's detention, he may be detained pending the conclusion of proceedings on the application.

(7) Where an application under paragraph 29 or 36 of Schedule 8 is granted in respect of a person's detention, he may be detained, subject to paragraph 37 of that Schedule, during the period specified in the warrant.

(8) The refusal of an application in respect of a person's detention under paragraph 29 or 36 of Schedule 8 shall not prevent his continued detention in accordance with this section.

(9) A person who has the powers of a constable in one Part of the United Kingdom may exercise the power under subsection (1) in any Part of the United Kingdom.

42   Search of premises

(1) A justice of the peace may on the application of a constable issue a warrant in relation to specified premises if he is satisfied that there are reasonable grounds for suspecting that a person whom the constable reasonably suspects to be a person falling within section 40(1)(b) is to be found there.

(2) A warrant under this section shall authorise any constable to enter and search the specified premises for the purpose of arresting the person referred to in subsection (1) under section 41.

(3) In the application of subsection (1) to Scotland—

(a) "justice of the peace" includes the sheriff, and

(b) the justice of the peace or sheriff can be satisfied as mentioned in that subsection only by having heard evidence on oath.

43   Search of persons

(1) A constable may stop and search a person whom he reasonably suspects to be a terrorist to discover whether he has in his possession anything which may constitute evidence that he is a terrorist.

(2) A constable may search a person arrested under section 41 to discover whether he has in his possession anything which may constitute evidence that he is a terrorist.

(3) A search of a person under this section must be carried out by someone of the same sex.

(4) A constable may seize and retain anything which he discovers in the course of a search of a person under subsection (1) or (2) and which he reasonably suspects may constitute evidence that the person is a terrorist.

(5) A person who has the powers of a constable in one Part of the United Kingdom may exercise a power under this section in any Part of the United Kingdom.

44–58   ***

Inciting terrorism overseas

59 England and Wales

(1) A person commits an offence if—

    (a) he incites another person to commit an act of terrorism wholly or partly outside the United Kingdom, and

    (b) the act would, if committed in England and Wales, constitute one of the offences listed in subsection (2).

(2) Those offences are—

    (a) murder,

    (b) an offence under section 18 of the Offences against the Person Act 1861 (wounding with intent),

    (c) an offence under section 23 or 24 of that Act (poison),

    (d) an offence under section 28 or 29 of that Act (explosions), and

    (e) an offence under section 1(2) of the Criminal Damage Act 1971 (endangering life by damaging property).

(3) A person guilty of an offence under this section shall be liable to any penalty to which he would be liable on conviction of the offence listed in subsection (2) which corresponds to the act which he incites.

(4) For the purposes of subsection (1) it is immaterial whether or not the person incited is in the United Kingdom at the time of the incitement.

(5) Nothing in this section imposes criminal liability on any person acting on behalf of, or holding office under, the Crown.

Note: There is equivalent provision for Northern Ireland in s 60 and for Scotland in s 61.

60–61 *****

Terrorist bombing and finance offences

62 Terrorist bombing: jurisdiction

(1) If—

    (a) a person does anything outside the United Kingdom as an act of terrorism or for the purposes of terrorism, and

    (b) his action would have constituted the commission of one of the offences listed in subsection (2) if it had been done in the United Kingdom,

he shall be guilty of the offence.

(2) The offences referred to in subsection (1)(b) are—

    (a) an offence under section 2, 3 or 5 of the Explosive Substances Act 1883 (causing explosions, &c.),

    (b) an offence under section 1 of the Biological Weapons Act 1974 (biological weapons), and

    (c) an offence under section 2 of the Chemical Weapons Act 1996 (chemical weapons).

63 *****

[63A Other terrorist offences under this Act: jurisdiction]

[(1) If—

    (a) a United Kingdom national or a United Kingdom resident does anything outside the United Kingdom, and

    (b) his action, if done in any part of the United Kingdom, would have constituted an offence under section 54 or any of sections 56 to 61,

he shall be guilty in that part of the United Kingdom of the offence.

(2) For the purposes of this section and sections 63B and 63C a "United Kingdom national" means an individual who is—

(a) a British citizen, a British overseas territories citizen, a British National (Overseas) or a British Overseas citizen.

(b) a person who under the British Nationality Act 1981 is a British subject, or

(c) a British protected person within the meaning of that Act.

(3) For the purposes of this section and sections 63B and 63C a "United Kingdom resident" means an individual who is resident in the United Kingdom.]

[63B   Terrorist attacks abroad by UK nationals or residents: jurisdiction]

[(1) If—

(a) a United Kingdom national or a United Kingdom resident does anything outside the United Kingdom as an act of terrorism or for the purposes of terrorism, and

(b) his action, if done in any part of the United Kingdom, would have constituted an offence listed in subsection (2).

he shall be guilty in that part of the United Kingdom of the offence.

(2) These are the offences—

(a) murder, manslaughter, culpable homicide, rape, assault causing injury, assault to injury, kidnapping, abduction or false imprisonment,

(b) an offence under section 4, 16, 18, 20, 21, 22, 23, 24, 28, 29, 30 or 64 of the Offences against the Person Act 1861,

(c) an offence under any of sections 1 to 5 of the Forgery and Counterfeiting Act 1981,

(d) the uttering of a forged document or an offence under section 46A of the Criminal Law (Consolidation) (Scotland) Act 1995,

(e) an offence under section 1 or 2 of the Criminal Damage Act 1971,

(f) an offence under Article 3 or 4 of the Criminal Damage (Northern Ireland) Order 1977,

(g) malicious mischief,

(h) wilful fire-raising.]

[63C   Terrorist attacks abroad on UK nationals, residents and diplomatic staff etc: jurisdiction]

[(1) If—

(a) a person does anything outside the United Kingdom as an act of terrorism or for the purposes of terrorism,

(b) his action is done to, or in relation to, a United Kingdom national, a United Kingdom resident or a protected person, and

(c) his action, if done in any part of the United Kingdom, would have constituted an offence listed in subsection (2),

he shall be guilty in that part of the United Kingdom of the offence.

(2) These are the offences—

(a) murder, manslaughter, culpable homicide, rape, assault causing injury, assault to injury, kidnapping, abduction or false imprisonment,

(b) an offence under section 4, 16, 18, 20, 21, 22, 23, 24, 28, 29, 30 or 64 of the Offences against the Person Act 1861,

(c) an offence under section 1, 2, 3, 4 or 5(1) or (3) of the Forgery and Counterfeiting Act 1981,

(d) the uttering of a forged document or an offence under section 46A(1) of the Criminal Law (Consolidation) (Scotland) Act 1995.

(3)–(5)*****

64–113   *****

PART VIII   GENERAL

114   Police powers
(1) A power conferred by virtue of this Act on a constable—
  (a) is additional to powers which he has at common law or by virtue of any other enactment, and
  (b) shall not be taken to affect those powers.

(2) A constable may if necessary use reasonable force for the purpose of exercising a power conferred on him by virtue of this Act (apart fromparagraphs 2 and 3 of Schedule 7).

(3) Where anything is seized by a constable under a power conferred by virtue of this Act, it may (unless the contrary intention appears) be retained for so long as is necessary in all the circumstances.

SCHEDULE 2   PROSCRIBED ORGANISATIONS

The Irish Republican Army
Cumann na mBan
Fianna na hEireann
The Red Hand Commando
Saor Eire
The Ulster Freedom Fighters
The Ulster Volunteer Force
The Irish National Liberation Army
The Irish People's Liberation Organisation
The Ulster Defence Association
The Loyalist Volunteer Force
The Continuity Army Council
The Orange Volunteers
The Red Hand Defenders
[Al-Qa'ida
Egyptian Islamic Jihad
Al-Gama'at al-Islamiya
Armed Islamic Group (Groupe Islamique Armée) (GIA)
Salafist Group for Call and Combat (Groupe Salafiste pour la Prédication et le Combat) (GSPC)
Babbar Khalsa
International Sikh Youth Federation
Harakat Mujahideen
Jaish e Mohammed
Lashkar e Tayyaba
Liberation Tigers of Tamil Eelam (LTTE)
Hizballah External Security Organisation
Hamas-Izz al-Din al-Qassem Brigades
Palestinian Islamic Jihad—Shaqaqi
Abu Nidal Organisation
Islamic Army of Aden
Mujaheddin e Khalq
Kurdistan Workers' Party (Partiya Karkeren Kurdistan) (PKK)
Revolutionary Peoples' Liberation Party—Front (Devrimci Halk Kurtulus Partisi-Cephesi) (DHKP-C)
Basque Homeland and Liberty (Euskadi ta Askatasuna) (ETA)
17 November Revolutionary Organisation (N17)]

[Abu Sayyaf Group
Asbat Al-Ansar
Islamic Movement of Uzbekistan
Jemaah Islamiyah]

Note

The entry for The Orange Volunteers refers to the organisation which uses that name and in the name of which a statement described as a press release was published on 14th October 1998.

[The entry for Jemaah Islamiyah refers to the organisation using that name that is based in south-east Asia, members of which were arrested by the Singapore authorities in December 2001 in connection with a plot to attack US and other Western targets in Singapore.]

SCHEDULE 3   THE PROSCRIBED ORGANISATIONS APPEAL COMMISSION

Constitution and administration

1.—(1) The Commission shall consist of members appointed by the Lord Chancellor.

(2) The Lord Chancellor shall appoint one of the members as chairman.

(3) A member shall hold and vacate office in accordance with terms of his appointment.

(4) A member may resign at any time by notice in writing to the Lord Chancellor.

2, 3   *****

Procedure

4.—(1) The Commission shall sit at such times and in such places as the Lord Chancellor may direct, [after consulting the following—

    (a) the Lord Chief Justice of England and Wales;

    (b) the Lord President of the Court of Session;

    (c) the Lord Chief Justice of Northern Ireland.]

(2) The Commission may sit in two or more divisions.

(3) At each sitting of the Commission—

    (a) three members shall attend,

    (b) one of the members shall be a person who holds or has held high judicial office (within the meaning of [Part 3 of the Constitutional Reform Act 2005) or has been a member of the Judicial Committee of the Privy Council], and

    (c) the chairman or another member nominated by him shall preside and report the Commission's decision.

(4)–(6)   *****

5.—(1) The Lord Chancellor may make rules—

    (a) regulating the exercise of the right of appeal to the Commission;

    (b) prescribing practice and procedure to be followed in relation to proceedings before the Commission;

    (c) providing for proceedings before the Commission to be determined without an oral hearing in specified circumstances;

    (d) making provision about evidence in proceedings before the Commission (including provision about the burden of proof and admissibility of evidence);

    (e) making provision about proof of the Commission's decisions.

(2) In making the rules the Lord Chancellor shall, in particular, have regard to the need to secure—

(a) that decisions which are the subject of appeals are properly reviewed, and

(b) that information is not disclosed contrary to the public interest.

(3) The rules shall make provision permitting organisations to be legally represented in proceedings before the Commission.

(4)–(6) *****

6.—(1) This paragraph applies to—

(a) proceedings brought by an organisation before the Commission, and

(b) proceedings arising out of proceedings to which paragraph (a) applies.

(2) Proceedings shall be conducted on behalf of the organisation by a person designated by the Commission (with such legal representation as he may choose to obtain).

(3) In [paragraph 5] of this Schedule a reference to an organisation includes a reference to a person designated under this paragraph.

7. *****

8. ...

SCHEDULE 3A–5 *****

SCHEDULE 6   FINANCIAL INFORMATION

Orders

1.—(1) Where an order has been made under this paragraph in relation to a terrorist investigation, a constable named in the order may require a financial institution [to which the order applies] to provide customer information for the purposes of the investigation.

(1A) *****

(2) The information shall be provided—

(a) in such manner and within such time as the constable may specify, and

(b) notwithstanding any restriction on the disclosure of information imposed by statute or otherwise.

(3) An institution which fails to comply with a requirement under this paragraph shall be guilty of an offence.

(4) It is a defence for an institution charged with an offence under sub-paragraph (3) to prove—

(a) that the information required was not in the institution's possession, or

(b) that it was not reasonably practicable for the institution to comply with the requirement.

(5) An institution guilty of an offence under sub-paragraph (3) shall be liable on summary conviction to a fine not exceeding level 5 on the standard scale.

2.–4. *****

Criteria for making order

5. An order under paragraph 1 may be made only if the person making it is satisfied that—

(a) the order is sought for the purposes of a terrorist investigation,

(b) the tracing of terrorist property is desirable for the purposes of the investigation, and

(c) the order will enhance the effectiveness of the investigation.

*****

Anti-terrorism, Crime and Security Act 2001
(2001, c. 24)

An Act to amend the Terrorism Act 2000; to make further provision about terrorism and security; to provide for the freezing of assets; to make provision about immigration and asylum; to amend or extend the criminal law and powers for preventing crime and enforcing that law: to make provision about the control of pathogens and toxins; to provide for the retention of communications data; to provide for implementation of Title VI of the Treaty on European Union; and for connected purposes   [14 December 2001]

Territorial extent: United Kingdom (provisions reproduced here)

1–3 *****

PART 2   FREEZING ORDERS

Orders

4   Power to make order

(1) The Treasury may make a freezing order if the following two conditions are satisfied.

(2) The first condition is that the Treasury reasonably believe that—

    (a) action to the detriment of the United Kingdom's economy (or part of it) has been or is likely to be taken by a person or persons, or

    (b) action constituting a threat to the life or property of one or more nationals of the United Kingdom or residents of the United Kingdom has been or is likely to be taken by a person or persons.

(3) If one person is believed to have taken or to be likely to take the action the second condition is that the person is—

    (a) the government of a country or territory outside the United Kingdom, or

    (b) a resident of a country or territory outside the United Kingdom.

(4) If two or more persons are believed to have taken or to be likely to take the action the second condition is that each of them falls within paragraph (a) or (b) of subsection (3); and different persons may fall within different paragraphs.

5   Contents of order

(1) A freezing order is an order which prohibits persons from making funds available to or for the benefit of a person or persons specified in the order.

(2) The order must provide that these are the persons who are prohibited—

    (a) all persons in the United Kingdom, and

    (b) all persons elsewhere who are nationals of the United Kingdom or are bodies incorporated under the law of any part of the United Kingdom or are Scottish partnerships.

(3) The order may specify the following (and only the following) as the person or persons to whom or for whose benefit funds are not to be made available—

    (a) the person or persons reasonably believed by the Treasury to have taken or to be likely to take the action referred to in section 4;

    (b) any person the Treasury reasonably believe has provided or is likely to provide assistance (directly or indirectly) to that person or any of those persons.

(4) A person may be specified under subsection (3) by—

    (a) being named in the order, or

    (b) falling within a description of persons set out in the order.

(5) The description must be such that a reasonable person would know whether he fell within it.

(6) Funds are financial assets and economic benefits of any kind.

6   *****

7   Review of order
The Treasury must keep a freezing order under review.

8   Duration of order
A freezing order ceases to have effect at the end of the period of 2 years starting with the day on which it is made.

9   *****

Orders: procedure etc.

10   Procedure for making freezing orders
(1) A power to make a freezing order is exercisable by statutory instrument.

(2) A freezing order—
   (a) must be laid before Parliament after being made;
   (b) ceases to have effect at the end of the relevant period unless before the end of that period the order is approved by a resolution of each House of Parliament (but without that affecting anything done under the order or the power to make a new order).

(3) The relevant period is a period of 28 days starting with the day on which the order is made.

   (4), (5) *****

11–14   *****

15   The Crown
(1) A freezing order binds the Crown, subject to the following provisions of this section.

(2) No contravention by the Crown of a provision of a freezing order makes the Crown criminally liable; but the High Court or in Scotland the Court of Session may, on the application of a person appearing to the Court to have an interest, declare unlawful any act or omission of the Crown which constitutes such a contravention.

(3) Nothing in this section affects Her Majesty in her private capacity; and this is to be construed as if section 38(3) of the Crown Proceedings Act 1947 (meaning of Her Majesty in her private capacity) were contained in this Act.

16–20   *****

21   . . .

22   *****

23–32   . . .

33–46   *****

PART 6   WEAPONS OF MASS DESTRUCTION

*****

Nuclear weapons

47   Use etc. of nuclear weapons
(1) A person who—

    (a) knowingly causes a nuclear weapon explosion;

    (b) develops or produces, or participates in the development or production of, a nuclear weapon;

    (c) has a nuclear weapon in his possession;

    (d) participates in the transfer of a nuclear weapon; or

    (e) engages in military preparations, or in preparations of a military nature, intending to use, or threaten to use, a nuclear weapon, is guilty of an offence.

(2) Subsection (1) has effect subject to the exceptions and defences in sections 48 and 49.

(3)–(9) *****

48   Exceptions

(1) Nothing in section 47 applies—

    (a) to an act which is authorised under subsection (2); or

    (b) to an act done in the course of an armed conflict.

(2) The Secretary of State may—

    (a) authorise any act which would otherwise contravene section 47 in such manner and on such terms as he thinks fit; and

    (b) withdraw or vary any authorisation given under this subsection.

(3) Any question arising in proceedings for an offence under section 47 as to whether anything was done in the course of an armed conflict shall be determined by the Secretary of State.

49   Defences

(1) In proceedings for an offence under section 47(1)(c) or (d) relating to an object it is a defence for the accused to show that he did not know and had no reason to believe that the object was a nuclear weapon.

(2) But he shall be taken to have shown that fact if—

    (a) sufficient evidence is adduced to raise an issue with respect to it; and

    (b) the contrary is not proved by the prosecution beyond reasonable doubt.

(3) In proceedings for such an offence it is also a defence for the accused to show that he knew or believed that the object was a nuclear weapon but, as soon as reasonably practicable after he first knew or believed that fact, he took all reasonable steps to inform the Secretary of State or a constable of his knowledge or belief.

*****

SCHEDULES

*****

SCHEDULE 3
FREEZING ORDERS

*****

Compensation

10.—(1) A freezing order may include provision for the award of compensation to or on behalf of a person on the grounds that he has suffered loss as a result of—

    (a) the order;

    (b) the fact that a licence has not been granted under the order;

    (c) the fact that a licence under the order has been granted on particular terms rather than others;

    (d) the fact that a licence under the order has been varied or revoked.

(2) In particular, the order may include—
  (a) provision about the person who may make a claim for an award;
  (b) provision about the person to whom a claim for an award is to be made (which may be provision that it is to be made to the High Court or, in Scotland, the Court of Session);
  (c) provision about the procedure for making and deciding a claim;
  (d) provision that no compensation is to be awarded unless the claimant has behaved reasonably (which may include provision requiring him to mitigate his loss, for instance by applying for a licence);
  (e) provision that compensation must be awarded in specified circumstances or may be awarded in specified circumstances (which may include provision that the circumstances involve negligence or other fault);
  (f) provision about the amount that may be awarded;
  (g) provision about who is to pay any compensation awarded (which may include provision that it is to be paid or reimbursed by the Treasury);
  (h) provision about how compensation is to be paid (which may include provision for payment to a person other than the claimant).

Treasury's duty to give reasons
  11.—A freezing order must include provision that if—
  (a) a person is specified in the order as a person to whom or for whose benefit funds are not to be made available, and
  (b) he makes a written request to the Treasury to give him the reason why he is so specified,
as soon as is practicable the Treasury must give the person the reason in writing.

*****

Criminal Justice and Police Act 2001
(2001, c. 16)

An Act to make provision for combating crime and disorder; to make provision about the disclosure of information relating to criminal matters and about powers of search and seizure; to amend the Police and Criminal Evidence Act 1984, the Police and Criminal Evidence (Northern Ireland) Order 1989 and the Terrorism Act 2000; to make provision about the police, the National Criminal Intelligence Service, and the National Crime Squad; to make provision about the powers of the Courts in relation to criminal matters; and for connected purposes [11 May 2001]

Territorial extent: England and Wales but Parts 2, 5 (National Criminal Intelligence Service) extend to the United Kingdom

1 Offences leading to penalties on the spot
  (1) For the purposes of this Chapter "penalty offence" means an offence committed under any of the provisions mentioned in the first column of the following Table and described, in general terms, in the second column:

Offence creating provision	Description of offence
Section 12 of the Licensing Act 1872 (c. 94)	Being drunk in a highway, other public place or licensed premises

. . .

Section 55 of the British Transport Commission Act 1949 (c. xxix)	Trespassing on a railway
Section 56 of the British Transport Commission Act 1949 (c. xxix)	Throwing stones etc. at trains or other things on railways
. . .	
[Section 169A of the Licensing Act 1964 (c.26)	Sale of alcohol to a person under 18]
[Section 169C(2) and (3) of the Licensing Act 1964	Buying or attempting to buy alcohol for . . . a person under 18]
[Section 169E of the Licensing Act 1964 (c.26)	Consumption of alcohol by a person under 18 or allowing such consumption
Section 169F of the Licensing Act 1964 (c.26)	Delivery of alcohol to a person under 18 or allowing such delivery]
Section 91 of the Criminal Justice Act 1967 (c. 80)	Disorderly behaviour while drunk in a public place
Section 5(2) of the Criminal Law Act 1967 (c. 58)	Wasting police time or giving false report
. . .	
[Section 1 of the Theft Act 1968 (c. 60)	Theft
Section 1(1) of the Criminal Damage Act 1971 (c. 48)	Destroying or damaging property]
[Section 5 of the Public Order Act 1986 (c. 64)	Behaviour likely to cause harassment, alarm or distress]
[Section 87 of the Environmental Protection Act 1990 (c. 43)	Depositing and leaving litter]
Section 12 of this Act	Consumption of alcohol in designated public place
[Section 127(2) of the Communications Act 2003	Using Public Electronic Communications network in order to cause annoyance, inconvenience or needless anxiety]
[Section 11 of the Fireworks Act 2003 (c. 22)	Contravention of a prohibition or failure to comply with a requirement imposed by or under fireworks regulations or making false statements]
[Section 149(4) of the Licensing Act 2003	Buying or attempting to buy alcohol for consumption on licensed premises, etc by child]
[Section 49 of the Fire and Rescue Services Act 2004 (c. 21)	Knowingly giving a false alarm of fire]

(2) The Secretary of State may by order amend an entry in the Table or add or remove an entry.

(3)–(5) *****

Penalty notices and penalties

2   Penalty notices

(1) A constable who has reason to believe that a person aged [10] or over has committed a penalty offence may give him a penalty notice in respect of the offence.

(2) Unless the notice is given in a police station, the constable giving it must be in uniform.

(3) At a police station, a penalty notice may be given only by an authorised constable.

(4) In this Chapter "penalty notice" means a notice offering the opportunity, by paying a penalty in accordance with this Chapter, to discharge any liability to be convicted of the offence to which the notice relates.

(5) "Authorised constable" means a constable authorised, on behalf of the chief officer of police for the area in which the police station is situated, to give penalty notices.

(6)–(9) *****

3   Amount of penalty and form of penalty notice

(1) The penalty payable in respect of a penalty offence is such amount as the Secretary of State may specify by order.

[(1A) The Secretary of State may specify different amounts for different ages.]

(2) But the Secretary of State may not specify an amount which is more than a quarter of the amount of the maximum fine for which a person is liable on [summary] conviction of the offence [plus a half of the relevant surcharge].

[(2A) The "relevant surcharge" in relation to a person of a given age, is the amount payable by way of surcharge under section 161A of the Criminal Justice Act 2003 by a person of that age who is fined the maximum amount for the offence.]

(3) A penalty notice must—

    (a) be in the prescribed form;

    (b) state the alleged offence;

    (c) give such particulars of the circumstances alleged to constitute the offence as are necessary to provide reasonable information about it;

    (d) specify the suspended enforcement period (as to which see section 5) and explain its effect;

    (e) state the amount of the penalty;

    (f) state the [designated officer for a local justice] area to whom, and the address at which, the penalty may be paid; and

    (g) inform the person to whom it is given of his right to ask to be tried for the alleged offence and explain how that right may be exercised.

(4)–(6) *****

4   Effect of penalty notice

(1) This section applies if a penalty notice is given to a person ("A") under section 2.

(2) If A asks to be tried for the alleged offence, proceedings may be brought against him.

(3) Such a request must be made by a notice given by A—

    (a) in the manner specified in the penalty notice; and

    (b) before the end of the period of suspended enforcement (as to which see section 5).

(4) A request which is made in accordance with subsection (3) is referred to in this Chapter as a "request to be tried".

(5) If, by the end of the suspended enforcement period–

    (a) the penalty has not been paid in accordance with this Chapter, and

    (b) A has not made a request to be tried,

a sum equal to one and a half times the amount of the penalty may be registered under section 8 for enforcement against A as a fine.

5   General restriction on proceedings

(1) Proceedings for the offence to which a penalty notice relates may not be brought until the end of the period of 21 days beginning with the date on which the notice was given ("the suspended enforcement period").

(2) If the penalty is paid before the end of the suspended enforcement period, no proceedings may be brought for the offence.

(3) Subsection (1) does not apply if the person to whom the penalty notice was given has made a request to be tried.

6–38   ***

39   Intimidation of witnesses

(1) A person commits an offence if—
  (a) he does an act which intimidates, and is intended to intimidate, another person ("the victim");
  (b) he does the act—
    (i) knowing or believing that the victim is or may be a witness in any relevant proceedings; and
    (ii) intending, by his act, to cause the course of justice to be obstructed, perverted or interfered with;
  and
  (c) the act is done after the commencement of those proceedings.

(2) For the purposes of subsection (1) it is immaterial—
  (a) whether or not the act that is done is done in the presence of the victim;
  (b) whether that act is done to the victim himself or to another person; and
  (c) whether or not the intention to cause the course of justice to be obstructed, perverted or interfered with is the predominating intention of the person doing the act in question.

(3) If, in proceedings against a person for an offence under this section, it is proved—
  (a) that he did any act that intimidated, and was intended to intimidate, another person, and
  (b) that he did that act knowing or believing that that other person was or might be a witness in any relevant proceedings that had already commenced,

he shall be presumed, unless the contrary is shown, to have done the act with the intention of causing the course of justice to be obstructed, perverted or interfered with.

(4) A person guilty of an offence under this section shall be liable—
  (a) on conviction on indictment, to imprisonment for a term not exceeding five years or to a fine, or to both;
  (b) on summary conviction, to imprisonment for a term not exceeding six months or to a fine not exceeding the statutory maximum, or to both.

(5)–(7)   *****

40   Harming witnesses etc.

(1) A person commits an offence if, in circumstances falling within subsection (2)—
  (a) he does an act which harms, and is intended to harm, another person; or
  (b) intending to cause another person to fear harm, he threatens to do an act which would harm that other person.

(2) The circumstances fall within this subsection if—
  (a) the person doing or threatening to do the act does so knowing or believing that some person (whether or not the person harmed or threatened or the person against whom harm is threatened) has been a witness in relevant proceedings; and
  (b) he does or threatens to do that act because of that knowledge or belief.

(3) If, in proceedings against a person for an offence under this section, it is proved that, within the relevant period—

(a) he did an act which harmed, and was intended to harm, another person, or

(b) intending to cause another person to fear harm, he threatened to do an act which would harm that other person,

and that he did the act, or (as the case may be) threatened to do the act, with the knowledge or belief required by paragraph (a) of subsection (2), he shall be presumed, unless the contrary is shown, to have done the act, or (as the case may be) threatened to do the act, because of that knowledge or belief.

(4) For the purposes of this section it is immaterial—

(a) whether or not the act that is done or threatened, or the threat that is made, is or would be done or is made in the presence of the person who is or would be harmed or of the person who is threatened;

(b) whether or not the motive mentioned in subsection (2)(b) is the predominating motive for the act or threat; and

(c) whether the harm that is done or threatened is physical or financial or is harm to a person or to his property.

(5) A person guilty of an offence under this section shall be liable—

(a) on conviction on indictment, to imprisonment for a term not exceeding five years or to a fine, or to both;

(b) on summary conviction, to imprisonment for a term not exceeding six months or to a fine not exceeding the statutory maximum, or to both.

(6) In this section "the relevant period", in relation to an act done, or threat made, with the knowledge or belief that a person has been a witness in any relevant proceedings, means the period that begins with the commencement of those proceedings and ends one year after they are finally concluded.

(7), (8) *****

41 Relevant proceedings

(1) A reference in section 39 or 40 to relevant proceedings is a reference to any proceedings in or before the Court of Appeal, the High Court, the Crown Court or any county court or magistrates' court which—

(a) are not proceedings for an offence; and

(b) were commenced after the coming into force of that section.

(2)–(5) *****

42 Police directions stopping the harassment etc of a person in his home

(1) Subject to the following provisions of this section, a constable who is at the scene may give a direction under this section to any person if—

(a) that person is present outside or in the vicinity of any premises that are used by any individual ("the resident") as his dwelling;

(b) that constable believes, on reasonable grounds, that that person is present there for the purpose (by his presence or otherwise) of representing to the resident or another individual (whether or not one who uses the premises as his dwelling), or of persuading the resident or such another individual—

(i)   that he should not do something that he is entitled or required to do; or

(ii) that he should do something that he is not under any obligation to do; and

(c) that constable also believes, on reasonable grounds, that the presence of that person (either alone or together with that of any other persons who are also present)—

(i)   amounts to, or is likely to result in, the harassment of the resident; or

(ii) is likely to cause alarm or distress to the resident.

(2) A direction under this section is a direction requiring the person to whom it is given to do all such things as the constable giving it may specify as the things he considers necessary to prevent one or both of the following—

(a) the harassment of the resident; or

(b) the causing of any alarm or distress to the resident.

(3) A direction under this section may be given orally; and where a constable is entitled to give a direction under this section to each of several persons outside, or in the vicinity of, any premises, he may give that direction to those persons by notifying them of his requirements either individually or all together.

[(4) The requirements that may be imposed by a direction under this section include—

(a) a requirement to leave the vicinity of the premises in question, and

(b) a requirement to leave that vicinity, and not to return to it within such period as the constable may specify, not being longer than 3 months;

and (in either case) the requirement to leave the vicinity may be to do so immediately or after a specified period of time.]

(5) A direction under this section may make exceptions to any requirement imposed by the direction, and may make any such exception subject to such conditions as the constable giving the direction thinks fit; and those conditions may include—

(a) conditions as to the distance from the premises in question at which, or otherwise as to the location where, persons who do not leave their vicinity must remain; and

(b) conditions as to the number or identity of the persons who are authorised by the exception to remain in the vicinity of those premises.

(6) The power of a constable to give a direction under this section shall not include–

(a) any power to give a direction at any time when there is a more senior-ranking police officer at the scene; or

(b) any power to direct a person to refrain from conduct that is lawful under section 220 of the Trade Union and Labour Relations (Consolidation) Act 1992 (c. 52) (right peacefully to picket a work place);

but it shall include power to vary or withdraw a direction previously given under this section.

(7) Any person who knowingly [fails to comply with a requirement in a direction given to him under this section (other than a requirement under subsection (4)(b))] shall be guilty of an offence and liable, on summary conviction, to imprisonment for a term not exceeding [51 weeks] or to a fine not exceeding level 4 on the standard scale, or to both.

[(7A) Any person to whom a constable has given a direction including a requirement under subsection (4)(b) commits an offence if he—

(a) returns to the vicinity of the premises in question within the period specified in the direction beginning with the date on which the direction is given; and

(b) does so for the purpose described in subsection (1)(b).

(7B) A person guilty of an offence under subsection (7A) shall be liable, on summary conviction, to imprisonment for a term not exceeding 51 weeks or to a fine not exceeding level 4 on the standard scale, or to both.]

(7C) *****

(8) . . .

(9) In this section "dwelling" has the same meaning as in Part 1 of the Public Order Act 1986 (c. 64).

42A–49 *****

PART 2   POWERS OF SEIZURE

Additional powers of seizure

50   Additional powers of seizure from premises

(1) Where—

(a) a person who is lawfully on any premises finds anything on those premises that he has reasonable grounds for believing may be or may contain something for which he is authorised to search on those premises,

    (b) a power of seizure to which this section applies or the power conferred by subsection (2) would entitle him, if he found it, to seize whatever it is that he has grounds for believing that thing to be or to contain, and

    (c) in all the circumstances, it is not reasonably practicable for it to be determined, on those premises—

        (i) whether what he has found is something that he is entitled to seize, or

        (ii) the extent to which what he has found contains something that he is entitled to seize,

that person's powers of seizure shall include power under this section to seize so much of what he has found as it is necessary to remove from the premises to enable that to be determined.

    (2) Where—

    (a) a person who is lawfully on any premises finds anything on those premises ("the seizable property") which he would be entitled to seize but for its being comprised in something else that he has (apart from this subsection) no power to seize,

    (b) the power under which that person would have power to seize the seizable property is a power to which this section applies, and

    (c) in all the circumstances it is not reasonably practicable for the seizable property to be separated, on those premises, from that in which it is comprised,

that person's powers of seizure shall include power under this section to seize both the seizable property and that from which it is not reasonably practicable to separate it.

    (3)–(6) *****

51 Additional powers of seizure from the person

    (1) Where—

    (a) a person carrying out a lawful search of any person finds something that he has reasonable grounds for believing may be or may contain something for which he is authorised to search,

    (b) a power of seizure to which this section applies or the power conferred by subsection (2) would entitle him, if he found it, to seize whatever it is that he has grounds for believing that thing to be or to contain, and

    (c) in all the circumstances it is not reasonably practicable for it to be determined, at the time and place of the search–

        (i) whether what he has found is something that he is entitled to seize, or

        (ii) the extent to which what he has found contains something that he is entitled to seize,

that person's powers of seizure shall include power under this section to seize so much of what he has found as it is necessary to remove from that place to enable that to be determined.

    (2)–(5) *****

52–58 *****

Remedies and safeguards

59 Application to the appropriate judicial authority

    (1) This section applies where anything has been seized in exercise, or purported exercise, of a relevant power of seizure.

    (2) Any person with a relevant interest in the seized property may apply to the appropriate judicial authority, on one or more of the grounds mentioned in subsection (3), for the return of the whole or a part of the seized property.

    (3) Those grounds are—

    (a) that there was no power to make the seizure;

  (b) that the seized property is or contains an item subject to legal privilege that is not comprised in property falling within section 54(2);

  (c) that the seized property is or contains any excluded material or special procedure material which—

  (i)   has been seized under a power to which section 55 applies;

  (ii) is not comprised in property falling within section 55(2) or (3); and

  (iii) is not property the retention of which is authorised by section 56;

  (d) that the seized property is or contains something seized under section 50 or 51 which does not fall within section 53(3);

and subsections (5) and (6) of section 55 shall apply for the purposes of paragraph (c) as they apply for the purposes of that section.

  (4) Subject to subsection (6), the appropriate judicial authority, on an application under subsection (2), shall—

  (a) if satisfied as to any of the matters mentioned in subsection (3), order the return of so much of the seized property as is property in relation to which the authority is so satisfied; and

  (b) to the extent that that authority is not so satisfied, dismiss the application.

  (5)–(7) *****

60–63 *****

64 Meaning of "appropriate judicial authority"

  (1) Subject to subsection (2), in this Part "appropriate judicial authority" means—

  (a) in relation to England and Wales and Northern Ireland, a judge of the Crown Court;

  (b) in relation to Scotland, a sheriff.

  (2), (3) *****

*****

International Criminal Court Act 2001

(2001, c. 17)

An Act to give effect to the Statute of the International Criminal Court; to provide for offences under the law of England and Wales and Northern Ireland corresponding to offences within the jurisdiction of that Court; and for connected purposes   [11 May 2001]

Territorial extent: The United Kingdom (but ss. 28 and 51 apply only to England and Wales)

PART 1   THE INTERNATIONAL CRIMINAL COURT

1 The ICC and the ICC Statute

  (1) In this Act—

  "the ICC" means the International Criminal Court established by the Statute of the International Criminal Court, done at Rome on 17th July 1998;

  "the ICC Statute" means that Statute; and

  "ICC crime" means a crime (other than the crime of aggression) over which the ICC has jurisdiction in accordance with the ICC Statute.

  (2) References in this Act to articles are, unless otherwise indicated, to articles of the ICC Statute.

  (3) Schedule 1 to this Act contains supplementary provisions relating to the ICC.

PART 2   ARREST AND DELIVERY OF PERSONS

Proceedings on request

2   Request for arrest and surrender

(1) Where the Secretary of State receives a request from the ICC for the arrest and surrender of a person alleged to have committed an ICC crime, or to have been convicted by the ICC, he shall transmit the request and the documents accompanying it to an appropriate judicial officer.

(2) If it appears to the Secretary of State that the request should be considered by an appropriate judicial officer in Scotland, he shall transmit the request and the documents accompanying it to the Scottish Ministers who shall transmit them to an appropriate judicial officer.

(3) If the request is accompanied by a warrant of arrest and the appropriate judicial officer is satisfied that the warrant appears to have been issued by the ICC, he shall endorse the warrant for execution in the United Kingdom.

(4) If in the case of a person convicted by the ICC the request is not accompanied by a warrant of arrest, but is accompanied by—

(a) a copy of the judgment of conviction,
(b) information to demonstrate that the person sought is the one referred to in the judgment of conviction, and
(c) where the person sought has been sentenced, a copy of the sentence imposed and a statement of any time already served and the time remaining to be served,

the officer shall issue a warrant for the arrest of the person to whom the request relates.

(5) In this Part a warrant endorsed or issued under this section is referred to as a "section 2 warrant".

3   Request for provisional arrest

(1) This section applies where the Secretary of State receives from the ICC a request for the provisional arrest of a person alleged to have committed an ICC crime or to have been convicted by the ICC.

(2) If it appears to the Secretary of State that application for a warrant should be made in England and Wales—

(a) he shall transmit the request to a constable and direct the constable to apply for a warrant for the arrest of that person, and
(b) on an application by a constable stating on oath that he has reason to believe—
    (i) that a request has been made on grounds of urgency by the ICC for the arrest of a person, and
    (ii) that the person is in, or on his way to, the United Kingdom, an appropriate judicial officer shall issue a warrant for the arrest of that person.

(3), (4) *****

(5) In this Part a warrant issued under this section is referred to as a "provisional warrant".

4   Dealing with person arrested under provisional warrant

(1) A person arrested under a provisional warrant shall be brought before a competent court as soon as is practicable.

(2) If there is produced to the court a section 2 warrant in respect of that person, the court shall proceed as if he had been arrested under that warrant.

(3) If no such warrant is produced, the court shall remand him pending the production of such a warrant.

(4)–(7) *****

5   Proceedings for delivery order

(1) A person arrested under a section 2 warrant shall be brought before a competent court as soon as is practicable.

(2) If the competent court is satisfied—
    (a) that the warrant—
        (i) is a warrant of the ICC and has been duly endorsed under section 2(3), or
        (ii) has been duly issued under section 2(4), and
    (b) that the person brought before the court is the person named or described in the warrant,
it shall make a delivery order.

(3) A "delivery order" is an order that the person be delivered up—
    (a) into the custody of the ICC, or
    (b) if the ICC so directs in the case of a person convicted by the ICC, into the custody of the state of enforcement,
in accordance with arrangements made by the Secretary of State.

(4) In the case of a person alleged to have committed an ICC crime, the competent court may adjourn the proceedings pending the outcome of any challenge before the ICC to the admissibility of the case or to the jurisdiction of the ICC.

(5) In deciding whether to make a delivery order the court is not concerned to enquire—
    (a) whether any warrant issued by the ICC was duly issued, or
    (b) in the case of a person alleged to have committed an ICC crime, whether there is evidence to justify his trial for the offence he is alleged to have committed.

(6)–(9) *****

6–22 *****

Supplementary provisions

23   Provisions as to state or diplomatic immunity

(1) Any state or diplomatic immunity attaching to a person by reason of a connection with a state party to the ICC Statute does not prevent proceedings under this Part in relation to that person.

(2) Where—
    (a) state or diplomatic immunity attaches to a person by reason of a connection with a state other than a state party to the ICC Statute, and
    (b) waiver of that immunity is obtained by the ICC in relation to a request for that person's surrender,
the waiver shall be treated as extending to proceedings under this Part in connection with that request.

(3) A certificate by the Secretary of State—
    (a) that a state is or is not a party to the ICC Statute, or
    (b) that there has been such a waiver as is mentioned in subsection (2),
is conclusive evidence of that fact for the purposes of this Part.

(4) The Secretary of State may in any particular case, after consultation with the ICC and the state concerned, direct that proceedings (or further proceedings) under this Part which, but for subsection (1) or (2), would be prevented by state or diplomatic immunity attaching to a person shall not be taken against that person.

(5), (6) *****

24–27 *****

28   Questioning

(1) This section applies where the Secretary of State receives a request from the ICC for assistance in questioning a person being investigated or prosecuted.

(2) The person concerned shall not be questioned in pursuance of the request unless—
    (a) he has been informed of his rights under article 55, and
    (b) he consents to be interviewed.

(3) The provisions of article 55 are set out in Schedule 3 to this Act.

(4) Consent for the purposes of subsection (2)(b) may be given—

(a) by the person himself, or

(b) in circumstances in which it is inappropriate for the person to act for himself, by reason of his physical or mental condition or his youth, by an appropriate person acting on his behalf.

(5) Such consent may be given orally or in writing, but if given orally it shall be recorded in writing as soon as is reasonably practicable.

29–50   ***

51   Genocide, crimes against humanity and war crimes

(1) It is an offence against the law of England and Wales for a person to commit genocide, a crime against humanity or a war crime.

(2) This section applies to acts committed—

(a) in England or Wales, or

(b) outside the United Kingdom by a United Kingdom national, a United Kingdom resident or a person subject to UK service jurisdiction.

*****

SCHEDULE 3   RIGHTS OF PERSONS DURING INVESTIGATION: ARTICLE 55

Article 55
Rights of persons during an investigation

In respect of an investigation under this Statute, a person:

(a) Shall not be compelled to incriminate himself or herself or to confess guilt;

(b) Shall not be subjected to any form of coercion, duress or threat, to torture or to any other form of cruel, inhuman or degrading treatment or punishment;

(c) Shall, if questioned in a language other than a language the person fully understands and speaks, have, free of any cost, the assistance of a competent interpreter and such translations as are necessary to meet the requirements of fairness; and

(d) Shall not be subjected to arbitrary arrest or detention, and shall not be deprived of his or her liberty except on such grounds and in accordance with such procedures as are established in this Statute.

Where there are grounds to believe that a person has committed a crime within the jurisdiction of the Court and that person is about to be questioned either by the Prosecutor, or by national authorities pursuant to a request made under Part 9, that person shall also have the following rights of which he or she shall be informed prior to being questioned:

(a) To be informed, prior to being questioned, that there are grounds to believe that he or she has committed a crime within the jurisdiction of the Court;

(b) To remain silent, without such silence being a consideration in the determination of guilt or innocence;

(c) To have legal assistance of the person's choosing, or, if the person does not have legal assistance, to have legal assistance assigned to him or her, in any case where the interests of justice so require, and without payment by the person in any such case if the person does not have sufficient means to pay for it; and

(d) To be questioned in the presence of counsel unless the person has voluntarily waived his or her right to counsel.

*****

European Communities (Amendment) Act 2002
(2002, c. 3)

An Act to make provision consequential on the Treaty signed at Nice on 26th February 2001 amending the Treaty on European Union, the Treaties establishing the European Communities and certain related Acts   [26 February 2002]

Territorial extent: United Kingdom

Note: This Act amends s. 1 of the European Communities Act 1972 by adding to the list of Treaties Articles 2 to 10 of the Treaty of Nice, and the other provisions of the Treaty so far as relating to those Articles, and the Protocols adopted on the occasion of the signing of the Treaty. That Treaty is also declared by s. 3 of the Act to be approved for the purpose of s. 6 of the European Parliamentary Elections Act 1978.

European Parliamentary Elections Act 2002
(2002, c. 24)

An Act to consolidate the European Parliamentary Elections Acts 1978, 1993 and 1999
[24 July 2002]

Territorial extent: United Kingdom, and Gibraltar (by virtue of the European Parliament (Representation) Act 2003, s. 19)

Introductory

[1   Number of MEPs and electoral regions
    (1) There shall be [78] members of the European Parliament ("MEPs") elected for the United Kingdom.
    (2) For the purposes of electing those MEPs—
        (a)   England is divided into the nine electoral regions specified in Schedule 1; and
        (b)   Scotland, Wales and Northern Ireland are each single electoral regions.
    [(3) The number of MEPs to be elected for each electoral region is as follows—

East Midlands	6
Eastern	7
London	9
North East	3
North West	9
South East	10
South West	7
West Midlands	7
Yorkshire and the Humber	6
Scotland	7
Wales	4
Northern Ireland	3.]]

1A   *****

General elections

2   Voting system in Great Britain [and Gibraltar]

(1) The system of election of MEPs in an electoral region [other than Northern Ireland] is to be a regional list system.

(2) The Secretary of State must by regulations—

    (a) make provision for the nomination of registered parties in relation to an election in such a region, and

    (b) require a nomination under paragraph (a) to be accompanied by a list of candidates numbering no more than the MEPs to be elected for the region.

(3) The system of election must comply with the following conditions.

(4) A vote may be cast for a registered party or an individual candidate named on the ballot paper.

(5) The first seat is to be allocated to the party or individual candidate with the greatest number of votes.

(6) The second and subsequent seats are to be allocated in the same way, except that the number of votes given to a party to which one or more seats have already been allocated are to be divided by the number of seats allocated plus one.

(7) In allocating the second or any subsequent seat there are to be disregarded any votes given to—

    (a) a party to which there has already been allocated a number of seats equal to the number of names on the party's list of candidates, and

    (b) an individual candidate to whom a seat has already been allocated.

(8) Seats allocated to a party are to be filled by the persons named on the party's list of candidates in the order in which they appear on that list.

(9) For the purposes of subsection (6) fractions are to be taken into account.

(10) In this section "registered party" means a party registered under Part 2 of the Political Parties, Elections and Referendums Act 2000.

3   Voting system in Northern Ireland

The system of election of MEPs in Northern Ireland is to be a single transferable vote system under which—

    (a) a vote is capable of being given so as to indicate the voter's order of preference for the candidates, and

    (b) a vote is capable of being transferred to the next choice—

        (i)   when the vote is not required to give a prior choice the necessary quota of votes, or

        (ii) when, owing to the deficiency in the number of votes given for a prior choice, that choice is eliminated from the list of candidates.

4–7   *****

Entitlement to vote

8   Persons entitled to vote

(1) A person is entitled to vote as an elector at an election to the European Parliament in an electoral region if he is within any of subsections (2) to (5).

(2) A person is within this subsection if on the day of the poll he would be entitled to vote as an elector at a parliamentary election in a parliamentary constituency wholly or partly comprised in the electoral region, and—

    (a) the address in respect of which he is registered in the relevant register of parliamentary electors is within the electoral region, or

    (b) his registration in the relevant register of parliamentary electors results from an overseas elector's declaration which specifies an address within the electoral region.

(3) A person is within this subsection if—

    (a) he is a peer who on the day of the poll would be entitled to vote at a local government election in an electoral area wholly or partly comprised in the electoral region, and

    (b) the address in respect of which he is registered in the relevant register of local government electors is within the electoral region.

(4) A person is within this subsection if he is entitled to vote in the electoral region by virtue of section 3 of the Representation of the People Act 1985 (peers resident outside the United Kingdom).

(5) A person is within this subsection if he is entitled to vote in the electoral region by virtue of the European Parliamentary Elections (Franchise of Relevant Citizens of the Union) Regulations 2001 (citizens of the European Union other than Commonwealth and Republic of Ireland citizens).

    (6)–(8) *****

9 *****

Entitlement to be MEP

10   Disqualification

(1) A person is disqualified for the office of MEP if—

    (a) he is disqualified for membership of the House of Commons, ...

(2) But a person is not disqualified for the office of MEP under subsection (1)(a) merely because—

    (a) he is a peer,

    (b) he is a Lord Spiritual,

    (c) he holds an office mentioned in section 4 of the House of Commons Disqualification Act 1975 (stewardship of Chiltern Hundreds etc), or

    (d) he holds any of the offices described in Part 2 or 3 of Schedule 1 to that Act which are designated by order by the Secretary of State for the purposes of this section.

(3) A citizen of the European Union who is resident in the United Kingdom [or Gibraltar] is not disqualified for the office of MEP under subsection (1)(a) merely because he is disqualified for membership of the House of Commons under section 3 of the Act of Settlement (disqualification of persons, other than Commonwealth and Republic of Ireland citizens, who are born outside Great Britain and Ireland and the dominions).

    (4)–(8) *****

11 *****

European Parliament

12   Ratification of treaties

(1) No treaty which provides for any increase in the powers of the European Parliament is to be ratified by the United Kingdom unless it has been approved by an Act of Parliament.

(2) In this section "treaty" includes—

    (a) any international agreement, and

    (b) any protocol or annex to a treaty or international agreement.

*****

Police Reform Act 2002
(2002, c. 30)

An Act to make new provision about the supervision, administration, functions and conduct of police forces, police officers, and other persons serving with, or carrying out functions in relation to, the police; to amend police powers and provide for the exercise of police powers by persons who are not police officers; to amend the law relating to anti-social behaviour orders; to amend the law relating to sex offender orders; and for connected purposes   [24 July 2002]

Territorial extent: England and Wales (material reproduced here)

1–7 *****

8 . . .

The Independent Police Complaints Commission

9   The Independent Police Complaints Commission
(1) There shall be a body corporate to be known as the Independent Police Complaints Commission (in this Part referred to as "the Commission").
(2) The Commission shall consist of—
 (a) a chairman appointed by Her Majesty; and
 (b) not less than ten other members appointed by the Secretary of State.
(3) A person shall not be appointed as the chairman of the Commission, or as another member of the Commission, if—
 (a) he holds or has held office as a constable in any part of the United Kingdom;
 (b) he is or has been under the direction and control of a chief officer or of any person holding an equivalent office in Scotland or Northern Ireland;
 (c)–(f) *****
(4)–(7) *****

10   General functions of the Commission
(1) The functions of the Commission shall be—
 (a) to secure the maintenance by the Commission itself, and by police authorities and chief officers, of suitable arrangements with respect to the matters mentioned in subsection (2);
 (b) to keep under review all arrangements maintained with respect to those matters;
 (c) to secure that arrangements maintained with respect to those matters comply with the requirements of the following provisions of this Part, are efficient and effective and contain and manifest an appropriate degree of independence;
 (d) to secure that public confidence is established and maintained in the existence of suitable arrangements with respect to those matters and with the operation of the arrangements that are in fact maintained with respect to those matters;
 (e) to make such recommendations, and to give such advice, for the modification of the arrangements maintained with respect to those matters, and also of police practice in relation to other matters, as appear, from the carrying out by the Commission of its other functions, to be necessary or desirable; . . .
 (f) to such extent as it may be required to do so by regulations made by the Secretary of State, to carry out functions in relation to . . . bodies of constables maintained otherwise than by police authorities which broadly correspond to those conferred on the Commission in relation to police forces by the preceding paragraphs of this subsection[; and
 (g) to carry out functions in relation to the Serious Organised Crime Agency which

correspond to those conferred on the Commission in relation to police forces by paragraph (e) of this subsection.]

(2) Those matters are—

(a) the handling of complaints made about the conduct of persons serving with the police;

(b) the recording of matters from which it appears that there may have been conduct by such persons which constitutes or involves the commission of a criminal offence or behaviour justifying disciplinary proceedings;

[(ba) the recording of matters from which it appears that a person has died or suffered serious injury during, or following, contact with a person serving with the police;]

(c) the manner in which any such complaints or any such matters as are mentioned in paragraph (b) [or (ba)] are investigated or otherwise handled and dealt with.

(3)–(7) *****

(8) Nothing in this Part shall confer any function on the Commission in relation to so much of any complaint or conduct matter as relates to the direction and control of a police force by—

(a) the chief officer of police of that force; or

(b) a person for the time being carrying out the functions of the chief officer of police of that force.

11   Reports to the Secretary of State

(1) As soon as practicable after the end of each of its financial years, the Commission shall make a report to the Secretary of State on the carrying out of its functions during that year.

(2) The Commission shall also make such reports to the Secretary of State about matters relating generally to the carrying out of its functions as he may, from time to time, require.

(3) The Commission may, from time to time, make such other reports to the Secretary of State as it considers appropriate for drawing his attention to matters which—

(a) have come to the Commission's notice; and

(b) are matters that it considers should be drawn to his attention by reason of their gravity or of other exceptional circumstances.

(4)–(11) *****

Application of Part 2

12   Complaints, matters and persons to which Part 2 applies

(1) In this Part references to a complaint are references (subject to the following provisions of this section) to any complaint about the conduct of a person serving with the police which is made (whether in writing or otherwise) by—

(a) a member of the public who claims to be the person in relation to whom the conduct took place;

(b) a member of the public not falling within paragraph (a) who claims to have been adversely affected by the conduct;

(c) a member of the public who claims to have witnessed the conduct;

(d) a person acting on behalf of a person falling within any of paragraphs (a) to (c).

(2) In this Part "conduct matter" means (subject to the following provisions of this section, paragraph 2(4) of Schedule 3 and any regulations made by virtue of section 23(2)(d)) any matter which is not and has not been the subject of a complaint but in the case of which there is an indication (whether from the circumstances or otherwise) that a person serving with the police may have—

(a) committed a criminal offence; or

(b) behaved in a manner which would justify the bringing of disciplinary proceedings.

[(2A) In this Part "death or serious injury matter" (or "DSI matter" for short) means any circumstances (other than those which are or have been the subject of a complaint or which amount to a conduct matter)—

(a) in or in consequence of which a person has died or has sustained serious injury; and

(b) in relation to which the requirements of either subsection (2B) or subsection (2C) are satisfied.

(2B) The requirements of this subsection are that at the time of the death or serious injury the person—

(a) had been arrested by a person serving with the police and had not been released from that arrest; or

(b) was otherwise detained in the custody of a person serving with the police.

(2C) The requirements of this subsection are that—

(a) at or before the time of the death or serious injury the person had contact (of whatever kind, and whether direct or indirect) with a person serving with the police who was acting in the execution of his duties; and

(b) there is an indication that the contact may have caused (whether directly or indirectly) or contributed to the death or serious injury.

(2D) In subsection (2A) the reference to a person includes a person serving with the police, but in relation to such a person "contact" in subsection (2C) does not include contact that he has whilst acting in the execution of his duties.]

(3)–(7) *****

13–14 *****

Co-operation, assistance and information

15   General duties of police authorities, chief officers and inspectors

(1)–(3) *****

(4) It shall be the duty of—

(a) every police authority maintaining a police force,

(b) the chief officer of police of every police force, [and

(c) the Serious Organised Crime Agency,]

to provide the Commission and every member of the Commission's staff with all such assistance as the Commission or that member of staff may reasonably require for the purposes of, or in connection with, the carrying out of any investigation by the Commission under this Part.

(5) It shall be the duty of—

(a) every police authority maintaining a police force,

(b) the chief officer of every police force, [and

(c) the Serious Organised Crime Agency,]

to ensure that a person appointed under paragraph 16, 17 or 18 of Schedule 3 to carry out an investigation is given all such assistance and co-operation in the carrying out of that investigation as that person may reasonably require.

(6), (7) *****

16   *****

17   Provision of information to the Commission

(1) It shall be the duty of—

(a) every police authority, and

(b) every chief officer,

at such times, in such circumstances and in accordance with such other requirements as may be set out in regulations made by the Secretary of State, to provide the Commission with all such information and documents as may be specified or described in regulations so made.

(2) It shall also be the duty of every police authority and of every chief officer—

- (a) to provide the Commission with all such other information and documents specified or described in a notification given by the Commission to that authority or chief officer, and
- (b) to produce or deliver up to the Commission all such evidence and other things so specified or described,

as appear to the Commission to be required by it for the purposes of the carrying out of any of its functions.

(3) Anything falling to be provided, produced or delivered up by any person in pursuance of a requirement imposed under subsection (2) must be provided, produced or delivered up in such form, in such manner and within such period as may be specified in—

- (a) the notification imposing the requirement; or
- (b) in any subsequent notification given by the Commission to that person for the purposes of this subsection.

(4), (5) *****

18 Inspections of police premises on behalf of the Commission

(1) Where—

- (a) the Commission requires—
    - (i) a police authority maintaining any police force, or
    - (ii) the chief officer of police of any such force,

    to allow a person nominated for the purpose by the Commission to have access to any premises occupied for the purposes of that force and to documents and other things on those premises, and
- (b) the requirement is imposed for any of the purposes mentioned in subsection (2),

it shall be the duty of the authority or, as the case may be, of the chief officer to secure that the required access is allowed to the nominated person.

(2) Those purposes are—

- (a) the purposes of any examination by the Commission of the efficiency and effectiveness of the arrangements made by the force in question for handling complaints or dealing with recordable conduct matters [or DSI matters];
- (b) the purposes of any investigation by the Commission under this Part or of any investigation carried out under its supervision or management.

(3) A requirement imposed under this section for the purposes mentioned in subsection (2)(a) must be notified to the authority or chief officer at least 48 hours before the time at which access is required.

(4) Where—

- (a) a requirement imposed under this section for the purposes mentioned in subsection (2)(a) requires access to any premises, document or thing to be allowed to any person, but
- (b) there are reasonable grounds for not allowing that person to have the required access at the time at which he seeks to have it,

the obligation to secure that the required access is allowed shall have effect as an obligation to secure that the access is allowed to that person at the earliest practicable time after there cease to be any such grounds as that person may specify.

(5) *****

19 Use of investigatory powers by or on behalf of the Commission

(1) The Secretary of State may by order make such provision as he thinks appropriate for the purpose of authorising—

- (a) the use of directed and intrusive surveillance, and
- (b) the conduct and use of covert human intelligence sources,

for the purposes of, or for purposes connected with, the carrying out of the Commission's functions.

(2)–(4) *****

20–21   *****

Guidance and regulations

22   Power of the Commission to issue guidance

(1) The Commission may issue guidance—

    (a) to police authorities,

    (b) to chief officers, and

    (c) to persons who are serving with the police otherwise than as chief officers,

concerning the exercise or performance, by the persons to whom the guidance is issued, of any of the powers or duties specified in subsection (2).

(2) Those powers and duties are—

    (a) those that are conferred or imposed by or under this Part; and

    (b) those that are otherwise conferred or imposed but relate to—

        (i)   the handling of complaints;

        (ii) the means by which recordable conduct matters [or DSI matters] are dealt with; or

        (iii) the detection or deterrence of misconduct by persons serving with the police.

(3) Before issuing any guidance under this section, the Commission shall consult with—

    (a) persons whom it considers to represent the interests of police authorities;

    (b) persons whom it considers to represent the interests of chief officers of police; and

    (c) such other persons as it thinks fit.

(4) The approval of the Secretary of State shall be required for the issue by the Commission of any guidance under this section.

(5) *****

(6) Nothing in this section shall authorise the issuing of any guidance about a particular case.

(7) It shall be the duty of every person to whom any guidance under this section is issued to have regard to that guidance in exercising or performing the powers and duties to which the guidance relates.

(8) A failure by a person to whom guidance under this section is issued to have regard to the guidance shall be admissible in evidence in any disciplinary proceedings or on any appeal from a decision taken in any such proceedings.

23–49 *****

Power to require name and address

50   Persons acting in an anti-social manner

(1) If a constable in uniform has reason to believe that a person has been acting, or is acting, in an anti-social manner (within the meaning of section 1 of the Crime and Disorder Act 1998 (anti-social behaviour orders)), he may require that person to give his name and address to the constable.

(2) Any person who—

    (a) fails to give his name and address when required to do so under subsection (1), or

    (b) gives a false or inaccurate name or address in response to a requirement under that subsection,

is guilty of an offence and shall be liable, on summary conviction, to a fine not exceeding level 3 on the standard scale.
*****

Proceeds of Crime Act 2002
(2002, c. 29)

An Act to establish the Assets Recovery Agency and make provision about the appointment of its Director and his functions (including Revenue functions), to provide for confiscation orders in relation to persons who benefit from criminal conduct and for restraint orders to prohibit dealing with property, to allow the recovery of property which is or represents property obtained through unlawful conduct or which is intended to be used in unlawful conduct, to make provision about money laundering, to make provision about investigations relating to benefit from criminal conduct or to property which is or represents property obtained through unlawful conduct or to money laundering, to make provision to give effect to overseas requests and orders made where property is found or believed to be obtained through criminal conduct, and for connected purposes
[24 July 2002]

Territorial extent: United Kingdom (ss. 1–4); England and Wales (remainder of sections printed). Part 3 of the Act makes equivalent provisions for Scotland and Part 4 for Northern Ireland; these are not reproduced for reasons of space

PART 1   ASSETS RECOVERY AGENCY

1   The Agency and its Director
(1) There shall be an Assets Recovery Agency (referred to in this Act as the Agency).

(2) The Secretary of State must appoint a Director of the Agency (referred to in this Act as the Director).

(3) The Director is a corporation sole.

(4) The Director may—
   (a) appoint such persons as members of staff of the Agency, and
   (b) make such arrangements for the provision of services,
as he considers appropriate for or in connection with the exercise of his functions.

(5)–(7) *****

2   Director's functions: general
(1) The Director must exercise his functions in the way which he considers is best calculated to contribute to the reduction of crime.

(2) In exercising his functions as required by subsection (1) the Director must—
   (a) act efficiently and effectively;
   (b) have regard to his current annual plan (as approved by the Secretary of State in accordance with Schedule 1).

(3) The Director may do anything (including the carrying out of investigations) which he considers is—
   (a) appropriate for facilitating, or
   (b) incidental or conducive to,
the exercise of his functions.

(4) But subsection (3) does not allow the Director to borrow money.

(5) In considering under subsection (1) the way which is best calculated to contribute to the reduction of crime the Director must have regard to any guidance given to him by the Secretary of State.

(6) The guidance must indicate that the reduction of crime is in general best secured by means of criminal investigations and criminal proceedings.

3 *****

4 Co-operation

(1) Persons who have functions relating to the investigation or prosecution of offences must co-operate with the Director in the exercise of his functions.

(2) The Director must co-operate with those persons in the exercise of functions they have under this Act.

5 Advice and assistance

The Director must give the Secretary of State advice and assistance which he reasonably requires and which—

(a) relate to matters connected with the operation of this Act, and

(b) are designed to help the Secretary of State to exercise his functions so as to reduce crime.

PART 2   CONFISCATION: ENGLAND AND WALES

Confiscation orders

6 Making of order

(1) The Crown Court must proceed under this section if the following two conditions are satisfied.

(2) The first condition is that a defendant falls within any of the following paragraphs—

(a) he is convicted of an offence or offences in proceedings before the Crown Court;

(b) he is committed to the Crown Court for sentence in respect of an offence or offences under [section 3, 3A, 3B, 3C, 4, 4A or 6] of the Sentencing Act;

(c) he is committed to the Crown Court in respect of an offence or offences under section 70 below (committal with a view to a confiscation order being considered).

(3) The second condition is that—

(a) the prosecutor or the Director asks the court to proceed under this section, or

(b) the court believes it is appropriate for it to do so.

(4) The court must proceed as follows—

(a) it must decide whether the defendant has a criminal lifestyle;

(b) if it decides that he has a criminal lifestyle it must decide whether he has benefited from his general criminal conduct;

(c) if it decides that he does not have a criminal lifestyle it must decide whether he has benefited from his particular criminal conduct.

(5) If the court decides under subsection (4)(b) or (c) that the defendant has benefited from the conduct referred to it must—

(a) decide the recoverable amount, and

(b) make an order (a confiscation order) requiring him to pay that amount.

(6) But the court must treat the duty in subsection (5) as a power if it believes that any victim of the conduct has at any time started or intends to start proceedings against the defendant in respect of loss, injury or damage sustained in connection with the conduct.

(7) The court must decide any question arising under subsection (4) or (5) on a balance of probabilities.

(8) The first condition is not satisfied if the defendant absconds (but section 27 may apply).

(9) References in this Part to the offence (or offences) concerned are to the offence (or offences) mentioned in subsection (2).

7   Recoverable amount

(1) The recoverable amount for the purposes of section 6 is an amount equal to the defendant's benefit from the conduct concerned.

(2) But if the defendant shows that the available amount is less than that benefit the recoverable amount is—

(a) the available amount, or

(b) a nominal amount, if the available amount is nil.

(3) But if section 6(6) applies the recoverable amount is such amount as—

(a) the court believes is just, but

(b) does not exceed the amount found under subsection (1) or (2) (as the case may be).

(4), (5) *****

8   *****

9   Available amount

(1) For the purposes of deciding the recoverable amount, the available amount is the aggregate of—

(a) the total of the values (at the time the confiscation order is made) of all the free property then held by the defendant minus the total amount payable in pursuance of obligations which then have priority, and

(b) the total of the values (at that time) of all tainted gifts.

(2) An obligation has priority if it is an obligation of the defendant—

(a) to pay an amount due in respect of a fine or other order of a court which was imposed or made on conviction of an offence and at any time before the time the confiscation order is made, or

(b) to pay a sum which would be included among the preferential debts if the defendant's bankruptcy had commenced on the date of the confiscation order or his winding up had been ordered on that date.

(3) "Preferential debts" has the meaning given by section 386 of the Insolvency Act 1986.

10   Assumptions to be made in case of criminal lifestyle

(1) If the court decides under section 6 that the defendant has a criminal lifestyle it must make the following four assumptions for the purpose of—

(a) deciding whether he has benefited from his general criminal conduct, and

(b) deciding his benefit from the conduct.

(2) The first assumption is that any property transferred to the defendant at any time after the relevant day was obtained by him—

(a) as a result of his general criminal conduct, and

(b) at the earliest time he appears to have held it.

(3) The second assumption is that any property held by the defendant at any time after the date of conviction was obtained by him—

(a) as a result of his general criminal conduct, and

(b) at the earliest time he appears to have held it.

(4) The third assumption is that any expenditure incurred by the defendant at any time after the relevant day was met from property obtained by him as a result of his general criminal conduct.

(5) The fourth assumption is that, for the purpose of valuing any property obtained (or assumed to have been obtained) by the defendant, he obtained it free of any other interests in it.

(6) But the court must not make a required assumption in relation to particular property or expenditure if—

(a) the assumption is shown to be incorrect, or

(b) there would be a serious risk of injustice if the assumption were made.

(7) If the court does not make one or more of the required assumptions it must state its reasons.

(8) The relevant day is the first day of the period of six years ending with—

    (a) the day when proceedings for the offence concerned were started against the defendant, or

    (b) if there are two or more offences and proceedings for them were started on different days, the earliest of those days.

(9), (10) *****

11–74   *****

Interpretation

75   Criminal lifestyle

(1) A defendant has a criminal lifestyle if (and only if) the following condition is satisfied.

(2) The condition is that the offence (or any of the offences) concerned satisfies any of these tests—

    (a) it is specified in Schedule 2;

    (b) it constitutes conduct forming part of a course of criminal activity;

    (c) it is an offence committed over a period of at least six months and the defendant has benefited from the conduct which constitutes the offence.

(3) Conduct forms part of a course of criminal activity if the defendant has benefited from the conduct and—

    (a) in the proceedings in which he was convicted he was convicted of three or more other offences, each of three or more of them constituting conduct from which he has benefited, or

    (b) in the period of six years ending with the day when those proceedings were started (or, if there is more than one such day, the earliest day) he was convicted on at least two separate occasions of an offence constituting conduct from which he has benefited.

(4) But an offence does not satisfy the test in subsection (2)(b) or (c) unless the defendant obtains relevant benefit of not less than £5000.

(5) Relevant benefit for the purposes of subsection (2)(b) is—

    (a) benefit from conduct which constitutes the offence;

    (b) benefit from any other conduct which forms part of the course of criminal activity and which constitutes an offence of which the defendant has been convicted;

    (c) benefit from conduct which constitutes an offence which has been or will be taken into consideration by the court in sentencing the defendant for an offence mentioned in paragraph (a) or (b).

(6) Relevant benefit for the purposes of subsection (2)(c) is—

    (a) benefit from conduct which constitutes the offence;

    (b) benefit from conduct which constitutes an offence which has been or will be taken into consideration by the court in sentencing the defendant for the offence mentioned in paragraph (a).

(7) The Secretary of State may by order amend Schedule 2.

(8) The Secretary of State may by order vary the amount for the time being specified in subsection (4).

76   Conduct and benefit

(1) Criminal conduct is conduct which—

    (a) constitutes an offence in England and Wales, or

    (b) would constitute such an offence if it occurred in England and Wales.

(2) General criminal conduct of the defendant is all his criminal conduct, and it is immaterial—

(a) whether conduct occurred before or after the passing of this Act;

(b) whether property constituting a benefit from conduct was obtained before or after the passing of this Act.

(3) Particular criminal conduct of the defendant is all his criminal conduct which falls within the following paragraphs—

(a) conduct which constitutes the offence or offences concerned;

(b) conduct which constitutes offences of which he was convicted in the same proceedings as those in which he was convicted of the offence or offences concerned;

(c) conduct which constitutes offences which the court will be taking into consideration in deciding his sentence for the offence or offences concerned.

(4)–(7) *****

77   Tainted gifts

(1) Subsections (2) and (3) apply if—

(a) no court has made a decision as to whether the defendant has a criminal lifestyle, or

(b) a court has decided that the defendant has a criminal lifestyle.

(2) A gift is tainted if it was made by the defendant at any time after the relevant day.

(3) A gift is also tainted if it was made by the defendant at any time and was of property—

(a) which was obtained by the defendant as a result of or in connection with his general criminal conduct, or

(b) which (in whole or part and whether directly or indirectly) represented in the defendant's hands property obtained by him as a result of or in connection with his general criminal conduct.

(4)–(9) *****

78–83   *****

84   Property: general provisions

(1) Property is all property wherever situated and includes—

(a) money;

(b) all forms of real or personal property;

(c) things in action and other intangible or incorporeal property.

(2) The following rules apply in relation to property—

(a) property is held by a person if he holds an interest in it;

(b) property is obtained by a person if he obtains an interest in it;

(c) property is transferred by one person to another if the first one transfers or grants an interest in it to the second;

(d) references to property held by a person include references to property vested in his trustee in bankruptcy, permanent or interim trustee (within the meaning of the Bankruptcy (Scotland) Act 1985) or liquidator;

(e) references to an interest held by a person beneficially in property include references to an interest which would be held by him beneficially if the property were not so vested;

(f) references to an interest, in relation to land in England and Wales or Northern Ireland, are to any legal estate or equitable interest or power;

(g) references to an interest, in relation to land in Scotland, are to any estate, interest, servitude or other heritable right in or over land, including a heritable security;

(h) references to an interest, in relation to property other than land, include references to a right (including a right to possession).

85–363   *****

364 Meaning of customer information

(1) "Customer information", in relation to a person and a financial institution, is information whether the person holds, or has held, an account or accounts at the financial institution (whether solely or jointly with another) and (if so) information as to—

    (a) the matters specified in subsection (2) if the person is an individual;

    (b) the matters specified in subsection (3) if the person is a company or limited liability partnership or a similar body incorporated or otherwise established outside the United Kingdom.

(2) The matters referred to in subsection (1)(a) are—

    (a) the account number or numbers;

    (b) the person's full name;

    (c) his date of birth;

    (d) his most recent address and any previous addresses;

    (e) the date or dates on which he began to hold the account or accounts and, if he has ceased to hold the account or any of the accounts, the date or dates on which he did so;

    (f) such evidence of his identity as was obtained by the financial institution under or for the purposes of any legislation relating to money laundering;

    (g) the full name, date of birth and most recent address, and any previous addresses, of any person who holds, or has held, an account at the financial institution jointly with him;

    (h) the account number or numbers of any other account or accounts held at the financial institution to which he is a signatory and details of the person holding the other account or accounts.

(3)–(5) *****

365–462   *****

Schedule 1   *****

Section 75
SCHEDULE 2
LIFESTYLE OFFENCES: ENGLAND AND WALES

Drug trafficking

1 (1) An offence under any of the following provisions of the Misuse of Drugs Act 1971 (c. 38)—

    (a) section 4(2) or (3) (unlawful production or supply of controlled drugs);

    (b) section 5(3) (possession of controlled drug with intent to supply);

    (c) section 8 (permitting certain activities relating to controlled drugs);

    (d) section 20 (assisting in or inducing the commission outside the UK of an offence punishable under a corresponding law).

(2) An offence under any of the following provisions of the Customs and Excise Management Act 1979 (c. 2) if it is committed in connection with a prohibition or restriction on importation or exportation which has effect by virtue of section 3 of the Misuse of Drugs Act 1971—

    (a) section 50(2) or (3) (improper importation of goods);

    (b) section 68(2) (exploration of prohibited or restricted goods);

    (c) section 170 (fraudulent evasion).

(3) An offence under either of the following provisions of the Criminal Justice (International Co-operation) Act 1990 (c. 5)—

  (a) section 12 (manufacture or supply of a substance for the time being specified in Schedule 2 to that Act);
  (b) section 19 (using a ship for illicit traffic in controlled drugs).

Money laundering

2   An offence under either of the following provisions of this Act—
  (a) section 327 (concealing etc criminal property);
  (b) section 328 (assisting another to retain criminal property).

Directing terrorism

3   An offence under section 56 of the Terrorism Act 2000 (c. 11) (directing the activities of a terrorist organisation).

People trafficking

[4(1)   An offence under section 25(1), 25A or 25B of the Immigration Act 1971 (c. 77) (assisting illegal entry etc).]
  [(2)   An offence under any of sections 57 to 59 of the Sexual Offences Act 2003 (trafficking for sexual exploitation).]

Arms trafficking

5   (1) An offence under either of the following provisions of the Customs and Excise Management Act 1979 if it is committed in connection with a firearm or ammunition—
  (a) section 68(2) (exportation of prohibited goods);
  (b) section 170 (fraudulent evasion).
(2) An offence under section 3(1) of the Firearms Act 1968 (c. 27) (dealing in firearms or ammunition by way of trade or business).
(3) In this paragraph "firearm" and "ammunition" have the same meanings as in section 57 of the Firearms Act 1968 (c. 27).

Counterfeiting

6   An offence under any of the following provisions of the Forgery and Counterfeiting Act 1981 (c. 45)—
  (a) section 14 (making counterfeit notes or coins);
  (b) section 15 (passing etc counterfeit notes or coins);
  (c) section 16 (having counterfeit notes or coins);
  (d) section 17 (making or possessing materials or equipment for counterfeiting).

Intellectual property

7   (1) An offence under any of the following provisions of the Copyright, Designs and Patents Act 1988 (c. 48)—
  (a) section 107(1) (making or dealing in an article which infringes copyright);
  (b) section 107(2) (making or possessing an article designed or adapted for making a copy of a copyright work);
  (c) section 198(1) (making or dealing in an illicit recording);
  (d) section 297A (making or dealing in unauthorised decoders).
(2) An offence under section 92(1), (2) or (3) of the Trade Marks Act 1994 (c. 26) (unauthorised use etc of trade mark).

[Prostitution and Child Sex

8   (1) An offence under section 33 or 34 of the Sexual Offences Act 1956 (keeping or letting premises for use as a brothel).

(2)   An offence under any of the following provisions of the Sexual Offences Act 2003—

  (a)   section 14 (arranging or facilitating commission of a child sex offence);
  (b)   section 48 (causing or inciting child prostitution or pornography);
  (c)   section 49 (controlling a child prostitute or a child involved in pornography);
  (d)   section 50 (arranging or facilitating child prostitution or pornography);
  (e)   section 52 (causing or inciting prostitution for gain);
  (f)   section 53 (controlling prostitution for gain).]

Blackmail

9   An offence under section 21 of the Theft Act 1968 (c. 60) (blackmail).

Inchoate offences

10   (1) An offence of attempting, conspiring or inciting the commission of an offence specified in this Schedule.

(2) An offence of aiding, abetting, counselling or procuring the commission of such an offence.

Scottish Parliamentary Standards Commissioner Act 2002

(2002, asp. 16)

An Act of the Scottish Parliament to establish a Scottish Parliamentary Standards Commissioner to investigate complaints about the conduct of members of the Parliament and to report upon the outcome of such investigations to the Parliament; and for connected purposes   [30 June 2002]

Territorial extent: Scotland

The Scottish Parliamentary Standards Commissioner

1   Appointment of the Scottish Parliamentary Standards Commissioner

(1) There shall be a Scottish Parliamentary Standards Commissioner (in this Act referred to as "the Commissioner").

(2) The Commissioner shall be appointed by the Parliamentary corporation with the agreement of the Parliament.

(3) A person shall not be eligible to be appointed as the Commissioner if that person—

  (a)   is a member of the Parliament or of the staff of the Parliament; or
  (b)   has been such a member at any time during the period of 2 years prior to the date when the appointment is to take effect.

(4)–(8) *****

2   ***

3   Functions of the Commissioner

(1) Subject to the provisions of this Act, where a complaint has been made to the Commissioner about the conduct of a member of the Parliament, it shall be the function of the Commissioner to—

(a) investigate whether the member has committed the conduct complained about and has, as a result of that conduct, breached a relevant provision; and

(b) report upon the outcome of that investigation to the Parliament.

(2) However, subject to section 12, the Commissioner shall not investigate any complaint which falls within a class of complaint which is excluded from the jurisdiction of the Commissioner by any provision in the standing orders or in the Code of Conduct; and any such complaint is referred to in this Act as an "excluded complaint".

(3) A "relevant provision" is any provision in force at the relevant time—

(a) in the standing orders;

(b) in the Code of Conduct;

(c) in the Scotland Act 1998 (Transitory and Transitional Provisions) (Members' Interests) Order 1999 (SI 1999/1350); or

(d) made by or under an Act of the Scottish Parliament in pursuance of section 39 (members' interests) of the Scotland Act.

(4) The "relevant time" is the time when the conduct in question is alleged to have taken place, whether before or after this section comes into force.

(5)–(7) *****

4   Directions to the Commissioner

(1) The Commissioner shall, in carrying out the functions of that office, comply with any directions given by the Parliament.

(2) Any direction to the Commissioner by the Parliament under this section may, in particular—

(a) make provision as to the procedure to be followed by the Commissioner when conducting—

(i) investigations generally into any complaint about the conduct of a member of the Parliament; or

(ii) investigations into complaints falling within such class or classes as may be specified in the direction (and different provision may be made in relation to different classes of complaint); or

(b) require the Commissioner to make a report to the Parliament upon such matter relating to the exercise of the functions of the Commissioner as may be specified in the direction.

(3) However, any direction to the Commissioner by the Parliament under this section shall not direct the Commissioner as to whether or how any particular investigation is to be carried out.

Investigation of complaints

5   General provisions relating to an investigation into a complaint

(1) There are two possible stages to any investigation by the Commissioner into a complaint, namely—

(a) Stage 1 which consists of investigating and determining whether a complaint is admissible; and

(b) if the complaint is admissible, Stage 2 which consists of further investigating the complaint and reporting upon it to the Parliament,

and any reference in this Act to "the stage of an investigation" or to "Stage 1" or "Stage 2" shall be construed accordingly.

(2) Each stage of an investigation into a complaint shall be conducted in private.

(3) The Commissioner may at any time make a report to the Parliament as to the progress of an investigation into a complaint.

(4) Subject to the provisions of this Act, it is for the Commissioner to decide when and how to carry out any investigation at each stage.

6 Stage 1: Admissibility of complaints

(1) At Stage 1, the Commissioner shall investigate and determine whether a complaint is admissible.

(2) A complaint is admissible if it appears to the Commissioner that the following three tests are satisfied, namely—

    (a) that the complaint is relevant;

    (b) that the complaint meets all the requirements specified in subsection (5) ("the specified requirements") or that the Parliament has, as under section 7(7)(b), directed the Commissioner to treat the complaint as if it had met all of those requirements; and

    (c) that the complaint warrants further investigation.

(3) The three tests mentioned in paragraphs (a), (b) and (c) of subsection (2) are referred to as the first, second and third tests respectively.

(4) For the purposes of the first test, a complaint is relevant if—

    (a) it is about the conduct of a member of the Parliament;

    (b) it is not an excluded complaint or, if it is, that the Commissioner has been directed under section 12 to investigate it; and

    (c) it appears at first sight that, if all or part of the conduct complained about is established to have been committed by that member, it might amount to a breach of a relevant provision or provisions identified by the Commissioner.

(5) For the purposes of the second test, the specified requirements are that the complaint—

    (a) is made in writing to the Commissioner;

    (b) is made by an individual person, is signed by that person and states that person's name and address;

    (c) names the member of the Parliament concerned;

    (d) sets out the facts relevant to the conduct complained about and is accompanied by any supporting evidence which the complainer wishes to submit; and

    (e) is made within one year from the date when the complainer could reasonably have become aware of the conduct complained about.

(6) For the purposes of the third test, a complaint warrants further investigation if it appears after an initial investigation that the evidence is sufficient to suggest that the conduct complained about may have taken place.

7 Procedures at Stage 1

(1) When the Commissioner receives a complaint about the conduct of a member of the Parliament, the Commissioner shall—

    (a) notify that member that a complaint has been made;

    (b) inform that member of the nature of the complaint; and

    (c) except where the Commissioner considers that it would be inappropriate to do so, inform that member of the name of the complainer.

(2) If the Commissioner considers that the complaint is admissible, the Commissioner shall proceed to Stage 2 of the investigation into the complaint and shall—

    (a) make a report to the Parliament informing it of that fact and of the relevant provision or provisions identified by the Commissioner for the purposes of the first test; and

    (b) inform the complainer and the member of the Parliament concerned accordingly.

(3) If the Commissioner considers that the complaint is inadmissible for failing to satisfy the first or the third test, the Commissioner shall dismiss the complaint and shall inform the complainer and the member of the Parliament concerned accordingly, together with the reasons for that view.

(4)–(11) *****

8   Stage 2: Investigation of an admissible complaint

(1) At Stage 2, the Commissioner shall investigate an admissible complaint with a view to—

(a) making findings of fact in relation to whether the member of the Parliament concerned (whether or not named in the complaint) has committed the conduct complained about; and

(b) reaching a conclusion as to whether that member has, as a result of that conduct, breached the relevant provision or provisions identified by the Commissioner for the purposes of the first test.

(2) The Commissioner may make a finding of fact if satisfied on a balance of probabilities that the fact is established.

(3) *****

9   Report

(1) At the conclusion of an investigation into a complaint at Stage 2, the Commissioner shall make a report to the Parliament upon the outcome of the investigation.

(2) The report shall include—

(a) details of the complaint;

(b) details of the investigation carried out by the Commissioner;

(c) the facts found by the Commissioner in relation to whether the member of the Parliament concerned (whether or not named in the complaint) has committed the conduct complained about;

(d) the conclusion reached by the Commissioner as to whether that member has, as a result of that conduct, breached the relevant provision or provisions identified by the Commissioner for the purposes of the first test and the reasons for that view,

but shall not express any view upon what sanction would be appropriate for any breach.

(3) No report concluding that a member of the Parliament, who is named in the report, has breached a relevant provision shall be made to the Parliament unless the member concerned has been given a copy of the draft report and an opportunity to make representations on the alleged breach and on the draft report; and there shall be annexed to the report made to the Parliament any representations made by that member which are not given effect to in that report.

10   Action on receipt of a report

(1) The Parliament is not bound by the facts found, or the conclusions reached, by the Commissioner in a report made under section 9.

(2) The Parliament may direct the Commissioner to carry out such further investigations as may be specified in the direction and to report on the outcome of these investigations to it.

(3) *****

*****

Anti-social Behaviour Act 2003

(2003, c. 38)

An Act to make provision in connection with anti-social behaviour   [20 November 2003]

Territorial Extent: England and Wales (material reproduced here)

PART 1   PREMISES WHERE DRUGS USED UNLAWFULLY

1   Closure notice

(1)   This section applies to premises if a police officer not below the rank of superintendent (the authorising officer) has reasonable grounds for believing—

  (a)   that at any time during the relevant period the premises have been used in connection with the unlawful use, production or supply of a Class A controlled drug, and

  (b)   that the use of the premises is associated with the occurrence of disorder or serious nuisance to members of the public.

(2)   The authorising officer may authorise the issue of a closure notice in respect of premises to which this section applies if he is satisfied—

  (a)   that the local authority for the area in which the premises are situated has been consulted;

  (b)   that reasonable steps have been taken to establish the identity of any person who lives on the premises or who has control of or responsibility for or an interest in the premises.

(3)   An authorisation under subsection (2) may be given orally or in writing, but if it is given orally the authorising officer must confirm it in writing as soon as it is practicable.

(4)   A closure notice must—

  (a)   give notice that an application will be made under section 2 for the closure of the premises;

  (b)   state that access to the premises by any person other than a person who habitually resides in the premises or the owner of the premises is prohibited;

  (c)   specify the date and time when and the place at which the application will be heard;

  (d)   explain the effects of an order made in pursuance of section 2;

  (e)   state that failure to comply with the notice amounts to an offence;

  (f)   give information about relevant advice providers.

(5)   The closure notice must be served by a constable.

(6)   Service is effected by—

  (a)   fixing a copy of the notice to at least one prominent place on the premises,

  (b)   fixing a copy of the notice to each normal means of access to the premises,

  (c)   fixing a copy of the notice to any outbuildings which appear to the constable to be used with or as part of the premises,

  (d)   giving a copy of the notice to at least one person who appears to the constable to have control of or responsibility for the premises, and

  (e)   giving a copy of the notice to the persons identified in pursuance of subsection (2)(b) and to any other person appearing to the constable to be a person of a description mentioned in that subsection.

(7)   The closure notice must also be served on any person who occupies any other part of the building or other structure in which the premises are situated if the constable reasonably believes at the time of serving the notice under subsection (6) that the person's access to the other part of the building or structure will be impeded if a closure order is made under section 2.

[(7A)   For the purposes of subsection (6)(a) a constable may enter any premises to which this section applies, using reasonable force if necessary.]

(8)   It is immaterial whether any person has been convicted of an offence relating to the use, production or supply of a controlled drug.

(9)   The Secretary of State may by regulations specify premises or descriptions of premises to which this section does not apply.

(10)   The relevant period is the period of three months ending with the day on which the authorising officer considers whether to authorise the issue of a closure notice in respect of the premises.

(11) Information about relevant advice providers is information about the names of and means of contacting persons and organisations in the area that provide advice about housing and legal matters.

2 Closure order

(1) If a closure notice has been issued under section 1 a constable must apply under this section to a magistrates' court for the making of a closure order.

(2) The application must be heard by the magistrates' court not later than 48 hours after the notice was served in pursuance of section 1(6)(a).

(3) The magistrates' court may make a closure order if and only if it is satisfied that each of the following paragraphs applies—

(a) the premises in respect of which the closure notice was issued have been used in connection with the unlawful use, production or supply of a Class A controlled drug;

(b) the use of the premises is associated with the occurrence of disorder or serious nuisance to members of the public;

(c) the making of the order is necessary to prevent the occurrence of such disorder or serious nuisance for the period specified in the order.

(4) A closure order is an order that the premises in respect of which the order is made are closed to all persons for such period (not exceeding three months) as the court decides.

(5) But the order may include such provision as the court thinks appropriate relating to access to any part of the building or structure of which the premises form part.

(6) The magistrates' court may adjourn the hearing on the application for a period of not more than 14 days to enable—

(a) the occupier of the premises,

(b) the person who has control of or responsibility for the premises, or

(c) any other person with an interest in the premises,

to show why a closure order should not be made.

(7) If the magistrates' court adjourns the hearing under subsection (6) it may order that the closure notice continues in effect until the end of the period of the adjournment.

(8) A closure order may be made in respect of all or any part of the premises in respect of which the closure notice was issued.

(9) It is immaterial whether any person has been convicted of an offence relating to the use, production or supply of a controlled drug.

3–29 *****

PART 4   DISPERSAL OF GROUPS ETC

30 Dispersal of groups and removal of persons under 16 to their place of residence

(1) This section applies where a relevant officer has reasonable grounds for believing—

(a) that any members of the public have been intimidated, harassed, alarmed or distressed as a result of the presence or behaviour of groups of two or more persons in public places in any locality in his police area (the "relevant locality"), and

(b) that anti-social behaviour is a significant and persistent problem in the relevant locality.

(2) The relevant officer may give an authorisation that the powers conferred on a constable in uniform by subsections (3) to (6) are to be exercisable for a period specified in the authorisation which does not exceed 6 months.

(3) Subsection (4) applies if a constable in uniform has reasonable grounds for believing that the presence or behaviour of a group of two or more persons in any public place in

the relevant locality has resulted, or is likely to result, in any members of the public being intimidated, harassed, alarmed or distressed.

(4) The constable may give one or more of the following directions, namely—

    (a) a direction requiring the persons in the group to disperse (either immediately or by such time as he may specify and in such way as he may specify),

    (b) a direction requiring any of those persons whose place of residence is not within the relevant locality to leave the relevant locality or any part of the relevant locality (either immediately or by such time as he may specify and in such way as he may specify), and

    (c) a direction prohibiting any of those persons whose place of residence is not within the relevant locality from returning to the relevant locality or any part of the relevant locality for such period (not exceeding 24 hours) from the giving of the direction as he may specify;

but this subsection is subject to subsection (5).

(5) A direction under subsection (4) may not be given in respect of a group of persons—

    (a) who are engaged in conduct which is lawful under section 220 of the Trade Union and Labour Relations (Consolidation) Act 1992 (c. 52), or

    (b) who are taking part in a public procession of the kind mentioned in section 11(1) of the Public Order Act 1986 (c. 64) in respect of which—

        (i) written notice has been given in accordance with section 11 of that Act, or

        (ii) such notice is not required to be given as provided by subsections (1) and (2) of that section.

(6) If, between the hours of 9pm and 6am, a constable in uniform finds a person in any public place in the relevant locality who he has reasonable grounds for believing—

    (a) is under the age of 16, and

    (b) is not under the effective control of a parent or a responsible person aged 18 or over,

he may remove the person to the person's place of residence unless he has reasonable grounds for believing that the person would, if removed to that place, be likely to suffer significant harm.

(7) In this section any reference to the presence or behaviour of a group of persons is to be read as including a reference to the presence or behaviour of any one or more of the persons in the group.

31 Authorisations: supplemental

(1) An authorisation—

    (a) must be in writing,

    (b) must be signed by the relevant officer giving it, and

    (c) must specify—

        (i) the relevant locality,

        (ii) the grounds on which the authorisation is given, and

        (iii) the period during which the powers conferred by section 30(3) to (6) are exercisable.

(2) An authorisation may not be given without the consent of the local authority or each local authority whose area includes the whole or part of the relevant locality.

(3) Publicity must be given to an authorisation by either or both of the following methods—

    (a) publishing an authorisation notice in a newspaper circulating in the relevant locality,

    (b) posting an authorisation notice in some conspicuous place or places within the relevant locality.

(4)–(10) *****

32   Powers under section 30: supplemental

(1) A direction under section 30(4)—

(a) may be given orally,

(b) may be given to any person individually or to two or more persons together, and

(c) may be withdrawn or varied by the person who gave it.

(2) A person who knowingly contravenes a direction given to him under section 30(4) commits an offence and is liable on summary conviction to—

(a) a fine not exceeding level 4 on the standard scale, or

(b) imprisonment for a term not exceeding 3 months,

or to both.

(3) ...

(4) *****

33–35 *****

36   Interpretation

In this Part—

"anti-social behaviour" means behaviour by a person which causes or is likely to cause harassment, alarm or distress to one or more other persons not of the same household as the person,

"local authority" means—

(a) in relation to England, a district council, a country council that is the council for a county in which there are no district councils, a London borough council, the Common Council of the City of London or the Council of the Isles of Scilly,

(b) in relation to Wales, a county council or a county borough council,

"public place" means—

(a) any highway, and

(b) any place to which at the material time the public or any section of the public has access, on payment or otherwise, as of right or by virtue of express or implied permission,

"relevant locality" has the same meaning as in section 30,

"relevant officer" means a police officer of or above the rank of superintendent.

*****

Communications Act 2003

(2003, c. 21)

An Act to confer functions on the Office of Communications; to make provision about the regulation of the provision of electronic communications networks and services and of the use of the electromagnetic spectrum; to make provision about the regulation of broadcasting and of the provision of television and radio services; to make provision about mergers involving newspaper and other media enterprises and, in that connection, to amend the Enterprise Act 2002; and for connected purposes [17 July 2003]

Territorial extent: The United Kingdom (and may be extended by Order in Council to any of the Channel Islands or the Isle of Man)

PART 1   FUNCTIONS OF OFCOM

Transferred and assigned functions

1 Functions and general powers of OFCOM

(1) The Office of Communications ("OFCOM") shall have the following functions—

    (a) the functions transferred to OFCOM under section 2; and

    (b) such other functions as may be conferred on OFCOM by or under any enactment (including this Act).

(2)–(8)*****

2 *****

General duties in carrying out functions

3 General duties of OFCOM

(1) It shall be the principal duty of OFCOM, in carrying out their functions—

    (a) to further the interests of citizens in relation to communications matters; and

    (b) to further the interests of consumers in relevant markets, where appropriate by promoting competition.

(2) The things which, by virtue of subsection (1), OFCOM are required to secure in the carrying out of their functions include, in particular, each of the following—

    (a) the optimal use for wireless telegraphy of the electro-magnetic spectrum;

    (b) the availability throughout the United Kingdom of a wide range of electronic communications services;

    (c) the availability throughout the United Kingdom of a wide range of television and radio services which (taken as a whole) are both of high quality and calculated to appeal to a variety of tastes and interests;

    (d) the maintenance of a sufficient plurality of providers of different television and radio services;

    (e) the application, in the case of all television and radio services, of standards that provide adequate protection to members of the public from the inclusion of offensive and harmful material in such services;

    (f) the application, in the case of all television and radio services, of standards that provide adequate protection to members of the public and all other persons from both—

        (i) unfair treatment in programmes included in such services; and

        (ii) unwarranted infringements of privacy resulting from activities carried on for the purposes of such services.

(3) In performing their duties under subsection (1), OFCOM must have regard, in all cases, to—

    (a) the principles under which regulatory activities should be transparent, accountable, proportionate, consistent and targeted only at cases in which action is needed; and

    (b) any other principles appearing to OFCOM to represent the best regulatory practice.

(4) OFCOM must also have regard, in performing those duties, to such of the following as appear to them to be relevant in the circumstances—

    (a) the desirability of promoting the fulfilment of the purposes of public service television broadcasting in the United Kingdom;

    (b) the desirability of promoting competition in relevant markets;

    (c) the desirability of promoting and facilitating the development and use of effective forms of self-regulation;

(d) the desirability of encouraging investment and innovation in relevant markets;

(e) the desirability of encouraging the availability and use of high speed data transfer services throughout the United Kingdom;

(f) the different needs and interests, so far as the use of the electro-magnetic spectrum for wireless telegraphy is concerned, of all persons who may wish to make use of it;

(g) the need to secure that the application in the case of television and radio services of standards falling within subsection (2)(e) and (f) is in the manner that best guarantees an appropriate level of freedom of expression;

(h) the vulnerability of children and of others whose circumstances appear to OFCOM to put them in need of special protection;

(i) the needs of persons with disabilities, of the elderly and of those on low incomes;

(j) the desirability of preventing crime and disorder;

(k) the opinions of consumers in relevant markets and of members of the public generally;

(l) the different interests of persons in the different parts of the United Kingdom, of the different ethnic communities within the United Kingdom and of persons living in rural and in urban areas;

(m) the extent to which, in the circumstances of the case, the furthering or securing of the matters mentioned in subsections (1) and (2) is reasonably practicable.

(5) In performing their duty under this section of furthering the interests of consumers, OFCOM must have regard, in particular, to the interests of those consumers in respect of choice, price, quality of service and value for money.

(6)–(14) *****

4–10   ***

Media literacy

11   Duty to promote media literacy

(1) It shall be the duty of OFCOM to take such steps, and to enter into such arrangements, as appear to them calculated—

(a) to bring about, or to encourage others to bring about, a better public understanding of the nature and characteristics of material published by means of the electronic media;

(b) to bring about, or to encourage others to bring about, a better public awareness and understanding of the processes by which such material is selected, or made available, for publication by such means;

(c) to bring about, or to encourage others to bring about, the development of a better public awareness of the available systems by which access to material published by means of the electronic media is or can be regulated;

(d) to bring about, or to encourage others to bring about, the development of a better public awareness of the available systems by which persons to whom such material is made available may control what is received and of the uses to which such systems may be put; and

(e) to encourage the development and use of technologies and systems for regulating access to such material, and for facilitating control over what material is received, that are both effective and easy to use.

(2) . . .

OFCOM's Content Board

12   Duty to establish and maintain Content Board

(1) It shall be the duty of OFCOM, in accordance with the following provisions of this section, to exercise their powers under paragraph 14 of the Schedule to the Office of Communications Act 2002 (c 11) (committees of OFCOM) to establish and maintain a committee to be known as "the Content Board".

(2) The Content Board shall consist of—

    (a) a chairman appointed by OFCOM; and

    (b) such number of other members appointed by OFCOM as OFCOM think fit.

(3)–(7) *****

(8) It shall be the duty of OFCOM when appointing members of the Content Board to secure, so far as practicable, that a majority of the members of the Board (counting the chairman) consists of persons who are neither members nor employees of OFCOM.

(9) The following shall be disqualified from being the chairman or another member of the Content Board—

    (a) governors and employees of the BBC;

    (b) members and employees of the Welsh Authority; and

    (c) members and employees of C4C.

(10)–(14) *****

13   Functions of the Content Board

(1) The Content Board shall have such functions as OFCOM, in exercise of their powers under the Schedule to the Office of Communications Act 2002 (c 11), may confer on the Board.

(2) The functions conferred on the Board must include, to such extent and subject to such restrictions and approvals as OFCOM may determine, the carrying out on OFCOM's behalf of—

    (a) functions in relation to matters that concern the contents of anything which is or may be broadcast or otherwise transmitted by means of electronic communications networks; and

    (b) functions in relation to the promotion of public understanding or awareness of matters relating to the publication of matter by means of the electronic media.

(3)–(7) *****

14–31   *****

PART 2   NETWORKS, SERVICES AND THE RADIO SPECTRUM

CHAPTER 1   ELECTRONIC COMMUNICATIONS NETWORKS AND SERVICES

Preliminary

32   Meaning of electronic communications networks and services

(1) In this Act "electronic communications network" means—

    (a) a transmission system for the conveyance, by the use of electrical, magnetic or electro-magnetic energy, of signals of any description; and

    (b) such of the following as are used, by the person providing the system and in association with it, for the conveyance of the signals—

        (i) apparatus comprised in the system;

        (ii) apparatus used for the switching or routing of the signals; and

        (iii) software and stored data.

(2) In this Act "electronic communications service" means a service consisting in, or having as its principal feature, the conveyance by means of an electronic communications network of signals, except in so far as it is a content service.

(3)–(10) *****

Notification by providers

33   Advance notification to OFCOM

(1) A person shall not—
- (a) provide a designated electronic communications network,
- (b) provide a designated electronic communications service, or
- (c) make available a designated associated facility,

unless, before beginning to provide it or to make it available, he has given a notification to OFCOM of his intention to provide that network or service, or to make that facility available.

(2) An electronic communications network, electronic communications service or associated facility is designated for the purposes of this section if it is of a description of networks, services of facilities that is for the time being designated by OFCOM as a description of networks, services or facilities for which notification under this section is required.

(3)–(12) *****

34–126 *****

127   Improper use of public electronic communications network

(1) A person is guilty of an offence if he—
- (a) sends by means of a public electronic communications network a message or other matter that is grossly offensive or of an indecent, obscene or menacing character; or
- (b) causes any such message or matter to be so sent.

(2) A person is guilty of an offence if, for the purpose of causing annoyance, inconvenience or needless anxiety to another, he—
- (a) sends by means of a public electronic communications network, a message that he knows to be false,
- (b) causes such a message to be sent; or
- (c) persistently makes use of a public electronic communications network.

(3) A person guilty of an offence under this section shall be liable, on summary conviction, to imprisonment for a term not exceeding six months or to a fine not exceeding level 5 on the standard scale, or to both.

(4) Subsections (1) and (2) do not apply to anything done in the course of providing a programme service (within the meaning of the Broadcasting Act 1990 (c. 42)).

Persistent misuse of network or service

128   Notification of misuse of networks and services

(1) Where OFCOM determine that there are reasonable grounds for believing that a person has persistently misused an electronic communications network or electronic communications services, they may give that person a notification under this section.

(2) A notification under this section is one which—
- (a) sets out the determination made by OFCOM;
- (b) specifies the use that OFCOM consider constitutes persistent misuse; and
- (c) specifies the period during which the person notified has an opportunity of making representations about the matters notified.

(3) That period must not be less than the following—
- (a) in an urgent case, seven days; and
- (b) in any other case, one month.

(4) A case is an urgent case for the purposes of subsection (3) if OFCOM consider—
- (a) that the misuse in question is continuing; and
- (b) that the harm it causes makes it necessary for it to be stopped as soon as possible.

(5) For the purposes of this Chapter a person misuses an electronic communications network or electronic communications service if—

  (a) the effect or likely effect of his use of the network or service is to cause another person unnecessarily to suffer annoyance, inconvenience or anxiety; or

  (b) he uses the network or service to engage in conduct the effect or likely effect of which is to cause another person unnecessarily to suffer annoyance, inconvenience or anxiety.

(6)–(8) *********

129 Enforcement notifications for stopping persistent misuse

(1) This section applies where—

  (a) a person ("the notified misuser") has been given a notification under section 128;

  (b) OFCOM have allowed the notified misuser an opportunity of making representations about the matters notified; and

  (c) the period allowed for the making of the representations has expired.

(2) OFCOM may give the notified misuser an enforcement notification if they are satisfied—

  (a) that he has, in one or more of the notified respects, persistently misused an electronic communications network or electronic communications service; and

  (b) that he has not, since the giving of the notification, taken all such steps as OFCOM consider appropriate for—

    (i) securing that his misuse is brought to an end and is not repeated; and

    (ii) remedying the consequences of the notified misuse.

(3) An enforcement notification is a notification which imposes a requirement on the notified misuser to take all such steps for—

  (a) securing that his misuse is brought to an end and is not repeated, and

  (b) remedying the consequences of the notified misuse,

as may be specified in the notification.

(4) A decision of OFCOM to give an enforcement notification to a person must fix a reasonable period for the taking of the steps required by the notification.

(5) It shall be the duty of a person to whom an enforcement notification has been given to comply with it.

(6) That duty shall be enforceable in civil proceedings by OFCOM—

  (a) for an injunction;

  (b) for specific performance of a statutory duty under section 45 of the Court of Session Act 1988 (c. 36); or

  (c) for any other appropriate remedy or relief.

(7) *********

130–197 *********

PART 3   TELEVISION AND RADIO SERVICES

CHAPTER 1   THE BBC, C4C THE WELSH AUTHORITY AND THE
GAELIC MEDIA SERVICE

The BBC

198 Functions of OFCOM in relation to the BBC

(1) It shall be a function of OFCOM, to the extent that provision for them to do so is contained in—

  (a) the BBC Charter and Agreement, and

  (b) the provisions of this Act and of Part 5 of the 1996 Act, to regulate the provision of the BBC's services and the carrying on by the BBC of other activities for purposes connected with the provision of those services.

(2) For the purposes of the carrying out of that function OFCOM—

(a) are to have such powers and duties as may be conferred on them by or under the BBC Charter and Agreement; and

(b) are entitled, to the extent that they are authorised to do so by the Secretary of State or under the terms of that Charter and Agreement, to act on his behalf in relation to that Charter and Agreement.

(3)–(9) *****

199–210 *****

CHAPTER 2   REGULATORY STRUCTURE FOR INDEPENDENT TELEVISION SERVICES

Preliminary

211   Regulation of independent television services

(1) It shall be a function of OFCOM to regulate the following services in accordance with this Act, the 1990 Act and the 1996 Act—

(a) services falling within subsection (2) that are provided otherwise than by the BBC or the Welsh Authority; and

(b) services falling within subsection (3) that are provided otherwise than by the BBC.

(2) The services referred to in subsection (1)(a) are—

(a) television broadcasting services that are provided from places in the United Kingdom with a view to their being broadcast otherwise than only from a satellite;

(b) television licensable content services that are provided by persons under the jurisdiction of the United Kingdom for the purposes of the Television without Frontiers Directive;

(c) digital television programme services that are provided by persons under the jurisdiction of the United Kingdom for the purposes of that Directive;

(d) restricted television services that are provided from places in the United Kingdom; and

(e) additional television services that are provided from places in the United Kingdom.

(3) *****

212–278 *****

News provision etc on public service television

279   News and current affairs programmes

(1) The regulatory regime for every licensed public service channel includes the conditions that OFCOM consider appropriate for securing—

(a) that the programmes included in the channel include news programmes and current affairs programmes;

(b) that the news programmes and current affairs programmes included in the service are of high quality and deal with both national and international matters; and

(c) that the news programmes so included are broadcast for viewing at intervals throughout the period for which the channel is provided.

(2) That regime also includes the conditions that OFCOM consider appropriate for securing that, in each year—

(a) the time allocated to the broadcasting of news programmes included in the service, and

(b) the time allocated to the broadcasting of current affairs programmes so included,
each constitutes no less than what appears to OFCOM to be an appropriate proportion of the
time allocated to the broadcasting of all the programmes included in the channel.

(3)–(7) *********

280–318 *********

Programme and fairness standards for television and radio

319 OFCOM's standards code

(1) It shall be the duty of OFCOM to set, and from time to time to review and revise, such
standards for the content of programmes to be included in television and radio services as
appear to them best calculated to secure the standards objectives.

(2) The standards objectives are—

(a) that persons under the age of eighteen are protected;

(b) that material likely to encourage or to incite the commission of crime or to lead to
disorder is not included in television and radio services;

(c) that news included in television and radio services is presented with due impartiality and that the impartiality requirements of section 320 are complied with;

(d) that news included in television and radio services is reported with due accuracy;

(e) that the proper degree of responsibility is exercised with respect to the content of
programmes which are religious programmes;

(f) that generally accepted standards are applied to the contents of television and
radio services so as to provide adequate protection for members of the public from
the inclusion in such services of offensive and harmful material;

(g) that advertising that contravenes the prohibition on political advertising set out
in section 321(2) is not included in television or radio services;

(h) that the inclusion of advertising which may be misleading, harmful or offensive in
television and radio services is prevented;

(i) that the international obligations of the United Kingdom with respect to
advertising included in television and radio services are complied with;

(j) that the unsuitable sponsorship of programmes included in television and radio
services is prevented;

(k) that there is no undue discrimination between advertisers who seek to have
advertisements included in television and radio services; and

(l) that there is no use of techniques which exploit the possibility of conveying a
message to viewers or listeners, or of otherwise influencing their minds, without
their being aware, or fully aware, of what has occurred.

(3) The standards set by OFCOM under this section must be contained in one or more codes.

(4) In setting or revising any standards under this section, OFCOM must have regard, in
particular and to such extent as appears to them to be relevant to the securing of the standards
objectives, to each of the following matters—

(a) the degree of harm or offence likely to be caused by the inclusion of any particular sort of material in programmes generally, or in programmes of a particular
description;

(b) the likely size and composition of the potential audience for programmes
included in television and radio services generally, or in television and radio
services of a particular description;

(c) the likely expectation of the audience as to the nature of a programme's content
and the extent to which the nature of a programme's content can be brought to
the attention of potential members of the audience;

(d) the likelihood of persons who are unaware of the nature of a programme's content
being unintentionally exposed, by their own actions, to that content;

(e) the desirability of securing that the content of services identifies when there is a change affecting the nature of a service that is being watched or listened to and, in particular, a change that is relevant to the application of the standards set under this section; and

(f) the desirability of maintaining the independence of editorial control over programme content.

(5) *****

(6) Standards set to secure the standards objective specified in subsection (2)(e) shall, in particular, contain provision designed to secure that religious programmes do not involve—

(a) any improper exploitation of any susceptibilities of the audience for such a programme; or

(b) any abusive treatment of the religious views and beliefs of those belonging to a particular religion or religious denomination.

(7), (8) *****

320   Special impartiality requirements

(1) The requirements of this section are—

(a) the exclusion, in the case of television and radio services (other than a restricted service within the meaning of section 245), from programmes included in any of those services of all expressions of the views or opinions of the person providing the service on any of the matters mentioned in subsection (2);

(b) the preservation, in the case of every television programme service, teletext service, national radio service and national digital sound programme service, of due impartiality, on the part of the person providing the service, as respects all of those matters;

(c) the prevention, in the case of every local radio service, local digital sound programme service or radio licensable content service, of the giving of undue prominence in the programmes included in the service to the views and opinions of particular persons or bodies on any of those matters.

(2) Those matters are—

(a) matters of political or industrial controversy; and

(b) matters relating to current public policy.

(3) Subsection (1)(a) does not require—

(a) the exclusion from television programmes of views or opinions relating to the provision of programme services; or

(b) the exclusion from radio programmes of views or opinions relating to the provision of programme services.

(4) For the purposes of this section—

(a) the requirement specified in subsection (1)(b) is one that (subject to any rules under subsection (5)) may be satisfied by being satisfied in relation to a series of programmes taken as a whole;

(b) the requirement specified in subsection (1)(c) is one that needs to be satisfied only in relation to all the programmes included in the service in question, taken as a whole.

(5)–(7) *****

321   Objectives for advertisements and sponsorship

(1) Standards set by OFCOM to secure the objectives mentioned in section 319(2)(a) and (g) to (j)—

(a) must include general provision governing standards and practice in advertising and in the sponsoring of programmes; and

(b) may include provision prohibiting advertisements and forms and methods of advertising or sponsorship (whether generally or in particular circumstances).

(2) For the purposes of section 319(2)(g) an advertisement contravenes the prohibition on political advertising if it is—

(a) an advertisement which is inserted by or on behalf of a body whose objects are wholly or mainly of a political nature;

(b) an advertisement which is directed towards a political end; or

(c) an advertisement which has a connection with an industrial dispute.

(3) For the purposes of this section objects of a political nature and political ends include each of the following—

(a) influencing the outcome of elections or referendums, whether in the United Kingdom or elsewhere;

(b) bringing about changes of the law in the whole or a part of the United Kingdom or elsewhere, or otherwise influencing the legislative process in any country or territory;

(c) influencing the policies or decisions of local, regional or national governments, whether in the United Kingdom or elsewhere;

(d) influencing the policies or decisions of persons on whom public functions are conferred by or under the law of the United Kingdom or of a country or territory outside the United Kingdom;

(e) influencing the policies or decisions of persons on whom functions are conferred by or under international agreements;

(f) influencing public opinion on a matter which, in the United Kingdom, is a matter of public controversy;

(g) promoting the interests of a party or other group of persons organised, in the United Kingdom or elsewhere, for political ends.

(4)–(8) *****

322–324 *****

325 Observance of standards code

(1) The regulatory regime for every programme service licensed by a Broadcasting Act licence includes conditions for securing—

(a) that standards set under section 319 are observed in the provision of that service; and

(b) that procedures for the handling and resolution of complaints about the observance of those standards are established and maintained.

(2) It shall be the duty of OFCOM themselves to establish procedures for the handling and resolution of complaints about the observance of standards set under section 319.

(3)–(6) *****

326–332 *****

333 Party political broadcasts

(1) The regulatory regime for every licensed public service channel, and the regulatory regime for every national radio service, includes—

(a) conditions requiring the inclusion in that channel or service of party political broadcasts and of referendum campaign broadcasts; and

(b) conditions requiring that licence holder to observe such rules with respect to party political broadcasts and referendum campaign broadcasts as may be made by OFCOM.

(2) The rules made by OFCOM for the purposes of this section may, in particular, include provision for determining—

(a) the political parties on whose behalf party political broadcasts may be made;

(b) in relation to each political party on whose behalf such broadcasts may be made, the length and frequency of the broadcasts; and

(c) in relation to each designated organisation on whose behalf referendum campaign broadcasts are required to be broadcast, the length and frequency of such broadcasts.

(3) Those rules are to have effect subject to sections 37 and 127 of the Political Parties, Elections and Referendums Act 2000 (c. 41) (only registered parties and designated organisations to be entitled to party political broadcasts or referendum campaign broadcasts).

(4)–(6) *****

*****

Courts Act 2003

(2003, c. 39)

An Act to make provision about the courts and their procedure and practice; about judges and magistrates; about fines and the enforcement processes of the courts; about periodical payments of damages; and for connected purposes   [20 November 2003]

Territorial extent: England and Wales

*****

PART 2   JUSTICES OF THE PEACE

THE COMMISSION OF THE PEACE AND LOCAL JUSTICE AREAS

Protection and indemnification of justices and justices' clerks

31   Immunity for acts within jurisdiction

(1) No action lies against a justice of the peace in respect of what he does or omits to do—

(a) in the execution of his duty as a justice of the peace, and

(b) in relation to a matter within his jurisdiction.

(2) No action lies against a justices' clerk or an assistant clerk in respect of what he does or omits to do—

(a) in the execution of his duty as a justices' clerk or assistant clerk exercising, by virtue of an enactment, a function of a single justice of the peace, and

(b) in relation to a matter within his jurisdiction.

32   Immunity for certain acts beyond jurisdiction

(1) An action lies against a justice of the peace in respect of what he does or omits to do—

(a) in the purported execution of his duty as a justice of the peace, but

(b) in relation to a matter not within his jurisdiction,

if, but only if, it is proved that he acted in bad faith.

(2) An action lies against a justices' clerk or an assistant clerk in respect of what he does or omits to do—

(a) in the purported execution of his duty as a justices' clerk or assistant clerk exercising, by virtue of an enactment, a function of a single justice of the peace, but

(b) in relation to a matter not within his jurisdiction,

if, but only if, it is proved that he acted in bad faith.

33   Striking out proceedings where action prohibited

(1) If an action is brought in circumstances in which section 31 or 32 provides that no action lies, a judge of the court in which the action is brought may, on the application of the defendant, strike out the proceedings in the action.

(2) If a judge strikes out proceedings under subsection (1), he may if he thinks fit order the person bringing the action to pay costs.

34   Costs in legal proceedings

(1) A court may not order a justice of the peace to pay costs in any proceedings in respect of what he does or omits to do in the execution (or purported execution) of his duty as a justice of the peace.

(2) A court may not order—

(a) a justices' clerk, or

(b) an assistant clerk,

to pay costs in any proceedings in respect of what he does or omits to do in the execution (or purported execution) of his duty as a justices' clerk or assistant clerk exercising, by virtue of an enactment, a function of a single justice of the peace.

(3) But subsections (1) and (2) do not apply in relation to any proceedings in which a justice of the peace, justices' clerk or assistant clerk—

(a) is being tried for an offence or is appealing against a conviction, or

(b) is proved to have acted in bad faith in respect of the matters giving rise to the proceedings.

(4) A court which is prevented by subsection (1) or (2) from ordering a justice of the peace, justices' clerk or assistant clerk to pay costs in any proceedings may instead order the Lord Chancellor to make a payment in respect of the costs of a person in the proceedings.

(5) *****

*****

Crime (International Co-operation) Act 2003

(2003, c. 32)

An Act to make provision for furthering co-operation with other countries in respect of criminal proceedings and investigations; to extend jurisdiction to deal with terrorist acts or threats outside the United Kingdom; to amend section 5 of the Forgery and Counterfeiting Act 1981 and make corresponding provision in relation to Scotland; and for connected purposes   [30 October 2003]

Territorial extent: England, Wales and Northern Ireland (Materials reproduced here; note that ss. 37–41 (not reproduced here) contain equivalent provisions for Scotland)

*****

CHAPTER 4   INFORMATION ABOUT BANKING TRANSACTIONS

Requests for information about banking transactions in England and Wales and Northern Ireland for use abroad

32   Customer information

(1) This section applies where the Secretary of State receives a request from an authority mentioned in subsection (2) for customer information to be obtained in relation to a person who appears to him to be subject to an investigation in a participating country into serious criminal conduct.

(2) The authority referred to in subsection (1) is the authority in that country which appears to the Secretary of State to have the function of making requests of the kind to which this section applies.

(3) The Secretary of State may—

    (a) direct a senior police officer to apply, or arrange for a constable to apply, for a customer information order,

    (b) direct a senior customs officer to apply, or arrange for a customs officer to apply, for such an order.

(4) A customer information order is an order made by a judge that a financial institution specified in the application for the order must, on being required to do so by notice in writing given by the applicant for the order, provide any such customer information as it has relating to the person specified in the application.

(5) A financial institution which is required to provide information under a customer information order must provide the information to the applicant for the order in such manner, and at or by such time, as the applicant requires.

(6) Section 364 of the Proceeds of Crime Act 2002 (c. 29) (meaning of customer information), except subsections (2)(f) and (3)(i), has effect for the purposes of this section as if this section were included in Chapter 2 of Part 8 of that Act.

(7) A customer information order has effect in spite of any restriction on the disclosure of information (however imposed).

(8) Customer information obtained in pursuance of a customer information order is to be given to the Secretary of State and sent by him to the authority which made the request.

33 Making, varying or discharging customer information orders

(1) A judge may make a customer information order, on an application made to him pursuant to a direction under section 32(3), if he is satisfied that—

    (a) the person specified in the application is subject to an investigation in the country in question,

    (b) the investigation concerns conduct which is serious criminal conduct,

    (c) the conduct constitutes an offence in England and Wales or (as the case may be) Northern Ireland, or would do were it to occur there, and

    (d) the order is sought for the purposes of the investigation.

(2) The application may be made ex parte to a judge in chambers.

(3) The application may specify—

    (a) all financial institutions,

    (b) a particular description, or particular descriptions, of financial institutions, or

    (c) a particular financial institution or particular financial institutions.

(4) *****

34 Offences

(1) A financial institution is guilty of an offence if without reasonable excuse it fails to comply with a requirement imposed on it under a customer information order.

(2) A financial institution is guilty of an offence under subsection (1) is liable on summary conviction to a fine not exceeding level 5 on the standard scale.

(3) A financial institution is guilty of an offence if, in purported compliance with a customer information order, it—

    (a) makes a statement which it knows to be false or misleading in a material particular, or

    (b) recklessly makes a statement which is false or misleading in a material particular.

(4) A financial institution guilty of an offence under subsection (3) is liable—

    (a) on summary conviction, to a fine not exceeding the statutory maximum, or

    (b) on conviction on indictment, to a fine.

35 Account information

(1) This section applies where the Secretary of State receives a request from an authority mentioned in subsection (2) for account information to be obtained in relation to an investigation in a participating country into criminal conduct.

(2) The authority referred to in subsection (1) is the authority in that country which appears to the Secretary of State to have the function of making requests of the kind to which this section applies.

(3) The Secretary of State may—

    (a) direct a senior police officer to apply, or arrange for a constable to apply, for an account monitoring order,

    (b) direct a senior customs officer to apply, or arrange for a customs officer to apply, for such an order.

(4) An account monitoring order is an order made by a judge that a financial institution specified in the application for the order must, for the period stated in the order, provide account information of the description specified in the order to the applicant in the manner, and at or by the time or times, stated in the order.

(5) Account information is information relating to an account or accounts held at the financial institution specified in the application by the person so specified (whether solely or jointly with another).

(6) An account monitoring order has effect in spite of any restriction on the disclosure of information (however imposed).

(7) Account information obtained in pursuance of an account monitoring order is to be given to the Secretary of State and sent by him to the authority which made the request.

36 Making, varying or discharging account monitoring orders

(1) A judge may make an account monitoring order, on an application made to him in pursuance of a direction under section 35(3), if he is satisfied that—

    (a) there is an investigation in the country in question into criminal conduct, and

    (b) the order is sought for the purposes of the investigation.

(2) The application may be made ex parte to a judge in chambers.

(3) The application may specify information relating to—

    (a) all accounts held by the person specified in the application for the order at the financial institution so specified.

    (b) a particular description, or particular descriptions, of accounts so held, or

    (c) a particular account, or particular accounts, so held.

(4) The court may discharge or vary an account monitoring order on an application made by—

    (a) the person who applied for the order,

    (b) a senior police officer,

    (c) a constable authorised by a senior police officer to make the application,

    (d) a senior customs officer,

    (e) a customs officer authorised by a senior customs officer to make the application.

(5) Account monitoring orders have effect as if they were orders of the court.

*****

Criminal Justice Act 2003

(2003, c. 44)

An Act to make provision about criminal justice (including the powers and duties of the police) and about dealing with offenders; to amend the law relating to jury service; to amend Chapter 1 of Part

1 of the Crime and Disorder Act 1998 and Part 5 of the Police Act 1997; to make provision about civil proceedings brought by offenders; and for connected purposes [20 November 2003]

Territorial extent: England and Wales (and Northern Ireland, subject to certain modifications)
*****

PART 10   RETRIAL FOR SERIOUS OFFENCES

Cases that may be retried

75   Cases that may be retried

(1) This Part applies where a person has been acquitted of a qualifying offence in proceedings—

   (a) on indictment in England and Wales,

   (b) on appeal against a conviction, verdict or finding in proceedings on indictment in England and Wales, or

   (c) on appeal from a decision on such an appeal.

(2) A person acquitted of an offence in proceedings mentioned in subsection (1) is treated for the purposes of that subsection as also acquitted of any qualifying offence of which he could have been convicted in the proceedings because of the first-mentioned offence being charged in the indictment, except an offence—

   (a) of which he has been convicted,

   (b) of which he has been found not guilty by reason of insanity, or

   (c) in respect of which, in proceedings where he has been found to be under a disability (as defined by section 4 of the Criminal Procedure (Insanity) Act 1964 (c. 84)), a finding has been made that he did the act or made the omission charged against him.

(3) References in subsections (1) and (2) to a qualifying offence do not include references to an offence which, at the time of the acquittal, was the subject of an order under section 77(1) or (3).

(4) This Part also applies where a person has been acquitted, in proceedings elsewhere than in the United Kingdom, of an offence under the law of the place where the proceedings were held, if the commission of the offence as alleged would have amounted to or included the commission (in the United Kingdom or elsewhere) of a qualifying offence.

(5) Conduct punishable under the law in force elsewhere than in the United Kingdom is an offence under that law for the purposes of subsection (4), however it is described in that law.

(6) This Part applies whether the acquittal was before or after the passing of this Act.

(7) References in this Part to acquittal are to acquittal in circumstances within subsection (1) or (4).

(8) In this Part "qualifying offence" means an offence listed in Part 1 of Schedule 5.

Application for retrial

76   Application to Court of Appeal

(1) A prosecutor may apply to the Court of Appeal for an order—

   (a) quashing a person's acquittal in proceedings within section 75(1), and

   (b) ordering him to be retried for the qualifying offence.

(2) A prosecutor may apply to the Court of Appeal, in the case of a person acquitted elsewhere than in the United Kingdom, for—

   (a) a determination whether the acquittal is a bar to the person being tried in England and Wales for the qualifying offence, and

   (b) if it is, an order that the acquittal is not to be a bar.

(3)–(5) *****

77 Determination by Court of Appeal

(1) On an application under section 76(1), the Court of Appeal—

    (a) if satisfied that the requirements of sections 78 and 79 are met, must make the order applied for;

    (b) otherwise, must dismiss the application.

(2) Subsections (3) and (4) apply to an application under section 76(2).

(3) Where the Court of Appeal determines that the acquittal is a bar to the person being tried for the qualifying offence, the court—

    (a) if satisfied that the requirements of sections 78 and 79 are met, must make the order applied for;

    (b) otherwise, must make a declaration to the effect that the acquittal is a bar to the person being tried for the offence.

(4) Where the Court of Appeal determines that the acquittal is not a bar to the person being tried for the qualifying offence, it must make a declaration to that effect.

78 New and compelling evidence

(1) The requirements of this section are met if there is new and compelling evidence against the acquitted person in relation to the qualifying offence.

(2) Evidence is new if it was not adduced in the proceedings in which the person was acquitted (nor, if those were appeal proceedings, in earlier proceedings to which the appeal related).

(3) Evidence is compelling if—

    (a) it is reliable,

    (b) it is substantial, and

    (c) in the context of the outstanding issues, it appears highly probative of the case against the acquitted person.

(4) The outstanding issues are the issues in dispute in the proceedings in which the person was acquitted and, if those were appeal proceedings, any other issues remaining in dispute from earlier proceedings to which the appeal related.

(5) For the purposes of this section, it is irrelevant whether any evidence would have been admissible in earlier proceedings against the acquitted person.

79 Interests of justice

(1) The requirements of this section are met if in all the circumstances it is in the interests of justice for the court to make the order under section 77.

(2) That question is to be determined having regard in particular to—

    (a) whether existing circumstances make a fair trial unlikely;

    (b) for the purposes of that question and otherwise, the length of time since the qualifying offence was allegedly committed;

    (c) whether it is likely that the new evidence would have been adduced in the earlier proceedings against the acquitted person but for a failure by an officer or by a prosecutor to act with due diligence or expedition;

    (d) whether, since those proceedings or, if later, since the commencement of this Part, any officer or prosecutor has failed to act with due diligence or expedition.

(3)–(4) *****

80–81 *****

82 Restrictions on publication in the interests of justice

(1) Where it appears to the Court of Appeal that the inclusion of any matter in a publication would give rise to a substantial risk of prejudice to the administration of justice in a retrial, the court may order that the matter is not to be included in any publication while the order has effect.

(2) In subsection (1) "retrial" means the trial of an acquitted person for a qualifying offence pursuant to any order made or that may be made under section 77.

(3) The court may make an order under this section only if it appears to it necessary in the interests of justice to do so.

(4) An order under this section may apply to a matter which has been included in a publication published before the order takes effect, but such an order—

  (a) applies only to the later inclusion of the matter in a publication (whether directly or by inclusion of the earlier publication), and

  (b) does not otherwise affect the earlier publication.

(5)–(11) *****

*****

Extradition Act 2003

(2003, c. 41)

An Act to make provision about extradition   [20 November 2003]

Territorial extent: The United Kingdom

PART 1   EXTRADITION TO CATEGORY 1 TERRITORIES

Introduction

1   Extradition to category 1 territories

(1) This Part deals with extradition from the United Kingdom to the territories designated for the purposes of this Part by order made by the Secretary of State.

(2) In this Act references to category 1 territories are to the territories designated for the purposes of this Part.

(3) A territory may not be designated for the purposes of this Part if a person found guilty in the territory of a criminal offence may be sentenced to death for the offence under the general criminal law of the territory.

2   Part 1 warrant and certificate

(1) This section applies if the designated authority receives a Part 1 warrant in respect of a person.

(2) A Part 1 warrant is an arrest warrant which is issued by a judicial authority of a category 1 territory and which contains—

  (a) the statement referred to in subsection (3) and the information referred to in subsection (4), or

  (b) the statement referred to in subsection (5) and the information referred to in subsection (6).

(3) The statement is one that—

  (a) the person in respect of whom the Part 1 warrant is issued is accused in the category 1 territory of the commission of an offence specified in the warrant, and

  (b) the Part 1 warrant is issued with a view to his arrest and extradition to the category 1 territory for the purpose of being prosecuted for the offence.

(4) The information is—

  (a) particulars of the person's identity;

  (b) particulars of any other warrant issued in the category 1 territory for the person's arrest in respect of the offence;

(c) particulars of the circumstances in which the person is alleged to have committed the offence, including the conduct alleged to constitute the offence, the time and place at which he is alleged to have committed the offence and any provision of the law of the category 1 territory under which the conduct is alleged to constitute an offence;

(d) particulars of the sentence which may be imposed under the law of the category 1 territory in respect of the offence if the person is convicted of it.

(5) The statement is one that—

(a) the person in respect of whom the Part 1 warrant is issued is alleged to be unlawfully at large after conviction of an offence specified in the warrant by a court in the category 1 territory, and

(b) the Part 1 warrant is issued with a view to his arrest and extradition to the category 1 territory for the purpose of being sentenced for the offence or of serving a sentence of imprisonment or another form of detention imposed in respect of the offence.

(6) The information is—

(a) particulars of the person's identity;

(b) particulars of the conviction;

(c) particulars of any other warrant issued in the category 1 territory for the person's arrest in respect of the offence;

(d) particulars of the sentence which may be imposed under the law of the category 1 territory in respect of the offence, if the person has not been sentenced for the offence;

(e) particulars of the sentence which has been imposed under the law of the category 1 territory in respect of the offence, if the person has been sentenced for the offence.

(7)–(10) *****

Arrest

3 Arrest under certified Part 1 warrant

(1) This section applies if a certificate is issued under section 2 in respect of a Part 1 warrant issued in respect of a person.

(2) The warrant may be executed by a constable or a customs officer in any part of the United Kingdom.

(3)–(6) *****

4 Person arrested under Part 1 warrant

(1) This section applies if a person is arrested under a Part 1 warrant.

(2) A copy of the warrant must be given to the person as soon as practicable after his arrest.

(3) The person must be brought as soon as practicable before the appropriate judge.

(4) If subsection (2) is not complied with and the person applies to the judge to be discharged, the judge may order his discharge.

(5) If subsection (3) is not complied with and the person applies to the judge to be discharged, the judge must order his discharge.

(6) A person arrested under the warrant must be treated as continuing in legal custody until he is brought before the appropriate judge under subsection (3) or he is discharged under subsection (4) or (5).

5 Provisional arrest

(1) A constable, a customs officer or a service policeman may arrest a person without a warrant if he has reasonable grounds for believing—

(a) that a Part 1 warrant has been or will be issued in respect of the person by an authority of a category 1 territory, and

(b) that the authority has the function of issuing arrest warrants in the category 1 territory.

(2) A constable or a customs officer may arrest a person under subsection (1) in any part of the United Kingdom.

(3)–(6) *****

6–9 *****

10 Initial stage of extradition hearing

(1) This section applies if a person in respect of whom a Part 1 warrant is issued appears or is brought before the appropriate judge for the extradition hearing.

(2) The judge must decide whether the offence specified in the Part 1 warrant is an extradition offence.

(3) If the judge decides the question in subsection (2) in the negative he must order the person's discharge.

(4) If the judge decides that question in the affirmative he must proceed under section 11.

11 Bars to extradition

(1) If the judge is required to proceed under this section he must decide whether the person's extradition to the category 1 territory is barred by reason of—

(a) the rule against double jeopardy;

(b) extraneous considerations;

(c) the passage of time;

(d) the person's age;

(e) hostage-taking considerations;

(f) speciality;

(g) the person's earlier extradition to the United Kingdom from another category 1 territory;

(h) the person's earlier extradition to the United Kingdom from a non-category 1 territory.

(2) Sections 12 to 19 apply for the interpretation of subsection (1).

(3) If the judge decides any of the questions in subsection (1) in the affirmative he must order the person's discharge.

(4) If the judge decides those questions in the negative and the person is alleged to be unlawfully at large after conviction of the extradition offence, the judge must proceed under section 20.

(5) If the judge decides those questions in the negative and the person is accused of the commission of the extradition offence but is not alleged to be unlawfully at large after conviction of it, the judge must proceed under section 21.

12 Rule against double jeopardy

A person's extradition to a category 1 territory is barred by reason of the rule against double jeopardy if (and only if) it appears that he would be entitled to be discharged under any rule of law relating to previous acquittal or conviction on the assumption—

(a) that the conduct constituting the extradition offence constituted an offence in the part of the United Kingdom where the judge exercises jurisdiction;

(b) that the person were charged with the extradition offence in that part of the United Kingdom.

13 Extraneous considerations

A person's extradition to a category 1 territory is barred by reason of extraneous considerations if (and only if) it appears that—

(a) the Part 1 warrant issued in respect of him (though purporting to be issued on account of the extradition offence) is in fact issued for the purpose of prosecuting or punishing him on account of his race, religion, nationality, gender, sexual orientation or political opinions, or

(b) if extradited he might be prejudiced at his trial or punished, detained or restricted in his personal liberty by reason of his race, religion, nationality, gender, sexual orientation or political opinions.

14   Passage of time

A person's extradition to a category 1 territory is barred by reason of the passage of time if (and only if) it appears that it would be unjust or oppressive to extradite him by reason of the passage of time since he is alleged to have committed the extradition offence or since he is alleged to have become unlawfully at large (as the case may be).

15   Age

A person's extradition to a category 1 territory is barred by reason of his age if (and only if) it would be conclusively presumed because of his age that he could not be guilty of the extradition offence on the assumption—

(a) that the conduct constituting the extradition offence constituted an offence in the part of the United Kingdom where the judge exercises jurisdiction;

(b) that the person carried out the conduct when the extradition offence was committed (or alleged to be committed);

(c) that the person carried out the conduct in the part of the United Kingdom where the judge exercises jurisdiction.

16   *****

17   Speciality

(1) A person's extradition to a category 1 territory is barred by reason of speciality if (and only if) there are no speciality arrangements with the category 1 territory.

(2) There are speciality arrangements with a category 1 territory if, under the law of that territory or arrangements made between it and the United Kingdom, a person who is extradited to the territory from the United Kingdom may be dealt with in the territory for an offence committed before his extradition only if—

(a) the offence is one falling within subsection (3), or

(b) the condition in subsection (4) is satisfied.

(3) The offences are—

(a) the offence in respect of which the person is extradited;

(b) an extradition offence disclosed by the same facts as that offence;

(c) an extradition offence in respect of which the appropriate judge gives his consent under section 55 to the person being dealt with;

(d) an offence which is not punishable with imprisonment or another form of detention;

(e) an offence in respect of which the person will not be detained in connection with his trial, sentence or appeal;

(f) an offence in respect of which the person waives the right that he would have (but for this paragraph) not to be dealt with for the offence.

(4) The condition is that the person is given an opportunity to leave the category 1 territory and—

(a) he does not do so before the end of the permitted period, or

(b) if he does so before the end of the permitted period, he returns there.

(5) The permitted period is 45 days starting with the day on which the person arrives in the category 1 territory.

(6), (7) *****

18–19   *****

20   Case where person has been convicted

(1) If the judge is required to proceed under this section (by virtue of section 11) he must decide whether the person was convicted in his presence.

(2) If the judge decides the question in subsection (1) in the affirmative he must proceed under section 21.

(3) If the judge decides that question in the negative he must decide whether the person deliberately absented himself from his trial.

(4) If the judge decides the question in subsection (3) in the affirmative he must proceed under section 21.

(5) If the judge decides that question in the negative he must decide whether the person would be entitled to a retrial or (on appeal) to a review amounting to a retrial.

(6) If the judge decides the question in subsection (5) in the affirmative he must proceed under section 21.

(7) If the judge decides that question in the negative he must order the person's discharge.

(8) The judge must not decide the question in subsection (5) in the affirmative unless, in any proceedings that it is alleged would constitute a retrial or a review amounting to a retrial, the person would have these rights—

(a) the right to defend himself in person or through legal assistance of his own choosing or, if he had not sufficient means to pay for legal assistance, to be given it free when the interests of justice so required;

(b) the right to examine or have examined witnesses against him and to obtain the attendance and examination of witnesses on his behalf under the same conditions as witnesses against him.

21   Human rights

(1) If the judge is required to proceed under this section (by virtue of section 11 or 20) he must decide whether the person's extradition would be compatible with the Convention rights within the meaning of the Human Rights Act 1998 (c. 42).

(2) If the judge decides the question in subsection (1) in the negative he must order the person's discharge.

(3) If the judge decides that question in the affirmative he must order the person to be extradited to the category 1 territory in which the warrant was issued.

(4) If the judge makes an order under subsection (3) he must remand the person in custody or on bail to wait for his extradition to the category 1 territory.

(5) If the judge remands the person in custody he may later grant bail.

22–68   *****

PART 2   EXTRADITION TO CATEGORY 2 TERRITORIES

Introduction

69   Extradition to category 2 territories

(1) This Part deals with extradition from the United Kingdom to the territories designated for the purposes of this Part by order made by the Secretary of State.

(2) In this Act references to category 2 territories are to the territories designated for the purposes of this Part.

70–79   *****

80   Rule against double jeopardy

A person's extradition to a category 2 territory is barred by reason of the rule against double jeopardy if (and only if) it appears that he would be entitled to be discharged under any rule of law relating to previous acquittal or conviction if he were charged with the extradition offence in the part of the United Kingdom where the judge exercises his jurisdiction.

81 Extraneous considerations

A person's extradition to a category 2 territory is barred by reason of extraneous considerations if (and only if) it appears that—

    (a) the request for his extradition (though purporting to be made on account of the extradition offence) is in fact made for the purpose of prosecuting or punishing him on account of his race, religion, nationality, gender, sexual orientation or political opinions, or

    (b) if extradited he might be prejudiced at his trial or punished, detained or restricted in his personal liberty by reason of his race, religion, nationality, gender, sexual orientation or political opinions.

82 Passage of time

A person's extradition to a category 2 territory is barred by reason of the passage of time if (and only if) it appears that it would be unjust or oppressive to extradite him by reason of the passage of time since he is alleged to have committed the extradition offence or since he is alleged to have become unlawfully at large (as the case may be).

83–86 *****

87 Human rights

(1) If the judge is required to proceed under this section (by virtue of section 84, 85 or 86) he must decide whether the person's extradition would be compatible with the Convention rights within the meaning of the Human Rights Act 1998 (c. 42).

(2) If the judge decides the question in subsection (1) in the negative he must order the person's discharge.

(3) If the judge decides that question in the affirmative he must send the case to the Secretary of State for his decision whether the person is to be extradited.

88–93 *****

94 Death penalty

(1) The Secretary of State must not order a person's extradition to a category 2 territory if he could be, will be or has been sentenced to death for the offence concerned in the category 2 territory.

(2) Subsection (1) does not apply if the Secretary of State receives a written assurance which he considers adequate that a sentence of death—

    (a) will not be imposed, or

    (b) will not be carried out (if imposed).

*****

Licensing Act 2003

(2003, c. 17)

An Act to make provision about the regulation of the sale and supply of alcohol, the provision of entertainment and the provision of late night refreshment, about offences relating to alcohol and for connected purposes   [10 July 2003]

Territorial extent: England and Wales

1–10 *****

PART 3   PREMISES LICENCES

Introductory

11   Premises licence

In this Act "premises licence" means a licence granted under this Part, in respect of any premises, which authorises the premises to be used for one or more licensable activities.

12   The relevant licensing authority

(1) For the purposes of this Part the "relevant licensing authority" in relation to any premises is determined in accordance with this section.

(2) Subject to subsection (3), the relevant licensing authority is the authority in whose area the premises are situated.

(3), (4)   *****

13–19   *****

20   Mandatory condition: exhibition of films

(1) Where a premises licence authorises the exhibition of films, the licence must include a condition requiring the admission of children to the exhibition of any film to be restricted in accordance with this section.

(2) Where the film classification body is specified in the licence, unless subsection (3)(b) applies, admission of children must be restricted in accordance with any recommendation made by that body.

(3) Where—

    (a) the film classification body is not specified in the licence, or

    (b) the relevant licensing authority has notified the holder of the licence that this subsection applies to the film in question,

admission of children must be restricted in accordance with any recommendation made by that licensing authority.

(4) In this section—

"children" means persons aged under 18; and

"film classification body" means the person or persons designated as the authority under section 4 of the Video Recordings Act 1984 (c. 39) (authority to determine suitability of video works for classification).

21   *****

22   Prohibited conditions: plays

(1) In relation to a premises licence which authorises the performance of plays, no condition may be attached to the licence as to the nature of the plays which may be performed, or the manner of performing plays, under the licence.

(2) But subsection (1) does not prevent a licensing authority imposing, in accordance with section 18(2)(a) or (3)(b), 35(3)(b) or 52(3), any condition which it considers necessary on the grounds of public safety.

23–159   *****

PART 8   CLOSURE OF PREMISES

Closure of premises in an identified area

160   Orders to close premises in area experiencing disorder

(1) Where there is or is expected to be disorder in any petty sessions area, a magistrates' court acting for the area may make an order requiring all premises—

    (a) which are situated at or near the place of the disorder or expected disorder, and

(b) in respect of which a premises licence or a temporary event notice has effect,
to be closed for a period, not exceeding 24 hours, specified in the order.

(2) A magistrates' court may make an order under this section only on the application of a police officer who is of the rank of superintendent or above.

(3) A magistrates' court may not make such an order unless it is satisfied that it is necessary to prevent disorder.

(4)–(7) *****

Closure of identified premises

161   Closure orders for identified premises

(1) A senior police officer may make a closure order in relation to any relevant premises if he reasonably believes that—

(a) there is, or is likely imminently to be, disorder on, or in the vicinity of and related to, the premises and their closure is necessary in the interests of public safety, or

(b) a public nuisance is being caused by noise coming from the premises and the closure of the premises is necessary to prevent that nuisance.

(2) A closure order is an order under this section requiring relevant premises to be closed for a period not exceeding 24 hours beginning with the coming into force of the order.

(3) In determining whether to make a closure order in respect of any premises, the senior police officer must have regard, in particular, to the conduct of each appropriate person in relation to the disorder or nuisance.

(4) A closure order must—

(a) specify the premises to which it relates,

(b) specify the period for which the premises are to be closed,

(c) specify the grounds on which it is made, and

(d) state the effect of sections 162 to 168.

(5) A closure order in respect of any relevant premises comes into force at the time a constable gives notice of it to an appropriate person who is connected with any of the activities to which the disorder or nuisance relates.

(6) A person commits an offence if, without reasonable excuse, he permits relevant premises to be open in contravention of a closure order or any extension of it.

(7) A person guilty of an offence under subsection (6) is liable on summary conviction to imprisonment for a term not exceeding three months or to a fine not exceeding £20,000, or to both.

(8) In this section—
"relevant premises" means premises in respect of which one or more of the following have effect—

(a) a premises licence,

(b) a temporary event notice; and
"senior police officer" means a police officer of, or above, the rank of inspector.

162–163   *****

164   Application to magistrates' court by police

(1) The responsible senior police officer must, as soon as reasonably practicable after a closure order comes into force in respect of any relevant premises, apply to a relevant magistrates court for it to consider the order and any extension of it.

(2) Where an application is made under this section in respect of licensed premises, the responsible senior officer must also notify the relevant licensing authority—

(a) that a closure order has come into force,

(b) of the contents of the order and of any extension of it, and

(c) of the application under subsection (1).

165   Consideration of closure order by magistrates' court

(1) A relevant magistrates' court must as soon as reasonably practicable after receiving an application under section 164(1)—

    (a) hold a hearing to consider whether it is appropriate to exercise any of the court's powers under subsection (2) in relation to the closure order or any extension of it, and

    (b) determine whether to exercise any of those powers.

(2) The relevant magistrates' court may—

    (a) revoke the closure order and any extension of it;

    (b) order the premises to remain, or to be, closed until such time as the relevant licensing authority has made a determination in respect of the order for the purposes of section 167;

    (c) order the premises to remain or to be closed until that time subject to such exceptions as may be specified in the order;

    (d) order the premises to remain or to be closed until that time unless such conditions as may be specified in the order are satisfied.

(3) In determining whether the premises will be, or will remain, closed the relevant magistrates' court must, in particular, consider whether—

    (a) in the case of an order made by virtue of section 161(1)(a), closure is necessary in the interests of public safety because of disorder or likely disorder on the premises, or in the vicinity of and related to, the premises;

    (b) in the case of an order made by virtue of section 161(1)(b), closure is necessary to ensure that no public nuisance is, or is likely to be, caused by noise coming from the premises.

(4)–(10) *****

166   Appeal from decision of magistrates' court

(1) Any person aggrieved by a decision of a magistrates' court under section 165 may appeal to the Crown Court against the decision.

(2) An appeal under subsection (1) must be commenced by notice of appeal given by the appellant to the justices' chief executive for the magistrates' court within the period of 21 days beginning with the day the decision appealed against was made.

167–168   *****

169   Enforcement of closure order

A constable may use such force as may be necessary for the purposes of closing premises in compliance with a closure order.

170   Exemption of police from liability for damages

(1) A constable is not liable for relevant damages in respect of any act or omission of his in the performance or purported performance of his functions in relation to a closure order or any extension of it.

(2) A chief officer of police is not liable for relevant damages in respect of any act or omission of a constable under his direction or control in the performance or purported performance of a function of the constable's in relation to a closure order or any extension of it.

(3) But neither subsection (1) nor (2) applies—

    (a) if the act or omission is shown to have been in bad faith, or

    (b) so as to prevent an award of damages in respect of an act or omission on the grounds that the act or omission was unlawful as a result of section 6(1) of the Human Rights Act 1998 (c. 42) (incompatibility of act or omission with Convention rights).

(4) This section does not affect any other exemption from liability for damages (whether at common law or otherwise).

(5) In this section, "relevant damages" means damages awarded in proceedings for judicial review, the tort of negligence or misfeasance in public office.

*****

Employment Equality (Religion or Belief) Regulations 2003
(SI 2003/1660)

Territorial extent: England and Wales, Scotland (Reg 12 applies only to England and Wales, but equivalent provisions applying to Scotland are in Reg 13)

PART 1   GENERAL

1   Citation, commencement and extent
(1) These Regulations may be cited as the Employment Equality (Religion or Belief) Regulations 2003, and shall come into force on 2nd December 2003.

(2) These Regulations do not extend to Northern Ireland.

2   Interpretation
(1) In these Regulations, "religion or belief" means any religion, religious belief, or similar philosophical belief.

(2) In these Regulations, references to discrimination are to any discrimination falling within regulation 3 (discrimination on grounds of religion or belief) or 4 (discrimination by way of victimisation) and related expressions shall be construed accordingly, and references to harassment shall be construed in accordance with regulation 5 (harassment on grounds of religion or belief).

(3) In these Regulations—

"act" includes a deliberate omission;

*****

"detriment" does not include harassment within the meaning of regulation 5;

references to "employer", in their application to a person at any time seeking to employ another, include a person who has no employees at that time;

"employment" means employment under a contract of service or of apprenticeship or a contract personally to do any work, and related expressions shall be construed accordingly;

*****

3   Discrimination on grounds of religion or belief
(1) For the purposes of these Regulations, a person ("A") discriminates against another person ("B") if—

(a) on grounds of religion or belief, A treats B less favourably than he treats or would treat other persons; or

(b) A applies to B a provision, criterion or practice which he applies or would apply equally to persons not of the same religion or belief as B, but—

(i) which puts or would put persons of the same religion or belief as B at a particular disadvantage when compared with other persons,

(ii) which puts B at that disadvantage, and

(iii) which A cannot show to be a proportionate means of achieving a legitimate aim.

(2) The reference in paragraph (1)(a) to religion or belief does not include A's religion or belief.

(3) A comparison of B's case with that of another person under paragraph (1) must be such that the relevant circumstances in the one case are the same, or not materially different, in the other.

4   Discrimination by way of victimisation

(1) For the purposes of these Regulations, a person ("A") discriminates against another person ("B") if he treats B less favourably than he treats or would treat other persons in the same circumstances, and does so by reason that B has—

(a) brought proceedings against A or any other person under these Regulations;

(b) given evidence or information in connection with proceedings brought by any person against A or any other person under these Regulations;

(c) otherwise done anything under or by reference to these Regulations in relation to A or any other person; or

(d) alleged that A or any other person has committed an act which (whether or not the allegation so states) would amount to a contravention of these Regulations,

or by reason that A knows that B intends to do any of those things, or suspects that B has done or intends to do any of them.

(2) Paragraph (1) does not to apply to treatment of B by reason of any allegation made by him, or evidence or information given by him, if the allegation, evidence or information was false and not made (or, as the case may be, given) in good faith.

5   Harassment on grounds of religion or belief

(1) For the purposes of these Regulations, a person ("A") subjects another person ("B") to harassment where, on grounds of religion or belief, A engages in unwanted conduct which has the purpose or effect of—

(a) violating B's dignity; or

(b) creating an intimidating, hostile, degrading, humiliating or offensive environment for B.

(2) Conduct shall be regarded as having the effect specified in paragraph (1)(a) or (b) only if, having regard to all the circumstances, including in particular the perception of B, it should reasonably be considered as having that effect.

PART II   DISCRIMINATION IN EMPLOYMENT AND VOCATIONAL TRAINING

6   Applicants and employees

(1) It is unlawful for an employer, in relation to employment by him at an establishment in Great Britain, to discriminate against a person—

(a) in the arrangements he makes for the purpose of determining to whom he should offer employment;

(b) in the terms on which he offers that person employment; or

(c) by refusing to offer, or deliberately not offering, him employment.

(2) It is unlawful for an employer, in relation to a person whom he employs at an establishment in Great Britain, to discriminate against that person—

(a) in the terms of employment which he affords him;

(b) in the opportunities which he affords him for promotion, a transfer, training, or receiving any other benefit;

(c) by refusing to afford him, or deliberately not affording him, any such opportunity; or

(d) by dismissing him, or subjecting him to any other detriment.

(3) It is unlawful for an employer, in relation to employment by him at an establishment in Great Britain, to subject to harassment a person whom he employs or who has applied to him for employment.

(4), (5) *****

7 Exception for genuine occupational requirement

(1) In relation to discrimination falling within regulation 3 (discrimination on grounds of religion or belief)—

    (a) regulation 6(1)(a) or (c) does not apply to any employment;

    (b) regulation 6(2)(b) or (c) does not apply to promotion or transfer to, or training for, any employment; and

    (c) regulation 6(2)(d) does not apply to dismissal from any employment,

where paragraph (2) or (3) applies.

(2) This paragraph applies where, having regard to the nature of the employment or the context in which it is carried out—

    (a) being of a particular religion or belief is a genuine and determining occupational requirement;

    (b) it is proportionate to apply that requirement in the particular case; and

    (c) either—

        (i) the person to whom that requirement is applied does not meet it, or

        (ii) the employer is not satisfied, and in all the circumstances it is reasonable for him not to be satisfied, that that person meets it,

and this paragraph applies whether or not the employer has an ethos based on religion or belief.

(3) This paragraph applies where an employer has an ethos based on religion or belief and, having regard to that ethos and to the nature of the employment or the context in which it is carried out—

    (a) being of a particular religion or belief is a genuine occupational requirement for the job;

    (b) it is proportionate to apply that requirement in the particular case; and

    (c) either—

        (i) the person to whom that requirement is applied does not meet it, or

        (ii) the employer is not satisfied, and in all the circumstances it is reasonable for him not to be satisfied, that that person meets it.

8 Contract workers

(1) It is unlawful for a principal, in relation to contract work at an establishment in Great Britain, to discriminate against a contract worker—

    (a) in the terms on which he allows him to do that work;

    (b) by not allowing him to do it or continue to do it;

    (c) in the way he affords him access to any benefits or by refusing or deliberately not affording him access to them; or

    (d) by subjecting him to any other detriment.

(2) It is unlawful for a principal, in relation to contract work at an establishment in Great Britain, to subject a contract worker to harassment.

(3) A principal does not contravene paragraph (1)(b) by doing any act in relation to a contract worker where, if the work were to be done by a person taken into the principal's employment, that act would be lawful by virtue of regulation 7 (exception for genuine occupational requirement).

(4), (5) *****

9 Meaning of employment and contract work at establishment in Great Britain

(1) For the purposes of this Part ("the relevant purposes"), employment is to be regarded as being at an establishment in Great Britain if the employee—

    (a) does his work wholly or partly in Great Britain; or

    (b) does his work wholly outside Great Britain and paragraph (2) applies.

(2) This paragraph applies if—

(a) the employer has a place of business at an establishment in Great Britain;

(b) the work is for the purposes of the business carried on at that establishment; and

(c) the employee is ordinarily resident in Great Britain—

(i) at the time when he applies for or is offered the employment, or

(ii) at any time during the course of the employment.

(3)–(7) *****

9A, 10   *****

11   Police

(1) For the purposes of this Part, the holding of the office of constable shall be treated as employment—

(a) by the chief officer of police as respects any act done by him in relation to a constable or that office;

(b) by the police authority as respects any act done by it in relation to a constable or that office.

(2) For the purposes of regulation 22 (liability of employers and principals)—

(a) the holding of the office of constable shall be treated as employment by the chief officer of police (and as not being employment by any other person); and

(b) anything done by a person holding such an office in the performance, or purported performance, of his functions shall be treated as done in the course of that employment.

12   Barristers

(1) It is unlawful for a barrister or barrister's clerk, in relation to any offer of a pupillage or tenancy, to discriminate against a person—

(a) in the arrangements which are made for the purpose of determining to whom the pupillage or tenancy should be offered;

(b) in respect of any terms on which it is offered; or

(c) by refusing, or deliberately not offering, it to him.

(2) It is unlawful for a barrister or barrister's clerk, in relation to a pupil or tenant in the set of chambers in question, to discriminate against him—

(a) in respect of any terms applicable to him as a pupil or tenant;

(b) in the opportunities for training, or gaining experience, which are afforded or denied to him;

(c) in the benefits which are afforded or denied to him; or

(d) by terminating his pupillage, or by subjecting him to any pressure to leave the chambers or other detriment.

(3) It is unlawful for a barrister or barrister's clerk, in relation to a pupillage or tenancy in the set of chambers in question, to subject to harassment a person who is, or has applied to be, a pupil or tenant.

(4) It is unlawful for any person, in relation to the giving, withholding or acceptance of instructions to a barrister, to discriminate against any person by subjecting him to a detriment, or to subject him to harassment.

(5), (6) *****

13   (Equivalent provisions as to Advocates) *****

14–19   *****

20   Institutions of further and higher education

(1) It is unlawful, in relation to an educational establishment to which this regulation applies, for the governing body of that establishment to discriminate against a person—

(a) in the terms on which it offers to admit him to the establishment as a student;

    (b) by refusing or deliberately not accepting an application for his admission to the establishment as a student; or

    (c) where he is a student of the establishment—

        (i)   in the way it affords him access to any benefits,

        (ii) by refusing or deliberately not affording him access to them, or

        (iii) by excluding him from the establishment or subjecting him to any other detriment.

(2) It is unlawful, in relation to an educational establishment to which this regulation applies, for the governing body of that establishment to subject to harassment a person who is a student at the establishment, or who has applied for admission to the establishment as a student.

(3) Paragraph (1) does not apply if the discrimination only concerns training which would help fit a person for employment which, by virtue of regulation 7 (exception for genuine occupational requirement), the employer could lawfully refuse to offer the person in question.

(4)–(6) *****

21 Relationships which have come to an end

(1) In this regulation a "relevant relationship" is a relationship during the course of which an act of discrimination against, or harassment of, one party to the relationship ("B") by the other party to it ("A") is unlawful by virtue of any preceding provision of this Part.

(2) Where a relevant relationship has come to an end, it is unlawful for A—

    (a) to discriminate against B by subjecting him to a detriment; or

    (b) to subject B to harassment,

where the discrimination or harassment arises out of and is closely connected to that relationship.

(3) *****

PART III OTHER UNLAWFUL ACTS

22 Liability of employers and principals

(1) Anything done by a person in the course of his employment shall be treated for the purposes of these Regulations as done by his employer as well as by him, whether or not it was done with the employer's knowledge or approval.

(2) Anything done by a person as agent for another person with the authority (whether express or implied, and whether precedent or subsequent) of that other person shall be treated for the purposes of these Regulations as done by that other person as well as by him.

(3) In proceedings brought under these Regulations against any person in respect of an act alleged to have been done by an employee of his it shall be a defence for that person to prove that he took such steps as were reasonably practicable to prevent the employee from doing that act, or from doing in the course of his employment acts of that description.

23 Aiding unlawful acts

(1) A person who knowingly aids another person to do an act made unlawful by these Regulations shall be treated for the purpose of these Regulations as himself doing an unlawful act of the like description.

(2) For the purposes of paragraph (1) an employee or agent for whose act the employer or principal is liable under regulation 22 (or would be so liable but for regulation 22(3)) shall be deemed to aid the doing of the act by the employer or principal.

(3), (4) *****

PART IV   GENERAL EXCEPTIONS FROM PARTS II AND III

24   Exception for national security

Nothing in Part II or III shall render unlawful an act done for the purpose of safeguarding national security, if the doing of the act was justified by that purpose.

25   Exceptions for positive action

(1) Nothing in Part II or III shall render unlawful any act done in or in connection with—

(a) affording persons of a particular religion or belief access to facilities for training which would help fit them for particular work; or

(b) encouraging persons of a particular religion or belief to take advantage of opportunities for doing particular work,

where it reasonably appears to the person doing the act that it prevents or compensates for disadvantages linked to religion or belief suffered by persons of that religion or belief doing that work or likely to take up that work.

(2), (3) *****

26   Protection of Sikhs from discrimination in connection with requirements as to wearing of safety helmets

(1) Where—

(a) any person applies to a Sikh any provision, criterion or practice relating to the wearing by him of a safety helmet while he is on a construction site; and

(b) at the time when he so applies the provision, criterion or practice that person has no reasonable grounds for believing that the Sikh would not wear a turban at all times when on such a site,

then, for the purposes of regulation 3(1)(b)(iii), the provision, criterion or practice shall be taken to be one which cannot be shown to be a proportionate means of achieving a legitimate aim.

(2) Any special treatment afforded to a Sikh in consequence of section 11(1) or (2) of the Employment Act 1989 (exemption of Sikhs from requirements as to wearing of safety helmets on construction sites) shall not be regarded as giving rise, in relation to any other person, to any discrimination falling within regulation 3.

PART V   ENFORCEMENT

27   Restriction of proceedings for breach of Regulations

(1) Except as provided by these Regulations no proceedings, whether civil or criminal, shall lie against any person in respect of an act by reason that the act is unlawful by virtue of a provision of these Regulations.

(2) Paragraph (1) does not prevent the making of an application for judicial review [or the investigation or determination of any matter in accordance with Part X (investigations: the Pensions Ombudsman) of the Pension Schemes Act 1993 by the Pensions Ombudsman].

28   Jurisdiction of employment tribunals

(1) A complaint by any person ("the complainant") that another person ("the respondent")—

(a) has committed against the complainant an act to which this regulation applies; or

(b) is by virtue of regulation 22 (liability of employers and principals) or 23 (aiding unlawful acts) to be treated as having committed against the complainant such an act,

may be presented to an employment tribunal.

(2) This regulation applies to any act of discrimination or harassment which is unlawful by virtue of any provision of Part II other than—

(a) where the act is one in respect of which an appeal or proceedings in the nature of an appeal may be brought under any enactment, regulation 16 (qualifications bodies);

(b) regulation 20 (institutions of further and higher education); or

(c) where the act arises out of and is closely connected to a relationship between the complainant and the respondent which has come to an end but during the course of which an act of discrimination against, or harassment of, the complainant by the respondent would have been unlawful by virtue of regulation 20, regulation 21 (relationships which have come to an end).

(3), (4) *****

29   Burden of proof: employment tribunals

(1) This regulation applies to any complaint presented under regulation 28 to an employment tribunal.

(2) Where, on the hearing of the complaint, the complainant proves facts from which the tribunal could, apart from this regulation, conclude in the absence of an adequate explanation that the respondent—

(a) has committed against the complainant an act to which regulation 28 applies; or

(b) is by virtue of regulation 22 (liability of employers and principals) or 23 (aiding unlawful acts) to be treated as having committed against the complainant such an act,

the tribunal shall uphold the complaint unless the respondent proves that he did not commit, or as the case may be, is not to be treated as having committed, that act.

30   Remedies on complaints in employment tribunals

(1) Where an employment tribunal finds that a complaint presented to it under regulation 28 is well-founded, the tribunal shall make such of the following as it considers just and equitable—

(a) an order declaring the rights of the complainant and the respondent in relation to the act to which the complaint relates;

(b) an order requiring the respondent to pay to the complainant compensation of an amount corresponding to any damages he could have been ordered by a county court or by a sheriff court to pay to the complainant if the complaint had fallen to be dealt with under regulation 31 (jurisdiction of county and sheriff courts);

(c) a recommendation that the respondent take within a specified period action appearing to the tribunal to be practicable for the purpose of obviating or reducing the adverse effect on the complainant of any act of discrimination or harassment to which the complaint relates.

(2)–(5) *****

31   Jurisdiction of county and sheriff courts

(1) A claim by any person ("the claimant") that another person ("the respondent")—

(a) has committed against the claimant an act to which this regulation applies; or

(b) is by virtue of regulation 22 (liability of employers and principals) or 23 (aiding unlawful acts) to be treated as having committed against the claimant such an act,

may be made the subject of civil proceedings in like manner as any other claim in tort or (in Scotland) in reparation for breach of statutory duty.

(2) Proceedings brought under paragraph (1) shall—

(a) in England and Wales, be brought only in a county court; and

(b) in Scotland, be brought only in a sheriff court.

(3) For the avoidance of doubt it is hereby declared that damages in respect of an unlawful act to which this regulation applies may include compensation for injury to feelings whether or not they include compensation under any other head.

(4) This regulation applies to any act of discrimination or harassment which is unlawful by virtue of—

(a) regulation 20 (institutions of further and higher education); or
(b) where the act arises out of and is closely connected to a relationship between the claimant and the respondent which has come to an end but during the course of which an act of discrimination against, or harassment of, the claimant by the respondent would have been unlawful by virtue of regulation 20, regulation 21 (relationships which have come to an end).

(5) *****

32   *****

33   Help for persons in obtaining information etc

(1) In accordance with this regulation, a person ("the person aggrieved") who considers he may have been discriminated against, or subjected to harassment, in contravention of these Regulations may serve on the respondent to a complaint presented under regulation 28 (jurisdiction of employment tribunals) or a claim brought under regulation 31 (jurisdiction of county and sheriff courts) questions in the form set out in Schedule 2 or forms to the like effect with such variation as the circumstances require; and the respondent may if he so wishes reply to such questions by way of the form set out in Schedule 3 or forms to the like effect with such variation as the circumstances require.

(2) Where the person aggrieved questions the respondent (whether in accordance with paragraph (1) or not)—
(a) the questions, and any reply by the respondent (whether in accordance with paragraph (1) or not) shall, subject to the following provisions of this regulation, be admissible as evidence in the proceedings;
(b) if it appears to the court or tribunal that the respondent deliberately, and without reasonable excuse, omitted to reply within eight weeks of service of the questions or that his reply is evasive or equivocal, the court or tribunal may draw any inference from that fact that it considers it just and equitable to draw, including an inference that he committed an unlawful act.

(3)–(7) *****

*****

Employment Equality (Sexual Orientation) Regulations 2003

(SI 2003/1661)

Territorial extent: England and Wales, Scotland (provisions reproduced)

Note: These Regulations are to a considerable extent worded identically to the equivalent provisions in the Employment Equality (Religion or Belief) Regulations 2003, above. In particular Regs 6, 8, 9, 11, 12, 20, 21, 22, 24, 27, 28, 29, 30, 31 and 33 of the Religion or Belief Regulations, as printed above, appear with identical wording in the Sexual Orientation Regulations. To save space they are not reproduced a second time.

PART I   GENERAL

1   Citation, commencement and extent

(1) These Regulations may be cited as the Employment Equality (Sexual Orientation) Regulations 2003, and shall come into force on 1st December 2003.
(2) These Regulations do not extend to Northern Ireland.

2   Interpretation

(1) In these Regulations, "sexual orientation" means a sexual orientation towards—

  (a) persons of the same sex;

  (b) persons of the opposite sex; or

  (c) persons of the same sex and of the opposite sex.

(2) In these Regulations, references to discrimination are to any discrimination falling within regulation 3 (discrimination on grounds of sexual orientation) or 4 (discrimination by way of victimisation) and related expressions shall be construed accordingly, and references to harassment shall be construed in accordance with regulation 5 (harassment on grounds of sexual orientation).

(3) In these Regulations—

"act" includes a deliberate omission;

*****

"detriment" does not include harassment within the meaning of regulation 5;

references to "employer", in their application to a person at any time seeking to employ another, include a person who has no employees at that time;

"employment" means employment under a contract of service or of apprenticeship or a contract personally to do any work, and related expressions shall be construed accordingly;

*****

3   Discrimination on grounds of sexual orientation

(1) For the purposes of these Regulations, a person ("A") discriminates against another person ("B") if—

  (a) on grounds of sexual orientation, A treats B less favourably than he treats or would treat other persons; or

  (b) A applies to B a provision, criterion or practice which he applies or would apply equally to persons not of the same sexual orientation as B, but—

    (i)   which puts or would put persons of the same sexual orientation as B at a particular disadvantage when compared with other persons,

    (ii) which puts B at that disadvantage, and

    (iii) which A cannot show to be a proportionate means of achieving a legitimate aim.

(2) A comparison of B's case with that of another person under paragraph (1) must be such that the relevant circumstances in the one case are the same, or not materially different, in the other.

4   Discrimination by way of victimisation

(1) For the purposes of these Regulations, a person ("A") discriminates against another person ("B") if he treats B less favourably than he treats or would treat other persons in the same circumstances, and does so by reason that B has—

  (a) brought proceedings against A or any other person under these Regulations;

  (b) given evidence or information in connection with proceedings brought by any person against A or any other person under these Regulations;

  (c) otherwise done anything under or by reference to these Regulations in relation to A or any other person; or

  (d) alleged that A or any other person has committed an act which (whether or not the allegation so states) would amount to a contravention of these Regulations,

or by reason that A knows that B intends to do any of those things, or suspects that B has done or intends to do any of them.

(2) Paragraph (1) does not apply to treatment of B by reason of any allegation made by him, or evidence or information given by him, if the allegation, evidence or information was false and not made (or, as the case may be, given) in good faith.

5   Harassment on grounds of sexual orientation

(1) For the purposes of these Regulations, a person ("A") subjects another person ("B") to harassment where, on grounds of sexual orientation, A engages in unwanted conduct which has the purpose or effect of—

(a) violating B's dignity; or

(b) creating an intimidating, hostile, degrading, humiliating or offensive environment for B.

(2) Conduct shall be regarded as having the effect specified in paragraph (1)(a) or (b) only if, having regard to all the circumstances, including in particular the perception of B, it should reasonably be considered as having that effect.

PART II   DISCRIMINATION IN EMPLOYMENT AND VOCATIONAL TRAINING

6   ***   (see general note above)**

7   Exception for genuine occupational requirement etc

(1) In relation to discrimination falling within regulation 3 (discrimination on grounds of sexual orientation)—

(a) regulation 6(1)(a) or (c) does not apply to any employment;

(b) regulation 6(2)(b) or (c) does not apply to promotion or transfer to, or training for, any employment; and

(c) regulation 6(2)(d) does not apply to dismissal from any employment,

where paragraph (2) or (3) applies.

(2) This paragraph applies where, having regard to the nature of the employment or the context in which it is carried out—

(a) being of a particular sexual orientation is a genuine and determining occupational requirement;

(b) it is proportionate to apply that requirement in the particular case; and

(c) either—

(i)   the person to whom that requirement is applied does not meet it, or

(ii) the employer is not satisfied, and in all the circumstances it is reasonable for him not to be satisfied, that that person meets it,

and this paragraph applies whether or not the employment is for purposes of an organised religion.

(3) This paragraph applies where—

(a) the employment is for purposes of an organised religion;

(b) the employer applies a requirement related to sexual orientation—

(i)   so as to comply with the doctrines of the religion, or

(ii) because of the nature of the employment and the context in which it is carried out, so as to avoid conflicting with the strongly held religious convictions of a significant number of the religion's followers; and

(c) either—

(i)   the person to whom that requirement is applied does not meet it, or

(ii) the employer is not satisfied, and in all the circumstances it is reasonable for him not to be satisfied, that that person meets it.

8–24   ***   (see general note above)**

25   Exception for benefits dependent on marital status

Nothing in Part II or III shall render unlawful anything which prevents or restricts access to a benefit by reference to marital status.

26   Exceptions for positive action
   (1) Nothing in Part II or III shall render unlawful any act done in or in connection with—
      (a)   affording persons of a particular sexual orientation access to facilities for training which would help fit them for particular work; or
      (b)   encouraging persons of a particular sexual orientation to take advantage of opportunities for doing particular work,
where it reasonably appears to the person doing the act that it prevents or compensates for disadvantages linked to sexual orientation suffered by persons of that sexual orientation doing that work or likely to take up that work.
   (2), (3) ****

*****   (see general note above)

Asylum and Immigration (Treatment of Claimants, etc.) Act 2004
(2004, c. 19)

An Act to make provision about asylum and immigration   [22 July 2004]

Territorial extent: United Kingdom; may be extended by Order to any of the Channel Islands and the Isle of Man

Offences

1   *****

2   Entering United Kingdom without passport, &c.
   (1) A person commits an offence if at a leave or asylum interview he does not have with him an immigration document which—
      (a) is in force, and
      (b) satisfactorily establishes his identity and nationality or citizenship.
   (2) A person commits an offence if at a leave or asylum interview he does not have with him, in respect of any dependent child with whom he claims to be travelling or living, an immigration document which—
      (a) is in force, and
      (b) satisfactorily establishes the child's identity and nationality or citizenship.
   (3) But a person does not commit an offence under subsection (1) or (2) if—
      (a) the interview referred to in that subsection takes place after the person has entered the United Kingdom, and
      (b) within the period of three days beginning with the date of the interview the person provides to an immigration officer or to the Secretary of State a document of the kind referred to in that subsection.
   (4) It is a defence for a person charged with an offence under subsection (1)—
      (a) to prove that he is an EEA national,
      (b) to prove that he is a member of the family of an EEA national and that he is exercising a right under the Community Treaties in respect of entry to or residence in the United Kingdom,
      (c) to prove that he has a reasonable excuse for not being in possession of a document of the kind specified in subsection (1),
      (d) to produce a false immigration document and to prove that he used that document as an immigration document for all purposes in connection with his journey to the United Kingdom, or

(e) to prove that he travelled to the United Kingdom without, at any stage since he set out on the journey, having possession of an immigration document.

(5) It is a defence for a person charged with an offence under subsection (2) in respect of a child—

(a) to prove that the child is an EEA national,

(b) to prove that the child is a member of the family of an EEA national and that the child is exercising a right under the Community Treaties in respect of entry to or residence in the United Kingdom,

(c) to prove that the person has a reasonable excuse for not being in possession of a document of the kind specified in subsection (2),

(d) to produce a false immigration document and to prove that it was used as an immigration document for all purposes in connection with the child's journey to the United Kingdom, or

(e) to prove that he travelled to the United Kingdom with the child without, at any stage since he set out on the journey, having possession of an immigration document in respect of the child.

(6) Where the charge for an offence under subsection (1) or (2) relates to an interview which takes place after the defendant has entered the United Kingdom—

(a) subsections (4)(c) and (5)(c) shall not apply, but

(b) it is a defence for the defendant to prove that he has a reasonable excuse for not providing a document in accordance with subsection (3).

(7) For the purposes of subsections (4) to (6)—

(a) the fact that a document was deliberately destroyed or disposed of is not a reasonable excuse for not being in possession of it or for not providing it in accordance with subsection (3), unless it is shown that the destruction or disposal was—

(i) for a reasonable cause, or

(ii) beyond the control of the person charged with the offence, and

(b) in paragraph (a)(i) "reasonable cause" does not include the purpose of—

(i) delaying the handling or resolution of a claim or application or the taking of a decision,

(ii) increasing the chances of success of a claim or application, or

(iii) complying with instructions or advice given by a person who offers advice about, or facilitates, immigration into the United Kingdom, unless in the circumstances of the case it is unreasonable to expect non-compliance with the instructions or advice.

(8) A person shall be presumed for the purposes of this section not to have a document with him if he fails to produce it to an immigration officer or official of the Secretary of State on request.

(9) A person guilty of an offence under this section shall be liable—

(a) on conviction on indictment, to imprisonment for a term not exceeding two years, to a fine or to both, or

(b) on summary conviction, to imprisonment for a term not exceeding twelve months, to a fine not exceeding the statutory maximum or to both.

(10)–(17) *****

3　*****

4　Trafficking people for exploitation

(1) A person commits an offence if he arranges or facilitates the arrival in the United Kingdom of an individual (the "passenger") and—

(a) he intends to exploit the passenger in the United Kingdom or elsewhere, or

(b) he believes that another person is likely to exploit the passenger in the United Kingdom or elsewhere.

(2) A person commits an offence if he arranges or facilitates travel within the United Kingdom by an individual (the "passenger") in respect of whom he believes that an offence under subsection (1) may have been committed and—

    (a) he intends to exploit the passenger in the United Kingdom or elsewhere, or

    (b) he believes that another person is likely to exploit the passenger in the United Kingdom or elsewhere.

(3) A person commits an offence if he arranges or facilitates the departure from the United Kingdom of an individual (the "passenger") and—

    (a) he intends to exploit the passenger outside the United Kingdom, or

    (b) he believes that another person is likely to exploit the passenger outside the United Kingdom.

(4) For the purposes of this section a person is exploited if (and only if)—

    (a) he is the victim of behaviour that contravenes Article 4 of the Human Rights Convention (slavery and forced labour),

    (b) he is encouraged, required or expected to do anything as a result of which he or another person would commit an offence under the Human Organ Transplants Act 1989 (c. 31) or the Human Organ Transplants (Northern Ireland) Order 1989 (S.I. 1989/2408 (N.I. 21)),

    (c) he is subjected to force, threats or deception designed to induce him—

        (i) to provide services of any kind,

        (ii) to provide another person with benefits of any kind, or

        (iii) to enable another person to acquire benefits of any kind, or

    (d) he is requested or induced to undertake any activity, having been chosen as the subject of the request or inducement on the grounds that—

        (i) he is mentally or physically ill or disabled, he is young or he has a family relationship with a person, and

        (ii) a person without the illness, disability, youth or family relationship would be likely to refuse the request or resist the inducement.

(5) A person guilty of an offence under this section shall be liable—

    (a) on conviction on indictment, to imprisonment for a term not exceeding 14 years, to a fine or to both, or

    (b) on summary conviction, to imprisonment for a term not exceeding twelve months, to a fine not exceeding the statutory maximum or to both.

5–7 *******

Treatment of claimants

8   Claimant's credibility

(1) In determining whether to believe a statement made by or on behalf of a person who makes an asylum claim or a human rights claim, a deciding authority shall take account, as damaging the claimant's credibility, of any behaviour to which this section applies.

(2) This section applies to any behaviour by the claimant that the deciding authority thinks—

    (a) is designed or likely to conceal information,

    (b) is designed or likely to mislead, or

    (c) is designed or likely to obstruct or delay the handling or resolution of the claim or the taking of a decision in relation to the claimant.

(3) *******

(4) This section also applies to failure by the claimant to take advantage of a reasonable opportunity to make an asylum claim or human rights claim while in a safe country.

(5) This section also applies to failure by the claimant to make an asylum claim or human

rights claim before being notified of an immigration decision, unless the claim relies wholly on matters arising after the notification.

(6) This section also applies to failure by the claimant to make an asylum claim or human rights claim before being arrested under an immigration provision, unless—

(a) he had no reasonable opportunity to make the claim before the arrest, or

(b) the claim relies wholly on matters arising after the arrest.

(7)–(11) *****

(12) This section shall not prevent a deciding authority from determining not to believe a statement on the grounds of behaviour to which this section does not apply.

(13) *****

9–32 ***

Removal and detention

33 Removing asylum seeker to safe country

(1) Schedule 3 (which concerns the removal of persons claiming asylum to countries known to protect refugees and to respect human rights) shall have effect.

(2), (3) *****

34 *****

35 Deportation or removal: cooperation

(1) The Secretary of State may require a person to take specified action if the Secretary of State thinks that—

(a) the action will or may enable a travel document to be obtained by or for the person, and

(b) possession of the travel document will facilitate the person's deportation or removal from the United Kingdom.

(2) In particular, the Secretary of State may require a person to—

(a) provide information or documents to the Secretary of State or to any other person;

(b) obtain information or documents;

(c) provide fingerprints, submit to the taking of a photograph or provide information, or submit to a process for the recording of information, about external physical characteristics (including, in particular, features of the iris or any other part of the eye);

(d) make, or consent to or cooperate with the making of, an application to a person acting for the government of a State other than the United Kingdom;

(e) cooperate with a process designed to enable determination of an application;

(f) complete a form accurately and completely;

(g) attend an interview and answer questions accurately and completely;

(h) make an appointment.

(3) A person commits an offence if he fails without reasonable excuse to comply with a requirement of the Secretary of State under subsection (1).

(4)–(8) *****

36 Electronic monitoring

(1) In this section—

(a) "residence restriction" means a restriction as to residence imposed under—

(i) paragraph 21 of Schedule 2 to the Immigration Act 1971 (c. 77) (control on entry) (including that paragraph as applied by another provision of the Immigration Acts), or

(ii) Schedule 3 to that Act (deportation),

(b) "reporting restriction" means a requirement to report to a specified person imposed under any of those provisions,

(c), (d) *****
(2) Where a residence restriction is imposed on an adult—
    (a) he may be required to cooperate with electronic monitoring, and
    (b) failure to comply with a requirement under paragraph (a) shall be treated for all purposes of the Immigration Acts as failure to observe the residence restriction.
(3) Where a reporting restriction could be imposed on an adult—
    (a) he may instead be required to cooperate with electronic monitoring, and
    (b) the requirement shall be treated for all purposes of the Immigration Acts as a reporting restriction.
(4) Immigration bail may be granted to an adult subject to a requirement that he cooperate with electronic monitoring; and the requirement may (but need not) be imposed as a condition of a recognizance or bail bond.
(5) In this section a reference to requiring an adult to cooperate with electronic monitoring is a reference to requiring him to cooperate with such arrangements as the person imposing the requirement may specify for detecting and recording by electronic means the location of the adult, or his presence in or absence from a location—
    (a) at specified times,
    (b) during specified periods of time, or
    (c) throughout the currency of the arrangements.
(6)–(12) *****

*****

SCHEDULE 3   REMOVAL OF ASYLUM SEEKER TO SAFE COUNTRY

PART 1   INTRODUCTORY

1 (1) In this Schedule—
"asylum claim" means a claim by a person that to remove him from or require him to leave the United Kingdom would breach the United Kingdom's obligations under the Refugee Convention,
"Convention rights" means the rights identified as Convention rights by section 1 of the Human Rights Act 1998 (c. 42) (whether or not in relation to a State that is a party to the Convention),
"human rights claim" means a claim by a person that to remove him from or require him to leave the United Kingdom would be unlawful under section 6 of the Human Rights Act 1998 (public authority not to act contrary to Convention) as being incompatible with his Convention rights,
"immigration appeal" means an appeal under section 82(1) of the Nationality, Immigration and Asylum Act 2002 (c. 41) (appeal against immigration decision), and
"the Refugee Convention" means the Convention relating to the Status of Refugees done at Geneva on 28th July 1951 and its Protocol.
    (2) In this Schedule a reference to anything being done in accordance with the Refugee Convention is a reference to the thing being done in accordance with the principles of the Convention, whether or not by a signatory to it.

PART 2   FIRST LIST OF SAFE COUNTRIES (REFUGEE CONVENTION AND HUMAN RIGHTS (1))

2 This Part applies to—
    (a) Austria,

(b) Belgium,

(c) Republic of Cyprus,

(d) Czech Republic,

(e) Denmark,

(f) Estonia,

(g) Finland,

(h) France,

(i) Germany,

(j) Greece,

(k) Hungary,

(l) Iceland,

(m) Ireland,

(n) Italy,

(o) Latvia,

(p) Lithuania,

(q) Luxembourg,

(r) Malta,

(s) Netherlands,

(t) Norway,

(u) Poland,

(v) Portugal,

(w) Slovak Republic,

(x) Slovenia,

(y) Spain, and

(z) Sweden.

3 (1) This paragraph applies for the purposes of the determination by any person, tribunal or court whether a person who has made an asylum claim or a human rights claim may be removed—

(a) from the United Kingdom, and

(b) to a State of which he is not a national or citizen.

(2) A State to which this Part applies shall be treated, in so far as relevant to the question mentioned in sub-paragraph (1), as a place—

(a) where a person's life and liberty are not threatened by reason of his race, religion, nationality, membership of a particular social group or political opinion,

(b) from which a person will not be sent to another State in contravention of his Convention rights, and

(c) from which a person will not be sent to another State otherwise than in accordance with the Refugee Convention.

4 Section 77 of the Nationality, Immigration and Asylum Act 2002 (c. 41) (no removal while claim for asylum pending) shall not prevent a person who has made a claim for asylum from being removed—

(a) from the United Kingdom, and

(b) to a State to which this Part applies;

provided that the Secretary of State certifies that in his opinion the person is not a national or citizen of the State.

5 (1)   This paragraph applies where the Secretary of State certifies that—

(a) it is proposed to remove a person to a State to which this Part applies, and

(b) in the Secretary of State's opinion the person is not a national or citizen of the State.

(2) The person may not bring an immigration appeal by virtue of section 92(2) or (3) of that Act (appeal from within United Kingdom: general).

(3) The person may not bring an immigration appeal by virtue of section 92(4)(a) of that Act (appeal from within United Kingdom: asylum or human rights) in reliance on—

(a) an asylum claim which asserts that to remove the person to a specified State to which this Part applies would breach the United Kingdom's obligations under the Refugee Convention, or

(b) a human rights claim in so far as it asserts that to remove the person to a specified State to which this Part applies would be unlawful under section 6 of the Human Rights Act 1998 because of the possibility of removal from that State to another State.

(4) The person may not bring an immigration appeal by virtue of section 92(4)(a) of that Act in reliance on a human rights claim to which this sub-paragraph applies if the Secretary of State certifies that the claim is clearly unfounded; and the Secretary of State shall certify a human rights claim to which this sub-paragraph applies unless satisfied that the claim is not clearly unfounded.

(5) Sub-paragraph (4) applies to a human rights claim if, or in so far as, it asserts a matter other than that specified in sub-paragraph (3)(b).

6 A person who is outside the United Kingdom may not bring an immigration appeal on any ground that is inconsistent with treating a State to which this Part applies as a place—

(a) where a person's life and liberty are not threatened by reason of his race, religion, nationality, membership of a particular social group or political opinion,

(b) from which a person will not be sent to another State in contravention of his Convention rights, and

(c) from which a person will not be sent to another State otherwise than in accordance with the Refugee Convention.

PART 3   SECOND LIST OF SAFE COUNTRIES (REFUGEE CONVENTION AND HUMAN RIGHTS (2))

7 (1) This Part applies to such States as the Secretary of State may by order specify.

(2) An order under this paragraph—

(a) shall be made by statutory instrument, and

(b) shall not be made unless a draft has been laid before and approved by resolution of each House of Parliament.

8 (1) This paragraph applies for the purposes of the determination by any person, tribunal or court whether a person who has made an asylum claim may be removed—

(a) from the United Kingdom, and

(b) to a State of which he is not a national or citizen.

(2) A State to which this Part applies shall be treated, in so far as relevant to the question mentioned in sub-paragraph (1), as a place—

(a) where a person's life and liberty are not threatened by reason of his race, religion, nationality, membership of a particular social group or political opinion, and

(b) from which a person will not be sent to another State otherwise than in accordance with the Refugee Convention.

9–16   *****

PART 5   COUNTRIES CERTIFIED AS SAFE FOR INDIVIDUALS

17   This Part applies to a person who has made an asylum claim if the Secretary of State certifies that—

(a) it is proposed to remove the person to a specified State,

(b) in the Secretary of State's opinion the person is not a national or citizen of the specified State, and

(c) in the Secretary of State's opinion the specified State is a place—

     (i) where the person's life and liberty will not be threatened by reason of his race, religion, nationality, membership of a particular social group or political opinion, and

     (ii) from which the person will not be sent to another State otherwise than in accordance with the Refugee Convention.

18 Where this Part applies to a person section 77 of the Nationality, Immigration and Asylum Act 2002 (c. 41) (no removal while claim for asylum pending) shall not prevent his removal to the State specified under paragraph 17.

19 Where this Part applies to a person—

    (a) he may not bring an immigration appeal by virtue of section 92(2) or (3) of that Act (appeal from within United Kingdom: general),

    (b) he may not bring an immigration appeal by virtue of section 92(4)(a) of that Act (appeal from within United Kingdom: asylum or human rights) in reliance on an asylum claim which asserts that to remove the person to the State specified under paragraph 17 would breach the United Kingdom's obligations under the Refugee Convention,

    (c) he may not bring an immigration appeal by virtue of section 92(4)(a) of that Act in reliance on a human rights claim if the Secretary of State certifies that the claim is clearly unfounded, and

    (d) he may not while outside the United Kingdom bring an immigration appeal on any ground that is inconsistent with the opinion certified under paragraph 17(c).

20, 21 *****

*****

Civil Contingencies Act 2004
(2004, c. 36)

An Act to make provision about civil contingencies   [18 November 2004]

Territorial extent: United Kingdom

1–18 *****

PART 2 EMERGENCY POWERS

19 Meaning of "emergency"

(1) In this Part "emergency" means—

    (a) an event or situation which threatens serious damage to human welfare in the United Kingdom or in a Part or region,

    (b) an event or situation which threatens serious damage to the environment of the United Kingdom or of a Part or region, or

    (c) war, or terrorism, which threatens serious damage to the security of the United Kingdom.

(2) For the purposes of subsection (1)(a) an event or situation threatens damage to human welfare only if it involves, causes or may cause—

    (a) loss of human life,

    (b) human illness or injury,

    (c) homelessness,

    (d) damage to property,

    (e) disruption of a supply of money, food, water, energy or fuel,

(f) disruption of a system of communication,

(g) disruption of facilities for transport, or

(h) disruption of services relating to health.

(3) For the purposes of subsection (1)(b) an event or situation threatens damage to the environment only if it involves, causes or may cause—

(a) contamination of land, water or air with biological, chemical or radio-active matter, or

(b) disruption or destruction of plant life or animal life.

(4)–(6) *****

20 Power to make emergency regulations

(1) Her Majesty may by Order in Council make emergency regulations if satisfied that the conditions in section 21 are satisfied.

(2) A senior Minister of the Crown may make emergency regulations if satisfied—

(a) that the conditions in section 21 are satisfied, and

(b) that it would not be possible, without serious delay, to arrange for an Order in Council under subsection (1).

(3) In this Part "senior Minister of the Crown" means—

(a) the First Lord of the Treasury (the Prime Minister),

(b) any of Her Majesty's Principal Secretaries of State, and

(c) the Commissioners of Her Majesty's Treasury.

(4) In this Part "serious delay" means a delay that might—

(a) cause serious damage, or

(b) seriously obstruct the prevention, control or mitigation of serious damage.

(5) *****

21 Conditions for making emergency regulations

(1) This section specifies the conditions mentioned in section 20.

(2) The first condition is that an emergency has occurred, is occurring or is about to occur.

(3) The second condition is that it is necessary to make provision for the purpose of preventing, controlling or mitigating an aspect or effect of the emergency.

(4) The third condition is that the need for provision referred to in subsection (3) is urgent.

(5), (6) *****

22 Scope of emergency regulations

(1) Emergency regulations may make any provision which the person making the regulations is satisfied is appropriate for the purpose of preventing, controlling or mitigating an aspect or effect of the emergency in respect of which the regulations are made.

(2) In particular, emergency regulations may make any provision which the person making the regulations is satisfied is appropriate for the purpose of—

(a) protecting human life, health or safety,

(b) treating human illness or injury,

(c) protecting or restoring property,

(d) protecting or restoring a supply of money, food, water, energy or fuel,

(e) protecting or restoring a system of communication,

(f) protecting or restoring facilities for transport,

(g) protecting or restoring the provision of services relating to health,

(h) protecting or restoring the activities of banks or other financial institutions,

(i) preventing, containing or reducing the contamination of land, water or air,

(j) preventing, reducing or mitigating the effects of disruption or destruction of plant life or animal life,

(k) protecting or restoring activities of Parliament, of the Scottish Parliament, of the Northern Ireland Assembly or of the National Assembly for Wales, or

(l) protecting or restoring the performance of public functions.

(3) Emergency regulations may make provision of any kind that could be made by Act of Parliament or by the exercise of the Royal Prerogative; in particular, regulations may—

(a) confer a function on a Minister of the Crown, on the Scottish Ministers, on the National Assembly for Wales, on a Northern Ireland department, on a coordinator appointed under section 24 or on any other specified person (and a function conferred may, in particular, be—

(i) a power, or duty, to exercise a discretion;

(ii) a power to give directions or orders, whether written or oral);

(b) provide for or enable the requisition or confiscation of property (with or without compensation);

(c) provide for or enable the destruction of property, animal life or plant life (with or without compensation);

(d) prohibit, or enable the prohibition of, movement to or from a specified place;

(e) require, or enable the requirement of, movement to or from a specified place;

(f) prohibit, or enable the prohibition of, assemblies of specified kinds, at specified places or at specified times;

(g) prohibit, or enable the prohibition of, travel at specified times;

(h) prohibit, or enable the prohibition of, other specified activities;

(i) create an offence of—

(i) failing to comply with a provision of the regulations;

(ii) failing to comply with a direction or order given or made under the regulations;

(iii) obstructing a person in the performance of a function under or by virtue of the regulations;

(j) disapply or modify an enactment or a provision made under or by virtue of an enactment;

(k) require a person or body to act in performance of a function (whether the function is conferred by the regulations or otherwise and whether or not the regulations also make provision for remuneration or compensation);

(l) enable the Defence Council to authorise the deployment of Her Majesty's armed forces;

(m) make provision (which may include conferring powers in relation to property) for facilitating any deployment of Her Majesty's armed forces;

(n) confer jurisdiction on a court or tribunal (which may include a tribunal established by the regulations);

(o) make provision which has effect in relation to, or to anything done in—

(i) an area of the territorial sea,

(ii) an area within British fishery limits, or

(iii) an area of the continental shelf;

(p) make provision which applies generally or only in specified circumstances or for a specified purpose;

(q) make different provision for different circumstances or purposes.

(4) In subsection (3) "specified" means specified by, or to be specified in accordance with, the regulations.

(5) A person making emergency regulations must have regard to the importance of ensuring that Parliament, the High Court and the Court of Session are able to conduct proceedings in connection with—

(a) the regulations, or

(b) action taken under the regulations.

23 Limitations of emergency regulations

(1) Emergency regulations may make provision only if and in so far as the person making the regulations is satisfied—

   (a) that the provision is appropriate for the purpose of preventing, controlling or mitigating an aspect or effect of the emergency in respect of which the regulations are made, and

   (b) that the effect of the provision is in due proportion to that aspect or effect of the emergency.

(2) Emergency regulations must specify the Parts of the United Kingdom or regions in relation to which the regulations have effect.

(3) Emergency regulations may not—

   (a) require a person, or enable a person to be required, to provide military service, or

   (b) prohibit or enable the prohibition of participation in, or any activity in connection with, a strike or other industrial action.

(4) Emergency regulations may not—

   (a) create an offence other than one of the kind described in section 22(3)(i),

   (b) create an offence other than one which is triable only before a magistrates' court or, in Scotland, before a sheriff under summary procedure,

   (c) create an offence which is punishable—

      (i) with imprisonment for a period exceeding three months, or

      (ii) with a fine exceeding level 5 on the standard scale, or

   (d) alter procedure in relation to criminal proceedings.

(5) Emergency regulations may not amend—

   (a) this Part of this Act, or

   (b) the Human Rights Act 1998 (c. 42).

24–25 *****

26 Duration

(1) Emergency regulations shall lapse—

   (a) at the end of the period of 30 days beginning with the date on which they are made, or

   (b) at such earlier time as may be specified in the regulations.

(2) Subsection (1)—

   (a) shall not prevent the making of new regulations, and

   (b) shall not affect anything done by virtue of the regulations before they lapse.

27 Parliamentary scrutiny

(1) Where emergency regulations are made—

   (a) a senior Minister of the Crown shall as soon as is reasonably practicable lay the regulations before Parliament, and

   (b) the regulations shall lapse at the end of the period of seven days beginning with the date of laying unless during that period each House of Parliament passes a resolution approving them.

(2) If each House of Parliament passes a resolution that emergency regulations shall cease to have effect, the regulations shall cease to have effect—

   (a) at such time, after the passing of the resolutions, as may be specified in them, or

   (b) if no time is specified in the resolutions, at the beginning of the day after that on which the resolutions are passed (or, if they are passed on different days, at the beginning of the day after that on which the second resolution is passed).

(3) If each House of Parliament passes a resolution that emergency regulations shall have effect with a specified amendment, the regulations shall have effect as amended, with effect from—

(a) such time, after the passing of the resolutions, as may be specified in them, or

(b) if no time is specified in the resolutions, the beginning of the day after that on which the resolutions are passed (or, if they are passed on different days, the beginning of the day after that on which the second resolution is passed).

(4) Nothing in this section—

(a) shall prevent the making of new regulations, or

(b) shall affect anything done by virtue of regulations before they lapse, cease to have effect or are amended under this section.

28   Parliamentary scrutiny: prorogation and adjournment

(1) If when emergency regulations are made under section 20 Parliament stands prorogued to a day after the end of the period of five days beginning with the date on which the regulations are made, Her Majesty shall by proclamation under the Meeting of Parliament Act 1797 (c. 127) require Parliament to meet on a specified day within that period.

(2) If when emergency regulations are made under section 20 the House of Commons stands adjourned to a day after the end of the period of five days beginning with the date on which the regulations are made, the Speaker shall arrange for the House to meet on a day during that period.

(3) If when emergency regulations are made under section 20 the House of Lords stands adjourned to a day after the end of the period of five days beginning with the date on which the regulations are made, the Lord Chancellor shall arrange for the House to meet on a day during that period.

(4) *****

*****

Civil Partnership Act 2004

(2004, c. 33)

An Act to make provision for and in connection with civil partnership   [18 November 2004]

Territorial extent: United Kingdom (s 1); England and Wales (remaining sections printed; equivalent provisions for Scotland and Northern Ireland respectively are in Parts 3 and 4 of the Act).

PART 1   INTRODUCTION

1   Civil partnership

(1) A civil partnership is a relationship between two people of the same sex ("civil partners")—

(a) which is formed when they register as civil partners of each other—

(i)   in England or Wales (under Part 2),

(ii) in Scotland (under Part 3),

(iii) in Northern Ireland (under Part 4), or

(iv) outside the United Kingdom under an Order in Council made under Chapter 1 of Part 5 (registration at British consulates etc. or by armed forces personnel), or

(b) which they are treated under Chapter 2 of Part 5 as having formed (at the time determined under that Chapter) by virtue of having registered an overseas relationship.

(2) Subsection (1) is subject to the provisions of this Act under or by virtue of which a civil partnership is void.

(3) A civil partnership ends only on death, dissolution or annulment.

(4) The references in subsection (3) to dissolution and annulment are to dissolution and annulment having effect under or recognised in accordance with this Act.

(5) References in this Act to an overseas relationship are to be read in accordance with Chapter 2 of Part 5.

PART 2   CIVIL PARTNERSHIP: ENGLAND AND WALES

CHAPTER 1   REGISTRATION

Formation, eligibility and parental etc. consent

2   Formation of civil partnership by registration

(1) For the purposes of section 1, two people are to be regarded as having registered as civil partners of each other once each of them has signed the civil partnership document—

    (a)   at the invitation of, and in the presence of, a civil partnership registrar, and

    (b)   in the presence of each other and two witnesses.

(2) Subsection (1) applies regardless of whether subsections (3) and (4) are complied with.

(3) After the civil partnership document has been signed under subsection (1), it must also be signed, in the presence of the civil partners and each other, by—

    (a)   each of the two witnesses, and

    (b)   the civil partnership registrar.

(4) After the witnesses and the civil partnership registrar have signed the civil partnership document, the relevant registration authority must ensure that—

    (a)   the fact that the two people have registered as civil partners of each other, and

    (b)   any other information prescribed by regulations,

is recorded in the register as soon as is practicable.

(5) No religious service is to be used while the civil partnership registrar is officiating at the signing of a civil partnership document.

(6) "The civil partnership document" has the meaning given by section 7(1).

(7) "The relevant registration authority" means the registration authority in whose area the registration takes place.

3   Eligibility

(1) Two people are not eligible to register as civil partners of each other if—

    (a)   they are not of the same sex,

    (b)   either of them is already a civil partner or lawfully married,

    (c)   either of them is under 16, or

    (d)   they are within prohibited degrees of relationship.

(2) Part 1 of Schedule 1 contains provisions for determining when two people are within prohibited degrees of relationship.

4-5   *****

Registration procedure: general

6   Place of registration

(1) The place at which two people may register as civil partners of each other—

    (a)   must be in England or Wales,

    (b)   must not be in religious premises, and

    (c)   must be specified in the notices, or notice, of proposed civil partnership required by this Chapter.

(2) "Religious premises" means premises which—

    (a)   are used solely or mainly for religious purposes, or

    (b)   have been so used and have not subsequently been used solely or mainly for other purposes.

(3) In the case of registration under the standard procedure (including that procedure modified as mentioned in section 5), the place—

    (a) must be one which is open to any person wishing to attend the registration, and

    (b) before being specified in a notice of proposed civil partnership, must be agreed with the registration authority in whose area that place is located.

(4) If the place specified in a notice is not so agreed, the notice is void.

(5) A registration authority may provide a place in its area for the registration of civil partnerships.

*****

Gender Recognition Act 2004
(2004, c. 7)

An Act to make provision for and in connection with change of gender　　　　　[1 July 2004]

Territorial extent: United Kingdom (provisions reproduced)

Applications for gender recognition certificate

1　Applications

(1) A person of either gender who is aged at least 18 may make an application for a gender recognition certificate on the basis of—

    (a) living in the other gender, or

    (b) having changed gender under the law of a country or territory outside the United Kingdom.

(2) In this Act "the acquired gender", in relation to a person by whom an application under subsection (1) is or has been made, means—

    (a) in the case of an application under paragraph (a) of that subsection, the gender in which the person is living, or

    (b) in the case of an application under paragraph (b) of that subsection, the gender to which the person has changed under the law of the country or territory concerned.

(3) An application under subsection (1) is to be determined by a Gender Recognition Panel.

(4) Schedule 1 (Gender Recognition Panels) has effect.

2　Determination of applications

(1) In the case of an application under section 1(1)(a), the Panel must grant the application if satisfied that the applicant—

    (a) has or has had gender dysphoria,

    (b) has lived in the acquired gender throughout the period of two years ending with the date on which the application is made,

    (c) intends to continue to live in the acquired gender until death, and

    (d) complies with the requirements imposed by and under section 3.

(2) In the case of an application under section 1(1)(b), the Panel must grant the application if satisfied—

    (a) that the country or territory under the law of which the applicant has changed gender is an approved country or territory, and

    (b) that the applicant complies with the requirements imposed by and under section 3.

(3) The Panel must reject an application under section 1(1) if not required by subsection (1) or (2) to grant it.

(4) In this Act "approved country or territory" means a country or territory prescribed by order made by the Secretary of State after consulting the Scottish Ministers and the Department of Finance and Personnel in Northern Ireland.

3 Evidence

(1) An application under section 1(1)(a) must include either—

(a) a report made by a registered medical practitioner practising in the field of gender dysphoria and a report made by another registered medical practitioner (who may, but need not, practise in that field), or

(b) a report made by a chartered psychologist practising in that field and a report made by a registered medical practitioner (who may, but need not, practise in that field).

(2) But subsection (1) is not complied with unless a report required by that subsection and made by—

(a) a registered medical practitioner, or

(b) a chartered psychologist,

practising in the field of gender dysphoria includes details of the diagnosis of the applicant's gender dysphoria.

(3) And subsection (1) is not complied with in a case where—

(a) the applicant has undergone or is undergoing treatment for the purpose of modifying sexual characteristics, or

(b) treatment for that purpose has been prescribed or planned for the applicant,

unless at least one of the reports required by that subsection includes details of it.

(4) An application under section 1(1)(a) must also include a statutory declaration by the applicant that the applicant meets the conditions in section 2(1)(b) and (c).

(5) An application under section 1(1)(b) must include evidence that the applicant has changed gender under the law of an approved country or territory.

(6)–(8) *****

4 Successful applications

(1) If a Gender Recognition Panel grants an application under section 1(1) it must issue a gender recognition certificate to the applicant.

(2) Unless the applicant is married, the certificate is to be a full gender recognition certificate.

(3) If the applicant is married, the certificate is to be an interim gender recognition certificate.

(4)–(5) *****

5 Subsequent issue of full certificates

(1) A court which—

(a) makes absolute a decree of nullity granted on the ground that an interim gender recognition certificate has been issued to a party to the marriage, or

(b) (in Scotland) grants a decree of divorce on that ground,

must, on doing so, issue a full gender recognition certificate to that party and send a copy to the Secretary of State.

(2) If an interim gender recognition certificate has been issued to a person and either—

(a) the person's marriage is dissolved or annulled (otherwise than on the ground mentioned in subsection (1)) in proceedings instituted during the period of six months beginning with the day on which it was issued, or

(b) the person's spouse dies within that period,

the person may make an application for a full gender recognition certificate at any time within the period specified in subsection (3) (unless the person is again married).

(3) That period is the period of six months beginning with the day on which the marriage is dissolved or annulled or the death occurs.

(4)–(7) *****

*****

Hunting Act 2004

(2004, c. 37)

An Act to make provision about hunting wild mammals with dogs; to prohibit hare coursing; and for connected purposes   [18 November 2004]

Territorial extent: England and Wales

BE IT ENACTED by The Queen's most Excellent Majesty, by and with the advice and consent of the Commons in this present Parliament assembled, in accordance with the provisions of the Parliament Acts 1911 and 1949, and by the authority of the same, as follows:—

PART 1   OFFENCES

1   Hunting wild mammals with dogs

A person commits an offence if he hunts a wild mammal with a dog, unless his hunting is exempt.

2   Exempt hunting

(1) Hunting is exempt if it is within a class specified in Schedule 1.

(2) The Secretary of State may by order amend Schedule 1 so as to vary a class of exempt hunting.

3   Hunting: assistance

(1) A person commits an offence if he knowingly permits land which belongs to him to be entered or used in the course of the commission of an offence under section 1.

(2) A person commits an offence if he knowingly permits a dog which belongs to him to be used in the course of the commission of an offence under section 1.

4   Hunting: defence

It is a defence for a person charged with an offence under section 1 in respect of hunting to show that he reasonably believed that the hunting was exempt.

5   *****

PART 2   ENFORCEMENT

6   Penalty

A person guilty of an offence under this Act shall be liable on summary conviction to a fine not exceeding level 5 on the standard scale.

7   *****

8   Search and seizure

(1) This section applies where a constable reasonably suspects that a person ("the suspect") is committing or has committed an offence under Part 1 of this Act.

(2) If the constable reasonably believes that evidence of the offence is likely to be found on the suspect, the constable may stop the suspect and search him.

(3) If the constable reasonably believes that evidence of the offence is likely to be found on or in a vehicle, animal or other thing of which the suspect appears to be in possession or control, the constable may stop and search the vehicle, animal or other thing.

(4) A constable may seize and detain a vehicle, animal or other thing if he reasonably believes that—

    (a) it may be used as evidence in criminal proceedings for an offence under Part 1 of this Act, or

    (b) it may be made the subject of an order under section 9.

(5) For the purposes of exercising a power under this section a constable may enter—

    (a) land;

    (b) premises other than a dwelling;

    (c) a vehicle.

(6) The exercise of a power under this section does not require a warrant.

9 Forfeiture

(1) A court which convicts a person of an offence under Part 1 of this Act may order the forfeiture of any dog or hunting article which—

    (a) was used in the commission of the offence, or

    (b) was in the possession of the person convicted at the time of his arrest.

(2) A court which convicts a person of an offence under Part 1 of this Act may order the forfeiture of any vehicle which was used in the commission of the offence.

(3) In subsection (1) "hunting article" means anything designed or adapted for use in connection with—

    (a) hunting a wild mammal, or

    (b) hare coursing.

(4)–(7) *****

*****

Constitutional Reform Act 2005
(2005, c. 4)

An Act to make provision for modifying the office of Lord Chancellor, and to make provision relating to the functions of that office; to establish a Supreme Court of the United Kingdom, and to abolish the appellate jurisdiction of the House of Lords; to make provision about the jurisdiction of the Judicial Committee of the Privy Council and the judicial functions of the President of the Council; to make other provision about the judiciary, their appointment and discipline; and for connected purposes   [24 March 2005]

Territorial extent: The United Kingdom

PART 1   THE RULE OF LAW

1 The rule of law

This Act does not adversely affect—

    (a) the existing constitutional principle of the rule of law, or

    (b) the Lord Chancellor's existing constitutional role in relation to that principle.

PART 2   ARRANGEMENTS TO MODIFY THE OFFICE OF LORD CHANCELLOR

Qualifications for office of Lord Chancellor

2 Lord Chancellor to be qualified by experience

(1) A person may not be recommended for appointment as Lord Chancellor unless he appears to the Prime Minister to be qualified by experience.

(2) The Prime Minister may take into account any of these—

    (a) experience as a Minister of the Crown;

   (b) experience as a member of either House of Parliament;

   (c) experience as a qualifying practitioner;

   (d) experience as a teacher of law in a university;

   (e) other experience that the Prime Minister considers relevant.

  (3) In this section "qualifying practitioner" means any of these—

   (a) a person who has a Senior Courts qualification, within the meaning of section 71 of the Courts and Legal Services Act 1990 (c. 41);

   (b) an advocate in Scotland or a solicitor entitled to appear in the Court of Session and the High Court of Justiciary;

   (c) a member of the Bar of Northern Ireland or a solicitor of the Court of Judicature of Northern Ireland.

Continued judicial independence

3 Guarantee of continued judicial independence

  (1) The Lord Chancellor, other Ministers of the Crown and all with responsibility for matters relating to the judiciary or otherwise to the administration of justice must uphold the continued independence of the judiciary.

  (2) Subsection (1) does not impose any duty which it would be within the legislative competence of the Scottish Parliament to impose.

  (3) A person is not subject to the duty imposed by subsection (1) if he is subject to the duty imposed by section 1(1) of the Justice (Northern Ireland) Act 2002 (c. 26).

  (4) The following particular duties are imposed for the purpose of upholding that independence.

  (5) The Lord Chancellor and other Ministers of the Crown must not seek to influence particular judicial decisions through any special access to the judiciary.

  (6) The Lord Chancellor must have regard to—

   (a) the need to defend that independence;

   (b) the need for the judiciary to have the support necessary to enable them to exercise their functions;

   (c) the need for the public interest in regard to matters relating to the judiciary or otherwise to the administration of justice to be properly represented in decisions affecting those matters.

  (7) In this section "the judiciary" includes the judiciary of any of the following—

   (a) the Supreme Court;

   (b) any other court established under the law of any part of the United Kingdom;

   (c) any international court.

  (8) *****

4 *****

Representations by senior judges

5 Representations to Parliament

  (1) The chief justice of any part of the United Kingdom may lay before Parliament written representations on matters that appear to him to be matters of importance relating to the judiciary, or otherwise to the administration of justice, in that part of the United Kingdom.

  (2)–(4) *****

  (5) In this section "chief justice" means—

   (a) in relation to England and Wales or Northern Ireland, the Lord Chief Justice of that part of the United Kingdom;

   (b) in relation to Scotland, the Lord President of the Court of Session.

6–18 *****

Functions subject to transfer, modification or abolition

19　Transfer, modification or abolition of functions by order

(1) The Lord Chancellor may by order make provision for any of these purposes—

    (a) to transfer an existing function of the Lord Chancellor to another person;

    (b) to direct that an existing function of the Lord Chancellor is to be exercisable concurrently with another person;

    (c) to direct that an existing function of the Lord Chancellor exercisable concurrently with another person is to cease to be exercisable by the Lord Chancellor;

    (d) to modify an existing function of the Lord Chancellor;

    (e) to abolish an existing function of the Lord Chancellor.

(2)–(8) *****

20–22　*****

PART 3　THE SUPREME COURT

The Supreme Court

23　The Supreme Court

(1) There is to be a Supreme Court of the United Kingdom.

(2) The Court consists of 12 judges appointed by Her Majesty by letters patent.

(3) Her Majesty may from time to time by Order in Council amend subsection (2) so as to increase or further increase the number of judges of the Court.

(4) No recommendation may be made to Her Majesty in Council to make an Order under subsection (3) unless a draft of the Order has been laid before and approved by resolution of each House of Parliament.

(5) Her Majesty may by letters patent appoint one of the judges to be President and one to be Deputy President of the Court.

(6) The judges other than the President and Deputy President are to be styled "Justices of the Supreme Court".

(7) The Court is to be taken to be duly constituted despite any vacancy among the judges of the Court or in the office of President or Deputy President.

24　First members of the Court

On the commencement of section 23—

    (a) the persons who immediately before that commencement are Lords of Appeal in Ordinary become judges of the Supreme Court,

    (b) the person who immediately before that commencement is the senior Lord of Appeal in Ordinary becomes the President of the Court, and

    (c) the person who immediately before that commencement is the second senior Lord of Appeal in Ordinary becomes the Deputy President of the Court.

Appointment of judges

25　Qualification for appointment

(1) A person is not qualified to be appointed a judge of the Supreme Court unless he has (at any time)—

    (a) held high judicial office for a period of at least 2 years, or

    (b) been a qualifying practitioner for a period of at least 15 years.

(2) A person is a qualifying practitioner for the purposes of this section at any time when—

    (a) he has a Senior Courts qualification, within the meaning of section 71 of the Courts and Legal Services Act 1990 (c. 41),

(b) he is an advocate in Scotland or a solicitor entitled to appear in the Court of Session and the High Court of Justiciary, or

(c) he is a member of the Bar of Northern Ireland or a solicitor of the Court of Judicature of Northern Ireland.

26 Selection of members of the Court

(1) This section applies to a recommendation for an appointment to one of the following offices—

(a) judge of the Supreme Court;

(b) President of the Court;

(c) Deputy President of the Court.

(2) A recommendation may be made only by the Prime Minister.

(3) The Prime Minister—

(a) must recommend any person whose name is notified to him under section 29;

(b) may not recommend any other person.

(4) A person who is not a judge of the Court must be recommended for appointment as a judge if his name is notified to the Prime Minister for an appointment as President or Deputy President.

(5) If there is a vacancy in one of the offices mentioned in subsection (1), or it appears to him that there will soon be such a vacancy, the Lord Chancellor must convene a selection commission for the selection of a person to be recommended.

(6) Schedule 8 is about selection commissions.

(7) Subsection (5) is subject to Part 3 of that Schedule.

(8) Sections 27 to 31 apply where a selection commission is convened under this section.

27 Selection process

(1) The commission must—

(a) determine the selection process to be applied,

(b) apply the selection process, and

(c) make a selection accordingly.

(2) As part of the selection process the commission must consult each of the following—

(a) such of the senior judges as are not members of the commission and are not willing to be considered for selection;

(b) the Lord Chancellor;

(c) the First Minister in Scotland;

(d) the Assembly First Secretary in Wales;

(e) the Secretary of State for Northern Ireland.

(3) If for any part of the United Kingdom no judge of the courts of that part is to be consulted under subsection (2)(a), the commission must consult as part of the selection process the most senior judge of the courts of that part who is not a member of the commission and is not willing to be considered for selection.

(4) Subsections (5) to (10) apply to any selection under this section or section 31.

(5) Selection must be on merit.

(6) A person may be selected only if he meets the requirements of section 25.

(7) A person may not be selected if he is a member of the commission.

(8) In making selections for the appointment of judges of the Court the commission must ensure that between them the judges will have knowledge of, and experience of practice in, the law of each part of the United Kingdom.

(9) The commission must have regard to any guidance given by the Lord Chancellor as to matters to be taken into account (subject to any other provision of this Act) in making a selection.

(10) Any selection must be of one person only.

28 Report
(1) After complying with section 27 the commission must submit a report to the Lord Chancellor.
(2) The report must—
    (a) state who has been selected;
    (b) state the senior judges consulted under section 27(2)(a) and any judge consulted under section 27(3);
    (c) contain any other information required by the Lord Chancellor.
(3) The report must be in a form approved by the Lord Chancellor.
(4) After submitting the report the commission must provide any further information the Lord Chancellor may require.
(5) When he receives the report the Lord Chancellor must consult each of the following—
    (a) the senior judges consulted under section 27(2)(a);
    (b) any judge consulted under section 27(3);
    (c) the First Minister in Scotland;
    (d) the Assembly First Secretary in Wales;
    (e) the Secretary of State for Northern Ireland.

29 The Lord Chancellor's options
(1) This section refers to the following stages—
Stage 1: where a person has been selected under section 27
Stage 2: where a person has been selected following a rejection or reconsideration at stage 1
Stage 3: where a person has been selected following a rejection or reconsideration at stage 2.
(2) At stage 1 the Lord Chancellor must do one of the following—
    (a) notify the selection;
    (b) reject the selection;
    (c) require the commission to reconsider the selection.
(3) At stage 2 the Lord Chancellor must do one of the following—
    (a) notify the selection;
    (b) reject the selection, but only if it was made following a reconsideration at stage 1;
    (c) require the commission to reconsider the selection, but only if it was made following a rejection at stage 1.
(4) At stage 3 the Lord Chancellor must notify the selection, unless subsection (5) applies and he makes a notification under it.
(5) If a person whose selection the Lord Chancellor required to be reconsidered at stage 1 or 2 was not selected again at the next stage, the Lord Chancellor may at stage 3 notify that person's name to the Prime Minister.
(6) In this Part references to the Lord Chancellor notifying a selection are references to his notifying to the Prime Minister the name of the person selected.

30 Exercise of powers to reject or require reconsideration
(1) The power of the Lord Chancellor under section 29 to reject a selection at stage 1 or 2 is exercisable only on the grounds that, in the Lord Chancellor's opinion, the person selected is not suitable for the office concerned.
(2) The power of the Lord Chancellor under section 29 to require the commission to reconsider a selection at stage 1 or 2 is exercisable only on the grounds that, in the Lord Chancellor's opinion—
    (a) there is not enough evidence that the person is suitable for the office concerned,
    (b) there is evidence that the person is not the best candidate on merit, or
    (c) there is not enough evidence that if the person were appointed the judges of the Court would between them have knowledge of, and experience of practice in, the law of each part of the United Kingdom.

(3) The Lord Chancellor must give the commission reasons in writing for rejecting or requiring reconsideration of a selection.

31 Selection following rejection or requirement to reconsider

(1) If under section 29 the Lord Chancellor rejects or requires reconsideration of a selection at stage 1 or 2, the commission must select a person in accordance with this section.

(2) If the Lord Chancellor rejects a selection, the commission—

(a) may not select the person rejected, and

(b) where the rejection is following reconsideration of a selection, may not select the person (if different) whose selection it reconsidered.

(3) If the Lord Chancellor requires a selection to be reconsidered, the commission—

(a) may select the same person or a different person, but

(b) where the requirement is following a rejection, may not select the person rejected.

(4) The commission must inform the Lord Chancellor of the person selected following a rejection or requirement to reconsider.

32 *****

33 Tenure

A judge of the Supreme Court holds that office during good behaviour, but may be removed from it on the address of both Houses of Parliament.

34 *****

35 Resignation and retirement

(1) A judge of the Supreme Court may at any time resign that office by giving the Lord Chancellor notice in writing to that effect.

(2) The President or Deputy President of the Court may at any time resign that office (whether or not he resigns his office as a judge) by giving the Lord Chancellor notice in writing to that effect.

(3) *****

36–39 *****

Jurisdiction, relation to other courts etc

40 Jurisdiction

(1) The Supreme Court is a superior court of record.

(2) An appeal lies to the Court from any order or judgment of the Court of Appeal in England and Wales in civil proceedings.

(3) An appeal lies to the Court from any order or judgment of a court in Scotland if an appeal lay from that court to the House of Lords at or immediately before the commencement of this section.

(4), (5) *****

(6) An appeal under subsection (2) lies only with the permission of the Court of Appeal or the Supreme Court; but this is subject to provision under any other enactment restricting such an appeal.

41 Relation to other courts etc

(1) Nothing in this Part is to affect the distinctions between the separate legal systems of the parts of the United Kingdom.

(2) A decision of the Supreme Court on appeal from a court of any part of the United Kingdom, other than a decision on a devolution matter, is to be regarded as the decision of a court of that part of the United Kingdom.

(3) A decision of the Supreme Court on a devolution matter—

(a) is not binding on that Court when making such a decision;

(b) otherwise, is binding in all legal proceedings.

(4) In this section "devolution matter" means—

(a) a question referred to the Supreme Court under section 33 of the Scotland Act 1998 (c. 46) or section 11 of the Northern Ireland Act 1998 (c. 47);

(b) a devolution issue as defined in Schedule 8 to the Government of Wales Act 1998 (c. 38), Schedule 6 to the Scotland Act 1998 or Schedule 10 to the Northern Ireland Act 1998.

Composition for proceedings

42   Composition

(1) The Supreme Court is duly constituted in any proceedings only if all of the following conditions are met—

(a) the Court consists of an uneven number of judges;

(b) the Court consists of at least three judges;

(c) more than half of those judges are permanent judges.

(2) Paragraphs (a) and (b) of subsection (1) are subject to any directions that in specified proceedings the Court is to consist of a specified number of judges that is both uneven and greater than three.

(3) Paragraph (b) of subsection (1) is subject to any directions that in specified descriptions of proceedings the Court is to consist of a specified minimum number of judges that is greater than three.

(4) This section is subject to section 43.

(5) In this section—

(a) "directions" means directions given by the President of the Court;

(b) "specified", in relation to directions, means specified in those directions;

(c) references to permanent judges are references to those judges of the Court who are not acting judges under section 38.

(6) This section and section 43 apply to the constitution of the Court in any proceedings from the time judges are designated to hear the proceedings.

43   Changes in composition

(1) This section applies if in any proceedings the Court ceases to be duly constituted in accordance with section 42, or in accordance with a direction under this section, because one or more members of the Court are unable to continue.

(2) The presiding judge may direct that the Court is still duly constituted in the proceedings.

(3) The presiding judge may give a direction under this section only if—

(a) the parties agree;

(b) the Court still consists of at least three judges (whether the number of judges is even or uneven);

(c) at least half of those judges are permanent judges.

(4) Subsections (2) and (3) are subject to directions given by the President of the Court.

(5), (6) *****

Practice and procedure

44   Specially qualified advisers

(1) If the Supreme Court thinks it expedient in any proceedings, it may hear and dispose of the proceedings wholly or partly with the assistance of one or more specially qualified advisers appointed by it.

(2) Any remuneration payable to such an adviser is to be determined by the Court unless agreed between the adviser and the parties to the proceedings.

(3) Any remuneration forms part of the costs of the proceedings.

45–60 *****

PART 4   JUDICIAL APPOINTMENTS AND DISCIPLINE

CHAPTER 1   COMMISSION AND OMBUDSMAN

61   The Judicial Appointments Commission

(1) There is to be a body corporate called the Judicial Appointments Commission.

(2) Schedule 12 is about the Commission.

62   Judicial Appointments and Conduct Ombudsman

(1) There is to be a Judicial Appointments and Conduct Ombudsman.

(2) Schedule 13 is about the Ombudsman.

[**Note:** Schedules 12 and 13 are not included in the text]

CHAPTER 2   APPOINTMENTS

General provisions

63   Merit and good character

(1) Subsections (2) and (3) apply to any selection under this Part by the Commission or a selection panel ("the selecting body").

(2) Selection must be solely on merit.

(3) A person must not be selected unless the selecting body is satisfied that he is of good character.

64   Encouragement of diversity

(1) The Commission, in performing its functions under this Part, must have regard to the need to encourage diversity in the range of persons available for selection for appointments.

(2) This section is subject to section 63.

65   Guidance about procedures

(1) The Lord Chancellor may issue guidance about procedures for the performance by the Commission or a selection panel of its functions of—

    (a)   identifying persons willing to be considered for selection under this Part, and

    (b)   assessing such persons for the purposes of selection.

(2) The guidance may, among other things, relate to consultation or other steps in determining such procedures.

(3) The purposes for which guidance may be issued under this section include the encouragement of diversity in the range of persons available for selection.

(4) The Commission and any selection panel must have regard to the guidance in matters to which it relates.

66–98 *****

Complaints and references

99   Complaints: interpretation

(1) This section applies for the purposes of this Part.

(2) A Commission complaint is a complaint by a qualifying complainant of maladministration by the Commission or a committee of the Commission.

(3) A departmental complaint is a complaint by a qualifying complainant of maladministration by the Lord Chancellor or his department in connection with any of the following—

(a) selection under this Part;

(b) recommendation for or appointment to an office listed in Schedule 14.

(4) A qualifying complainant is a complainant who claims to have been adversely affected, as an applicant for selection or as a person selected under this Part, by the maladministration complained of.

100   Complaints to the Commission or the Lord Chancellor

(1) The Commission must make arrangements for investigating any Commission complaint made to it.

(2) The Lord Chancellor must make arrangements for investigating any departmental complaint made to him.

(3) Arrangements under this section need not apply to a complaint made more than 28 days after the matter complained of.

101   Complaints to the Ombudsman

(1) Subsections (2) and (3) apply to a complaint which the complainant—

(a) has made to the Commission or the Lord Chancellor in accordance with arrangements under section 100, and

(b) makes to the Ombudsman not more than 28 days after being notified of the Commission's or Lord Chancellor's decision on the complaint.

(2) If the Ombudsman considers that investigation of the complaint is not necessary, he must inform the complainant.

(3) Otherwise he must investigate the complaint.

(4) The Ombudsman may investigate a complaint which the complainant—

(a) has made to the Commission or the Lord Chancellor in accordance with arrangements under section 100, and

(b) makes to the Ombudsman at any time.

(5) The Ombudsman may investigate a transferred complaint made to him, and no such complaint may be made under the Judicial Appointments Order after the commencement of this section.

(6) The Judicial Appointments Order is the Judicial Appointments Order in Council 2001, which sets out the functions of Her Majesty's Commissioners for Judicial Appointments.

(7) A transferred complaint is a complaint that lay to those Commissioners (whether or not it was made to them) in respect of the application of appointment procedures before the commencement of this section, but not a complaint that those Commissioners had declined to investigate or on which they had concluded their investigation.

(8) Any complaint to the Ombudsman under this section must be in a form approved by him.

102   Report and recommendations

(1) The Ombudsman must prepare a report on any complaint he has investigated under section 101.

(2) The report must state—

(a) what findings the Ombudsman has made;

(b) whether he considers the complaint should be upheld in whole or part;

(c) if he does, what if any action he recommends should be taken by the Commission or the Lord Chancellor as a result of the complaint.

(3) The recommendations that may be made under subsection (2)(c) include recommendations for the payment of compensation.

(4) Such a recommendation must relate to loss which appears to the Ombudsman to have been suffered by the complainant as a result of maladministration and not as a result of any failure to be appointed to an office to which the complaint related.

103   Report procedure

(1) This section applies to a report under section 102.

(2) The Ombudsman must submit a draft of the report—

(a) to the Lord Chancellor, and

(b) if the complaint was a Commission complaint, to the Commission.

(3) In finalising the report the Ombudsman—

(a) must have regard to any proposal by the Lord Chancellor or the Commission for changes in the draft report;

(b) must include in the report a statement of any such proposal not given effect to.

(4) The report must be signed by the Ombudsman.

(5) If the complaint was a Commission complaint the Ombudsman must send the report in duplicate to the Lord Chancellor and the Commission.

(6) Otherwise the Ombudsman must send the report to the Lord Chancellor.

(7) The Ombudsman must send a copy of the report to the complainant, but that copy must not include information—

(a) which relates to an identified or identifiable individual other than the complainant, and

(b) whose disclosure by the Ombudsman to the complainant would (apart from this subsection) be contrary to section 139.

104   References by the Lord Chancellor

(1) If the Lord Chancellor refers to the Ombudsman any matter relating to the procedures of the Commission or a committee of the Commission, the Ombudsman must investigate it.

(2) The matter may relate to such procedures generally or in a particular case.

(3) The Ombudsman must report to the Lord Chancellor on any investigation under this section.

(4) The report must state—

(a) what findings the Ombudsman has made;

(b) what if any action he recommends should be taken by any person in relation to the matter.

(5) The report must be signed by the Ombudsman.

105   Information

The Commission and the Lord Chancellor must provide the Ombudsman with such information as he may reasonably require relating to the subject matter of any investigation by him under section 101 or 104.

106–107   ***

CHAPTER 3   DISCIPLINE

Disciplinary powers

108   Disciplinary powers

(1) Any power of the Lord Chancellor to remove a person from an office listed in Schedule 14 is exercisable only after the Lord Chancellor has complied with prescribed procedures (as well as any other requirements to which the power is subject).

(2) The Lord Chief Justice may exercise any of the following powers but only with the agreement of the Lord Chancellor and only after complying with prescribed procedures.

(3) The Lord Chief Justice may give a judicial office holder formal advice, or a formal warning or reprimand, for disciplinary purposes (but this section does not restrict what he may do informally or for other purposes or where any advice or warning is not addressed to a particular office holder).

(4) He may suspend a person from a judicial office for any period during which any of the following applies—

    (a) the person is subject to criminal proceedings;

    (b) the person is serving a sentence imposed in criminal proceedings;

    (c) the person has been convicted of an offence and is subject to prescribed procedures in relation to the conduct constituting the offence.

  (5) He may suspend a person from a judicial office for any period if—

    (a) the person has been convicted of a criminal offence,

    (b) it has been determined under prescribed procedures that the person should not be removed from office, and

    (c) it appears to the Lord Chief Justice with the agreement of the Lord Chancellor that the suspension is necessary for maintaining confidence in the judiciary.

  (6) He may suspend a person from office as a senior judge for any period during which the person is subject to proceedings for an Address.

  (7) He may suspend the holder of an office listed in Schedule 14 for any period during which the person—

    (a) is under investigation for an offence, or

    (b) is subject to prescribed procedures.

  (8) While a person is suspended under this section from any office he may not perform any of the functions of the office (but his other rights as holder of the office are not affected).

[**Note:** Schedule 14 is not reproduced in this text]

109 *****

Applications for review and references

110 Applications to the Ombudsman

  (1) This section applies if an interested party makes an application to the Ombudsman for the review of the exercise by any person of a regulated disciplinary function, on the grounds that there has been—

    (a) a failure to comply with prescribed procedures, or

    (b) some other maladministration.

  (2) The Ombudsman must carry out a review if the following three conditions are met.

  (3) The first condition is that the Ombudsman considers that a review is necessary.

  (4) The second condition is that—

    (a) the application is made within the permitted period,

    (b) the application is made within such longer period as the Ombudsman considers appropriate in the circumstances, or

    (c) the application is made on grounds alleging undue delay and the Ombudsman considers that the application has been made within a reasonable time.

  (5) The third condition is that the application is made in a form approved by the Ombudsman.

  (6) But the Ombudsman may not review the merits of a decision made by any person.

  (7) If any of the conditions in subsections (3) to (5) is not met, or if the grounds of the application relate only to the merits of a decision, the Ombudsman—

    (a) may not carry out a review, and

    (b) must inform the applicant accordingly.

  (8)–(10) *****

111–114 *****

General

115 Regulations about procedures

The Lord Chief Justice may, with the agreement of the Lord Chancellor, make regulations providing for the procedures that are to be followed in—

    (a) the investigation and determination of allegations by any person of misconduct by judicial office holders;

    (b) reviews and investigations (including the making of applications or references) under sections 110 to 112.

116–136   *********

PART 6   OTHER PROVISIONS RELATING TO THE JUDICIARY

137   Parliamentary disqualification

    (1), (2) *********

    (3) A member of the House of Lords is, while he holds any disqualifying judicial office, disqualified for sitting or voting in—

    (a) the House of Lords,

    (b) a committee of that House, or

    (c) a joint committee of both Houses.

    (4) *********

    (5) A member of the House of Lords who is disqualified under subsection (3) is not for that reason disqualified for receiving a writ of summons to attend that House, but any such writ is subject to that subsection.

*****

Inquiries Act 2005
(2005, c. 12)

An Act to make provision about the holding of inquiries   [7 April 2005]

Territorial extent: The United Kingdom (sections reproduced here)

Constitution of inquiry

1   Power to establish inquiry

    (1) A Minister may cause an inquiry to be held under this Act in relation to a case where it appears to him that—

    (a) particular events have caused, or are capable of causing, public concern, or

    (b) there is public concern that particular events may have occurred.

    (2) In this Act "Minister" means—

    (a) a United Kingdom Minister;

    (b) the Scottish Ministers;

    (c) a Northern Ireland Minister;

and references to a Minister also include references to the National Assembly for Wales.

    (3) References in this Act to an inquiry, except where the context requires otherwise, are to an inquiry under this Act.

2   No determination of liability

    (1) An inquiry panel is not to rule on, and has no power to determine, any person's civil or criminal liability.

    (2) But an inquiry panel is not to be inhibited in the discharge of its functions by any likelihood of liability being inferred from facts that it determines or recommendations that it makes.

3 The inquiry panel

(1) An inquiry is to be undertaken either—

(a) by a chairman alone, or

(b) by a chairman with one or more other members.

(2) References in this Act to an inquiry panel are to the chairman and any other member or members.

4 Appointment of inquiry panel

(1) Each member of an inquiry panel is to be appointed by the Minister by an instrument in writing.

(2) The instrument appointing the chairman must state that the inquiry is to be held under this Act.

(3) Before appointing a member to the inquiry panel (otherwise than as chairman) the Minister must consult the person he has appointed, or proposes to appoint, as chairman.

5 Setting-up date and terms of reference

(1) In the instrument under section 4 appointing the chairman, or by a notice given to him within a reasonable time afterwards, the Minister must—

(a) specify the date that is to be the setting-up date for the purposes of this Act; and

(b) before that date—

(i) set out the terms of reference of the inquiry;

(ii) state whether or not the Minister proposes to appoint other members to the inquiry panel, and if so how many.

(2) An inquiry must not begin considering evidence before the setting-up date.

(3) The Minister may at any time after setting out the terms of reference under this section amend them if he considers that the public interest so requires.

(4) Before setting out or amending the terms of reference the Minister must consult the person he proposes to appoint, or has appointed, as chairman.

(5) Functions conferred by this Act on an inquiry panel, or a member of an inquiry panel, are exercisable only within the inquiry's terms of reference.

(6) In this Act "terms of reference", in relation to an inquiry under this Act, means—

(a) the matters to which the inquiry relates;

(b) any particular matters as to which the inquiry panel is to determine the facts;

(c) whether the inquiry panel is to make recommendations;

(d) any other matters relating to the scope of the inquiry that the Minister may specify.

6 Minister's duty to inform Parliament or Assembly

(1) A Minister who proposes to cause an inquiry to be held, or who has already done so without making a statement under this section, must as soon as is reasonably practicable make a statement to that effect to the relevant Parliament or Assembly.

(2) A statement under subsection (1) must state—

(a) who is to be, or has been, appointed as chairman of the inquiry;

(b) whether the Minister has appointed, or proposes to appoint, any other members to the inquiry panel, and if so how many;

(c) what are to be, or are, the inquiry's terms of reference.

(3) Where the terms of reference of an inquiry are amended under section 5(3), the Minister must, as soon as is reasonably practicable, make a statement to the relevant Parliament or Assembly setting out the amended terms of reference.

(4) A statement under this section may be oral or written.

7 *****

8 Suitability of inquiry panel

(1) In appointing a member of the inquiry panel, the Minister must have regard—

(a) to the need to ensure that the inquiry panel (considered as a whole) has the necessary expertise to undertake the inquiry;

(b) in the case of an inquiry panel consisting of a chairman and one or more other members, to the need for balance (considered against the background of the terms of reference) in the composition of the panel.

(2) For the purposes of subsection (1)(a) the Minister may have regard to the assistance that may be provided to the inquiry panel by any assessor whom the Minister proposes to appoint, or has appointed, under section 11.

9   Requirement of impartiality

(1) The Minister must not appoint a person as a member of the inquiry panel if it appears to the Minister that the person has—

(a) a direct interest in the matters to which the inquiry relates, or

(b) a close association with an interested party,

unless, despite the person's interest or association, his appointment could not reasonably be regarded as affecting the impartiality of the inquiry panel.

(2) Before a person is appointed as a member of an inquiry panel he must notify the Minister of any matters that, having regard to subsection (1), could affect his eligibility for appointment.

(3) If at any time (whether before the setting-up date or during the course of the inquiry) a member of the inquiry panel becomes aware that he has an interest or association falling within paragraph (a) or (b) of subsection (1), he must notify the Minister.

(4) A member of the inquiry panel must not, during the course of the inquiry, undertake any activity that could reasonably be regarded as affecting his suitability to serve as such.

10   Appointment of judge as panel member

(1) If the Minister proposes to appoint as a member of an inquiry panel a particular person who is a judge of a description specified in the first column of the following table, he must first consult the person specified in the second column.

Description of judge	Person to be consulted
Lord of Appeal in Ordinary	The senior Lord of Appeal in Ordinary
Judge of the Supreme Court of England and Wales, or Circuit judge	The Lord Chief Justice of England and Wales
Judge of the Court of Session, sheriff principal or sheriff	The Lord President of the Court of Session
Judge of the Supreme Court of Northern Ireland, or county court judge in Northern Ireland	The Lord Chief Justice of Northern Ireland

(2) In this section "sheriff principal" and "sheriff" have the same meaning as in the Sheriff Courts (Scotland) Act 1971 (c. 58).

11   Assessors

(1) One or more persons may be appointed to act as assessors to assist the inquiry panel.

(2) The power to appoint assessors is exercisable—

(a) before the setting-up date, by the Minister;

(b) during the course of the inquiry, by the chairman (whether or not the Minister has appointed assessors).

(3) Before exercising his powers under subsection (2)(a) the Minister must consult the person he proposes to appoint, or has appointed, as chairman.

(4) A person may be appointed as an assessor only if it appears to the Minister or the chairman (as the case requires) that he has expertise that makes him a suitable person to provide assistance to the inquiry panel.

(5) The chairman may at any time terminate the appointment of an assessor, but only with the consent of the Minister in the case of an assessor appointed by the Minister.

12   Duration of appointment of members of inquiry panel

(1) Subject to the following provisions of this section, a member of an inquiry panel remains a member until the inquiry comes to an end (or until his death if he dies before then).

(2) A member of an inquiry panel may at any time resign his appointment by notice to the Minister.

(3) The Minister may at any time by notice terminate the appointment of a member of an inquiry panel—

    (a) on the ground that, by reason of physical or mental illness or for any other reason, the member is unable to carry out the duties of a member of the inquiry panel;

    (b) on the ground that the member has failed to comply with any duty imposed on him by this Act;

    (c) on the ground that the member has—

        (i)   a direct interest in the matters to which the inquiry relates, or

        (ii) a close association with an interested party,

    such that his membership of the inquiry panel could reasonably be regarded as affecting its impartiality;

    (d) on the ground that the member has, since his appointment, been guilty of any misconduct that makes him unsuited to membership of the inquiry panel.

(4) In determining whether subsection (3)(a) applies in a case where the inability to carry out the duties is likely to be temporary, the Minister may have regard to the likely duration of the inquiry.

(5) The Minister may not terminate a member's appointment under subsection (3)(c) if the Minister was aware of the interest or association in question when appointing him.

(6) Before exercising his powers under subsection (3) in relation to a member other than the chairman, the Minister must consult the chairman.

(7) Before exercising his powers under subsection (3) in relation to any member of the inquiry panel, the Minister must—

    (a) inform the member of the proposed decision and of the reasons for it, and take into account any representations made by the member in response, and

    (b) if the member so requests, consult the other members of the inquiry panel (to the extent that no obligation to consult them arises under subsection (6)).

13   Power to suspend inquiry

(1) The Minister may at any time, by notice to the chairman, suspend an inquiry for such period as appears to him to be necessary to allow for—

    (a) the completion of any other investigation relating to any of the matters to which the inquiry relates, or

    (b) the determination of any civil or criminal proceedings (including proceedings before a disciplinary tribunal) arising out of any of those matters.

(2) The power conferred by subsection (1) may be exercised whether or not the investigation or proceedings have begun.

(3) Before exercising that power the Minister must consult the chairman.

(4)–(7) *****

14   End of inquiry

(1) For the purposes of this Act an inquiry comes to an end—

    (a) on the date, after the delivery of the report of the inquiry, on which the chairman notifies the Minister that the inquiry has fulfilled its terms of reference, or

    (b) on any earlier date specified in a notice given to the chairman by the Minister.

(2) The date specified in a notice under subsection (1)(b) may not be earlier than the date on which the notice is sent.

(3) Before exercising his power under subsection (1)(b) the Minister must consult the chairman.

(4) Where the Minister gives a notice under subsection (1)(b) he must—

    (a) set out in the notice his reasons for bringing the inquiry to an end;

    (b) lay a copy of the notice, as soon as is reasonably practicable, before the relevant Parliament or Assembly.

15–17 *****

18   Public access to inquiry proceedings and information

(1) Subject to any restrictions imposed by a notice or order under section 19, the chairman must take such steps as he considers reasonable to secure that members of the public (including reporters) are able—

    (a) to attend the inquiry or to see and hear a simultaneous transmission of proceedings at the inquiry;

    (b) to obtain or to view a record of evidence and documents given, produced or provided to the inquiry or inquiry panel.

(2)–(4) *****

19   Restrictions on public access etc

(1) Restrictions may, in accordance with this section, be imposed on—

    (a) attendance at an inquiry, or at any particular part of an inquiry;

    (b) disclosure or publication of any evidence or documents given, produced or provided to an inquiry.

(2) Restrictions may be imposed in either or both of the following ways—

    (a) by being specified in a notice (a "restriction notice") given by the Minister to the chairman at any time before the end of the inquiry;

    (b) by being specified in an order (a "restriction order") made by the chairman during the course of the inquiry.

(3) A restriction notice or restriction order must specify only such restrictions—

    (a) as are required by any statutory provision, enforceable Community obligation or rule of law, or

    (b) as the Minister or chairman considers to be conducive to the inquiry fulfilling its terms of reference or to be necessary in the public interest, having regard in particular to the matters mentioned in subsection (4).

(4) Those matters are—

    (a) the extent to which any restriction on attendance, disclosure or publication might inhibit the allaying of public concern;

    (b) any risk of harm or damage that could be avoided or reduced by any such restriction;

    (c) any conditions as to confidentiality subject to which a person acquired information that he is to give, or has given, to the inquiry;

    (d) the extent to which not imposing any particular restriction would be likely—

        (i)   to cause delay or to impair the efficiency or effectiveness of the inquiry, or

        (ii) otherwise to result in additional cost (whether to public funds or to witnesses or others).

(5) In subsection (4)(b) "harm or damage" includes in particular—

    (a) death or injury;

    (b) damage to national security or international relations;

    (c) damage to the economic interests of the United Kingdom or of any part of the United Kingdom;

    (d) damage caused by disclosure of commercially sensitive information.

20   *****

21   Powers of chairman to require production of evidence etc

(1) The chairman of an inquiry may by notice require a person to attend at a time and place stated in the notice—

(a) to give evidence;

(b) to produce any documents in his custody or under his control that relate to a matter in question at the inquiry;

(c) to produce any other thing in his custody or under his control for inspection, examination or testing by or on behalf of the inquiry panel.

(2) The chairman may by notice require a person, within such period as appears to the inquiry panel to be reasonable—

(a) to provide evidence to the inquiry panel in the form of a written statement;

(b) to provide any documents in his custody or under his control that relate to a matter in question at the inquiry;

(c) to produce any other thing in his custody or under his control for inspection, examination or testing by or on behalf of the inquiry panel.

(3) A notice under subsection (1) or (2) must—

(a) explain the possible consequences of not complying with the notice;

(b) indicate what the recipient of the notice should do if he wishes to make a claim within subsection (4).

(4) A claim by a person that—

(a) he is unable to comply with a notice under this section, or

(b) it is not reasonable in all the circumstances to require him to comply with such a notice,

is to be determined by the chairman of the inquiry, who may revoke or vary the notice on that ground.

(5) In deciding whether to revoke or vary a notice on the ground mentioned in subsection (4)(b), the chairman must consider the public interest in the information in question being obtained by the inquiry, having regard to the likely importance of the information.

(6) For the purposes of this section a thing is under a person's control if it is in his possession or if he has a right to possession of it.

22   Privileged information etc

(1) A person may not under section 21 be required to give, produce or provide any evidence or document if—

(a) he could not be required to do so if the proceedings of the inquiry were civil proceedings in a court in the relevant part of the United Kingdom, or

(b) the requirement would be incompatible with a Community obligation.

(2) The rules of law under which evidence or documents are permitted or required to be withheld on grounds of public interest immunity apply in relation to an inquiry as they apply in relation to civil proceedings in a court in the relevant part of the United Kingdom.

23–24   ***

25   Publication of reports

(1) It is the duty of the Minister, or the chairman if subsection (2) applies, to arrange for reports of an inquiry to be published.

(2) This subsection applies if—

(a) the Minister notifies the chairman before the setting-up date that the chairman is to have responsibility for arranging publication, or

(b) at any time after that date the chairman, on being invited to do so by the Minister, accepts responsibility for arranging publication.

(3) Subject to subsection (4), a report of an inquiry must be published in full.

(4) The person whose duty it is to arrange for a report to be published may withhold material in the report from publication to such extent—

(a) as is required by any statutory provision, enforceable Community obligation or rule of law, or

(b) as the person considers to be necessary in the public interest, having regard in particular to the matters mentioned in subsection (5).

(5) Those matters are—

(a) the extent to which withholding material might inhibit the allaying of public concern;

(b) any risk of harm or damage that could be avoided or reduced by withholding any material;

(c) any conditions as to confidentiality subject to which a person acquired information that he has given to the inquiry.

(6) In subsection (5)(b) "harm or damage" includes in particular—

(a) death or injury;

(b) damage to national security or international relations;

(c) damage to the economic interests of the United Kingdom or of any part of the United Kingdom;

(d) damage caused by disclosure of commercially sensitive information.

(7) Subsection (4)(b) does not affect any obligation of the Minister, or any other public authority or Scottish public authority, that may arise under the Freedom of Information Act 2000 (c. 36) or the Freedom of Information (Scotland) Act 2002 (asp 13).

(8) In this section "report" includes an interim report.

26 Laying of reports before Parliament or Assembly

Whatever is required to be published under section 25 must be laid by the Minister, either at the time of publication or as soon afterwards as is reasonably practicable, before the relevant Parliament or Assembly.

*****

Prevention of Terrorism Act 2005

(2005, c. 2)

An Act to provide for the making against individuals involved in terrorism-related activity of orders imposing obligations on them for purposes connected with preventing or restricting their further involvement in such activity; to make provision about appeals and other proceedings relating to such orders; and for connected purposes   [14 March 2005]

Territorial extent: The United Kingdom – with power by Order in Council to extend to any of the Channel Islands or the Isle of Man

Control orders

1 Power to make control orders

(1) In this Act "control order" means an order against an individual that imposes obligations on him for purposes connected with protecting members of the public from a risk of terrorism.

(2) The power to make a control order against an individual shall be exercisable—

(a) except in the case of an order imposing obligations that are incompatible with the individual's right to liberty under Article 5 of the Human Rights Convention, by the Secretary of State; and

(b) in the case of an order imposing obligations that are or include derogating obligations, by the court on an application by the Secretary of State.

(3) The obligations that may be imposed by a control order made against an individual are any obligations that the Secretary of State or (as the case may be) the court considers necessary for purposes connected with preventing or restricting involvement by that individual in terrorism-related activity.

(4) Those obligations may include, in particular—

    (a) a prohibition or restriction on his possession or use of specified articles or substances;

    (b) a prohibition or restriction on his use of specified services or specified facilities, or on his carrying on specified activities;

    (c) a restriction in respect of his work or other occupation, or in respect of his business;

    (d) a restriction on his association or communications with specified persons or with other persons generally;

    (e) a restriction in respect of his place of residence or on the persons to whom he gives access to his place of residence;

    (f) a prohibition on his being at specified places or within a specified area at specified times or on specified days;

    (g) a prohibition or restriction on his movements to, from or within the United Kingdom, a specified part of the United Kingdom or a specified place or area within the United Kingdom;

    (h) a requirement on him to comply with such other prohibitions or restrictions on his movements as may be imposed, for a period not exceeding 24 hours, by directions given to him in the specified manner, by a specified person and for the purpose of securing compliance with other obligations imposed by or under the order;

    (i) a requirement on him to surrender his passport, or anything in his possession to which a prohibition or restriction imposed by the order relates, to a specified person for a period not exceeding the period for which the order remains in force;

    (j) a requirement on him to give access to specified persons to his place of residence or to other premises to which he has power to grant access;

    (k) a requirement on him to allow specified persons to search that place or any such premises for the purpose of ascertaining whether obligations imposed by or under the order have been, are being or are about to be contravened;

    (l) a requirement on him to allow specified persons, either for that purpose or for the purpose of securing that the order is complied with, to remove anything found in that place or on any such premises and to subject it to tests or to retain it for a period not exceeding the period for which the order remains in force;

    (m) a requirement on him to allow himself to be photographed;

    (n) a requirement on him to co-operate with specified arrangements for enabling his movements, communications or other activities to be monitored by electronic or other means;

    (o) a requirement on him to comply with a demand made in the specified manner to provide information to a specified person in accordance with the demand;

    (p) a requirement on him to report to a specified person at specified times and places.

(5) Power by or under a control order to prohibit or restrict the controlled person's movements includes, in particular, power to impose a requirement on him to remain at or within a particular place or area (whether for a particular period or at particular times or generally).

(6) The reference in subsection (4)(n) to co-operating with specified arrangements for monitoring includes a reference to each of the following—

    (a) submitting to procedures required by the arrangements;

    (b) wearing or otherwise using apparatus approved by or in accordance with the arrangements;

    (c) maintaining such apparatus in the specified manner;

(d) complying with directions given by persons carrying out functions for the purposes of those arrangements.

(7) The information that the controlled person may be required to provide under a control order includes, in particular, advance information about his proposed movements or other activities.

(8) A control order may provide for a prohibition, restriction or requirement imposed by or under the order to apply only where a specified person has not given his consent or approval to what would otherwise contravene the prohibition, restriction or requirement.

(9) For the purposes of this Act involvement in terrorism-related activity is any one or more of the following—

(a) the commission, preparation or instigation of acts of terrorism;

(b) conduct which facilitates the commission, preparation or instigation of such acts, or which is intended to do so;

(c) conduct which gives encouragement to the commission, preparation or instigation of such acts, or which is intended to do so;

(d) conduct which gives support or assistance to individuals who are known or believed to be involved in terrorism-related activity;

and for the purposes of this subsection it is immaterial whether the acts of terrorism in question are specific acts of terrorism or acts of terrorism generally.

(10) In this Act—

"derogating obligation" means an obligation on an individual which—

(a) is incompatible with his right to liberty under Article 5 of the Human Rights Convention; but

(b) is of a description of obligations which, for the purposes of the designation of a designated derogation, is set out in the designation order;

"designated derogation" has the same meaning as in the Human Rights Act 1998 (c. 42) (see section 14(1) of that Act);

"designation order", in relation to a designated derogation, means the order under section 14(1) of the Human Rights Act 1998 by which the derogation is designated.

2   Making of non-derogating control orders

(1) The Secretary of State may make a control order against an individual if he—

(a) has reasonable grounds for suspecting that the individual is or has been involved in terrorism-related activity; and

(b) considers that it is necessary, for purposes connected with protecting members of the public from a risk of terrorism, to make a control order imposing obligations on that individual.

(2) The Secretary of State may make a control order against an individual who is for the time being bound by a control order made by the court only if he does so—

(a) after the court has determined that its order should be revoked; but

(b) while the effect of the revocation has been postponed for the purpose of giving the Secretary of State an opportunity to decide whether to exercise his own powers to make a control order against the individual.

(3) A control order made by the Secretary of State is called a non-derogating control order.

(4) A non-derogating control order—

(a) has effect for a period of 12 months beginning with the day on which it is made; but

(b) may be renewed on one or more occasions in accordance with this section.

(5) A non-derogating control order must specify when the period for which it is to have effect will end.

(6) The Secretary of State may renew a non-derogating control order (with or without modifications) for a period of 12 months if he—

(a) considers that it is necessary, for purposes connected with protecting members of the public from a risk of terrorism, for an order imposing obligations on the controlled person to continue in force; and

(b) considers that the obligations to be imposed by the renewed order are necessary for purposes connected with preventing or restricting involvement by that person in terrorism-related activity.

(7)–(9) *****

3   Supervision by court of making of non-derogating control orders

(1) The Secretary of State must not make a non-derogating control order against an individual except where—

(a) having decided that there are grounds to make such an order against that individual, he has applied to the court for permission to make the order and has been granted that permission;

(b) the order contains a statement by the Secretary of State that, in his opinion, the urgency of the case requires the order to be made without such permission; or

(c) the order is made before 14th March 2005 against an individual who, at the time it is made, is an individual in respect of whom a certificate under section 21(1) of the Anti-terrorism, Crime and Security Act 2001 (c. 24) is in force.

(2) Where the Secretary of State makes an application for permission to make a non-derogating control order against an individual, the application must set out the order for which he seeks permission and—

(a) the function of the court is to consider whether the Secretary of State's decision that there are grounds to make that order is obviously flawed;

(b) the court may give that permission unless it determines that the decision is obviously flawed; and

(c) if it gives permission, the court must give directions for a hearing in relation to the order as soon as reasonably practicable after it is made.

(3) Where the Secretary of State makes a non-derogating control order against an individual without the permission of the court—

(a) he must immediately refer the order to the court; and

(b) the function of the court on the reference is to consider whether the decision of the Secretary of State to make the order he did was obviously flawed.

(4) The court's consideration on a reference under subsection (3)(a) must begin no more than 7 days after the day on which the control order in question was made.

(5) The court may consider an application for permission under subsection (1)(a) or a reference under subsection (3)(a)—

(a) in the absence of the individual in question;

(b) without his having been notified of the application or reference; and

(c) without his having been given an opportunity (if he was aware of the application or reference) of making any representations to the court;

but this subsection is not to be construed as limiting the matters about which rules of court may be made in relation to the consideration of such an application or reference.

(6) On a reference under subsection (3)(a), the court—

(a) if it determines that the decision of the Secretary of State to make a non-derogating control order against the controlled person was obviously flawed, must quash the order;

(b) if it determines that that decision was not obviously flawed but that a decision of the Secretary of State to impose a particular obligation by that order was obviously flawed, must quash that obligation and (subject to that) confirm the order and give directions for a hearing in relation to the confirmed order; and

(c) in any other case, must confirm the order and give directions for a hearing in relation to the confirmed order.

(7) The directions given under subsection (2)(c) or (6)(b) or (c) must include arrangements for the individual in question to be given an opportunity within 7 days of the court's giving permission or (as the case may be) making its determination on the reference to make representations about—

(a) the directions already given; and

(b) the making of further directions.

(8) On a reference under subsection (3)(a), the court may quash a certificate contained in the order for the purposes of subsection (1)(b) if it determines that the Secretary of State's decision that the certificate should be contained in the order was flawed.

(9) The court must ensure that the controlled person is notified of its decision on a reference under subsection (3)(a).

(10)–(14) *****

4 Power of court to make derogating control orders

(1) On an application to the court by the Secretary of State for the making of a control order against an individual, it shall be the duty of the court—

(a) to hold an immediate preliminary hearing to determine whether to make a control order imposing obligations that are or include derogating obligations (called a "derogating control order") against that individual; and

(b) if it does make such an order against that individual, to give directions for the holding of a full hearing to determine whether to confirm the order (with or without modifications).

(2) The preliminary hearing under subsection (1)(a) may be held—

(a) in the absence of the individual in question;

(b) without his having had notice of the application for the order; and

(c) without his having been given an opportunity (if he was aware of the application) of making any representations to the court;

but this subsection is not to be construed as limiting the matters about which rules of court may be made in relation to that hearing.

(3) At the preliminary hearing, the court may make a control order against the individual in question if it appears to the court—

(a) that there is material which (if not disproved) is capable of being relied on by the court as establishing that the individual is or has been involved in terrorism-related activity;

(b) that there are reasonable grounds for believing that the imposition of obligations on that individual is necessary for purposes connected with protecting members of the public from a risk of terrorism;

(c) that the risk arises out of, or is associated with, a public emergency in respect of which there is a designated derogation from the whole or a part of Article 5 of the Human Rights Convention; and

(d) that the obligations that there are reasonable grounds for believing should be imposed on the individual are or include derogating obligations of a description set out for the purposes of the designated derogation in the designation order.

(4) The obligations that may be imposed by a derogating control order in the period between—

(a) the time when the order is made, and

(b) the time when a final determination is made by the court whether to confirm it,

include any obligations which the court has reasonable grounds for considering are necessary as mentioned in section 1(3).

(5) At the full hearing under subsection (1)(b), the court may—

(a) confirm the control order made by the court; or

(b) revoke the order;

and where the court revokes the order, it may (if it thinks fit) direct that this Act is to have effect as if the order had been quashed.

(6) In confirming a control order, the court—

(a) may modify the obligations imposed by the order; and

(b) where a modification made by the court removes an obligation, may (if it thinks fit) direct that this Act is to have effect as if the removed obligation had been quashed.

(7) At the full hearing, the court may confirm the control order (with or without modifications) only if—

(a) it is satisfied, on the balance of probabilities, that the controlled person is an individual who is or has been involved in terrorism-related activity;

(b) it considers that the imposition of obligations on the controlled person is necessary for purposes connected with protecting members of the public from a risk of terrorism;

(c) it appears to the court that the risk is one arising out of, or is associated with, a public emergency in respect of which there is a designated derogation from the whole or a part of Article 5 of the Human Rights Convention; and

(d) the obligations to be imposed by the order or (as the case may be) by the order as modified are or include derogating obligations of a description set out for the purposes of the designated derogation in the designation order.

(8) A derogating control order ceases to have effect at the end of the period of 6 months beginning with the day on which it is made unless—

(a) it is previously revoked (whether at the hearing under subsection (1)(b) or otherwise under this Act);

(b) it ceases to have effect under section 6; or

(c) it is renewed.

(9) The court, on an application by the Secretary of State, may renew a derogating control order (with or without modifications) for a period of 6 months from whichever is the earlier of—

(a) the time when the order would otherwise have ceased to have effect; and

(b) the beginning of the seventh day after the date of renewal.

(10) The power of the court to renew a derogating control order is exercisable on as many occasions as the court thinks fit; but, on each occasion, it is exercisable only if—

(a) the court considers that it is necessary, for purposes connected with protecting members of the public from a risk of terrorism, for a derogating control order to continue in force against the controlled person;

(b) it appears to the court that the risk is one arising out of, or is associated with, a public emergency in respect of which there is a designated derogation from the whole or a part of Article 5 of the Human Rights Convention;

(c) the derogating obligations that the court considers should continue in force are of a description that continues to be set out for the purposes of the designated derogation in the designation order; and

(d) the court considers that the obligations to be imposed by the renewed order are necessary for purposes connected with preventing or restricting involvement by that person in terrorism-related activity.

(11)–(13) *****

5   Arrest and detention pending derogating control order

(1) A constable may arrest and detain an individual if—

(a) the Secretary of State has made an application to the court for a derogating control order to be made against that individual; and

(b) the constable considers that the individual's arrest and detention is necessary to ensure that he is available to be given notice of the order if it is made.

(2) A constable who has arrested an individual under this section must take him to the designated place that the constable considers most appropriate as soon as practicable after the arrest.

(3) An individual taken to a designated place under this section may be detained there until the end of 48 hours from the time of his arrest.

(4) If the court considers that it is necessary to do so to ensure that the individual in question is available to be given notice of any derogating control order that is made against him, it may, during the 48 hours following his arrest, extend the period for which the individual may be detained under this section by a period of no more than 48 hours.

(5)–(8) *****

(9) The power to detain an individual under this section includes power to detain him in a manner that is incompatible with his right to liberty under Article 5 of the Human Rights Convention if, and only if—

(a) there is a designated derogation in respect of the detention of individuals under this section in connection with the making of applications for derogating control orders; and

(b) that derogation and the designated derogation relating to the power to make the orders applied for are designated in respect of the same public emergency.

(10) *****

6 Duration of derogating control orders

(1) A derogating control order has effect at a time only if—

(a) the relevant derogation remains in force at that time; and

(b) that time is not more than 12 months after—

(i) the making of the order under section 14(1) of the Human Rights Act 1998 (c. 42) designating that derogation; or

(ii) the making by the Secretary of State of an order declaring that it continues to be necessary for him to have power to impose derogating obligations by reference to that derogation.

(2) The power of the Secretary of State to make an order containing a declaration for the purposes of subsection (1)(b)(ii) is exercisable by statutory instrument.

(3) No order may be made by the Secretary of State containing such a declaration unless a draft of it has been laid before Parliament and approved by a resolution of each House.

(4) Subsection (3) does not apply to an order that contains a statement by the Secretary of State that the order needs, by reason of urgency, to be made without the approval required by that subsection.

(5) An order under this section that contains such a statement—

(a) must be laid before Parliament after being made; and

(b) if not approved by a resolution of each House before the end of 40 days beginning with the day on which the order was made, ceases to have effect at the end of that period.

(6) Where an order ceases to have effect in accordance with subsection (5), that does not—

(a) affect anything previously done in reliance on the order; or

(b) prevent the Secretary of State from exercising any power of his to make a new order for the purposes of subsection (1)(b)(ii) to the same or similar effect.

(7) *****

7 Modification, notification and proof of orders etc.

(1) If while a non-derogating control order is in force the controlled person considers that there has been a change of circumstances affecting the order, he may make an application to the Secretary of State for—

(a) the revocation of the order; or

(b) the modification of an obligation imposed by the order;

and it shall be the duty of the Secretary of State to consider the application.

(2) The Secretary of State may, at any time (whether or not in response to an application by the controlled person)—

(a) revoke a non-derogating control order;

(b) relax or remove an obligation imposed by such an order;

(c) with the consent of the controlled person, modify the obligations imposed by such an order; or

(d) make to the obligations imposed by such an order any modifications which he considers necessary for purposes connected with preventing or restricting involvement by the controlled person in terrorism-related activity.

(3) The Secretary of State may not make to the obligations imposed by a control order any modification the effect of which is that a non-derogating control order becomes an order imposing a derogating obligation.

(4) An application may be made at any time to the court—

(a) by the Secretary of State, or

(b) by the controlled person,

for the revocation of a derogating control order or for the modification of obligations imposed by such an order.

(5) On such an application, the court may modify the obligations imposed by the derogating control order only where—

(a) the modification consists in the removal or relaxation of an obligation imposed by the order;

(b) the modification has been agreed to by both the controlled person and the Secretary of State; or

(c) the modification is one which the court considers necessary for purposes connected with preventing or restricting involvement by the controlled person in terrorism-related activity.

(6)–(11) *****

8 *****

9 Offences

(1) A person who, without reasonable excuse, contravenes an obligation imposed on him by a control order is guilty of an offence.

(2), (3) *****

(4) A person guilty of an offence under subsection (1) or (2) shall be liable—

(a) on conviction on indictment, to imprisonment for a term not exceeding 5 years or to a fine, or to both;

(b) on summary conviction in England and Wales, to imprisonment for a term not exceeding 12 months or to a fine not exceeding the statutory maximum, or to both;

(c) on summary conviction in Scotland or Northern Ireland, to imprisonment for a term not exceeding 6 months or to a fine not exceeding the statutory maximum, or to both.

(5)–(10) *****

10–12 *****

Supplemental

13 Duration of sections 1 to 9

(1) Except so far as otherwise provided under this section, sections 1 to 9 expire at the end of the period of 12 months beginning with the day on which this Act is passed.

(2) The Secretary of State may, by order made by statutory instrument—
  (a) repeal sections 1 to 9;
  (b) at any time revive those sections for a period not exceeding one year; or
  (c) provide that those sections—
    (i) are not to expire at the time when they would otherwise expire under subsection (1) or in accordance with an order under this subsection; but
    (ii) are to continue in force after that time for a period not exceeding one year.
(3) Before making an order under this section the Secretary of State must consult—
  (a) the person appointed for the purposes of section 14(2);
  (b) the Intelligence Services Commissioner; and
  (c) the Director-General of the Security Service.
(4) No order may be made by the Secretary of State under this section unless a draft of it has been laid before Parliament and approved by a resolution of each House.
(5) Subsection (4) does not apply to an order that contains a declaration by the Secretary of State that the order needs, by reason of urgency, to be made without the approval required by that subsection.
(6) An order under this section that contains such a declaration—
  (a) must be laid before Parliament after being made; and
  (b) if not approved by a resolution of each House before the end of 40 days beginning with the day on which the order was made, ceases to have effect at the end of that period.
(7)–(10) *****

14   Reporting and review

(1) As soon as reasonably practicable after the end of every relevant 3 month period, the Secretary of State must—
  (a) prepare a report about his exercise of the control order powers during that period; and
  (b) lay a copy of that report before Parliament.
(2) The Secretary of State must also appoint a person to review the operation of this Act.
(3) As soon as reasonably practicable after the end of—
  (a) the period of 9 months beginning with the day on which this Act is passed, and
  (b) every 12 month period which ends with the first or a subsequent anniversary of the end of the period mentioned in the preceding paragraph and is a period during the whole or a part of which sections 1 to 9 of this Act were in force,
the person so appointed must carry out a review of the operation of this Act during that period.
(4) The person who conducts a review under this section must send the Secretary of State a report on its outcome as soon as reasonably practicable after completing the review.
(5) That report must also contain the opinion of the person making it on—
  (a) the implications for the operation of this Act of any proposal made by the Secretary of State for the amendment of the law relating to terrorism; and
  (b) the extent (if any) to which the Secretary of State has made use of his power by virtue of section 3(1)(b) to make non-derogating control orders in urgent cases without the permission of the court.
(6) On receiving a report under subsection (4), the Secretary of State must lay a copy of it before Parliament.
(7), (8) *****

*****

Serious Organised Crime and Police Act 2005
(2005, c. 15)

An Act to provide for the establishment and functions of the Serious Organised Crime Agency; to make provision about investigations, prosecutions, offenders and witnesses in criminal proceedings and the protection of persons involved in investigations or proceedings; to provide for the implementation of certain international obligations relating to criminal matters; to amend the proceeds of Crime Act 2002; to make further provision for combating crime and disorder, including new provision about powers of arrest and search warrants and about parental compensation orders; to make further provision about the police and policing and persons supporting the police; to make provision for protecting certain organisations from interference with their activities; to make provision about criminal records; to provide for the Private Security Industry Act 2001 to extend to Scotland; and for connected purposes   [7 April 2005]

Territorial extent: See section 179 (reproduced below)

PART 1   THE SERIOUS ORGANISED CRIME AGENCY

CHAPTER 1   SOCA: ESTABLISHMENT AND ACTIVITIES

Establishment of SOCA

1   Establishment of Serious Organised Crime Agency

(1) There shall be a body corporate to be known as the Serious Organised Crime Agency ("SOCA").

(2) *******

(3) Each of the following bodies shall cease to exist on such date as the Secretary of State appoints by order—

    (a) the National Criminal Intelligence Service and its Service Authority, and

    (b) the National Crime Squad and its Service Authority.

Functions

2   Functions of SOCA as to serious organised crime

(1) SOCA has the functions of—

    (a) preventing and detecting serious organised crime, and

    (b) contributing to the reduction of such crime in other ways and to the mitigation of its consequences.

(2) SOCA's functions under subsection (1) are exercisable subject to subsections (3) to (5) (but subsection (3) does not apply to Scotland).

(3) If, in exercising its function under subsection (1)(a), SOCA becomes aware of conduct appearing to SOCA to involve serious or complex fraud, SOCA may thereafter exercise that function in relation to the fraud in question only—

    (a) with the agreement of the Director, or an authorised officer, of the Serious Fraud Office, or

    (b) if the Serious Fraud Office declines to act in relation to it.

(4) If, in exercising its function under subsection (1)(a), SOCA becomes aware of conduct appearing to SOCA to involve revenue fraud, SOCA may thereafter exercise that function in relation to the fraud in question only with the agreement of the Commissioners.

(5) Before exercising its function under subsection (1)(b) in any way in relation to revenue fraud, SOCA must consult the Commissioners.

(6) The issue of whether SOCA's function under subsection (1)(a) continued to be

exercisable in any circumstances within subsection (3) or (4) may not be raised in any criminal proceedings.

(7) In this section "revenue fraud" includes fraud relating to taxes, duties and national insurance contributions.

(8) In this Chapter "the Commissioners" means the Commissioners for Her Majesty's Revenue and Customs.

3   Functions of SOCA as to information relating to crime

(1) SOCA has the function of gathering, storing, analysing and disseminating information relevant to—

(a) the prevention, detection, investigation or prosecution of offences, or

(b) the reduction of crime in other ways or the mitigation of its consequences.

(2) SOCA may disseminate such information to—

(a) police forces within subsection (3),

(b) special police forces,

(c) law enforcement agencies, or

(d) such other persons as it considers appropriate in connection with any of the matters mentioned in subsection (1)(a) or (b).

(3)–(5) *****

4   ***

General powers

5   SOCA's general powers

(1) SOCA has the general powers conferred by this section.

(2) SOCA may—

(a) institute criminal proceedings in England and Wales or Northern Ireland;

(b) at the request of the chief officer of a police force within section 3(3) or of a special police force, act in support of any activities of that force;

(c) at the request of any law enforcement agency, act in support of any activities of that agency;

(d) enter into other arrangements for co-operating with bodies or persons (in the United Kingdom or elsewhere) which it considers appropriate in connection with the exercise of any of SOCA's functions under section 2 or 3 or any activities within subsection (3).

(3) Despite the references to serious organised crime in section 2(1), SOCA may carry on activities in relation to other crime if they are carried on for the purposes of any of the functions conferred on SOCA by section 2 or 3.

(4)–(7) *****

6–59   ***

PART 2   INVESTIGATIONS, PROSECUTIONS, PROCEEDINGS AND PROCEEDS OF CRIME

CHAPTER 1   INVESTIGATORY POWERS OF DPP, ETC.

Introductory

60   Investigatory powers of DPP etc.

(1) This Chapter confers powers on—

(a) the Director of Public Prosecutions,

(b) the Director of Revenue and Customs Prosecutions, and

(c) the Lord Advocate,

in relation to the giving of disclosure notices in connection with the investigation of offences to which this Chapter applies.

(2)–(6) *****

61 Offences to which this Chapter applies

(1) This Chapter applies to the following offences—

(a) any offence listed in Schedule 2 to the Proceeds of Crime Act 2002 (c. 29) (lifestyle offences: England and Wales);

(b) any offence listed in Schedule 4 to that Act (lifestyle offences: Scotland);

(c) any offence under sections 15 to 18 of the Terrorism Act 2000 (c. 11) (offences relating to fund-raising, money laundering etc.);

(d) any offence under section 170 of the Customs and Excise Management Act 1979 (c. 2) (fraudulent evasion of duty) or section 72 of the Value Added Tax Act 1994 (c. 23) (offences relating to VAT) which is a qualifying offence;

(e) any offence under section 17 of the Theft Act 1968 (c. 60) (false accounting), or any offence at common law of cheating in relation to the public revenue, which is a qualifying offence;

(f) any offence under section 1 of the Criminal Attempts Act 1981 (c. 47), or in Scotland at common law, of attempting to commit any offence in paragraph (c) or any offence in paragraph (d) or (e) which is a qualifying offence;

(g) any offence under section 1 of the Criminal Law Act 1977 (c. 45), or in Scotland at common law, of conspiracy to commit any offence in paragraph (c) or any offence in paragraph (d) or (e) which is a qualifying offence.

(2) For the purposes of subsection (1) an offence in paragraph (d) or (e) of that subsection is a qualifying offence if the Investigating Authority certifies that in his opinion—

(a) in the case of an offence in paragraph (d) or an offence of cheating the public revenue, the offence involved or would have involved a loss, or potential loss, to the public revenue of an amount not less than £5,000;

(b) in the case of an offence under section 17 of the Theft Act 1968 (c. 60), the offence involved or would have involved a loss or gain, or potential loss or gain, of an amount not less than £5,000.

(3)–(5) *****

Disclosure notices

62 Disclosure notices

(1) If it appears to the Investigating Authority—

(a) that there are reasonable grounds for suspecting that an offence to which this Chapter applies has been committed,

(b) that any person has information (whether or not contained in a document) which relates to a matter relevant to the investigation of that offence, and

(c) that there are reasonable grounds for believing that information which may be provided by that person in compliance with a disclosure notice is likely to be of substantial value (whether or not by itself) to that investigation,

he may give, or authorise an appropriate person to give, a disclosure notice to that person.

(2) In this Chapter "appropriate person" means—

(a) a constable,

(b) a member of the staff of SOCA who is for the time being designated under section 43, or

(c) an officer of Revenue and Customs.

(3) In this Chapter "disclosure notice" means a notice in writing requiring the person to whom it is given to do all or any of the following things in accordance with the specified requirements, namely—

(a) answer questions with respect to any matter relevant to the investigation;

(b) provide information with respect to any such matter as is specified in the notice;

(c) produce such documents, or documents of such descriptions, relevant to the investigation as are specified in the notice.

(4)–(6) *****

63 Production of documents

(1) This section applies where a disclosure notice has been given under section 62.

(2) An authorised person may—

(a) take copies of or extracts from any documents produced in compliance with the notice, and

(b) require the person producing them to provide an explanation of any of them.

(3) Documents so produced may be retained for so long as the Investigating Authority considers that it is necessary to retain them (rather than copies of them) in connection with the investigation for the purposes of which the disclosure notice was given.

(4)–(7) *****

64 Restrictions on requiring information etc.

(1) A person may not be required under section 62 or 63—

(a) to answer any privileged question,

(b) to provide any privileged information, or

(c) to produce any privileged document,

except that a lawyer may be required to provide the name and address of a client of his.

(2) A "privileged question" is a question which the person would be entitled to refuse to answer on grounds of legal professional privilege in proceedings in the High Court.

(3) "Privileged information" is information which the person would be entitled to refuse to provide on grounds of legal professional privilege in such proceedings.

(4) A"privileged document" is a document which the person would be entitled to refuse to produce on grounds of legal professional privilege in such proceedings.

(5) A person may not be required under section 62 to produce any excluded material (as defined by section 11 of the Police and Criminal Evidence Act 1984 (c. 60)).

(6)–(7) *****

(8) A person may not be required under section 62 or 63 to disclose any information or produce any document in respect of which he owes an obligation of confidence by virtue of carrying on any banking business, unless—

(a) the person to whom the obligation of confidence is owed consents to the disclosure or production, or

(b) the requirement is made by, or in accordance with a specific authorisation given by, the Investigating Authority.

(9) Subject to the preceding provisions, any requirement under section 62 or 63 has effect despite any restriction on disclosure (however imposed).

65 *****

Enforcement

66 Power to enter and seize documents

(1) A justice of the peace may issue a warrant under this section if, on an information on oath laid by the Investigating Authority, he is satisfied—

(a) that any of the conditions mentioned in subsection (2) is met in relation to any documents of a description specified in the information, and

(b) that the documents are on premises so specified.

(2) The conditions are—

(a) that a person has been required by a disclosure notice to produce the documents but has not done so;

    (b) that it is not practicable to give a disclosure notice requiring their production;

    (c) that giving such a notice might seriously prejudice the investigation of an offence to which this Chapter applies.

(3) A warrant under this section is a warrant authorising an appropriate person named in it—

    (a) to enter and search the premises, using such force as is reasonably necessary;

    (b) to take possession of any documents appearing to be documents of a description specified in the information, or to take any other steps which appear to be necessary for preserving, or preventing interference with, any such documents;

    (c) in the case of any such documents consisting of information recorded otherwise than in legible form, to take possession of any computer disk or other electronic storage device which appears to contain the information in question, or to take any other steps which appear to be necessary for preserving, or preventing interference with, that information;

    (d) to take copies of or extracts from any documents or information falling within paragraph (b) or (c);

    (e) to require any person on the premises to provide an explanation of any such documents or information or to state where any such documents or information may be found;

    (f) to require any such person to give the appropriate person such assistance as he may reasonably require for the taking of copies or extracts as mentioned in paragraph (d).

(4) A person executing a warrant under this section may take other persons with him, if it appears to him to be necessary to do so.

(5) A warrant under this section must, if so required, be produced for inspection by the owner or occupier of the premises or anyone acting on his behalf.

(6) If the premises are unoccupied or the occupier is temporarily absent, a person entering the premises under the authority of a warrant under this section must leave the premises as effectively secured against trespassers as he found them.

(7)–(10) *****

67–70 *****

CHAPTER 2 OFFENDERS ASSISTING INVESTIGATIONS AND PROSECUTIONS

71 Assistance by offender: immunity from prosecution

(1) If a specified prosecutor thinks that for the purposes of the investigation or prosecution of any offence it is appropriate to offer any person immunity from prosecution he may give the person a written notice under this subsection (an "immunity notice").

(2) If a person is given an immunity notice, no proceedings for an offence of a description specified in the notice may be brought against that person in England and Wales or Northern Ireland except in circumstances specified in the notice.

(3) An immunity notice ceases to have effect in relation to the person to whom it is given if the person fails to comply with any conditions specified in the notice.

(4) Each of the following is a specified prosecutor—

    (a) the Director of Public Prosecutions;

    (b) the Director of Revenue and Customs Prosecutions;

    (c) the Director of the Serious Fraud Office;

    (d) the Director of Public Prosecutions for Northern Ireland;

    (e) a prosecutor designated for the purposes of this section by a prosecutor mentioned in paragraphs (a) to (d).

(5)–(7) *****

72   Assistance by offender: undertakings as to use of evidence

(1) If a specified prosecutor thinks that for the purposes of the investigation or prosecution of any offence it is appropriate to offer any person an undertaking that information of any description will not be used against the person in any proceedings to which this section applies he may give the person a written notice under this subsection (a "restricted use undertaking").

(2) This section applies to—
  (a) criminal proceedings;
  (b) proceedings under Part 5 of the Proceeds of Crime Act 2002 (c. 29).

(3) If a person is given a restricted use undertaking the information described in the undertaking must not be used against that person in any proceedings to which this section applies brought in England and Wales or Northern Ireland except in the circumstances specified in the undertaking.

(4) A restricted use undertaking ceases to have effect in relation to the person to whom it is given if the person fails to comply with any conditions specified in the undertaking.

(5)–(7) *****

73   Assistance by defendant: reduction in sentence

(1) This section applies if a defendant—
  (a) following a plea of guilty is either convicted of an offence in proceedings in the Crown Court or is committed to the Crown Court for sentence, and
  (b) has, pursuant to a written agreement made with a specified prosecutor, assisted or offered to assist the investigator or prosecutor in relation to that or any other offence.

(2) In determining what sentence to pass on the defendant the court may take into account the extent and nature of the assistance given or offered.

(3) If the court passes a sentence which is less than it would have passed but for the assistance given or offered, it must state in open court—
  (a) that it has passed a lesser sentence than it would otherwise have passed, and
  (b) what the greater sentence would have been.

(4) Subsection (3) does not apply if the court thinks that it would not be in the public interest to disclose that the sentence has been discounted; but in such a case the court must give written notice of the matters specified in paragraphs (a) and (b) of subsection (3) to both the prosecutor and the defendant.

(5)–(10) *****

74   Assistance by defendant: review of sentence

(1) This section applies if—
  (a) the Crown Court has passed a sentence on a person in respect of an offence, and
  (b) the person falls within subsection (2).

(2) A person falls within this subsection if—
  (a) he receives a discounted sentence in consequence of his having offered in pursuance of a written agreement to give assistance to the prosecutor or investigator of an offence but he knowingly fails to any extent to give assistance in accordance with the agreement;
  (b) he receives a discounted sentence in consequence of his having offered in pursuance of a written agreement to give assistance to the prosecutor or investigator of an offence and, having given the assistance in accordance with the agreement, in pursuance of another written agreement gives or offers to give further assistance;
  (c) he receives a sentence which is not discounted but in pursuance of a written agreement he subsequently gives or offers to give assistance to the prosecutor or investigator of an offence.

(3) A specified prosecutor may at any time refer the case back to the court by which the sentence was passed if—

(a) the person is still serving his sentence, and

(b) the specified prosecutor thinks it is in the interests of justice to do so.

(4) A case so referred must, if possible, be heard by the judge who passed the sentence to which the referral relates.

(5) If the court is satisfied that a person who falls within subsection (2)(a) knowingly failed to give the assistance it may substitute for the sentence to which the referral relates such greater sentence (not exceeding that which it would have passed but for the agreement to give assistance) as it thinks appropriate.

(6) In a case of a person who falls within subsection (2)(b) or (c) the court may—

(a) take into account the extent and nature of the assistance given or offered;

(b) substitute for the sentence to which the referral relates such lesser sentence as it thinks appropriate.

(7) Any part of the sentence to which the referral relates which the person has already served must be taken into account in determining when a greater or lesser sentence imposed by subsection (5) or (6) has been served.

(8) A person in respect of whom a reference is made under this section and the specified prosecutor may with the leave of the Court of Appeal appeal to the Court of Appeal against the decision of the Crown Court.

(9)–(15) *****

75   Proceedings under section 74: exclusion of public

(1) This section applies to—

(a) any proceedings relating to a reference made under section 74(3), and

(b) any other proceedings arising in consequence of such proceedings.

(2) The court in which the proceedings will be or are being heard may make such order as it thinks appropriate—

(a) to exclude from the proceedings any person who does not fall within subsection (4);

(b) to give such directions as it thinks appropriate prohibiting the publication of any matter relating to the proceedings (including the fact that the reference has been made).

(3) An order under subsection (2) may be made only to the extent that the court thinks—

(a) that it is necessary to do so to protect the safety of any person, and

(b) that it is in the interests of justice.

(4), (5) *****

76–127   *****

Trespass on designated site

128   Offence of trespassing on designated site

(1) A person commits an offence if he enters, or is on, any designated site in England and Wales or Northern Ireland as a trespasser.

(2) A "designated site" means a site—

(a) specified or described (in any way) in an order made by the Secretary of State, and

(b) designated for the purposes of this section by the order.

(3) The Secretary of State may only designate a site for the purposes of this section if—

(a) it is comprised in Crown land; or

(b) it is comprised in land belonging to Her Majesty in Her private capacity or to the immediate heir to the Throne in his private capacity; or

(c) it appears to the Secretary of State that it is appropriate to designate the site in the interests of national security.

(4) It is a defence for a person charged with an offence under this section to prove that he did not know, and had no reasonable cause to suspect, that the site in relation to which the offence is alleged to have been committed was a designated site.

(5) A person guilty of an offence under this section is liable on summary conviction—

    (a) to imprisonment for a term not exceeding 51 weeks, or

    (b) to a fine not exceeding level 5 on the standard scale, or to both.

(6)–(10) *****

129 Corresponding Scottish offence

(1) A person commits an offence if he enters, or is on, any designated Scottish site without lawful authority.

(2) A "designated Scottish site" means a site in Scotland—

    (a) specified or described (in any way) in an order made by the Secretary of State, and

    (b) designated for the purposes of this section by the order.

(3) The Secretary of State may only designate a site for the purposes of this section if it appears to him that it is appropriate to designate the site in the interests of national security.

(4)–(7) *****

130–131 *****

Demonstrations in vicinity of Parliament

132 Demonstrating without authorisation in designated area

(1) Any person who—

    (a) organises a demonstration in a public place in the designated area, or

    (b) takes part in a demonstration in a public place in the designated area, or

    (c) carries on a demonstration by himself in a public place in the designated area,

is guilty of an offence if, when the demonstration starts, authorisation for the demonstration has not been given under section 134(2).

(2) It is a defence for a person accused of an offence under subsection (1) to show that he reasonably believed that authorisation had been given.

(3) Subsection (1) does not apply if the demonstration is—

    (a) a public procession of which notice is required to be given under subsection (1) of section 11 of the Public Order Act 1986 (c. 64), or of which (by virtue of subsection (2) of that section) notice is not required to be given, or

    (b) a public procession for the purposes of section 12 or 13 of that Act.

(4) Subsection (1) also does not apply in relation to any conduct which is lawful under section 220 of the Trade Union and Labour Relations (Consolidation) Act 1992 (c. 52).

(5), (6) *****

(7) In this section and in sections 133 to 136—

    (a) "the designated area" means the area specified in an order under section 138,

    (b) "public place" means any highway or any place to which at the material time the public or any section of the public has access, on payment or otherwise, as of right or by virtue of express or implied permission,

    (c) references to any person organising a demonstration include a person participating in its organisation,

    (d) references to any person organising a demonstration do not include a person carrying on a demonstration by himself,

    (e) references to any person or persons taking part in a demonstration (except in subsection (1) of this section) include a person carrying on a demonstration by himself.

133 Notice of demonstrations in designated area

(1) A person seeking authorisation for a demonstration in the designated area must give written notice to that effect to the Commissioner of Police of the Metropolis (referred to in this section and section 134 as "the Commissioner").

(2) The notice must be given—

(a) if reasonably practicable, not less than 6 clear days before the day on which the demonstration is to start, or

(b) if that is not reasonably practicable, then as soon as it is, and in any event not less than 24 hours before the time the demonstration is to start.

(3) The notice must be given—

(a) if the demonstration is to be carried on by more than one person, by any of the persons organising it,

(b) if it is to be carried on by a person by himself, by that person.

(4) The notice must state—

(a) the date and time when the demonstration is to start,

(b) the place where it is to be carried on,

(c) how long it is to last,

(d) whether it is to be carried on by a person by himself or not,

(e) the name and address of the person giving the notice.

(5), (6) *****

134 Authorisation of demonstrations in designated area

(1) This section applies if a notice complying with the requirements of section 133 is received at a police station in the metropolitan police district by the time specified in section 133(2).

(2) The Commissioner must give authorisation for the demonstration to which the notice relates.

(3) In giving authorisation, the Commissioner may impose on the persons organising or taking part in the demonstration such conditions specified in the authorisation and relating to the demonstration as in the Commissioner's reasonable opinion are necessary for the purpose of preventing any of the following—

(a) hindrance to any person wishing to enter or leave the Palace of Westminster,

(b) hindrance to the proper operation of Parliament,

(c) serious public disorder,

(d) serious damage to property,

(e) disruption to the life of the community,

(f) a security risk in any part of the designated area,

(g) risk to the safety of members of the public (including any taking part in the demonstration).

(4) The conditions may, in particular, impose requirements as to—

(a) the place where the demonstration may, or may not, be carried on,

(b) the times at which it may be carried on,

(c) the period during which it may be carried on,

(d) the number of persons who may take part in it,

(e) the number and size of banners or placards used,

(f) maximum permissible noise levels.

(5) The authorisation must specify the particulars of the demonstration given in the notice under section 133 pursuant to subsection (4) of that section, with any modifications made necessary by any condition imposed under subsection (3) of this section.

(6) The Commissioner must give notice in writing of—

(a) the authorisation,

(b) any conditions imposed under subsection (3), and

(c) the particulars mentioned in subsection (5),

to the person who gave the notice under section 133.

(7) Each person who takes part in or organises a demonstration in the designated area is guilty of an offence if —

(a) he knowingly fails to comply with a condition imposed under subsection (3) which is applicable to him (except where it is varied under section 135), or

(b) he knows or should have known that the demonstration is carried on otherwise than in accordance with the particulars set out in the authorisation by virtue of subsection (5).

(8) It is a defence for a person accused of an offence under subsection (7) to show—

(a) (in a paragraph (a) case) that the failure to comply, or

(b) (in a paragraph (b) case) that the divergence from the particulars,

arose from circumstances beyond his control, or from something done with the agreement, or by the direction, of a police officer.

(9)–(10) *****

135   Supplementary directions

(1) This section applies if the senior police officer reasonably believes that it is necessary, in order to prevent any of the things mentioned in paragraphs (a) to (g) of subsection (3) of section 134—

(a) to impose additional conditions on those taking part in or organising a demonstration authorised under that section, or

(b) to vary any condition imposed under that subsection or under paragraph (a) (including such a condition as varied under subsection (2)).

(2) The senior police office may give directions to those taking part in or organising the demonstration imposing such additional conditions or varying any such condition already imposed.

(3) A person taking part in or organising the demonstration who knowingly fails to comply with a condition which is applicable to him and which is imposed or varied by a direction under this section is guilty of an offence.

(4) It is a defence for him to show that the failure to comply arose from circumstances beyond his control.

(5) In this section, "the senior police officer" means the most senior in rank of the police officers present at the scene (or any one of them if there are more than one of the same rank).

136   *****

137   Loudspeakers in designated area

(1) Subject to subsection (2), a loudspeaker shall not be operated, at any time or for any purpose, in a street in the designated area.

(2)–(6) *****

138   The designated area

(1) The Secretary of State may by order specify an area as the designated area for the purposes of sections 132 to 137.

(2) The area may be specified by description, by reference to a map or in any other way.

(3) No point in the area so specified may be more than one kilometre in a straight line from the point nearest to it in Parliament Square.

139–144   *****

PART 5   MISCELLANEOUS

Protection of activities of certain organisations

145   Interference with contractual relationships so as to harm animal research organisation

(1) A person (A) commits an offence if, with the intention of harming an animal research organisation, he—

(a) does a relevant act, or

(b) threatens that he or somebody else will do a relevant act,

in circumstances in which that act or threat is intended or likely to cause a second person (B) to take any of the steps in subsection (2).

(2) The steps are—

(a) not to perform any contractual obligation owed by B to a third person (C) (whether or not such non-performance amounts to a breach of contract);

(b) to terminate any contract B has with C;

(c) not to enter into a contract with C.

(3) For the purposes of this section, a "relevant act" is—

(a) an act amounting to a criminal offence, or

(b) a tortious act causing B to suffer loss or damage of any description;

but paragraph (b) does not include an act which is actionable on the ground only that it induces another person to break a contract with B.

(4) For the purposes of this section, "contract" includes any other arrangement (and "contractual" is to be read accordingly).

(5) For the purposes of this section, to "harm" an animal research organisation means—

(a) to cause the organisation to suffer loss or damage of any description, or

(b) to prevent or hinder the carrying out by the organisation of any of its activities.

(6) This section does not apply to any act done wholly or mainly in contemplation or furtherance of a trade dispute.

(7) *****

146   Intimidation of persons connected with animal research organisation

(1) A person (A) commits an offence if, with the intention of causing a second person (B) to abstain from doing something which B is entitled to do (or to do something which B is entitled to abstain from doing)—

(a) A threatens B that A or somebody else will do a relevant act, and

(b) A does so wholly or mainly because B is a person falling within subsection (2).

(2) A person falls within this subsection if he is—

(a) an employee or officer of an animal research organisation;

(b) a student at an educational establishment that is an animal research organisation;

(c) a lessor or licensor of any premises occupied by an animal research organisation;

(d) a person with a financial interest in, or who provides financial assistance to, an animal research organisation;

(e) a customer or supplier of an animal research organisation;

(f) a person who is contemplating becoming someone within paragraph (c), (d) or (e);

(g) a person who is, or is contemplating becoming, a customer or supplier of someone within paragraph (c), (d), (e) or (f);

(h) an employee or officer of someone within paragraph (c), (d), (e), (f) or (g);

(i) a person with a financial interest in, or who provides financial assistance to, someone within paragraph (c), (d), (e), (f) or (g);

(j) a spouse, civil partner, friend or relative of, or a person who is known personally to, someone within any of paragraphs (a) to (i);

(k) a person who is, or is contemplating becoming, a customer or supplier of someone within paragraph (a), (b), (h), (i) or (j); or

(l) an employer of someone within paragraph (j).

(3)–(4) *****

(5) For the purposes of this section, a "relevant act" is—

(a) an act amounting to a criminal offence, or

(b) a tortious act causing B or another person to suffer loss or damage of any description.

(6) *****

(7) This section does not apply to any act done wholly or mainly in contemplation or furtherance of a trade dispute.

(8) *****

147　Penalty for offences under sections 145 and 146

(1) A person guilty of an offence under section 145 or 146 is liable—

(a) on summary conviction, to imprisonment for a term not exceeding 12 months or to a fine not exceeding the statutory maximum, or to both;

(b) on conviction on indictment, to imprisonment for a term not exceeding five years or to a fine, or to both.

(2) No proceedings for an offence under either of those sections may be instituted except by or with the consent of the Director of Public Prosecutions.

148　*****

149　Extension of sections 145 to 147

(1) The Secretary of State may by order provide for sections 145, 146 and 147 to apply in relation to persons or organisations of a description specified in the order as they apply in relation to animal research organisations.

(2) The Secretary of State may, however, only make an order under this section if satisfied that a series of acts has taken place and—

(a) that those acts were directed at persons or organisations of the description specified in the order or at persons having a connection with them, and

(b) that, if those persons or organisations had been animal research organisations, those acts would have constituted offences under section 145 or 146.

(3) In this section "organisation" and "animal research organisation" have the meanings given by section 148.

150–178　*****

179　Short title and extent

(1) This Act may be cited as the Serious Organised Crime and Police Act 2005.

(2) Subject to the following provisions, this Act extends to England and Wales only.

(3) The following extend also to Scotland—

(a) sections 1 to 54, 57 and 58,

(b) sections 60 to 68, 70, 79 to 96, 98 to 106, 107(1) and (4) and 108,

(c) section 123,

(d) section 131,

(e) sections 150 to 153, 156(6), 158, 163(1) and (2), 164, 165(1) and (2), 166(2), 167 and 171(1),

(f) sections 172, 173, 176 to 178 and this section,

(g) Schedules 1, 3, 5 and 15.

(4) The following extend to Scotland only—

(a) section 77 and 107(3),

(b) sections 129 and 130(3),

    (c) sections 156(1) to (5), 166(1) and 171(2).

(5) The following extend also to Northern Ireland—

    (a) sections 1 to 54, 57 and 58,

    (b) sections 68, 71 to 75, 79 to 106, 107(1), (2) and (4) and 108,

    (c) section 123(1),

    (d) sections 128, 131 and 144,

    (e)–(g) *****

(6)–(10) *****

*****

PART II

Other constitutional materials

The Constitution of the United States

We the People of the United States, in order to form a more perfect Union, establish Justice, ensure Domestic Tranquillity, provide for the common Defence, promote the general Welfare, and secure the Blessings of Liberty to ourselves and our Posterity, do ordain and establish this CONSTITUTION for the United States of America.

Articles I–VII
*****

AMENDMENTS TO THE CONSTITUTION

Article I

Congress shall make no law respecting an establishment of religion, or prohibiting the free exercise thereof; or abridging the freedom of speech or of the press; or the right of the people peaceably to assemble, and to petition the government for a redress of grievances.

Article II

A well-regulated militia being necessary to the security of a free state, the right of the people to keep and bear arms shall not be infringed.

Article III

No soldier shall, in time of peace, be quartered in any house without the consent of the owner, nor in time of war but in a manner to be prescribed by law.

Article IV

The right of the people to be secure in their persons, houses, papers, and effects, against unreasonable searches and seizures, shall not be violated, and no warrants shall issue but upon probable cause, supported by oath or affirmation, and particularly describing the place to be searched, and the persons or things to be seized.

Article V

No person shall be held to answer for a capital or other infamous crime unless on a presentment or indictment of a grand jury, except in cases arising in the land or naval forces, or in the militia, when in actual service, in time of war or public danger; nor shall any person be subject for the same offence to be twice put in jeopardy of life or limb; nor shall be compelled in any criminal case to be a witness against himself, nor be deprived of life, liberty, or property, without due process of law; nor shall private property be taken for public use without just compensation.

Article VI

In all criminal prosecutions, the accused shall enjoy the right to a speedy and public trial, by an impartial jury of the state and district wherein the crime shall have been committed, which district shall have been previously ascertained by law, and to be informed of the nature and cause of the accusation; to be confronted with the witnesses against him; to have compulsory process for obtaining witnesses in his favor, and to have the assistance of counsel for his defence.

Article VII

In suits at common law, where the value in controversy shall exceed twenty dollars, the right of trial by jury shall be preserved, and no fact tried by a jury shall be otherwise re-examined in any court of the United States than according to the rules of the common law.

Article VIII

Excessive bail shall not be required, nor excessive fines imposed, nor cruel and unusual punishments inflicted.

Article IX

The enumeration in the constitution of certain rights shall not be construed to deny or disparage others retained by the people.

Article X

The powers not delegated to the United States by the constitution, nor prohibited by it to the states, are reserved to the states respectively, or to the people.

[*The foregoing ten amendments were adopted at the first session of Congress, and were declared to be in force, December 15, 1791.*]

Articles XI–XIII

*****

Article XIV

1. All persons born or naturalized in the United States, and subject to the jurisdiction thereof, are citizens of the United States and of the state wherein they reside. No state shall make or enforce any law which shall abridge the privileges or immunities of citizens of the United States; nor shall any state deprive any person of life, liberty, or property without due process of law; nor deny to any person within its jurisdiction the equal protection of the law.

2.–4.   *****

5. The Congress shall have power to enforce, by appropriate legislation, the provisions of this article.

[*Declared in force, July 28, 1868.*]

*****

United Nations Universal Declaration of Human Rights, December 1948

Preamble

Whereas recognition of the inherent dignity and of the equal and inalienable rights of all members of the human family is the foundation of freedom, justice and peace in the world,

Whereas disregard and contempt for human rights have resulted in barbarous acts which have outraged the conscience of mankind, and the advent of a world in which human beings shall enjoy freedom of speech and belief and freedom from fear and want has been proclaimed as the highest aspiration of the common people,

Whereas it is essential, if man is not to be compelled to have recourse, as a last resort, to rebellion against tyranny and oppression, that human rights should be protected by the rule of law,

Whereas it is essential to promote the development of friendly relations between nations,

Whereas the peoples of the United Nations have in the Charter reaffirmed their faith in fundamental human rights, in the dignity and worth of the human person and in the equal rights of men and women and have determined to promote social progress and better standards of life in larger freedom,

Whereas Member States have pledged themselves to achieve, in co-operation with the United Nations, the promotion of universal respect for and observance of human rights and fundamental freedoms,

Whereas a common understanding of these rights and freedoms is of the greatest importance for the full realization of this pledge,

Now, Therefore THE GENERAL ASSEMBLY proclaims THIS UNIVERSAL DECLAR-ATION OF HUMAN RIGHTS as a common standard of achievement for all peoples and all nations, to the end that every individual and every organ of society, keeping this Declaration constantly in mind, shall strive by teaching and education to promote respect for these rights and freedoms and by progressive measures, national and international, to secure their universal and effective recognition and observance, both among the peoples of Member States themselves and among the peoples of territories under their jurisdiction.

Article 1
All human beings are born free and equal in dignity and rights. They are endowed with reason and conscience and should act towards one another in a spirit of brotherhood.

Article 2
Everyone is entitled to all the rights and freedoms set forth in this Declaration, without distinction of any kind, such as race, colour, sex, language, religion, political or other opinion, national or social origin, property, birth or other status. Furthermore, no distinction shall be made on the basis of the political, jurisdictional or international status of the country or territory to which a person belongs, whether it be independent, trust, non-self-governing or under any other limitation of sovereignty.

Article 3
Everyone has the right to life, liberty and security of person.

Article 4
No one shall be held in slavery or servitude; slavery and the slave trade shall be prohibited in all their forms.

Article 5
No one shall be subjected to torture or to cruel, inhuman or degrading treatment or punishment.

Article 6
Everyone has the right to recognition everywhere as a person before the law.

Article 7
All are equal before the law and are entitled without any discrimination to equal protection of the law. All are entitled to equal protection against any discrimination in violation of this Declaration and against any incitement to such discrimination.

Article 8
Everyone has the right to an effective remedy by the competent national tribunals for acts violating the fundamental rights granted him by the constitution or by law.

Article 9

No one shall be subjected to arbitrary arrest, detention or exile.

Article 10

Everyone is entitled in full equality to a fair and public hearing by an independent and impartial tribunal, in the determination of his rights and obligations and of any criminal charge against him.

Article 11

(1) Everyone charged with a penal offence has the right to be presumed innocent until proved guilty according to law in a public trial at which he has had all the guarantees necessary for his defence.

(2) No one shall be held guilty of any penal offence on account of any act or omission which did not constitute a penal offence, under national or international law, at the time when it was committed. Nor shall a heavier penalty be imposed than the one that was applicable at the time the penal offence was committed.

Article 12

No one shall be subjected to arbitrary interference with his privacy, family, home or correspondence, nor to attacks upon his honour and reputation. Everyone has the right to the protection of the law against such interference or attacks.

Article 13

(1) Everyone has the right to freedom of movement and residence within the borders of each state.

(2) Everyone has the right to leave any country, including his own, and to return to his country.

Article 14

(1) Everyone has the right to seek and to enjoy in other countries asylum from persecution.

(2) This right may not be invoked in the case of prosecutions genuinely arising from non-political crimes or from acts contrary to the purposes and principles of the United Nations.

Article 15

(1) Everyone has the right to a nationality.

(2) No one shall be arbitrarily deprived of his nationality nor denied the right to change his nationality.

Article 16

(1) Men and women of full age, without any limitation due to race, nationality or religion, have the right to marry and to found a family. They are entitled to equal rights as to marriage, during marriage and at its dissolution.

(2) Marriage shall be entered into only with the free and full consent of the intending spouses.

(3) The family is the natural and fundamental group unit of society and is entitled to protection by society and the State.

Article 17

(1) Everyone has the right to own property alone as well as in association with others.

(2) No one shall be arbitrarily deprived of his property.

Article 18

Everyone has the right to freedom of thought, conscience and religion; this right includes freedom to change his religion or belief, and freedom, either alone or in community with others and in public or private, to manifest his religion or belief in teaching, practice, worship and observance.

Article 19

Everyone has the right to freedom of opinion and expression; this right includes freedom to hold opinions without interference and to seek, receive and impart information and ideas through any media and regardless of frontiers.

Article 20

(1) Everyone has the right to freedom of peaceful assembly and association.

(2) No one may be compelled to belong to an association.

Article 21

(1) Everyone has the right to take part in the government of his country, directly or through freely chosen representatives.

(2) Everyone has the right of equal access to public service in his country.

(3) The will of the people shall be the basis of the authority of government; this will shall be expressed in periodic and genuine elections which shall be by universal and equal suffrage and shall be held by secret vote or by equivalent free voting procedures.

Article 22

Everyone, as a member of society, has the right to social security and is entitled to realization, through national effort and international co-operation and in accordance with the organization and resources of each State, of the economic, social and cultural rights indispensable for his dignity and the free development of his personality.

Article 23

(1) Everyone has the right to work, to free choice of employment, to just and favourable conditions of work and to protection against unemployment.

(2) Everyone, without any discrimination, has the right to equal pay for equal work.

(3) Everyone who works has the right to just and favourable remuneration ensuring for himself and his family an existence worthy of human dignity, and supplemented, if necessary, by other means of social protection.

(4) Everyone has the right to form and to join trade unions for the protection of his interests.

Article 24

Everyone has the right to rest and leisure, including reasonable limitation of working hours and periodic holidays with pay.

Article 25

(1) Everyone has the right to a standard of living adequate for the health and well-being of himself and of his family, including food, clothing, housing and medical care and necessary social services, and the right to security in the event of unemployment, sickness, disability, widowhood, old age or other lack of livelihood in circumstances beyond his control.

(2) Motherhood and childhood are entitled to special care and assistance. All children, whether born in or out of wedlock, shall enjoy the same social protection.

Article 26

(1) Everyone has the right to education. Education shall be free, at least in the elementary and fundamental stages. Elementary education shall be compulsory. Technical and professional education shall be made generally available and higher education shall be equally accessible to all on the basis of merit.

(2) Education shall be directed to the full development of the human personality and to the strengthening of respect for human rights and fundamental freedoms. It shall promote understanding, tolerance and friendship among all nations, racial or religious groups, and shall further the activities of the United Nations for the maintenance of peace.

(3) Parents have a prior right to choose the kind of education that shall be given to their children.

Article 27
(1) Everyone has the right freely to participate in the cultural life of the community, to enjoy the arts and to share in scientific advancement and its benefits.

(2) Everyone has the right to the protection of the moral and material interests resulting from any scientific, literary or artistic production of which he is the author.

Article 28
Everyone is entitled to a social and international order in which the rights and freedoms set forth in this Declaration can be fully realized.

Article 29
(1) Everyone has duties to the community in which alone the free and full development of his personality is possible.

(2) In the exercise of his rights and freedoms, everyone shall be subject only to such limitations as are determined by law solely for the purpose of securing due recognition and respect for the rights and freedoms of others and of meeting the just requirements of morality, public order and the general welfare in a democratic society.

(3) These rights and freedoms may in no case be exercised contrary to the purposes and principles of the United Nations.

Article 30
Nothing in this Declaration may be interpreted as implying for any State, group or person any right to engage in any activity or to perform any act aimed at the destruction of any of the rights and freedoms set forth herein.

European Convention for the Protection of Human Rights and Fundamental Freedoms (1950)

[The European Convention on Human Rights]

The Governments signatory hereto, being Members of the Council of Europe,

Considering the Universal Declaration of Human Rights proclaimed by the General Assembly of the United Nations on 10 December 1948;

Considering that this Declaration aims at securing the universal and effective recognition and observance of the Rights therein declared;

Considering that the aim of the Council of Europe is the achievement of greater unity between its Members and that one of the methods by which the aim is to be pursued is the maintenance and further realization of Human Rights and Fundamental Freedoms;

Reaffirming their profound belief in those Fundamental Freedoms which are the foundation of justice and peace in the world and are best maintained on the one hand by an effective political democracy and on the other by a common understanding and observance of the Human Rights upon which they depend;

Being resolved, as the Governments of European countries which are like-minded and have a common heritage of political traditions, ideals, freedom and the rule of law to take the first steps for the collective enforcement of certain of the Rights stated in the Universal Declaration;

Have agreed as follows:

Article 1   Obligation to respect human rights
The High Contracting Parties shall secure to everyone within their jurisdiction the rights and freedoms defined in Section I of this Convention.

SECTION I   RIGHTS AND FREEDOMS

Article 2   Right to life

1.   Everyone's right to life shall be protected by law. No one shall be deprived of his life intentionally save in the execution of a sentence of a court following his conviction of a crime for which this penalty is provided by law.

2.   Deprivation of life shall not regarded as inflicted in contravention of this article when it results from the use of force which is no more than absolutely necessary:

(a)   in defence of any person from unlawful violence;
(b)   in order to effect a lawful arrest or to prevent the escape of a person lawfully detained;
(c)   in action lawfully taken for the purpose of quelling a riot or insurrection.

Article 3   Prohibition of torture

No one shall be subjected to torture or to inhuman or degrading treatment or punishment.

Article 4   Prohibition of slavery and forced labour

1.   No one shall be held in slavery or servitude.

2.   No one shall be required to perform forced or compulsory labour.

3.   For the purpose of this article the term "forced or compulsory labour' shall not include:

(a)   any work required to be done in the ordinary course of detention imposed according to the provisions of Article 5 of this Convention or during conditional release from such detention;
(b)   any service of a military character or, in case of conscientious objectors in countries where they are recognized, service exacted instead of compulsory military service;
(c)   any service exacted in case of an emergency or calamity threatening the life or well-being of the community;
(d)   any work or service which forms part of normal civic obligations.

Article 5   Right to liberty and security

1.   Everyone has the right to liberty and security of person.

No one shall be deprived of his liberty save in the following cases and in accordance with a procedure prescribed by law:

(a)   the lawful detention of a person after conviction by a competent court;
(b)   the lawful arrest or detention of a person for non-compliance with the lawful order of a court or in order to secure the fulfilment of any obligation prescribed by law;
(c)   the lawful arrest or detention of a person effected for the purpose of bringing him before the competent legal authority on reasonable suspicion of having committed an offence or when it is reasonably considered necessary to prevent his committing an offence or fleeing after having done so;
(d)   the detention of a minor by lawful order for the purpose of educational supervision or his lawful detention for the purpose of bringing him before the competent legal authority;
(e)   the lawful detention of persons for the prevention of the spreading of infectious diseases, of persons of unsound mind, alcoholics or drug addicts, or vagrants;
(f)   the lawful arrest or detention of a person to prevent his effecting an unauthorized entry into the country or of a person against whom action is being taken with a view to deportation or extradition.

2.   Everyone who is arrested shall be informed promptly, in a language which he understands, of the reasons for his arrest and of any charge against him.

3.   Everyone arrested or detained in accordance with the provisions of paragraph 1(c) of this article shall be brought promptly before a judge or other officer authorized by law to exercise judicial power and shall be entitled to trial within a reasonable time or to release pending trial. Release may be conditioned by guarantees to appear for trial.

4.   Everyone who is deprived of his liberty by arrest or detention shall be entitled to take proceedings by which the lawfulness of his detention shall be decided speedily by a court and his release ordered if the detention is not lawful.

5.   Everyone who has been the victim of arrest or detention in contravention of the provisions of this article shall have an enforceable right to compensation.

Article 6   Right to a fair trial

1.   In the determination of his civil rights and obligations or of any criminal charge against him, everyone is entitled to a fair and public hearing within a reasonable time by an independent and impartial tribunal established by law. Judgment shall be pronounced publicly but the press and public may be excluded from all or part of the trial in the interest of morals, public order or national security in a democratic society, where the interests of juveniles or the protection of the private life of the parties so require, or to the extent strictly necessary in the opinion of the court in special circumstances where publicity would prejudice the interests of justice.

2.   Everyone charged with a criminal offence shall be presumed innocent until proved guilty according to law.

3.   Everyone charged with a criminal offence has the following minimum rights:
   (a) to be informed promptly, in a language which he understands and in detail, of the nature and cause of the accusation against him;
   (b) to have adequate time and facilities for the preparation of his defence;
   (c) to defend himself in person or through legal assistance of his own choosing or, if he has not sufficient means to pay for legal assistance, to be given it free when the interests of justice so require;
   (d) to examine or have examined witnesses against him and to obtain the attendance and examination of witnesses on his behalf under the same conditions as witnesses against him;
   (e) to have the free assistance of an interpreter if he cannot understand or speak the language used in court.

Article 7   No punishment without law

1.   No one shall be held guilty of any criminal offence on account of any act or omission which did not constitute a criminal offence under national or international law at the time when it was committed. Nor shall a heavier penalty be imposed than the one that was applicable at the time the criminal offence was committed.

2.   This article shall not prejudice the trial and punishment of any person for any act or omission which, at the time when it was committed, was criminal according to the general principles of law recognized by civilized nations.

Article 8   Right to respect for private and family life

1.   Everyone has the right to respect for his private and family life, his home and his correspondence.

2.   There shall be no interference by a public authority with the exercise of this right except such as is in accordance with the law and is necessary in a democratic society in the interests of national security, public safety or the economic well-being of the country, for the prevention of disorder or crime, for the protection of health or morals, or for the protection of the rights and freedoms of others.

Article 9   Freedom of thought, conscience and religion

1.   Everyone has the right to freedom of thought, conscience and religion; this right

includes freedom to change his religion or belief, and freedom, either alone or in community with others and in public or private, to manifest his religion or belief, in worship, teaching, practice and observance.

2.   Freedom to manifest one's religion or beliefs shall be subject only to such limitations as are prescribed by law and are necessary in a democratic society in the interests of public safety, for the protection of public order, health or morals, or for the protection of the rights and freedoms of others.

Article 10   Freedom of expression

1.   Everyone has the right to freedom of expression. This right shall include freedom to hold opinions and to receive and impart information and ideas without interference by public authority and regardless of frontiers. This article shall not prevent States from requiring the licensing of broadcasting, television or cinema enterprises.

2.   The exercise of these freedoms, since it carries with it duties and responsibilities, may be subject to such formalities, conditions, restrictions or penalties as are prescribed by law and are necessary in a democratic society, in the interests of national security, territorial integrity or public safety, for the prevention of disorder or crime, for the protection of health or morals, for the protection of the reputation or rights of others, for preventing the disclosure of information received in confidence, or for maintaining the authority and impartiality of the judiciary.

Article 11   Freedom of assembly and association

1.   Everyone has the right to freedom of peaceful assembly and to freedom of association with others, including the right to form and to join trade unions for the protection of his interests.

2.   No restrictions shall be placed on the exercise of these rights other than such as are prescribed by law and are necessary in a democratic society in the interests of national security or public safety, for the prevention of disorder or crime, of the protection of health or morals or for the protection of the rights and freedoms of others. This article shall not prevent the imposition of lawful restrictions on the exercise of these rights by members of the armed forces, of the police or of the administration of the State.

Article 12   Right to marry

Men and women of marriageable age have the right to marry and to found a family, according to the national laws governing the exercise of this right.

Article 13   Right to an effective remedy

Everyone whose rights and freedoms as set forth in this Convention are violated shall have an effective remedy before a national authority notwithstanding that the violation has been committed by persons acting in an official capacity.

Article 14   Prohibition of discrimination

The enjoyment of the rights and freedoms set forth in this Convention shall be secured without discrimination on any ground such as sex, race, colour, language, religion, political or other opinion, national or social origin, association with a national minority, property, birth or other status.

Article 15   Derogation in time of emergency

1.   In time of war or other public emergency threatening the life of the nation any High Contracting Party may take measures derogating from its obligations under this Convention to the extent strictly required by the exigencies of the situation, provided that such measures are not inconsistent with its other obligations under international law.

2.   No derogation from Article 2, except in respect of deaths resulting from lawful acts of war, or from Articles 3, 4 (paragraph 1) and 7 shall be made under this provision.

3.   Any High Contracting Party availing itself of this right of derogation shall keep the Secretary-General of the Council of Europe fully informed of the measures which it has taken and the reasons therefor. It shall also inform the Secretary-General of the Council of Europe when such measures have ceased to operate and the provisions of the Convention are again being fully executed.

Article 16   Restrictions on political activity of aliens
Nothing in Articles 10, 11, and 14 shall be regarded as preventing the High Contracting Parties from imposing restrictions on the political activity of aliens.

Article 17   Prohibition of abuse of rights
Nothing in this Convention may be interpreted as implying for any State, group or person any right to engage in any activity or perform any act aimed at the destruction of any of the rights and freedoms set forth herein or at their limitation to a greater extent than is provided for in the Convention.

Article 18   Limitation on use of restrictions on rights
The restrictions permitted under this Convention to the said rights and freedoms shall not be applied for any purpose other than those for which they have been prescribed.

SECTION II   EUROPEAN COURT OF HUMAN RIGHTS

Article 19   Establishment of the court
To ensure the observance of the engagements undertaken by the High Contracting Parties in the Convention and the protocols thereto, there shall be set up a European Court of Human Rights, hereinafter referred to as "the Court". It shall function on a permanent basis.

Article 20   Number of judges
The Court shall consist of a number of judges equal to that of the High Contracting Parties.

Article 21   Criteria for office
1.   The judges shall be of high moral character and must either possess the qualifications required for appointment to high judicial office or be jurisconsults of recognised competence.
2.   The judges shall sit on the Court in their individual capacity.
3.   During their term of office the judges shall not engage in any activity which is incompatible with their independence, impartiality or with the demands of a full-time office; all questions arising from the application of this paragraph shall be decided by the Court.

Article 22   Election of judges
1.   The judges shall be elected by the Parliamentary Assembly with respect to each High Contracting Party by a majority of votes cast from a list of three candidates nominated by the High Contracting Party.
2.   The same procedure shall be followed to complete the Court in the event of the accession of new High Contracting Parties and in filling casual vacancies.

Article 23   Terms of office
1.   The judges shall be elected for a period of six years. They may be re-elected. However, the terms of office of one-half of the judges elected at the first election shall expire at the end of three years.
2.   The judges whose terms of office are to expire at the end of the initial period of three years shall be chosen by lot by the Secretary General of the Council of Europe immediately after their election.
3.   In order to ensure that, as far as possible, the terms of office of one-half of the judges are renewed every three years, the Parliamentary Assembly may decide, before proceeding to

any subsequent election, that the term or terms of office of one or more judges to be elected shall be for a period other than six years but not more than nine and not less than three years.

4.   In cases where more than one term of office is involved and where the Parliamentary Assembly applies the preceding paragraph, the allocation of the terms of office shall be effected by a drawing of lots by the Secretary General of the Council of Europe immediately after the election.

5.   A judge elected to replace a judge whose term of office has not expired shall hold office for the remainder of his predecessor's term.

6.   The terms of office of judges shall expire when they reach the age of 70.

7.   The judges shall hold office until replaced. They shall, however, continue to deal with such cases as they already have under consideration.

Article 24   Dismissal
No judge may be dismissed from his office unless the other judges decide by a majority of two-thirds that he has ceased to fulfil the required conditions.

Article 25   Registry and legal secretaries
The Court shall have a registry, the functions and organisation of which shall be laid down in the rules of the Court. The Court shall be assisted by legal secretaries.

Article 26   Plenary court
The plenary court shall:
  (a)   elect its President and one or two Vice-Presidents for a period of three years; they may be re-elected;
  (b)   set up Chambers, constituted for a fixed period of time;
  (c)   elect the Presidents of the Chambers of the Court; they may be re-elected;
  (d)   adopt the rules of the Court; and
  (e)   elect the Registrar and one or more Deputy Registrars.

Article 27   Committees, Chambers and Grand Chamber
1.   To consider cases brought before it, the Court shall sit in committees of three judges, in Chambers of seven judges and in a Grand Chamber of seventeen judges. The Court's Chambers shall set up committees for a fixed period of time.

2.   There shall sit as an *ex officio* member of the Chamber and the Grand Chamber the judge elected in respect of the State Party concerned or, if there is none or if he is unable to sit, a person of its choice who shall sit in the capacity of judge.

3.   The Grand Chamber shall also include the President of the Court, the Vice-Presidents, the Presidents of the Chambers and other judges chosen in accordance with the rules of the Court. When a case is referred to the Grand Chamber under Article 43, no judge from the Chamber which rendered the judgment shall sit in the Grand Chamber, with the exception of the President of the Chamber and the judge who sat in respect of the State Party concerned.

Article 28   Declarations of inadmissibility by committees
A committee may, by a unanimous vote, declare inadmissible or strike out of its list of cases an individual application submitted under Article 34 where such a decision can be taken without further examination. The decision shall be final.

Article 29   Decisions by Chambers on admissibility and merits
1.   If no decision is taken under Article 28, a Chamber shall decide on the admissibility and merits of individual applications submitted under Article 34.

2.   A Chamber shall decide on the admissibility and merits of inter-State applications submitted under Article 33.

3.   The decision on admissibility shall be taken separately unless the court, in exceptional cases, decides otherwise.

Article 30 Relinquishment of jurisdiction to the Grand Chamber

Where a case pending before a Chamber raises a serious question affecting the interpretation of the Convention or the protocols thereto, or where the resolution of a question before the Chamber might have a result inconsistent with a judgment previously delivered by the Court, the Chamber may, at any time before it has rendered its judgment, relinquish jurisdiction in favour of the Grand Chamber, unless one of the parties to the case objects.

Article 31 Powers of the Grand Chamber

The Grand Chamber shall:

(a) determine applications submitted either under Article 33 or Article 34 when a Chamber has relinquished jurisdiction under Article 30 or when the case has been referred to it under Article 43; and

(b) consider requests for advisory opinions submitted under Article 47.

Article 32 Jurisdiction of the Court

1. The jurisdiction of the Court shall extend to all matters concerning the interpretation and application of the Convention and the protocols thereto which are referred to it as provided in Articles 33, 34 and 47.

2. In the event of dispute as to whether the Court has jurisdiction, the Court shall decide.

Article 33 Inter-state cases

Any High Contracting Party may refer to the Court any alleged breach of the provisions of the Convention and the protocols thereto by another High Contracting Party.

Article 34 Individual applications

The Court may receive applications from any person, non-governmental organisation or group of individuals claiming to be the victim of a violation by one of the High Contracting Parties of the rights set forth in the Convention or the protocols thereto. The High Contracting Parties undertake not to hinder in any way the effective exercise of this right.

Article 35 Admissibility criteria

1. The Court may only deal with the matter after all domestic remedies have been exhausted, according to the generally recognised rules of international law, and within a period of six months from the date on which the final decision was taken.

2. The Court shall not deal with any individual application submitted under Article 34 that:

(a) is anonymous; or

(b) is substantially the same as a matter that has already been examined by the Court or has already been submitted to another procedure of international investigation or settlement and contains no relevant new information.

3. The Court shall declare inadmissible any individual application submitted under Article 34 which it considers incompatible with the provisions of the Convention or the protocols thereto, manifestly ill-founded, or an abuse of the right of application.

4. The Court shall reject any application which it considers inadmissible under this Article. It may do so at any stage of the proceedings.

Article 36 Third-party intervention

1. In all cases before a Chamber or the Grand Chamber, a High Contracting Party one of whose nationals is an applicant shall have the right to submit written comments and to take part in hearings.

2. The President of the Court may, in the interest of the proper administration of justice, invite any High Contracting Party which is not a party to the proceedings or any person concerned who is not the applicant to submit written comments or take part in hearings.

Article 37   Striking out applications

1.   The Court may at any stage of the proceedings decide to strike an application out of its list of cases where the circumstances lead to the conclusion that:
   (a) the applicant does not intend to pursue his application; or
   (b) the matter has been resolved; or
   (c) for any other reason established by the Court, it is no longer justified to continue the examination of the application.

However, the Court shall continue the examination of the application if respect for human rights as defined in the Convention and the protocols thereto so requires.

2.   The Court may decide to restore an application to its list of cases if it considers that the circumstances justify such a course.

Article 38   Examination of the case and friendly settlement proceedings

1.   If the Court declares the application admissible, it shall:
   (a) pursue the examination of the case, together with the representatives of the parties, and if need be, undertake an investigation, for the effective conduct of which the States concerned shall furnish all necessary facilities;
   (b) place itself at the disposal of the parties concerned with a view to securing a friendly settlement of the matter on the basis of respect of human rights as defined in the Convention and the protocols thereto.

2.   Proceedings conducted under paragraph 1(b) shall be confidential.

Article 39   Finding of a friendly settlement

If a friendly settlement is effected, the Court shall strike the case out of its list by means of a decision which shall be confined to a brief statement of the facts and of the solution reached.

Article 40   Public hearings and access to documents

1.   Hearings shall be public unless the Court in exceptional circumstances decides otherwise.

2.   Documents deposited with the Registrar shall be accessible to the public unless the President of the Court decides otherwise.

Article 41   Just satisfaction

If the Court finds that there has been a violation of the Convention or the protocols thereto, and if the internal law of the High Contracting Party concerned allows only partial reparation to be made, the Court shall, if necessary, afford just satisfaction to the injured party.

Article 42   Judgments of Chambers

Judgments of Chambers shall become final in accordance with the provisions of Article 44, paragraph 2.

Article 43   Referral to the Grand Chamber

1.   Within a period of three months from the date of the judgment of the Chamber, any party to the case may, in exceptional cases, request that the case be referred to the Grand Chamber.

2.   A panel of five judges of the Grand Chamber shall accept the request if the case raises a serious question affecting the interpretation or application of the Convention or the protocols thereto, or a serious issue of general importance.

3.   If the panel accepts the request, the Grand Chamber shall decide the case by means of a judgment.

Article 44   Final judgments

1.   The judgment of the Grand Chamber shall be final.
2.   The judgment of a Chamber shall become final:
   (a) when the parties declare that they will not request that the case be referred to the Grand Chamber; or

(b) three months after the date of the judgment, if reference of the case to the Grand Chamber has not been requested; or

(c) when the panel of the Grand Chamber rejects the request to refer under Article 43.

3. The final judgment shall be published.

Article 45 Reasons for judgments and decisions

1. Reasons shall be given for judgments as well as for decisions declaring applications admissible or inadmissible.

2. If a judgment does not represent, in whole or in part, the unanimous opinion of the judges, any judge shall be entitled to deliver a separate opinion.

Article 46 Binding force and execution of judgments

1. The High Contracting Parties undertake to abide by the final judgment of the Court in any case to which they are parties.

2. The final judgment of the Court shall be transmitted to the Committee of Ministers, which shall supervise its execution.

Article 47 Advisory opinions

1. The Court may, at the request of the Committee of Ministers, give advisory opinions on legal questions concerning the interpretation of the Convention and the protocols thereto.

2. Such opinions shall not deal with any question relating to the content or scope of the rights or freedoms defined in Section I of the Convention and the protocols thereto, or with any other question which the Court or the Committee of Ministers might have to consider in consequence of any such proceedings as could be instituted in accordance with the Convention.

3. Decisions of the Committee of Ministers to request an advisory opinion of the Court shall require a majority vote of the representatives entitled to sit on the Committee.

Article 48 Advisory jurisdiction of the Court

The Court shall decide whether a request for an advisory opinion submitted by the Committee of Ministers is within its competence as defined in Article 47.

Article 49 Reasons for advisory opinions

1. Reasons shall be given for advisory opinions of the Court.

2. If the advisory opinion does not represent, in whole or in part, the unanimous opinion of the judges, any judge shall be entitled to deliver a separate opinion.

3. Advisory opinions of the Court shall be communicated to the Committee of Ministers.

Article 50 Expenditure on the Court

The expenditure on the Court shall be borne by the Council of Europe.

Article 51 Privileges and immunities of judges

The judges shall be entitled, during the exercise of their functions, to the privileges and immunities provided for in Article 40 of the Statute of the Council of Europe and in the agreements made thereunder.

SECTION III   MISCELLANEOUS PROVISIONS

Article 52
*****

Article 53 Safeguard for existing human rights

Nothing in this Convention shall be construed as limiting or derogating from any of the human rights and fundamental freedoms which may be ensured under the laws of any High Contracting Party or under any other agreement to which it is a Party.

Articles 54–56
*****

Article 57   Reservations

1.   Any State may, when signing this Convention or when depositing its instrument of ratification, make a reservation in respect of any particular provision of the Convention to the extent that any law then in force in its territory is not in conformity with the provision. Reservations of a general character shall not be permitted under this article.

2.   Any reservation made under this article shall contain a brief statement of the law concerned.
*****

PROTOCOLS

Enforcement of certain Rights and Freedoms not included in Section I of the Convention

The Governments signatory hereto, being Members of the Council of Europe,

Being resolved to take steps to ensure the collective enforcement of certain rights and freedoms other than those already included in Section I of the Convention for the Protection of Human Rights and Fundamental Freedoms signed at Rome on 4th November 1950 (hereinafter referred to as 'the Convention'),

Have agreed as follows:

Article 1   Protection of property

Every natural or legal person is entitled to the peaceful enjoyment of his possessions. No one shall be deprived of his possessions except in the public interest and subject to the conditions provided for by law and by the general principles of international law.

The preceding provisions shall not, however, in any way impair the right of a State to enforce such laws as it deems necessary to control the use of property in accordance with the general interest or to secure the payment of taxes or other contributions or penalties.

Article 2   Right to education

No person shall be denied the right to education. In the exercise of any functions which it assumes in relation to education and to teaching, the State shall respect the right of parents to ensure such education and teaching in conformity with their own religious and philosophical convictions.

Article 3   Right to free elections

The High Contracting Parties undertake to hold free elections at reasonable intervals by secret ballot, under conditions which will ensure the free expression of the opinion of the people in the choice of the legislature.

*****

4.   Protecting certain Additional Rights

The Governments signatory hereto, being Members of the Council of Europe.

Being resolved to take steps to ensure the collective enforcement of certain rights and freedoms other than those already included in Section I of the Convention for the Protection of Human Rights and Fundamental Freedoms signed at Rome on 4 November 1950 (hereinafter referred to as 'the Convention') and in Articles 1 to 3 of the First Protocol to the Convention, signed at Paris on 20 March 1952,

Have agreed as follows:

Article 1   Prohibition of imprisonment for debt

No one shall be deprived of his liberty merely on the ground of inability to fulfil a contractual obligation.

Article 2   Freedom of movement

1.   Everyone lawfully within the territory of a State shall, within that territory, have the right to liberty of movement and freedom to choose his residence.

2.   Everyone shall be free to leave any country, including his own.

3.   No restrictions shall be placed on the exercise of these rights other than such as are in accordance with law and are necessary in a democratic society in the interests of national security or public safety, for the maintenance of 'order public', for the prevention of crime, for the protection of the rights and freedoms of others.

4.   The rights set forth in paragraph 1 may also be subject, in particular areas, to restrictions imposed in accordance with law and justified by the public interest in a democratic society.

Article 3   Prohibition of expulsion of nationals

1.   No one shall be expelled, by means either of an individual or of a collective measure, from the territory of the State of which he is a national.

2.   No one shall be deprived of the right to enter the territory of the State of which he is a national.

Article 4   Prohibition of collective expulsion of aliens

Collective expulsion of aliens is prohibited.
*****

Note: This Protocol has not yet been ratified by the United Kingdom.

6.   Concerning the Abolition of the Death Penalty

The member States of the Council of Europe, signatory to this Protocol to the Convention for the Protection of Human Rights and Fundamental Freedoms, signed at Rome on 4 November 1950 (hereinafter referred to as 'the Convention').

Considering that the evolution that has occurred in several member States of the Council of Europe expresses a general tendency in favour of abolition of the death penalty.

Have agreed as follows:

Article 1   Abolition of the death penalty

The death penalty shall be abolished. No one shall be condemned to such penalty or executed.

Article 2   Death penalty in time of war

A state may make provision in its law for the death penalty in respect of acts committed in time of war or of imminent threat of war; such penalty shall be applied only in the instance laid down in the law and in accordance with its provisions. The State shall communicate to the Secretary General of the Council of Europe the relevant provisions of that law.

Article 3   Prohibition of derogations

No derogation from the provision of this Protocol shall be made under Article 15 of the Convention.

Article 4   Prohibition of reservations

No reservation may be made under Article 57 of the Convention in respect of the provisions of this Protocol.

Note: Protocol 7 is not included as it is not yet in force and has not been ratified by the UK.

International Convention on the Elimination of All Forms of Racial Discrimination (December 1965)

The States Parties to this Convention,

Considering that the Charter of the United Nations is based on the principles of the dignity and equality inherent in all human beings, and that all Member States have pledged themselves to take joint and separate action, in co-operation with the Organization, for the achievement of one of the purposes of the United Nations which is to promote and encourage universal respect for and observance of human rights and fundamental freedoms for all, without distinction as to race, sex, language or religion,

Considering that the Universal Declaration of Human Rights proclaims that all human beings are born free and equal in dignity and rights and that everyone is entitled to all the rights and freedoms set out therein, without distinction of any kind, in particular as to race, colour or national origin,

Considering that all human beings are equal before the law and are entitled to equal protection of the law against any discrimination and against any incitement to discrimination,

*****

Convinced that any doctrine of superiority based on racial differentiation is scientifically false, morally condemnable, socially unjust and dangerous, and that there is no justification for racial discrimination, in theory or in practice, anywhere,

Reaffirming that discrimination between human beings on the grounds of race, colour or ethnic origin is an obstacle to friendly and peaceful relations among nations and is capable of disturbing peace and security among peoples and the harmony of persons living side by side even within one and the same State,

Convinced that the existence of racial barriers is repugnant to the ideals of any human society,

*****

Desiring to implement the principles embodied in the United Nations Declaration on the Elimination of All Forms of Racial Discrimination and to secure the earliest adoption of practical measures to that end,

Have agreed as follows:

PART I

Article 1

1. In this Convention, the term "racial discrimination" shall mean any distinction, exclusion, restriction or preference based on race, colour, descent, or national or ethnic origin which has the purpose or effect of nullifying or impairing the recognition, enjoyment or exercise, on an equal footing, of human rights and fundamental freedoms in the political, economic, social, cultural or any other field of public life.

2. This Convention shall not apply to distinctions, exclusions, restrictions or preferences made by a State Party to this Convention between citizens and non-citizens.

3. Nothing in this Convention may be interpreted as affecting in any way the legal provisions of States Parties concerning nationality, citizenship or naturalization, provided that such provisions do not discriminate against any particular nationality.

4. Special measures taken for the sole purpose of securing adequate advancement of certain racial or ethnic groups or individuals requiring such protection as may be necessary in order to ensure such groups or individuals equal enjoyment or exercise of human rights and fundamental freedoms shall not be deemed racial discrimination, provided, however,

that such measures do not, as a consequence, lead to the maintenance of separate rights for different racial groups and that they shall not be continued after the objectives for which they were taken have been achieved.

Article 2

1.   States Parties condemn racial discrimination and undertake to pursue by all appropriate means and without delay a policy of eliminating racial discrimination in all its forms and promoting understanding among all races, and, to this end:

(a) Each State Party undertakes to engage in no act or practice of racial discrimination against persons, groups of persons or institutions and to ensure that all public authorities and public institutions, national and local, shall act in conformity with this obligation;

(b) Each State Party undertakes not to sponsor, defend or support racial discrimination by any persons or organizations;

(c) Each State Party shall take effective measures to review governmental, national and local policies, and to amend, rescind or nullify any laws and regulations which have the effect of creating or perpetuating racial discrimination wherever it exists;

(d) Each State Party shall prohibit and bring to an end, by all appropriate means, including legislation as required by circumstances, racial discrimination by any persons, group or organization;

(e) Each State Party undertakes to encourage, where appropriate, integrationist multiracial organizations and movements and other means of eliminating barriers between races, and to discourage anything which tends to strengthen racial division.

2.   States Parties shall, when the circumstances so warrant, take, in the social, economic, cultural and other fields, special and concrete measures to ensure the adequate development and protection of certain racial groups or individuals belonging to them, for the purpose of guaranteeing them the full and equal enjoyment of human rights and fundamental freedoms. These measures shall in no case entail as a consequence the maintenance of unequal or separate rights for different racial groups after the objectives for which they were taken have been achieved.

Article 3

States Parties particularly condemn racial segregation and apartheid and undertake to prevent, prohibit and eradicate all practices of this nature in territories under their jurisdiction.

Article 4

States Parties condemn all propaganda and all organizations which are based on ideas or theories of superiority of one race or group of persons of one colour or ethnic origin, or which attempt to justify or promote racial hatred and discrimination in any form, and undertake to adopt immediate and positive measures designed to eradicate all incitement to, or acts of, such discrimination and, to this end, with due regard to the principles embodied in the Universal Declaration of Human Rights and the rights expressly set forth in article 5 of this Convention, inter alia:

(a) Shall declare an offence punishable by law all dissemination of ideas based on racial superiority or hatred, incitement to racial discrimination, as well as all acts of violence or incitement to such acts against any race or group of persons of another colour or ethnic origin, and also the provision of any assistance to racist activities, including the financing thereof;

(b) Shall declare illegal and prohibit organizations, and also organized and all other propaganda activities, which promote and incite racial discrimination, and shall recognize participation in such organizations or activities as an offence punishable by law;

(c) Shall not permit public authorities or public institutions, national or local, to promote or incite racial discrimination.

Article 5

In compliance with the fundamental obligations laid down in article 2 of this Convention, States Parties undertake to prohibit and to eliminate racial discrimination in all its forms and to guarantee the right of everyone, without distinction as to race, colour, or national or ethnic origin, to equality before the law, notably in the enjoyment of the following rights:

(a) The right to equal treatment before the tribunals and all other organs administering justice;

(b) The right to security of person and protection by the State against violence or bodily harm, whether inflicted by government officials or by any individual group or institution;

(c) Political rights, in particular the right to participate in elections to vote and to stand for election on the basis of universal and equal suffrage, to take part in the Government as well as in the conduct of public affairs at any level and to have equal access to public service;

(d) Other civil rights, in particular:

  (i) The right to freedom of movement and residence within the border of the State;

  (ii) The right to leave any country, including one's own, and to return to one's country;

  (iii) The right to nationality;

  (iv) The right to marriage and choice of spouse;

  (v) The right to own property alone as well as in association with others;

  (vi) The right to inherit;

  (vii) The right to freedom of thought, conscience and religion;

  (viii) The right to freedom of opinion and expression;

  (ix) The right to freedom of peaceful assembly and association;

(e) Economic, social and cultural rights, in particular:

  (i) The rights to work, to free choice of employment, to just and favourable conditions of work, to protection against unemployment, to equal pay for equal work, to just and favourable remuneration;

  (ii) The right to form and join trade unions;

  (iii) The right to housing;

  (iv) The right to public health, medical care, social security and social services;

  (v) The right to education and training;

  (vi) The right to equal participation in cultural activities;

(f) The right of access to any place or service intended for use by the general public, such as transport, hotels, restaurants, cafes, theatres and parks.

Article 6

States Parties shall assure to everyone within their jurisdiction effective protection and remedies, through the competent national tribunals and other State institutions, against any acts of racial discrimination which violate his human rights and fundamental freedoms contrary to this Convention, as well as the right to seek from such tribunals just and adequate reparation or satisfaction for any damage suffered as a result of such discrimination.

Article 7

States Parties undertake to adopt immediate and effective measures, particularly in the fields of teaching, education, culture and information, with a view to combating prejudices which lead to racial discrimination and to promoting understanding, tolerance and friendship among nations and racial or ethnical groups, as well as to propagating the purposes and principles of the Charter of the United Nations, the Universal Declaration of Human Rights, the United Nations Declaration on the Elimination of All Forms of Racial Discrimination, and this Convention.

Articles 8–25   ***

International Covenant on Civil and Political Rights (December 1966)

Preamble

The States Parties to the present Covenant,

Considering that, in accordance with the principles proclaimed in the Charter of the United Nations, recognition of the inherent dignity and of the equal and inalienable rights of all members of the human family is the foundation of freedom, justice and peace in the world,

Recognizing that these rights derive from the inherent dignity of the human person,

Recognizing that, in accordance with the Universal Declaration of Human Rights, the ideal of free human beings enjoying civil and political freedom and freedom from fear and want can only be achieved if conditions are created whereby everyone may enjoy his civil and political rights, as well as his economic, social and cultural rights,

Considering the obligation of States under the Charter of the United Nations to promote universal respect for, and observance of, human rights and freedoms,

Realizing that the individual, having duties to other individuals and to the community to which he belongs, is under a responsibility to strive for the promotion and observance of the rights recognized in the present Covenant,

Agree upon the following articles:

PART I

Article 1

1. All peoples have the right of self-determination. By virtue of that right they freely determine their political status and freely pursue their economic, social and cultural development.

PART II

Article 2

1. Each State Party to the present Covenant undertakes to respect and to ensure to all individuals within its territory and subject to its jurisdiction the rights recognized in the present Covenant, without distinction of any kind, such as race, colour, sex, language, religion, political or other opinion, national or social origin, property, birth or other status.

2. Where not already provided for by existing legislative or other measures, each State Party to the present Covenant undertakes to take the necessary steps, in accordance with its constitutional processes and with the provisions of the present Covenant, to adopt such laws or other measures as may be necessary to give effect to the rights recognized in the present Covenant.

3. Each State Party to the present Covenant undertakes:

(a) To ensure that any person whose rights or freedoms as herein recognized are violated shall have an effective remedy,

notwithstanding that the violation has been committed by persons acting in an official capacity;

(b) To ensure that any person claiming such a remedy shall have his right thereto determined by competent judicial, administrative or legislative authorities, or by any other competent authority provided for by the legal system of the State, and to develop the possibilities of judicial remedy;

(c) To ensure that the competent authorities shall enforce such remedies when granted.

Article 3

The States Parties to the present Covenant undertake to ensure the equal right of men and women to the enjoyment of all civil and political rights set forth in the present Covenant.

Article 4

1. In time of public emergency which threatens the life of the nation and the existence of which is officially proclaimed, the States Parties to the present Covenant may take measures derogating from their obligations under the present Covenant to the extent strictly required by the exigencies of the situation, provided that such measures are not inconsistent with their other obligations under international law and do not involve discrimination solely on the ground of race, colour, sex, language, religion or social origin.

2. No derogation from articles 6, 7, 8 (paragraphs 1 and 2), 11, 15, 16 and 18 may be made under this provision.

3. Any State Party to the present Covenant availing itself of the right of derogation shall immediately inform the other States Parties to the present Covenant, through the intermediary of the Secretary-General of the United Nations, of the provisions from which it has derogated and of the reasons by which it was actuated. A further communication shall be made, through the same intermediary, on the date on which it terminates such derogation.

Article 5

1. Nothing in the present Covenant may be interpreted as implying for any State, group or person any right to engage in any activity or perform any act aimed at the destruction of any of the rights and freedoms recognized herein or at their limitation to a greater extent than is provided for in the present Covenant.

2. There shall be no restriction upon or derogation from any of the fundamental human rights recognized or existing in any State Party to the present Covenant pursuant to law, conventions, regulations or custom on the pretext that the present Covenant does not recognize such rights or that it recognizes them to a lesser extent.

PART III

Article 6

1. Every human being has the inherent right to life. This right shall be protected by law. No one shall be arbitrarily deprived of his life.

2. In countries which have not abolished the death penalty, sentence of death may be imposed only for the most serious crimes in accordance with the law in force at the time of the commission of the crime and not contrary to the provisions of the present Covenant and to the Convention on the Prevention and Punishment of the Crime of Genocide. This penalty can only be carried out pursuant to a final judgement rendered by a competent court.

3. When deprivation of life constitutes the crime of genocide, it is understood that nothing in this article shall authorize any State Party to the present Covenant to derogate in any way from any obligation assumed under the provisions of the Convention on the Prevention and Punishment of the Crime of Genocide.

4. Anyone sentenced to death shall have the right to seek pardon or commutation of the sentence. Amnesty, pardon or commutation of the sentence of death may be granted in all cases.

5.   Sentence of death shall not be imposed for crimes committed by persons below eighteen years of age and shall not be carried out on pregnant women.

6.   Nothing in this article shall be invoked to delay or to prevent the abolition of capital punishment by any State Party to the present Covenant.

Article 7

No one shall be subjected to torture or to cruel, inhuman or degrading treatment or punishment. In particular, no one shall be subjected without his free consent to medical or scientific experimentation.

Article 8

1.   No one shall be held in slavery; slavery and the slave-trade in all their forms shall be prohibited.

2.   No one shall be held in servitude.

3.   (a) No one shall be required to perform forced or compulsory labour;

(b) Paragraph 3 (a) shall not be held to preclude, in countries where imprisonment with hard labour may be imposed as a punishment for a crime, the performance of hard labour in pursuance of a sentence to such punishment by a competent court;

(c) For the purpose of this paragraph the term "forced or compulsory labour" shall not include:

(i)   Any work or service, not referred to in subparagraph (b), normally required of a person who is under detention in consequence of a lawful order of a court, or of a person during conditional release from such detention;

(ii) Any service of a military character and, in countries where conscientious objection is recognized, any national service required by law of conscientious objectors;

(iii) Any service exacted in cases of emergency or calamity threatening the life or well-being of the community;

(iv) Any work or service which forms part of normal civil obligations.

Article 9

1.   Everyone has the right to liberty and security of person. No one shall be subjected to arbitrary arrest or detention. No one shall be deprived of his liberty except on such grounds and in accordance with such procedure as are established by law.

2.   Anyone who is arrested shall be informed, at the time of arrest, of the reasons for his arrest and shall be promptly informed of any charges against him.

3.   Anyone arrested or detained on a criminal charge shall be brought promptly before a judge or other officer authorized by law to exercise judicial power and shall be entitled to trial within a reasonable time or to release. It shall not be the general rule that persons awaiting trial shall be detained in custody, but release may be subject to guarantees to appear for trial, at any other stage of the judicial proceedings, and, should occasion arise, for execution of the judgement.

4.   Anyone who is deprived of his liberty by arrest or detention shall be entitled to take proceedings before a court, in order that court may decide without delay on the lawfulness of his detention and order his release if the detention is not lawful.

5.   Anyone who has been the victim of unlawful arrest or detention shall have an enforceable right to compensation.

Article 10

1.   All persons deprived of their liberty shall be treated with humanity and with respect for the inherent dignity of the human person.

2. (a) Accused persons shall, save in exceptional circumstances, be segregated from convicted persons and shall be subject to separate treatment appropriate to their
status as unconvicted persons;

(b) Accused juvenile persons shall be separated from adults and brought as speedily as
possible for adjudication.

3. The penitentiary system shall comprise treatment of prisoners the essential aim
of which shall be their reformation and social rehabilitation. Juvenile offenders shall be
segregated from adults and be accorded treatment appropriate to their age and legal status.

Article 11

No one shall be imprisoned merely on the ground of inability to fulfil a contractual
obligation.

Article 12

1. Everyone lawfully within the territory of a State shall, within that territory, have the
right to liberty of movement and freedom to choose his residence.

2. Everyone shall be free to leave any country, including his own.

3. The above-mentioned rights shall not be subject to any restrictions except those
which are provided by law, are necessary to protect national security, public order (ordre
public), public health or morals or the rights and freedoms of others, and are consistent with
the other rights recognized in the present Covenant.

4. No one shall be arbitrarily deprived of the right to enter his own country.

Article 13

An alien lawfully in the territory of a State Party to the present Covenant may be expelled
therefrom only in pursuance of a decision reached in accordance with law and shall, except
where compelling reasons of national security otherwise require, be allowed to submit the
reasons against his expulsion and to have his case reviewed by, and be represented for
the purpose before, the competent authority or a person or persons especially designated by
the competent authority.

Article 14

1. All persons shall be equal before the courts and tribunals. In the determination of any
criminal charge against him, or of his rights and obligations in a suit at law, everyone shall be
entitled to a fair and public hearing by a competent, independent and impartial tribunal
established by law. The press and the public may be excluded from all or part of a trial for
reasons of morals, public order (ordre public) or national security in a democratic society,
or when the interest of the private lives of the parties so requires, or to the extent strictly
necessary in the opinion of the court in special circumstances where publicity would
prejudice the interests of justice; but any judgement rendered in a criminal case or in a suit at
law shall be made public except where the interest of juvenile persons otherwise requires or
the proceedings concern matrimonial disputes or the guardianship of children.

2. Everyone charged with a criminal offence shall have the right to be presumed
innocent until proved guilty according to law.

3. In the determination of any criminal charge against him, everyone shall be entitled to
the following minimum guarantees, in full equality:

(a) To be informed promptly and in detail in a language which he understands of the
nature and cause of the charge against him;

(b) To have adequate time and facilities for the preparation of his defence and to
communicate with counsel of his own choosing;

(c) To be tried without undue delay;

(d) To be tried in his presence, and to defend himself in person or through legal
assistance of his own choosing; to be informed, if he does not have legal assistance, of this right; and to have legal assistance assigned to him, in any case where

the interests of justice so require, and without payment by him in any such case if he does not have sufficient means to pay for it;

(e) To examine, or have examined, the witnesses against him and to obtain the attendance and examination of witnesses on his behalf under the same conditions as witnesses against him;

(f) To have the free assistance of an interpreter if he cannot understand or speak the language used in court;

(g) Not to be compelled to testify against himself or to confess guilt.

4.   In the case of juvenile persons, the procedure shall be such as will take account of their age and the desirability of promoting their rehabilitation.

5.   Everyone convicted of a crime shall have the right to his conviction and sentence being reviewed by a higher tribunal according to law.

6.   When a person has by a final decision been convicted of a criminal offence and when subsequently his conviction has been reversed or he has been pardoned on the ground that a new or newly discovered fact shows conclusively that there has been a miscarriage of justice, the person who has suffered punishment as a result of such conviction shall be compensated according to law, unless it is proved that the non-disclosure of the unknown fact in time is wholly or partly attributable to him.

7.   No one shall be liable to be tried or punished again for an offence for which he has already been finally convicted or acquitted in accordance with the law and penal procedure of each country.

Article 15

1.   No one shall be held guilty of any criminal offence on account of any act or omission which did not constitute a criminal offence, under national or international law, at the time when it was committed. Nor shall a heavier penalty be imposed than the one that was applicable at the time when the criminal offence was committed. If, subsequent to the commission of the offence, provision is made by law for the imposition of the lighter penalty, the offender shall benefit thereby.

2.   Nothing in this article shall prejudice the trial and punishment of any person for any act or omission which, at the time when it was committed, was criminal according to the general principles of law recognized by the community of nations.

Article 16

Everyone shall have the right to recognition everywhere as a person before the law.

Article 17

1.   No one shall be subjected to arbitrary or unlawful interference with his privacy, family, home or correspondence, nor to unlawful attacks on his honour and reputation.

2.   Everyone has the right to the protection of the law against such interference or attacks.

Article 18

1.   Everyone shall have the right to freedom of thought, conscience and religion. This right shall include freedom to have or to adopt a religion or belief of his choice, and freedom, either individually or in community with others and in public or private, to manifest his religion or belief in worship, observance, practice and teaching.

2.   No one shall be subject to coercion which would impair his freedom to have or to adopt a religion or belief of his choice.

3.   Freedom to manifest one's religion or beliefs may be subject only to such limitations as are prescribed by law and are necessary to protect public safety, order, health, or morals or the fundamental rights and freedoms of others.

4.   The States Parties to the present Covenant undertake to have respect for the liberty

of parents and, when applicable, legal guardians to ensure the religious and moral education of their children in conformity with their own convictions.

Article 19

1.   Everyone shall have the right to hold opinions without interference.

2.   Everyone shall have the right to freedom of expression; this right shall include freedom to seek, receive and impart information and ideas of all kinds, regardless of frontiers, either orally, in writing or in print, in the form of art, or through any other media of his choice.

3.   The exercise of the rights provided for in paragraph 2 of this article carries with it special duties and responsibilities. It may therefore be subject to certain restrictions, but these shall only be such as are provided by law and are necessary:
   (a)   For respect of the rights or reputations of others;
   (b)   For the protection of national security or of public order (ordre public), or of public health or morals.

Article 20

1.   Any propaganda for war shall be prohibited by law.

2.   Any advocacy of national, racial or religious hatred that constitutes incitement to discrimination, hostility or violence shall be prohibited by law.

Article 21

The right of peaceful assembly shall be recognized. No restrictions may be placed on the exercise of this right other than those imposed in conformity with the law and which are necessary in a democratic society in the interests of national security or public safety, public order (ordre public), the protection of public health or morals or the protection of the rights and freedoms of others.

Article 22

1.   Everyone shall have the right to freedom of association with others, including the right to form and join trade unions for the protection of his interests.

2.   No restrictions may be placed on the exercise of this right other than those which are prescribed by law and which are necessary in a democratic society in the interests of national security or public safety, public order (ordre public), the protection of public health or morals or the protection of the rights and freedoms of others. This article shall not prevent the imposition of lawful restrictions on members of the armed forces and of the police in their exercise of this right.

3.   Nothing in this article shall authorize States Parties to the International Labour Organisation Convention of 1948 concerning Freedom of Association and Protection of the Right to Organize to take legislative measures which would prejudice, or to apply the law in such a manner as to prejudice, the guarantees provided for in that Convention.

Article 23

1.   The family is the natural and fundamental group unit of society and is entitled to protection by society and the State.

2.   The right of men and women of marriageable age to marry and to found a family shall be recognized.

3.   No marriage shall be entered into without the free and full consent of the intending spouses.

4.   States Parties to the present Covenant shall take appropriate steps to ensure equality of rights and responsibilities of spouses as to marriage, during marriage and at its dissolution. In the case of dissolution, provision shall be made for the necessary protection of any children.

Article 24

1. Every child shall have, without any discrimination as to race, colour, sex, language, religion, national or social origin, property or birth, the right to such measures of protection as are required by his status as a minor, on the part of his family, society and the State.
2. Every child shall be registered immediately after birth and shall have a name.
3. Every child has the right to acquire a nationality.

Article 25

Every citizen shall have the right and the opportunity, without any of the distinctions mentioned in article 2 and without unreasonable restrictions:

(a) To take part in the conduct of public affairs, directly or through freely chosen representatives;

(b) To vote and to be elected at genuine periodic elections which shall be by universal and equal suffrage and shall be held by secret ballot, guaranteeing the free expression of the will of the electors;

(c) To have access, on general terms of equality, to public service in his country.

Article 26

All persons are equal before the law and are entitled without any discrimination the equal protection of the law. In this respect, the law shall prohibit any discrimination and guarantee to all persons equal and effective protection against discrimination on any ground such as race, colour, sex, language, religion, political or other opinion, national or social origin, property, birth or other status.

Article 27

In those States in which ethnic, religious or linguistic minorities exist, persons belonging to such minorities shall not be denied the right, in community with the other members of their group, to enjoy their own culture, to profess and practise their own religion, or to use their own language.

Articles 28–53***

Constitution of the Republic of South Africa 1996

(As adopted on 8 May 1996 and amended on 11 October 1996 by the Constitutional Assembly)

Preamble

We, the people of South Africa,

Recognise the injustices of our past;

Honour those who suffered for justice and freedom in our land;

Respect those who have worked to build and develop our country; and

Believe that South Africa belongs to all who live in it, united in our diversity.

We therefore, through our freely elected representatives, adopt this Constitution as the supreme law of the Republic so as to:

- Heal the divisions of the past and establish a society based on democratic values, social justice and fundamental human rights;
- Lay the foundations for a democratic and open society in which government is based on the will of the people and every citizen is equally protected by law;
- Improve the quality of life of all citizens and free the potential of each person; and
- Build a united and democratic South Africa able to take its rightful place as a sovereign state in the family of nations.

May God protect our people.

Nkosi Sikelel' iAfrika. Morena boloka setjhaba sa heso.

God seën Suid-Afrika. God bless South Africa.

Mudzimu fhatutshedza Afurika. Hosi katekisa Afrika.

CHAPTER 1   FOUNDING PROVISIONS

Republic of South Africa

1.   The Republic of South Africa is one, sovereign, democratic state founded on the following values:

- (a) Human dignity, the achievement of equality and the advancement of human rights and freedoms.
- (b) Non-racialism and non-sexism.
- (c) Supremacy of the constitution and the rule of law.
- (d) Universal adult suffrage, a national common voters roll, regular elections and a multi-party system of democratic government, to ensure accountability, responsiveness and openness.

Supremacy of Constitution

2.   This Constitution is the supreme law of the Republic; law or conduct inconsistent with it is invalid, and the obligations imposed by it must be fulfilled.

Citizenship

3.—(1)   There is a common South African citizenship.

(2) All citizens are:

- (a) equally entitled to the rights, privileges and benefits of citizenship; and
- (b) equally subject to the duties and responsibilities of citizenship.

(3) National legislation must provide for the acquisition, loss and restoration of citizenship.

4.–6.   *****

CHAPTER 2   BILL OF RIGHTS

Rights

7.—(1)   This Bill of Rights is a cornerstone of democracy in South Africa. It enshrines the rights of all people in our country and affirms the democratic values of human dignity, equality and freedom.

(2) The state must respect, protect, promote and fulfil the rights in the Bill of Rights.

(3) The rights in the Bill of Rights are subject to the limitations contained or referred to in section 36, or elsewhere in the Bill.

Application

8.—(1)   The Bill of Rights applies to all law, and binds the legislature, the executive, the judiciary and all organs of state.

(2) A provision of the Bill of Rights binds a natural or a juristic person if, and to the extent that, it is applicable, taking into account the nature of the right and the nature of any duty imposed by the right.

(3) When applying a provision of the Bill of Rights to a natural or juristic person in terms of subsection (2), a court:

- (a) in order to give effect to a right in the Bill, must apply, or if necessary develop, the common law to the extent that legislation does not give effect to that right; and
- (b) may develop rules of the common law to limit the right, provided that the limitation is in accordance with section 36(1).

(4) A juristic person is entitled to the rights in the Bill of Rights to the extent required by the nature of the rights and the nature of that juristic person.

Equality

9.—(1) Everyone is equal before the law and has the right to equal protection and benefit of the law.

(2) Equality includes the full and equal enjoyment of all rights and freedoms. To promote the achievement of equality, legislative and other measures designed to protect or advance persons, or categories of persons, disadvantaged by unfair discrimination may be taken.

(3) The state may not unfairly discriminate directly or indirectly against anyone on one or more grounds, including race, gender, sex, pregnancy, marital status, ethnic or social origin, colour, sexual orientation, age, disability, religion, conscience, belief, culture, language and birth.

(4) No person may unfairly discriminate directly or indirectly against anyone on one or more grounds in terms of subsection (3). National legislation must be enacted to prevent or prohibit unfair discrimination.

(5) Discrimination on one or more of the grounds listed in subsection (3) is unfair unless it is established that the discrimination is fair.

Human dignity

10. Everyone has inherent dignity and the right to have their dignity respected and protected.

Life

11. Everyone has the right to life.

Freedom and security of the person

12.—(1) Everyone has the right to freedom and security of the person, which includes the right:

(a) not to be deprived of freedom arbitrarily or without just cause;
(b) not to be detained without trial;
(c) to be free from all forms of violence from either public or private sources;
(d) not to be tortured in any way; and
(e) not to be treated or punished in a cruel, inhuman or degrading way.

(2) Everyone has the right to bodily and psychological integrity, which includes the right:

(a) to make decisions concerning reproduction;
(b) to security in and control over their body; and
(c) not to be subjected to medical or scientific experiments without their informed consent.

Slavery, servitude and forced labour

13. No one may be subjected to slavery, servitude or forced labour.

Privacy

14. Everyone has the right to privacy, which includes the right not to have:

(a) their person or home searched;
(b) their property searched;
(c) their possessions seized; or
(d) the privacy of their communications infringed.

Freedom of religion, belief and opinion

15.—(1) Everyone has the right to freedom of conscience, religion, thought, belief and opinion.

(2) Religious observances may be conducted at state or state-aided institutions, provided that:

(a) those observances follow rules made by the appropriate public authorities;
(b) they are conducted on an equitable basis; and
(c) attendance at them is free and voluntary.
(3) (a) This section does not prevent legislation recognising:
(b)
   (i) marriages concluded under any tradition, or a system of religious, personal or family law; or
   (ii) systems of personal and family law under any tradition, or adhered to by persons professing a particular religion.
(c) Recognition in terms of paragraph (a) must be consistent with this section and the other provisions of the Constitution.

Freedom of expression

16.—(1)   Everyone has the right to freedom of expression, which includes:
(a) freedom of the press and other media;
(b) freedom to receive or impart information or ideas;
(c) freedom of artistic creativity; and
(d) academic freedom and freedom of scientific research.
(2) The right in subsection (1) does not extend to:
(a) propaganda for war;
(b) incitement of imminent violence; or
(c) advocacy of hatred that is based on race, ethnicity, gender or religion, and that constitutes incitement to cause harm.

Assembly, demonstration, picket and petition

17.   Everyone has the right, peacefully and unarmed, to assemble, to demonstrate, to picket and to present petitions.

Freedom of association

18.   Everyone has the right to freedom of association.

Political rights

19.—(1)   Every citizen is free to make political choices, which includes the right:
(a) to form a political party;
(b) to participate in the activities of, or recruit members for, a political party; and
(c) to campaign for a political party or cause.
(2) Every citizen has the right to free, fair and regular elections for any legislative body established in terms of the Constitution.
(3) Every adult citizen has the right:
(a) to vote in elections for any legislative body established in terms of the Constitution, and to do so in secret; and
(b) to stand for public office and, if elected, to hold office.

Citizenship

20.—(1)   No citizen may be deprived of citizenship.

Freedom of movement and residence

21.—(1)   Everyone has the right to freedom of movement.
(2) Everyone has the right to leave the Republic.
(3) Every citizen has the right to enter, to remain in and to reside anywhere in, the Republic.
(4) Every citizen has the right to a passport.

Freedom of trade, occupation and profession

22.   Every citizen has the right to choose their trade, occupation or profession freely. The practice of a trade, occupation or profession may be regulated by law.

Labour relations

23.—(1) Everyone has the right to fair labour practices.

(2) Every worker has the right:
- (a) to form and join a trade union;
- (b) to participate in the activities and programmes of a trade union; and
- (c) to strike.

(3) Every employer has the right:
- (a) to form and join an employers' organisation; and
- (b) to participate in the activities and programmes of an employers' organisation.

(4) Every trade union and every employers' organisation has the right:
- (a) to determine its own administration, programmes and activities;
- (b) to organise; and
- (c) to form and join a federation.

(5) Every trade union, employers' organisation and employer has the right to engage in collective bargaining. National legislation may be enacted to regulate collective bargaining. To the extent that the legislation may limit a right in this Chapter, the limitation must comply with section 36(1).

(6) National legislation may recognise union security arrangements contained in collective agreements. To the extent that the legislation may limit a right in this Chapter, the limitation must comply with section 36(1).

Environment

24. Everyone has the right:
- (a) to an environment that is not harmful to their health or well-being; and
- (b) to have the environment protected, for the benefit of present and future generations, through reasonable legislative and other measures that:
- (c)
  - (i) prevent pollution and ecological degradation;
  - (ii) promote conservation; and
  - (iii) secure ecologically sustainable development and use of natural resources while promoting justifiable economic and social development.

Property

25.—(1) No one may be deprived of property except in terms of law of general application, and no law may permit arbitrary deprivation of property.

(2) Property may be expropriated only in terms of law of general application:
- (a) for a public purpose or in the public interest; and
- (b) subject to compensation, the amount of which and the time and manner of payment of which have either been agreed to by those affected or decided or approved by a court.

(3) The amount of the compensation and the time and manner of payment must be just and equitable, reflecting an equitable balance between the public interest and the interests of those affected, having regard to all relevant circumstances, including:
- (a) the current use of the property;
- (b) the history of the acquisition and use of the property;
- (c) the market value of the property;
- (d) the extent of direct state investment and subsidy in the acquisition and beneficial capital improvement of the property; and
- (e) the purpose of the expropriation.

(4) For the purposes of this section:
- (a) the public interest includes the nation's commitment to land reform, and to reforms to bring about equitable access to all South Africa's natural resources; and
- (b) property is not limited to land.

(5) The state must take reasonable legislative and other measures, within its available resources, to foster conditions which enable citizens to gain access to land on an equitable basis.

(6) A person or community whose tenure of land is legally insecure as a result of past racially discriminatory laws or practices is entitled, to the extent provided by an Act of Parliament, either to tenure which is legally secure or to comparable redress.

(7) A person or community dispossessed of property after 19 June 1913 as a result of past racially discriminatory laws or practices is entitled, to the extent provided by an Act of Parliament, either to restitution of that property or to equitable redress.

(8) No provision of this section may impede the state from taking legislative and other measures to achieve land, water and related reform, in order to redress the results of past racial discrimination, provided that any departure from the provisions of this section is in accordance with the provisions of section 36(1).

(9) Parliament must enact the legislation referred to in subsection (6).

Housing

26.—(1)   Everyone has the right to have access to adequate housing.

(2) The state must take reasonable legislative and other measures, within its available resources, to achieve the progressive realisation of this right.

(3) No one may be evicted from their home, or have their home demolished, without an order of court made after considering all the relevant circumstances. No legislation may permit arbitrary evictions.

Health care, food, water and social security

27.—(1)   Everyone has the right to have access to:
  (a) health care services, including reproductive health care;
  (b) sufficient food and water; and
  (c) social security, including, if they are unable to support themselves and their dependants, appropriate social assistance.

(2) The state must take reasonable legislative and other measures, within its available resources, to achieve the progressive realisation of each of these rights.

(3) No one may be refused emergency medical treatment.

28., 29.   *****

Language and culture

30.   Everyone has the right to use the language and to participate in the cultural life of their choice, but no one exercising these rights may do so in a manner inconsistent with any provision of the Bill of Rights.

Cultural, religious and linguistic communities

31.—(1)   Persons belonging to a cultural, religious or linguistic community may not be denied the right, with other members of that community:
  (a) to enjoy their culture, practise their religion and use their language; and
  (b) to form, join and maintain cultural, religious and linguistic associations and other organs of civil society.

(2) The rights in subsection (1) may not be exercised in a manner inconsistent with any provision of the Bill of Rights.

Access to information

32.—(1)   Everyone has the right of access to:
  (a) any information held by the state; and
  (b) any information that is held by another person and that is required for the exercise or protection of any rights.

(2) National legislation must be enacted to give effect to this right, and may provide for reasonable measures to alleviate the administrative and financial burden on the state.

Just administrative action

33.—(1) Everyone has the right to administrative action that is lawful, reasonable and procedurally fair.

(2) Everyone whose rights have been adversely affected by administrative action has the right to be given written reasons.

(3) National legislation must be enacted to give effect to these rights, and must:

    (a) provide for the review of administrative action by a court or, where appropriate, an independent and impartial tribunal;

    (b) impose a duty on the state to give effect to the rights in subsections (1) and (2); and

    (c) promote an efficient administration.

Access to courts

34. Everyone has the right to have any dispute that can be resolved by the application of law decided in a fair public hearing before a court or, where appropriate, another independent and impartial tribunal or forum.

Arrested, detained and accused persons

35.—(1) Everyone who is arrested for allegedly committing an offence has the right:

    (a) to remain silent;

    (b) to be informed promptly:

    (c)

        (i) of the right to remain silent; and

        (ii) of the consequences of not remaining silent;

    (d) not to be compelled to make any confession or admission that could be used in evidence against that person;

    (e) to be brought before a court as soon as reasonably possible, but not later than:

    (f)

        (i) 48 hours after the arrest; or

        (ii) the end of the first court day after the expiry of the 48 hours, if the 48 hours expire outside ordinary court hours or on a day which is not an ordinary court day;

    (g) at the first court appearance after being arrested, to be charged or to be informed of the reason for the detention to continue, or to be released; and

    (h) to be released from detention if the interests of justice permit, subject to reasonable conditions.

(2) Everyone who is detained, including every sentenced prisoner, has the right:

    (a) to be informed promptly of the reason for being detained;

    (b) to choose, and to consult with, a legal practitioner, and to be informed of this right promptly;

    (c) to have a legal practitioner assigned to the detained person by the state and at state expense, if substantial injustice would otherwise result, and to be informed of this right promptly;

    (d) to challenge the lawfulness of the detention in person before a court and, if the detention is unlawful, to be released;

    (e) to conditions of detention that are consistent with human dignity, including at least exercise and the provision, at state expense, of adequate accommodation, nutrition, reading material and medical treatment; and

    (f) to communicate with, and be visited by, that person's:

(g)
  (i)   spouse or partner;
  (ii) next of kin;
  (iii) chosen religious counsellor; and
  (iv) chosen medical practitioner.

(3) Every accused person has a right to a fair trial, which includes the right:
  (a) to be informed of the charge with sufficient detail to answer it;
  (b) to have adequate time and facilities to prepare a defence;
  (c) to a public trial before an ordinary court;
  (d) to have their trial begin and conclude without unreasonable delay;
  (e) to be present when being tried;
  (f) to choose, and be represented by, a legal practitioner, and to be informed of this right promptly;
  (g) to have a legal practitioner assigned to the accused person by the state and at state expense, if substantial injustice would otherwise result, and to be informed of this right promptly;
  (h) to be presumed innocent, to remain silent, and not to testify during the proceedings;
  (i) to adduce and challenge evidence;
  (j) not to be compelled to give self-incriminating evidence;
  (k) to be tried in a language that the accused person understands or, if that is not practicable, to have the proceedings interpreted in that language;
  (l) not to be convicted for an act or omission that was not an offence under either national or international law at the time it was committed or omitted;
  (m) not to be tried for an offence in respect of an act or omission for which that person has previously been either acquitted or convicted;
  (n) to the benefit of the least severe of the prescribed punishments if the prescribed punishment for the offence has been changed between the time that the offence was committed and the time of sentencing; and
  (o) of appeal to, or review by, a higher court.

(4) Whenever this section requires information to be given to a person, that information must be given in a language that the person understands.

(5) Evidence obtained in a manner that violates any right in the Bill of Rights must be excluded if the admission of that evidence would render the trial unfair or otherwise be detrimental to the administration of justice.

Limitation of rights

36.—(1) The rights in the Bill of Rights may be limited only in terms of law of general application to the extent that the limitation is reasonable and justifiable in an open and democratic society based on human dignity, equality and freedom, taking into account all relevant factors, including:
  (a) the nature of the right;
  (b) the importance of the purpose of the limitation;
  (c) the nature and extent of the limitation;
  (d) the relation between the limitation and its purpose; and
  (e) less restrictive means to achieve the purpose.

(2) Except as provided in subsection (1) or in any other provision of the Constitution, no law may limit any right entrenched in the Bill of Rights.

37. *****

Enforcement of rights

38. Anyone listed in this section has the right to approach a competent court, alleging that a right in the Bill of Rights has been infringed or threatened, and the court may grant

appropriate relief, including a declaration of rights. The persons who may approach a court are—

    (a) anyone acting in their own interest;

    (b) anyone acting on behalf of another person who cannot act in their own name;

    (c) anyone acting as a member of, or in the interest of, a group or class of persons;

    (d) anyone acting in the public interest; and

    (e) an association acting in the interest of its members.

Interpretation of Bill of Rights

39.—(1) When interpreting the Bill of Rights, a court, tribunal or forum:

    (a) must promote the values that underlie an open and democratic society based on human dignity, equality and freedom;

    (b) must consider international law; and

    (c) may consider foreign law.

(2) When interpreting any legislation, and when developing the common law or customary law, every court, tribunal or forum must promote the spirit, purport and objects of the Bill of Rights.

(3) The Bill of Rights does not deny the existence of any other rights or freedoms that are recognised or conferred by common law, customary law or legislation, to the extent that they are consistent with the Bill.

*****

CHAPTER 8   COURTS AND ADMINISTRATION OF JUSTICE

Judicial authority

165.—(1) The judicial authority of the Republic is vested in the courts.

(2) The courts are independent and subject only to the Constitution and the law, which they must apply impartially and without fear, favour or prejudice.

(3) No person or organ of state may interfere with the functioning of the courts.

(4) Organs of state, through legislative and other measures, must assist and protect the courts to ensure the independence, impartiality, dignity, accessibility and effectiveness of the courts.

(5) An order or decision issued by a court binds all persons to whom and organs of state to which it applies.

Judicial system

166. The courts are:

    (a) the Constitutional Court;

    (b) the Supreme Court of Appeal;

    (c) the High Courts, including any high court of appeal that may be established by an Act of Parliament to hear appeals from High Courts;

    (d) the Magistrates' Courts; and

    (e) any other court established or recognised in terms of an Act of Parliament, including any court of a status similar to either the High Courts or the Magistrates' Courts.

Constitutional Court

167.—(1) The Constitutional Court consists of a President, a Deputy President and nine other judges.

(2) A matter before the Constitutional Court must be heard by at least eight judges.

(3) The Constitutional Court:

    (a) is the highest court in all constitutional matters;

    (b) may decide only constitutional matters, and issues connected with decisions on constitutional matters; and

(c) makes the final decision whether a matter is a constitutional matter or whether an issue is connected with a decision on a constitutional matter.

(4) Only the Constitutional Court may:

(a) decide disputes between organs of state in the national or provincial sphere concerning the constitutional status, powers or functions of any of those organs of state;

(b) decide on the constitutionality of any parliamentary or provincial Bill, but may do so only in the circumstances anticipated in section 79 or 121;

(c) decide applications envisaged in section 80 or 122;

(d) decide on the constitutionality of any amendment to the Constitution;

(e) decide that Parliament or the President has failed to fulfil a constitutional obligation; or

(f) certify a provincial constitution in terms of section 144.

(5) The Constitutional Court makes the final decision whether an Act of Parliament, a provincial Act or conduct of the President is constitutional, and must confirm any order of invalidity made by the Supreme Court of Appeal, a High Court, or a court of similar status, before that order has any force.

(6) National legislation or the rules of the Constitutional Court must allow a person, when it is in the interests of justice and with leave of the Constitutional Court:

(a) to bring a matter directly to the Constitutional Court; or

(b) to appeal directly to the Constitutional Court from any other court.

(7) A constitutional matter includes any issue involving the interpretation, protection or enforcement of the Constitution.

168.–171. *****

Powers of courts in constitutional matters

172.—(1) When deciding a constitutional matter within its power, a court:

(a) must declare that any law or conduct that is inconsistent with the Constitution is invalid to the extent of its inconsistency; and

(b) may make any order that is just and equitable, including:

(c)

(i) an order limiting the retrospective effect of the declaration of invalidity; and

(ii) an order suspending the declaration of invalidity for any period and on any conditions, to allow the competent authority to correct the defect.

(2) (a) The Supreme Court of Appeal, a High Court or a court of similar status may make an order concerning the constitutional validity of an Act of Parliament, a provincial Act or any conduct of the President, but an order of constitutional invalidity has no force unless it is confirmed by the Constitutional Court.

(b) A court which makes an order of constitutional invalidity may grant a temporary interdict or other temporary relief to a party, or may adjourn the proceedings, pending a decision of the Constitutional Court on the validity of that Act or conduct.

(c) National legislation must provide for the referral of an order of constitutional invalidity to the Constitutional Court.

(d) Any person or organ of state with a sufficient interest may appeal, or apply, directly to the Constitutional Court to confirm or vary an order of constitutional invalidity by a court in terms of this subsection.

Inherent power

173. The Constitutional Court, Supreme Court of Appeal and High Courts have the inherent power to protect and regulate their own process, and to develop the common law, taking into account the interests of justice.

Appointment of judicial officers

174.—(1)   Any appropriately qualified woman or man who is a fit and proper person may be appointed as a judicial officer. Any person to be appointed to the Constitutional Court must also be a South African citizen.

(2) The need for the judiciary to reflect broadly the racial and gender composition of South Africa must be considered when judicial officers are appointed.

(3) The President as head of the national executive, after consulting the Judicial Service Commission and the leaders of parties represented in the National Assembly, appoints the President and Deputy President of the Constitutional Court and, after consulting the Judicial Service Commission, appoints the Chief Justice and Deputy Chief Justice.

(4) The other judges of the Constitutional Court are appointed by the President, as head of the national executive, after consulting the President of the Constitutional Court and the leaders of parties represented in the National Assembly, in accordance with the following procedure:

  (a) The Judicial Service Commission must prepare a list of nominees with three names more than the number of appointments to be made, and submit the list to the President.

  (b) The President may make appointments from the list, and must advise the Judicial Service Commission, with reasons, if any of the nominees are unacceptable and any appointment remains to be made.

  (c) The Judicial Service Commission must supplement the list with further nominees and the President must make the remaining appointments from the supplemented list.

(5) At all times, at least four members of the Constitutional Court must be persons who were judges at the time they were appointed to the Constitutional Court.

(6) The President must appoint the judges of all other courts on the advice of the Judicial Service Commission.

(7) Other judicial officers must be appointed in terms of an Act of Parliament which must ensure that the appointment, promotion, transfer or dismissal of, or disciplinary steps against, these judicial officers take place without favour or prejudice.

(8) Before judicial officers begin to perform their functions, they must take an oath or affirm, in accordance with Schedule 2, that they will uphold and protect the Constitution.

175   *****

Terms of office and remuneration

176.—(1)   A Constitutional Court judge is appointed for a non-renewable term of 12 years, but must retire at the age of 70.

(2) Other judges hold office until they are discharged from active service in terms of an Act of Parliament.

(3) The salaries, allowances and benefits of judges may not be reduced.

Removal

177.—(1)   A judge may be removed from office only if:

  (a) the Judicial Service Commission finds that the judge suffers from an incapacity, is grossly incompetent or is guilty of gross misconduct; and

  (b) the National Assembly calls for that judge to be removed, by a resolution adopted with a supporting vote of at least two thirds of its members.

(2) The President must remove a judge from office upon adoption of a resolution calling for that judge to be removed.

(3) The President, on the advice of the Judicial Service Commission, may suspend a judge who is the subject of a procedure in terms of subsection (1).

Judicial Service Commission

178.—(1)   There is a Judicial Service Commission consisting of:

   (a) the Chief Justice, who presides at meetings of the Commission;
   (b) the President of the Constitutional Court;
   (c) one Judge President designated by the Judges President;
   (d) the Cabinet member responsible for the administration of justice, or an alternate designated by that Cabinet member;
   (e) two practising advocates nominated from within the advocates' profession to represent the profession as a whole, and appointed by the President;
   (f) two practising attorneys nominated from within the attorneys' profession to represent the profession as a whole, and appointed by the President;
   (g) one teacher of law designated by teachers of law at South African universities;
   (h) six persons designated by the National Assembly from among its members, at least three of whom must be members of opposition parties represented in the Assembly;
   (i) four permanent delegates to the National Council of Provinces designated together by the Council with a supporting vote of at least six provinces;
   (j) four persons designated by the President as head of the national executive, after consulting the leaders of all the parties in the National Assembly; and
   (k) when considering matters specifically relating to a provincial or local division of the High Court, the Judge President of that division and the Premier, or an alternate designated by the Premier, of the province concerned.

(2) If the number of persons nominated from within the advocates' or attorneys' profession in terms of subsection (1)(e) or (f) equals the number of vacancies to be filled, the President must appoint them. If the number of persons nominated exceeds the number of vacancies to be filled, the President, after consulting the relevant profession, must appoint sufficient of the nominees to fill the vacancies, taking into account the need to ensure that those appointed represent the profession as a whole.

(3) Members of the Commission designated by the National Council of Provinces serve until they are replaced together, or until any vacancy occurs in their number. Other members who were designated or nominated to the Commission serve until they are replaced by those who designated or nominated them.

(4) The Judicial Service Commission has the powers and functions assigned to it in the Constitution and national legislation.

(5) The Judicial Service Commission may advise the national government on any matter relating to the judiciary or the administration of justice, but when it considers any matter except the appointment of a judge, it must sit without the members designated in terms of subsection (1)(h) and (i).

(6) The Judicial Service Commission may determine its own procedure, but decisions of the Commission must be supported by a majority of its members.

*****

Treaty Establishing the European Community (Treaty of Rome)

(25 March 1957)

Note: The Treaty is printed as amended (with effect from 1 February 2003) by the Nice Treaty and as further amended by the Act of Accession of the 10 additional member states; the full texts of the Consolidated Treaties are published in the Official Journal of the European

Communities OJ(C) 325, 24 December 2002. Articles amended or added by the Nice Treaty and the Act of Accession are printed in square brackets.

EC TREATY (NICE VERSION) PART ONE (PRINCIPLES)

Article 1
By this Treaty, the High Contracting Parties establish among themselves a EUROPEAN COMMUNITY.

Article 2
The Community shall have as its task, by establishing a common market and an economic and monetary union and by implementing the common policies or activities referred to in Articles 3 and 4, to promote throughout the Community a harmonious, balanced and sustainable development of economic activities, a high level of employment and of social protection, equality between men and women, sustainable and non-inflationary growth, a high degree of competitiveness and convergence of economic performance, a high level of protection and improvement of the quality of the environment, the raising of the standard of living and quality of life, and economic and social cohesion and solidarity among Member States.

Article 3
1. For the purposes set out in Article 2, the activities of the Community shall include, as provided in this Treaty and in accordance with the timetable set out therein:
    (a) the prohibition, as between Member States, of customs duties and quantitative restrictions on the import and export of goods, and of all other measures having equivalent effect;
    (b) a common commercial policy;
    (c) an internal market characterised by the abolition, as between Member States, of obstacles to the free movement of goods, persons, services and capital;
    (d) measures concerning the entry and movement of persons as provided for in Title IV;
    (e) a common policy in the sphere of agriculture and fisheries;
    (f) a common policy in the sphere of transport;
    (g) a system ensuring that competition in the internal market is not distorted;
    (h) the approximation of the laws of Member States to the extent required for the functioning of the common market;
    (i) the promotion of co-ordination between employment policies of the Member States with a view to enhancing their effectiveness by developing a co-ordinated strategy for employment;
    (j) a policy in the social sphere comprising a European Social Fund;
    (k) the strengthening of economic and social cohesion;
    (l) a policy in the sphere of the environment;
    (m) the strengthening of the competitiveness of Community industry;
    (n) the promotion of research and technological development;
    (o) encouragement for the establishment and development of trans-European networks;
    (p) a contribution to the attainment of a high level of health protection;
    (q) a contribution to education and training of quality and to the flowering of the cultures of the Member States;
    (r) a policy in the sphere of development cooperation;
    (s) the association of the overseas countries and territories in order to increase trade and promote jointly economic and social development;
    (t) a contribution to the strengthening of consumer protection;
    (u) measures in the spheres of energy, civil protection and tourism.

2.   In all the activities referred to in this Article, the Community shall aim to eliminate inequalities, and to promote equality between men and women.

Article 4

1.   For the purposes set out in Article 2, the activities of the Member States and the Community shall include, as provided in this Treaty and in accordance with the timetable set out therein, the adoption of an economic policy which is based on the close coordination of Member States' economic policies, on the internal market and on the definition of common objectives, and conducted in accordance with the principle of an open market economy with free competition.

2.   Concurrently with the foregoing, and as provided in this Treaty and in accordance with the timetable and the procedures set out therein, these activities shall include the irrevocable fixing of exchange rates leading to the introduction of a single currency, the ECU, and the definition and conduct of a single monetary policy and exchange-rate policy the primary objective of both of which shall be to maintain price stability and, without prejudice to this objective, to support the general economic policies in the Community, in accordance with the principle of an open market economy with free competition.

3.   These activities of the Member States and the Community shall entail compliance with the following guiding principles: stable prices, sound public finances and monetary conditions and a sustainable balance of payments.

Article 5

The Community shall act within the limits of the powers conferred upon it by this Treaty and of the objectives assigned to it therein.

In areas which do not fall within its exclusive competence, the Community shall take action, in accordance with the principle of subsidiarity, only if and in so far as the objectives of the proposed action cannot be sufficiently achieved by the Member States and can therefore, by reason of the scale or effects of the proposed action, be better achieved by the Community.

Any action by the Community shall not go beyond what is necessary to achieve the objectives of this Treaty.

Article 6

Environmental protection requirements must be integrated into the definition and implementation of the Community policies and activities referred to in Article 3, in particular with a view to promoting sustainable development.

Article 7

1.   The tasks entrusted to the Community shall be carried out by the following institutions:
  — a EUROPEAN PARLIAMENT,
  — a COUNCIL,
  — a COMMISSION,
  — a COURT OF JUSTICE,
  — a COURT OF AUDITORS.
Each institution shall act within the limits of the powers conferred upon it by this Treaty.

2.   The Council and the Commission shall be assisted by an Economic and Social Committee and a Committee of the Regions acting in an advisory capacity.

Articles 8, 9   *****

Article 10

Member States shall take all appropriate measures, whether general or particular, to ensure fulfilment of the obligations arising out of this Treaty or resulting from action taken by the institutions of the Community. They shall facilitate the achievement of the Community's tasks.

They shall abstain from any measure which could jeopardise the attainment of the objectives of this Treaty.

Article 11

[1.   Member States which intend to establish enhanced cooperation between themselves in one of the areas referred to in this Treaty shall address a request to the Commission, which may submit a proposal to the Council to that effect. In the event of the Commission not submitting a proposal, it shall inform the Member States concerned of the reasons for not doing so.

2.   Authorisation to establish enhanced cooperation as referred to in paragraph I shall be granted, in compliance with Article 43 to 45 of the Treaty on European Union, by the Council, acting by a qualified majority on a proposal from the Commission and after consulting the European Parliament. When enhanced cooperation relates to an area covered by the procedure referred to in Article 251 of this Treaty, the assent of the European Parliament shall be required.

A member of the Council may request that the matter be referred to the European Council. After that matter has been raised before the European Council, the Council may act in accordance with the first subparagraph of this paragraph.

3.   The acts and decisions necessary for the implementation of enhanced cooperation activities shall be subject to all the relevant provisions of this Treaty, save as otherwise provided in this Article and in Articles 43 to 45 of the Treaty on European Union.]

Article 11a

[Any Member State which wishes to participate in enhanced cooperation established in accordance with Article 11 shall notify its intention to the Council and to the Commission, which shall give an opinion to the Council within three months of the date of receipt of that notification. Within four months of the date of receipt of that notification, the Commission shall take a decision on it, and on such specific arrangements as it may deem necessary.]

Article 12

Within the scope of application of this Treaty, and without prejudice to any special provisions contained therein, any discrimination on grounds of nationality shall be prohibited.

The Council, acting in accordance with the procedure referred to in Article 251, may adopt rules designed to prohibit such discrimination.

Article 13

[1.   Without prejudice to the other provisions of this Treaty and within the limits of the powers conferred by it upon the Community, the Council, acting unanimously on a proposal from the Commission and after consulting the European Parliament, may take appropriate action to combat discrimination based on sex, racial or ethnic origin, religion or belief, disability, age or sexual orientation.

2.   By way of derogation from paragraph 1, when the Council adopts Community incentive measures, excluding any harmonisation of the laws and regulations of the Member States, to support action taken by the Member States in order to contribute to the achievement of the objectives referred to in paragraph 1, it shall act in accordance with the procedure referred to in Article 251.]

Article 14

1.   The Community shall adopt measures with the aim of progressively establishing the internal market over a period expiring on 31 December 1992, in accordance with the provisions of this Article and of Articles 15, 26, 47(2), 49, 80, 93 and 95 and without prejudice to the other provisions of this Treaty.

2. The internal market shall comprise an area without internal frontiers in which the free movement of goods, persons, services and capital is ensured in accordance with the provisions of this Treaty.

3. The Council, acting by a qualified majority on a proposal from the Commission, shall determine the guidelines and conditions necessary to ensure balanced progress in all the sectors concerned.

Article 15
When drawing up its proposals with a view to achieving the objectives set out in Article 14, the Commission shall take into account the extent of the effort that certain economies showing differences in development will have to sustain during the period of establishment of the internal market and it may propose appropriate provisions.

If these provisions take the form of derogations, they must be of a temporary nature and must cause the least possible disturbance to the functioning of the common market.

Article 16
Without prejudice to Articles 73, 86 and 87, and given the place occupied by services of general economic interest in the shared values of the Union as well as their role in promoting social and territorial cohesion, the Community and the Member States, each within their respective powers and within the scope of application of this Treaty, shall take care that such services operate on the basis of principles and conditions which enable them to fulfil their missions.

PART TWO   (CITIZENSHIP OF THE UNION)

Article 17
1. Citizenship of the Union is hereby established. Every person holding the nationality of a Member State shall be a citizen of the Union. Citizenship of the Union shall complement and not replace national citizenship.

2. Citizens of the Union shall enjoy the rights conferred by this Treaty and shall be subject to the duties imposed thereby.
*****

PART THREE   (COMMUNITY POLICIES)

CHAPTER 2—(PROHIBITION OF QUANTITATIVE RESTRICTIONS BETWEEN MEMBER STATES)

Article 28
Quantitative restrictions on imports and all measures having equivalent effect shall be prohibited between Member States.

*****

Article 30
The provisions of Articles 28 and 29 shall not preclude prohibitions or restrictions on imports, exports or goods in transit justified on grounds of public morality, public policy or public security; the protection of health and life of humans, animals or plants; the protection of national treasures possessing artistic, historic or archaeological value; or the protection of industrial and commercial property. Such prohibitions or restrictions shall not, however, constitute a means of arbitrary discrimination or a disguised restriction on trade between Member States.
*****

TITLE III   FREE MOVEMENT OF PERSONS, SERVICES AND CAPITAL

CHAPTER 1—(WORKERS)

Article 39

1.   Freedom of movement for workers shall be secured within the Community.

2.   Such freedom of movement shall entail the abolition of any discrimination based on nationality between workers of the Member States as regards employment, remuneration and other conditions of work and employment.

3.   It shall entail the right, subject to limitations justified on grounds of public policy, public security or public health:

   (a)   to accept offers of employment actually made;
   (b)   to move freely within the territory of Member States for this purpose;
   (c)   to stay in a Member State for the purpose of employment in accordance with the provisions governing the employment of nationals of that State laid down by law, regulation or administrative action;
   (d)   to remain in the territory of a Member State after having been employed in that State, subject to conditions which shall be embodied in implementing regulations to be drawn up by the Commission.

4.   The provisions of this Article shall not apply to employment in the public service.
*****

CHAPTER 2—(RIGHT OF ESTABLISHMENT)

*****

Article 43

Within the framework of the provisions set out below, restrictions on the freedom of establishment of nationals of a Member State in the territory of another Member State shall be prohibited. Such prohibition shall also apply to restrictions on the setting up of agencies, branches or subsidiaries by nationals of any Member State established in the territory of any Member State.

Freedom of establishment shall include the right to take up and pursue activities as self-employed persons and to set up and manage undertakings, in particular companies or firms within the meaning of the second paragraph of Article 58, under the conditions laid down for its own nationals by the law of the country where such establishment is effected, subject to the provisions of the Chapter relating to capital.
*****

Article 48

Companies or firms formed in accordance with the law of a Member State and having their registered office, central administration or principal place of business within the Community shall, for the purposes of this Chapter, be treated in the same way as natural persons who are nationals of Member States.

"Companies or firms" means companies or firms constituted under civil or commercial law, including co-operative societies, and other legal persons governed by public or private law, save for those which are non-profit-making.

CHAPTER 3—(SERVICES)

Article 49

Within the framework of the provisions set out below, restrictions on freedom to provide services within the Community shall be prohibited in respect of nationals of Member States who are established in a State of the Community other than that of the person for whom the services are intended.

The Council may, acting by a qualified majority on a proposal from the Commission, extend the provisions of the Chapter to nationals of a third country who provide services and who are established within the Community.

Article 50

Services shall be considered to be "services" within the meaning of this Treaty where they are normally provided for remuneration, in so far as they are not governed by the provisions relating to freedom of movement for goods, capital and persons.

"Services" shall in particular include:

    (a) activities of an industrial character;

    (b) activities of a commercial character;

    (c) activities of craftsmen;

    (d) activities of the professions.

Without prejudice to the provisions of the Chapter relating to the right of establishment, the person providing a service may, in order to do so, temporarily pursue his activity in the State where the service is provided, under the same conditions as are imposed by that State on its own nationals.

*****

TITLE IV   VISAS, ASYLUM, IMMIGRATION AND OTHER POLICIES RELATED TO FREE MOVEMENT OF PERSONS

Article 61

In order to establish progressively an area of freedom, security and justice, the Council shall adopt:

    (a) within a period of five years after the entry into force of the Treaty of Amsterdam, measures aimed at ensuring the free movement of persons in accordance with Article 14, in conjunction with directly related flanking measures with respect to external border controls, asylum and immigration, in accordance with the provisions of Article 62(2) and (3) and Article 63(1)(a) and (2)(a), and measures to prevent and combat crime in accordance with the provisions of Article 31(e) of the Treaty on European Union;

    (b) other measures in the fields of asylum, immigration and safeguarding the rights of nationals of third countries, in accordance with the provisions of Article 63;

    (c) measures in the field of judicial cooperation in civil matters as provided for in Article 65;

    (d) appropriate measures to encourage and strengthen administrative cooperation, as provided for in Article 66;

    (e) measures in the field of police and judicial cooperation in criminal matters aimed at a high level of security by preventing and combating crime within the Union in accordance with the provisions of the Treaty on European Union.

Article 62

The Council, acting in accordance with the procedure referred to in Article 67, shall, within a period of five years after the entry into force of the Treaty of Amsterdam, adopt:

    1.   measures with a view to ensuring, in compliance with Article 14, the absence of any controls on persons, be they citizens of the Union or nationals of third countries, when crossing internal borders;

    2.   measures on the crossing of the external borders of the Member States which shall establish:

    (a) standards and procedures to be followed by Member States in carrying out checks on persons at such borders;

    (b) rules on visas for intended stays of no more than three months, including:

        (i) the list of third countries whose nationals must be in possession of visas when crossing the external borders and those whose nationals are exempt from that requirement;

        (ii) the procedures and conditions for issuing visas by Member States;

        (iii) a uniform format for visas;

        (iv) rules on a uniform visa;

    3. measures setting out the conditions under which nationals of third countries shall have the freedom to travel within the territory of the Member States during a period of no more than three months.

Article 63

The Council, acting in accordance with the procedure referred to in Article 67, shall, within a period of five years after the entry into force of the Treaty of Amsterdam, adopt:

    1. measures on asylum, in accordance with the Geneva Convention of 28 July 1951 and the Protocol of 31 January 1967 relating to the status of refugees and other relevant treaties, withint he following areas:

    (a) criteria and mechanisms for determining which Member State is responsible for considering an application for asylum submitted by a national of a third country in one of the Member States,

    (b) minimum standards on the reception of asylum seekers in Member States,

    (c) minimum standards with respect to the qualification of nationals of third countries as refugees,

    (d) minimum standards on procedures in Member States for granting or withdrawing refugee status;

    2. measures on refugees and displaced persons within the following areas:

    (a) minimum standards for giving temporary protection to displaced persons from third countries who cannot return to their country of origin and for persons who otherwise need international protection,

    (b) promoting a balance of effort between Member States in receiving and bearing the consequences of receiving refugees and displaced persons;

    3. measures on immigration policy within the following areas:

    (a) conditions of entry and residence, and standards on procedures for the issue by Member States of long-term visas and residence permits, including those for the purpose of family reunion,

    (b) illegal immigration and illegal residence, including repatriation of illegal residents;

    4. measures defining the rights and conditions under which nationals of third countries who are legally resident in a Member State may reside in other Member States.

Measures adopted by the Council pursuant to points 3 and 4 shall not prevent any Member State from maintaining or introducing in the areas concerned national provisions which are compatible with this Treaty and with international agreements.

Measures to be adopted pursuant to points 2(b), 3(a) and 4 shall not be subject to the five-year period referred to above.

Article 64

    1. This title shall not affect the exercise of the responsibilities incumbent upon Member States with regard to the maintenance of law and order and the safeguarding of internal security.

    2. In the event of one or more Member States being confronted with an emergency situation characterised by a sudden inflow of nationals of third countries and without prejudice to paragraph 1, the Council may, acting by qualified majority on a proposal from

the Commission, adopt provisional measures of a duration not exceeding six months for the benefit of the Member States concerned.

Article 65

Measures in the field of judicial cooperation in civil matters having cross-border implications, to be taken in accordance with Article 67 and in so far as necessary for the proper functioning of the internal market, shall include:

- (a) improving and simplifying:
  - — the system for cross-border service of judicial and extrajudicial documents,
  - — cooperation in the taking of evidence,
  - — the recognition and enforcement of decisions in civil and commercial cases, including decisions in extrajudicial cases;
- (b) promoting the compatibility of the rules applicable in the Member States concerning the conflict of laws and of jurisdiction;
- (c) eliminating obstacles to the good functioning of civil proceedings, if necessary by promoting the compatibility of the rules on civil procedure applicable in the Member States.

*****

Article 69

The application of this title shall be subject to the provisions of the Protocol on the position of the United Kingdom and Ireland and to the Protocol on the position of Denmark and without prejudice to the Protocol on the application of certain aspects of Article 14 of the Treaty establishing the European Community to the United Kingdom and to Ireland.
*****

TITLE VI   COMMON RULES ON COMPETITION, TAXATION AND APPROXIMATION OF LAWS

CHAPTER 1—(RULES ON COMPETITION)

Section 1—Rules applying to undertakings

Article 81

1.   The following shall be prohibited as incompatible with the common market: all agreements between undertakings, decisions by associations of undertakings and concerted practices which may affect trade between Member States and which have as their object or effect the prevention, restriction or distortion of competition within the common market, and in particular those which:

- (a) directly or indirectly fix purchase or selling prices or any other trading conditions;
- (b) limit or control production, markets, technical development, or investment;
- (c) share markets or sources of supply;
- (d) apply dissimilar conditions to equivalent transactions with other trading parties, thereby placing them at a competitive disadvantage;
- (e) make the conclusion of contracts subject to acceptance by the other parties of supplementary obligations which, by their nature or according to commercial usage, have no connection with the subject of such contracts.

2.   Any agreements or decisions prohibited pursuant to this Article shall be automatically void.

3.   The provisions of paragraph 1 may, however, be declared inapplicable in the case of:

- — any agreement or category of agreements between undertakings;

— any decision or category of decisions by associations of undertakings;
— any concerted practice or category of concerted practices;

which contributes to improving the production or distribution of goods or to promoting technical or economic progress, while allowing consumers a fair share of the resulting benefit, and which does not:

(a) impose on the undertakings concerned restrictions which are not indispensable to the attainment of these objectives;

(b) afford such undertakings the possibility of eliminating competition in respect of a substantial part of the products in question.

Article 82

Any abuse by one or more undertakings of a dominant position within the common market or in a substantial part of it shall be prohibited as incompatible with the common market in so far as it may affect trade between Member States.

Such abuse may, in particular, consist in:

(a) directly or indirectly imposing unfair purchase or selling prices or other unfair trading conditions;

(b) limiting production, markets or technical development to the prejudice of consumers;

(c) applying dissimilar conditions to equivalent transactions with other trading parties, thereby placing them at a competitive disadvantage;

(d) making the conclusion of contracts subject to acceptance by the other parties of supplementary obligations which, by their nature or according to commercial usage, have no connection with the subject of such contracts.

*****

CHAPTER 3—(APPROXIMATION OF LAWS)

Article 94

The Council shall, acting unanimously on a proposal from the Commission and after consulting the European Parliament and the Economic and Social Committee, issue directives for the approximation of such laws, regulations or administrative provisions of the Member States as directly affect the establishment or functioning of the common market.

Article 95

1. By way of derogation from Article 94 and save where otherwise provided in this Treaty, the following provisions shall apply for the achievement of the objectives set out in Article 14. The Council shall, acting in accordance with the procedure referred to in Article 251 and after consulting the Economic and Social Committee, adopt the measures for the approximation of the provisions laid down by law, regulation or administrative action in Member States which have as their object the establishment and functioning of the internal market.

2. Paragraph 1 shall not apply to fiscal provisions, to those relating to the free movement of persons nor to those relating to the rights and interests of employed persons.

3. The Commission, in its proposals envisaged in paragraph 1 concerning health, safety, environmental protection and consumer protection, will take as a base a high level of protection, taking into account in particular any new development based on scientific facts within their relevant powers, the European Parliament and Council will also seek to achieve this objective.

4. If, after the adoption by the Council or the Commission of a harmonisation measure a Member State deems it necessary to apply national provisions on grounds of major needs referred to in Article 30, or relating to protection of the environment or the working

environment, it shall notify the Commission of these provisions as well as the grounds for maintaining them.

5.–10. *****

*****

TITLE XI SOCIAL POLICY, EDUCATION, VOCATIONAL TRAINING AND YOUTH

CHAPTER 1—(SOCIAL PROVISIONS)

Article 136

The Community and the Member States, having in mind fundamental social rights such as those set out in the European Social Charter signed at Turin on 18 October 1961 and in the 1989 Community Charter of the Fundamental Social Rights of Workers, shall have as their objectives the promotion of employment, improved living and working conditions, so as to make possible their harmonisation while the improvement is being maintained, proper social protection, dialogue between management and labour, the development of human resources with a view to lasting high employment and the combating of exclusion.

To this end the Community and the Member States shall implement measures which take account of the diverse forms of national practices, in particular in the field of contractual relations, and the need to maintain the competitiveness of the Community economy.

They believe that such a development will ensue not only from the functioning of the common market, which will favour the harmonisation of social systems, but also from the procedures provided for in this Treaty and from the approximation of provisions laid down by law, regulation or administrative action.

Article 137

[1. With a view to achieving the objectives of Article 136, the Community shall support and complement the activities of the Member States in the following fields:

(a) improvement in particular of the working environment to protect workers' health and safety;

(b) working conditions;

(c) social security and social protection of workers;

(d) protection of workers where their employment contract is terminated;

(e) the information and consultation of workers;

(f) representation and collective defence of the interests of workers and employers, including co-determination, subject to paragraph 5;

(g) conditions of employment for third-country nationals legally residing in Community territory;

(h) the integration of persons excluded from the labour market, without prejudice to Article 150;

(i) equality between men and women with regard to labour market opportunities and treatment at work;

(j) the combating of social exclusion;

(k) the modernisation of social protection systems without prejudice to point (c).

2. To this end, the Council:

(a) may adopt measures designed to encourage cooperation between Member States through initiatives aimed at improving knowledge, developing exchanges of information and best practices, promoting innovative approaches and evaluating experiences, excluding any harmonisation of the laws and regulations of the Member States;

(b) may adopt, in the fields referred to in paragraph 1(a) to (i), by means of directives, minimum requirements for gradual implementation, having regard to the conditions and technical rules obtaining in each of the Member States. Such directives shall avoid imposing administrative, financial and legal constraints in a way which would hold back the creation and development of small and medium-sized undertakings.

The Council shall act in accordance with the procedure referred to in Article 251 after consulting the Economic and Social Committee and the Committee of the Regions, except in the fields referred to in paragraph 1(c), (d), (f) and (g) of this article, where the Council shall act unanimously on a proposal from the Commission, after consulting the European Parliament and the said Committees. The Council, acting unanimously on a proposal from the Commission, after consulting the European Parliament, may decide to render the procedure referred to in Article 251 applicable to paragraph 1(d), (f) and (g) of this article.

3. A Member State may entrust management and labour, at their joint request, with the implementation of directives adopted pursuant to paragraph 2.

In this case, it shall ensure that, no later than the date on which a directive must be transposed in accordance with Article 249, management and labour have introduced the necessary measures by agreement, the Member State concerned being required to take any necessary measure enabling it at any time to be in a position to guarantee the results imposed by that directive.

4. The provisions adopted pursuant to this article:
— shall not affect the right of Member States to define the fundamental principles of their social security systems and must not significantly affect the financial equilibrium thereof,
— shall not prevent any Member State from maintaining or introducing more stringent protective measures compatible with this Treaty.

5. The provisions of this article shall not apply to pay, the right of association, the right to strike or the right to impose lock-outs.]

Article 138

1. The Commission shall have the task of promoting the consultation of management and labour at Community level and shall take any relevant measure to facilitate their dialogue by ensuring balanced support for the parties.

2. To this end, before submitting proposals in the social policy field, the Commission shall consult management and labour on the possible direction of Community action.

3. If, after such consultation, the Commission considers Community action advisable, it shall consult management and labour on the content of the envisaged proposal. Management and labour shall forward to the Commission an opinion or, where appropriate, a recommendation.

4. On the occasion of such consultation, management and labour may inform the Commission of their wish to initiate the process provided for in Article 139. The duration of the procedure shall not exceed nine months, unless the management and labour concerned and the Commission decide jointly to extend it.

Article 139

1. Should management and labour so desire, the dialogue between them at Community level may lead to contractual relations, including agreements.

2. Agreements concluded at Community level shall be implemented either in accordance with the procedures and practices specific to management and labour and the Member States or, in matters covered by Article 137, at the joint request of the signatory parties, by a Council decision on a proposal from the Commission.

The Council shall act by qualified majority, except where the agreement in question contains one or more provisions relating to one of the areas [for which unanimity is required pursuant to Article 137(2). In that] case it shall act unanimously.

Article 140

With a view to achieving the objectives of Article 136 and without prejudice to the other provisions of this Treaty, the Commission shall encourage cooperation between the Member States and facilitate the coordination of their action in all social policy fields under this chapter, particularly in matters relating to:

— employment;
— labour law and working conditions;
— basic and advanced vocational training;
— social security;
— prevention of occupational accidents and diseases;
— occupational hygiene;
— the right of association and collective bargaining between employers and workers.

To this end, the Commission shall act in close contact with Member States by making studies, delivering opinions and arranging consultations both on problems arising at national level and on those of concern to international organisations.

Before delivering the opinions provided for in this Article, the Commission shall consult the Economic and Social Committee.

Article 141

1.   Each Member State shall ensure that the principle of equal pay for male and female workers for equal work or work of equal value is applied.

2.   For the purpose of this Article 'pay' means the ordinary basic or minimum wage or salary and any other consideration, whether in cash or in kind, which the worker receives directly or indirectly, in respect of his employment, from his employer.

Equal pay without discrimination based on sex means:

(a) that pay for the same work at piece rates shall be calculated on the basis of the same unit of measurement;
(b) that pay for work at time rates shall be the same for the same job.

3.   The Council, acting in accordance with the procedure referred to in Article 251, and after consulting the Economic and Social Committee, shall adopt measures to ensure the application of the principle of equal opportunities and equal treatment of men and women in matters of employment and occupation, including the principle of equal pay for equal work or work of equal value.

4.   With a view to ensuring full equality in practice between men and women in working life, the principle of equal treatment shall not prevent any Member State from maintaining or adopting measures providing for specific advantages in order to make it easier for the under-represented sex to pursue a vocational activity or to prevent or compensate for disadvantages in professional careers.

*****

TITLE XVI   INDUSTRY

Article 157

1.   The Community and the Member States shall ensure that the conditions necessary for the competitiveness of the Community's industry exist.

For that purpose, in accordance with a system of open and competitive markets, their action shall be aimed at:

— speeding up the adjustment of industry to structural changes;
— encouraging an environment favourable to initiative and to the development of undertakings throughout the Community, particularly small and medium-sized undertakings;
— encouraging an environment favourable to co-operation between undertakings;
— fostering better exploitation of the industrial potential of policies of innovation, research and technological development.

2.   The Member States shall consult each other in liaison with the Commission and, where necessary, shall co-ordinate their action. The Commission may take any useful initiative to promote such co-ordination.

3.   The Community shall contribute to the achievement of the objectives set out in paragraph 1 through the policies and activities it pursues under other provisions of this Treaty. The Council, acting [in accordance with the procedure referred to in Article 251 and], after consulting ... the Economic and Social Committee, may decide on specific measures in support of action taken in the Member States to achieve the objectives set out in paragraph 1.

This Title shall not provide a basis for the introduction by the Community of any measure which could lead to a distortion of competition [or contains tax provisions or provisions relating to the rights and interests of employed persons].

*****

PART FIVE   (INSTITUTIONS OF THE COMMUNITY)
TITLE I   PROVISIONS GOVERNING THE INSTITUTIONS

CHAPTER 1—(THE INSTITUTIONS)

Section 1—The European Parliament

Article 189
The European Parliament, which shall consist of representatives of the peoples of the States brought together in the Community, shall exercise the powers conferred upon it by this Treaty. The number of Members of the European Parliament shall not exceed [732].

Article 190
1.   The representatives in the European Parliament of the peoples of the States brought together in the Community shall be elected by direct universal suffrage.

2.   The number of representatives elected in each Member State is as follows:

```
[Belgium . . . . . . . . . . . . . . . . . . . . . . . . . . . . . . . . . . 24
Czech Republic . . . . . . . . . . . . . . . . . . . . . . . . . . . . 24
Denmark . . . . . . . . . . . . . . . . . . . . . . . . . . . . . . . . . 14
Germany . . . . . . . . . . . . . . . . . . . . . . . . . . . . . . . . . 99
Estonia . . . . . . . . . . . . . . . . . . . . . . . . . . . . . . . . . . . 6
Greece . . . . . . . . . . . . . . . . . . . . . . . . . . . . . . . . . . . 24
Spain . . . . . . . . . . . . . . . . . . . . . . . . . . . . . . . . . . . . 54
France . . . . . . . . . . . . . . . . . . . . . . . . . . . . . . . . . . . 78
Ireland . . . . . . . . . . . . . . . . . . . . . . . . . . . . . . . . . . 13
Italy . . . . . . . . . . . . . . . . . . . . . . . . . . . . . . . . . . . . 78
Cyprus . . . . . . . . . . . . . . . . . . . . . . . . . . . . . . . . . . . 6
Latvia . . . . . . . . . . . . . . . . . . . . . . . . . . . . . . . . . . . . 9
Lithuania . . . . . . . . . . . . . . . . . . . . . . . . . . . . . . . . 13
Luxembourg . . . . . . . . . . . . . . . . . . . . . . . . . . . . . . . 6
```

Hungary 24
Malta 5
Netherlands 27
Austria 18
Poland 54
Portugal 24
Slovenia 7
Slovakia 14
Finland 14
Sweden 19
United Kingdom . . . . 78]

In the event of amendments to this paragraph, the number of representatives elected in each Member State must ensure appropriate representation of the peoples of the States brought together in the Community.

3.   Representatives shall be elected for a term of five years.

4.   The European Parliament shall draw up a proposal for elections by direct universal suffrage in accordance with a uniform procedure in all Member States or in accordance with principles common to all Member States.

The Council shall, acting unanimously after obtaining the assent of the European Parliament, which shall act by a majority of its component members, lay down the appropriate provisions, which it shall recommend to Member States for adoption in accordance with their respective constitutional requirements.

5.   The European Parliament shall, after seeking an opinion from the Commission and with the approval of the Council acting unanimously, lay down the regulations and general conditions governing the performance of the duties of its Members.

Article 191

Political parties at European level are important as a factor for integration within the Union. They contribute to forming a European awareness and to expressing the political will of the citizens of the Union.

[The Council, acting in accordance with the procedure referred to in Article 251, shall lay down the regulations governing political parties at European level and in particular the rules regarding their funding.]

Article 192

In so far as provided in this Treaty, the European Parliament shall participate in the process leading up to the adoption of Community acts by exercising its powers under the procedures laid down in Articles 251 and 253 and by giving its assent or delivering advisory opinions.

The European Parliament may, acting by a majority of its Members, request the Commission to submit any appropriate proposal on matters on which it considers that a Community act is required for the purpose of implementing this Treaty.

Article 193

In the course of its duties, the European Parliament may, at the request of a quarter of its Members, set up a temporary Committee of Inquiry to investigate, without prejudice to the powers conferred by this Treaty on other institutions or bodies, alleged contraventions or maladministration in the implementation of Community law, except where the alleged facts are being examined before a court and while the case is still subject to legal proceedings.

The temporary Committee of Inquiry shall cease to exist on the submission of its report.

The detailed provisions governing the exercise of the right of inquiry shall be determined by common accord of the European Parliament, the Council and the Commission.

Article 194

Any citizen of the Union, and any natural or legal person residing or having its registered office in a Member State, shall have the right to address, individually or in association with other citizens or persons, a petition to the European Parliament on a matter which comes within the Community's fields of activity and which affects him, her or it directly.

Article 195

1. The European Parliament shall appoint an Ombudsman empowered to receive complaints from any citizen of the Union or any natural or legal person residing or having its registered office in a Member State concerning instances of maladministration in the activities of the Community institutions or bodies, with the exception of the Court of Justice and the Court of First Instance acting in their judicial role.

In accordance with his duties, the Ombudsman shall conduct inquiries for which he finds grounds, either on his own initiative or on the basis of complaints submitted to him direct or through a member of the European Parliament, except where the alleged facts are or have been the subject of legal proceedings. Where the Ombudsman establishes an instance of maladministration, he shall refer the matter to the institution concerned, which shall have a period of three months in which to inform him of its views.

The Ombudsman shall then forward a report to the European Parliament and the institution concerned. The person lodging the complaint shall be informed of the outcome of such inquiries.

The Ombudsman shall submit an annual report to the European Parliament on the outcome of his inquiries.

2. The Ombudsman shall be appointed after each election of the European Parliament for the duration of its term of office. The Ombudsman shall be eligible for re-appointment.

The Ombudsman may be dismissed by the Court of Justice at the request of the European Parliament if he no longer fulfils the conditions required for the performance of his duties or if he is guilty of serious misconduct.

3. The Ombudsman shall be completely independent in the performance of his duties. In the performance of those duties he shall neither seek nor take instructions from any body.

The Ombudsman may not, during his term of office, engage in any other occupation, whether gainful or not.

4. The European Parliament shall, after seeking an opinion from the Commission and with the approval of the Council acting by a qualified majority, lay down the regulations and general conditions governing the performance of the Ombudsman's duties.

Article 196

The European Parliament shall hold an annual session. It shall meet, without requiring to be convened, on the second Tuesday in March.

The European Parliament may meet in extraordinary session at the request of a majority of its members or at the request of the Council or of the Commission.

Article 197

The European Parliament shall elect its President and its officers from among its members.

Members of the Commission may attend all meetings and shall, at their request, be heard on behalf of the Commission.

The Commission shall reply orally or in writing to questions put to it by the European Parliament or by its members.

The Council shall be heard by the European Parliament in accordance with the conditions laid down by the Council in its rules of procedure.

Article 198

Save as otherwise provided in this Treaty, the European Parliament shall act by an absolute majority of the votes cast.

The Rules of Procedure shall determine the quorum.

Article 199

The European Parliament shall adopt its Rules of Procedure, acting by a majority of its Members.

The proceedings of the European Parliament shall be published in the manner laid down in its Rules of Procedure.

Article 200

The European Parliament shall discuss in open session the annual general report submitted to it by the Commission.

Article 201

If a motion of censure on the activities of the Commission is tabled before it, the European Parliament shall not vote thereon until at least three days after the motion has been tabled and only by open vote.

If the motion of censure is carried by a two-third majority of the votes cast, representing a majority of the members of the European Parliament, the members of the Commission shall resign as a body. They shall continue to deal with current business until they are replaced in accordance with Article 214. In this case, the term of office of the members of the Commission appointed to replace them shall expire on the date on which the term of office of the members of the Commission obliged to resign as a body would have expired.

Section 2—The Council

Article 202

To ensure that the objectives set out in the Treaty are attained, the Council shall, in accordance with the provisions of this Treaty:
 — ensure co-ordination of the general economic policies of the Member States;
 — have power to take decisions;
 — confer on the Commission, in the acts which the Council adopts, powers for the implementation of the rules which the Council lays down. The Council may impose certain requirements in respect of the exercise of these powers. The Council may also reserve the right, in specific cases, to exercise directly implementing powers itself. The procedures referred to above must be consonant with principles and rules to be laid down in advance by the Council, acting unanimously on a proposal from the Commission and after obtaining the Opinion of the European Parliament.

*****

Article 205

1. Save as otherwise provided in this Treaty, the Council shall act by a majority of its members.

2. Where the Council is required to act by a qualified majority, the votes of its members shall be weighted as follows:

> [Belgium 12
> Czech Republic 12
> Denmark 7
> Germany 29

Estonia 4
Greece 12
Spain 27
France 29
Ireland 7
Italy 29
Cyprus 4
Latvia 4
Lithuania 7
Luxembourg 4
Hungary 12
Malta 3
Netherlands 13
Austria 10
Poland 27
Portugal 12
Slovenia 4
Slovakia 7
Finland 7
Sweden 10
United Kingdom . . . . 29]

[Acts of the Council shall require for their adoption at least 232 votes in favour cast by a majority of the members where this Treaty requires them to be adopted on a proposal from the Commission.

In other cases, for their adoption acts of the Council shall require at least 232 votes in favour, cast by at least two-thirds of the members.]

3. Abstentions by members present in person or represented shall not prevent the adoption by the Council of acts which require unanimity.

[4.   When a decision is to be adopted by the Council by a qualified majority, a member of the Council may request verification that the Member States constituting the qualified majority represent at least 62% of the total population of the Union. If that condition is shown not to have been met, the decision in question shall not be adopted.]

*****

Section 3—The Commission

Article 211
In order to ensure the proper functioning and development of the common market, the Commission shall:

— ensure that the provisions of this Treaty and the measures taken by the institutions pursuant thereto are applied;

— formulate recommendations or deliver opinions on matters dealt with in this Treaty, if it expressly so provides or if the Commission considers it necessary;

— have its own power of decision and participate in the shaping of measures taken by the Council and by the European Parliament in the manner provided for in this Treaty;

— exercise the powers conferred on it by the Council for the implementation of the rules laid down by the latter.

*****

Section 4—The Court of Justice

Article 220
[The Court of Justice and the Court of First Instance, each within its jurisdiction, shall ensure that in the interpretation and application of this Treaty the law is observed.

In addition, judicial panels may be attached to the Court of First Instance under the conditions laid down in Article 225a in order to exercise, in certain specific areas, the judicial competence laid down in this Treaty.]

Article 221
[The Court of Justice shall consist of one judge per Member State.

The Court of Justice shall sit in chambers or in a Grand Chamber, in accordance with the rules laid down for that purpose in the Statute of the Court of Justice.

When provided for in the Statute, the Court of Justice may also sit as a full Court.]

Article 222
[The Court of Justice shall be assisted by eight Advocates-General. Should the Court of Justice so request, the Council, acting unanimously, may increase the number of Advocates-General.

It shall be the duty of the Advocate-General, acting with complete impartiality and independence, to make, in open court, reasoned submissions on cases which, in accordance with the Statute of the Court of Justice, require his involvement.]

Article 223
[The Judges and Advocates-General of the Court of Justice shall be chosen from persons whose independence is beyond doubt and who possess the qualifications required for appointment to the highest judicial offices in their respective countries or who are jurisconsults of recognised competence; they shall be appointed by common accord of the governments of the Member States for a term of six years.

Every three years there shall be a partial replacement of the Judges and Advocates-General, in accordance with the conditions laid down in the Statute of the Court of Justice.

The Judges shall elect the President of the Court of Justice from among their number for a term of three years. He may be re-elected.

Retiring Judges and Advocates-General may be reappointed.

The Court of Justice shall appoint its Registrar and lay down the rules governing his service.

The Court of Justice shall establish its Rules of Procedure. Those Rules shall require the approval of the Council, acting by a qualified majority.]

Article 224
[The Court of First Instance shall comprise at least one judge per Member State. The number of Judges shall be determined by the Statute of the Court of Justice. The Statute may provide for the Court of First Instance to be assisted by Advocates-General.

The members of the Court of First Instance shall be chosen from persons whose independence is beyond doubt and who possess the ability required for appointment to high judicial office. They shall be appointed by common accord of the governments of the Member States for a term of six years. The membership shall be partially renewed every three years. Retiring members shall be eligible for reappointment.

The Judges shall elect the President of the Court of First Instance from among their number for a term of three years. He may be re-elected.

The Court of First Instance shall appoint its Registrar and lay down the rules governing his service.

The Court of First Instance shall establish its Rules of Procedure in agreement with the Court of Justice. Those Rules shall require the approval of the Council, acting by a qualified majority.

Unless the Statute of the Court of Justice provides otherwise, the provisions of this Treaty relating to the Court of Justice shall apply to the Court of First Instance.]

Article 225

[1. The Court of First Instance shall have jurisdiction to hear and determine at first instance actions or proceedings referred to in Articles 230, 232, 235, 236 and 238, with the exception of those assigned to a judicial panel and those reserved in the Statute for the Court of Justice. The Statute may provide for the Court of First Instance to have jurisdiction for other classes of action or proceeding.

Decisions given by the Court of First Instance under this paragraph may be subject to a right of appeal to the Court of Justice on points of law only, under the conditions and within the limits laid down by the Statute.

2.   The Court of First Instance shall have jurisdiction to hear and determine actions or proceedings brought against decisions of the judicial panels set up under Article 225a.

Decisions given by the Court of First Instance under this paragraph may exceptionally be subject to review by the Court of Justice, under the conditions and within the limits laid down by the Statute, where there is a serious risk of the unity or consistency of Community law being affected.

3.   The Court of First Instance shall have jurisdiction to hear and determine questions referred for a preliminary ruling under Article 234, in specific areas laid down by the Statute.

Where the Court of First Instance considers that the case requires a decision of principle likely to affect the unity or consistency of Community law, it may refer the case to the Court of Justice for a ruling.

Decisions given by the Court of First Instance on questions referred for a preliminary ruling may exceptionally be subject to review by the Court of Justice, under the conditions and within the limits laid down by the Statute, where there is a serious risk of the unity or consistency of Community law being affected.]

Article 225a

[The Council, acting unanimously on a proposal from the Commission and after consulting the European Parliament and the Court of Justice or at the request of the Court of Justice and after consulting the European Parliament and the Commission, may create judicial panels to hear and determine at first instance certain classes of action or proceeding brought in specific arcas.

The decision establishing a judicial panel shall lay down the rules on the organisation of the panel and the extent of the jurisdiction conferred upon it.

Decisions given by judicial panels may be subject to a right of appeal on points of law only or, when provided for in the decision establishing the panel, a right of appeal also on matters of fact, before the Court of First Instance.

The members of the judicial panels shall be chosen from persons whose independence is beyond doubt and who possess the ability required for appointment to judicial office. They shall be appointed by the Council, acting unanimously.

The judicial panels shall establish their Rules of Procedure in agreement with the Court of Justice. Those Rules shall require the approval of the Council, acting by a qualified majority.

Unless the decision establishing the judicial panel provides otherwise, the provisions of this Treaty relating to the Court of Justice and the provisions of the Statute of the Court of Justice shall apply to the judicial panels.]

Article 226

If the Commission considers that a Member State has failed to fulfil an obligation under this Treaty, it shall deliver a reasoned opinion on the matter after giving the State concerned the opportunity to submit its observations.

If the State concerned does not comply with the opinion within the period laid down by the Commission, the latter may bring the matter before the Court of Justice.

Article 227

A Member State which considers that another Member State has failed to fulfil an obligation under this Treaty may bring the matter before the Court of Justice.

Before a Member State brings an action against another Member State for an alleged infringement of an obligation under this Treaty, it shall bring the matter before the Commission.

The Commission shall deliver a reasoned opinion after each of the States concerned has been given the opportunity to submit its own case and its observations on the other party's case both orally and in writing.

*****

Article 228

1.   If the Court of Justice finds that a Member State has failed to fulfil an obligation under this Treaty, the State shall be required to take the necessary measures to comply with the judgment of the Court of Justice.

2.   If the Commission considers that the Member State concerned has not taken such measures it shall, after giving that State the opportunity to submit its observations, issue a reasoned opinion specifying the points on which the Member State concerned has not complied with the judgment of the Court of Justice.

If the Member State concerned fails to take the necessary measures to comply with the Court's judgment within the time-limit laid down by the Commission, the latter may bring the case before the Court of Justice. In so doing it shall specify the amount of the lump sum or penalty payment to be paid by the Member State concerned which it considers appropriate in the circumstances.

If the Court of Justice finds that the Member State concerned has not complied with its judgment it may impose a lump sum or penalty payment on it.

This procedure shall be without prejudice to Article 227.

Article 229

Regulations adopted jointly by the European Parliament and the Council, and by the Council, pursuant to the provisions of this Treaty, may give the Court of Justice unlimited jurisdiction with regard to the penalties provided for in such regulations.

Article 229a *****

Article 230

The Court of Justice shall review the legality of acts adopted jointly by the European Parliament and the Council, of acts of the Council, of the Commission and of the ECB, other than recommendations and opinions, and of acts of the European Parliament intended to produce legal effects *vis-à-vis* third parties.

It shall for this purpose have jurisdiction in actions brought by a Member State, the Council or the Commission on grounds of lack of competence, infringement of an essential procedural requirement, infringement of this Treaty or of any rule of law relating to its application, or misuse of powers.

The Court shall have jurisdiction under the same conditions in actions brought by the . . . Court of Auditors and by the ECB for the purpose of protecting their prerogatives.

Any natural or legal person may, under the same conditions, institute proceedings against a decision addressed to that person or against a decision which, although in the form of a regulation or a decision addressed to another person, is of direct and individual concern to the former.

The proceedings provided for in this Article shall be instituted within two months of the publication of the measure, or of its notification to the plaintiff, or, in the absence thereof, of the day on which it came to the knowledge of the latter, as the case may be.

Article 231

If the action is well founded, the Court of Justice shall declare the act concerned to be void.

In the case of a regulation, however, the Court of Justice shall, if it considers this necessary, state which of the effects of the regulation which it has declared void shall be considered as definitive.

*****

Article 234

The Court of Justice shall have jurisdiction to give preliminary rulings concerning:
- (a) the interpretation of this Treaty;
- (b) the validity and interpretation of acts of the institutions of the Community and of the ECB;
- (c) the interpretation of the statutes of bodies established by an act of the Council, where those statutes so provide.

Where such a question is raised before any court or tribunal of a Member State, that court or tribunal may, if it considers that a decision on the question is necessary to enable it to give judgment, request the Court of Justice to give a ruling thereon.

Where any such question is raised in a case pending before a court or tribunal of a Member State against whose decisions there is no judicial remedy under national law, that court or tribunal shall bring the matter before the Court of Justice.

CHAPTER 2—(PROVISIONS COMMON TO SEVERAL INSTITUTIONS)

Article 249

In order to carry out their task and in accordance with the provisions of this Treaty, the European Parliament acting jointly with the Council, the Council and the Commission shall make regulations and issue directives, take decisions, make recommendations or deliver opinions.

A regulation shall have general application. It shall be binding in its entirety and directly applicable in all Member States.

A directive shall be binding, as to the result to be achieved, upon each Member State to which it is addressed, but shall leave to the national authorities the choice of form and methods.

A decision shall be binding in its entirety upon those to whom it is addressed. Recommendations and opinions shall have no binding force.

Article 250

1. Where, in pursuance of this Treaty, the Council acts on a proposal from the Commission, unanimity shall be required for an act constituting an amendment to that proposal, subject to Article 251(4) and (5).

2. As long as the Council has not acted, the Commission may alter its proposal at any time during the procedures leading to the adoption of a Community act.

Article 251

1. Where reference is made in this Treaty to this Article for the adoption of an act, the following procedure shall apply.

2. The Commission shall submit a proposal to the European Parliament and the Council.

The Council, acting by a qualified majority after obtaining the opinion of the European Parliament,
- — if it approves all the amendments contained in the European Parliament's opinion, may adopt the proposed act thus amended;

— if the European Parliament does not propose any amendments, may adopt the proposed act;

— shall otherwise adopt a common position and communicate it to the European Parliament. The Council shall inform the European Parliament fully of the reasons which led it to adopt its common position. The Commission shall inform the European Parliament fully of its position.

If, within three months of such communication, the European Parliament:

(a) approves the common position or has not taken a decision, the act in question shall be deemed to have been adopted in accordance with that common position;

(b) rejects, by an absolute majority of its component members, the common position, the proposed act shall be deemed not to have been adopted;

(c) proposes amendments to the common position by an absolute majority of its component members, the amended text shall be forwarded to the Council and to the Commission, which shall deliver an opinion on those amendments.

3.   If, within three months of the matter being referred to it, the Council, acting by a qualified majority, approves all the amendments of the European Parliament, the act in question shall be deemed to have been adopted in the form of the common position thus amended; however, the Council shall act unanimously on the amendments on which the Commission has delivered a negative opinion. If the Council does not approve all the amendments, the President of the Council, in agreement with the President of the European Parliament, shall within six weeks convene a meeting of the Conciliation Committee.

4.   The Conciliation Committee, which shall be composed of the members of the Council or their representatives and an equal number of representatives of the European Parliament, shall have the task of reaching agreement on a joint text, by a qualified majority of the members of the Council or their representatives and by a majority of the representatives of the European Parliament. The Commission shall take part in the Conciliation Committee's proceedings and shall take all the necessary initiatives with a view to reconciling the positions of the European Parliament and the Council. In fulfilling this task, the Conciliation Committee shall address the common position on the basis of the amendments proposed by the European Parliament.

5.   If, within six weeks of its being convened, the Conciliation Committee approves a joint text, the European Parliament, acting by an absolute majority of the votes cast, and the Council, acting by a qualified majority, shall have a period of six weeks from that approval in which to adopt the act in question in accordance with the joint text. If either of the two institutions fails to approve the proposed act, it shall be deemed not to have been adopted.

6.   Where the Conciliation Committee does not approve a joint text, the proposed act shall be deemed not to have been adopted.

7.   The periods of three months and six weeks referred to in this Article may be extended by a maximum of one month and two weeks respectively at the initiative of the European Parliament or the Council.

Article 252

Where reference is made in this Treaty to this Article for the adoption of an act, the following procedure shall apply:

(a) The Council, acting by a qualified majority on a proposal from the Commission and after obtaining the Opinion of the European Parliament, shall adopt a common position.

(b) The Council's common position shall be communicated to the European Parliament. The Council and the Commission shall inform the European Parliament fully of the reasons which led the Council to adopt its common position and also of the Commission's position.

If, within three months of such communication, the European Parliament approves this common position or has not taken a decision within that period, the Council shall definitively adopt the act in question in accordance with the common position.

    (c) The European Parliament may, within the period of three months referred to in point (b), by an absolute majority of its component Members, propose amendments to the Council's common position.

The European Parliament may also, by the same majority, reject the Council's common position. The result of the proceedings shall be transmitted to the Council and the Commission.

If the European Parliament has rejected the Council's common position, unanimity shall be required for the Council to act on a second reading.

    (d) The Commission shall, within a period of one month, re-examine the proposal on the basis of which the Council adopted its common position, by taking into account the amendments proposed by the European Parliament.

The Commission shall forward to the Council, at the same time as its re-examined proposal, the amendments of the European Parliament which it has not accepted, and shall express its opinion on them. The Council may adopt these amendments unanimously.

    (e) The Council, acting by a qualified majority, shall adopt the proposal as re-examined by the Commission.

Unanimity shall be required for the Council to amend the proposal as re-examined by the Commission.

    (f) In the cases referred to in points (c), (d) and (e), the Council shall be required to act within a period of three months. If no decision is taken within this period, the Commission proposal shall be deemed not to have been adopted.

    (g) The periods referred to in points (b) and (f) may be extended by a maximum of one month by common accord between the Council and the European Parliament.

*****

PART SIX   (GENERAL AND FINAL PROVISIONS)

*****

Article 308

If action by the Community should prove necessary to attain, in the course of the operation of the common market, one of the objectives of the Community and this Treaty has not provided the necessary powers, the Council shall, acting unanimously on a proposal from the Commission and after consulting the European Parliament, take the appropriate measures.

*****

Article 311

The Protocols annexed to this Treaty by common accord of the Member States shall form an integral part thereof.

Article 312

This Treaty is concluded for an unlimited period.

Treaty on European Union

ADOPTED BY THE EU MEMBER STATES

(Done at Maastricht) 7 February 1992

Entry into force: 1 November 1993. The text is printed as amended by the Nice Treaty.

TITLE I   COMMON PROVISIONS

Article 1

By this Treaty, the HIGH CONTRACTING PARTIES establish among themselves a EUROPEAN UNION, hereinafter called the Union.

This Treaty marks a new stage in the process of creating an ever closer union among the peoples of Europe, in which decisions are taken as openly as possible and as closely as possible to the citizen.

The Union shall be founded on the European Communities, supplemented by the policies and forms of co-operation established by this Treaty. Its task shall be to organise, in a manner demonstrating consistency and solidarity, relations between the Member States and between their peoples.

Article 2

The Union shall set itself the following objectives:

— to promote economic and social progress and a high level of employment and to achieve balanced and sustainable development, in particular through the creation of an area without internal frontiers, through the strengthening of economic and social cohesion and through the establishment of economic and monetary union, ultimately including a single currency in accordance with the provisions of this Treaty;

— to assert its identity on the international scene, in particular through the implementation of a common foreign and security policy including the framing of a common defence policy, which might in time lead to a common defence in accordance with the provisions of Article 17;

— to strengthen the protection of the rights and interests of the nationals of its Member States through the introduction of a citizenship of the Union;

— to maintain and develop the Union as an area of freedom, security and justice, in which the free movement of persons is assured in conjunction with appropriate measures with respect to external border controls, asylum, immigration and the prevention and combating of crime;

— to maintain in full the *"acquis communautaire"* and build on it with a view to considering to what extent the policies and forms of co-operation introduced by this Treaty may need to be revised with the aim of ensuring the effectiveness of the mechanisms and the institutions of the Community.

The objectives of the Union shall be achieved as provided in this Treaty and in accordance with the conditions and the timetable set out therein while respecting the principle of subsidiarity as defined in Article 5 of the Treaty establishing the European Community.

Article 3

The Union shall be served by a single institutional framework which shall ensure the consistency and the continuity of the activities carried out in order to attain its objectives while respecting and building upon the *"acquis communautaire"*.

The Union shall in particular ensure the consistency of its external activities as a whole in the context of its external relations, security, economic and development policies. The Council and the Commission shall be responsible for ensuring such consistency and shall co-operate to this end. They shall ensure the implementation of these policies, each in accordance with its respective powers.

Article 4

The European Council shall provide the Union with the necessary impetus for its development and shall define the general political guidelines thereof.

The European Council shall bring together the Heads of State or of Government of the Member States and the President of the Commission.

They shall be assisted by the Ministers for Foreign Affairs of the Member States and by a Member of the Commission. The European Council shall meet at least twice a year, under the chairmanship of the Head of State or of Government of the Member State which holds the Presidency of the Council.

The European Council shall submit to the European Parliament a report after each of its meetings and a yearly written report on the progress achieved by the Union.

Article 5

The European Parliament, the Council, the Commission, the Court of Justice and the Court of Auditors shall exercise their powers under the conditions and for the purposes provided for, on the one hand, by the provisions of the Treaties establishing the European Communities and of the subsequent Treaties and Acts modifying and supplementing them and, on the other hand, by the other provisions of this Treaty.

Article 6

1. The Union is founded on the principles of liberty, democracy, respect for human rights and fundamental freedoms and the rule of law, principles which are common to Member States.

2. The Union shall respect fundamental rights, as guaranteed by the European Convention for the Protection of Human Rights and Fundamental Freedoms signed in Rome on 4 November 1950 and as they result from the constitutional traditions common to the Member States, as general principles of Community law.

3. The Union shall respect the national identities of its Member States.

4. The Union shall provide itself with the means necessary to attain its objectives and carry through its policies.

*****

TITLE VI   PROVISIONS ON POLICE AND JUDICIAL COOPERATION IN CRIMINAL MATTERS

Article 29

Without prejudice to the powers of the European Community, the Union's objective shall be to provide citizens with a high level of safety within an area of freedom, security and justice by developing common action among the Member States in the fields of police and judicial cooperation in criminal matters and by preventing and combating racism and xenophobia.

That objective shall be achieved by preventing and combating crime, organised or other-wise, in particular terrorism, trafficking in persons and offences against children, illicit drug trafficking and illicit arms trafficking, corruption and fraud, through:

— closer cooperation between police forces, customs authorities and other competent authorities in the Member States, both directly and through the European Police Office (Europol), in accordance with the provisions of Articles 30 and 32;

— closer cooperation between judicial and other competent authorities of the Member States [including cooperation through the European Judicial Co-operation Unit ('Eurojust') in accordance with the provisions of Articles 31 and 32].

— approximation, where necessary, of rules on criminal matters in the Member States, in accordance with the provisions of Article 31(e).

Article 30

1. Common action in the field of police cooperation shall include:
    (a) operational cooperation between the competent authorities, including the police, customs and other specialised law enforcement services of the Member States in relation to the prevention, detection and investigation of criminal offences;
    (b) the collection, storage, processing, analysis and exchange of relevant information, including information held by law enforcement services on reports on suspicious financial transactions, in particular through Europol, subject to appropriate provisions on the protection of personal data;
    (c) cooperation and joint initiatives in training, the exchange of liaison officers, secondments, the use of equipment, and forensic research;
    (d) the common evaluation of particular investigative techniques in relation to the detection of serious forms of organised crime.

2. The Council shall promote cooperation through Europol and shall in particular, within a period of five years after the date of entry into force of the Treaty of Amsterdam:
    (a) enable Europol to facilitate and support the preparation, and to encourage the coordination and carrying out, of specific investigative actions by the competent authorities of the Member States, including operational actions of joint teams comprising representatives of Europol in a support capacity;
    (b) adopt measures allowing Europol to ask the competent authorities of the Member States to conduct and coordinate their investigations in specific cases and to develop specific expertise which may be put at the disposal of Member States to assist them in investigating cases of organised crime;
    (c) promote liaison arrangements between prosecuting/investigating officials specialising in the fight against organised crime in close cooperation with Europol;
    (d) establish a research, documentation and statistical network on cross-border crime.

*****

European Union Charter of Fundamental Rights (2000)

Preamble

The peoples of Europe, in creating an ever closer union among them, are resolved to share a peaceful future based on common values.

Conscious of its spiritual and moral heritage, the Union is founded on the indivisible, universal values of human dignity, freedom, equality and solidarity; it is based on the principles of democracy and the rule of law. It places the individual at the heart of its activities, by establishing the citizenship of the Union and by creating an area of freedom, security and justice.

The Union contributes to the preservation and to the development of these common values while respecting the diversity of the cultures and traditions of the peoples of Europe as well as the national identities of the Member States and the organisation of their public authorities at national, regional and local levels; it seeks to promote balanced and sustainable development and ensures free movement of persons, goods, services and capital, and the freedom of establishment.

To this end, it is necessary to strengthen the protection of fundamental rights in the light of changes in society, social progress and scientific and technological developments by making those rights more visible in a Charter.

This Charter reaffirms, with due regard for the powers and tasks of the Community and the Union and the principle of subsidiarity, the rights as they result, in particular, from the constitutional traditions and international obligations common to the Member States, the Treaty on European Union, the Community Treaties, the European Convention for the Protection of Human Rights and Fundamental Freedoms, the Social Charters adopted by the Community and by the Council of Europe and the case law of the Court of Justice of the European Communities and of the European Court of Human Rights.

Enjoyment of these rights entails responsibilities and duties with regard to other persons, to the human community and to future generations.

The Union therefore recognises the rights, freedoms and principles set out hereafter.

CHAPTER I   DIGNITY

Article 1   Human dignity
Human dignity is inviolable. It must be respected and protected.

Article 2   Right to life
1.   Everyone has the right to life.
2.   No one shall be condemned to the death penalty, or executed.

Article 3   Right to the integrity of the person
1.   Everyone has the right to respect for his or her physical and mental integrity.
2.   In the fields of medicine and biology, the following must be respected in particular:
   •   the free and informed consent of the person concerned, according to the procedures laid down by law,
   •   the prohibition of eugenic practices, in particular those aiming at the selection of persons,
   •   the prohibition on making the human body and its parts as such a source of financial gain,
   •   the prohibition of the reproductive cloning of human beings.

Article 4   Prohibition of torture and inhuman or degrading treatment or punishment
No one shall be subjected to torture or to inhuman or degrading treatment or punishment.

Article 5   Prohibition of slavery and forced labour
1.   No one shall be held in slavery or servitude.
2.   No one shall be required to perform forced or compulsory labour.
3.   Trafficking in human beings is prohibited.

CHAPTER II   FREEDOMS

Article 6   Right to liberty and security
Everyone has the right to liberty and security of person.

Article 7   Respect for private and family life
Everyone has the right to respect for his or her private and family life, home and communications.

Article 8   Protection of personal data

1. Everyone has the right to the protection of personal data concerning him or her.

2. Such data must be processed fairly for specified purposes and on the basis of the consent of the person concerned or some other legitimate basis laid down by law. Everyone has the right of access to data which has been collected concerning him or her, and the right to have it rectified.

3. Compliance with these rules shall be subject to control by an independent authority.

Article 9   Right to marry and right to found a family

The right to marry and the right to found a family shall be guaranteed in accordance with the national laws governing the exercise of these rights.

Article 10   Freedom of thought, conscience and religion

1. Everyone has the right to freedom of thought, conscience and religion. This right includes freedom to change religion or belief and freedom, either alone or in community with others and in public or in private, to manifest religion or belief, in worship, teaching, practice and observance.

2. The right to conscientious objection is recognised, in accordance with the national laws governing the exercise of this right.

Article 11   Freedom of expression and information

1. Everyone has the right to freedom of expression. This right shall include freedom to hold opinions and to receive and impart information and ideas without interference by public authority and regardless of frontiers.

2. The freedom and pluralism of the media shall be respected.

Article 12   Freedom of assembly and of association

1. Everyone has the right to freedom of peaceful assembly and to freedom of association at all levels, in particular in political, trade union and civic matters, which implies the right of everyone to form and to join trade unions for the protection of his or her interests.

2. Political parties at Union level contribute to expressing the political will of the citizens of the Union.

Article 13   Freedom of the arts and sciences

The arts and scientific research shall be free of constraint. Academic freedom shall be respected.

Article 14   Right to education

1. Everyone has the right to education and to have access to vocational and continuing training.

2. This right includes the possibility to receive free compulsory education.

3. The freedom to found educational establishments with due respect for democratic principles and the right of parents to ensure the education and teaching of their children in conformity with their religious, philosophical and pedagogical convictions shall be respected, in accordance with the national laws governing the exercise of such freedom and right.

Article 15   Freedom to choose an occupation and right to engage in work

1. Everyone has the right to engage in work and to pursue a freely chosen or accepted occupation.

2. Every citizen of the Union has the freedom to seek employment, to work, to exercise the right of establishment and to provide services in any Member State.

3. Nationals of third countries who are authorised to work in the territories of the Member States are entitled to working conditions equivalent to those of citizens of the Union.

Article 16   Freedom to conduct a business
The freedom to conduct a business in accordance with Community law and national laws and practices is recognised.

Article 17   Right to property
1. Everyone has the right to own, use, dispose of and bequeath his or her lawfully acquired possessions. No one may be deprived of his or her possessions, except in the public interest and in the cases and under the conditions provided for by law, subject to fair compensation being paid in good time for their loss. The use of property may be regulated by law insofar as is necessary for the general interest.
2. Intellectual property shall be protected.

Article 18   Right to asylum
The right to asylum shall be guaranteed with due respect for the rules of the Geneva Convention of 28 July 1951 and the Protocol of 31 January 1967 relating to the status of refugees and in accordance with the Treaty establishing the European Community.

Article 19   Protection in the event of removal, expulsion or extradition
1. Collective expulsions are prohibited.
2. No one may be removed, expelled or extradited to a State where there is a serious risk that he or she would be subjected to the death penalty, torture or other inhuman or degrading treatment or punishment.

CHAPTER III   EQUALITY

Article 20   Equality before the law
Everyone is equal before the law.

Article 21   Non-discrimination
1. Any discrimination based on any ground such as sex, race, colour, ethnic or social origin, genetic features, language, religion or belief, political or any other opinion, membership of a national minority, property, birth, disability, age or sexual orientation shall be prohibited.
2. Within the scope of application of the Treaty establishing the European Community and of the Treaty on European Union, and without prejudice to the special provisions of those Treaties, any discrimination on grounds of nationality shall be prohibited.

Article 22   Cultural, religious and linguistic diversity
The Union shall respect cultural, religious and linguistic diversity.

Article 23   Equality between men and women
Equality between men and women must be ensured in all areas, including employment, work and pay.

The principle of equality shall not prevent the maintenance or adoption of measures providing for specific advantages in favour of the under-represented sex.

Article 24   The rights of the child
1. Children shall have the right to such protection and care as is necessary for their well-being. They may express their views freely. Such views shall be taken into consideration on matters which concern them in accordance with their age and maturity.
2. In all actions relating to children, whether taken by public authorities or private institutions, the child's best interests must be a primary consideration.
3. Every child shall have the right to maintain on a regular basis a personal relationship and direct contact with both his or her parents, unless that is contrary to his or her interests.

Article 25   **The rights of the elderly**
The Union recognises and respects the rights of the elderly to lead a life of dignity and independence and to participate in social and cultural life.

Article 26   **Integration of persons with disabilities**
The Union recognises and respects the right of persons with disabilities to benefit from measures designed to ensure their independence, social and occupational integration and participation in the life of the community.

CHAPTER IV   SOLIDARITY

Article 27   **Workers' right to information and consultation within the undertaking**
Workers or their representatives must, at the appropriate levels, be guaranteed information and consultation in good time in the cases and under the conditions provided for by Community law and national laws and practices.

Article 28   **Right of collective bargaining and action**
Workers and employers, or their respective organisations, have, in accordance with Community law and national laws and practices, the right to negotiate and conclude collective agreements at the appropriate levels and, in cases of conflicts of interest, to take collective action to defend their interests, including strike action.

Article 29   **Right of access to placement services**
Everyone has the right of access to a free placement service.

Article 30   **Protection in the event of unjustified dismissal**
Every worker has the right to protection against unjustified dismissal, in accordance with Community law and national laws and practices.

Article 31   **Fair and just working conditions**
   1.   Every worker has the right to working conditions which respect his or her health, safety and dignity.
   2.   Every worker has the right to limitation of maximum working hours, to daily and weekly rest periods and to an annual period of paid leave.

Article 32   **Prohibition of child labour and protection of young people at work**
The employment of children is prohibited. The minimum age of admission to employment may not be lower than the minimum school-leaving age, without prejudice to such rules as may be more favourable to young people and except for limited derogations.
   Young people admitted to work must have working conditions appropriate to their age and be protected against economic exploitation and any work likely to harm their safety, health or physical, mental, moral or social development or to interfere with their education.

Article 33   **Family and professional life**
   1.   The family shall enjoy legal, economic and social protection.
   2.   To reconcile family and professional life, everyone shall have the right to protection from dismissal for a reason connected with maternity and the right to paid maternity leave and to parental leave following the birth or adoption of a child.

Article 34   **Social security and social assistance**
   1.   The Union recognises and respects the entitlement to social security benefits and social services providing protection in cases such as maternity, illness, industrial accidents, dependency or old age, and in the case of loss of employment, in accordance with the procedures laid down by Community law and national laws and practices.

2.   Everyone residing and moving legally within the European Union is entitled to social security benefits and social advantages in accordance with Community law and national laws and practices.

3.   In order to combat social exclusion and poverty, the Union recognises and respects the right to social and housing assistance so as to ensure a decent existence for all those who lack sufficient resources, in accordance with the procedures laid down by Community law and national laws and practices.

Article 35   Health care
Everyone has the right of access to preventive health care and the right to benefit from medical treatment under the conditions established by national laws and practices. A high level of human health protection shall be ensured in the definition and implementation of all Union policies and activities.

Article 36   Access to services of general economic interest
The Union recognises and respects access to services of general economic interest as provided for in national laws and practices, in accordance with the Treaty establishing the European Community, in order to promote the social and territorial cohesion of the Union.

Article 37   Environmental protection
A high level of environmental protection and the improvement of the quality of the environment must be integrated into the polices of the Union and ensured in accordance with the principle of sustainable development.

Article 38   Consumer protection
Union policies shall ensure a high level of consumer protection.

CHAPTER V   CITIZEN'S RIGHTS

Article 39   Right to vote and to stand as a candidate at elections to the European Parliament
1.   Every citizen of the Union has the right to vote and to stand as a candidate at elections to the European Parliament in the Member State in which he or she resides, under the same conditions as nationals of that State.

2.   Members of the European Parliament shall be elected by direct universal suffrage in a free and secret ballot.

Article 40   Right to vote and to stand as a candidate at municipal elections
Every citizen of the Union has the right to vote and to stand as a candidate at municipal elections in the Member State in which he or she resides under the same conditions as nationals of that State.

Article 41   Right to good administration
1.   Every person has the right to have his or her affairs handled impartially, fairly and within a reasonable time by the institutions and bodies of the Union.

2.   This right includes:
   - the right of every person to be heard, before any individual measure which would affect him or her adversely is taken;
   - the right of every person to have access to his or her file, while respecting the legitimate interests of confidentiality and of professional and business secrecy;
   - the obligation of the administration to give reasons for its decisions.

3.   Every person has the right to have the Community make good any damage caused by its institutions or by its servants in the performance of their duties, in accordance with the general principles common to the laws of the Member States.

4.   Every person may write to the institutions of the Union in one of the languages of the Treaties and must have an answer in the same language.

Article 42   Right of access to documents

Any citizen of the Union, and any natural or legal person residing or having its registered office in a Member State, has a right of access to European Parliament, Council and Commission documents.

Article 43   Ombudsman

Any citizen of the Union and any natural or legal person residing or having its registered office in a Member State has the right to refer to the Ombudsman of the Union cases of maladministration in the activities of the Community institutions or bodies, with the exception of the Court of Justice and the Court of First Instance acting in their judicial role.

Article 44   Right to petition

Any citizen of the Union and any natural or legal person residing or having its registered office in a Member State has the right to petition the European Parliament.

Article 45   Freedom of movement and of residence

1.   Every citizen of the Union has the right to move and reside freely within the territory of the Member States.

2.   Freedom of movement and residence may be granted, in accordance with the Treaty establishing the European Community, to nationals of third countries legally resident in the territory of a Member State.

Article 46   Diplomatic and consular protection

Every citizen of the Union shall, in the territory of a third country in which the Member State of which he or she is a national is not represented, be entitled to protection by the diplomatic or consular authorities of any Member State, on the same conditions as the nationals of that Member State.

CHAPTER VI   JUSTICE

Article 47   Right to an effective remedy and to a fair trial

Everyone whose rights and freedoms guaranteed by the law of the Union are violated has the right to an effective remedy before a tribunal in compliance with the conditions laid down in this Article. Everyone is entitled to a fair and public hearing within a reasonable time by an independent and impartial tribunal previously established by law. Everyone shall have the possibility of being advised, defended and represented.

Legal aid shall be made available to those who lack sufficient resources insofar as such aid is necessary to ensure effective access to justice.

Article 48   Presumption of innocence and right of defence

1.   Everyone who has been charged shall be presumed innocent until proved guilty according to law.

2.   Respect for the rights of the defence of anyone who has been charged shall be guaranteed.

Article 49   Principles of legality and proportionality of criminal offences and penalties

1.   No one shall be held guilty of any criminal offence on account of any act or omission which did not constitute a criminal offence under national law or international law at the time when it was committed. Nor shall a heavier penalty be imposed than that which was applicable at the time the criminal offence was committed. If, subsequent to the

commission of a criminal offence, the law provides for a lighter penalty, that penalty shall be applicable.

2.   This Article shall not prejudice the trial and punishment of any person for any act or omission which, at the time when it was committed, was criminal according to the general principles recognised by the community of nations.

3.   The severity of penalties must not be disproportionate to the criminal offence.

Article 50   Right not to be tried or punished twice in criminal proceedings for the same criminal offence

No one shall be liable to be tried or punished again in criminal proceedings for an offence for which he or she has already been finally acquitted or convicted within the Union in accordance with the Law.

CHAPTER VII   GENERAL PROVISIONS

Article 51   Scope

1.   The provisions of this Charter are addressed to the institutions and bodies of the Union with due regard for the principle of subsidiarity and to the Member States only when they are implementing Union law. They shall therefore respect the rights, observe the principles and promote the application thereof in accordance with their respective powers.

2.   This Charter does not establish any new power or task for the Community or the Union, or modify powers and tasks defined by the Treaties.

Article 52   Scope of guaranteed rights

1.   Any limitation on the exercise of the rights and freedoms recognised by this Charter must be provided for by law and respect the essence of those rights and freedoms. Subject to the principle of proportionality, limitations may be made only if they are necessary and genuinely meet objectives of general interest recognized by the Union or the need to protect the rights and freedoms of others.

2.   Rights recognised by this Charter which are based on the Community Treaties or the Treaty on European Union shall be exercised under the conditions and within the limits defined by those Treaties.

3.   Insofar as this Charter contains rights which correspond to rights guaranteed by the Convention for the Protection of Human Rights and Fundamental Freedoms, the meaning and scope of those rights shall be the same as those laid down by the said Convention. This provision shall not prevent Union law providing more extensive protection.

Article 53   Level of protection

Nothing in this Charter shall be interpreted as restricting or adversely affecting human rights and fundamental freedoms as recognised, in their respective fields of application, by Union law and international law and by international agreements to which the Union, the Community or all the Member States are party, including the European Convention for the Protection of Human Rights and Fundamental Freedoms, and by the Member States' constitutions.

Article 54   Prohibition of abuse of rights

Nothing in this Charter shall be interpreted as implying any right to engage in any activity or to perform any act aimed at the destruction of any of the rights and freedoms recognised in this Charter or at their limitation to a greater extent than is provided for herein.

Police and Criminal Evidence Act 1984 Revised Codes of Practice A–C

Note: For the legal status of the Codes and other issues relating to them, see ss. 66 and 67 of the Police and Criminal Evidence Act 1984 (*supra*). The Codes have been revised on a number of occasions in accordance with s. 67(7) of the Act. The most recent revised version of each Code, which in each case came into force on 1 April 2003, is printed below (except for Codes D and E which are not reproduced). The Codes apply only to England and Wales.

Code A   Code of Practice for the Exercise by Police Officers of Statutory Powers of Stop and Search

General
This code of practice must be readily available at all police stations for consultation by police officers, detained persons and members of the public.

The notes for guidance included are not provisions of this code, but are guidance to police officers and others about its application and interpretation. Provisions in the annexes to the code are provisions of this code.
*****

1   Principles governing stop and search
1.1   Powers to stop and search must be used fairly, responsibly, with respect for people being searched and without unlawful discrimination. The Race Relations (Amendment) Act 2000 makes it unlawful for police officers to discriminate on the grounds of race, colour, ethnic origin, nationality or national origins when using their powers.

1.2   The intrusion on the liberty of the person stopped or searched must be brief and detention for the purposes of a search must take place at or near the location of the stop.

1.3   If these fundamental principles are not observed the use of powers to stop and search may be drawn into question. Failure to use the powers in the proper manner reduces their effectiveness. Stop and search can play an important role in the detection and prevention of crime, and using the powers fairly makes them more effective.

1.4   The primary purpose of stop and search powers is to enable officers to allay or confirm suspicions about individuals without exercising their power of arrest. Officers may be required to justify the use or authorisation of such powers, in relation both to individual searches and the overall pattern of their activity in this regard, to their supervisory officers or in court. Any misuse of the powers is likely to be harmful to policing and lead to mistrust of the police. Officers must also be able to explain their actions to the member of the public searched. The misuse of these powers can lead to disciplinary action.

1.5   An officer must not search a person, even with his or her consent, where no power to search is applicable. Even where a person is prepared to submit to a search voluntarily, the person must not be searched unless the necessary legal power exists, and the search must be in accordance with the relevant power and the provisions of this Code. The only exception, where an officer does not require a specific power, applies to searches of persons entering sports grounds or other premises carried out with their consent given as a condition of entry.

2   Explanation of powers to stop and search
2.1   This code applies to powers of stop and search as follows:
(a) powers which require reasonable grounds for suspicion, before they may be exer-

cised; that articles unlawfully obtained or possessed are being carried, or under section 43 of the Terrorism Act 2000 that a person is a terrorist;

(b) authorised under section 60 of the Criminal Justice and Public Order Act 1994, based upon a reasonable belief that incidents involving serious violence may take place or that people are carrying dangerous instruments or offensive weapons within any locality in the police area;

(c) authorised under section 44(1) and (2) of the Terrorism Act 2000 based upon a consideration that the exercise of one or both powers is expedient for the prevention of acts of terrorism;

(d) powers to search a person who has not been arrested in the exercise of a power to search premises (see Code B paragraph 1.3a).

Searches requiring reasonable grounds for suspicion

2.2   Reasonable grounds for suspicion depend on the circumstances in each case. There must be an objective basis for that suspicion based on facts, information, and/or intelligence which are relevant to the likelihood of finding an article of a certain kind or, in the case of searches under section 43 of the Terrorism Act 2000, to the likelihood that the person is a terrorist. Reasonable suspicion can never be supported on the basis of personal factors alone without reliable supporting intelligence or information or some specific behaviour by the person concerned. For example, a person's race, age, appearance, or the fact that the person is known to have a previous conviction, cannot be used alone or in combination with each other as the reason for searching that person. Reasonable suspicion cannot be based on generalisations or stereotypical images of certain groups or categories of people as more likely to be involved in criminal activity.

2.3   Reasonable suspicion can sometimes exist without specific information or intelligence and on the basis of some level of generalisation stemming from the behaviour of a person. For example, if an officer encounters someone on the street at night who is obviously trying to hide something, the officer may (depending on the other surrounding circumstances) base such suspicion on the fact that this kind of behaviour is often linked to stolen or prohibited articles being carried. Similarly, for the purposes of section 43 of the Terrorism Act 2000, suspicion that a person is a terrorist may arise from the person's behaviour at or near a location which has been identified as a potential target for terrorists.

2.4   However, reasonable suspicion should normally be linked to accurate and current intelligence or information, such as information describing an article being carried, a suspected offender, or a person who has been seen carrying a type of article known to have been stolen recently from premises in the area. Searches based on accurate and current intelligence or information are more likely to be effective. Targeting searches in a particular area at specified crime problems increases their effectiveness and minimises inconvenience to law-abiding members of the public. It also helps in justifying the use of searches both to those who are searched and to the general public. This does not however prevent stop and search powers being exercised in other locations where such powers may be exercised and reasonable suspicion exists.

2.5   Searches are more likely to be effective, legitimate, and secure public confidence when reasonable suspicion is based on a range of factors. The overall use of these powers is more likely to be effective when up to date and accurate intelligence or information is communicated to officers and they are well-informed about local crime patterns.

2.6   Where there is reliable information or intelligence that members of a group or gang habitually carry knives unlawfully or weapons or controlled drugs, and wear a distinctive item of clothing or other means of identification to indicate their membership of the group or gang, that distinctive item of clothing or other means of identification may provide reasonable grounds to stop and search a person. [See *Note 9*]

2.7   A police officer may have reasonable grounds to suspect that a person is in innocent possession of a stolen or prohibited article or other item for which he or she is empowered to search. In that case the officer may stop and search the person even though there would be no power of arrest.

2.8   Under section 43(1) of the Terrorism Act 2000 a constable may stop and search a person whom the officer reasonably suspects to be a terrorist to discover whether the person is in possession of anything which may constitute evidence that the person is a terrorist. These searches may only be carried out by an officer of the same sex as the person searched.

2.9   An officer who has reasonable grounds for suspicion may detain the person concerned in order to carry out a search. Before carrying out a search the officer may ask questions about the person's behaviour or presence in circumstances which gave rise to the suspicion. As a result of questioning the detained person, the reasonable grounds for suspicion necessary to detain that person may be confirmed or, because of a satisfactory explanation, be eliminated. [See *Notes 2* and *3*] Questioning may also reveal reasonable grounds to suspect the possession of a different kind of unlawful article from that originally suspected. Reasonable grounds for suspicion however cannot be provided retrospectively by such questioning during a person's detention or by refusal to answer any questions put.

2.10   If, as a result of questioning before a search, or other circumstances which come to the attention of the officer, there cease to be reasonable grounds for suspecting that an article is being carried of a kind for which there is a power to stop and search, no search may take place. [See *Note 3*] In the absence of any other lawful power to detain, the person is free to leave at will and must be so informed.

2.11   There is no power to stop or detain a person in order to find grounds for a search. Police officers have many encounters with members of the public which do not involve detaining people against their will. If reasonable grounds for suspicion emerge during such an encounter, the officer may search the person, even though no grounds existed when the encounter began. If an officer is detaining someone for the purpose of a search, he or she should inform the person as soon as detention begins.

2.12–2.26   *****

Powers to search in the exercise of a power to search premises

2.27   The following powers to search premises also authorise the search of a person, not under arrest, who is found on the premises during the course of the search:

(a)   section 139B of the Criminal Justice Act 1988 under which a constable may enter school premises and search the premises and any person on those premises for any bladed or pointed article or offensive weapon; and

(b)   under a warrant issued under section s. 23(3) of the Misuse of Drugs Act 1971 to search premises for drugs or documents but only if the warrant specifically authorises the search of persons found on the premises.

2.28   Before the power under section 139B of the Criminal Justice Act 1988 may be exercised, the constable must have reasonable grounds to believe that an offence under section 139A of the Criminal Justice Act 1988 (having a bladed or pointed article or offensive weapon on school premises) has been or is being committed. A warrant to search premises and persons found therein may be issued under section s. 23(3) of the Misuse of Drugs Act 1971 if there are reasonable grounds to suspect that controlled drugs or certain documents are in the possession of a person on the premises.

2.29   The powers in paragraph 2.27(a) or (b) do not require prior specific grounds to suspect that the person to be searched is in possession of an item for which there is an existing power to search. However, it is still necessary to ensure that the selection and treatment of those searched under these powers is based upon objective factors connected with the search of the premises, and not upon personal prejudice.

3 Conduct of searches

3.1 All stops and searches must be carried out with courtesy, consideration and respect for the person concerned. This has a significant impact on public confidence in the police. Every reasonable effort must be made to minimise the embarrassment that a person being searched may experience. [See *Note 4*]

3.2 The co-operation of the person to be searched must be sought in every case, even if the person initially objects to the search. A forcible search may be made only if it has been established that the person is unwilling to co-operate or resists. Reasonable force may be used as a last resort if necessary to conduct a search or to detain a person or vehicle for the purposes of a search.

3.3 The length of time for which a person or vehicle may be detained must be reasonable and kept to a minimum. Where the exercise of the power requires reasonable suspicion, the thoroughness and extent of a search must depend on what is suspected of being carried, and by whom. If the suspicion relates to a particular article which is seen to be slipped into a person's pocket, then, in the absence of other grounds for suspicion or an opportunity for the article to be moved elsewhere, the search must be confined to that pocket. In the case of a small article which can readily be concealed, such as a drug, and which might be concealed anywhere on the person, a more extensive search may be necessary. In the case of searches mentioned in paragraph 2.1(b), (c), and (d), which do not require reasonable grounds for suspicion, officers may make any reasonable search to look for items for which they are empowered to search. [See *Note 5*]

3.4 The search must be carried out at or near the place where the person or vehicle was first detained. [See *Note 6*]

3.5 There is no power to require a person to remove any clothing in public other than an outer coat, jacket or gloves except under section 45(3) of the Terrorism Act 2000 (which empowers a constable conducting a search under section 44(1) or 44(2) of that Act to require a person to remove headgear and footwear in public) and under section 60AA of the Criminal Justice and Public Order Act 1994 (which empowers a constable to require a person to remove any item worn to conceal identity). [See *Notes 4* and *6*] A search in public of a person's clothing which has not been removed must be restricted to superficial examination of outer garments. This does not, however, prevent an officer from placing his or her hand inside the pockets of the outer clothing, or feeling round the inside of collars, socks and shoes if this is reasonably necessary in the circumstances to look for the object of the search or to remove and examine any item reasonably suspected to be the object of the search. For the same reasons, subject to the restrictions on the removal of headgear, a person's hair may also be searched in public (see paragraphs 3.1 and 3.3).

3.6 Where on reasonable grounds it is considered necessary to conduct a more thorough search (e.g. by requiring a person to take off a T-shirt), this must be done out of public view, for example, in a police van unless paragraph 3.7 applies, or police station if there is one nearby. [See *Note 6*] Any search involving the removal of more than an outer coat, jacket, gloves, headgear or footwear, or any other item concealing identity, may only be made by an officer of the same sex as the person searched and may not be made in the presence of anyone of the opposite sex unless the person being searched specifically requests it. [See *Notes 4, 7* and *8*]

3.7 Searches involving exposure of intimate parts of the body must not be conducted as a routine extension of a less thorough search, simply because nothing is found in the course of the initial search. Searches involving exposure of intimate parts of the body may be carried out only at a nearby police station or other nearby location which is out of public view (but not a police vehicle). These searches must be conducted in accordance with paragraph 11 of Annex A to Code C except that an intimate search mentioned in paragraph 11(f) of Annex A to Code C may not be authorised or carried out under any stop and search powers. The other provisions of Code C do not apply to the conduct and recording of searches of persons detained at police stations in the exercise of stop and search powers. [See *Note 7*]

Steps to be taken prior to a search

3.8   Before any search of a detained person or attended vehicle takes place the officer must take reasonable steps to give the person to be searched or in charge of the vehicle the following information:

(a) that they are being detained for the purposes of a search;

(b) the officer's name (except in the case of enquiries linked to the investigation of terrorism, or otherwise where the officer reasonably believes that giving his or her name might put him or her in danger, in which case a warrant or other identification number shall be given) and the name of the police station to which the officer is attached;

(c) the legal search power which is being exercised; and

(d) a clear explanation of:

(i) the purpose of the search in terms of the article or articles for which there is a power to search; and

(ii) in the case of powers requiring reasonable suspicion (see paragraph 2.1(a)), the grounds for that suspicion; or

(iii) in the case of powers which do not require reasonable suspicion (see paragraph 2.1(b), and (c)), the nature of the power and of any necessary authorisation and the fact that it has been given.

3.9   Officers not in uniform must show their warrant cards. Stops and searches under the power mentioned in paragraphs 2.1(b), and (c) may be undertaken only by a constable in uniform.

3.10   Before the search takes place the officer must inform the person (or the owner or person in charge of the vehicle that is to be searched) of his or her entitlement to a copy of the record of the search, including his entitlement to a record of the search if an application is made within 12 months, if it is wholly impracticable to make a record at the time. If a record is not made at the time the person should also be told how a copy can be obtained (see section 4). The person should also be given information about police powers to stop and search and the individual's rights in these circumstances.

3.11   If the person to be searched, or in charge of a vehicle to be searched, does not appear to understand what is being said, or there is any doubt about the person's ability to understand English, the officer must take reasonable steps to bring information regarding the person's rights and any relevant provisions of this Code to his or her attention. If the person is deaf or cannot understand English and is accompanied by someone, then the officer must try to establish whether that person can interpret or otherwise help the officer to give the required information.

4   Recording requirements

4.1   An officer who has carried out a search in the exercise of any power to which this Code applies, must make a record of it at the time, unless there are exceptional circumstances which would make this wholly impracticable (e.g. in situations involving public disorder or when the officer's presence is urgently required elsewhere). If a record is not made at the time, the officer must do so as soon as practicable afterwards. There may be situations in which it is not practicable to obtain the information necessary to complete a record, but the officer should make every reasonable effort to do so.

4.2   A copy of a record made at the time must be given immediately to the person who has been searched. The officer must ask for the name, address and date of birth of the person searched, but there is no obligation on a person to provide these details and no power of detention if the person is unwilling to do so.

4.3   The following information must always be included in the record of a search even if the person does not wish to provide any personal details:

(i)   the name of the person searched, or (if it is withheld) a description;
(ii)   a note of the person's self-defined ethnic background;
(iii)   when a vehicle is searched, its registration number;
(iv)   the date, time, and place that the person or vehicle was first detained;
(v)   the date, time and place the person or vehicle was searched (if different from (iv));
(vi)   the purpose of the search;
(vii)   the grounds for making it, or in the case of those searches mentioned in paragraph 2.1(b) and (c), the nature of the power and of any necessary authorisation and the fact that it has been given;
(viii) its outcome (e.g. arrest or no further action);
(ix)   a note of any injury or damage to property resulting from it;
(x)   subject to paragraph 3.8(a), the identity of the officer making the search.

4.4   Nothing in paragraph 4.3(x) requires the names of police officers to be shown on the search record or any other record required to be made under this code in the case of enquiries linked to the investigation of terrorism or otherwise where an officer reasonably believes that recording names might endanger the officers. In such cases the record must show the officers' warrant or other identification number and duty station.

4.5   A record is required for each person and each vehicle searched. However, if a person is in a vehicle and both are searched, and the object and grounds of the search are the same, only one record need be completed. If more than one person in a vehicle is searched, separate records for each search of a person must be made. If only a vehicle is searched, the name of the driver and his or her self-defined ethnic background must be recorded, unless the vehicle is unattended.

4.6   The record of the grounds for making a search must, briefly but informatively, explain the reason for suspecting the person concerned, by reference to the person's behaviour and/or other circumstances.

4.7   Where officers detain an individual with a view to performing a search, but the search is not carried out due to the grounds for suspicion being eliminated as a result of questioning the person detained, a record must still be made in accordance with the procedure outlined above.

4.8   After searching an unattended vehicle, or anything in or on it, an officer must leave a notice in it (or on it, if things on it have been searched without opening it) recording the fact that it has been searched.

4.9   The notice must include the name of the police station to which the officer concerned is attached and state where a copy of the record of the search may be obtained and where any application for compensation should be directed.

4.10   The vehicle must if practicable be left secure.

5   Monitoring and supervising the use of stop and search powers

5.1   Supervising officers must monitor the use of stop and search powers and should consider in particular whether there is any evidence that they are being exercised on the basis of stereotyped images or inappropriate generalisations. Supervising officers should satisfy themselves that the practice of officers under their supervision in stopping, searching and recording is fully in accordance with this Code. Supervisors must also examine whether the records reveal any trends or patterns which give cause for concern, and if so take appropriate action to address this

5.2   Senior officers with area or force-wide responsibilities must also monitor the broader use of stop and search powers and, where necessary, take action at the relevant level.

5.3   Supervision and monitoring must be supported by the compilation of comprehensive statistical records of stops and searches at force, area and local level. Any apparently disproportionate use of the powers by particular officers or groups of officers or in relation to specific sections of the community should be identified and investigated.

5.4   In order to promote public confidence in the use of the powers, forces in consultation with police authorities must make arrangements for the records to be scrutinised by representatives of the community, and to explain the use of the powers at a local level.

Notes for guidance

Officers exercising stop and search powers

1   This code does not affect the ability of an officer to speak to or question a person in the ordinary course of the officer's duties without detaining the person or exercising any element of compulsion. It is not the purpose of the code to prohibit such encounters between the police and the community with the co-operation of the person concerned and neither does it affect the principle that all citizens have a duty to help police officers to prevent crime and discover offenders. This is a civic rather than a legal duty; but when a police officer is trying to discover whether, or by whom, an offence has been committed he or she may question any person from whom useful information might be obtained, subject to the restrictions imposed by Code C. A person's unwillingness to reply does not alter this entitlement, but in the absence of a power to arrest, or to detain in order to search, the person is free to leave at will and cannot be compelled to remain with the officer.

2   In some circumstances preparatory questioning may be unnecessary, but in general a brief conversation or exchange will be desirable not only as a means of avoiding unsuccessful searches, but to explain the grounds for the stop/search, to gain cooperation and reduce any tension there might be surrounding the stop/search.

3   Where a person is lawfully detained for the purpose of a search, but no search in the event takes place, the detention will not thereby have been rendered unlawful.

4   Many people customarily cover their heads or faces for religious reasons – for example, Muslim women, Sikh men, Sikh or Hindu women, or Rastarfarian men or women. A police officer cannot order the removal of a head or face covering except where there is reason to believe that the item is being worn by the individual wholly or mainly for the purpose of disguising identity, not simply because it disguises identity. Where there may be religious sensitivities about ordering the removal of such an item, the officer should permit the item to be removed out of public view. Where practicable, the item should be removed in the presence of an officer of the same sex as the person and out of sight of anyone of the opposite sex.

5   A search of a person in public should be completed as soon as possible.

6   A person may be detained under a stop and search power at a place other than where the person was first detained, only if that place, be it a police station or elsewhere, is nearby. Such a place should be located within a reasonable travelling distance using whatever mode of travel (on foot or by car) is appropriate. This applies to all searches under stop and search powers, whether or not they involve the removal of clothing or exposure of intimate parts of the body (see paragraphs 3.6 and 3.7) or take place in or out of public view. It means, for example, that a search under the stop and search power in section 23 of the Misuse of Drugs Act 1971 which involves the compulsory removal of more than a person's outer coat, jacket or gloves cannot be carried out unless a place which is both nearby the place they were first detained and out of public view, is available. If a search involves exposure of intimate parts of the body and a police station is not nearby, particular care must be taken to ensure that the location is suitable in that it enables the search to be conducted in accordance with the requirements of paragraph 11 of Annex A to Code C.

7   A search in the street itself should be regarded as being in public for the purposes of paragraphs 3.6 and 3.7 above, even though it may be empty at the time a search begins. Although there is no power to require a person to do so, there is nothing to prevent an officer from asking a person voluntarily to remove more than an outer coat, jacket or gloves (and headgear or footwear under section 45(3) of the Terrorism Act 2000) in public.

8   *Where there may be religious sensitivities about asking someone to remove headgear using a power under section 45(3) of the Terrorism Act 2000, the police officer should offer to carry out the search out of public view (for example, in a police van or police station if there is one nearby).*

9   *Other means of identification might include jewellery, insignias, tattoos or other features which are known to identify members of the particular gang or group.*

Code B   Code of Practice for Searches of Premises by, Police Officers and the Seizure of Property Found, by Police Officers on Persons or Premises

1   Introduction

1.1   This Code of Practice deals with police powers to:
- search premises
- seize and retain property found on premises and persons

1.1A   These powers may be used to find:
- property and material relating to a crime
- wanted persons
- children who abscond from local authority accommodation where they have been remanded or committed by a court

1.2   A justice of the peace may issue a search warrant granting powers of entry, search and seizure, e.g. warrants to search for stolen property, drugs, firearms and evidence of serious offences. Police also have powers without a search warrant. The main ones provided by the Police and Criminal Evidence Act 1984 (PACE) include powers to search premises:
- to make an arrest
- after an arrest

1.3   The right to privacy and respect for personal property are key principles of the Human Rights Act 1998. Powers of entry, search and seizure should be fully and clearly justified before use because they may significantly interfere with the occupier's privacy. Officers should consider if the necessary objectives can be met by less intrusive means.

1.4   In all cases, police should:
- exercise their powers courteously and with respect for persons and property
- only use reasonable force when this is considered necessary and proportionate to the circumstances

1.5   If the provisions of PACE and this Code are not observed, evidence obtained from a search may be open to question.

2   General

2.1   This Code must be readily available at all police stations for consultation by:
- police officers
- detained persons
- members of the public

2.2   The *Notes for Guidance* included are not provisions of this Code.

2.3   This Code applies to searches of premises:
(a) by police for the purposes of an investigation into an alleged offence, with the occupier's consent, other than:
- routine scene of crime searches;
- calls to a fire or burglary made by or on behalf of an occupier or searches following the activation of fire or burglar alarms or discovery of insecure premises;

- searches when *paragraph 5.4* applies;
- bomb threat calls;

(b) under powers conferred on police officers by PACE, sections 17, 18 and 32;

(c) undertaken in pursuance of search warrants issued to and executed by constables in accordance with PACE, sections 15 and 16;

(d) subject to *paragraph 2.6*, under any other power given to police to enter premises with or without a search warrant for any purpose connected with the investigation into an alleged or suspected offence.

For the purposes of this Code, 'premises' as defined in PACE, section 23, includes any place, vehicle, vessel, aircraft, hovercraft, tent or movable structure and any offshore installation as defined in the Mineral Workings (Offshore Installations) Act 1971, section 1.

2.4–2.13 *****

3 Search warrants and production orders

(a) Before making an application

3.1   When information appears to justify an application, the officer must take reasonable steps to check the information is accurate, recent and not provided maliciously or irresponsibly. An application may not be made on the basis of information from an anonymous source if corroboration has not been sought. See *Note 3A*

3.2   The officer shall ascertain as specifically as possible the nature of the articles concerned and their location.

3.3   The officer shall make reasonable enquiries to:

(i) establish if:
- anything is known about the likely occupier of the premises and the nature of the premises themselves;
- the premises have been searched previously and how recently;

(ii) obtain any other relevant information.

3.4   An application:

(a) to a justice of the peace for a search warrant or to a circuit judge for a search warrant or production order under PACE, Schedule 1 must be supported by a signed written authority from an officer of inspector rank or above;
Note: If the case is an urgent application to a justice of the peace and an inspector or above is not readily available, the next most senior officer on duty can give the written authority.

(b) to a circuit judge under the Terrorism Act 2000, Schedule 5 for
- a production order;
- search warrant; or
- an order requiring an explanation of material seized or produced under such a warrant or production order

must be supported by a signed written authority from an officer of superintendent rank or above.

3.5   Except in a case of urgency, if there is reason to believe a search might have an adverse effect on relations between the police and the community, the officer in charge shall consult the local police/community liaison officer:
- before the search; or
- in urgent cases, as soon as practicable after the search

(b) Making an application

3.6   A search warrant application must be supported in writing, specifying:

(a) the enactment under which the application is made;

(b) the premises to be searched;

(c) the object of the search, see *Note 3B*;

(d) the grounds for the application, including, when the purpose of the proposed search is to find evidence of an alleged offence, an indication of how the evidence relates to the investigation;

(e) there are no reasonable grounds to believe the material to be sought, when making application to a:

(i) justice of the peace or a circuit judge, consists of or includes items subject to legal privilege;

(ii) justice of the peace, consists of or includes excluded material or special procedure material;

Note: this does not affect the additional powers of seizure in the Criminal Justice and Police Act 2001, Part 2 covered in paragraph 7.7, see *Note 3B*;

(f) if applicable, a request for the warrant to authorise a person or persons to accompany the officer who executes the warrant, see *Note 3C*.

3.7 A search warrant application under PACE, Schedule 1, paragraph 12(a), shall if appropriate indicate why it is believed service of notice of an application for a production order may seriously prejudice the investigation. Applications for search warrants under the Terrorism Act 2000, Schedule 5, paragraph 11 must indicate why a production order would not be appropriate.

3.8 If a search warrant application is refused, a further application may not be made for those premises unless supported by additional grounds.

Notes for guidance

3A The identity of an informant need not be disclosed when making an application, but the officer should be prepared to answer any questions the magistrate or judge may have about:

- *the accuracy of previous information from that source*
- *any other related matters*

3B The information supporting a search warrant application should be as specific as possible, particularly in relation to the articles or persons being sought and where in the premises it is suspected they may be found. The meaning of 'items subject to legal privilege', 'special procedure material' and 'excluded material' are defined by PACE, sections 10, 11 and 14 respectively.

3C Under PACE, section 16(2), a search warrant may authorise persons other than police officers to accompany the constable who executes the warrant. This includes, e.g. any suitably qualified or skilled person or an expert in a particular field whose presence is needed to help accurately identify the material sought or to advise where certain evidence is most likely to be found and how it should be dealt with. It does not give them any right to force entry, to search for or seize property but it gives them the right to be on the premises during the search without the occupier's permission.

4 *****

5 Search with consent

5.1 Subject to *paragraph 5.4*, if it is proposed to search premises with the consent of a person entitled to grant entry the consent must, if practicable, be given in writing on the Notice of Powers and Rights before the search. The officer must make any necessary enquiries to be satisfied the person is in a position to give such consent. See *Notes 5A and 5B*

5.2 Before seeking consent the officer in charge of the search shall state the purpose of the proposed search and its extent. This information must be as specific as possible, particularly regarding the articles or persons being sought and the parts of the premises to be searched. The person concerned must be clearly informed they are not obliged to consent and anything seized may be produced in evidence. If at the time the person is not suspected of an offence, the officer shall say this when stating the purpose of the search.

5.3 An officer cannot enter and search or continue to search premises under *paragraph 5.1* if consent is given under duress or withdrawn before the search is completed.

5.4   It is unnecessary to seek consent under *paragraphs 5.1* and *5.2* if this would cause disproportionate inconvenience to the person concerned. See *Note 5C*

Notes for guidance

5A   In a lodging house or similar accommodation, every reasonable effort should be made to obtain the consent of the tenant, lodger or occupier. A search should not be made solely on the basis of the landlord's consent unless the tenant, lodger or occupier is unavailable and the matter is urgent.

5B   If the intention is to search premises under the authority of a warrant or a power of entry and search without warrant, and the occupier of the premises co-operates in accordance with paragraph 6.4, there is no need to obtain written consent.

5C   Paragraph 5.4 is intended to apply when it is reasonable to assume innocent occupiers would agree to, and expect, police to take the proposed action, e.g. if:

- *a suspect has fled the scene of a crime or to evade arrest and it is necessary quickly to check surrounding gardens and readily accessible places to see if the suspect is hiding*
- *police have arrested someone in the night after a pursuit and it is necessary to make a brief check of gardens along the pursuit route to see if stolen or incriminating articles have been discarded*

6   Searching premises – general considerations

(a) Time of searches

6.1   Searches made under warrant must be made within one calendar month of the date of the warrant's issue.

6.2   Searches must be made at a reasonable hour unless this might frustrate the purpose of the search.

6.3   A warrant authorises an entry on one occasion only. When the extent or complexity of a search mean it is likely to take a long time, the officer in charge of the search may consider using the seize and sift powers referred to in *section 7*.

(b) Entry other than with consent

6.4   The officer in charge of the search shall first try to communicate with the occupier, or any other person entitled to grant access to the premises, explain the authority under which entry is sought and ask the occupier to allow entry, unless:

- (i)   the search premises are unoccupied;
- (ii) the occupier and any other person entitled to grant access are absent;
- (iii) there are reasonable grounds for believing that alerting the occupier or any other person entitled to grant access would frustrate the object of the search or endanger officers or other people.

6.5   Unless *sub-paragraph 6.4(iii)* applies, if the premises are occupied the officer, subject to *paragraph 2.9*, shall, before the search begins:

- (i)   identify him or herself, show their warrant card (if not in uniform) and state the purpose of and grounds for the search;
- (ii) identify and introduce any person accompanying the officer on the search (such persons should carry identification for production on request) and briefly describe that person's role in the process.

6.6   Reasonable and proportionate force may be used if necessary to enter premises if the officer in charge of the search is satisfied the premises are those specified in any warrant, or in exercise of the powers described in *paragraphs 4.1 to 4.3*, and if:

- (i)   the occupier or any other person entitled to grant access has refused entry;
- (ii) it is impossible to communicate with the occupier or any other person entitled to grant access; or
- (iii) any of the provisions of *paragraphs 6.4* apply.

6.7, 6.8   *****

(d) Conduct of searches

6.9   Premises may be searched only to the extent necessary to achieve the object of the search, having regard to the size and nature of whatever is sought.

6.9A   A search may not continue under:

- a warrant's authority once all the things specified in that warrant have been found
- any other power once the object of that search has been achieved

6.9B   No search may continue once the officer in charge of the search is satisfied whatever is being sought is not on the premises. This does not prevent a further search of the same premises if additional grounds come to light supporting a further application for a search warrant or exercise or further exercise of another power. For example, when, as a result of new information, it is believed articles previously not found or additional articles are on the premises.

6.10   Searches must be conducted with due consideration for the property and privacy of the occupier and with no more disturbance than necessary. Reasonable force may be used only when necessary and proportionate because the co-operation of the occupier cannot be obtained or is insufficient for the purpose.

6.11   A friend, neighbour or other person must be allowed to witness the search if the occupier wishes unless the officer in charge of the search has reasonable le grounds for believing the presence of the person asked for would seriously hinder the investigation or endanger officers or other people. A search need not be unreasonably delayed for this purpose. A record of the action taken should be made on the premises search record including the grounds for refusing the occupier's request.

6.12   A person is not required to be cautioned prior to being asked questions that are solely necessary for the purpose of furthering the proper and effective conduct of a search, see Code C, *paragraph 10.1(c)*. For example, questions to discover the occupier of specified premises, to find a key to open a locked drawer or cupboard or to otherwise seek co-operation during the search or to determine if a particular item is liable to be seized.

6.12A   If questioning goes beyond what is necessary for the purpose of the exemption in Code C, the exchange is likely to constitute an interview as defined by Code C, *paragraph 11.1A* and would require the associated safeguards included in Code C, *section 10*.

(e) Leaving premises

6.13   If premises have been entered by force, before leaving the officer in charge of the search must make sure they are secure by:

- arranging for the occupier or their agent to be present
- any other appropriate means

6.14, 6.15   *****

Notes for guidance

6A   Whether compensation is appropriate depends on the circumstances in each case. Compensation for damage caused when effecting entry is unlikely to be appropriate if the search was lawful, and the force used can be shown to be reasonable, proportionate and necessary to effect entry. If the wrong premises are searched by mistake everything possible should be done at the earliest opportunity to allay any sense of grievance and there should normally be a strong presumption in favour of paying compensation.
*****

7   Seizure and retention of property

(a) Seizure

7.1   Subject to *paragraph 7.2*, an officer who is searching any person or premises under any statutory power or with the consent of the occupier may seize anything:

(a) covered by a warrant

(b) the officer has reasonable grounds for believing is evidence of an offence or has been obtained in consequence of the commission of an offence but only if seizure is necessary to prevent the items being concealed, lost, disposed of, altered, damaged, destroyed or tampered with

(c) covered by the powers in the Criminal Justice and Police Act 2001, Part 2 allowing an officer to seize property from persons or premises and retain it for sifting or examination elsewhere.

7.2   No item may be seized which an officer has reasonable grounds for believing to be subject to legal privilege, as defined in PACE, section 10, other than under the Criminal Justice and Police Act 2001, Part 2.

7.3–7.13   *****

(c) Retention

7.14   Subject to *paragraph 7.15*, anything seized in accordance with the above provisions may be retained only for as long as is necessary. It may be retained, among other purposes:

(i)   for use as evidence at a trial for an offence;

(ii)   to facilitate the use in any investigation or proceedings of anything to which it is inextricably linked;

(iii)   for forensic examination or other investigation in connection with an offence;

(iv)   in order to establish its lawful owner when there are reasonable grounds for believing it has been stolen or obtained by the commission of an offence.

7.15   Property shall not be retained under *paragraph 7.14(i), (ii)* or *(iii)* if a copy or image would be sufficient.

(d) Rights of owners etc

7.16   If property is retained, the person who had custody or control of it immediately before seizure must, on request, be provided with a list or description of the property within a reasonable time.

7.17   That person or their representative must be allowed supervised access to the property to examine it or have it photographed or copied, or must be provided with a photograph or copy, in either case within a reasonable time of any request and at their own expense, unless the officer in charge of an in vestigation has reasonable grounds for believing this would:

(i)   prejudice the investigation of any offence or criminal proceedings; or

(ii)   lead to the commission of an offence by providing access to unlawful material such as pornography;

A record of the grounds shall be made when access is denied.

8, 9   *****

Code C   Code of Practice for the Detention, Treatment and Questioning of Persons by Police Officers

1   General

1.1   All persons in custody must be dealt with expeditiously, and released as soon as the need for detention no longer applies.

1.1A   A custody officer must perform the functions in this Code as soon as practicable. A custody officer will not be in breach of this Code if delay is justifiable and reasonable steps are taken to prevent unnecessary delay. The custody record shall show when a delay has occurred and the reason.

1.2   This Code of Practice must be readily available at all police stations for consultation by:

- police officers
- detained persons
- members of the public.

1.3   The provisions of this Code:

- include the *Annexes*
- do not include the *Notes for Guidance*.

1.4   If an officer has any suspicion, or is told in good faith, that a person of any age may be mentally disordered or otherwise mentally vulnerable, in the absence of clear evidence to dispel that suspicion, the person shall be treated as such for the purposes of this Code.

1.5   If anyone appears to be under 17, they shall be treated as a juvenile for the purposes of this Code in the absence of clear evidence that they are older.

1.6   If a person appears to be blind, seriously visually impaired, deaf, unable to read or speak or has difficulty orally because of a speech impediment, they shall be treated as such for the purposes of this Code in the absence of clear evidence to the contrary.

1.7   'The appropriate adult' means, in the case of a:

  (a) juvenile:

    (i)   the parent, guardian or, if the juvenile is in local authority or voluntary organisation care, or is otherwise being looked after under the Children Act 1989, a person representing that authority or organisation;

    (ii) a social worker of a local authority social services department;

    (iii) failing these, some other responsible adult aged 18 or over who is not a police officer or employed by the police.

  (b) person who is mentally disordered or mentally vulnerable:

    (i)   a relative, guardian or other person responsible for their care or custody;

    (ii) someone experienced in dealing with mentally disordered or mentally vulnerable people but who is not a police officer or employed by the police;

    (iii) failing these, some other responsible adult aged 18 or over who is not a police officer or employed by the police.

1.8   If this Code requires a person be given certain information, they do not have to be given it if at the time they are incapable of understanding what is said, are violent or may become violent or in urgent need of medical attention, but they must be given it as soon as practicable.

1.9–1.17   *****

Notes for guidance

1A   Although certain sections of this Code apply specifically to people in custody at police stations, those there voluntarily to assist with an investigation should be treated with no less consideration, e.g. offered refreshments at appropriate times, and enjoy an absolute right to obtain legal advice or communicate with anyone outside the police station.
*****

2   Custody records

2.1   A separate custody record must be opened as soon as practicable for each person brought to a police station under arrest or arrested at the station having gone there voluntarily. All information recorded under this Code must be recorded as soon as practicable in the custody record unless otherwise specified. Any audio or video recording made in the custody area is not part of the custody record.

2.2   If any action requires the authority of an officer of a specified rank, subject to *paragraph 2.6A*, their name and rank must be noted in the custody record.

2.3   The custody officer is responsible for the custody record's accuracy and com-
pleteness and for making sure the record or copy of the record accompanies a detainee if
they are transferred to another police station. The record shall show the:
- time and reason for transfer;
- time a person is released from detention.

2.4   A solicitor or appropriate adult must be permitted to consult a detainee's custody
record as soon as practicable after their arrival at the station and at any other time whilst the
person is detained. Arrangements for this access must be agreed with the custody officer and
may not unreasonably interfere with the custody officer's duties.

2.4A   When a detainee leaves police detention or is taken before a court they, their legal
representative or appropriate adult shall be given, on request, a copy of the custody record
as soon as practicable. This entitlement lasts for 12 months after release.

2.5   The detainee, appropriate adult or legal representative shall be permitted to
inspect the original custody record after the detainee has left police detention provided
they give reasonable notice of their request. Any such inspection shall be noted in the custody
record.

2.6–2.7   *****

3   Initial action

(a) Detained persons – normal procedure

3.1   When a person is brought to a police station under arrest or arrested at the station
having gone there voluntarily, the custody officer must make sure the person is told clearly
about the following continuing rights which may be exercised at any stage during the period
in custody:
- (i)   the right to have someone informed of their arrest as in *section 5*;
- (ii) the right to consult privately with a solicitor and that free independent legal
  advice is available;
- (iii) the right to consult these Codes of Practice.

3.2   The detainee must also be given:
- a written notice setting out:
  - ~ the above three rights;
  - ~ the arrangements for obtaining legal advice;
  - ~ the right to a copy of the custody record as in *paragraph 2.4A*;
  - ~ the caution in the terms prescribed in *section 10*.
- an additional written notice briefly setting out their entitlements while in custody.

Note: The detainee shall be asked to sign the custody record to acknowledge receipt of these
notices. Any refusal must be recorded on the custody record.

3.3   A citizen of an independent Commonwealth country or a national of a foreign
country, including the Republic of Ireland, must be informed as soon as practicable
about their rights of communication with their High Commission, Embassy or Consulate. See
section 7

3.4   The custody officer shall:
- note on the custody record any comment the detainee makes in relation to the
  arresting officer's account but shall not invite comment. If the custody officer
  authorises a person's detention the detainee must be informed of the grounds as
  soon as practicable and before they are questioned about any offence;
- note any comment the detainee makes in respect of the decision to detain them
  but shall not invite comment;
- not put specific questions to the detainee regarding their involvement in any
  offence, nor in respect of any comments they may make in response to the

arresting officer's account or the decision to place them in detention. Such an exchange is likely to constitute an interview as in *paragraph 11.1A* and require the associated safeguards in *section 11*.

See *paragraph 11.13* in respect of unsolicited comments.

    3.5   The custody officer shall:

   (a) ask the detainee, whether at this time, they:

     (i) would like legal advice, see *paragraph 6.5*;

    (ii) want someone informed of their detention, see *section 5*;

   (b) ask the detainee to sign the custody record to confirm their decisions in respect of (*a*);

   (c) determine whether the detainee:

     (i) is, or might be, in need of medical treatment or attention, see *section 9*;

    (ii) requires:

- an appropriate adult;
- help to check documentation;
- an interpreter;

   (d) record the decision in respect of (*c*).

    3.6–3.10 *****

    3.11 If video cameras are installed in the custody area, notices shall be prominently displayed showing cameras are in use. Any request to have video cameras switched off shall be refused.

    3.12–3.20 *****

(c) Persons attending a police station voluntarily

    3.21 Anybody attending a police station voluntarily to assist with an investigation may leave at will unless arrested. If it is decided they shall not be allowed to leave, they must be informed at once that they are under arrest and brought before the custody officer, who is responsible for making sure they are notified of their rights in the same way as other detainees. If they are not arrested but are cautioned as in *section 10*, the person who gives the caution must, at the same time, inform them they are not under arrest, they are not obliged to remain at the station but if they remain at the station they may obtain free and independent legal advice if they want. They shall be told the right to legal advice includes the right to speak with a solicitor on the telephone and be asked if they want to do so.

    3.22 If a person attending the police station voluntarily asks about their entitlement to legal advice, they shall be given a copy of the notice explaining the arrangements for obtaining legal advice. See *paragraph 3.2*

    3.23–3.24 *****

4 Detainee's property

(a) Action

    4.1 The custody officer is responsible for:

   (a) ascertaining what property a detainee:

     (i) has with them when they come to the police station, whether on:

- arrest or re-detention on answering to bail;
- commitment to prison custody on the order or sentence of a court;
- lodgement at the police station with a view to their production in court from prison custody;
- transfer from detention at another station or hospital;
- detention under the Mental Health Act 1983, section 135 or 136;

    (ii) might have acquired for an unlawful or harmful purpose while in custody;

   (b) the safekeeping of any property taken from a detainee which remains at the police station.

The custody officer may search the detainee or authorise their being searched to the extent they consider necessary, provided a search of intimate parts of the body or involving the removal of more than outer clothing is only made as in *Annex A*. A search may only be carried out by an officer of the same sex as the detainee.

4.2   Detainees may retain clothing and personal effects at their own risk unless the custody officer considers they may use them to cause harm to themselves or others, interfere with evidence, damage property, effect an escape or they are needed as evidence. In this event the custody officer may withhold such articles as they consider necessary and must tell the detainee why.

4.3   Personal effects are those items a detainee may lawfully need, use or refer to while in detention but do not include cash and other items of value.

(b) Documentation

4.4   The custody officer is responsible for recording all property brought to the police station which a detainee had with them, or had taken from them on arrest. The detainee shall be allowed to check and sign the record of property as correct. Any refusal to sign shall be recorded.

4.5   If a detainee is not allowed to keep any article of clothing or personal effects, the reason must be recorded.

5   Right not to be held incommunicado

(a) Action

5.1   Any person arrested and held in custody at a police station or other premises may, on request, have one person known to them or likely to take an interest in their welfare informed at public expense of their whereabouts as soon as practicable. If the person cannot be contacted the detainee may choose up to two alternatives. If they cannot be contacted, the person in charge of detention or the investigation has discretion to allow further attempts until the information has been conveyed.

5.2   The exercise of the above right in respect of each person nominated may be delayed only in accordance with *Annex B*.

5.3   The above right may be exercised each time a detainee is taken to another police station.

5.4   The detainee may receive visits at the custody officer's discretion.

5.5   If a friend, relative or person with an interest in the detainee's welfare enquires about their whereabouts, this information shall be given if the suspect agrees and *Annex B* does not apply.

5.6   The detainee shall be given writing materials, on request, and allowed to telephone one person for a reasonable time. Either or both these privileges may be denied or delayed if an officer of inspector rank or above considers sending a letter or making a telephone call may result in any of the consequences in:

    (a)   *Annex B paragraphs 1* and *2* and the person is detained in connection with an arrestable or serious arrestable offence; or

    (b)   *Annex B paragraphs 8* and *9* and the person is detained under the Terrorism Act 2000, Schedule 7 or section 41

For the purposes of this paragraph, any reference to a serious arrestable offence in *Annex B* includes an arrestable offence. However, nothing in this paragraph permits the restriction or denial of the rights in *paragraphs 5.1* and *6.1*.

5.7   Before any letter or message is sent, or telephone call made, the detainee shall be informed that what they say in any letter, call or message (other than in a communication to a solicitor) may be read or listened to and may be given in evidence. A telephone call may be terminated if it is being abused. The costs can be at public expense at the custody officer's discretion.

5.8   *******

6 Right to legal advice

(a) Action

6.1   Unless *Annex B* applies, all detainees must be informed that they may at any time consult and communicate privately with a solicitor, whether in person, in writing or by telephone, and that free independent legal advice is available from the duty solicitor. See *paragraph 3.1*

6.2   Not Used

6.3   A poster advertisting the right to legal advice must be prominently displayed in the charging area of every police station.

6.4   No police officer should, at any time, do or say anything with the intention of dissuading a detainee from obtaining legal advice.

6.5   The exercise of the right of access to legal advice may be delayed only as in *Annex B*. Whenever legal advice is requested, and unless *Annex B* applies, the custody officer must act without delay to secure the provision of such advice. If, on being informed or reminded of this right, the detainee declines to speak to a solicitor in person, the officer should point out that the right includes the right to speak with a solicitor on the telephone. If the detainee continues to waive this right the officer should ask them why and any reasons should be recorded on the custody record or the interview record as appropriate. Reminders of the right to legal advice must be given as in *paragraphs 3.5, 11.2, 15.4, 16.4* and *16.5* and Code D, *paragraphs 3.17(ii)* and *6.3*. Once it is clear a detainee does not want to speak to a solicitor in person or by telephone they should cease to be asked their reasons.

6.6   A detainee who wants legal advice may not be interviewed or continue to be interviewed until they have received such advice unless:

(a)   *Annex B* applies, when the restriction on drawing adverse inferences from silence in *Annex C* will apply because the detainee is not allowed an opportunity to consult a solicitor; or

(b)   an officer of superintendent rank or above has reasonable grounds for believing that:

(i)   the consequent delay might:
   - lead to interference with, or harm to, evidence connected with an offence;
   - lead to interference with, or physical harm to, other people;
   - lead to serious loss of, or damage to, property;
   - lead to alerting other people suspected of having committed an offence but not yet arrested for it;
   - hinder the recovery of property obtained in consequence of the commission of an offence.

(ii)   when a solicitor, including a duty solicitor, has been contacted and has agreed to attend, awaiting their arrival would cause unreasonable delay to the process of investigation.

Note: In these cases the restriction on drawing adverse inferences from silence in *Annex C* will apply because the detainee is not allowed an opportunity to consult a solicitor;

(c)   the solicitor the detainee has nominated or selected from a list:

(i)   cannot be contacted;

(ii)   has previously indicated they do not wish to be contacted; or

(iii)   having been contacted, has declined to attend; and
   the detainee has been advised of the Duty Solicitor Scheme but has declined to ask for the duty solicitor.

In these circumstances the interview may be started or continued without further delay provided an officer of inspector rank or above has agreed to the interview proceeding.

Note: The restriction on drawing adverse inferences from silence in *Annex C* will not apply because the detainee is allowed an opportunity to consult the duty solicitor;

    (d) the detainee changes their mind, about wanting legal advice.

          In these circumstances the interview may be started or continued without delay provided that:

        (i) the detainee agrees to do so, in writing or on tape; and

       (ii) an officer of inspector rank or above has inquired about the detainee's reasons for their change of mind and gives authority for the interview to proceed.

Confirmation of the detainee's agreement, their change of mind, the reasons for it if given and, subject to *paragraph 2.6A*, the name of the authorising officer shall be recorded in the taped or written interview record.

Note: In these circumstances the restriction on drawing adverse inferences from silence in *Annex C* will not apply because the detainee is allowed an opportunity to consult a solicitor if they wish.

    6.7   If *paragraph 6.6(b)(i)* applies, once sufficient information has been obtained to avert the risk, questioning must cease until the detainee has received legal advice unless *paragraph 6.6(a), (b)(ii), (c)* or *(d)* applies.

    6.8   A detainee who has been permitted to consult a solicitor shall be entitled on request to have the solicitor present when they are interviewed unless one of the exceptions in *paragraph 6.6* applies.

    6.9   The solicitor may only be required to leave the interview if their conduct is such that the interviewer is unable properly to put questions to the suspect.

    6.10   If the interviewer considers a solicitor is acting in such a way, they will stop the interview and consult an officer not below superintendent rank, if one is readily available, and otherwise an officer not below inspector rank not connected with the investigation. After speaking to the solicitor, the officer consulted will decide if the interview should continue in the presence of that solicitor. If they decide it should not, the suspect will be given the opportunity to consult another solicitor before the interview continues and that solicitor given an opportunity to be present at the interview.

    6.11   The removal of a solicitor from an interview is a serious step and, if it occurs, the officer of superintendent rank or above who took the decision will consider if the incident should be reported to the Law Society. If the decision to remove the solicitor has been taken by an officer below superintendent rank, the facts must be reported to an officer of superintendent rank or above who will similarly consider whether a report to the Law Society would be appropriate. When the solicitor concerned is a duty solicitor, the report should be both to the Law Society and to the Legal Services Commission.

    6.12–6.17   *****

Notes for guidance

    6A   In considering if paragraph 6.6(b) applies, the officer should, if practicable, ask the solicitor for an estimate of how long it will take to come to the station and relate this to the time detention is permitted, the time of day (i.e. whether the rest period under paragraph 12.2 is imminent) and the requirements of other investigations. If the solicitor is on their way or is to set off immediately, it will not normally be appropriate to begin an interview before they arrive. If it appears necessary to begin an interview before the solicitor's arrival, they should be given an indication of how long the police would be able to wait before 6.6(b) applies so there is an opportunity to make arrangements for someone else to provide legal advice.

    6B   A detainee who asks for legal advice should be given an opportunity to consult a specific solicitor or another solicitor from that solicitor's firm or the duty solicitor. If advice is not available by these means, or they do not want to consult the duty solicitor, the detainee should be given an opportunity to choose a solicitor from a list of those willing to provide legal advice. If this solicitor is unavailable, they may choose up to two alternatives. If these attempts are unsuccessful, the custody officer has discretion to allow further attempts until a solicitor has been contacted and agrees to provide legal advice. Apart from carrying out these duties, an officer must not advise the suspect about any particular firm of solicitors.

6C   *Not Used*

6D   *A detainee has a right to free legal advice and to be represented by a solicitor. The solicitor's only role in the police station is to protect and advance the legal rights of their client. On occasions this may require the solicitor to give advice which has the effect of the client avoiding giving evidence which strengthens a prosecution case. The solicitor may intervene in order to seek clarification, challenge an improper question to their client or the manner in which it is put, advise their client not to reply to particular questions, or if they wish to give their client further legal advice. Paragraph 6.9 only applies if the solicitor's approach or conduct prevents or unreasonably obstructs proper questions being put to the suspect or the suspect's response being recorded. Examples of unacceptable conduct include answering questions on a suspect's behalf or providing written replies for the suspect to quote.*

7   Citizens of independent Commonwealth countries or foreign nationals

(a) Action

7.1   Any citizen of an independent Commonwealth country or a national of a foreign country, including the Republic of Ireland, may communicate at any time with the appropriate High Commission, Embassy or Consulate. The detainee must be informed as soon as practicable of:

- this right;
- their right, upon request, to have their High Commission, Embassy or Consulate told of their whereabouts and the grounds for their detention. Such a request should be acted upon as soon as practicable.

7.2   *****

7.3   Consular officers may visit one of their nationals in police detention to talk to them and, if required, to arrange for legal advice. Such visits shall take place out of the hearing of a police officer.

7.4   Notwithstanding the provisions of consular conventions, if the detainee is a political refugee whether for reasons of race, nationality, political opinion or religion, or is seeking political asylum, consular officers shall not be informed of the arrest of one of their nationals or given access or information about them except at the detainee's express request.

7.5   *****

8   Conditions of detention

(a) Action

8.1   So far as it is practicable, not more than one detainee should be detained in each cell.

8.2   Cells in use must be adequately heated, cleaned and ventilated. They must be adequately lit, subject to such dimming as is compatible with safety and security to allow people detained overnight to sleep. No additional restraints shall be used within a locked cell unless absolutely necessary and then only restraint equipment, approved for use in that force by the Chief Officer, which is reasonable and necessary in the circumstances having regard to the detainee's demeanour and with a view to ensuring their safety and the safety of others. If a detainee is deaf, mentally disordered or otherwise mentally vulnerable, particular care must be taken when deciding whether to use any form of approved restraints.

8.3   Blankets, mattresses, pillows and other bedding supplied shall be of a reasonable standard and in a clean and sanitary condition.

8.4   Access to toilet and washing facilities must be provided.

8.5   If it is necessary to remove a detainee's clothes for the purposes of investigation, for hygiene, health reasons or cleaning, replacement clothing of a reasonable standard of comfort and cleanliness shall be provided. A detainee may not be interviewed unless adequate clothing has been offered.

8.6   At least two light meals and one main meal should be offered in any 24 hour period. Drinks should be provided at meal times and upon reasonable request between meals. Whenever necessary, advice shall be sought from the appropriate health care professional, on medical and dietary matters. As far as practicable, meals provided shall offer a varied diet and meet any specific dietary needs or religious beliefs the detainee may have. The detainee may, at the custody officer's discretion, have meals supplied by their family or friends at their expense.

8.7   Brief outdoor exercise shall be offered daily if practicable.

8.8   A juvenile shall not be placed in a police cell unless no other secure accommodation is available and the custody officer considers it is not practicable to supervise them if they are not placed in a cell or that a cell provides more comfortable accommodation than other secure accommodation in the station. A juvenile may not be placed in a cell with a detained adult.

8.9–8.11   *****

9   Care and treatment of detained persons

(a) General

9.1   Nothing in this section prevents the police from calling the police surgeon or, if appropriate, some other health care professional, to examine a detainee for the purposes of obtaining evidence relating to any offence in which the detainee is suspected of being involved. See *Note 9A*

9.2   If a complaint is made by, or on behalf of, a detainee about their treatment since their arrest, or it comes to notice that a detainee may have been treated improperly, a report must be made as soon as practicable to an officer of inspector rank or above not connected with the investigation. If the matter concerns a possible assault or the possibility of the unnecessary or unreasonable use of force, an appropriate health care professional must also be called as soon as practicable.

9.3–9.4   *****

(b) Clinical treatment and attention

9.5   The custody officer must make sure a detainee receives appropriate clinical attention as soon as reasonably practicable if the person:

(a)   appears to be suffering from physical illness; or
(b)   is injured; or
(c)   appears to be suffering from a mental disorder; or
(d)   appears to need clinical attention.

This applies even if the detainee makes no request for clinical attention and whether or not they have already received clinical attention elsewhere. If the need for attention appears urgent, e.g. when indicated as in *Annex H*, the nearest available health care professional or an ambulance must be called immediately.

9.6–9.17   *****

10   Cautions

(a) When a caution must be given

10.1   A person whom there are grounds to suspect of an offence, see *Note 10A*, must be cautioned before any questions about an offence, or further questions if the answers provide the grounds for suspicion, are put to them if either the suspect's answers or silence, (i.e. failure or refusal to answer or answer satisfactorily) may be given in evidence to a court in a prosecution. A person need not be cautioned if questions are for other necessary purposes, e.g.:

(a)   solely to establish their identity or ownership of any vehicle;
(b)   to obtain information in accordance with any relevant statutory requirement, see *paragraph 10.9;*

(c) in furtherance of the proper and effective conduct of a search, e.g. to determine the need to search in the exercise of powers of stop and search or to seek co-operation while carrying out a search;

(d) to seek verification of a written record as in *paragraph 11.13*;

(e) when examining a person in accordance with the Terrorism Act 2000, Schedule 7 and the Code of Practice for Examining Officers issued under that Act, Schedule 14, paragraph 6.

10.2 Whenever a person not under arrest is initially cautioned, or reminded they are under caution, that person must at the same time be told they are not under arrest and are free to leave if they want to. See *Note 10C*

10.3 A person who is arrested, or further arrested, must be informed at the time, or as soon as practicable thereafter, that they are under arrest and the grounds for their arrest, see *Note 10B*.

10.4 A person who is arrested, or further arrested, must also be cautioned unless:

(a) it is impracticable to do so by reason of their condition or behaviour at the time;

(b) they have already been cautioned immediately prior to arrest as in *paragraph 10.1*.

(b) Terms of the cautions

10.5 The caution which must be given on:

(a) arrest;

(b) all other occasions before a person is charged or informed they may be prosecuted, see *section 16*,

should, unless the restriction on drawing adverse inferences from silence applies, see *Annex C*, be in the following terms:

"You do not have to say anything. But it may harm your defence if you do not mention when questioned something which you later rely on in Court. Anything you do say may be given in evidence."

10.6 *Annex C, paragraph 2* sets out the alternative terms of the caution to be used when the restriction on drawing adverse inferences from silence applies.

10.7 Minor deviations from the words of any caution given in accordance with this Code do not constitute a breach of this Code, provided the sense of the relevant caution is preserved. See *Note 10D*

10.8 After any break in questioning under caution, the person being questioned must be made aware they remain under caution. If there is any doubt the relevant caution should be given again in full when the interview resumes. See *Note 10E*

10.9 When, despite being cautioned, a person fails to co-operate or to answer particular questions which may affect their immediate treatment, the person should be informed of any relevant consequences and that those consequences are not affected by the caution. Examples are when a person's refusal to provide:

• their name and address when charged may make them liable to detention;

• particulars and information in accordance with a statutory requirement, e.g. under the Road Traffic Act 1988, may amount to an offence or may make the person liable to a further arrest.

10.10–10.11   *****

(d) Juveniles and persons who are mentally disordered or otherwise mentally vulnerable

10.12 If a juvenile or a person who is mentally disordered or otherwise mentally vulner able is cautioned in the absence of the appropriate adult, the caution must be repeated in the adult's presence.

(e) Documentation

10.13 A record shall be made when a caution is given under this section, either in the interviewer's pocket book or in the interview record.

Notes for guidance

10A   There must be some reasonable, objective grounds for the suspicion, based on known facts or information which are relevant to the likelihood the offence has been committed and the person to be questioned committed it.

10B   An arrested person must be given sufficient information to enable them to understand they have been deprived of their liberty and the reason they have been arrested, e.g. when a person is arrested on suspicion of committing an offence they must be informed of the suspected offence's nature, when and where it was committed. If the arrest is made under the general arrest conditions in PACE, section 25, the grounds for arrest must include an explanation of the conditions which make the arrest necessary. Vague or technical language should be avoided.

10C   The restriction on drawing inferences from silence, see Annex C, paragraph 1, does not apply to a person who has not been detained and who therefore cannot be prevented from seeking legal advice if they want, see paragraph 3.21.

10D   If it appears a person does not understand the caution, the person giving it should explain it in their own words.

10E   It may be necessary to show to the court that nothing occurred during an interview break or between interviews which influenced the suspect's recorded evidence. After a break in an interview or at the beginning of a subsequent interview, the interviewing officer should summarise the reason for the break and confirm this with the suspect.

*****

11   Interviews – general

(a) Action

11.1   Following a decision to arrest a suspect, they must not be interviewed about the relevant offence except at a police station or other authorised place of detention, unless the consequent delay would be likely to:

- (a) lead to:
  - • interference with, or harm to, evidence connected with an offence;
  - • interference with, or physical harm to, other people; or
  - • serious loss of, or damage to, property;
- (b) lead to alerting other people suspected of committing an offence but not yet arrested for it; or
- (c) hinder the recovery of property obtained in consequence of the commission of an offence.

Interviewing in any of these circumstances shall cease once the relevant risk has been averted or the necessary questions have been put in order to attempt to avert that risk.

11.2   Immediately prior to the commencement or re-commencement of any interview at a police station or other authorised place of detention, the interviewer should remind the suspect of their entitlement to free legal advice and that the interview can be delayed for legal advice to be obtained, unless one of the exceptions in *paragraph 6.6* applies. It is the interviewer's responsibility to make sure all reminders are recorded in the interview record.

11.3   Not Used

11.4   At the beginning of an interview the interviewer, after cautioning the suspect, see *section 10*, shall put to them any significant statement or silence which occurred in the presence and hearing of a police officer or civilian interviewer before the start of the interview and which have not been put to the suspect in the course of a previous interview. See *Note 11A*. The interviewer shall ask the suspect whether they confirm or deny that earlier statement or silence and if they want to add anything.

11.4A   A significant statement is one which appears capable of being used in evidence against the suspect, in particular a direct admission of guilt. A significant silence is a failure or refusal to answer a question or answer satisfactorily when under caution, which might, allowing for the restriction on drawing adverse inferences from silence, see *Annex C*, give rise to an inference under the Criminal Justice and Public Order Act 1994, Part III.

11.5   No interviewer may try to obtain answers or elicit a statement by the use of oppression. Except as in *paragraph 10.9*, no interviewer shall indicate, except to answer a direct question, what action will be taken by the police if the person being questioned answers questions, makes a statement or refuses to do either. If the person asks directly what action will be taken if they answer questions, make a statement or refuse to do either, the interviewer may inform them what action the police propose to take provided that action is itself proper and warranted.

11.6   The interview or further interview of a person about an offence with which that person has not been charged or for which they have not been informed they may be prosecuted, must cease when the officer in charge of the investigation:

(a) is satisfied all the questions they consider relevant to obtaining accurate and reliable information about the offence have been put to the suspect, this includes allowing the suspect an opportunity to give an innocent explanation and asking questions to test if the explanation is accurate and reliable, e.g. to clear up ambiguities or clarify what the suspect said;

(b) has taken account of any other available evidence; and

(c) the officer in charge of the investigation, or in the case of a detained suspect, the custody officer, see *paragraph 16.1*, reasonably believes there is sufficient evidence to provide a realistic prospect of conviction for that offence if the person was prosecuted for it. See *Note 11B*

This paragraph does not prevent officers in revenue cases or acting under the confiscation provisions of the Criminal Justice Act 1988 or the Drug Trafficking Act 1994 from inviting suspects to complete a formal question and answer record after the interview is concluded.

(b) Interview records

11.7   (a)   An accurate record must be made of each interview, whether or not the interview takes place at a police station

(b) The record must state the place of interview, the time it begins and ends, any interview breaks and, subject to *paragraph 2.6A*, the names of all those present; and must be made on the forms provided for this purpose or in the interviewer's pocket book or in accordance with the Codes of Practice E or F;

(c) Any written record must be made and completed during the interview, unless this would not be practicable or would interfere with the conduct of the interview, and must constitute either a verbatim record of what has been said or, failing this, an account of the interview which adequately and accurately summarises it.

11.8–11.14   *****

(c) Juveniles and mentally disordered or otherwise mentally vulnerable people

11.15   A juvenile or person who is mentally disordered or otherwise mentally vulnerable must not be interviewed regarding their involvement or suspected involvement in a criminal offence or offences, or asked to provide or sign a written statement under caution or record of interview, in the absence of the appropriate adult unless *paragraphs 11.1, 11.18 to 11.20* apply. See *Note 11C*

11.16   Juveniles may only be interviewed at their place of education in exceptional circumstances and only when the principal or their nominee agrees. Every effort should be made to notify the parent(s) or other person responsible for the juvenile's welfare and the appropriate adult, if this is a different person, that the police want to interview the juvenile and reasonable time should be allowed to enable the appropriate adult to be present at the interview. If awaiting the appropriate adult would cause unreasonable delay, and unless the juvenile is suspected of an offence against the educational establishment, the principle or their nominee can act as the appropriate adult for the purposes of the interview.

11.17   If an appropriate adult is present at an interview, they shall be informed:

- they are not expected to act simply as an observer; and
- the purpose of their presence is to:
  - ~ advise the person being interviewed;
  - ~ observe whether the interview is being conducted properly and fairly;
  - ~ facilitate communication with the person being interviewed.

11.18–11.20   *****

11.19   These interviews may not continue once sufficient information has been obtained to avert the consequences in *paragraph 11.1(a)* to *(c)*.

11.20   A record shall be made of the grounds for any decision to interview a person under *paragraph 11.18*.

Notes for guidance

11A   Paragraph 11.4 does not prevent the interviewer from putting significant statements and silences to a suspect again at a later stage or a further interview.

11B   The Criminal Procedure and Investigations Act 1996 Code of Practice, paragraph 3.4 states 'In conducting an investigation, the investigator should pursue all reasonable lines of enquiry, whether these point towards or away from the suspect. What is reasonable will depend on the particular circumstances.' Interviewers should keep this in mind when deciding what questions to ask in an interview.

11C   Although juveniles or people who are mentally disordered or otherwise mentally vulnerable are often capable of providing reliable evidence, they may, without knowing or wishing to do so, be particularly prone in certain circumstances to provide information that may be unreliable, misleading or self-incriminating. Special care should always be taken when questioning such a person, and the appropriate adult should be involved if there is any doubt about a person's age, mental state or capacity. Because of the risk of unreliable evidence it is also important to obtain corroboration of any facts admitted whenever possible.

11D   Juveniles should not be arrested at their place of education unless this is unavoidable. When a juvenile is arrested at their place of education, the principal or their nominee must be informed.

11E   Significant statements described in paragraph 11.4 will always be relevant to the offence and must be recorded. When a suspect agrees to read records of interviews and other comments and sign them as correct, they should be asked to endorse the record with, e.g. 'I agree that this is a correct record of what was said' and add their signature. If the suspect does not agree with the record, the interviewer should record the details of any disagreement and ask the suspect to read these details and sign them to the effect that they accurately reflect their disagreement. Any refusal to sign should be recorded.

12   Interviews in police stations

(a) Action

12.1   If a police officer wants to interview or conduct enquiries which require the presence of a detainee, the custody officer is responsible for deciding whether to deliver the detainee into the officer's custody.

12.2   Except as below, in any period of 24 hours a detainee must be allowed a continuous period of at least 8 hours for rest, free from questioning, travel or any interruption in connection with the investigation concerned. This period should normally be at night or other appropriate time which takes account of when the detainee last slept or rested. If a detainee is arrested at a police station after going there voluntarily, the period of 24 hours runs from the time of their arrest and not the time of arrival at the police station. The period may not be interrupted or delayed, except:

    (a) when there are reasonable grounds for believing not delaying or interrupting the period would:

        (i)   involve a risk of harm to people or serious loss of, or damage to, property;

        (ii) delay unnecessarily the person's release from custody;

        (iii) otherwise prejudice the outcome of the investigation;

    (b) at the request of the detainee, their appropriate adult or legal representative;

    (c) when a delay or interruption is necessary in order to:

        (i)   comply with the legal obligations and duties arising under *section 15*;

        (ii) to take action required under *section 9* or in accordance with medical advice.

If the period is interrupted in accordance with *(a)*, a fresh period must be allowed. interruptions under *(b)* and *(c)*, do not require a fresh period to be allowed.

    12.4   As far as practicable interviews shall take place in interview rooms which are adequately heated, lit and ventilated.

    12.5   A suspect whose detention without charge has been authorised under PACE, because the detention is necessary for an interview to obtain evidence of the offence for which they have been arrested, may choose not to answer questions but police do not require the suspect's consent or agreement to interview them for this purpose. If a suspect takes steps to prevent themselves being questioned or further questioned, e.g. by refusing to leave their cell to go to a suitable interview room or by trying to leave the interview room, they shall be advised their consent or agreement to interview is not required. The suspect shall be cautioned as in *section 10*, and informed if they fail or refuse to co-operate, the interview may take place in the cell and that their failure or refusal to co-operate may be given in evidence. The suspect shall then be invited to co-operate and go into the interview room.

    12.6   People being questioned or making statements shall not be required to stand.

    12.7   before the interview commences each interviewer shall, subject to *paragraph 2.6A*, identify themselves and any other persons present to the interviewee.

    12.8   Breaks from interviewing should be made at recognised meal times or at other times that take account of when an interviewee last had a meal. Short refreshment breaks shall be provided at approximately two hour intervals, subject to the interviewer's discretion to delay a break if there are reasonable grounds for believing it would:

        (i)   involve a:

           • risk of harm to people;

           • serious loss of, or damage to, property;

        (ii) unnecessarily delay the detainee's release;

        (iii) otherwise prejudice the outcome of the investigation.

    12.9   If during the interview a complaint is made by or on behalf of the interviewee concerning the provisions of this Code, the interviewer should:

        (i)   record it in the interview record;

        (ii) inform the custody officer, who is then responsible for dealing with it as in *section 9*.

    12.10–12.14 *****

13–15 *****

16 Charging detained persons

(a) Action

    16.1   When the officer in charge of the investigation reasonably believes there is sufficient evidence to provide a realistic prospect of the detainee's conviction, see *paragraph 11.6*, they shall without delay, and subject to the following qualification, inform the custody officer who will be responsible for considering whether the detainee should be charged. When a person is detained in respect of more than one offence it is permissible to delay informing the custody officer until the above conditions are satisfied in respect of all the offences, but see *paragraph 11.6.* If the detainee is a juvenile, mentally disordered or otherwise mentally vulnerable, any resulting action shall be taken in the presence of the appropriate adult if they are present at the time.

16.2   When a detainee is charged with or informed they may be prosecuted for an offence, they shall, unless the restriction on drawing adverse inferences from silence applies, see *Annex C*, be cautioned as follows:

'You do not have to say anything. But it may harm your defence if you do not mention now something which you later rely on in court. Anything you do say may be given in evidence.'

Annex C, paragraph 2 sets out the alternative terms of the caution to be used when the restriction on drawing adverse inferences from silence applies.

16.3   When a detainee is charged they shall be given a written notice showing particulars of the offence and, subject to *paragraph 2.6A*, the officer's name and the case reference number. As far as possible the particulars of the charge shall be stated in simple terms, but they shall also show the precise offence in law with which the detainee is charged. The notice shall begin:

'You are charged with the offence(s) shown below.' Followed by the caution.

If the detainee is a juvenile, mentally disordered or otherwise mentally vulner able, the notice should be given to the appropriate adult.

16.4   If, after a detainee has been charged with or informed they may be prosecuted for an offence, an officer wants to tell them about any written statement or interview with another person relating to such an offence, the detainee shall either be handed a true copy of the written statement or the content of the interview record brought to their attention. Nothing shall be done to invite any reply or comment except to:

(a)   caution the detainee, *'You do not have to say anything, but anything you do say may be given in evidence.'*; and

(b)   remind the detainee about their right to legal advice.

16.4A   If the detainee:

- cannot read, the document may be read to them
- is a juvenile, mentally disordered or otherwise mentally vulner able, the appro-priate adult shall also be given a copy, or the interview record shall be brought to their attention

16.5   A detainee may not be interviewed about an offence after they have been charged with, or informed they may be prosecuted for it, unless the interview is necessary:

- to prevent or minimise harm or loss to some other person, or the public
- to clear up an ambiguity in a previous answer or statement
- in the interests of justice for the detainee to have put to them, and have an opportunity to comment on, information concerning the offence which has come to light since they were charged or informed they might be prosecuted

Before any such interview, the interviewer shall:

(a)   caution the detainee, *'You do not have to say anything, but anything you do say may be given in evidence.'*;

(b)   remind the detainee about their right to legal advice.

16.6–16.10   *****

ANNEX A   *****

ANNEX B   DELAY IN NOTIFYING ARREST OR ALLOWING ACCESS TO LEGAL ADVICE

A   Persons detained under PACE

1.   The exercise of the rights in *Section 5* or *Section 6*, or both, may be delayed if the person is in police detention, as in PACE, section 118(2), in connection with a serious arrestable

offence, has not yet been charged with an offence and an officer of superintendent rank or above, or inspector rank or above only for the rights in *Section 5*, has reasonable grounds for believing their exercise will:

    (i)   lead to:

- interference with, or harm to, evidence connected with a serious arrestable offence; or
- interference with, or physical harm to, other people; or

    (ii) lead to alerting other people suspected of having committed a serious arrestable offence but not yet arrested for it; or

    (iii) hinder the recovery of property obtained in consequence of the commission of such an offence.

2.   These rights may also be delayed if the serious arrestable offence is:

    (i)   a drug trafficking offence and the officer has reasonable grounds for believing the detainee has benefited from drug trafficking, and the recovery of the value of the detainee's proceeds from drug trafficking will be hindered by the exercise of either right;

    (ii) an offence to which the Criminal Justice Act 1988, Part VI (confiscation orders) applies and the officer has reasonable grounds for believing the detainee has benefited from the offence, and the exercise of either right will hinder the recovery of the value of the:

- property obtained by the detainee from or in connection with the offence
- pecuniary advantage derived by the detainee from or in connection with it.

3.   Authority to delay a detainee's right to consult privately with a solicitor may be given only if the authorising officer has reasonable grounds to believe the solicitor the detainee wants to consult will, inadvertently or otherwise, pass on a message from the detainee or act in some other way which will have any of the consequences specified under *paragraph 1 or 2*. In these circumstances the detainee must be allowed to choose another solicitor.

4.   If the detainee wishes to see a solicitor, access to that solicitor may not be delayed on the grounds they might advise the detainee not to answer questions or the solicitor was initially asked to attend the police station by someone else. In the latter case the detainee must be told the solicitor has come to the police station at another person's request, and must be asked to sign the custody record to signify whether they want to see the solicitor.

5.   The fact the grounds for delaying notification of arrest may be satisfied does not automatically mean the grounds for delaying access to legal advice will also be satisfied.

6.   These rights may be delayed only for as long as grounds exist and in no case beyond 36 hours after the relevant time as in PACE, section 41. If the grounds cease to apply within this time, the detainee must, as soon as practicable, be asked if they want to exercise either right, the custody record must be noted accordingly, and action taken in accordance with the relevant section of the Code.

7.   A detained person must be permitted to consult a solicitor for a reasonable time before any court hearing.

*****

ANNEXES C–E *****

INDEX